THE
HOMEOWNER'S
DIRECTORY

A COMPLETE GUIDE TO THE BEST EQUIPMENT
AVAILABLE FOR BUILDING, REMODELING, AND
REPAIRING YOUR HOME
BY

Stanley Schuler

SIMON AND SCHUSTER · NEW YORK

PUBLISHED BY SIMON AND SCHUSTER
A DIVISION OF GULF & WESTERN CORPORATION
SIMON & SCHUSTER BUILDING
ROCKEFELLER CENTER
1230 AVENUE OF THE AMERICAS
NEW YORK, NEW YORK 10020
DESIGNED BY EVE METZ
MANUFACTURED IN THE UNITED STATES OF AMERICA

1 2 3 4 5 6 7 8 9 10

LIBRARY OF CONGRESS CATALOGING IN PUBLICATION DATA
SCHULER, STANLEY.
    THE HOMEOWNER'S DICTIONARY.
    1. BUILDING MATERIALS—DICTIONARIES. 2. BUILDING
FITTINGS—DICTIONARIES. 3. DWELLINGS—ELECTRIC
EQUIPMENT—DICTIONARIES. I. TITLE.
TH4811.s38   691'.03   77-21877
ISBN 0-671-22597-9

CONTENTS

Contents

Contents

Introduction

Finding out what materials and equipment are on the market for building, remodeling, and repairing houses has always been a problem for homeowners.

Architects and builders have long had access to special books describing the simple and amazing products they use or recommend in their work. But the homeowner—the fellow who pays the bills—has been kept in the dark. Whatever information he is able to pick up comes largely from magazines, which report only on the newest products and completely ignore the old products that are the staples of all building operations, and from assorted retail outlets, which are interested only in the products they sell and do not mention competitive products that may be better.

This book changes the picture. Now you, the homeowner, can find out all that the professionals presumably know about homebuilding, remodeling, and repair products—and then some.

If you don't know what's available in, say, roofing materials or bathroom fixtures, you can find out here.

If you don't know what kind of water pump or wall covering or electrical outlet you should use, you can find out here.

If you don't know who makes a specific kind of air conditioner or door or fire-alarm system, you can find out here.

If you have a vague recollection that you have heard about a sewage system that doesn't require a large disposal area but don't know whether it's still on the market, you will find the answer here.

In short, this is a book about what's available and where to find it.

More than that, it covers the sizes, colors, and features of products; details their principal advantages, disadvantages, and limitations; and describes how they should and should not be used.

And for good measure, it tells you what products you can install yourself and how to go about it.

But before you start digging into the book, you should understand several points about the listings of who sells what at the end of each chapter.

1. Most of the companies listed are manufacturers; some are suppliers. As a rule, manufacturers don't sell direct to homeowners. But if you can't find their products in any of your local stores, they will gladly tell you where else to look. The suppliers, on the other hand, generally are happy to sell to anyone. Some make their own products; others buy them from foreign firms or companies so

small that they have no outlets of the normal kind. Many unusual products, such as special decorative hardware and pivot windows, are available only from these sources.

2. No manufacturers or suppliers are listed for certain basic products, such as lumber, structural plywood, cement, and piping, for the simple reason that products of this kind are available everywhere and you can't tell one from the other.

3. The lists of manufacturers and suppliers are by no means all-inclusive. I've asked hundreds and hundreds of companies for information about their products. Many, for reasons of their own, didn't answer; and since they didn't, I am reluctant to say that John Brown & Sons makes heat pumps—even though I'm sure they do—because maybe they don't. Manufacturers today go in and out of product lines so fast that no one can keep up with them. I prefer to list a relatively few companies that I am sure are making a certain kind of product —because they told me they did—rather than a lot of companies I'm not sure about. And anyway, you'll find more companies and products to choose among than you need.

4. The source lists at the end of each chapter not only complement but also supplement the text of the chapter. By that I mean that while a few types of product may not be mentioned in the text, you will find them in the lists. In addition, all products mentioned in the text are also covered in the lists.

5. To save space, no addresses are given for manufacturers and suppliers in the end-of-chapter lists. For this information, see the alphabetical listing of all companies at the back of the book.

STANLEY SCHULER

1

Lumber, Plywood, and Cement

Of all the things used in home construction, lumber, plywood, and Portland cement are the most important. They not only compose the structure of a house but also much of its exterior and interior skin. Given nothing else except a keg of nails, you could build a house which would be habitable, although not very comfortable.

LUMBER

Lumber is categorized in so many ways that only a few people have a full understanding of the names and terms applied to it. This need not be cause for concern to the do-it-yourselfer. If you have a general grasp of the more important lumber classifications, you will never have trouble buying what you need for any given project.

KINDS OF WOOD. All lumber is cut either from softwood trees with needlelike evergreen leaves or from hardwood trees with broad leaves which fall in winter; consequently, the lumber itself is described either as a softwood or a hardwood. This does not mean, however, that all softwoods are soft and all hardwoods are hard. As a rule, they are; but there are exceptions (after all, what is a rule without exceptions?). Yellow pine, for example, is a very hard wood even though it is classified as a softwood, whereas basswood and poplar are softer than many softwoods although they are classified as hardwoods.

Most of the lumber used in building is softwood. The principal species are Douglas fir, hemlock, fir, spruce, western larch, and yellow pine, which are used primarily in the basic structure of the house; redwood and cypress, which are used in the basic structure as well as for finishing; western red cedar, which is used for siding

and shingles; and white pine (including ponderosa pine), which is used for interior and exterior finishing.

Hardwoods were used in colonial times for framing and siding, but their principal uses today are for flooring, paneling, and cabinets. The most important species are oak, maple, birch, and walnut.

HOW LUMBER IS CUT. Softwood lumber is cut from logs in two ways. If it is plain-sawed, the growth rings form an angle of less than 45° with the sides of the boards. If it is quarter-sawed, on the other hand, the growth rings form an angle of more than 45° with the sides of the boards. The difference is most apparent if you look at the end of a board, but it also shows up quite clearly in the surface. In a plain-sawed board, the growth rings visible in the surface are widely spaced, whereas in a quarter-sawed board, they are close together as if they had been drawn with a comb.

Quarter-sawed board (left); plain-sawed (right).

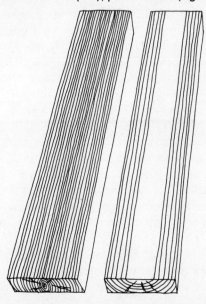

Hardwood lumber is cut in the same ways. However, plain-sawed lumber is called flat-grain lumber, while quarter-sawed lumber is called edge-grain lumber.

Plain-sawed, or flat-grain, lumber is less expensive than quarter-sawed, or edge-grain, lumber but is more likely to warp, split, and check and does not wear as evenly. Quarter-sawed lumber is therefore preferable when it is to be used for finishing work.

BASIC LUMBER CLASSIFICATIONS. The lumber which results after a log has gone through a sawmill is classified in one of five ways according to the extent that it has been manufactured:

Rough lumber is sawed to size but not dressed (planed smooth).

Dressed, or surfaced, lumber has been dressed on a sound and tight. (This grade is usually available only code indicates the extent of dressing. For example, if S1S is printed on a piece of lumber, it means that it has been surfaced on only one side. S2S means surfaced on two sides; S4S, surfaced on all four sides; S1E, surfaced one edge; S1S2E, surfaced one side and two edges; and so on.

Matched lumber is dressed lumber in which a tongue has been worked into one edge and a matching groove has been cut in the other edge to produce a close-fitting tongue-and-groove joint between adjacent boards. If a board is tongued and grooved at the ends, it is said to be end-matched.

Shiplapped lumber is dressed lumber which has been rabbeted on both edges.

Patterned lumber is dressed lumber which has been milled to a pattern. Moldings and more elaborate forms of siding are patterned lumber.

(Matched, shiplapped, and patterned lumber are grouped under the broad heading of "worked lumber"; but this is not a frequently used term in lumberyards.)

SEASONING OF LUMBER. Green lumber should never be used in building, because as it dries it contracts and tends to warp. Fortunately, such lumber is not handled by lumberyards, although a great deal of the lumber which is sold is only partially seasoned.

Federal Housing Administration standards require that rough lumber less than 8 in. wide should not contain more than 19% moisture; in wider boards, the moisture content should be only 15%. In finish lumber, the average moisture content should be about 10%.

The manner in which lumber is seasoned is immaterial. It can be either air-dried or kiln-dried. Individual opinions to the contrary, one type of lumber is just as strong, durable, and resistant to warping as the other.

GRADES OF LUMBER. One of the worst mistakes people make when buying lumber is to ask for a board or timber of a certain size without specifying the grade.

As a result, they often wind up with an expensive board which is much better than they actually need. Probably the most important rule for all lumber buyers is never to ask for a better grade than the job warrants.

Softwood boards up to 1½ in. thick are sorted into three select grades and five common grades. The specific grades are:

B & Better or 1 & 2 Clear. To all intents and purposes, such lumber is free of blemishes.

C Select. Has a few minor blemishes.

D Select. Has small knots, checks, and other minor blemishes.

No. 1 Common. With fairly large knots, but all sound and tight. (This grade is usually available only on special order.)

No. 2 Common. Much like No. 1. The boards are suitable for exterior trim and knotty paneling.

No. 3 Common. The knots are more numerous and larger, but the lumber is suitable for shelving, paneling, siding, etc. Selected boards can be used for knotty paneling.

No. 4 Common. The poorest grade you should buy. It is used for sheathing, in subfloors, and wherever else it is concealed and not subject to stress.

No. 5 Common. Used mainly for industrial purposes.

Softwood framing lumber of nominal 2-in. thickness or greater is graded as follows:

Select Structural. For exposed use and wherever extra strength is required.

Construction. Also suitable for exposed use, although it has more knots. The strength is excellent.

Standard. Normal grade used for joists, rafters, and planks.

Utility. Can be used only in short horizontal spans and for studs.

Economy. Not suitable for use in the framing of a house, but sometimes a timber can be cut into sound lengths suitable for use in walls.

Hardwood lumber is similarly graded. The top grade is FAS (Firsts & Seconds). Then come, in descending order, Selects, No. 1 Common, No. 2 Common, and No. 3 Common.

LUMBER SIZES. After it has been dressed, all lumber is smaller than its stated size. For example, if you go to a lumberyard and ask for a 1×6-in. board, you will be given one which measures ¾ × 5½ in. This is the actual size of the board; 1×6 is the nominal size.

The standard sizes for boards and timbers are as follows:

Nominal thickness	Actual thickness	Nominal width	Actual width
¾ in.	⅝ in.	2 in.	1½ in.
1	¾		
1¼	1⁵⁄₃₂	3	2½
1½	1¹³⁄₃₂	4	3½
1¾	1¹⁹⁄₃₂	5	4½
2	1¹³⁄₁₆	6	5½
3	2¾	7	6½
4	3¾	8 and wider	deduct ¾ in. from nominal

In all other dressed lumber, including matched, ship-lapped, and patterned lumber, the situation is the same. The actual width and thickness are always less than the nominal width and thickness.

Lengths are as stated, however. Standard lengths of boards, timbers, strips, etc. range from 6 to 20 ft. in multiples of 1 ft. But in lumberyards, lumber is usually available only in 2-ft. multiples.

EXTRA-LARGE LUMBER. The average lumberyard rarely carries timbers over 8×8 in. However, much larger lumber is available, although it may not be obtainable through the yard you ordinarily deal with or even from one of the huge lumber companies that supply a high percentage of the lumber sold throughout the country.

A number of small mills specializing in oversize timbers are scattered around the country. If you can't find one of these or if they can't give you exactly what is needed, you can have timbers produced to your specifications by firms which make laminated beams, arches, trusses, etc. Such timbers are made by gluing small timbers together under pressure. These are not only tremendously strong but also very beautiful when sanded smooth.

HOW LUMBER IS PRICED. All lumber except moldings, interior trim, furring strips, grounds, and material less than ½ in. thick is sold by the board foot. A board foot measures 1×12×12 in. To find the board feet in a piece of lumber, multiply the nominal thickness in inches by the nominal width in inches by the length in feet, and divide the answer by 12.

For example, to find the board feet in a 14-ft. length of 2×8:

$$\frac{2\times8\times14}{12} = 18\tfrac{2}{3} \text{ ft.}$$

Thus, if that particular grade of lumber sells at 50 cents a board foot, the board will cost you $9.34.

Lumber not sold by the board foot is sold by the lineal foot.

HOW TO BUY LUMBER. Because much of the lumber available today is of dubious quality, the only way to buy boards, timbers, moldings, siding, etc. is to visit a lumberyard and ask to be allowed to go through the stacks, picking out the pieces you want yourself.

After discarding the pieces that are too green (they actually look and feel a little damp), sort out those which are more or less free of the following defects:

Knots. The more knots there are in a board or the bigger they are, the weaker the board is. However, unless you're buying select lumber, you can't completely avoid knots. Just beware of very large knots or knots which are loose or entirely missing.

Warps. Lumber which is bent or twisted along the edges is impossible to work with. One-in. or thinner boards which are bent or slightly cupped on the face can usually be used if you nail them firmly to a base.

Splits. Splits weaken lumber and make it hard to handle. But if a board is to be nailed to a base and the split is slight, it may be possible to force the split edges together.

Shakes. A shake is a separation of the wood along the grain and between the growth rings. You encounter this problem especially in plain-sawed boards. Repairing the defect is difficult.

Pitch pockets. These are cavities filled with pitch. If they are deep, they weaken lumber like a knot. Deep or shallow, they cause problems, because unless you succeed in sealing in the pitch, it will bleed through paint.

Bark pockets. Cavities containing bark also weaken wood to some extent.

Pitch streaks. Pitch streaks show up in the form of slightly yellow streaks which feel bumpy as you run your fingers over them. They do not weaken the lumber but will bleed through paint and are hard to seal off.

Decay. Decayed wood is soft, fibrous, stringy-looking. Small spots can be cut out. Boards with large spots should definitely be discarded.

Wanes. A wane is a missing piece of wood, usually along the edge or end of a board. It's a nuisance, because unless the board can be used upside down, the gap must be filled. But it does little harm otherwise.

Honeycombing. This is characterized by tiny white pockets in the wood. They are unsightly in a board used for paneling or trim but do not affect the usefulness of the board otherwise.

Blue stain. Bluish or grayish stains in wood are caused by fungi, but outside of spoiling the appearance of the wood, they do no harm.

Gouges. Caused by mishandling of lumber, these can be easily concealed if the wood is to be painted but will be highly visible—whether filled or left as is—in wood with a natural finish.

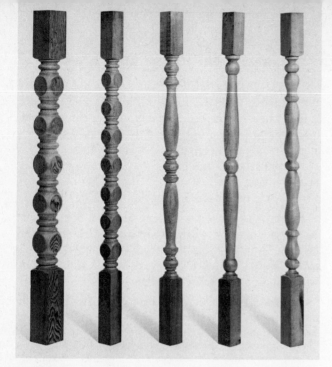

Wood turnings. Angelus Consolidated Industries.

Saw marks. Saw marks on one side of a board are unimportant if only one surface is to be exposed. Boards with saw marks on both sides should be avoided.

WOOD SPECIALTIES. Wood specialties include such things as boards and timbers of rare and exotic woods; veneers; nonstandard moldings and trims; turnings for use in balustrades, room dividers, window grilles, and furniture; and carved appliqués.

Many lumberyards carry turnings, but other specialties are difficult if not impossible to find in all except the largest cities where there are usually a few firms which cater to woodworkers. Some of these firms, however, also sell by mail.

WOOD PRESERVATIVES. Moisture and termites are the principal enemies of lumber, and while you don't have to worry about their effect on the wood (and plywood) used in most parts of the house, only a fool ignores what they can do to sills, joists, subfloors, sheathing, posts, steps, etc., which are close to the ground or in actual contact with the ground. The only way to protect yourself against costly damage to these parts of the house is to use wood which has natural resistance to decay (if it's resistant to decay, it's also resistant to termites) or to treat nonresistant wood with a wood preservative.

Only three woods commonly used in construction have natural resistance to decay and termites. They are redwood, cypress, and the cedars. In all three cases, the heartwood from the center of a tree has slightly better resistance than the sapwood cut from just inside the bark. (This is also generally true of other woods.) Even these woods, however, will eventually decay if exposed to constant dampness.

Other woods, such as pine, spruce, and Douglas fir, vary in their resistance to decay and termites, but none can be trusted for very long unless treated with a preservative. This can increase the life expectancy of the wood dramatically. For example, tests made by the U.S. Forest Products Laboratory show that while untreated southern-pine stakes driven into the ground in Mississippi have an average life of only 1.8 to 3.6 years, 50% of similar stakes which had been pressure-treated with one of the more common preservatives were still in serviceable condition after 26 years.

Many materials are used for preserving wood and plywood, but only four are generally available to the homeowner through lumberyards, hardware stores, and paint stores: creosote, pentachlorophenol, copper naphthanate, and zinc naphthanate.

Creosote, an old standby, is excellent but is generally applied only to wood which is buried in the ground, because it has an unpleasant odor, discolors the wood, and bleeds through finishes applied over it.

Copper naphthanate stains wood green, and for this reason is also rarely used in houses.

Zinc naphthanate and pentachlorophenol have no odor when dry and do not color wood unless they are premixed—as they sometimes are—with a stain. Both give good protection against decay and termites. They can, accordingly, be used anywhere inside or outside a house. But not all formulations can be painted over, so

Deck built of preservative-treated lumber. Koppers Co.

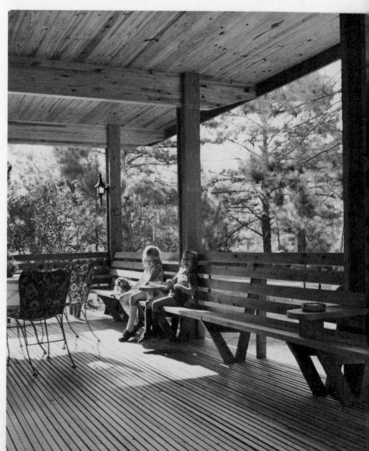

if you are planning to paint the wood you treat, make sure you buy a preservative which is labeled paintable.

No matter how good a preservative may be, however, its effectiveness depends on the way it is applied.

For maximum durability, preservative must be injected into wood under pressure. This can be done only in a factory, but wood treated in this way is sold through most lumberyards.

Wood that you treat yourself by brushing or dipping has a shorter life expectancy than pressure-treated wood, but is still far superior to untreated wood. Of the two methods, dipping is the better, provided you leave the wood immersed for about 24 hours. However, dipping often requires such huge containers and enormous quantities of preservative that it is not always practical.

Ideally, if you apply preservative yourself, you should make all cuts and holes in the wood before treatment. If you fail to do this, the cut surfaces must be treated separately. Cut surfaces in pressure-treated lumber must also be treated.

PLYWOOD

Plywood used for siding and paneling is discussed in other chapters.

Structural plywood is the ordinary material used for sheathing, subfloors, roof decks, painted cabinets, etc. Because it comes in large sheets, it can be installed much faster than solid lumber. It is extremely strong and rigid and eliminates need for bracing the framework to which it is applied. The quality is uniform.

Structural plywood was known for years as Douglas-fir plywood because it was made exclusively of this species of wood. If you ask for Douglas-fir plywood today, however, you may be given sheets of some 30 other species of wood. The majority are softwoods; a few are hardwoods. They are divided into four groups according to their stiffness.

Group 1 (stiffest)	*Group 2* (second stiffest)
Douglas fir	Port Orford cedar
Western larch	California red fir
Southern pine	Grand fir
Tanoak	Noble fir
	Pacific silver fir
	White fir
	Western hemlock
	Lauan
	Western white pine
	Sitka spruce
	Douglas fir from Nevada, Utah, Colorado, Arizona, New Mexico

Group 3 (third stiffest)	*Group 4* (least stiff)
Red alder	Incense cedar
Alaska yellow cedar	Western red cedar
Lodgepole pine	Subalpine fir
Ponderosa pine	Sugar pine
Redwood	Western poplar
	Englemann spruce

Plywood is made of three, five, or seven layers of wood, each at right angles to the next. The outer layers are called faces; the layers next below are called crossbands. All other inside layers are cores. Thus a three-ply panel has two faces and a core, while a five-ply panel has two faces, two crossbands, and a core.

The standard size of plywood panels is 4×8 ft. This is both the nominal and the actual size. Panels 10 and 12 ft. long are available, but not in all grades. Available thicknesses are ¼, ⁵⁄₁₆, ⅜, ½, ⅝, ¾, ⅞, 1, and 1⅛ in. (also not in all grades). The thicknesses are also actual.

The adhesive used in plywood determines whether the plywood is an interior grade, which must be used indoors only, or an exterior grade, which can be used outdoors as well as indoors in very damp locations.

Selecting the right grade of plywood for a project is easy if you understand the coding system used by American manufacturers. First consult the tables below; then examine the information stamped on the back of each panel. (Similar information is stamped on the edge of plywood construction-grade panels.) The stamp looks like this:

Grade of veneer on panel face

Special group
number

Shows where plywood
can be used

Product standard
governing manufacture

Grade of veneer on panel back

Grading seal used by the
American Plywood Assn.

Six letters are used to designate the veneer grades (indicated by the large hyphenated letters on the label):

N stands for "natural finish" veneer, all heartwood or sapwood. Free of open defects.

A means the veneer is smooth and paintable with neatly made repairs. The letter is also applied to natural-finish veneer in less demanding applications.

B stands for solid surface veneer with circular repair plugs and tight knots.

C means the veneer has knotholes up to 1 in. in diameter and occasional slightly larger knotholes. It may also have a few splits. No veneer of lesser grade is permitted in exterior plywood.

C Plugged is a C veneer which has been improved by plugging the largest knotholes. The veneer may, however, have knotholes and borer holes no larger than $\frac{1}{4} \times \frac{1}{2}$ in. Splits must not be more than $\frac{1}{8}$ in. wide.

D stands for veneer with knotholes up to $2\frac{1}{2}$ in. in diameter and a bit larger in some circumstances. It may also have splits.

Plywood used strictly for structural purposes is graded according to the following chart.

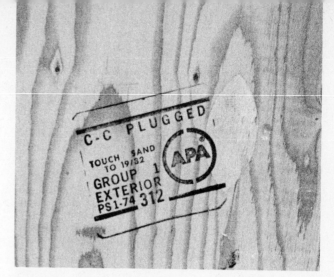

In the C-Plugged grade of plywood, the largest knotholes are cut out and replaced with patches of veneer like the light-colored oval plug just to right of label. American Plywood Assn.

GRADE-USE GUIDE FOR CONSTRUCTION AND INDUSTRIAL PLYWOOD

Interior type

Use these symbols when you specify plywood (1) (2)	Description and most common uses	Face	Back	Inner Plys
STANDARD INT-DFPA (3)	Unsanded interior sheathing grade for floors, walls, and roofs. Limited exposure crates, bins, containers, and pallets.	C	D	D
STANDARD INT-DFPA (3) (with exterior glue)	Same as standard sheathing but has exterior glue. For construction where unusual moisture conditions may be encountered. Often used for pallets, crates, bins, etc. that may be exposed to the weather.	C	D	D
STRUCTURAL I and STRUCTURAL II INT-DFPA	Unsanded structural grades where plywood design properties are of maximum importance. Structural diaphragms, box beams, gusset plates, stressed skin panels. Also for containers, pallets, bins. Made only with exterior glue. Structural I limited to Group 1 species for face, back and inner plies. Structural II permits Group 1, 2, or 3 species.	C	D	D
UNDERLAYMENT INT-DPFA (3)	For underlayment or combination subfloor-underlayment under resilient floor coverings, carpeting. Used in homes, apartments, mobile homes, commercial buildings. Ply beneath face is C or better veneer. Sanded or touch-sanded as specified.	C Plugged	D	C & D
C-D PLUGGED INT-DFPA (3)	For utility built-ins, backing for wall and ceiling tile. Not a substitute for underlayment. Ply beneath face permits D grade veneer. Also for cable reels, walkways, separator boards. Unsanded or touch-sanded as specified.	C Plugged	D	D
2-4-1 INT-DFPA (4)	Combination subfloor-underlayment. Quality base for resilient floor coverings, carpeting, wood strip flooring. Use 2-4-1 with exterior glue in areas subject to excessive moisture. Unsanded or touch-sanded as specified.	C Plugged	C	C & D

Exterior type

Use these symbols when you specify plywood (1) (2)	Description and most common uses	Face	Back	Inner Plys
C-C EXT-DFPA (3)	Unsanded grade with waterproof bond for subflooring and roof decking, siding on service and farm buildings. Backing, crating, pallets, pallet bins, cable reels.	C	C	C
C-C PLUGGED EXT-DFPA (3)	Use as a base for resilient floors and tile backing where unusual moisture conditions exist. For refrigerated or controlled atmosphere rooms. Also for pallets, fruit pallet bins, reusable cargo containers, tanks and boxcar and truck floors and linings. Sanded or touch-sanded as specified.	C Plugged	C	C

Use these symbols when you specify plywood (1) (2)	Description and most common uses	Face	Back	Inner Plys
STRUCTURAL I C-C EXT-DFPA	For engineered applications in construction and industry where full exterior type panels made with all Group 1 woods are required. Unsanded.	C	C	C
PLYFORM CLASS I & II B-B EXT-DFPA	Concrete form grades with high re-use factor. Sanded both sides. Edge-sealed and mill-oiled unless otherwise specified. Special restrictions on species.	B	B	C

Notes:
(1) All interior grades shown are also available with exterior glue
(2) All grades except Plyform available tongued and groove panels ½ in. and thicker
(3) Available in Group 1, 2, 3, or 4
(4) Available in Group 1, 2, or 3 only

Appearance grades of plywood which are exposed to view are graded according to the following chart. The plywood is sanded on both sides and available in Group 1, 2, 3, or 4 unless noted otherwise.

GRADE-USE GUIDE FOR APPEARANCE GRADES OF PLYWOOD

Interior type

Use these symbols when you specify plywood	Description and most common uses	Face	Back	Inner Plys
N-N, N-A, N-B, N-D INT-DFPA	Natural finish cabinet quality. One or both sides, select all heartwood or all sapwood veneer. For furniture having a natural finish, cabinet doors, built-ins. Use N-D for natural finish paneling. Special order items.	N	N, A B or D	C or D
A-A INT-DPFA	For interior applications where both sides will be on view. Built-ins, cabinets, furniture and partitions. Face is smooth and suitable for painting.	A	A	D
A-B INT-DFPA	For uses similar to Interior A-A but where the appearance of one side is less important and two smooth solid surfaces are necessary.	A	B	D
A-D INT-DFPA	For interior uses where the appearance of only one side is important. Paneling, built-ins, shelving, partitions and flow racks.	A	D	D

Use these symbols when you specify plywood	Description and most common uses	Face	Back	Inner Plys
B-B INT-DFPA	Interior utility panel used where two smooth sides are desired. Permits circular plugs. Paintable.	B	B	D
B-D INT-DFPA	Interior utility panel for use where one smooth side is required. Good for backing, sides or built-ins. Industry: shelving, slip sheets, separator boards and bins.	B	D	D
DECORATIVE PANELS	Rough-sawn, brushed, grooved or striated faces. Good for interior accent walls, built-ins, or counter facing, displays and btr. exhibits.	B or btr.	D	D
PLYRON INT-DFPA	Hardboard face on both sides. For counter tops, shelving, cabinet doors, flooring. Hardboard faces may be tempered, untempered, smooth or screened.			C & D

GRADE-USE GUIDE FOR APPEARANCE GRADES OF PLYWOOD

Exterior type

Use these symbols when you specify plywood	Description and most common uses	Face	Back	Inner Plys
A-A EXT-DFPA	Use where the appearance of both sides is important. Fences, built-ins, signs, boats, cabinets, commercial refrigerators, shipping containers, tote boxes, tanks and ducts.	A	A	C
A-B EXT-DFPA	For use similar to A-A EXT panels but where the appearance of one side is less important.	A	B	C
A-C EXT-DFPA	Exterior use where the appearance of only one side is important. Sidings, soffits, fences, structural uses, boxcar and truck lining and farm buildings. Tanks, trays, commercial refrigerators.	A	C	C
B-C EXT-DFPA	An outdoor utility panel for farm service and work buildings, box car and truck linings, containers, tanks, agricultural equipment.	B	C	C
B-B EXT-DFPA	An outdoor utility panel with solid paintable faces for uses where higher quality is not necessary.	B	B	C
HDO EXT-DFPA	Exterior type high-density-overlay plywood with hard, semi-opaque resin-fiber overlay. Abrasion resistant. Painting not ordinarily required. For concrete forms, signs, acid tanks, cabinets, counter tops.	A or B	A or B	C Plugged
MDO EXT-DFPA	Exterior type medium-density-overlay with smooth, opaque resin fiber overlay heat-fused to one or both panel faces. Ideal base for paint. Highly recommended for siding and other outdoor applications. Also good for built-ins, signs and displays.	B	B or C	C

Use these symbols when you specify plywood	Description and most common uses	Face	Back	Inner Plys
303 SPECIAL SIDING EXT-DFPA	Grade designation covers proprietary plywood products for exterior siding, fencing, etc., with special surface treatment such as V-groove, channel groove, striated, brushed, rough sawn.	B or btr.	C	C
T 1-11 EXT-DFPA	Exterior type, sanded or unsanded, shiplapped edges with parallel grooves ¼" deep. ⅜" wide. Grooves 2" or 4" o.c. Available in 8' and 10' lengths and MD overlay. For siding and accent paneling.	C or btr.	C	C
PLYRON EXT-DFPA	Exterior panel surfaced both sides with hardboard for use in exterior applications. Faces are tempered, smooth or screened.			C
MARINE EXT-DFPA	Exterior type plywood made only with Douglas fir or western larch. Special solid jointed core construction. Subject to special limitations on core gaps and number of face repairs. Ideal for boat hulls. Also available with overlaid faces.	A or B	A or B	B
SPECIAL EXTERIOR	Premium exterior panel similar to marine grade but permits any species covered under PS 1-66.	A or B	A or B	B

Charts from American Plywood Assn.

CEMENT

Most of the cement used in construction is Portland cement, which is so named because, when it hardens, it resembles the stone found in various quarries on the Isle of Portland, England. But several other cements are used for repair work.

The types of cement you are most likely to use are the following. The first three are sold in sacks containing 1 cu. ft. and weighing 94 lb. The others are sold in small packages.

Type 1 Portland cement is used in the great majority of masonry projects. The standard color is gray, but white cement can be purchased at a slightly higher price.

Type 1A Portland cement is an air-entrained cement which forms millions of microscopic air bubbles in concrete. These greatly increase the resistance of the concrete to damage by severe frost and by heavy applications of salt for snow removal.

Masonry cement is a Portland cement to which a small amount of lime is added at the factory (you can make your own masonry cement by adding hydrated lime to Type 1 Portland cement). It is used for laying bricks, concrete blocks, and other masonry units.

Hydraulic cement is a dark-gray cement which hardens in the presence of moisture. It is used for plugging active leaks in masonry walls and floors.

Latex, epoxy, vinyl, and acrylic cements have the unique ability of adhering tightly—without cracking—to masonry surfaces even when troweled to a feather edge about $\frac{1}{16}$ in. thick. (By contrast, Portland cement cannot be used in thickness of much less than $\frac{1}{2}$ in.) They are therefore recommended for leveling uneven surfaces as well as for repairing cracks.

Hydraulic, latex, epoxy, vinyl, and acrylic cements are used as they come from the package. You just mix them with water (or in the case of latex and epoxy cements, with a special liquid) and apply them.

Portland and masonry cements, on the other hand, must be mixed with an aggregate in addition to water. Two aggregates are used with Types 1 and 1A Portland cement: builder's sand (never sea sand) and clean pebbles or crushed rocks between $\frac{1}{4}$ and $1\frac{1}{2}$ in. in diameter. The amounts used depend on the purpose of the cement.

Masonry cement is mixed with sand alone. The most common mixture contains 1 part cement and 3 parts sand.

If you don't feel up to preparing your own concrete, you can buy ready-mixes in sacks to which you merely add water. The mixes are formulated for different purposes, such as laying masonry or pouring a slab. Each sack holds somewhat less than 1 cu. ft., so if you need a specific quantity of cement, you should make sure beforehand exactly how much a sack holds and figure accordingly.

For large pouring jobs—if, for example, you are pouring a concrete base for a new brick terrace—the best way to buy concrete is from a company which mixes it in the plant and delivers it in concrete trucks ready for pouring. Most companies, unfortunately, limit deliveries to batches of 5 cu. yd. or more. A few, however, will sell as little as 1 cu. yd. All deliveries are made at the time you set. Before calling for a delivery, you must have the forms for the concrete in place so you can pour the concrete as soon as it arrives. If kept in the truck too long, it is useless. Furthermore, you must pay a waiting charge if you don't get the concrete into the forms within the time specified by the company.

Mixing your own concrete is a tiring job but not difficult. You can use a rented mixer which is turned by hand or an electric motor, or do the job with a hoe and shovel on a large wood or plywood platform. In either case, you should build a box exactly $12 \times 12 \times 12$ in. on the inside to measure out the ingredients.

Mix the cement and sand first until they are blended to an even gray. Then work in the coarse aggregate until it is distributed evenly through the mixture. Finally, add water in measured amounts according to the mixture you're making.

To color concrete, buy a special powdered pigment from a masonry supplies dealer and mix it with the cement and sand before the aggregate and water are added. With the pigments you can produce blue, brown, buff, green, red, gray, and black concrete. For white concrete, use white Portland cement.

The amount of pigment used must be carefully controlled, because a little goes a long way and too much may affect the strength of the concrete. It should not exceed more than 10% of the weight of the cement (in other words, for each sack of cement use no more than 9.4 lb. of pigment). To produce the purest colors, use white cement.

Concrete can also be colored when dry by brushing on special concrete stains. The color, however, is rarely uniform over the entire surface.

An annoying problem with many concrete floors, whether colored or natural, is their tendency to give off a fine dust as they are subjected to wear. This cannot be predicted and is difficult to prevent during construction. But it can be stopped if it does start by swabbing the floor with chemical hardeners and dustproofers containing fluosilicates.

WHO MAKES IT

Angelus Consolidated Industries, Inc. · Wood turnings in many designs up to 6 ft. long. Finials.

Anti-Hydro Waterproofing Co. · Concrete hardener and dustproofer.

Bondex International, Inc. · Fast-setting cement for anchoring metal in masonry. Latex cement. Vinyl cement.

CGM, Inc. · E-Z concrete dustproofer and hardener.

Albert Constantine & Son. · 101 kinds of natural wood veneers; also dyed veneers. Wood inlay strips. Hardwood boards in nominal 8- and 10-in. widths up to 6 ft. long. Carved wood appliqués.

Darworth Co. · Cuprinol zinc and copper naphthanate; also with stains added.

Flair-Fold, Inc. · Walnut-stained, rough-hewn boards in 8-ft. lengths and 3-, 4-, and 5-in. widths.

Gibson-Homans Co. · Pentachlorophenol wood preservative.

Homecraft Veneer. · 140 natural wood veneers plus dyed veneers.

Koppers Co. · Wolmanized lumber, plywood, poles, and posts pressure-treated with preservative.

Morgan Co. · Turned spindles up to 8 ft. long.

Morgan Veneers. · Innumerable natural wood veneers plus crotch, burl and swirl veneers. Wood inlay strips. Decorated inlays and overlays.

E. A. Nord Co. · Wood turnings in many designs from 2½×7½ in. to 4×96 in.

Potlatch Corp. · Plywood panels with flakeboard cores.

Savogran. · Pentachlorophenol wood preservative.

Sears Roebuck & Co. · Latex cement.

Sonoco Products Co. · Fiberboard tubes used to form concrete piers and columns from 8 to 36 in. in diameter and from 32 in. to 25 ft. in length.

Standard Dry Wall Products. · Latex cement. Concrete hardener. Concrete leveler.

United Gilsonite Laboratories. · Drylok latex cement. Concrete hardener.

Waterlox Chemical & Coatings Corp. · Pentachlorophenol wood preservative, clear or with stain added.

Woodcraft Millwork Specialties. · Hardwood appliqués.

Woodcraft Supply Corp. · Hardwood boards in 6- and 8-in. widths to 3 ft. long.

2

Exterior Walls

Hardly a month goes by that the homeowner doesn't receive an unsolicited reminder that his house should be re-sided. The air waves and newspapers are full of advertisers pushing their favorite brands of siding; and even if you're able to ignore these, you will sooner or later get a phone call: "Mr. Schuler, do you own your home? Well, then, I'd like to tell you about our new aluminum siding that never needs painting, keeps out the cold. . . ." and on and on.

The truth is that the majority of houses do not have such dilapidated exterior walls that they need to be rebuilt. Nevertheless, siding manufacturers and suppliers flourish because hundreds of thousands of homeowners either are fed up with maintaining their present siding or think that something else will look better and perhaps be more practical. In addition, there are countless others who suddenly find themselves thinking about siding because they are adding a room or a garage or perhaps simply a dormer.

SHEATHING. Only a handful of houses have solid masonry walls. Most of these are made of concrete block; a very few are made of brick or stone.

In standard construction, exterior walls are framed with 2×4s, which are covered on the outside with sheathing and a layer of building paper. The siding, if nailable, is applied directly over the paper. Masonry veneer is separated from the sheathing by a narrow air space and held secure with metal ties nailed to the sheathing.

In addition to serving as the base for siding, sheathing stiffens and strengthens the walls, increases their insulating value, and helps to keep out air and water. It is omitted only in low-cost houses which are sided with plywood or hardboard.

To reduce cost, building paper is also eliminated sometimes. But it is essential in houses sheathed with boards and is highly desirable in all quality construction because it seals out moisture, air, and dust.

In the past, all sheathing was made of 1-in. boards nailed diagonally or horizontally to the studs (in the latter case, long boards are notched into the studs at the corners of the house to brace the framing). Today, plywood, particleboard, fiberboard, urethane board, or gypsum board is normally used.

Plywood for sheathing is a rough exterior grade, preferably $\frac{1}{2}$ in. thick; $\frac{5}{16}$- and $\frac{3}{8}$-in. thicknesses are also used but do not hold nails as well. Because of plywood's exceptional strength, no bracing is needed.

Particleboard sheathing is an inexpensive material made of wood chips or flakes which are coated with phenolic resin and bonded together under pressure. It is used under any nail-on siding and stucco in $\frac{1}{2}$-in. thicknesses. Bracing of the frame is recommended.

Fiberboard sheathing is a water-resistant panel made of compressed wood fibers. It is $\frac{1}{2}$, $\frac{5}{8}$, or $\frac{25}{32}$ in. thick. If the walls are shingled, the sheathing should be of a type suitable for holding nails. Standard fiberboard sheathing can be used only with larger siding materials which can be nailed through it into the studs. Diagonal bracing of the framing is required if the fiberboard is installed horizontally but not, as a rule, if it is installed vertically. One advantage of this kind of sheathing is its insulating value; however, this is not enough to obviate the need for mineral-wool or fiberglass insulation in the stud spaces. Some boards are treated for fire resistance.

Urethane-foam sheathing, made with a rigid foam core faced on both sides with paper or aluminum foil, has such high insulating value that no other insulation is required. (A $\frac{7}{10}$-in. board covered with $\frac{3}{4}$-in. wood siding has an R value of 11.8; used with brick veneer, an R value of 14.3. R values are explained in Chapter 4.) It comes in standard thicknesses of $\frac{2}{5}$ to $1\frac{1}{4}$ in. The framing must be braced.

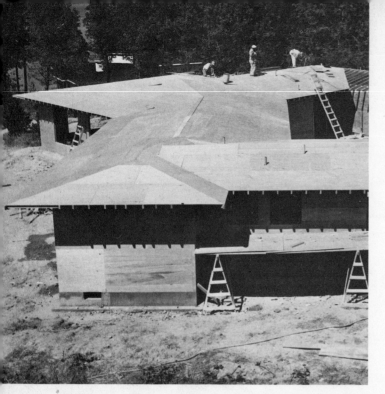

A new house with walls and roof sheathed with plywood. American Plywood Assn.

Gypsum-board sheathing, unlike interior gypsum board, has an asphalted core faced on both sides with water-repellent paper. It is ½ inch thick and can be installed vertically without bracing of the frame, but bracing is needed if it is used horizontally. The material retards fire.

TYPES OF SIDING

WOOD SHINGLES. Exterior walls have been surfaced with wood shingles since colonial times; and even though the shingles do not last forever and usually require more maintenance than other sidings, it's not likely that they will ever disappear from the scene, simply because their textured beauty has so much appeal and is so well suited to houses of most designs.

Almost all shingles are made of western red cedar, but some are of eastern white cedar or redwood. Standard rectangular shingles are sold in bundles of random widths (up to a maximum of 14 in.) and uniform lengths of either 16, 18, or 24 in. Red-cedar shingles are graded No. 1 Blue Label (the best), No. 2 Red Label, No. 3 Black Label, and No. 4 Undercoursing. Two other types of shingle are called rebutted-rejointed shingles (available in No. 1 and No. 2 grades) and grooved sidewall shakes (available in No. 1 grade). The former differ from standard shingles in that they are machine-trimmed to precise rectangles to produce tightly fitting joints between shingles. Units with smoothly sanded faces are available. Grooved sidewall shakes, despite their name, are like rebutted-rejointed shingles except that their faces have been grooved.

They are available in natural cedar color as well as in a variety of factory-applied colors.

Grooved shakes as well as conventional shingles and rough-sawn shingles can also be had in assembled 4- or 8-ft.-long panels which permit rapid installation over sheathing or directly to studs. Two-ply panels are made with an insulating backer board; three-ply panels with a plywood backing. Both are available with matching corner pieces.

A more unusual red-cedar shingle is the fancy butt type, which is so called because, instead of being squared off, the butts are cut into some 14 different shapes ranging from simple Vs and diagonals to intriguing wave and acorn patterns. These measure a standard 5×15 in.

Wood shingles can be applied directly over old walls which will hold nails, but when this is done they usually project beyond the door and window casings; consequently, you must nail moldings around the edges of the casings to increase their thickness. For this reason, you may prefer to remove the old siding—especially if it is made of easy-to-rip-off shingles—and nail the new shingles to the sheathing.

On non-nailable walls and stucco, install horizontal furring strips and nail the shingles to these. Moldings must be applied around the edges of the casings.

Shingles are applied in either a single or double course. In a single-coursed wall there are two layers of shingles at every point. The shingle area which is exposed to the weather should not exceed half the length of the shingles minus ½ in. In other words, maximum exposure for 16-in. shingles is 7½ in.; for 18-inchers, 8½ in.; and for 24-inchers, 11½ in.

In double coursing, the wall is covered with a layer of inexpensive undercoursing-grade shingles over which the finish shingles are laid. This method of construction permits you to increase the exposures to a maximum of 12 in. for 16-in. shingles, 14 in. for 18-in. shingles, and 16 in. for 24-in. shingles. In addition, the shadow lines at the butts are deepened and the insulating value of the siding is increased.

To shingle a wall, use rust-resistant shingle nails and place them about ¾ in. in from the two edges of each shingle. On shingles more than 8 in. wide, center a third nail between the others. In single coursing, the nails are driven in 1 in. above the butts of the next higher course. In double coursing, they are placed 2 in. above the butt of the shingle being nailed. Don't try to countersink them, since this may split the shingles.

The bottom or starter course on a single-coursed wall is two shingles thick; on a double-coursed wall, three shingles thick. Throughout both walls, the vertical joints between shingles must be offset at least 1½ in. In double coursing, the under layer of shingles is placed ½ in. higher than the surface layer.

Outside corners are made by butting the edge of a

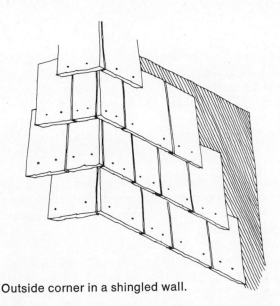

Outside corner in a shingled wall.

A pleasant blending of three types of wood siding: clapboards, board-and-batten, and shiplap.

shingle on one wall to the back of the shingle on the other wall. The overlap alternates between successive courses. Inside corners are most easily made by nailing 1½-in.-square strips of wood into them and butting the shingles to the sides.

At the heads of doors and windows, the butts of the shingles on both sides should be aligned with the top edges of the casings so that the shingles above the casings do not have to be cut off at the bottom. The shingle exposure should be calculated to permit this.

Completed walls can be allowed to weather to a silvery but nonuniform gray, treated with a water repellent, stained, or painted.

SHAKES. Shakes are thick, handsplit shingles usually made of western red cedar. In addition to having a longer life and greater insulating value than wood shingles, they produce a rugged, rustic effect totally unlike that of any other siding.

Shakes are sold in bundles of random widths and uniform 18- or 24-in. lengths. There are three grades. No. 1 Handsplit and Resawn have split faces and sawn backs so they lie flat on the subwall. No. 1 Tapersplit is rough-split on both sides. No. 1 Straight-Split is also rough-split on both sides but is the same thickness from end to end. Preassembled 4- and 8-ft. shake panels are also available.

Walls are usually single-coursed, with a maximum exposure of 8½ in. for 18-in. shakes and 11½ in. for 24-in. shakes. But double coursing is used. In one system, the shakes are applied over ordinary wood shingles and given an exposure of up to 14 and 20 in. respectively. In the other system, 18-in. straight-split shakes are laid over themselves with 16-in. exposure; and 24-in. straight-split shakes are given 22-in. exposure.

Installation is like that for wood shingles. Finishing is also similar; however, paint should not be used because it wears off more rapidly on the ridges than in the grooves.

WOOD SIDING. Because of its generally greater thickness, board siding has more durability and insulating value than wood shingles. Some types are thick enough to be nailed directly to studs, although this method of application is limited to garages and accessory buildings.

The patterns available are so numerous that lumberyards do not attempt to carry all. A recent publication by the Western Wood Products Association shows 21, of which probably no more than half a dozen can be delivered immediately from any one yard. They fall into eight basic but confusing categories. *Plain square-edged boards* are installed vertically with battens nailed over the joints. *Bevel siding,* including clapboards, is wedge-shaped and is installed horizontally with the thick butts overlapping the thin top edges. *Rabbeted bevel siding* is made with a rabbet behind the butts so the siding lies flat against the sheathing. *Anzac siding* is a modified form of bevel siding. *Shiplap* is an ordinary board (sometimes with chamfered edges) with rabbets cut in both sides so the adjoining boards can be interlocked. *Rustic siding* is a form of shiplap with the surfaces milled to a few special designs. *Drop siding* is made with either tongue-and-groove or rabbeted edges and has a considerable variety of patterns cut into the surface. And *log-cabin siding* has a rounded contour and one rabbeted edge which overlaps an adjacent squared edge. All sidings which are rabbeted or tongue-and-groove can be installed vertically as well as horizontally, although the latter installation is more common.

The woods used for siding are the common softwoods as well as western red cedar and redwood. Use select grades when the pocketbook permits. Antique

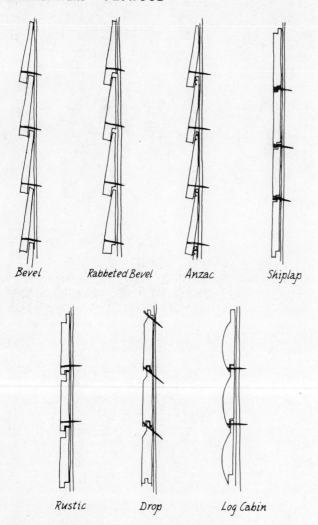

Bevel   Rabbeted Bevel   Anzac   Shiplap

Rustic   Drop   Log Cabin

Seven types of horizontal board siding.

and artificially weathered barn boards are available.

All wood sidings, as a rule, should be applied to sheathing or a level nailable finish wall. It is possible, however, to apply wide bevel siding over old shingles or bevel siding; and any vertical siding can also be applied over shingles or bevel siding. Horizontal siding can be applied directly over stucco if care is taken to position the boards so they can be nailed at the ends and between the ends to the studs; but vertical siding must be nailed to horizontal furring strips nailed over the stucco. Masonry walls must also be furred out.

A number of sidings, particularly the bevel type, are finished so that either side can be exposed. One side is smooth; the other rough-sawn. The latter is especially suited for staining.

Use rust-resistant nails. On bevel and rabbeted sidings, these are driven through the face of the boards about 1 in. above the butts. Countersink the heads and cover them with putty. In tongue-and-groove sidings, the nails are driven through the tongues so they are concealed. On plain board siding, the nails are placed near the edges and concealed by battens.

When installing horizontal siding, stagger the end joints. Position the boards so that the edge joints align with the tops of door and window casings. At inside corners, butt the boards to a square strip of wood nailed into the corner. At outside corners, the boards may be butted to vertical corner boards, lapped like shingles, mitered, or covered with special metal corner pieces.

In vertical siding, use boards which are long enough to span from the bottom to the top of the wall in order to eliminate end joints (but this is not always possible on very tall houses).

Board-and-batten siding is made, as a rule, with 12-in. boards nailed vertically and with 1×2-in. or 1×3-in. boards (battens) nailed over the joints. In batten-and-board siding, this arrangement is reversed: the battens are nailed to the sheathing and the boards are laid over these so that about 1 in. of the battens is exposed. Board-and-board siding is made entirely of 12-in. boards with every other board nailed to the sheathing and the alternate boards overlapping their edges.

Diagonal siding, which has become popular in recent years, is made with flush tongue-and-groove boards.

All sidings can be allowed to weather or can be finished with a water repellent, stain, or paint. Stains, however, achieve maximum durability when used on rough-sawn lumber.

PLYWOOD. Plywood siding imparts greater strength to the structure than solid wood, but has lower insulating value. When installed in large 4×8-, 4×9-, or 4×10-ft. panels, it reduces construction time. Medium-density-overlaid (MDO) plywoods, made by bonding a phenolic-resin-impregnated fiber sheet to the plywood, holds paint better than bare wood or plywood; and coated sidings have a tough factory finish which is guaranteed for many years.

To the purist, plywood's principal deficiency—which it shares with all other sidings—is that it lacks the full textured beauty of solid wood. This is not to say, however, that it is unattractive. Although it is not available in the more elaborate patterns of drop siding, there is a great variety of styles and textures. Panel sidings are most often made to resemble vertical board or board-and-batten siding, but also come in smooth panels as well as in panels surfaced with small stone chips to look like rough stucco or concrete. Lap sidings measuring 6 to 12 in. wide and 6 to 16 ft. long are installed like solid bevel siding and look almost exactly like it except that the exposure is generally greater.

The woods used to make plywood siding are the same as those used for structural plywood. Some sidings have redwood and cedar faces.

As noted earlier, in new construction, plywood siding can be installed directly over studs. Panels ⅜ in. thick require a stud spacing of 16 in.; ½-in. and ⅝-in. panels can be used with a stud spacing of 24 in. But the use of sheathing is recommended.

For re-siding, the panels can be nailed over any level, nailable wall, including stucco; but if the wall is shingled or surfaced with bevel siding, the old material should be removed. Masonry walls must be furred out. Lap plywood sidings are applied to the sheathing or to vertical furring strips.

Apply large plywood panels with rust-resistant nails spaced 6 in. apart around the edges and 12 in. apart over intermediate studs. Lap sidings are nailed 16 in. on center 1 in. up from the bottom edge.

Allow a $\frac{1}{16}$-in. space between all plywood sheets. This does not have to be caulked if the edges of the sheets are shiplapped (as they usually are) or backed by building paper. But all corner joints must be caulked.

For lap siding, inside corners are made by butting the strips to a square corner block; outside corners are usually covered with metal corner pieces. Large panels are simply scribed and butted at inside corners. At outside corners, they are covered with thin wood strips or butted to corner boards.

Painting of unfinished textured plywoods is generally not recommended. Use a penetrating stain on fir panels. Cedar and redwood can be allowed to weather or are treated with a water repellent.

On unfinished smooth-surfaced plywood, use an oil-base primer followed by one or two coats of oil-base or latex paint. Medium-density-overlaid sidings are finished in the same way (but the prime coat is omitted if the plywood was primed at the factory).

Three types of hardboard siding: vertical boards applied in 4×8-ft. panels, Georgia-Pacific Corp.; horizontal lap siding, Masonite Corp.; panels textured to resemble stucco, Masonite Corp.

HARDBOARD. Looking at hardboard and plywood siding panels for the first time in a big "home center," you would probably be hard put to see any differences between them. But there are some:

Although the wood (and other) textures given hardboard panels are remarkably true to life, they do not quite capture the texture of unfinished plywood. But neither does medium-density-overlaid plywood. The spitting likeness that so many people see between hardboard and plywood siding is actually between hardboard and MDO plywood.

Hardboard siding does not weather to wood's pleas-

ing gray, nor can it be given a transparent penetrating stain so the texture and character of the "wood" shows through. The only way you can finish hardboard siding is with paint or an opaque stain.

Because hardboard is made of cellulose fibers which are heated and pressed together, it is much denser than wood or plywood and has greater resistance to the transmission of sound. It also has greater dimensional stability and resistance to moisture, and has no grain which can raise or check. On the other hand, although it is a very strong material, it does not stiffen or strengthen walls to the same extent as plywood, nor does it have as much resistance to impact.

Finally, hardboard is more flexible than plywood and can therefore be formed into simple bends and curves.

Hardboard sidings are made in 4×8-ft. or 4×9-ft. panels and in lap sidings up to 12 in. wide and 16 ft. long. Both are $7/16$ in. thick. They are available unfinished, primed, or with a complete factory finish which is guaranteed for years. Most of the sidings resemble wood; one looks like rough stucco.

They are installed like plywood over the same kind of base. Unfinished sidings are coated with an oil-base primer followed by one or two coats of oil-base or latex house paint; or they may be stained with an opaque stain. Primed sidings are painted in the same way or may be finished with a heavy-bodied stain.

PARTICLEBOARD.
The conventional particleboard siding is a low-cost $3/8$-in. or $5/8$-in. sheet consisting of a particleboard core overlaid on both sides with a resin-impregnated fiber sheet. Made in 4-ft.-wide panels which are installed vertically and in strips which are lapped horizontally, it has the texture of solid wood and is handled and finished like plywood siding.

Standard 4×8-ft. particleboard panels without an overlay can also be used for siding. These are generally smooth-surfaced but are available with grooves. They should be finished with an oil-base primer under an oil-

Overlaid particleboard siding. Georgia-Pacific Corp.

base or latex top coat. They give a more interesting and attractive effect if stained, but stains do not give as much protection against the weather, with the result that some of the chips or flakes may fall out.

FIBERBOARD.
Although panels made of compressed cellulose fibers can be dented with a fingernail and lack the impact resistance of plywood and other materials, they are used on exterior walls because they are relatively low in cost and have above-average insulating value. They are resistant to moisture, termites, and rot. The same panels can be used on interior walls, for porch and carport ceilings, and for sheathing.

Fiberboard grades vary from standard to extra strong. The normal size is 4×8 ft., $1/2$ in. thick, but you can also buy 8-ft. widths; 6-, 7-, 10-, 12-, and 14-ft. lengths; and $5/8$-in. thickness.

All the panels have a linenlike texture. They come unfinished (you must apply an oil-base primer and top-coat of oil-base house paint); primed and ready for finishing with oil-base or latex paint; or factory-finished with an acrylic film in several colors which is guaranteed for ten years.

Fiberboard siding can be nailed directly to studs or over sheathing. Joints are gapped $1/4$ in., caulked, and covered with battens.

ASBESTOS-CEMENT.
One of the oldest prefinished sidings, asbestos-cement—which is also called mineral-fiber—has been considerably improved since its early days. It was always an extremely durable, fireproof material but had a tendency to powder or crack. Today these defects have been eliminated. In addition, most of the sidings are given a tough, colorful acrylic coating that is easy to clean and rarely needs refinishing.

The sidings are produced in three forms: shingles striated to resemble wood and measuring 12×24×$3/16$ in.; clapboards measuring 9×32×$3/16$ in.; and panels with a smooth or pebbled texture measuring 4 ft. wide, 4, 8, 9, 10, or 12 ft. long, and $1/8$ (standard) to $3/8$ in. thick. The panels are available with or without a factory finish.

All asbestos-cement sidings should be applied over a sound, level base that holds nails and will support the heavy weight of the sidings. Board and $1/2$-in. plywood and particleboard sheathing meet these requirements; other sheathings do not unless special application methods are used. If you are re-siding, you can apply asbestos-cement materials directly to level wood siding as well as to any other level, nailable material (plywood or particleboard, for example) provided that it is laid over wood, plywood, or particleboard sheathing. To re-side over bevel siding, beveled wood strips must be nailed below the butts of the old siding to provide a level surface. Stucco usually should be removed but need not be if special application methods are used.

Asbestos-cement shingles. GAF Corp.

The average do-it-yourselfer should attempt to install asbestos-cement shingles or clapboards only if the subwall is level and nailable. In this case, start by nailing a ¼ × 1½-in. wood strip along the bottom edge of the sheathing to give the necessary cant to the first strip of shingles.

Arrange the shingles or clapboards so that the vertical joints between one course bisect the shingles or clapboards in the adjoining courses. Lap courses 1 in. Use the colored nails which come with the siding and drive them through the predrilled holes. Insert asphalt-saturated backer strips (also provided by the manufacturer) behind all vertical joints.

Inside corners are made by butting the siding courses together or to a square corner strip. At outside corners, the courses are lapped like shingles, butted to corner boards, or covered with metal corner pieces.

Cut asbestos-cement with a crosscut saw. Nail holes are most safely made by drilling.

Large panels are applied with special rust-resistant screw nails spaced 8 in. apart around the perimeter and 16 in. over intermediate studs. Holes for the nails do not have to be drilled or punched. Allow ⅟₁₆ in. space between vertical joints; center asphalt backer strips behind them, and cover them with wood battens. The alternative is to finish the joints with extruded aluminum strips available with a porcelain enamel finish to match prefinished panels.

METAL. The extraordinary success of aluminum and, to a lesser extent, steel siding is attributable to two compelling sales appeals: Maintenance problems will be reduced and you'll save fuel. There can be little doubt about the first proposition; but the second, while true, is exaggerated.

Both aluminum and steel siding are made of relatively thin-gauge metal covered at the factory with a tough, colored plastic or baked-on finish which is guaranteed against chipping, flaking, cracking, or peeling—everything except fading—for up to 30 years. As a re-

sult, there is no need for periodic refinishing; to keep your house looking fresh, you just wash it occasionally. You have no worries about splitting, warping, or decay.

The insulating value of the siding is attributable not to the siding itself but to the way in which it's installed. Two methods are used. In the less expensive and less effective, the subwall is covered with aluminum foil. In the better method, rigid insulating board about ⅜ in. thick is applied to the back of the siding. But unfortunately, this does not have sufficient R value to make a major dent in fuel costs. You still need to pack insulation into the stud spaces to achieve significant savings.

The differences between aluminum and steel sidings are minor. Steel is considerably stronger and more resistant to damage if struck a blow. But if the finish is damaged, the base metal will start to rust, whereas the aluminum will not. Both materials tend to be noisy in driving storms and high winds. And both may create an electrical hazard if, through some mishap, they are energized by faulty wiring or appliances. For this reason, some building codes require that they be grounded with No. 8 wire to a copper ground rod.

The most popular materials look like smooth or textured bevel wood siding. In some patterns, each siding strip is a single wide clapboard; others have two narrow clapboards per strip. There are also strips which are textured like cedar shingles or shakes, and others which are textured and installed vertically to resemble board-and-batten construction.

When buying metal siding, you should use the type with an insulation backing, not only because it adds to the comfort of your home but also because the backing helps to stiffen the metal and make it quieter.

Installation of metal siding is generally left to a professional, because while the strips and various necessary accessories such as corners and casing trims are designed to interlock securely to keep out water, one mistake can bring on trouble. However, it is perfectly feasible to do the job yourself if you follow the manu-

Steel siding during installation. Lumaside, Inc.

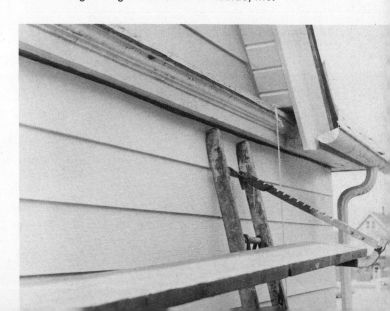

facturer's directions, which vary slightly among brands.

You can apply the siding directly over sheathing as well as over old sidings which are level and nailable. If your house is shingled or clapboarded, install wedge-shaped feathering strips as necessary below the butts. Masonry walls must be furred out with 1×3-in. strips installed vertically for lap siding or horizontally for vertical siding.

Before applying the siding strips, install a starter course at the base of the walls, inside and outside corner strips, door and window trim, and gable trim. The first siding panel is then set in the starter strip, locked in place, and nailed along the top edge. Use aluminum nails with aluminum siding, and galvanized steel nails with steel siding. The nails are centered in nailing slots provided by the manufacturer. They must not be driven tight; otherwise the strips cannot move laterally as they expand and contract.

Interlock the butts in each course with the flanges in the top edges of the course below. Lap end joints between strips 1 in. At corners, doors, and windows, fit the strips into the previously installed accessory strips, and allow ¼-in. space for expansion and contraction. Despite such gaps, water cannot enter. There is usually no need for caulking.

Vertical panels are applied in the same way. However, the installation must be planned so that only the end strips at the corners have to be cut. (In other words, install the first strip in the center of the wall and work from this toward the corners.) Unless exposed joints are interlocked, they cannot be made reliably watertight.

Both aluminum and steel siding can be cut with a rotary saw, hacksaw, and/or snips; but in cases where this is likely to damage the finish, special cutting tools must be borrowed or rented from the dealer.

INSULATED METAL PANELS. Large panels made of two sheets of aluminum or steel with rigid urethane or polystyrene foam sandwiched in between are generally used in industrial and commercial buildings, but there is no reason why they should not be used in homes. Designed for post-and-beam construction (see Chapter 3), they are strong, rigid, weathertight, and easily installed and have excellent insulation value.

The panels are made in standard sizes 46 in. wide and 8, 9, 10, and 12 ft. long. They are 2, 3, or 4 in. thick. The colorful exterior face sheets are smooth or embossed to resemble rough-sawn lumber or stucco. Other materials such as plywood, plastic laminates, and gypsum board can be laminated to either the front or back of the panels on special order. Almost identical panels are available for covering roofs.

The panels are suitable for replacement of exterior wall materials in old post-and-beam houses, but are primarily adapted to new construction. They should, as a rule, be installed only by professionals.

VINYL. Vinyl siding came along after aluminum had proved there is a tremendous market in the U.S. for a relatively easily applied re-siding material that requires little maintenance. If anything, it outperforms aluminum because it has no surface coating. The color is an integral part of the vinyl and extends all the way through, so even if it is gouged, you don't have to touch it up or worry about corrosion.

In addition, because of vinyl's resilience (except in very cold weather), it does not dent if struck a blow, and it is less noisy when pounded with hail or rain or rattled by wind.

There is no danger of electrical shock.

On the other hand, vinyl costs more than the best-quality metal. And although it does not support combustion, it will soften and droop if you let a grass or brush fire burn too close.

In all other respects, however, vinyl siding is difficult to distinguish from its metal competitors. It's available in the same horizontal and vertical patterns, and it is installed in the same way.

FIBERGLASS. Fiberglass-reinforced plastic siding enables you to cover your exterior walls with realistic imitation bricks or cut stones or somewhat less realistic imitation wood shakes in about half the time it would normally take to install the real thing. Made in panels 4 or 5 ft. long and 10 to 17 in. wide, depending on the design, the siding is applied to any nailable, level wall or to vertical furring strips. Edges are interlocked to keep out water. Outside corners are covered with L-shaped pieces which match the flat panels. Edge joints in brick and stone siding are filled with sealer to match the built-in "mortar" joints.

All the sidings come in several colors.

Walls need little maintenance, since the fiberglass is integrally colored and has relatively few joints which might leak. Most soil and stains are easy to wash off. Air spaces behind the panels have some insulating value. However, the panels are only moderately resistant to heat and impact.

BRICK. Re-siding a house with genuine clay brick can be much easier than most people suspect. You can do it yourself with 1-in.-thick nail-on bricks or ¼-in.-thick glue-on bricks. The installation procedure is described in Chapter 8.

Standard bricks are another matter. Even though you may have built garden walls, installation of brick veneer should be made only by a mason to ensure that it won't collapse or leak.

If the existing wall is concrete or concrete block, the

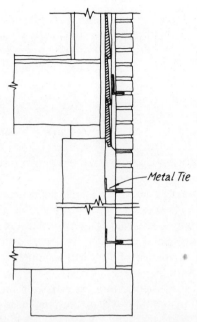

A 1-inch air gap separates new brick veneer from old wood siding.

brick can be plastered to it with cement mortar. Over a frame wall (and also over a concrete or concrete-block wall), the brick is separated from the old wall surface by a 1-in. air gap, which increases insulation value and allows for the escape of moisture which may pass through the veneer. Because of this gap, it is unnecessary to remove the old siding—even though it may not be level—provided that it is sound enough for metal ties to be nailed to it securely. The ties, which are inserted in the mortar joints between bricks, hold the veneer firmly upright.

Regardless of how well the veneer is anchored to the old wall, it must be supported from below. This is usually done by trenching out around the foundation walls and carrying the bricks—or 4-in.-thick concrete blocks—down to the footing.

Doors and windows are not affected by the addition of the veneer except that the jambs are recessed approximately 5 in. behind the face of the walls. The casings are left on and the space between them and the back of the veneer is filled with wood strips.

The bricks used for veneering are usually a nominal 4×8×2¼-in., but may be 12 in. long. You can use ordinary common, or building, bricks; old bricks, although these are likely to produce a weaker, less durable, and less water-resistant wall than new bricks; facing bricks, which are specially treated for color and texture; or glazed bricks with a hard, smooth, self-cleaning surface available in many colors and patterns.

STONE. Stone is used like brick to re-side houses. The only type you can install yourself is a square-cut slab 1 in. thick. This is made in several sizes (also in L-shaped pieces for covering outside corners) and is usually laid up in a random pattern. Several kinds of stone, such as bluestone and rough-cut marble, are available.

The stone can be applied to any level, sound, nailable surface. You simply screw metal clips to the wall at the top and bottom of each stone and fit the flanges into grooves which have been cut in the edges of the stone by the quarry. To fill the joints, mix 1 part masonry cement and 3 parts sand to a soupy consistency and squirt it in with a caulking gun. As soon as it sets, tool it to a concave profile with a piece of pipe and remove the excess mortar and mortar stains.

Conventional stone veneer is made of stones roughly 2 to 4 in. thick which are flat on the back and range from flat to irregular (depending on how they are cut) on the face. Almost any variety of stone found in the U.S. is used.

Ashlar stones, which are cut into rectangles, are laid up over frame and masonry walls with a 1-in. air space behind them. Rubble stones, which are irregular, can usually be installed only over masonry because they must be firmly embedded in mortar.

MANUFACTURED STONE. Manufactured stone is composed of cement, lightweight aggregates, and colored oxides. If well made, it is difficult to distinguish from real stone and has similar characteristics; but it costs about half as much and is much lighter in weight, so no footings are required. You can buy it in colors and textures resembling several of nature's products, and in both rubble and ashlar patterns. Thicknesses vary from 1 to 4 in. L-shaped stones which fit around outside corners are available in most patterns.

The stones can be applied directly to clean concrete block, poured concrete, or brick; but if the masonry has been painted, it must be covered with metal lath. Level wood surfaces are covered with building paper, metal lath, and a scratch coat of 2 parts Portland cement, 1 part masonry cement, and 4 parts sand.

To install the stones, work from the top to the bottom of the wall. Butter the back of each stone with mortar like that for the scratch coat and press it firmly into position. Grout the joints any time after the mortar has set. The job is most easily done by making a cone of vinyl fabric, filling it partially with mortar, and squeezing the mortar into the joints much as a baker puts decorative icing on a cake. Fill the joints completely; then, after the mortar has dried somewhat, tool it to a firm, smooth contour and clean out the excess with a whisk broom. Clean off mortar stains in the stones with a damp rag. This must be done well, because you cannot go back later with muriatic acid, which damages the stones. After the wall has dried for a month, apply a couple of coats of silicone water repellent.

STUCCO. Stucco is a Portland-cement plaster. It is not such a popular wall finish today as it used to be, mainly because it must be applied by a qualified stucco mason over a period of several days, and because it cracks—sometimes badly—if the house settles. It is, however, the only siding material which can be applied in unbroken sheets over an entire wall.

Stucco can be applied to any relatively smooth masonry wall and over any kind of sheathing on a wood-frame wall. It goes on directly over masonry, but a frame wall must first be covered with building paper and expanded metal lath. Three coats of stucco are used. The first is a $\frac{3}{8}$-in. scratch coat, which is allowed to cure for 48 hours. This is followed by a $\frac{3}{8}$-in. brown coat, which is cured for a week. Finally comes a $\frac{1}{8}$-in. finish coat.

The finish coat is best made with a prepared mix to which color pigments (if desired) are added at the factory. Texturing is done by the mason. The finish can be smooth, stippled, sandy, scored, rough, etc. You can also achieve a pebbled effect by pressing or literally throwing small pebbles or marble chips into the stucco while wet.

CEMENT-COATED WALL FABRIC. This is a new material similar to gypsum-coated wall fabric (see Chapter 8) but made with a cement coating on a fiberglass backing. It is applied in the same way over exterior concrete, concrete block, brick, or plywood walls to produce a smooth, durable, colorful surface.

CONCRETE BLOCKS. The biggest use for concrete

Types of ornamental concrete block used in walls.

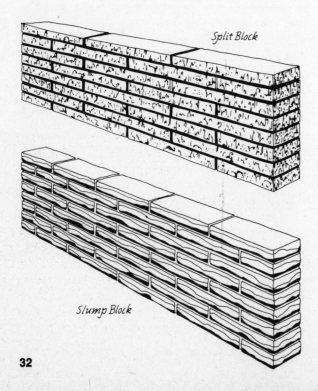

Split Block

Slump Block

Grille Block

Patterned Block

blocks is in foundation walls. They are also used—but less commonly—in building exterior and interior walls, fireplace walls, and garden walls. As a re-siding material, they are virtually unknown, although they can be installed like brick veneer.

Blocks are classified as lightweight or heavyweight. The latter are required when they are used to bear a load, as in a foundation wall. Both types have nominal dimensions of $16 \times 8 \times 8$ in. (actual dimensions are $15\frac{5}{8} \times 7\frac{5}{8} \times 7\frac{5}{8}$ in., so that when laid with $\frac{3}{8}$-in. mortar joints, they fill a space exactly 16 in. long and 8 in. high). There are also half-length blocks, half-width blocks, and half-height blocks. The great majority have hollow cores; some are solid. Blocks used for making corners have flat rather than partially cored ends.

The standard concrete block has no more beauty than a gray cube of concrete; and except in foundation walls, it is usually finished with a coat of cement plaster or paint. But a wide range of decorative blocks is available. These include patterned blocks with textured or sculptured faces; split blocks only 4 in. wide which are surfaced to resemble stone or brick and may also be integrally colored; slump blocks resembling weathered stone or adobe, also available in colors; grille blocks, which are pierced in interesting patterns from front to back; screen blocks, which are similar to grille blocks but have larger openings; and glazed blocks, which are surfaced with a thick, hard glaze available in many colors.

All concrete-block walls must be built up from poured concrete footings which are below the frost line

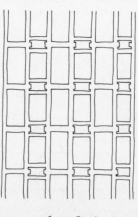

Screen Block

in cold climates, and at least 18 in. deep in frost-free climates. The blocks are laid either in a common bond, in which the vertical joints in one course are centered on the blocks in the adjacent courses, or in a stack bond, in which the vertical joints in all courses are aligned. Lay the blocks from the two ends of the wall toward the middle. For mortar use a mixture of 1 part masonry cement and 3 parts sand, and apply it in two separate strips along the horizontal edges and vertical ends (in other words, it is not applied to the cross strips between cores or in the cores). For solid blocks, however, the mortar is spread across the entire horizontal or vertical surface.

In a new construction method, concrete mortar is not used except to bed the first course on the footings. The blocks are simply stacked tightly together in a common bond; and the wall is then plastered on both sides with a mixture of cement, lime, fiberglass fibers, and water. The resulting wall has greater flexural strength and better water resistance than a conventional wall. And unlike a conventional wall, it can be constructed in freezing weather.

WHO MAKES IT

Alcan Aluminum Corp. · Vinyl siding. Aluminum siding. Fiberglass siding in stone pattern.

Alcoa Building Products, Inc. · Aluminum siding.

Allegheny Natural Stone Co. · Stone and marble veneer in ashlar pattern applied with metal clips.

Bird & Son, Inc. · Vinyl siding.

Julius Blum & Co. · Gorgeous treillage—traditional designs in malleable iron; modern designs in iron and aluminum.

Burns & Russell Co. · Glazed concrete blocks in plain and many patterned designs.

Celotex Corp. · Vinyl siding. Hardboard siding. Fiberboard siding. Urethane-foam sheathing panels.

Certain-Teed Products Corp. · Vinyl siding.

Colonial Hand Split Shingles, Inc. · Red-cedar shakes.

Design-Technics Ceramics, Inc. · Large glazed and unglazed ceramic tiles with sculptured faces. Pierced tiles for use in solar screens.

Diamond K Co. · Genuine old weathered pine boards. Old weathered clapboards. Antique bricks.

Eldorado Stone Co. · Manufactured stones and concrete bricks for veneer.

Flintkote Co. · Fiberboard sheathing.

GAF Corp. · Vinyl siding. Asbestos-cement shingles, clapboards, and panels.

Georgia Marble Co. · Stone and marble veneer in ashlar and rubble pattern.

Georgia-Pacific Corp. · Redwood and cedar plywood siding. Softwood plywood siding in variety. Hardboard siding. Particleboard siding. Redwood shingles and shakes. Gypsum sheathing.

Hanley Co. · Glazed bricks and conventional bricks.

Homasote Co. · Fiberboard sheathing. Fiberboard siding, unfinished, primed, or prefinished.

Homestead Mills, Ltd. · Fancy butt red-cedar shingles. Red-cedar shakes. Conventional red-cedar shingles.

INCA Distributing Co. · Cement-fiberglass bonding material for concrete-block construction.

Johns-Manville Sales Corp. · Vinyl siding.

Ludowici-Celadon Co. · Nail-on bricks.

Lumaside, Inc. · Steel siding.

MacMillan Bloedel, Ltd. · Particleboard sheathing. Unfinished particleboard siding.

Masonite Corp. · Hardboard siding in great variety, including stucco finish.

Masonite Corp., Roxite Div. · Fiberglass siding in brick and stone patterns.

Maybrik. · Glazed and unglazed bricks $\frac{1}{4}$-in. thick in several colors.

Montgomery Ward & Co. · Enameled aluminum vertical siding of board-and-batten design.

National Gypsum Co. · Asbestos-cement shingles, clapboards and panels.

Owens-Corning Fiberglas Corp. · Cement-fiberglass bonding material for putting up concrete block walls.

W. H. Porter, Inc. · Insulated metal panels.

Revere Aluminum Building Products, Inc. · Aluminum siding. Steel siding. Vinyl siding. Fiberglass siding in brick and stone patterns.

Sears Roebuck & Co. · Aluminum siding.

Shakertown Corp. · Red-cedar shingle and shake panels. Fancy butt red-cedar shingles.

Simpson Timber Co. · Plywood siding in variety. Redwood plywood siding.

United States Gypsum Co. · Gypsum sheathing board.

U.S. Steel Corp., Alside Div. · Steel siding. Aluminum siding. Vinyl siding. Fiberglass siding in brick, stone, and cedar-shake patterns.

Vermont Weatherboard, Inc. · Artificially weathered barn board siding.

Victor Oolitic Stone Co. · Indiana limestone in several colors, cut and uncut, for random and patterned ashlar veneers.

Wall & Floor Treatments, Inc., Flexi-Wall Systems Div. · Cement-coated wall fabric.

Wolverine-Pentronix, Inc. · Aluminum siding.

Plain and sculptured tiles make an unusual but handsome siding material. Design-Technics Ceramics, Inc.

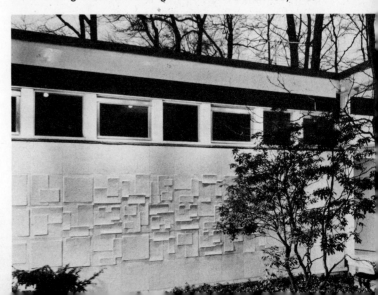

3

Roofs

Roofs normally don't command much attention until they start to leak. Then suddenly they mean possible ruin for everything—your walls and floors, your furnishings, your comfort, your sleep, even your health.

There in a nutshell is the main reason why a new roof—whether it be for an existing house or for a new house or addition—should be selected and installed more carefully than it usually is. Not that one accepted roofing material is more waterproof than another. But their life expectancies vary (pretty much in direct ratio to their cost). And what is suitable for one roof slope or configuration is not necessarily suitable for all.

A second reason why you shouldn't automatically reroof with the same material which has been on your house for the past 20 years is that a roof has a greater effect on the appearance of a house than is often realized. If it is incompatible with the architectural style of your house, it can completely negate the effect the architect labored to achieve. If it's the wrong color, it can make the house look taller or wider, smaller or larger, than it should. If it's the wrong pattern or texture, it can upset the harmony of the house.

Other reasons for exploring and pondering on the several available roofing materials are:

· The need for fire protection. Time was when the combustibility of a roofing material influenced the fire-insurance rate you paid. This is rarely true today, when most of us have fire departments within easy reach and telephones to call them. But if you live in a closely built-up neighborhood or on the edge of a forest or in chapparal-studded hills, the danger of flying embers igniting your roof greatly increases the need for a fire-resistant roofing material.

· The effect that sunlight can have on the comfort of your house. In the summer, more heat enters the house through the roof than by any other avenue. It follows that, if you live in a warm climate where air conditioning is a necessity, you would be well advised to install a light-colored roofing material that will reflect at least some of the sun's rays back into the atmosphere so they don't raise the temperature of your attic—and indirectly, that of the rooms below. On the other hand, you should not overlook the fact that if trees overhang a light-colored roof, they are likely to turn it into a streaked, blotchy, discolored mess. Many southerners with white roofs have switched to darker colors for this reason.

· Your need to cut costs by installing the roofing yourself. Since the cost of labor contributes substantially to the final bill paid for reroofing a house, it's natural that you may want to make the installation yourself. Unless you're a seasoned handyman, however, only a few types of roofing are within your scope. And even these should be approached with a certain amount of trepidation, because of the hazards of working on any roof and because of the back-breaking labor involved simply in transferring bundles of roofing from the ground up a ladder to the rooftop.

ROOF CONSTRUCTION. The underpinnings of most residential roofs consist of rafters or, in the case of flat or almost flat roofs, roof joists spaced 16 in. on center. These are covered with sheathing—also called a deck —which is usually made of plywood or boards but may also be made of fiberboard, hardboard, or panels of urethane foam. The sheathing is like that on exterior walls and is installed in the same way to provide a smooth, continuous base for the roofing. Under wood-shingle or tile roofs, however, the sheathing sometimes is made with boards which are spaced several inches apart.

In houses of post-and-beam construction, closely spaced rafters are replaced by large beams spaced 4 or more feet apart. These may run up and down the roof slope or across it. The deck is made of 2-in. or thicker wood or composition planks laid tight together. The

A plank-and-beam roof built with 2-in. planks over widely spaced beams. Potlatch Corp.

planks frequently form the ceiling surface in the rooms below. If necessary, as it usually is, rigid insulation board is laid on top of wood planks. The composition planks, however, have insulating value in their own right.

Most roof decks should be covered with asphalt-saturated building paper.

A problem which is peculiar to sloping shingled roofs in cold climates occurs when ice dams form along the eaves and block the melted snow from flowing off the roof to the ground. With no way to escape, the water backs up under the shingles, seeps through cracks in the sheathing, and drips down into the house. Most builders make no attempt to stop this, although the preventive measures are relatively simple and inexpensive to take at the time a roof is being constructed or when it is stripped of old roofing prior to reroofing. Simply lay an eaves flashing strip of asphalt roll roofing along the edges of the roof over the building paper, to lie directly under the finish roofing. The strip should overhang the roof edges about $\frac{1}{4}$ in. and should extend up the roof to a point well inside the interior wall line. If the roof has a pitch of 4 in. or more per foot, the upper edge of the strip should be at least 1 ft. inside the wall line; on a roof with a lower pitch, it should be at least 2 ft. inside the wall line. If 36-in.-wide roll roofing is too narrow to meet these requirements, use two strips, overlap the edges 4 in., and fasten them together with a continuous ribbon of asphalt roofing cement.

TYPES OF ROOFING

WOOD SHINGLES. Although wood shingles are no longer the most widely used roofing material, they will forever be favored by many homeowners because of their inherent mellow beauty and because they produce strong horizontal shadow lines that break the monotony of large roof expanses. If exposed to the sun, they have a life expectancy of 25 to 30 years (in deep shade, however, this may be reduced as much as ten years). And if they are damaged, repairs are easily made.

On the other hand, the shingles are combustible, and in damp, shady locations, they tend to collect a coating of moss. Fortunately, both of these problems can be forestalled. Shingles which are pressure-impregnated with certain fire-retardant chemicals are given a Class C rating by Underwriters' Laboratories when laid in the conventional manner, and a Class B rating when laid over a $\frac{1}{2}$-in. plywood or 2-in. board deck covered with plastic-coated steel foil.* Moss can be prevented by treating the shingles with pentachlorophenol wood preservative.

Individual shingles used for roofing are square-butt units similar to those for exterior walls. They are sold in assorted widths and uniform lengths in bundles

---

* Roofing materials are classified as follows: Class A materials are effective against severe fire exposures and possess no flying-brand hazard. Class B materials are effective against moderate fire exposures and possess no flying-brand hazard. Class C materials are effective against light fire exposure and possess no flying-brand hazard.

An eaves flashing strip prevents leaks through lower part of roof.

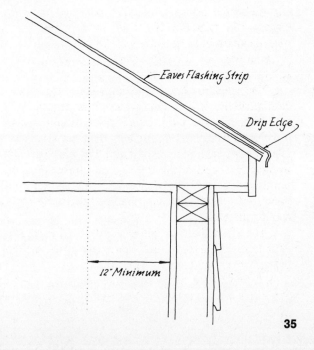

Because 8-ft. strips of cedar shingles come fastened to a plywood backing, they can be nailed directly to rafters. Shakertown Corp.

which cover 25 sq. ft. of roof area. Shingles are also available in 4-ft. or 8-ft. strips with ½-in. plywood backing for fast installation to rafters.

Roofs to be shingled must have a minimum pitch of 3 in. in 12 in. On a roof with a 3-in. to 5-in. pitch, the maximum exposure for 16-in. shingles is 3¾ in.; for 18-inchers, 4½ in.; and for 24-inchers, 5¾ in. On a roof with a pitch of over 5 in., the maximum exposures are 5, 5½, and 7½ in. respectively.

In new construction, shingles are installed either on solid or spaced sheathing. The former is generally preferred in cold climates because of its greater insulating value. It may or may not be covered with building paper. Spaced sheathing is made of 3-in., 4-in., or 6-in. boards spaced the same distance apart as the planned shingle exposure.

In reroofing, the shingles can be laid directly over an old roof of wood or asphalt shingles or roll roofing, but only if the old roofing is sound and no more than one layer thick. To prepare a shingled roof, rip off the ridge strip of shingles and replace it with bevel siding boards installed with the butts uppermost. Cut out and replace the eaves course of shingles with 1-in. boards; and cut out a 6-in. strip of shingles along each rake and nail in 1-in. boards. Nail down all broken and buckled shingles.

Lay the shingles along the eaves and rakes with a 1-in. overhang. Double the first course at the eaves. Space all shingles ¼ in. apart and place them so the joints in adjacent courses are offset at least 1½ in. and so those in alternate courses do not align exactly.

Use galvanized steel shingle nails—two nails per shingle regardless of its width. Drive the nails ¾ in.

from the edges of each shingle and at least ¾ in. above the butts of the overlapping shingles. Don't drive any nails through flashing, however.

To cover the roof ridge and hips, use factory-assembled ridge and hip pieces if available. Otherwise, lay flat shingles parallel to and on each side of the peak, and shape the edges so they butt securely. Alternate the direction of the joint in each course. Provide the same shingle exposure as in the rest of the roof.

Wood shingles are normally allowed to weather, but you can apply a transparent stain. Some shingles are factory-stained.

SHAKES. Thick, handsplit wood shakes impart more texture to roofs than any other material except barrel tiles. They have become particularly popular for contemporary houses with vast expanses of low-pitched roof, mainly because of their appearance but partly because their greater thickness gives a little extra protection against the sun. In all other respects, however, they are like wood shingles.

The same shakes which are used on exterior walls are used on roofs. Some are fire-resistant. In addition, you can buy strips of shakes bonded to ½-in. plywood. These are used primarily in new construction for nailing directly to rafters.

The minimum recommended roof pitch for shakes is 4 in. Maximum weather exposure is 7½ in. for 18-in. shakes and 10 in. for 24-in. shakes. With these exposures you get a roof which is two plies thick at all points. A superior three-ply roof is constructed by reducing the exposures to 5½ in. for 18-in. shakes and 7½ in. for 24-in. shakes.

You can lay shakes over the same type of new or old roof that is required for wood shingles; but because of their irregularity, special steps must be taken to ensure against leaks. First lay a 36-in.-wide strip of 30-lb. roofing felt over the deck at the eaves. Double the starting course of shakes. After this (and all succeeding courses) is laid, place an 18-in. strip of roofing felt over the upper part of the course. This is positioned so

Cedar shakes are applied with strips of roofing felt laid over the upper end of each course.

that the bottom edge is parallel with the butts in the second course of shakes above. For example, if you're laying 18-in. shakes with 7½-in. exposure, the bottom edge of the felt should be 15 in. above the butts of the shakes it covers. Let the upper edge of the felt lap over the sheathing and fasten it with a few nails.

Space all shakes ¼ to ⅜ in. apart. As in a wood shingle roof, the joints are offset at least 1½ in. in adjacent courses and should not align exactly in alternate courses. Fasten each shake with a pair of galvanized nails placed ¾ in. from the edges and at least ¾ in. above the butts of the overlying course. Don't nail through flashing.

Ridges and hips are covered with prefabricated units or with individual 6-in. shakes which are beveled and butted side to side. Before laying the shakes, fold 30-lb. roofing felt over the peak. Double the first course of shakes at the starting end of the ridge or hip. If the ridge is unbroken from gable end to gable end, lay the cap strip from the two ends toward the middle and double the courses at both ends.

The completed roof is allowed to weather or can be stained.

ASPHALT SHINGLES.

ASPHALT SHINGLES. There are some homeowners who don't like asphalt shingles because they think they lack character—are simply drab, though often colorful, materials which have no texture themselves and lie so flat that the entire roof appears textureless, too. The feeling is not entirely justified. True, the great majority of shingles are simple, flat, thin, granular-coated rectangles. But more and more are being given a pressed-in grain effect which from a distance has a reasonable resemblance to wood. Others are being assembled in double-thick strips with butts of random size and shape to resemble wood shakes. In still others, the size of the granules is increased to give a more uneven texture and color. A few giant (16×16-in.) shingles are made as in the past for Dutch lap and hexagonal installation. And in almost every instance, shingle colors have been improved and new ones added.

In short, if you have been against asphalt shingles, you ought to take another look. In doing so, you will discover that several other asphalt-shingle weaknesses have also been improved.

For one thing, you no longer need worry about the shingles being curled back or even torn off by strong winds. Almost all have seal-down butts.

The tendency of white shingles to collect algae and stain badly has been minimized in some shingles by surfacing them with a new kind of granule.

Finally, fire resistance has been improved so much in some—not all—shingles that they carry a Class A rating. This has been accomplished either by substituting fiberglass for felt in the backing or by inserting a layer

Newest type of asphalt shingle produces an interesting roof with a strong texture. Celotex Corp.

of fiberglass in the backing. All other asphalt shingles carry a Class C rating.

The average life of an asphalt-shingle roof is about 20 years. You can increase this somewhat by applying a roof coating before the shingles become brittle with age and start to crack. But a much easier way to prolong life is to start out with top-grade shingles which are covered by a guarantee of 25 years.

Asphalt shingles are graded by the weight of a square (the quantity of shingles required to cover 100 sq. ft.). The 3-ft.-strip shingles—by far the most common type—start at 210 lb. and range to 390 lb. Large individual shingles, which are rarely used, are lighter. Generally speaking, the heavier the shingles, the longer they will last.

Strip shingles measure 3 ft. long by 1 ft. wide. In the simpler designs, the lower portion of each strip is divided into three 12-in.-wide tabs. Some strips, however, have only two tabs; some are not cut at all; and still others—those made to look like wood shakes—have more than three tabs.

Asphalt roofing must be laid on a solid, reasonably smooth roof with a minimum pitch of 4 in. In new construction, cover the sheathing with 15-lb. asphalt-saturated roofing felt; nail metal drip edges along the eaves and rakes to force water to drip straight to the ground or into the gutters; and apply eaves flashing strips.

Old roofs can be reroofed with asphalt only if they are laid on a solid deck and covered with a single layer of wood or asphalt shingles, roll roofing, or flat metal sheets. All other materials must be ripped off. On old asphalt roofs, nail down bulges and torn or curled shingles. On wood-shingle roofs, remove ridge and hip strips; cut out the shingles within 6 in. of eaves and rakes and replace them with boards. Then, to provide a smooth surface, nail beveled boards—thick end up—under each row of butts.

For the first course, nail a starter strip along the eave and let it overhang about ¼ in. This can be made of a narrow strip of roll roofing if it is the same color as the shingles; otherwise, use shingles with the tabs cut off. Lay a course of full-size shingles over this. Then lay succeeding courses on up the roof, using a board or chalk line to control the placement of the butts. The cutouts between tabs in each adjacent course must, of course, be offset. As a rule, they are centered over the tabs in the course below; but with imitation-shake designs, follow the manufacturer's directions.

Most shingles now on the market are designed for a 5-in. exposure; a few require less. Follow the manufacturer's nailing instructions, which generally call for four galvanized asphalt-shingle nails per strip. These are placed in a straight line 5⅝ in. above the butts. No steps need be taken to seal down the tabs, for as the sun warms the roof, it softens the strips of cement applied to the shingles so they automatically adhere to the underlying shingles.

Ridge and hip strips are made in some cases with special shingles provided by the manufacturers. If these are unavailable, cut rectangular shingles into 1-ft. lengths, bend them over the peak, and fasten them with a single nail on each side. Each piece is exposed 5 in.

Seal-down asphalt shingles can also be laid on roofs with a pitch of as little as 2 in. if the entire roof is covered with a double thickness of roofing felt. This thickness is provided by lapping each 36-in.-wide felt strip over the preceding strip 19 in. (At the eaves, start with a 19-in. strip and cover it completely with a 36-in. strip.) In cold climates, to keep water from backing up the roof, the first two or three strips are embedded in roofing cement; then there is no need for an additional eaves flashing strip.

ASPHALT ROLL ROOFING.

Roll roofing is a dull-gray, featureless, and seamless material which is not suitable for houses simply because it is not attractive enough. You might use it, however, on roofs which are not exposed to view or on simple vacation homes.

Ordinary roofing is produced in long 3-ft.-wide rolls which are completely mineral-surfaced. They can be laid on roof pitches down to 1 in. if the strips are overlapped 3 in. and the nails concealed. Another type, known as double-coverage roofing, has granules applied to only the bottom half of the strip. The upper half is smooth. When laid, each course is overlapped and cemented to the smooth surface of the preceding course. This results in two-ply coverage which is excellent for use on roofs with a pitch of as little as ⅛ in.

Roll roofing is applied horizontally over solid sheathing or old roll roofing, asphalt shingles, or smooth metal roofs. It should give good protection for about 15 years if one layer thick, 20 years if two layers thick.

ASBESTOS-CEMENT SHINGLES.

Asbestos-cement shingles are the only reasonably lightweight man-made material which can give the homeowner a fireproof roof that will last indefinitely. But they are not widely used because of their cost. They are also fairly difficult to replace if shattered by falling tree limbs.

The shingles are made in several colors to resemble wood shingles or slates. The latter, though less common, are the more realistic. Individual shingles measure 9⅓ in. wide by 16 in. long and are laid with a standard 7-in. exposure. Strips are 30×14 in. and laid with 6-in. exposure. Minimum roof pitch for both types is 5 in., but a 3-in. pitch is permissible if special installation methods are followed.

The deck or old roof should be prepared as for asphalt shingles; however, it is inadvisable, though possible, to lay the shingles over old roof shingles.

Start the installation with a double course which overhangs the eaves ¾ in. In succeeding courses, center the shingles on the joints in the course below. Drive rust-resistant nails through predrilled holes 2 in. above the butts in the overlapping courses. At ridges and hips, butt wood strips to the roof shingles to form a nailing base for the cap units. Cover them with roofing felt.

BUILT-UP ROOFING.

Also called tar-and-gravel roofing, built-up roofing is made of alternate layers of building felt or fiberglass and asphaltic material topped with gravel, slag, or stone chips. The result is a seamless covering which can be safely used on dead-level roofs as well as on those with a pitch of up to 3 in. With special installation methods, it can also be used on 6-in. pitches.

The life expectancy of a built-up roof is about 20 years. Depending on the construction, it carries either a Class C or Class A fire rating.

Despite the fact that a built-up roof has no joints which produce shadow lines, the rough texture of the gravel topping is surprisingly attractive. The color depends on the color of the gravel used. Whites and light colors are most popular, primarily because the roofing is best adapted to the low-pitched roofs which are particularly prevalent in warmer climates. However, because of their roughness, such roofs are not well washed by rains and tend to show dirt and stains.

The roofing must be applied to solid sheathing by professionals. Simple repairs can be easily made by the homeowner, however.

URETHANE.

As a roofing material, urethane foam has to date been used mainly on large buildings, but it is equally suitable for houses. It is of particular interest because it is the only roofing with high insulating value.

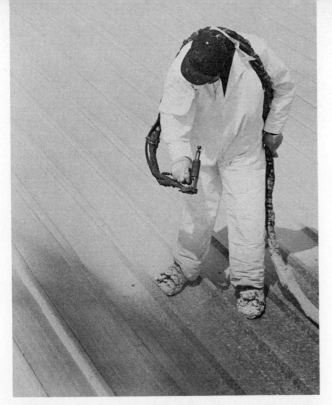

Urethane roofing is applied by spray gun. Witco Chemical Corp.

thickness is $\frac{3}{16}$ in.; standard lengths, 10, 11, 12, 14, 16, 18, 20, 22, 24, and 26 in. Widths range from 6 to 16 in. You can buy slates all of the same width so the vertical joints in each course are centered on the slates in the adjacent courses, or in random widths to produce a wood-shingled effect.

Minimum roof pitch is 4 in. The amount of exposure is determined by deducting the head lap (which is usually 3 in. but which may be reduced to 2 in. on very steep roofs) from the length of the slates and dividing by two. Thus a 20-in. slate should show an exposure of no more than $8\frac{1}{2}$ in.

Despite the fact that standard slates weigh about 7 lbs. per square foot, it is not necessary to reinforce the roof framing or use special sheathing. But the deck must be smooth, sound, and covered with 30-lb. roofing felt.

Installation should be made by experienced roofers with copper nails. It is also advisable to have a roofer make repairs if a slate is broken. On steep roofs, because of the smoothness of the slates, snow guards should be installed to prevent heavy snow from catapulting off the roof onto shrubbery below.

TILE. Roofing tiles have the same practical advantages as slates; and from the aesthetic standpoint, they are just as attractive, though in a different way.

Tiles are exceedingly colorful—available in nonfading hues of just about every primary color. They are available with and without a tough, glistening glaze that defies fungus growth. Textures range from smooth to rough. And in addition to flat tiles which resemble very thick slates or wood shingles, there are special configurations which have no counterparts among other roofing materials. Spanish and Mission tiles, for example, are barrel-shaped and laid in vertical rows with wide concave troughs between them. French, from a distance, suggests a washboard with complexly shaped corrugations standing on one edge. Greek and Roman consist of flat tiles with high rounded or tent-shaped pieces covering the vertical joints. Scandia is like a sea with waves marching in close procession toward the beach.

The most beautiful tiles are ceramic—very strong, dense, heavy, and durable. Concrete tiles are thinner, lighter, and reinforced with steel, but are also very strong and durable. They are made only in flat units which must be coated with paint to give them color.

The roof pitch required for tile varies. Flat tiles designed to interlock at the horizontal joints can be laid on a 3-in. pitch; noninterlocking flat tiles require a 5-in. pitch; while specially shaped tiles can be used on a 4-in. pitch. Maximum allowable exposures range from roughly 5 to 13 in.

Tiles which weigh about 8 lbs. per square foot do not require special framing; but for heavier units, it is nec-

A 1-in. thickness has an R value of approximately 7 yet weighs only two-hundredths of a pound per square foot.

Professionally applied by spray gun to roofs of any configuration, the foam forms an unbroken sheet which fills in and seals any cracks or holes that may exist in the deck and which actually helps to reinforce the deck against expansion and contraction. Thus it provides unusual protection against leaks. But because it is damaged by ultraviolet rays and is neither fire-resistant nor completely watertight, it must be given a final protective coating, usually of vinyl, silicone, or rubber. This results in a smooth white or colored surface unlike that of any other roofing material.

In new construction, urethane goes directly over a solid deck (which is sometimes covered with a polyethylene vapor barrier). For reroofing, it can be applied to any surface which is sound, clean, and dry. It is put down so rapidly that an entire roof can be completed within a few hours.

SLATE. Slate is one of the oldest, most beautiful, and most practical roofing materials. It is also one of the most costly. Primarily handcut from rock of great toughness and durability, it produces a roof which is impervious to weather and contaminants in the atmosphere, noncombustible, and permanent. To the would-be home buyer, it is a mark of excellence; and if for some reason it ever should be removed, it has considerable salvage value.

Generally, roofing slates are smooth, but if you prefer a rough texture, you can have it. They are available in black, gray, green, purple, and red. Some of the colors tend to fade slightly; others are fast. Standard

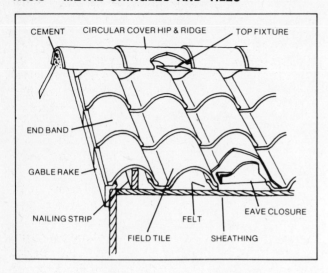

Two of several types of ceramic roofing tile: Spanish, above; Scandia, below. Ludowici-Celadon Co.

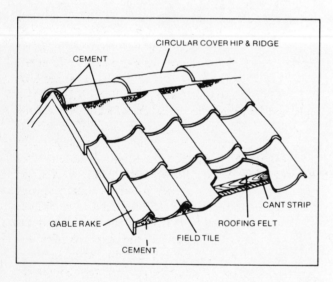

essary to increase the size or reduce the spacing of the rafters. All tiles can be laid on conventional sheathing covered with 30-lb. roofing felt. Installation and major repairs should be made by a professional.

METAL SHINGLES AND TILES. These are essentially the same as metal sidings. Made of aluminum or steel, they are factory-treated with a colorful, tough, baked-on plastic finish which is guaranteed not only against chipping, peeling, or cracking but also, in some instances, against fading.

The shingles, which are striated to resemble wood, come in long strips and have a 10-in. exposure. Tiles, which resemble barrel-shaped Mission-style ceramic tiles are individual units laid with 14-in. exposure.

Both require a roof pitch of at least 3 in. and are laid on a solid deck covered with 30-lb. asphalt-saturated felt or over an old asphalt roof. Install shingles according to the manufacturer's directions. The job entails a number of special accessories but is perfectly straightforward. Installation of the tiles, however, is sufficiently complex to require a roofing contractor.

METAL SHEETS. The old "tin" roof which is so often seen on farms and in small communities (especially in the South) has been modernized for urban use; but if you like it in its original form, you can still have it. In either case, you wind up with a strong, fire-resistant roof of excellent durability.

The newest materials are 2×16-ft. flat aluminum or steel sheets which are laid up and down a roof with pronounced joints between them. In some cases, the joints are high, thin standing seams; in other cases, they are shaped like wood battens. Both impart an effect similar to that of a board-and-batten wall. Unlike such a wall, however, the sheets are factory-coated with a smooth, tough, baked-on finish which rarely needs repainting.

The old-style galvanized-steel and aluminum sheets are of approximately the same size but are either corrugated, totally flat, or flat with small tent-shaped ribs. They are available only in their natural finish; if you want to color them (you must paint steel sheets to guard against rust), apply a couple of coats of house paint.

All sheet roofings require a minimum roof pitch of 3 in. Although they are often laid directly on the rafters (with purlins installed at 3-ft. intervals between each pair of rafters), they are so noisy in storms that you should protect yourself against the pitter-patter as well as against the sun by putting down sheathing and covering it with building felt. Let a professional install the roofing; making watertight joints calls for some experience.

Metal roof shingles resemble wood. Architectural Engineering Products Co.

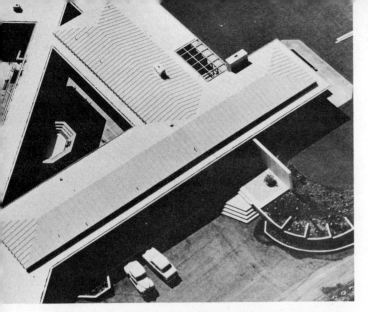

Terne roof with batten seams. Follansbee Steel Corp.

TERNE. Terne is an alloy of lead and tin which is applied either to copper-bearing steel or stainless steel to produce a smooth, fireproof, durable roofing material. This differs from galvanized steel and aluminum roofing in that it comes in rolls as well as in sheets, and is hand-formed at the building site.

A terne roof may be designed in several ways. The metal can be applied up and down a 3-in.-pitch roof in flat strips (up to about 24 in. wide) which are separated by 1-in.-high standing or batten seams. On roofs with 3½-in. pitch, it can be laid in horizontal strips in a low steplike arrangement. And on roofs with almost no pitch, it can be laid with flat-locked seams which are barely discernible from a distance.

Terne-coated stainless steel does not require painting; it weathers to a dark gray. Conventional terne roofing, however, must be primed with a red iron-oxide linseed-oil paint and finished with a coat of oil-base exterior paint.

Because of the complexities of the work, a terne roof must be installed by a trained mechanic. A smooth deck covered with rosin-sized building paper is required.

COPPER. In the past, copper was often used to roof porticos, bay windows, and flat or almost flat roof areas which were otherwise difficult to make watertight. Today, its high cost has pretty well driven it from the roofing market. But it is the most durable of all metal roofing materials. Because of its malleability, it is readily shaped to unusual configurations. And as it weathers, it develops a soft green patina of rare beauty.

A roof covered with copper requires only enough pitch to assure runoff of water. The deck must be smooth, solid, and covered with roofing felt. The copper itself can be put down in the same patterns as terne, but here again you must rely on a skilled sheet-metal worker to make the installation.

FIBERGLASS. In house construction, fiberglass-rein-forced plastic panels are used only for roofing terraces, porches, carports, and greenhouses. (They are also used in fences and room dividers.) Such roofs are easily constructed by the homeowner; require practically no maintenance; are resistant to chemicals, weather, and fire; and despite their seeming fragility, are remarkably durable. One of the special advantages—and also drawbacks—of the panels is their translucence; because of this, they give shade from the blinding sun without cutting off light. Even so, there is considerable build-up of heat in the space below. To minimize this, some panels are now formulated to block out ultraviolet rays.

Fiberglass panels are generally corrugated to increase their strength and rigidity, but flat and ribbed panels are available. Colors include white, greens, and yellows. The best grades are .045 in. thick and weigh 6 oz. per square foot. Other grades are .037 in. thick (5 oz.) and .03 in. (4 oz.). The panels are available in lengths of 8, 10, 12, 14, 15, and 16 ft. and in nominal widths of 24 and 48 in. Flat panels also come in 24-in. widths and 50-ft. rolls.

The framing for a fiberglass roof is built of 2×6-in. rafters spaced 24 in. on center with 2×4-in. cross blocks between each pair. The entire structure is supported on 4×4-in. posts and/or ledger strips spiked to the house walls. The roof should be pitched at least 1 in. per foot.

Lay the panels parallel with the rafters, drill holes for nails, and fasten them to the rafters with aluminum screw nails which are driven through neoprene washers to keep out water. Overlap adjoining panels approximately 2 in. and seal the joints with the clear mastic provided by the manufacturer or, in very windy areas, with vinyl strips. If corrugated panels are used, rounded wood strips are nailed to the rafters under the corrugations to provide a solid nailing base, and corrugated wood strips are inserted under the panels at the cross blocks and headers. Corrugated aluminum flashing strips keep out moisture along the edges of the roof where it adjoins the house walls.

The panels are cut, as necessary, with any fine-toothed saw.

INSULATED METAL PANELS. See Chapter 2.

CANVAS ROOF DECKS. No completely satisfactory covering has been developed for flat roof decks which are used as porches. Heavy deck canvas is the best available material, but it has a comparatively short life unless protected from sun and rain by a roof.

The canvas is available from marine suppliers and sometimes local awning makers. The base on which it is laid must be made as smooth as possible. Remove loose paint and dirt, countersink nails, and fill holes with wood plastic. Then apply a thick coat of high-grade oil-base deck paint and smooth the canvas into this while it is still wet. Overlap the edges of the strips 1 in. and coat them with paint. Tack the strips down with ½-in. copper tacks spaced 1 in. apart. When the paint is dry, apply two or three more coats of deck paint. Use a brush to work it well into the canvas.

OTHER ROOF COMPONENTS

ROOF FLASHING. One of the most important parts of every roof is the flashing which seals the joints in valleys, between the roof and walls rising above the roof surface, and around the chimney and plumbing stacks. When you are reroofing, this should always be checked to make sure it is sound and watertight; when you build a new roof, it must be installed.

Aluminum, which is produced in long rolls in several widths, is the most widely used flashing material because it is inexpensive, lightweight, and resistant to corrosion except in industrial areas and near the seacoast. Copper, galvanized steel, and terne-coated stainless steel are also used. Asphalt roll roofing is sometimes used for valley flashing. Plumbing stacks are generally flashed with special neoprene or plastic collars.

In valleys, use 20-in. aluminum. Fold it lengthwise down the middle, smooth it into the valley directly on the sheathing, and nail it at the top edge with aluminum nails.

Where a shed roof slants away from a wall, use 9-in. or wider flashing and fold it lengthwise along a line 4 in. from one edge. Fasten the 4-in. leg to the wall. If possible, it should be inserted under the siding. If the wall is of masonry, however, it is nailed to the surface and the joint along the top is caulked. The 5-in. leg is laid over the roofing and cemented down with fibered asphalt roofing cement.

Where a roof abuts the wall of a dormer or similar side wall, 9-in. flashing is cut into pieces the length of the shingles, and folded into 4-in. and 5-in. legs. The pieces are then inserted under each shingle course and nailed to the side wall.

To flash around a plumbing stack, lay the shingles up to the stack. Cut a large square of asphalt roll roofing, make a hole in the center, and fit it around the stack on the roof. Then slip a preformed vent flashing down over the stack and cement it to the roll roofing, and continue laying shingles on up the roof.

Chimney flashing should be installed only by a professional.

GUTTERS AND LEADERS. Of the six materials used for gutters, only two are in wide use today. Copper, the best of the materials, has become so expensive that you can buy it only through a few outlets. Terne-coated stainless steel, also expensive, is even harder to find.

Aluminum gutter hung with strap hangers. Joints at connectors must be sealed with silicone caulking to prevent leaks.

Wood never has been very popular, because even though it makes the most attractive guttering, it is heavy and rather difficult to install and is likely to develop leaks. Galvanized steel, once the most widely used material and still one of the cheapest, has lost popularity because it rusts out and needs to be replaced.

This leaves aluminum and vinyl, both comparative newcomers to the field. Neither has the strength of the materials they have replaced, but both have two compelling advantages: They are economical (this is especially true of aluminum) and durable. If unpainted, aluminum will corrode when exposed to salt air or air laden with chemical contaminants; but if you use the type which is finished at the factory with baked-on enamel, it presents few problems—and also is a great deal more attractive than the unfinished metal. Vinyl tends to be brittle in very cold weather, but because it is integrally colored, it never requires refinishing.

The standard aluminum and vinyl gutters are of the so-called K design—with flat bottoms and attractively molded fronts. The leaders are rectangular. For durability, select the heaviest available grades. Avoid the lightest aluminum even though it is now available in seamless lengths that will span from one end of your house to the other.

The gutters and leaders suitable for do-it-yourself installation come in 10-ft. lengths. You also need some or all of the following fittings: hangers, gutter connectors, outside and inside corner troughs, gutter outlets, right- and left-hand gutter end caps, leader elbows, and leader straps. The type of hanger required depends on the construction of your eaves. If there is a fascia board just back from the edges of the eaves, use fascia brackets which are nailed to the board. (You can also use spikes and ferrules which are driven through the top edges of the gutters into the fascia board.) If there is no fascia board, use wrap-around strap hangers.

Gutters should be sloped 1/16 in. per foot. For each 35-ft. length you need one leader, which can be located at either end of the gutter or somewhere between.

As much as possible, join the gutter sections together on the ground, and have a helper lift the entire length into place and fasten it. (However, you will probably have to put exceptionally long lengths together in two or three shorter runs.) To seal the joints, don't depend on the gutter connectors alone: you must squeeze silicone caulking into them. Anchor the end caps with caulking compound, too.

Install the gutter hangers at 2-ft. to 3-ft. intervals. When wraparound strap hangers are used, the straps should be installed under the roofing. On an existing roof, however, you cannot avoid nailing on top.

After the gutters are in place, install the leaders against the house walls. Unless the eaves have virtually no overhang, you will need two elbows between the gutter outlet and the top of each leader. The upper elbow is bent toward the wall; the lower elbow is bent down toward the leader. If it is necessary to shift a leader to either side of a gutter outlet, use a side elbow, which is bent across the narrow side, rather than a standard elbow, which is bent across the wide side. No connectors are required on either elbows or leaders. Simply push the lower section up over the end of the upper section. Fasten the leaders by bending leader straps around them and nailing to the walls. At the foot of each leader, install an elbow to direct the water away from the foundation walls. A superior way to divert the water is to slip the bottom of the leader into a 4-in. drainpipe which leads either into the footing drains or to a drywell.

SOFFITS. A soffit is a flat, painted surface under a roof overhang. It conceals the bottom sides of the rafters (just as the fascia conceals the rafter ends). In the past it was made of boards or plywood, and it is still often made in this way. But the trend today—especially among developers—is to use panels of aluminum, vinyl, hardboard, or asbestos-cement board. These have two advantages. Because they are prefinished (vinyl panels are integrally colored), they do not require repainting for many years. And they are available not only with a smooth unbroken surface but also with a perforated or slotted surface to permit ventilation of the attic or roof space.

CUPOLAS. Cupolas are installed on roofs for the effect and/or to provide better ventilation of the attic. There's no need to go to the trouble of building one because they are available—ready for fast installation—in several square and hexagonal designs and a wide range of sizes. Made of wood, they come completely or partially assembled. All you have to do is cut the base to fit the roof, then embed the cupola in a thick bed of caulking compound and nail it to the roof. If the cupola is used for ventilation, a hole is cut through the roof on either

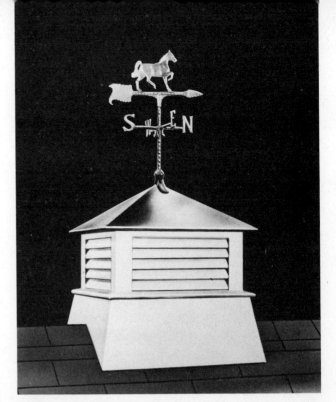

Prefabricated cupola. Stephenson Co.

side of the ridge pole and covered with screen wire to keep out insects which may enter through the louvered sides of the cupola.

ROOF COATINGS. Paintlike roof coatings are used on old asphalt, built-up, and metal roofs for four reasons: to extend the life of a roof which is starting to wear out; to change the color of the roof; to stop minor leaks; or to increase the reflectivity of the roof and thus to lower temperatures in the spaces underneath. Not all coatings will satisfy all purposes. The following are available:

Fibered asphalt coatings are viscous materials made of asphalt and mineral fibers. Available either in black or aluminum, they are used mainly for stopping leaks and preserving roofing.

Non-fibered asphalt coatings, also in black or aluminum, are thinner materials used only for refreshing dried-out asphalt roofing and protecting metal roofs against corrosion.

Asphalt-emulsion coatings are used as preservatives only. They are black.

Colored aluminum coatings consist of aluminum flakes, pigments, fibers, and a vehicle of asphalt, resinous binders, or synthetic rubber. Made in several colors, the coatings are used primarily to change the appearance of a roof and to increase its insulating value. They also help to lengthen the life of the roof.

With the exception of the emulsions, all roof coatings should be applied only to clean, dry roofs which are not badly blistered or scaling. Depending on the coating, application is made with a brush, roller, or spray gun. One coat is usually sufficient, but on asphalt roofs which are badly dried out, two may be required. Normally you need one or two gallons to cover 100 sq. ft. with one coat. Fibered and emulsion coatings cover only about half as much area. A generous coating of a top-grade material will add several years to the life of a roof.

For longer-lasting repairs, a lightweight fiberglass or heavy felt layer may be applied. This is rolled out into a layer of non-fibered asphalt coating and then covered with an additional application of asphalt or colored aluminum coating.

COLUMNS. Depending on their construction, unsupported roofs can overhang the sidewalls of a house a considerable distance. But beyond a certain point, they must be supported around the outside edges on columns.

Although wood columns—except in very small sizes —are hollow, they have the strength to bear a substantial load. But they are so intricately made that they also cost a substantial sum.

Aluminum columns, on the other hand, cost considerably less, but since they are made of very thin metal, they have little more support value than a cardboard tube. So unless they are used strictly for ornament, they are built around a wood or steel post.

This is just one of the differences between the two types of column. There are others:

Aluminum columns are available only with fluted shafts and the simplest type of capitals and bases. (Since the shafts are made in three narrow sections, the flutes are required to conceal the joints between sections.) Wood columns are available with smooth as well as fluted shafts and almost every kind of capital and base which was ever used.

Aluminum columns are the same diameter from top

to bottom. Wood columns may also be the same diameter or may be given the entasis which early Greek and Roman architects realized was necessary to counteract the illusion that tall, straight columns curve inward at the top. (Entasis is a gradual outward swelling of a shaft from bottom to top.)

Aluminum columns are made in standard diameters of 6, 8, 10, and 12 in. and in a number of lengths. The largest stock wood columns are 10 in. across, but you can have them made to order to any dimensions.

WHO MAKES IT

Alcan Aluminum Corp. · Aluminum shakes in 2-ft. panels, six colors. Aluminum soffits vented and solid. Aluminum guttering.

Architectural Engineering Products Co. · Prefinished steel and aluminum sheets. Prefinished steel and aluminum shingles and tiles.

Arctic Roofings, Inc. · Asphalt shingles.

Atlantic Asphalt & Asbestos, Inc. · Asphalt shingles.

Barclay Industries, Inc. · Fiberglass panels, corrugated and flat.

Billy Penn Corp. · Aluminum guttering and gutter guards. Aluminum drip edges. Corrugated aluminum sheets. Aluminum and galvanized steel flashing.

Bird & Son, Inc. · Asphalt shingles, including shake pattern. Vinyl guttering.

Julius Blum & Co. · Malleable iron ornamental load-bearing "columns" made of two or three slender posts joined by decorative cross pieces. Great variety.

Bondex International, Inc. · Roof coatings.

Buckingham-Virginia Slate Corp. · Unfading black slate.

Celotex Corp. · Asphalt shingles including shake pattern. Some Class A. Fungus-resistant white shingles. Roof coatings.

Certain-Teed Products Corp. · Asphalt shingles, some Class A, including shake pattern.

Colonial Hand Split Shingles, Inc. · Red-cedar shakes.

Cook Paint & Varnish Co. · Roof coatings.

Evode, Inc. · Self-sticking aluminum strips for flashing, sealing joints and holes in gutters, etc.

Flintkote Co. · Asphalt shingles, including wood-shingle pattern and self-locking shingles.

Follansbee Steel Corp. · Terne roofing and terne-coated stainless steel.

GAF Corp. · Asphalt shingles including wood-shingle pattern. Some Class A. Self-locking shingles. Built-up roofing. Asphalt roll roofing. Roof coatings.

Genova, Inc. · Neoprene vent-stack flashing.

Georgia Marble Co. · White marble chips for built-up roofs.

Gibson-Homans Co. · All kinds of roof coatings. Roofing cements.

Glasteel. · Fiberglass panels, corrugated and ridged.

Globe Industries, Inc. · Asphalt shingles, including self-locking types. Asphalt roll roofing in eleven colors. Some can be installed either edge up to produce a smooth or irregular shadow line. Roof coatings.

Open ornamental steel columns used to support porch roofs are available in flat and corner designs. Versa Products Co.

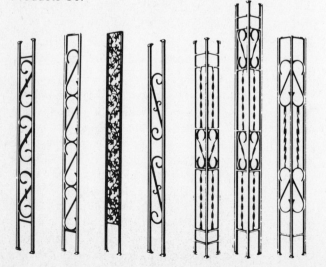

Homasote Co. · Composition roof deck planks, some fire-resistant.

Homestead Mills, Ltd. · Cedar shakes and shingles. Hip and ridge strips.

Howmet Corp. · Aluminum guttering. Galvanized-steel guttering. Aluminum and galvanized-steel flashing. Aluminum soffits vented and solid. Aluminum drip edges.

Johns-Manville. · Asphalt shingles including wood-shingle pattern. Some Class A. Asbestos-cement clapboards and shingles, including slate pattern. Asphalt roll roofing in several colors; some Class A.

Karnak Chemical Corp. · Fiberglass roof mat. All kinds of roof coating.

Kool-O-Matic Corp. · Redwood cupola with built-in power attic fan.

Koppers Co. · Red-cedar shingles and shakes treated for fire resistance.

Logan-Long Co. · Asphalt shingles in shake pattern.

Ludowici-Celadon Co. · Ceramic tiles in five designs.

Masonite Corp. · Asphalt shingles. Fungus-resistant white shingles. Class A rated. Vented hardboard soffits.

Montgomery Ward & Co. · Corrugated fiberglass panels. Corrugated and ridged aluminum panels in natural finish or colored enamel. White aluminum patio roofs. Aluminum gable carport roofs. Decorative iron columns. Aluminum and galvanized-steel guttering. Roof coatings.

Morgan Co. · 4×4-, 5×5-, and 6×6-in. turned wood porch posts. Plain and fluted round wood columns with entasis. Square plain and fluted columns.

Mortell Co. · Roof coatings and cements.

National Gypsum Co. · Composition roof deck planks, some with urethane-foam insulation. Vented asbestos-cement soffits.

North Bangor Slate Co. · Black slate.

Phifer Wire Products. · Aluminum gutter guards.

W. H. Porter, Inc. · Insulated metal panels.

Porter-Hadley Co. · Classic aluminum columns, capitals, and bases to 15 in. by 30 ft.

Potlatch Corp. · Wood deck planks textured and stained for exposure in ceilings.

Revere Aluminum Building Products, Inc. · Aluminum guttering. Vented and solid aluminum soffits. Aluminum flashing.

Rising & Nelson Slate Co. · Slate in assorted colors, some unfading.

F. E. Schumacher Co. · Aluminum soffit vents.

A. F. Schwerd Manufacturing Co. · Classic wood columns, capitals, and bases to any size.

SCM Corp., Macco Adhesive Div. · Roofing cement.

Sears Roebuck & Co. · Redwood and aluminum cupolas. Flat white aluminum roofs for patios. Steel or aluminum flat carport roofs. Steel gable carport roofs. Aluminum columns to 15 in. by 24 ft. Decorative iron columns. Asphalt roof coatings. Aluminum guttering.

Shakertown Corp. · Red-cedar shingle and shake panels.

Sheffield Bronze Paint Corp. · Aluminum roof coating.

Standard Equipment, Inc., Elite Products Div. · Ornamental wrought-iron load-bearing columns.

Stephenson Co. · Redwood cupolas.

Thermwell Products Co. · Plastic gutter guards.

United States Gypsum Co. · Asphalt shingles, including shake pattern. Some Class A.

United States Steel Corp., Alside Div. · Aluminum guttering. Vented and solid aluminum soffits.

Upjohn Co., CPR Div. · Spray-on urethane-foam roofing.

Versa Products Co. · Ornamental wrought-iron load-bearing columns.

Witco Chemical Corp. · Spray-on urethane-foam roofing.

Wolverine-Pentronix, Inc. · Aluminum drip edges. Aluminum guttering in assorted colors. Vented and solid aluminum soffits.

4

Insulation

It makes no difference where you live, Key West, Omaha, or Fairbanks—your house should be insulated to increase your comfort and cut your skyrocketing fuel bills. In the warmest parts of the country you need insulation to keep out heat and hold down air-conditioning costs; in the coldest parts you need it to keep in heat and hold down heating costs.

Since most heat escapes or enters through the roof, the thickest insulation is required either in the roof or the attic floor. Slightly less insulation is required in outside walls and in floors over unheated spaces, and still less is required in walls around a heated basement.

(Windows and exterior doors should also be insulated by installing double-pane insulating glass or covering them with storm windows. But this subject is covered in chapters 6 and 7.)

How much insulation you need depends on where you live and how much fuel costs. If you're looking for maximum savings, send to the Superintendent of Documents, U.S. Government Printing Office, Washington, D.C. 20402 for the U.S. Commerce Department's booklet c13.53:8, "Making the Most of Your Energy Dollars in Home Heating and Cooling." It costs 70 cents. This contains tables which give a precise answer to insulation requirements in all parts of the country. Unfortunately it is likely to be an expensive answer because so much insulation is called for.

If you'll settle for a more practical, not-too-expensive answer to the question, however, you should put in insulation with the following R values:

Roof or attic floor—R-19 to R-22

Outside walls and walls next to unheated spaces such as attached garages—R-11 to R-13

Floors over unheated spaces such as crawl spaces and overhangs—R-11

Walls in heated basements—R-7

R value (standing for resistance value) is a measure of a material's ability to resist the flow of heat. The higher the R value, the more effective the insulation. Since different types of insulation have different R values, the thickness of the insulation required to produce a desired R value varies.

To give this R value . . .   *. . . you need approximately this many inches of insulation*

	Mineral-wool batts, blankets	Fiberglass batts, blankets	Mineral-wool loose fill	Fiberglass loose fill	Cellulose-fiber loose fill	Vermiculite	Urethane board	Styrene board	Wood-fiber board	Urethane spray	Urea-formaldehyde spray
R-7	2¼	2¼	3	3½	2	3½	1	1¾	6¾	1	1½
R-11	3	3½	3¾	5	3	5½	1½	2½	10	1½	2
R-13	3½	3¾	4½	6	3¾	6¼	2	3	11½	2	2½
R-19	5¼	6	6½	8¾	5	9	2½	4¼	17	2½	3½
R-22	6	6½	7½	10	6	10¼	3	4¾	20	3	4

As the table indicates, there are many more kinds of insulation than most people realize. They are not, however, applicable to all purposes.

MINERAL-WOOL AND FIBERGLASS BATTS. Mineral wool and fiberglass are similar, although the former is made from rock or slag while the latter is glass. Both are resistant to fire and vermin. While the fibers themselves absorb very little water, any thickness of insulation can become water-soaked and lose effectiveness; but when it dries out, it is as good as new.

Batts of mineral wool and fiberglass have a vague resemblance to huge, thick wood planks, but they're so flexible that they can be bent double. They are made in 4-ft. or 8-ft. lengths and in 15-in. or 23-in. widths to fit between studs and joists. Thicknesses range from 1 to 7 in. Some batts are unfaced: the insulation is exposed on both the front and back. Others are faced on one side with a tough, vaporproof paper.

Because of their short length, batts are easy to handle and can be installed anywhere, but are particularly suited for use in attic floors, under floors over unheated spaces, and between roof rafters.

MINERAL-WOOL AND FIBERGLASS BLANKETS. The only difference between blankets and batts is in their shape. The blankets come in rolls up to 100 ft. long in 15-in. or 23-in. widths and 1-in. to 7-in. thicknesses. They may be unfaced; faced on one side with a paper vapor barrier; or faced on one side with a vapor barrier and the other side with an ordinary paper backing. Although they are usable anywhere, they are best for installation in walls and attic floors because it takes only one person to handle them. In overhead installations, you do better if you have a helper.

FIBROUS LOOSE FILL. Loose-fill insulation comes in large bags from which it is poured into joist spaces in an attic floor. It is made of mineral wool or fiberglass like that in batts and blankets, or of cellulose material, which is a fancy name for ground-up newspapers. As the table indicates, the cellulose insulation is somewhat more effective than the wools. It's also a little cheaper. It is treated to make it fire-resistant, but it soaks up water and vermin find it to their liking.

The main advantage of all loose fill is that you can control the thickness you need in the attic floor. For instance, if you want a resistance value of R-38 in the attic, you can achieve it just by pouring out a foot or more of loose fill; or if you want to add only a couple of inches to the insulation you already have, you can do that just as easily. Furthermore, you can work loose fill into awkward places—far under the eaves, for example —where you would have trouble installing other forms of insulation. A major disadvantage of the fill is that you must install a separate vapor barrier.

Probably the most common use for loose fill, however, is in walls of existing houses. The material must be installed professionally. This is done by cutting holes into a wall between each pair of studs, just below each floor level, and blowing the insulation in through a large hose until the spaces are filled. If there are obstructions in the stud spaces, the spaces below them are filled by cutting additional holes. All holes are then closed so you can't tell they have been made. Unfortunately, the insulation may settle somewhat, leaving small empty spaces and thus reducing the effectiveness of the insulation a little.

VERMICULITE. This is an expanded mica with a general resemblance to coarse white sand. It is fire-resistant and verminproof, and does not retain moisture. Unlike fiberglass and mineral wool, it doesn't irritate the skin when you handle it.

Vermiculite comes in bags and is poured into attic floors in any desired thickness. It is exceptionally easy to work into awkward places. It is also the only material which, when poured into the cores of concrete-block walls, can be counted on to fill the cores from top to bottom. As in the case of other loose fills, however, you must apply a separate vapor barrier.

URETHANE FOAM. Urethane foam forms a more effective barrier against heat and cold than any other insulation. It is disliked by vermin; does not soak up water; and has some value as a vapor barrier. But while it is slow to catch fire, it does burn and in doing so gives off lethal fumes. It's also expensive.

The foam must be applied by trained workmen. It can be used in an attic floor or exterior walls, and because it sticks like glue, it can also be applied to the underside of roofs and floors over unheated spaces. Next to its thermal efficiency, its greatest value is that it can be sprayed into every crack and crevice so the house is completely enveloped.

UREA-COPOLYMER FOAM. This is a recent variation of urea-formaldehyde foam-locking the formaldehyde. It is installed and performs in the same general ways but has a slightly higher R value and is even more

Urea-formaldehyde insulation is injected into walls by hose. Rapperswill Corp.

resistant to fire and the transmission of moisture (nevertheless, a vapor barrier should be used with it).

UREA-FORMALDEHYDE FOAM. This is another extremely effective insulation used in the same way as urethane foam. Its principal advantage is its good fire resistance. In fact, fire officials in one major city credit the foam with stopping a recent garage fire from consuming the house to which the garage was attached. But it must be installed with a separate vapor barrier.

Like urethane foam, urea-formaldehyde must be applied by trained workmen. It flows up and down through walls and across other surfaces like shaving cream and fills all voids but then shrinks slightly as it dries.

URETHANE BOARDS. The urethane used in rigid board insulation has the same characteristics as foam. The boards are made in standard 4×8-ft. panels and are also available in 24-in. widths and 10-ft. and 12-ft. lengths. Thicknesses range from ¾ to 4 in.

In new construction, the boards are used primarily for roof and wall sheathing and for insulating the perimeters of slabs. In existing homes, they can be used to cover attic ceilings, interior walls, and walls of heated basements. When applied to the ceiling or walls of occupied rooms, they must be covered with gypsum board, plaster, etc. to protect them from fire, gouging, denting, and breaking.

STYRENE BOARDS. The thermal efficiency of styrene is somewhat below that of urethane; otherwise boards made of the two materials have similar characteristics and are used in the same way. Styrene is somewhat less expensive.

The boards come in thicknesses of 1 in. to 4 in.; widths of 12, 16, 24, and 48 in.; and lengths of 4, 8, and 12 ft. Like urethane, the boards can be applied with nails or adhesive. They must then be covered with gypsum board or other wall-surfacing material to protect against fire and damage.

WOOD-FIBER BOARDS. As the preceding table indicates, wood-fiber boards are the least efficient insulators, and are therefore never used strictly to cut down heat loss and heat gain. They are, instead, used principally as a roof or wall sheathing material or for surfacing interior walls. Consequently, they are made only in ½-in. or ⅝-in. thicknesses having an R value of only 1.11.

The boards come in widths of 4 ft. and 8 ft. and in lengths of 8, 9, 10, and 12 ft. They are resistant to moisture, rot, fungi, and termites, but unless specially treated, are not fire-resistant.

FOIL INSULATION. Foil insulation made of several sheets of aluminum prevents heat from entering and leaving a house largely by radiation and, secondarily, by creating dead-air spaces within stud and joist spaces. It is particularly effective in preventing heat build-up under roofs in summer. It doesn't burn, discourages mice and rats from gnawing through walls, and is an outstanding vapor barrier.

The insulation is produced in 250-ft. and 500-ft. rolls, in widths of 12, 16, 20, and 24 in. Several types are available. These differ from one another only in the number of reflective layers and air spaces they contain.

The foil is installed in roofs, walls of new houses, and floors over unheated spaces. It is stapled along the edges either to the faces or sides of rafters and studs. Care must be taken to stretch it tightly between framing members so it will expand to its full thickness.

INSTALLING INSULATION

INSULATING ATTICS. In an attic, the insulation can be installed either in the roof or in the floor. If the attic is used for any purpose other than storage, or if it may be occupied at some time, or if it has a floor, roof insulation is called for. Otherwise, it is generally better to insulate the floor. This greatly reduces the amount of insulation needed and simplifies installation. It also reduces fuel consumption because heated and cooled air is held within the living spaces; none of it is wasted through leakage into the attic.

Insulation for the roof must either incorporate a built-in vapor barrier or be covered with a vapor barrier so that moisture escaping from the house cannot come in contact with the roof where it will condense and cause decay of sheathing and rafters.

Insulation in the attic floor must also have a vapor barrier on the warm (under) side. This is the best reason for using batts or blankets which are faced with a vapor barrier or foam which requires no vapor barrier. If loose fill is used, it must be laid over sheets of polyethylene film which lap up on the sides of the joists for several inches. The alternative is to paint the ceilings with a vapor-resistant paint.

Floor insulation must not be laid within 3 in. of recessed light fixtures projecting up between the joists; and if ventilation is provided in the roof overhangs, the insulation must not extend all the way into the eaves. Screened and louvered openings should be installed in the gable ends of the roof or in small dormers or a cupola so that air can circulate freely through the attic space at all times. As a rule of thumb, you need 1 sq. ft. of louvered opening for each 300 sq. ft. of attic floor area.

If you want to increase the thickness of existing attic-

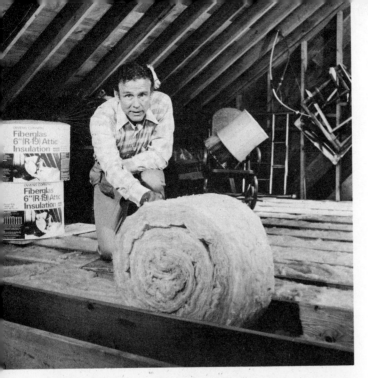

Easiest way to increase the thickness of insulation in an attic floor is to lay unfaced fiberglass or mineral-wool blankets between joists. GAF Corp.

floor insulation, use loose fill or unfaced batts and blankets. If for some reason the only insulation you can lay hands on is faced, the vapor barriers must be slashed so that any moisture entering the lower layer is not trapped.

Increasing the thickness of roof insulation is difficult because there is rarely any space within the rafter spaces for an extra thickness of batt or blanket insulation. The best procedure is to slash the vapor barriers of the existing insulation and nail rigid board insulation to the rafters.

INSULATING A ROOF THAT FORMS THE CEILING OF A ROOM.

If the underside of the roof serves as the ceiling surface, the insulation is installed above the roof deck or is incorporated in the roof deck (see Chapter 3). Increasing the thickness of the existing insulation can be done only by tearing off the roof covering and adding the insulation underneath, or by nailing rigid insulating boards to the ceiling.

If the ceiling surface is separate from the roof and applied to the under edges of the rafters, the insulation—with a vapor barrier on the underside—is installed between the two surfaces. To increase the thickness of insulation in an old house, your best bet is to have it blown into the rafter spaces above the present insulation. If this is impossible (as it may well be), nail insulation board to the underside of the ceiling.

INSULATING WALLS.

In a new house or addition, exterior walls are easily insulated with blankets, boards, foam, or foil. Install a vapor barrier on the warm side.

The most practical way of insulating walls in an old house—provided they are not already partially insu-

lated—is to have loose fill or foam blown in. The only other way of insulating existing walls or of adding insulation to poorly insulated walls is to install rigid boards over the interior wall surfaces.

INSULATING FLOORS OVER UNHEATED SPACES.

There are two ways of handling this problem. One is to install faced batts—with the vapor barrier on the upper side—between the joists. To support them, nail chicken wire to the bottoms of the joists or lace a straight wire back and forth across the joists. The alternative is to have foam blown against the underside of the floor.

The other way to insulate floors—but only those over a crawl space—is to apply unfaced batts or blankets to the walls of the crawl space. The insulation

To insulate floors over unheated spaces, lay batts over chicken wire. The insulation must also cover the headers at the exterior walls.

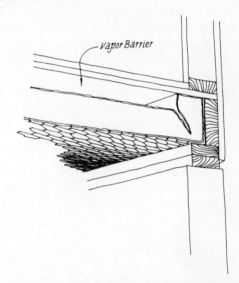

Walls which have been closed in are usually insulated with blankets or batts. Vapor barrier is always on the warm side of the wall. Johns-Manville Corp.

starts at the subfloor and is pressed into the space against the header, continues down over the foundation wall, and extends at least 2 ft. out over the bottom of the crawl space. The floor above the crawl space should be finished or covered with a vapor-resistant material to prevent condensation from forming on the floor joists and sills. In addition, the bottom of the crawl space should be completely covered with polyethylene film to prevent moisture in the ground from entering the house above. A continuous sheet of film is preferred. If narrow strips are used, lap the edges 6 in. and tape the joints. In both cases, lap the film up on the sides of the foundation walls several inches.

No matter how crawl spaces are insulated, all should be ventilated with screened vents installed high in the foundation walls. At least two vents are needed to provide a through draft. The vents are opened in the summer, closed in winter.

INSULATING HEATED BASEMENTS.

Basement insulation can be installed inside or outside the foundation walls. It should extend from the level of the ceiling down at least 2 ft. below the ground line.

For exterior insulation, use urethane or styrene boards and glue them to the walls with foamboard adhesive. To protect the exposed face of the boards against damage, cover them with $\frac{1}{4}$-in. asbestos-cement board or Portland-cement plaster.

To insulate the walls on the inside, use faced batts or blankets, or urethane or styrene boards. Line the space between the top of the foundation walls and the underside of the subfloor with insulation, and cover the upper part of the walls. If batts or blankets are used, you must install studs against the walls and install the insulation between the studs. Then cover the walls from top to bottom with gypsum board, plywood, etc.

Rigid boards can be glued to the foundation walls. Then the finish wall surface is glued to them. A better

Plywood paneling being applied over rigid styrene insulating boards which are cemented to basement wall. W. R. Grace & Co.

approach, if the foundation walls are the least bit damp, is to lay the boards against the walls and hold them in place with wood or special steel furring strips which are anchored by driving hardened steel studs into the concrete. The finish wall surface is then nailed to the furring strips.

INSULATING CONCRETE SLABS.

Slab floors must be insulated around the edges, not only to prevent the loss of heat through them but also to keep them from feeling icy cold underfoot. In new construction, the insulation should be installed before the slab is poured. It consists of rigid styrene or urethane boards laid against the edges of the slab and extending 2 ft. under the slab. Just 1-in. insulation is enough except in very cold climates, where 2-in. should be used.

To insulate the slab in an existing house, install styrene or urethane boards against the exposed edges of the slab or against the foundations in which the slab rests. The boards should extend from the top to the bottom of a floating slab or from the top of the slab to 2 ft. below ground if the slab rests on foundations. Cement the boards to the concrete and cover them with asbestos-cement board or Portland-cement plaster.

INSULATING PIPES AND DUCTS.

All pipes and ducts passing through unheated spaces should be insulated. Pipes are normally covered with 3-ft. lengths of preshaped cellular insulation held in place with metal straps. Joints are covered with furnace cement.

Ducts should be covered with fiberglass duct insulation or ordinary fiberglass or mineral-wool batts. Use at least a 2-in. thickness; 4 in. is recommended in colder areas. On ducts used for cooling, a vapor barrier on the outside of the insulation is essential.

VAPOR BARRIERS.

Insulating a house has one drawback. Coupled with the improved construction techniques now in use, it makes a house so tight that moisture given off by cooking, washing, bathing, floor-mopping, etc. cannot readily escape to the outdoors. Instead, it condenses into visible moisture on and within the exterior walls, roof, and floors over unheated spaces and causes exterior paint to peel, wood to rot, insulation to become sodden and ineffective.

There are three ways to prevent this:

1. Reduce the amount of moisture in the air by changing your cooking, laundering, and floor-mopping habits; installing mixing valves in bathtubs and showers (see Chapter 14); and covering the bottoms of crawl spaces with polyethylene film (see above).

2. Exhaust the moisture-laden air to the outdoors by venting automatic clothes dryers (see Chapter 15) and installing ducted ventilating fans in bathrooms and kitchens (see Chapters 14 and 15).

3. Install vapor barriers on the warm side of all ex-

terior walls, the roof or upstairs ceilings, and floors over unheated spaces.

As noted earlier, a number of insulating materials have built-in vapor barriers or serve as vapor barriers in their own right. If these are not used, you have two alternatives. One is to staple large sheets of heavy polyethylene film to studs, rafters, and/or ceiling joists after the insulation has been installed. In floors over unheated spaces, insert the film between the subfloor and finish floor. The film must form a complete envelope around the house (except, of course, for doors and windows). Lap the edges of adjoining sheets at least 6 in. and drive staples through the laps into the framing members.

Surfaces which cannot be covered with polyethylene must be covered with two coats of latex or alkyd paint, varnish, or sealer; vinyl wallcovering; or waterproof materials such as resilient flooring and ceramic tile.

WHO MAKES IT

Alfol, Inc. · Aluminum-foil insulation providing two, three, or four reflective air spaces.

Borden, Inc., Borden Chemical Div. · Urea-formaldehyde foam.

Celotex Corp. · Urethane board in 4×8-ft. panels. Metal furring channels.

Certain Teed Products Corp. · Fiberglass batt and blanket insulation.

C. P. Chemical Co. · Urea-copolymer insulation.

Diversified Insulation, Inc. · Cellulose-fiber loose-fill insulation.

Dyrelite Corp. · Rigid styrene foam panels in 1-ft. to 8-ft. lengths and 1-ft. to 4-ft. widths.

Fomo Products, Inc. · Urethane foam in small spray cans for do-it-yourself insulating around doors, windows, plumbing, etc.

W. R. Grace & Co., Construction Products Div. · Zonolite rigid styrene foam panels from 1 to 4 ft. wide and 4, 8, and 12 ft. long. Metal furring channels. Vermiculite loose fill.

Howmet Corp. · Foil insulation and vapor barriers.

Johns-Manville Sales Corp. · Fiberglass batt and blanket insulation.

Owens-Corning Fiberglas Corp. · Fiberglass batts, blankets and loose fill.

Rapperswill Corp. · Urea-formaldehyde foam.

Rockwool Industries, Inc. · Mineral wool loose-fill insulation, batts and blankets.

Thermo/Foam, Inc. · Urea-formaldehyde foam.

U.S. Fiber Corp. · Cellulose-fiber loose-fill insulation.

U.S. Mineral Products Co. · Mineral Wool loose fill, batts and blankets. Urethane board.

Upjohn Co., CPR Div. · Urethane foam panels up to 4×12 ft. for installation on roof decks under built-up roofing.

5

Waterproofing

For some homeowners water is a relentless enemy which never stops causing problems. For others water is of no concern until one day, without warning, a leak develops in the roof, an outside wall, or the basement.

No home is immune to leaks and water damage. You must anticipate trouble from water when you build. And you must be ready to take steps to control it ever after.

Two of the most important waterproofing materials—roofing and flashing—are covered in Chapter 3. Others, such as the sheathing paper in exterior walls and weatherstripping around doors and windows, contribute substantially to a dry house and are also discussed in other chapters.

The materials and equipment described below are those made with the specific purpose of keeping water out or getting rid of it when it sneaks in.

CAULKS AND SEALANTS. Caulks and sealants are essentially the same thing and can be substituted for each other. They are thick mastics applied with a tube, caulking gun, or putty knife to all cracks and joints through which water may enter the structure of the house—around doors, windows and tub rims; between dissimilar siding materials or metal flashings and walls; in translucent-plastic roofs, gutters, and leaders; and so on.

To be effective, caulks and sealants must (1) stick tightly to the materials to which they are applied; (2) expand and contract even in extreme temperatures to maintain a watertight seal; (3) hold paint without bleeding through and staining the paint; (4) resist cracking and disintegration for years.

Until comparatively recently, all caulks and sealants were oil-base materials much like a very soft putty. Frequently called painter's caulks, these are still available and because of their low cost are widely used by both professionals and do-it-yourselfers. But they be-

come brittle in a few years, fall out, and need to be replaced.

Caulks and sealants containing rubber are far superior. They cost more but they retain their flexibility for a very long time. Formulas vary. If you hunt through the racks of a well-stocked hardware store or building-supplies outlet, you will find latex, acrylic (meaning acrylic latex), polysulfide, butyl, hypalon, and neoprene caulks. There are differences between them, but they are, as a rule, relatively unimportant. Examine the labels carefully and select the kind which comes closest to your requirements. Acrylic caulk, for instance, sticks exceptionally well to glass. Butyl caulk is resistant to unusually low and high temperatures. If you are uncertain about the caulk to use, let price be your guide. The higher it is, the better the material.

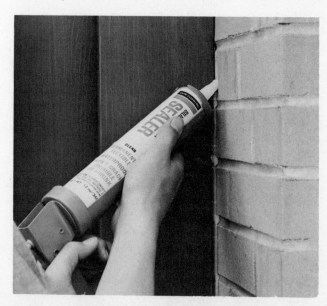

For large waterproofing jobs, buy caulking compound in cylinders and apply with a gun. Dow Corning Corp.

Latex caulks are generally white. Some are black, gray, or translucent. Use the gray or black, obviously, where it isn't going to show or blends with the background. The translucent caulk is used primarily in translucent-fiberglass roofs.

Urethane caulk has outstanding resistance to abrasion and puncturing and therefore is of particular value in sealing joints between walks, terraces, and decks and the house. A special primer must first be applied. Then the caulk, which comes in two containers, must be mixed.

Silicone caulk, most commonly sold as bathtub caulk, is outstanding for all purposes. It's very flexible, can bridge large gaps, sticks tenaciously, and wears forever. But because of its high cost, it is not usually used for general purposes. In addition, most of the caulks are unpaintable.

To use any caulk, clean the joint well and let it dry before filling it. Scrape off any caulk which gets on surrounding surfaces immediately. Once it sets, removal requires special solvents.

MASONRY WATERPROOFERS.

Portland-cement paint has some moisture-stopping ability but is used primarily for decorative purposes. Furthermore, it is tedious to work with since the powder must be mixed with water and then scrubbed into a damp wall surface (the paint does not have enough abrasion resistance to be used on floors). It must then be kept damp for 48 hours before a second coat is applied in the same way.

Cementitious coatings are of much heavier consistency than cement paints, and it usually takes only a couple of coats to stop any seepage of water through a masonry wall. But they cannot be counted on to seal off leaks through large cracks or holes. They are used mainly to waterproof the inside of basement and crawl-space walls. Like cement paint, they are not resistant to foot traffic.

The coatings, which come in white and several pastel colors, should be applied to concrete, blocks, bricks, etc. from which dirt, grease, and paint have been removed. Dampen the walls with water before application. Mix the cementitious powder with water to the consistency of thick cream (the exact quantity of water is specified on the bag). Then lay the coating on the walls with a whitewash brush. Do not brush it out. After the first coat has cured for 24 hours, repeat the process. For severe problems, you can apply as many additional coats as are needed.

Epoxy waterproofers are another answer to the basement wall which oozes water but does not have active leaks. They are clear coatings which stick tenaciously to all cleaned surfaces, but because they dry very rapidly once they are mixed, they do not cover very much ground. They are also expensive.

One kind of epoxy which can be used underwater

Waterproofing a concrete block wall with epoxy. Woodhill Chemical Sales Corp.

can be applied straight from the can or mixed with sand to increase coverage on porous surfaces.

Bituminous coatings are made of asphalt or coal-tar pitch which is sometimes reinforced with asbestos fibers. The coatings are applied to the outside of basement and foundation walls. Application should, of course, be made at the time the house is being built, before the trenches around the walls have been backfilled with soil. In dry locations, one coat of fibered coating or two coats of nonfibered coating well brushed into the pores of masonry usually stop all leaks. In wet locations, however, the coated walls should be parged (covered) with two 1/4-in. layers of Portland-cement plaster.

In an existing home, basement walls are waterproofed in this fashion only if all attempts to stop the leaks from inside fail. The cost is high because of the extent of the work. If the foundation walls are cracked, asphalt-saturated building felt or fiberglass fabric is embedded between two or three coats of bituminous material. Then, after the walls have been parged, 4-in.-diameter perforated composition drainpipes should be laid in a continuous row around the footings to collect water and carry it off through solid drainpipes to a storm sewer or other disposal point. The pipes are covered with 12 in. of crushed rock before the trenches are filled.

If a basement floor leaks badly over much of its area, the easiest way to correct matters is to mop it with asphalt primer in which overlapping strips of asphalt-saturated felt or a continuous sheet of heavy polyethylene film is embedded. A 2-in. or thicker slab of concrete is then poured on top.

Silicone water repellents are sometimes called waterproofers but are effective only as damp-proofers. They turn away moisture but do not stop persistent seepage.

The sealers are colorless, transparent coatings applied to the exterior of above-ground masonry walls. Use a brush or spray gun. One coat is enough but it must be renewed about every five years.

Copolymer sealers are similar in appearance to silicone water repellents but penetrate well into the pores of masonry so it does not absorb moisture and is not weakened by it. In the home, sealers are particularly useful for stopping used bricks from spalling and disintegrating. They can also be used to protect wood siding and gypsum board which serves as the base for ceramic tiles over bathtubs and in shower stalls.

PATCHING MATERIALS. Stopping water from trickling or actually gushing through cracks and holes in masonry is a relatively simple job. The standard procedure is to chip the crack open to a depth and width of at least ½ in. Cut the sides of the opening straight up and down or, better, bevel them backward. Then mix 1 part Portland cement with 3 parts sand and enough water to make a workable mix, and press this firmly into the hole.

There are other types of cement, however, which simplify this operation or are needed in cases where the incoming water loosens the cement before it hardens in place.

Latex cement is made by mixing cement with liquid latex. It is sold in small packages containing a powder and a liquid which are mixed together before use.

Unlike Portland cement, latex cement has the unusual property of adhering tightly to an existing masonry surface even when applied in a layer only a fraction of an inch thick. Because of this, it is unnecessary to open cracks and holes very wide. Simply scrape them out and cram the cement into them.

To repair cracks in joints between a basement wall and floor, clean them out well. Then trowel latex cement into the corners in a triangular shape. The cement should extend up the wall and out over the floor at least 1 in.

Acrylic, vinyl, and epoxy cements also stick tight in very thin layers. The acrylics and vinyls are mixed with water; the epoxies, with a special liquid. They can be used instead of latex cement for patching work.

Hydraulic cement sets up into rock-hard consistency even in the presence of flowing water. It is therefore

Latex cement is useful for filling holes quickly. Bondex International, Inc.

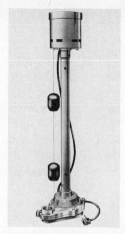

Left, upright sump pump, Jacuzzi Bros., Inc.; right, submersible sump pump, Flotec, Inc.

used to stop leaks through which water flows more or less constantly.

After chipping the crack or hole open to a depth of a couple of inches, mix a small amount of cement with water and mold it in your hand for several minutes until it feels warm. Press it into the hole immediately and hold it until it hardens enough to stop the leak.

Conventional Portland cement can also be used for plugging active leaks if it is mixed with a copolymer sealer rather than water.

SUMP PUMPS. If for some reason it is impossible to keep water out of a basement no matter what steps you take to waterproof the walls and floors, install a sump pump. It cannot prevent the entrance of water but will remove the water before you have a flood.

Sump pumps are designed to be installed in sumps—holes about a foot deep located at the lowest point in a basement floor. To be fully effective in removing all water, the floor must be sloped slightly toward the hole. The hole is lined either with concrete or with a prefabricated crock of polyethylene, fiberglass, or tile. The pump is then set into the sump and plugged into a 120-volt, 15-amp electrical circuit. A pipe carries the water from the pump into a drain or up to ground level. The pump turns on and off automatically as the sump fills and empties.

One type of sump pump is designed with the motor mounted above the sump on a short length of pipe. Operation is controlled by a float ball hanging from the motor. A second type of pump is a submersible unit with the motor enclosed in a watertight housing installed inside the sump. If equipped with a handle, the pump can be removed from the sump at any time and used for pumping out swimming pools, boats, etc.

WHO MAKES IT

Absolute Coatings, Inc. · Silicone water repellent.
Anti-Hydro Waterproofing Co. · Hydraulic cement. Cementitious coatings. Silicone water repellent.
Bondex International, Inc. · Cementitious coatings. Silicone

water repellent. Hydraulic cement. Oil-base, latex, and butyl caulks.

Borden, Inc., Borden Chemical Div. · Bathtub caulk.

Celotex Corp. · Silicone water repellent. Bituminous waterproofers.

DAP, Inc. · Oil-base, latex, butyl, and polysulfide caulks. Bathtub caulk.

Darworth Co. · Oil-base and latex caulks.

Ditrek Corp. · Epoxy waterproofer; can be applied to wet surfaces.

Dow Corning Corp. · Silicone caulk.

Flotec, Inc. · Submersible sump pumps.

H. B. Fuller Co. · Oil-base, butyl, and silicone caulks.

Genova, Inc. · Upright and submersible sump pumps. Polyethylene sump crocks.

Gibson-Homans Co. · Silicone water repellent. Oil-base, latex, hypalon rubber, butyl, acrylic, and urethane caulks. Bituminous waterproofers.

Goulds Pumps, Inc. · Upright and submersible sump pumps.

Jacuzzi Bros. Inc. · Upright and submersible sump pumps.

Karnak Chemical Corp. · Bituminous waterproofers and damp-proofers. Silicone water repellent. Butyl caulk.

Miracle Adhesives Corp. · Acrylic caulk.

Montgomery Ward & Co. · Upright and submersible sump pumps and fiberglass sump crocks.

Peabody Barnes. · Upright and submersible sump pumps.

Red Devil, Inc. · Acrylic, butyl, and oil-base caulks.

SCM Corp., Macco Adhesive Div. · Oil-base, latex, acrylic, butyl, and polysulfide caulks.

Sears Roebuck & Co. · Upright and submersible sump pumps. Epoxy waterproofer.

Standard Dry Wall Products. · Thoroseal cementitious coatings and exterior foundation coatings. Waterplug hydraulic cement. Acrylic, butyl, and polysulfide caulks. Silicone water repellent.

E. A. Thompson Co. · Copolymer sealers.

United Gilsonite Laboratories. · Cementitious coatings. Hydraulic cement. Silicone water repellent.

Waterlox Chemical & Coatings Corp. · Silicone water repellent.

Woodhill Chemical Sales Corp. · Duro epoxy waterproofers.

6

Windows

The natural tendency is to think of windows as a highly desirable feature of the home—which they are. They admit light, air, and view, and by breaking up what would otherwise be blank walls, they add to the interest and, if well designed, to the beauty of the house. But how often do you ever stop to think—as many architects have—how much trouble windows cause?

For example, in winter they lower house temperature by simultaneously letting cold air enter and warm air escape.

In summer, they bring in the sun, which makes the house uncomfortably warm and fades the color of almost everything it strikes.

In addition to permitting a view, which is not always pretty, windows turn the house into a goldfish bowl.

They require fairly frequent washing—a chore no one enjoys—and every now and then they are broken and need to be replaced.

They are the first surfaces in the house which fog up when the indoor humidity rises; and they often stream with water, which ruins the finish on the sills.

Finally, windows let in annoying neighborhood noises. They become ugly black mirrors when you turn on the lights at night. They afford easy access for intruders. They require expensive curtains and blinds, which also need periodic cleaning. And all too often, instead of improving the appearance of a house, they actually detract from it.

It's true that many of the shortcomings of windows can be corrected—though not without cost. But they cannot be ignored when you're building or remodeling. Your comfort, convenience, and pleasure depend far more on finding the right windows for any given wall than, say, on choosing the right interior wall finish or even on building a perfect kitchen.

WINDOW INSTALLATION. Installing a window in a new or existing wall is similar to installing a door. The rough opening is made as shown in the drawing with double studs on the sides, a rough sill (also called a header) formed of one or, in the case of large windows, a pair of 2×4s; and a large header (usually consisting of a pair of 2×4s) above. The opening should be approximately 1 in. wider than the window frame and ¾ in. higher.

Almost all wood windows on the market are partially assembled as they come from the factory. The sash is mounted in the frame with the outside casings attached. Thus it is necessary to add only the interior casings and sill after a window is in place.

Installation of windows is made from outside the house and usually requires two persons. Without removing the sash or bracing temporarily applied to the

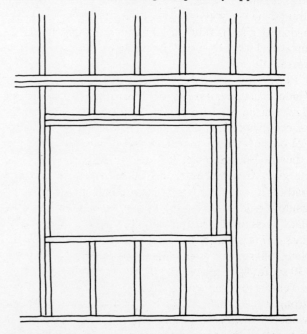

Framing for a large window that doesn't quite fill four stud spaces.

frame, set the frame in the rough opening with the casings hard against the sheathing. Wedge the frame up from the rough sill to the correct height. Level it carefully and install shims around the sides and top. Then fasten it in place with galvanized or aluminum casing nails driven through the casings into the framing.

Metal windows which come without casings are installed similarly except that after they are leveled, they are screwed through the sides to the frame. The installation is then completed by adding the casings.

Fixed windows of medium size are installed like operating wood windows. For large fixed windows you should have your lumber dealer make a jamb frame to fit the window. After nailing this into the rough opening, nail 1-in.-thick stops around the inside edges. Place the window—if framed—against these and nail additional stops around the outside edges.

If the window is unframed—merely a large pane of glass—a generous bed of glazing compound is applied to the outside edges of the inside stops and also to the frame. Neoprene spacer strips are then fastened to the edges of the glass, and the glass is firmly embedded in the glazing compound and held in place with outside stops.

Bay and bow windows are installed like conventional wood windows but must be supported on brackets or an extension of the floor framing, and covered with a slanting roof. This calls for a carpenter.

Dormers should also be constructed by a carpenter, although if you are simply replacing the windows in existing dormers, you can do the work yourself.

GLAZING. The standard glass for small-paned windows is single-strength (SS) glass of B quality. Double-strength (DS) glass may be used in larger panes, but A-quality glass is rarely used because window manufacturers feel it is not enough better than B-quality glass to warrant the extra cost.

Plate glass is generally recommended for picture windows because it is free of distortion, but heavy sheet glass can be used if you are willing to sacrifice clarity for economy. The thickness of the glass depends on the size of the window and the wind pressure to which it is exposed. For example, if your building code requires the glass area and thickness to be based on a design load of 25 lbs. per square foot, the maximum area of a window made with $3/16$-in. heavy sheet glass or $1/8$-in. plate glass is approximately 28 sq. ft.; $7/32$-in. sheet glass, 37 sq. ft.; $1/4$-in. plate glass, 43 sq. ft.; $5/16$-in. plate, 62 sq. ft.; $3/8$-in. plate, 87 sq. ft.; $1/2$-in. plate, 130 sq. ft.; $5/8$-in. plate, 170 sq. ft.

Tempered plate glass, which is three to five times stronger than ordinary plate, should be used in picture windows if they are located where there is any chance of people walking into them.

The insulating glass used in most stock windows is

Heat-absorbing glass used in sliding glass doors and windows. The effect is barely noticeable in a black-and-white photo, but the hills seen through the glass are darker than those seen through open door in center.

made of two panes of sheet glass with a $1/2$-in. air space between them. But in some cases, the glass has two panes with only $1/4$-in. air space; while in other cases, it consists of three panes of glass with approximately $1/4$-in. air space between each pair of panes.

Insulated picture windows can be glazed in the same way. However, glass made of two sheets of $1/4$-in. plate glass with a $1/2$-in. air space is preferable because it reduces heat loss and eliminates distortions which can spoil the view.

The newest development in insulating glass is a pane filled with dry gas rather than the dehydrated air normally used. The result is an increase of about 20% in insulating value. The glass, designated by the trademark Xi (which is printed on the corner of every pane), is being used in a number of stock windows and is also available for use in picture windows.

Another type of glass which can be specified for picture windows (it is not available in stock windows) is heat-absorbing glass. This is a conventional or tempered $1/4$-in. glass which is tinted brown, gray, or blue. It reduces both glare and heat as well as the amount of light entering a room. The actual effect depends on the color.

Blue glass reduces heat transmission approximately 40% and total light approximately 25%. The comparable figures for gray glass are 40% and 56%; for brown glass, 44% and 52%. Glare reduction roughly parallels the reduction in total light transmission.

Because of their color, all heat-absorbing glasses distort the colors of the landscape to some extent. Many architects feel that brown glass is least disturbing in this respect, but that is a matter of personal preference.

Two more types of glass which can be used in windows—although they must usually be installed by the homeowner—are patterned glass, which lets in light while obscuring the view in either direction; and mirror glass, which is reflective and opaque on the outside and transparent inside.

Some homeowners who live in high-crime-rate areas or who are bothered by children breaking windows with baseballs have replaced window glass in vulnerable locations with transparent or translucent plastics. Of the five materials used, the best in all-round performance are the polycarbonates, which are so tough that even the most determined burglar finds them difficult to break. They also have excellent resistance to abrasion and weathering.

Specially coated acrylics are only slightly less desirable. Then come coated vinyls and polystyrene. Fiberglass-reinforced plastic, which ranks with the polycarbonates in resistance to breaking, is available only in translucent sheets.

WINDOW FRAMES. Residential windows are framed either with wood or aluminum. Steel frames are available, but since their superior strength is generally not required in houses, they rarely are used.

To most homeowners, the principal advantage of wood-framed windows is their appearance. They look less clinical than aluminum sash; and unlike aluminum sash, they complement all architectural styles. Furthermore, if you prefer multi-paned windows, it is much easier to find exactly what you want in wood than in aluminum.

The other advantage of wood frames is that they are poor conductors; consequently, in winter they bar the entrance of cold, and condensation does not form on them.

On the other side of the coin, however, wood frames sometimes decay (to prevent this, most are treated with wood preservative before they leave the factory). Because they swell and contract, they sometimes stick. And they require periodic refinishing unless they are given a polyurea finish or sheathed in vinyl at the factory. (The vinyl sheathing also prevents decay and swelling.)

Aluminum-framed windows became popular largely because it was thought that they suffered from none of the problems associated with wood windows—they didn't rot, swell, contract, or need refinishing. Actually, this isn't altogether true. Near the seacoast and in corrosive industrial atmospheres, aluminum frames may corrode so badly that they must be painted to protect them; if not painted, they disintegrate and need to be replaced. For this reason, it is advisable to buy aluminum windows which are protected by a factory-applied finish.

The principal drawback of aluminum, however, is its poor insulating value. In winter, it not only transmits cold but is also covered with the moisture condensing

on it. Happily, this problem has now been corrected to a large extent by a number of manufacturers. In so-called thermalized windows (and sliding doors), the frames are designed to eliminate metal-to-metal contacts between the outside and inside. In some cases, this is done by inserting urethane, epoxy, or vinyl strips between the exterior and interior parts of the frames; in other cases, the frames are entirely covered on the inside with a rigid vinyl sheath which is separated from the aluminum by air spaces.

SINGLE-PANED AND MULTI-PANED WINDOWS. In sharp contrast to the many-paned windows which were in use before World War II, the great majority of stock windows now on the market have single panes. Three things brought this change about: Manufacturers found they could mass-produce single-paned windows at much lower cost than multi-paned windows; homeowners got fed up with washing small window panes; and insulating glass, which cannot be economically produced in small sizes, came into widespread use.

This development does not mean that if you want a double-hung window with 12 lights over 12, or a casement window with eight lights, or a horizontal sliding

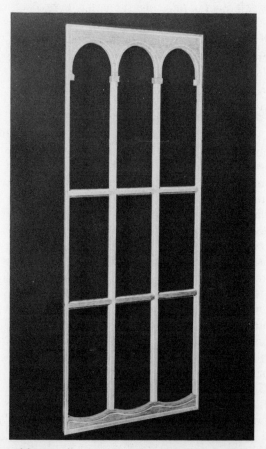

Removable wood muntins of decorative design for a casement window. National Woodwork Manufacturers Assn.

window with diamond panes, you cannot have them. Such windows are available in a number of standard sizes, and they can be made to any size by a local millwork shop. But the more common alternative today is to buy a single-paned window and turn it into a multi-paned window with snap-in muntins.

The muntins are made of plastic or wood. You can take them out quickly when you wash the windows, then snap them back into the sash when the glass is clean. Seen from inside the house, they are difficult to distinguish from permanent muntins; from outside, although you can tell that they do not project through the glass, they impart the effect of the real thing.

While snap-in muntins are usually made only for new windows, some can be installed in old single-paned windows which date to Victorian days, when big panes were also in vogue.

WINDOW SIZES. Windows are not made to exact standard sizes. Each manufacturer's units differ slightly, although most double-hung windows come fairly close to the sizes given below.

In general, the size of a window is designated by the actual size of its opening—that is, the size of the sash. For example, if a 24×28-in. window is called for on a plan, the figures refer to the size of the sash opening. The size of the glass is less; that of the frame, greater. And the size of the rough opening required in a wood-framed or masonry wall is greater still.

The sash opening width of double-hung and single-hung windows ranges, as a rule, from 20 in. upward in 4-in. increments to 40 in. Heights are 34, 38, 46, 50, 54, and 62 in.

Casement windows are available in roughly the same —but not so many—heights. Sash openings for a single sash are approximately 20, 24, or 32 in. wide. The narrow widths are available in groupings of two, three, four, or five sashes. Thus it is possible to have a bank of casements up to roughly 10 ft. wide.

Awning windows are made in two ways. One variety is composed of two to five relatively narrow horizontal panes which swing open and shut in unison as you turn a crank. The windows are made in widths ranging from 18 to 52 in., and heights from about 37 to 73 in. The other kind of awning window is a single, independently controlled sash which is installed by itself or in combination with two or three more independently controlled awning windows. The single-unit widths also range from 18 to 52 in. but heights are only 18 to 39 in.

Horizontal sliding windows—the last of the four most commonly used window types—are, as a rule, wider than high. Approximate widths are 36, 48, 60, and 72 in.; heights, 24, 34, 42, 48, 56, and 60 in.

When windows are installed in a house, all types and sizes are lined up at the top with the head jambs of the doors. Thus, most are hung at a height of 6 ft. 8 in. above the floors; and if there is any difference in their lengths, it is only the sill height which varies up and down. However, the head jambs of some windows (for example, picture windows) may be higher than the door jambs, while those of other windows (strip windows installed between kitchen counters and wall cabinets, for example) may be lower.

WINDOW TYPES

When building new homes, most people stick to a single type of window throughout. Aside from the sometimes real but sometimes questionable aesthetic value of this practice, however, there is little to be gained by it. Of the 12 basic window types now sold, none is free of shortcomings. Consequently, there is no reason why you cannot use two or three types as long as they look well together. Neither is there any reason why you cannot combine one type of movable window with a fixed window or even with another type of movable window in the same opening. More and more of the units installed in new and old houses are combinations.

DOUBLE-HUNG WINDOWS. The double-hung window has been the most popular since about 1750; and despite the fact that it is not so widely used today as before World War II, it still outnumbers all others. Although generally associated with traditional architectural styles, it is equally well suited to contemporary styles.

The double-hung window has two sashes which slide up and down in channels called stiles. As a rule, the sashes are the same size; but in some cases, the bottom sash is taller than the top sash. In the past, movement of the sashes was normally controlled by cords which ran over pulleys and were tied to weights hidden in pockets in either side of the window frame. This system of balancing has now been replaced by modern mechanisms which are not only more attractive but also a great deal more reliable and free of problems.

Because they are held firmly in place, double-hung windows do not warp or sag; and unless they are painted shut, they are easy to open and close as long as you can stand close to them (but if you must reach over a counter or piece of furniture, they are difficult to operate and should not be used). Relatively little air leaks in around the edges of the sashes even when they are not well weatherstripped.

Air is admitted either at the bottom or the top of the window or at both levels at the same time. But the windows can never be opened for more than half of their total area; and even when they are open only an inch or two, hard-driven rain is likely to blow in. This,

Aluminum double-hung window with tilt-in sash can be entirely washed from indoors. Thermal-Barrier Products, Inc.

however, is a relatively minor drawback compared with the difficulty of washing the windows. There simply is no safe way to get at the outside of the average window except by going outdoors and climbing a ladder. This problem has been corrected by the development of a few new designs in which the sash can be removed from inside or swung inward so you can wash both sides from within the house.

SINGLE-HUNG WINDOWS. The single-hung window looks exactly like the double-hung but differs from it in that the top sash is fixed. As a result, ventilation is limited to the bottom of the opening; but since half of the window is sealed, there is somewhat less maintenance and less chance of air leakage. Only the bottom half of the window is screened. And the total cost of the window is reduced. Washing, however, is a problem unless the lower sash is removable.

TRIPLE-HUNG WINDOWS. These have three sashes which slide up and down. You can open the window—to as much as two-thirds of its area—at the top, bottom, or top and bottom simultaneously.

The windows are either 69 or 81 in. high and range from 25 to 39 in. wide. The aluminum sashes are glazed only with single-thickness glass and are set in wood frames. Storm sashes available from the manufacturers are installed inside the windows in the positions occupied by the screens.

HORIZONTAL SLIDING WINDOWS. In effect, a horizontal sliding window is a double-hung or single-hung window laid on its side. In some units, both sashes slide from side to side; in others, only one sash (usually the right sash) slides; while in still others,

made with three panels of glass, the two outer sashes slide to the center over a fixed sash which is twice the width of each sliding sash.

The principal use for sliding windows is in locations where you want an operating sash with a large expanse of glass and a minimum number of framing members to obstruct the view. No other operating unit fills this requirement as well.

The advantages of the window are similar to those of a double-hung unit. Washing, however, is usually easier, since most sashes can be removed from inside the house. On the other hand, the window cannot be opened more than 50% and it admits driving rain. In addition, the breeze always blows straight in—it cannot be split as in a double-hung window.

CASEMENTS. The casement window was the first type of operating window used in buildings. It is a miniature version of a hinged door but is opened and closed by a crank or lever mounted on the sill. Thus you do not have to disturb the screen, installed inside the window (by contrast, in order to open old-style casements, you first had to open the screens and then push the windows open). Because of this method of operation, casements are ideal for installation behind counters and hard-to-move furniture; but they should not open out onto terraces, porches, or walks where people can bump into them.

Almost all casements open outward. In-swinging units, if required, usually must be made to order.

Since the entire sash opens, a casement window admits 100% of the available breeze. Even in storms, it can be cracked open an inch or two without letting in water (but if it is accidentally left wide open, it can cause a flood).

Washing is a problem in varying degrees. If the window frame is tightly hinged to the jamb, the only thing you can do is to go outdoors to get at the outer surface.

Horizontal sliding windows are ideal for installation above kitchen counters. Window frames are of ponderosa pine. National Woodwork Manufacturers Assn.

To eliminate this step, some manufacturers have designed their windows either so the sash can be removed or so you can reach through a gap between the sash and hinge jamb. While both ideas improve matters, neither is a perfect solution. Removable sashes are awkward to handle and often too heavy for a woman. Sashes which move away from the hinge jambs are difficult to dry with a squeegee.

The most serious drawback of casements, however, stems from the fact that they hang open and have relatively little support. As a result, they may be badly buffeted by wind and collect about as much dirt on the inside as on the outside. They tend to sag and warp. And the operating mechanism needs rather frequent cleaning and oiling to make it move freely.

AWNING WINDOWS. Awning windows consist of one or more framed horizontal sashes which swing outward and upward when you turn a crank or lever or simply give them a push. The screens are installed inside.

Although the design of the windows is best suited to contemporary architectural styles, they can be used in many ways. Multi-sash units can not only be substituted for other types of window of the same size but are also furnished by manufacturers in assembled units to fill openings up to 12 ft. wide. Single-sash windows are frequently installed underneath and/or above fixed picture windows to provide ventilation. Used as clerestory windows, they are placed high in walls to provide light and ventilation while assuring privacy. And because they are short and wide, they are made to order for installation between kitchen counters and wall cabinets. They should not, however, be installed overlooking porches, terraces, or walks, because someone might run into the projecting sash.

Aside from their usefulness, the principal advantage of awning windows is that they can be opened wide so you get almost 100% ventilation without letting in

Awning windows are made with one or more outward-opening sashes. Evans Products Co.

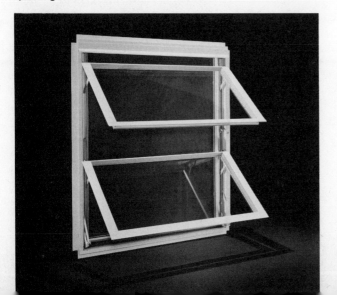

Picture window flanked by jalousies. International Window Corp.

rain. On the other hand, because the slanting open sashes are so exposed, they become dirty in short order and require more frequent washing than any other type of window. This means that unless the windows are designed so you can reach out under the head jamb to wash the outer surface of the glass, you must spend a good many hours each year trotting around outside your house with a bucket and sponge.

Another disadvantage of awning windows is their tendency to warp, sag, or operate crankily. This is particularly true of multi-sash units, which must be kept finely adjusted to ensure that all the sashes will operate in coordination.

HOPPER WINDOWS. These are the reverse of awning windows. Hinged or pivoted at the bottom, they open inward and downward from the top so that the entering air flows upward. They are most commonly used in basements and clerestories.

Hopper windows give almost 100% ventilation, and both the inner and outer surfaces are easily washed from indoors. They interfere with curtains, however, and are impossible to darken with shades when open. Screens are installed on the outside.

The standard hopper window is about 30 in. wide and 12, 15, or 18 in. high.

JALOUSIES. No other type of window has captured the interest of so many people and at the same time disappointed so many of them as the jalousie. This strange contradiction stems from the way in which the unit is constructed.

In essence, the jalousie is an awning window with numerous 4-in.-high, horizontal, slatlike panes that are held in metal clips at the ends but have no framing on the top and bottom edges. When opened and closed by a crank, the panes move in unison. They can be adjusted to any downward angle, pointing straight out, or to an upward angle. As a result, the window not only gives 100% ventilation but also permits you to deflect the incoming breezes upward, downward, or at right angles to the wall. Herein lies the jalousie's great appeal. In warm climates, where it originated, it is a god-send. But in cold climates, where it is sometimes sold by overzealous manufacturers, it is a horror because there is no way to keep cold air and moisture from seeping through the overlapping edges of the panes. (They cannot be weatherstripped without spoiling the appearance of the window.) True, a storm sash can be installed inside the window; but this is only partially effective because so much air comes through the slats.

Another disadvantage of the jalousie—even in warm climates—is that the overlapping panes break the view into disconcerting strips. In addition, there are so many moving parts that operation may become balky. On the other hand, washing the panes from inside is an easy though lengthy process.

Jalousies are made in widths of approximately 19, 26, 30, 37, and 53 in., and in lengths of 26, 39, 51, 63, 77, and 84 in. Screens are installed on the inside.

PIVOT WINDOWS.

Pivot windows consist of one large aluminum-, steel-, wood-, or polyvinyl-chloride-framed sash pivoted at the center so it turns from top to bottom or, in rare cases, from side to side. They are most often used in factories and commercial buildings but are going into more and more houses of modern design. They permit excellent two-way ventilation and are very easy to operate, and they are also easy to wash, since they are more or less fully reversible. But they are impossible to screen.

Windows suitable for home use are generally built to order in sizes up to 8 ft. high by 12 ft. wide.

HOPPER-CASEMENT WINDOWS.

These are ingenious windows which can be opened inward either like a hopper window hinged at the bottom or like a casement window hinged at one side. Thus you can adjust room ventilation to suit your preferences. A single handle controls the entire operation.

The windows have wood frames and double-thick insulating glass. Window sizes range from approximately 16×16 in. to 55×91 in.

A hopper-casement window in closed and open positions. I.M.M.S., Inc.

SLIP-HEAD WINDOWS.

The slip-head window is a rare and very economical type suitable only for garages, barns, simple vacation homes, and similar structures in which the interior walls are not covered. It consists of a simple wood frame with a one-piece, two-light sash that moves up and down in channels. You can slide the sash up to any height or even right out of the frame. Because there is no balancing mechanism, the sash must be held open by a peg driven into holes. If you tire of this arrangement, you can hinge the sash to the front of the frame like a casement.

The frame, which measures 22 in. wide by 32 in. high, is designed for installation between studs spaced at least 24 in. on center.

FIXED WINDOWS.

Fixed windows, including picture windows as well as much smaller units, are made with a single pane of glass and also with several small panes. Their sole purpose is to let in light and view. Since they are inoperable, they do not provide ventilation. In fact, if they are properly installed, not even a whisper of air can enter around the sides. But washing is a chore, since after finishing the inside you must trot around to the outside. To make matters worse, a large window may have many panes, which are tiresome to wash, and if it is a solid sheet of glass, you must take extra care to eliminate streaks and smudges which otherwise stand out like sore thumbs.

WINDOW TYPES IN COMBINATIONS.

As noted earlier, many windows are composed of several sashes of two basic types. One of the sashes is fixed; the other—or in some cases, others—is an awning unit, casement, double-hung or single-hung, or slider.

The drawings illustrate several of the more common combinations available. Sizes are not standardized.

BAY WINDOWS.

Bay windows are used when you want to increase the apparent side of a room and/or to add a grace note to a rather severe facade. But they have other virtues. They open up a 180° view. They not only increase ventilation but also enable you to scoop in breezes traveling parallel to the house walls. They form a delightful niche for sitting or dining. And they provide an excellent place for growing house plants.

In the past, bay windows were always specially designed, and if your requirements are unusual, you can have them designed and built (probably with stock windows) the same way today. Normal practice, however, is to use one of the stock bay windows which have recently flooded the market. Made of wood, these are designed to fit rough openings ranging from approxi-

Windows can be assembled in various combinations such as these.

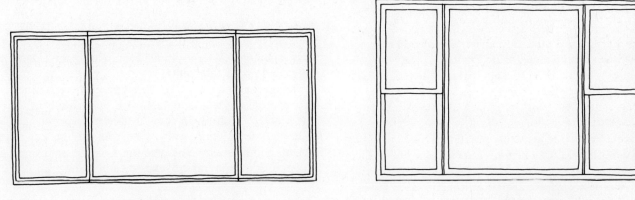

Casement Picture Window

Double Hung and Picture

Picture and Awning

Casement Awning

Casement Awning

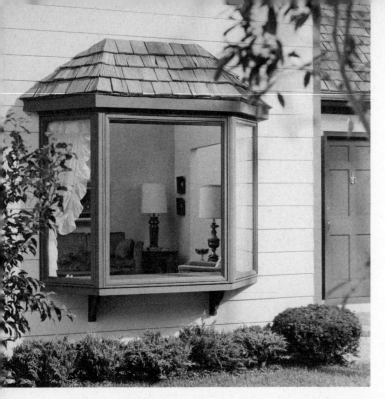

Bay window with fixed center sash and casements on the sides. Andersen Corp.

mately 6 to 12 ft. wide and 3½ to 5½ ft. high. The windows in the sides of the bay are set at an angle of 30°, 45°, or 90° to the house wall. The widest bays are angled at 30°.

The type of sash used in bay windows varies. In most units, the large center opening is filled with a fixed sash made with either one large pane or numerous small

A plant window, or window greenhouse, is a form of bay window with a glass roof. General Aluminum Corp.

panes; but in some cases it is filled with a large double-hung or single-hung window. The side panels are always operable, incorporating double-hung or single-hung windows or casements.

The normal practice in constructing a bay is to cantilever it from the wall and support it on brackets or an extension of the floor. In some instances, however, it is built atop foundation walls. The roof of the bay is hipped. Some window manufacturers offer precut roofs which include the rafters and sheathing but not the roofing.

BOW WINDOWS. The bow window is a close relative of the bay. Because it is gently curved rather than angled, it is of more graceful appearance. But it is usually not such an effective ventilator because it does not project as far. It does not open up the view so completely. And it provides little extra space for seating, dining, or growing plants.

Because of their shape, bow windows are necessarily made up of relatively narrow sashes or of many fixed small panes. When sashes are used, they are of the casement or, occasionally, the double-hung type. In casemented windows, all the sashes open, or only the two end panels open, or only the end panels and every other intermediate panel open. In double-hung bow windows, only the end panels open. There are also bow windows in which none of the sashes opens.

Bow windows with small panes are even more vari-

Bow window with five opening casements. Andersen Corp.

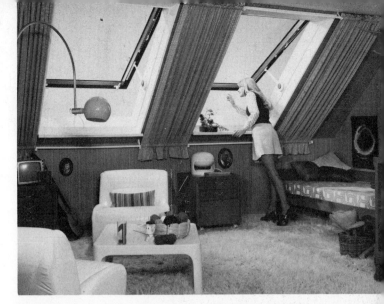

Two types of roof window. Below, the sash is pivoted. Velux-America, Inc. Above, the sash raises like an awning window. I.M.M.S., Inc.

Bow window composed of numerous fixed small panes with small awning windows at both sides. Joseph C. Klein, Inc.

able. In some units all the panes are fixed. Others have small-paned casements or double-hung sashes at the ends. In still others, small awning windows are substituted for fixed panes.

Small-paned windows are also available with either conventional slender muntins or with 3½-in.-deep muntins on which small flower pots can be placed.

Rough opening sizes for bow windows range from approximately 7 to 14 ft. wide and 3 to 6½ ft. high. Precut roofs are sold by some manufacturers.

ROOF WINDOWS. The roof window is designed to bring light into attics and even to take the place of dormers. It is usually installed only on fairly steep roofs. (Skylights are used on pitched as well as flat roofs.)

One type of roof window consists of a single sash which is pivoted at the sides about a third of the way down from the top; thus, when opened, the bottom swings out and the top swings in. It can be held open at any angle, completely reversed for easy washing from inside. A small ventilating flap can be opened to admit air while the sash is closed. The sash is glazed with insulating glass but cannot be screened.

In another type of roof window, the sash is hinged at the top and raises like an awning window to give an unobstructed view while keeping out rain. The sash is glazed with insulating glass and has a wood or aluminum frame. The outside is washed with a special tool provided by the manufacturer. Window sizes range from approximately 21×34 in. to 41×57 in. Venetian blinds to fit the windows are available.

DECORATIVE WINDOWS. These include small, odd-shaped windows which are used when, for one reason or another, a rectangular unit would be inappropriate. They have wood frames and are glazed with either single glass or insulating glass.

Round windows are available in 18-in. to 35-in. diameters. The glass is normally fixed. Some units, however, incorporate two half-round sashes; the top is fixed and the bottom can be rotated to admit air. A removable screen covers the opening on the inside.

Octagonal windows are for the most part fixed-glass

units measuring 14, 20, 24, or 32 in. across. One window has a 20-in. sash which can be hinged for opening.

Half-round windows, more commonly called fanlights, are installed either in gable ends of attics or directly over doors or conventional windows. Although the glass is usually fixed, it can be hinged to open inward. The windows measure 30, 36, 40, or 48 in. across.

Quarter-round windows are used in gables which are bisected by chimneys. They are 18 in. wide.

REPLACEMENT WINDOWS. Here is the easy way to replace windows when they are in serious need of repair, or when you want better protection against cold but object to conventional storm windows, or when you require a different type of window—say, an awning unit instead of a double-hung.

Formerly, when the homeowner was faced with the need for replacing a window, the only thing he could do was to rip out the old unit with its entire frame and put in a new one. But with modern aluminum-framed replacement units, this is no longer necessary. You simply remove the old sash and balancing mechanism and set a complete new unit in between the old jambs.

Replacement windows are made to fit most standard-size openings. Available types include double-hung, sliding, and awning.

WINDOW ACCESSORIES

REPLACEMENT STILES. If you have double-hung wood windows which are in good repair but which leak too much air around the edges or don't operate properly because of a faulty balancing mechanism, the simple way to correct matters once and for all is to rehang them in metal replacement stiles which seal out the weather and assure easy operation without pulleys that break or springs that kink.

The stiles can be used only on windows with 1⅜-in.-thick frames. To install them, remove the sash, inside stops, parting strips, and balancing hardware. Fit the stiles on each side of the sash and set the entire bundle into the jambs. Then nail the stiles into place and replace the stops.

WINDOWSILLS. Windowsills are in two parts: the thick, sloping exterior sill and the flat interior sill, which is properly called a stool. Both pieces are subject to damage and often need to be replaced.

Unfortunately, the outer sill is installed in such a way that it is impossible to remove without taking out the entire window frame. So when it is split or starts to rot, the only thing you can do is to fill the bad spots with

If old windows don't fit well, you can take them out and reinstall them in replacement stiles. Quaker City Manufacturing Co.

wood putty and cover the entire sill with fiberglass mat and polyester resin.

To replace an interior sill, remove the apron under it and the casings above; then pry or cut it out. Cut the new sill to the same pattern and nail it in.

Interior sills are most often made of wood with a triangular rabbet cut in the underside to fit over the top edge of the exterior sill. You can purchase them in any length from a lumberyard.

The only other material commonly used for interior sills is marble. This is popular in Pittsburgh, Cleveland, and several other mid-country cities because it can be wiped clean with a damp cloth whenever it becomes encrusted with soot. It never wears out or needs refinishing. Marble contractors and dealers in such areas often carry sills in stock, but any marble contractor or dealer can order them for you from the quarry and make the installation.

VENTILATORS. Ventilators are often installed in walls under or alongside fixed windows. Generally these are simple louvered and screened openings covered on the inside with a hinged door. Now from Europe comes a prefabricated aluminum ventilator with a concealed sliding door that is opened and closed with a lever.

The ventilators are made in three heights—2⅔, 4, and 5 in.—for installation above or below fixed windows or operating windows which you may prefer to keep closed because of extremely bad weather or for security reasons. They can be supplied in any length specified.

SCREENS. Window manufacturers provide screens for all their windows as optional accessories. They are made with white-painted aluminum frames and, depending on the manufacturer, aluminum or fiberglass screencloth.

If you have to provide your own screens for new or existing windows, your best bet is to have them made of wood by a local millwork shop or of aluminum by a supplier of storm and screen windows. But you can make your own with do-it-yourself aluminum framing sold in hardware stores and lumberyards. Whichever course you follow, it's well to remember that there is more than one kind of screencloth you can use.

Copper and bronze, which should be used only in wood frames, have outstanding durability but are so expensive that they have become hard to find. They develop a green coating which may stain the sills and walls below when washed off by rain.

Galvanized screencloth has also pretty well disappeared from the scene, not because of its cost, which is low, but because it rusts out rapidly unless painted or varnished almost every year. It too can be used only in wood frames.

The screencloth now in general use is made either of aluminum or fiberglass. Both are very durable and fire-resistant. They are available in several colors and suitable for installation in aluminum as well as wood frames. Aluminum has greater resistance to impact, but cannot be straightened when struck a sharp blow or raked by a dog's toenails. Fiberglass bellies fairly readily but can be pulled flat and smooth again with little trouble.

Like all metal screening, aluminum is made in rolls 2 to 4 ft. wide. Fiberglass comes in rolls 2 to 7 ft. wide. The standard mesh for both materials is 18×16, meaning that there are 18 squares per inch in the vertical direction, 16 in the horizontal direction. An 18×14 mesh is also available. In addition, fiberglass screening is made in fine 20×20 mesh and coarse 8×8 mesh.

Solar screening made of aluminum with a baked-on, colored finish differs from conventional screening in that the horizontal wires are flat—like tiny slats. In one brand of screening, these are laid on edge parallel to the window surface; in another brand they are laid at a 45° outward and downward angle. The vertical wires are round and of approximately the same width as the slats. The mesh is 12×4½.

Designed to reduce glare and heat inside the house, the screening actually blocks out over 50% of the direct and indirect sun rays. In daytime, it also prevents passersby from looking into the house but does not materially affect the view out.

STORM WINDOWS. Since most new windows can be glazed with double-pane or sometimes triple-pane insulating glass in place of single-thick glass, independent storm windows are not required. Even so, a number of manufacturers design their insulated windows so that homeowners in very cold climates can insert a third layer of glass in each sash over the insulating glass. This is the ideal way to secure maximum protection against cold without going to the expense and trouble of installing separate storm windows, which detract from the appearance of the primary windows.

If windows are not glazed with insulating glass, triple glazing is impossible (unless you have storm windows with insulating glass built to order). However, double glazing is easily secured by installing conventional storm windows or combination windows which cover the entire window opening.

On most types of window (double-hung, single-hung, awning, sliding, and jalousie), conventional storm windows are put up in the fall and taken down in the spring. On casements, they are permanently fastened to the outside of the sash. The units are made either with thick wood or slender aluminum frames. Wood-framed sashes are stocked by some building-supplies outlets in a few standard sizes; aluminum-framed sashes must, as a rule, be specially made.

Aluminum combination storm windows are used on double-hung, single-hung, and sliding windows. In

Solar screening has little effect on view out of a window, but the tiny horizontal slats cut out much of the sun. Phifer Wire Products, Inc.

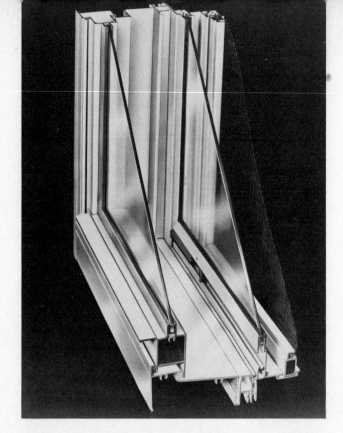

Some windows come with built-in storm sash and screens. Season-All Industries, Inc.

the North, they have generally replaced conventional storm windows because they are left in place the year round. In winter they keep out the cold; in summer they keep out insects.

Two kinds of combination window are available—double-track and triple-track. Both incorporate an upper and lower panel of glass and a single screen panel. In the two-track window, both glass panels are fitted into separate channels so they can be moved up and down independently. In summer, the bottom glass is pushed to the top of the frame and a screen panel of the same size is inserted in its place. In winter, the screen is removed entirely.

The three-track combination window eliminates the necessity for putting in and taking out the screen, because each glass panel fits into its own channel and the screen slides up and down in a third channel. Thus you can convert from a storm-glazed to screened opening simply by pushing the panels up and down. In winter, the screen is stored in the top of the frame.

Combination windows are designed so the frame is screwed either to the face of the casings or is set inside the casings and screwed to the stops. The latter are more attractive and should be used wherever possible.

Other points to note when buying combinations are: (1) Make sure that drip holes are provided in the bottom of the frame so that whatever water may accumulate on the windowsill behind the frame can seep out. However, if the frame lacks holes, you can drill a couple with a ¼-in. drill. (2) Make sure also that the meeting rails between the top and bottom glass panels

are at the same level as the meeting rails in the primary window. If the primary window has sash of unequal height, the storm windows should also have sash of unequal height. (3) To prevent corrosion and improve the appearance of the windows, select units which are finished with baked enamel.

Installation of combination windows is simple enough for any handyman who can balance a ladder. Apply a continuous bead of caulking to the stops (or casings) at the sides and top of the window. Without removing the sash or bracing from the storm window, press the frame firmly into the caulking. Center and level it carefully. Then drive screws through the frame into the stops.

WEATHERSTRIPPING. You don't have to worry about weatherstripping new windows that you buy. The manufacturers have done it for you better than you could do it yourself.

Old double-hung and wood casement windows are weatherstripped around the edges like doors (see Chapter 7) with spring metal or gasketed strips. Astragals are required to seal the joint between two-sash casements. Around the perimeter of metal casements, use spring-metal strips which clip over the edges.

EXTERIOR SHUTTERS. If you are one of the millions of homeowners who think the only purpose of shutters is to beautify the facade of the house, you will save money by using shutters made of plastic or aluminum. They are less expensive than wood and for the most part do not require costly operating hardware.

Shutters of both materials are made in louvered and raised-panel designs—usually in black, white, green, or brown. Aluminum units are the stronger; but since the finish is only baked on (as is the case with some of the

The vinyl shutters on this double-hung window, unlike most, are hinged so they can be closed. Andersen Corp.

Roll-down shutters on a city dwelling. I.M.M.S., Inc.

plastics), they eventually need to be repainted. Vinyl shutters, on the other hand, are integrally colored so that even when damaged they do not have to be touched up.

The shutters have two drawbacks, however. For one thing, only a few manufacturers offer a wide assortment of widths as well as heights. This means that the shutters may in many cases look too narrow or too wide for the windows they adorn. Proper shutter width is, of course, one-half the width of the window opening.

In the second place, the shutters are normally installed simply by screwing them to the window casings and adjacent wall surfaces (a few are hinged, however). This cuts installation time and cost; but it means there is no easy way to clean out wasp nests, bats, and debris behind the shutters. And when painting the house walls, you run the risk of slopping paint on the shutters, too.

Wood shutters also present problems. They rot if not adequately treated with wood preservative (fortunately, most stock units are). They require frequent painting. And like any site-painted building material, they cannot be washed as easily as factory-finished shutters.

But because wood shutters are available in many widths and are hung on pivots, they can be used not only to improve the appearance of a house but also to close the windows against the sun and hurricanes. This is their principal advantage. In addition, stock units are made with louvers, raised panels (like doors), or in a Spanish design composed of raised panels at the bottom and baluster-like turnings at the top. Other designs can be turned out by local millwork shops.

A new and totally different type of shutter which is

being imported from Europe rolls down over the window like a window shade. It is made of narrow wood, aluminum, or polyvinyl chloride slats which are closely linked together. When not in use, the blind rolls up into a housing at the head of the window. When pulled down, it is held securely in channels screwed to the sides of the window. It can be lowered to any height. An electric motor which is controlled from a switch indoors moves the shutter. The shutter can also be hand-operated.

Unlike conventional shutters, the new units are used not for decorative purposes, but strictly to provide protection against the sun and intruders. They also have considerable insulating value in cold winter weather. They are made to order in many colors to fit any window up to 12 ft. wide and 15 ft. high.

INTERIOR SHUTTERS. Used in place of draperies and shades, interior shutters not only ornament windows but also provide privacy from neighbors and protection against the sun. They come in a wide range of sizes with fixed or adjustable louvers. Also available are shutter frames into which you can insert fabrics or plastic or hardboard panels to create an original effect.

The shutters are made of ¾-in.-thick or 1⅛-in.-

Two kinds of interior shutter. The size of the openings in the wood shutter below can be adjusted. Cannon Craft Manufacturing Co.

thick wood which is either natural, primed for painting, or stained. You can assemble them yourself or buy them with hinges attached.

AWNINGS. Canvas awnings are fabricated only to order. Stock awnings are made of aluminum or steel with baked-on enamel, redwood, or fiberglass. Widths range from 30 to 96 in., and there are several projections and heights to provide shading for windows of different heights. For example, an awning with a 20-in. projection is generally suitable for shading windows up to 48 in. high, but a greater projection is required for windows, say, 60 in. high. The tops of the awnings are either straight or curved. Some have sides; others do not.

The standard awning is stationary and made with interlocking slats which lie parallel to the window surface or at right angles to it. For hurricane regions, however, spaced slats are preferred to reduce resistance to wind. The spacing also keeps overheated air from being trapped beneath the awning.

Two other types of awning are adjustable. In the simpler design, the canopy is hinged to the wall and supported on adjustable arms. It can be used on windows of any height. The second type has a flexible top which can be rolled up against the wall when not in use, and rolled down to any desired height at other times.

PLASTIC FILMS TO CONTROL THE SUN. In addition to awnings and heat-absorbing glass, there are three ways of keeping the sun from flooding through your windows. One is to plant trees—an excellent method but slow to produce results. The second is to build projecting eyebrows above the windows; but this generally requires an architect to ensure that the structures do not detract from the appearance of the house. Furthermore, eyebrows are effective only on south windows—not on west windows in the late afternoon. The third is to cover windows with a thin plastic film which allows full visibility from inside the house but reflects the sun rays on the outside.

Although the film has the somewhat objectionable characteristic of making windows look like mirrors from the street, it cuts indoor glare and contributes to a reduction of up to 60% in heat gain. It also minimizes fading of fabrics and other materials, prevents neighbors from seeing in, and makes the windows more shatter-resistant.

The film can be applied to the inner surface of any clear window glass but not to plastic. After cleaning a window, spray it with water, wet the film, and smooth it on the glass. Remove the backing on the film and smooth the film further with a squeegee. The film can be washed repeatedly thereafter with any common nonabrasive washing solution. It can be removed from the window without damage to the glass.

Woven Roman shade made of wood and colorful yarns. Liken, Inc.

SHADES. Like everything else in the home-building and home-furnishing field, the simple roller shade has been improved. It is no longer just a piece of coated white or dark-green fabric. You can buy it in many colors, patterns, and textures.

Least expensive of the materials used is solid vinyl. Vinyl-coated cotton is better. Fiberglass laminated to vinyl is best of all. While most of these materials are translucent, some are treated to give complete darkness. Also available are shades which are coated on the back to reflect the incoming sun.

The alternatives to fabric shades are those made of slender strips of wood, metal, or semi-rigid vinyl. In the earliest design, which is still available, stained wood strips were held together with cotton twine. In the newest and more decorative versions—called woven shades—the horizontal strips are interwoven with multi-colored nubby, satiny, chenille, or twisted yarns.

The new woven materials are available in spring roller shades, cord-and-pulley shades which operate like porch shades, and Roman shades which gather in soft folds as they are raised. The last are unique because they can be hung below a sloping ceiling over a triangular fixed window. Matching cornices are available for most types of woven shade.

VENETIAN AND VERTICAL BLINDS. Unlike shades, blinds permit almost total control of light and air because they can be opened to any degree and in any direction and closed completely.

Venetian blinds with horizontal wood, metal, or plastic louvers are made in two styles: the standard blind with 2-in.-wide slats held in place by wide cloth tapes, and the mini-blind with 1-in. slats held by slender cords. Simply because it is made of heavier material, the standard blind is more rugged, flaps less in the breeze, and can be used to darken rooms more completely. But the mini-blind is more attractive in every way, and when it is open wide, it is almost invisible. Both units come in a great range of colors and sizes up to a maximum of about 100 sq. ft.

Venetian blinds are also custom-made for just about any window shape. You can, for instance, use them on angle-headed cathedral windows or the tent-shaped windows in an A-frame house. You can also have blinds made to fit neatly around window air conditioners instead of bunching up on top of them.

Even more unusual than special-shape blinds is a motorized mini-blind which allows you to open and close the louvers simply by pushing a switch. Though hardly something you would want in every room of the house, it is useful in bedrooms—especially those occupied by invalids.

Vertical blind with fabric louvers. NCI, Inc.

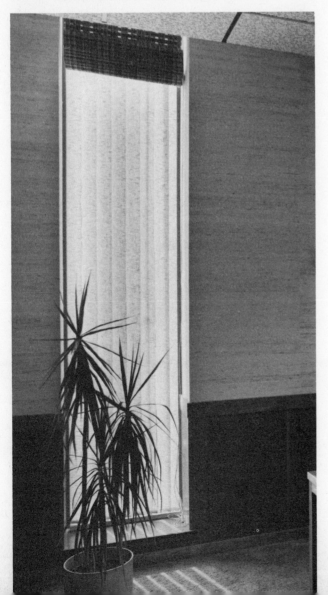

The motor, which is installed in the headrail of the blind in place of the normal tilting hardware, is battery-operated but can be connected to the house wiring if a power converter or voltage regulator is installed. The control unit can be operated from a distance of 30 ft. The blind itself should not exceed 50 sq. ft. in area if battery-run. It is installed in a free-hanging position or between glass in fixed windows.

Vertical blinds are, in effect, Venetian blinds turned on edge. They take the place of draperies and conventional blinds or shades on windows of above-average size, and are particularly suited to unusually tall or unusually wide windows. They are ideal for sliding glass doors because they can be set to shut out glare without barring the view, and do not catch in the doors like draperies.

The louvers in vertical blinds are made of fabric, metal, or vinyl in widths from 2 to 6 in. They rotate 180°. In addition, the majority of blinds are designed to traverse from one side of the window to the other. Thus, as with Venetian blinds, you can draw the blind across a window as far as you like and adjust the louvers to admit as much light as you like. The control mechanism is concealed in a housing at the head of the window. Some blinds hang free (but are weighted so they don't flap in the breeze); others are held at the bottom in tracks or by slender bead chains.

All verticals are made to order to any height. Maximum width is 12 ft.

DRAPERY HARDWARE. Drapery hardware includes the rods and accessories, such as tiebacks, used to hang curtains and draperies. There are five basic types of rod.

The least expensive are made of thin sheet steel formed into two very much flattened tubes which slide together. In the standard rod, which is rather flimsy, the seam in the back of the rod is open; in heavy-duty rods, the seam is locked for greater strength. The ends of the rods are generally bent at right angles for attachment to brackets mounted on the head casing. But other types are available. These include (1) straight rods for mounting curtains directly on window sash and doors; (2) short swinging rods used primarily for hanging curtains over doors; (3) bay window rods; and (4) corner rods.

Brass rods (which are now made of steel or aluminum) are straight ¼-in. rods which are cut to any required length and mounted in brackets with screw-on barrel-like holders. The rods can be hung very close to the casings or several inches away. They can be shaped by hand to fit bow and bay windows.

Spring extension rods are small, straight rods which are held inside window openings by spring tension.

Café rods are decorative metal or wood rods up to 1¾ in. in diameter. Curtains are hung from them in

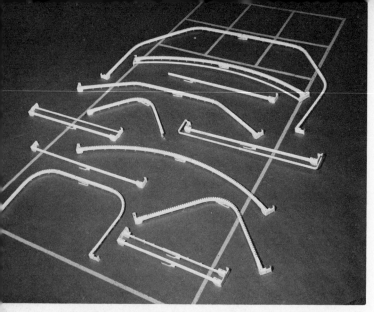

Traverse rods come in many shapes. Kirsch Co.

large rings. The rods themselves are mounted in U-shaped brackets screwed to the head casing. The metal rods are extendable.

Traverse rods were originally developed to hang large draw draperies but are today used wherever you want smooth, even operation of draperies and/or curtains. Mounted on the casing or wall to the sides or above a window, the rods generally hold a drapery panel at each end but are also made to draw a single drapery to right or left. The standard traverse rod is a smooth, rectangular, white-enameled unit which is completely concealed when the draperies are closed. Decorative rods are fancily shaped and colored so they can be exposed above the draperies. In all cases, the draperies are opened and closed by a pair of cords running through pulleys and hanging from one end of the rod. One cord closes the draperies; the other opens them. An electric control which permits you to operate the draperies from a distance is on the market.

The most commonly used type of rod is a single traverse which holds a pair of draw draperies. This

Traverse rod with accordion-type linkage. Baker Drapery Corp.

same type is also made to hold—in addition to the draperies—a pair of curtains which are drawn by hand, or a valance, or a pair of curtains and a valance.

Double traverse rods hold a pair of draw draperies as well as a pair of draw curtains. Some incorporate a rod for a valance.

Like most of the simple rods, traverse rods are extendable to roughly twice their collapsed length. The longest pulls out to 26 ft. Mounting brackets are, as a rule, placed at the ends of a rod, but if you want a drapery to extend beyond the sides of a window, special brackets can be installed in from the ends of the rod. Curved and angled rods in several shapes are made for hanging draperies in bow and bay windows and around corners.

In the newest kind of traverse rod, draperies are hung not from plastic guides, but from a folding, accordion-type linkage which eliminates the need for making pleats in the draperies and prevents the draperies from sagging away from the rod. When the draperies are taken down for cleaning, there is no need to take out drapery hooks; they lie perfectly flat so you can iron them like a sheet, without working around pleats.

ALTERNATIVES TO WINDOWS

GLASS BLOCK. Even though architects have long maintained that with year-round air conditioning there is no need to put in windows for ventilation, it is unlikely that homeowners will ever replace all their windows with glass block. But for windows in problem locations, glass block does offer advantages. It provides privacy without restricting natural illumination. It greatly reduces heat loss and heat gain. It keeps out noise. And it virtually defies entrance by burglars.

New designs in glass block. Pittsburgh Corning Corp.

Glass block is available in preassembled panels with a central jalousie or hopper window. Pittsburgh Corning Corp.

Domed skylights can be installed on sloping as well as flat roofs. Ventarama Skylight Corp.

Of course, if you can recall the days when glass block was introduced, you may think, "That's all well and good; but the blocks are hideous." But that is no longer true. New decorative designs have a sculptured look rivaling the glass objects made in Corning, N.Y., and Sweden. More functional blocks, which have also been improved in appearance, are designed either in clear glass which does not interfere with the view or in patterned glass which diffuses the light and, in some cases, controls its direction. Blocks are also available with fiberglass inserts to reduce glare and heat still further.

All standard blocks, which are hollow, are $3\frac{7}{8}$ in. thick. Available sizes are $5\frac{3}{4}$ in. square, $7\frac{3}{4}$ in. square, $11\frac{3}{4}$ in. square, $3\frac{3}{4} \times 11\frac{3}{4}$ in., and $3\frac{3}{4} \times 7\frac{3}{8}$ in. Solid bricks, used for maximum protection against vandalism and forced entry, are $7\frac{5}{8} \times 7\frac{5}{8} \times 3$ in., $5 \times 5 \times 2\frac{5}{8}$ in., $8 \times 3\frac{3}{4} \times 2\frac{3}{8}$ in., and $5\frac{7}{8} \times 8\frac{7}{8} \times 2\frac{5}{16}$ in.

Despite their strength, glass blocks cannot be used in load-bearing panels. The openings for them should be framed like conventional window openings. Actual installation of blocks should generally be made by professionals, but you can put in small preassembled panels yourself. These are made in three styles: with a hopper window in the center, with a jalousie in the center, or without any ventilator. (Hopper windows and jalousies can also be incorporated in large, site-constructed glass-block openings.)

SKYLIGHTS. Because skylights admit more light and distribute it more evenly than windows, they make the rooms in which they are used look larger than they really are. They help to equalize the light in a room

which has windows on only one side. They permit installation of fewer and smaller windows and thus simplify the arrangement of furniture and make for better utilization of space. They illuminate inside bathrooms, halls, and stairs. They give privacy without any reduction in room brightness. And they make for complete flexibility in the planning of a house or large addition because you don't have to worry about providing windows in every room and can lay the house out in a compact shape that cuts construction costs and makes for better utilization of land.

On the other hand, if not properly selected, skylights can mar the appearance of a house, create glare, raise room temperatures on sunny days, and allow heat to escape in winter.

Prefabricated skylights are glazed with clear or translucent plastic or, sometimes, glass set in an aluminum frame. In addition to the designs illustrated, flat-topped and wedge-shaped units are available. The smallest size is 19 in. square (inside dimensions); the largest, 75×75

Or if you need a skylight of unusual size or shape, you can have it built to order. Fisher Skylights, Inc.

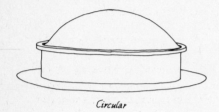

Continuous Vaulted

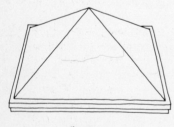

Circular

Low Profile Curb

Skylights are made in several styles.

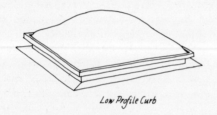

Pyramid

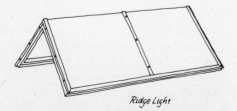

Ridge Light

in. and 57½×89½ in. Continuous vaulted skylights can be up to 120 in. wide and any length. Still larger skylights are made to order.

To reduce heat loss, any skylight you use should be double-glazed (not all are). Provision should be made in the skylight to drain off moisture which condenses on the plastic. Some units can be opened to provide ventilation. A few have built-in exhaust fans.

Depending on their design, skylights can be installed on roofs ranging from dead level to nearly vertical. They do not have to open directly into the rooms they are intended to illuminate. If there is an attic between the roof and room ceiling, you can construct a plywood shaft which carries the light down through the attic into the room.

Installation must be made according to the manufacturer's directions. In essence, all you have to do is cut an opening in the roof and frame it on the underside with lumber matching the rafters. Cut back the roofing around the hole and nail the skylight in place. Then cover the flanges on the skylight and surrounding sheathing with roofing cement in which roofing felt is embedded. Finally, replace the roofing.

WHO MAKES IT

Acorn Building Components, Inc. · Windowsills made of a blend of marble dust and polyester.

Afco, Inc. · Three-track aluminum combination storm-screen windows. Fiberglass and aluminum awnings.

Alcan Aluminum Corp. · Aluminum shutters. Motorized aluminum Venetian blinds.

Andersen Corp. · Wood windows unfinished, finished with polyurea, or sheathed in vinyl. Double-hung, single-hung, horizontal sliding, casement, awning, hopper, and fixed windows and combinations thereof. Removable vinyl grilles. Basement window convertible from top to bottom opening or completely removable. 30°- and 45°-angle bay windows with casements or double-hung windows. Casemented bow windows. Vinyl shutters.

APC Corp. · Fixed domed skylights with vinyl-covered aluminum frames to stop sweating; up to 46½ in. square.

Baker Drapery Corp. · Traverse rods with accordion-type linkage.

Billy Penn Corp. · Galvanized steel window wells.

Biltbest Corp. · Wood casement windows. Casemented bow windows. Bow windows with fixed panes of insulating glass and snap-in vinyl grilles. Wood picture windows with snap-in vinyl grilles. Wood awning windows. Wood double-hung windows with tilt-in and removable sash. Wood horizontal sliding windows with removable sash. Three-paned insulating glass available. Windows in combinations.

Bird & Son, Inc. · Vinyl shutters.

Buckingham-Virginia Slate Corp. · Natural cleft or honed-finish black slate windowsills.

Cabanarama Industries, Inc. · Interior shutters of wood in

numerous styles to heights of 108 in. Multi-paned aluminum awning windows. Aluminum and redwood solid and ventilated awnings. Steel and aluminum storm shutters.

Cannon Craft Manufacturing Co. · Inside wood shutters in enormous variety, including a selection of special insert panels and custom-made heads to fit windows of unusual shape. Full-length shutters for floor-to-ceiling windows and doors. Outside shutters.

Emco Specialties, Inc. · Plastic shutters.

Evans Products Co., Remington Aluminum Div. · Aluminum single and multi-paned awning windows for new construction and replacement.

Fisher Skylights, Inc. · All kinds of large skylights built to order.

GAF Corp. · Plastic shutters.

Gallatin Aluminum Products Co. · Aluminum single-hung windows with removable sash available with combination storm-screen windows built into frame. Aluminum horizontal sliding windows with combination storm-screen windows available to be built into frame. If equipped with insulating glass, mullions are inserted between panes. Aluminum picture windows with single or multiple panes and storm sash for insertion in frame if desired. Two-track and three-track combination storm-screen windows.

General Aluminum Corp. · Single-hung and horizontal sliding aluminum windows, some with thermalized frames. Aluminum bay windows designed specifically for growing plants, with shelves included. Window has 90° corners; glazed shed roof which opens for ventilation and is screened in summer. Single-hung aluminum windows with rounded tops as in Palladian windows. Aluminum multi-panel picture windows. Aluminum bow windows with small fixed panes. Aluminum 45°-angle bay windows with single-hung sashes at sides. Windows in combinations.

General Electric Co., Plastics Business Div. · Lexan polycarbonate sheets for glazing.

HC Products Co. · ABS plastic shutters.

Howmet Corp. · Galvanized-steel window wells.

Ideal Co. · Wood double-hung windows with tilt-in and removable sashes. Wood casement windows. Windows in combinations. Wood awning windows move to center of frame when opened wide for washing both sides. Wood shutters including Spanish design.

I.M.M.S., Inc., Roto International Div. · Roof windows with sash hinged at top. Hopper-casement windows. Pivot windows. Horizontal sliding windows which lift off the bottom track, slide to the side, and drop back into track so firmly that they cannot be moved. Roll-down shutters. Adjustable strip ventilators.

International Window Corp. · Jalousies for insertion in double-hung and casement window frames. Aluminum jalousie windows. Aluminum horizontal sliding windows with reversible sash, some with removable sash. Aluminum single-hung windows.

Keller Industries, Inc. · Aluminum jalousie windows. Aluminum single-hung windows. Aluminum horizontal sliding windows with removable sash. Aluminum single-hung windows with built-in storm sash. Aluminum

awning windows. Double- and triple-track combination storm-screen windows with aluminum frames.

Kirsch Co. · Simple rods, café rods, and traverse rods in enormous variety, including traverse rods that fit around corners and in bay and bow windows.

Joseph C. Klein, Inc. · Wood bow windows with casements or small awning windows. Snap-in wood grilles. Multi-paned casement windows with or without small awning windows.

Larson Manufacturing Co. · Aluminum replacement double-hung windows with tilt-in sash. Thermalized aluminum double-hung windows with tilt-in sash.

Leslie-Locke. · Plastic shutters.

Liken, Inc., Del Mar Div. · Woven wood shades in variety. Matching valances.

Louisiana-Pacific Corp. · Wood casement windows. Wood horizontal sliding windows with removable sash. Wood awning windows. Aluminum replacement windows custom-made for double-hung and horizontal sliding windows; double-hungs have tilt-in sash. Wood double-hung windows, some with tilt-in sash, some with removable sash. Casemented bow windows. Awning bow windows. Windows in combinations. Combination storm-screen windows for double-hung and sliding windows. Storm panels for fixed windows.

Marvin Windows Industries. · Wood double-hung windows, some with tilt-in and removable sash, some with removable sash only. Wood single-hung windows with lower sash removable. Wood horizontal sliding windows with removable sash. Wood multi-paned picture windows. Wood casement windows with removable storm sash on outside of sash. Wood awning windows. Casemented bow windows. 30°- and 45°-angle bay windows with double-hung sash at ends. Wood and vinyl removable grilles. Windows in combinations. Combination storm-screen windows for double-hungs and sliders have ponderosa-pine frames and aluminum frames on the panels.

Maywood, Inc. · Interior shutters of wood, some with open panels for special inserts.

Milgard Manufacturing, Inc. · Thermalized aluminum horizontal sliding windows.

Mon-Ray Windows, Inc. · Aluminum combination storm-screen windows snap into window opening for easy removable or can be permanently built into windows without casings. Frame has snap-in color strips. Also conventional combination storm-screen windows. Thermalized aluminum replacement double-hung windows with tilt-in sash; sliders with lift-out sash. Aluminum triple-hung windows with removable sash and full-length screens.

Montgomery Ward & Co. · Aluminum screen porch panels. Aluminum awning, sliding, and jalousie windows. Aluminum awnings, one of roll-up type. Another folds down completely over window. Plastic sun-control film. Wood and plastic shutters; interior wood shutters. Traverse and simple curtain rods. Woven wood shades.

Morgan Co. · Round, half-round, and octagonal windows. Wood shutters. One design is reversible—louvered on one side, flat on reverse.

Naturalite, Inc. · All types of skylight.

NCI, Inc. · Vertical blinds with metal, fabric, or vinyl louvers. Free-hanging or with bottom track. Woven wood shades. Woven wood canopies, cornices, and valances.

Northrop Architectural Systems. · Aluminum horizontal sliding windows with two, three, and four sashes, all removable.

Pemko Manufacturing Co. · Weatherstripping in great variety.

Phifer Wire Products, Inc. · Solar screening in gray and green. Fiberglass and aluminum screening, including 20×20-mesh fiberglass.

Pittsburgh Corning Corp. · All kinds of glass block. Pre-assembled glass-block panels. Jalousie and hopper ventilators for installation in glass-block panels.

Porter-Hadley Co. · Thermalized aluminum double-hung and horizontal sliding windows. Double-hungs with removable sash.

PPG Industries. · Gas-filled Xi insulating glass.

Quaker City Manufacturing Co. · Replacement window stiles.

Fred Reuten, Inc. · Wood bow windows with casements or double-hung windows in end sections, large fixed panes, small fixed panes in conventional or deep mullions. Awning windows can be used in place of small panes. Multi-paned wood picture windows with deep mullions. 45°-angle bay windows with casement or double-hung windows. Wood casement windows. Snap-in wood grilles.

Revere Aluminum Building Products, Inc. · Vinyl shutters.

Rodman Industries, Inc. · Wood double-hung windows with tilt-in sash. Wood casements. Casemented bow windows. Wood awning windows. Wood horizontal sliding windows. Wood single-hung windows with tilt-in sash. Windows in combinations. Removable wood grilles.

Rolleze, Inc. · Horizontal sliding windows with aluminum frames.

Rolscreen Co. · Wood double-hung windows with pivoting sash for easy washing. Wood casement windows move to center of frame when opened 90° for washing both sides. Wood awning windows also move to center of frame for washing. All windows designed to hold storm sash on inside of operating sash.

Rusco Industries, Inc., Ador/Hilite Div. · Reversible aluminum sliding windows.

F. E. Schumacher Co. · Wood slip-head windows. Screened aluminum hopper windows, one model with two fixed panes under opening pane. Aluminum jalousie windows, including small basement jalousies. Wood basement window reversible for use as awning or hopper window. Wood shutters. Aluminum and wood shutters.

Scovill Manufacturing Co., Caradco Window & Door Div. · Wood casement windows. Wood awning windows. Casemented wood bow windows. Casemented 30°- and 45°-angle bay windows with fixed center sash. Wood double-hung windows with removable sash. Wood horizontal sliding windows with removable sash. Windows in combination. Snap-in vinyl grilles. All windows designed for addition of storm panels in each sash.

Seal Rite Windows, Inc. · Wood awning windows. Wood casement windows. Wood double-hung windows with tilt-in sash. Casemented bow windows. Wood horizontal sliding windows with removable sash. Wood single-hung windows with tilt-in sash. Windows in combinations.

Sears Roebuck & Co. · Aluminum awning, jalousie, and sliding windows, some of the last with acrylic panes. Aluminum triple-track combination storm-screen double-hung windows; double-track horizontal sliding windows; single-pane sash for picture windows. Aluminum awnings. Plastic shutters. Domed 30×30-in. skylight. Plastic sun-control film. Aluminum screen panels to enclose porches. Traverse and simple curtain rods.

Season-All Industries, Inc. · Thermalized aluminum double-hung windows with built-in storm windows (primary windows can be double-glazed). Aluminum replacement windows for double-hung and sliding windows on order. Triple-track combination storm-screen windows, some units with thermalized aluminum frames. Aluminum combination storm-screen windows for horizontal sliding windows. Aluminum-framed panels for enclosing porches, with glass and screen inserts.

Semling-Menke Co. · Wood awning windows. Wood horizontal sliding windows with removable sash. Wood double-hung windows with tilt-in or removable sash. Wood casements. Casemented bow windows. Windows in combinations. Removable wood grilles.

Stanley Works, Drapery Hardware Div. · Simple extension rods, brass rods, spring extension rods, café rods, traverse rods. Electric traverse rod control.

Suntint of New York, Inc. · Plastic sun-control film.

Swedlow, Inc. · Acrylic sheets for glazing in clear, translucent white and translucent or transparent colors.

Tel-o-Post Co. · Steel areaway walls with grates to cover tops for safety.

Thermal-Barrier Products, Inc. · Thermalized aluminum double-hung windows with tilt-in sash and built-in full or half screens. Thermalized aluminum horizontal sliding windows with swing-in sash for easy cleaning.

Thermwell Products Co. · Weatherstripping.

3M Co. · Plastic sun-control film.

Three Rivers Aluminum Co. · Thermalized aluminum double-hung windows with tilt-in sash. Aluminum replacement double-hung windows with tilt-in sash. Three-track aluminum combination storm-screen windows for double-hung windows. Combination storm-screen windows for horizontal sliding windows. Aluminum storm windows for basement and fixed windows.

Thru-Vu Vertical Blind Corp. · Vertical blinds with aluminum or fabric louvers. Free-hanging with beaded chains at bottom. Fabric valances.

Unique Window Products Corp. · Replacement window stiles.

United States Metals & Manufacturing Co. · Thermalized aluminum single-hung, horizontal sliding and casement windows. Sliding windows have removable sash.

United States Steel Corp., Alside Div. · Aluminum and polystyrene shutters.

U.S. Plywood. · Plastic shutters.

Velux-America, Inc. · Pivoted roof windows.

Ventarama Skylight Corp. · Domed skylights with screens can be motorized for easy operation. Up to 45½ in. square.

Vermont Marble Co. · Marble windowsills.

Verticals, Inc. · Vertical blinds with metal or fabric louvers; also with perforated vinyl louvers to absorb sound. Free-hanging or with floor track.

Vestal Manufacturing Co. · Steel hopper windows, some with the opening sash above a fixed sash. Aluminum horizontal sliding windows installed in steel frames for installation in foundation walls. Steel areaway walls.

Warp Brothers. · Acrylic sheets for glazing windows.

Webb Manufacturing, Inc. · Ponderosa-pine snap-in grilles to fit all types of window. Rectangular or diamond panes. Also Mediterranean style with arched tops. Round, half-round, quarter-round, and octagonal wood windows.

Winter Seal of Flint, Inc. · Thermalized aluminum horizontal sliding windows with insulating glass. In multi-paned windows, muntins are sandwiched between the insulated panes.

Wolverine-Pentronix, Inc. · Aluminum shutters.

Woodco Corp. · Wood casement windows. Casemented bow windows. 30°-, 45°-, and 90°-angle casemented bay windows. Bronze heat-absorbing glass available. Wood awning windows. Wood double-hung windows with removable sash. Windows in combinations. Snap-in wood grilles.

Woodcraft Millwork Specialties, Inc. · Wood interior shutters. Wood and aluminum exterior shutters.

7

Doors

A door is not just something that closes an opening. It moves, gets in the way, takes up space, batters walls and furniture and gets battered in turn, seals out weather and dirt, lets in air, requires considerable maintenance, even pulls teeth. Selection of the right door for any given location therefore requires more thought than you may think.

The appearance of a door, though important, is only one point to be considered. Others are:

· Does it operate easily and reliably?
· Does it close securely?
· Does it permit easy passage?
· Does it interfere with use of the spaces on either side?
· Does it effectively close off whatever is supposed to be closed off?
· Does it retard the spread of fire?
· Does it minimize the transmission of sound?

In addition, you must also consider the unusual requirements of doors in specific situations. For example:

· Does it allow you to see through to the other side?
· Can you hang things on the back?
· Does it give you full access to whatever is behind it?
· Does it permit ventilation of the closed-off space even when shut?
· Can it be easily broken down even when locked?
· Does it keep out heat and cold?
· Will it cause injury if someone walks into it?

DOORWAY CONSTRUCTION. The drawing shows how a doorway is built. The important thing to note is that the studs on either side of the opening are doubled and that the timber across the top of the opening—the header, or lintel—is also made of two timbers or one extra-thick timber. The wider the opening, the larger the header must be. Over 8-ft.-wide sliding doors, for

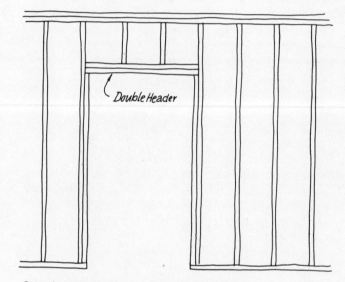

Opening made in a frame wall for a door.

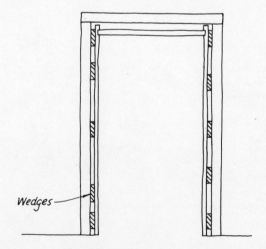

Doorway with jambs installed. The door will be hinged to the left jamb. Note difference in the way wedges are installed at the two side jambs.

instance, it should be made of a pair of 2×10s in order to support the joists in the floor above.

The jambs constituting the door frame are installed in the rough opening as shown in the second drawing. Normally the jambs are made of boards which are pre-cut at a mill and sold in a kit. To order the kit, you simply tell the lumberyard the size of the door to be installed. As long as the door is a standard size, there is no need to trim the jambs. Just nail the head jamb into the dados in the side jambs; then, after plumbing the frame and driving in wedges on either side, nail it into place and hang the door.

An even simpler way to install a door is to order one which is prehung in the frame (which is sometimes made of steel).

After a door frame is in place, the casings, which cover the gaping joints between the jambs and surrounding wall, are installed. The joints in the upper corners of the casings are either mitered or butted. In the latter case, the vertical pieces are butted to the bottom of the top piece; then, to conceal the end grain of the top pieces, a molding called a backband is fitted around the three sides of the cased opening.

DOOR SIZES. The standard thickness of interior doors is $1\frac{3}{8}$ in.; of exterior doors, $1\frac{3}{4}$ in.

Hinged doors—the most commonly used type—are available in stock widths of 18, 24, 28, 30, 32, 36, and 40 in. Double doors, which are used primarily at the front entrance, are 60, 64, and 72 in. wide. The standard height is 6 ft. 8 in. Other available heights are 6 ft., 6 ft. 6 in., 7 ft., 7 ft. 6 in., and 8 ft.

Bifold, sliding, folding, and accordion doors are made in even greater widths.

The recommended minimum widths for the doors in a house are:

Front door	3 ft.
Other exterior doors	2 ft. 6 in.
Room doors	2 ft. 6 in.
Bathroom doors	2 ft.
Inside basement door	2 ft. 6 in.
Doors closing stairways	2 ft. 6 in.
Closet doors	2 ft.

DOOR DESIGN. The design of the doors you install is largely dictated by personal preference and the style of your house. However, you must remember that the design also, in certain cases, affects the utility of doors.

Panel doors are the traditional design and also the most attractive. They are composed of several parts: rails (the horizontal members framing the panels), stiles (the vertical framing members at either side of the door), mullions or muntins (the vertical framing members between the stiles), and panels.

Raised-panel wood door of special design. Arabesque.

In a raised-panel door, the panels are set into the frame but have a raised center section. In a recessed-panel door, which is less attractive, the panels are completely flat.

A practical advantage of all raised-panel doors is that they give better protection against fire than recessed-panel doors and the most widely used kind of flush door. On the other hand, the panels can easily be kicked in by a burglar intent on ransacking a house.

Flush doors are simple smooth-surfaced slabs consisting of a wood frame covered on both sides with thin sheets of plywood. They are the most popular type of door in modern construction because of their low cost, but unless they are covered with choice hardwood veneers, they are totally lacking in charm.

Flush doors are classified as hollow-core and solid-core doors. The former, although not completely hollow, are so lightly constructed that they are quickly consumed by fire and have next to no sound-stopping ability. Despite their higher cost, solid-core doors are preferable. They should always be chosen for exterior doorways.

Louver doors have shutterlike louvers between the stiles and top and bottom rails. Their ostensible purpose is to permit circulation of air. For this reason, they are commonly used on closets to prevent mildewing of clothes. They are often used as room doors, and in very hot climates, they may even be used as exterior doors. Before buying louver doors for ventilation, however, you should make sure that there actually are open spaces between the louvers. In some of the new plastic doors, there are not.

Louver doors have a hard-to-explain charm, and many people buy them for this reason alone. But they can quickly lose their appeal when they require painting because they are so difficult to wash, sand, and repaint.

Jalousie doors are equipped with glass jalousies similar to those used in windows. The 4-in.-wide glass louvers can be adjusted with a crank to any angle to let in air. The doors are also screened and can be fitted with storm sash if used in cold climates (without storm sash, they are suitable only for warm climates).

Dutch doors—which are also called cottage doors—might be of flush or louvered design but are almost always paneled. At a distance they resemble a conventional hinged door. In actuality they are cut horizontally into two approximately equal pieces which can be opened and closed independent of each other. Usually installed in outside walls, the doors permit you to let in air while keeping out (or in) dogs and children.

French doors are conventional hinged doors with small glass panes pretty much from top to bottom. They are always hung in pairs. The two doors are hinged to the opposite sides of the door opening and come together at the center of the opening. Used primarily in traditional architecture, they usually open onto terraces but are also found between living areas. Wherever they are installed, they must be wide enough to permit a person to walk through one side of the door opening without twisting his body (you don't always open both sides). This means that each door should be at least 24 in. wide. A serious drawback of French doors is that they can be easily forced by intruders.

Café doors are used in the house to provide a modicum of privacy without totally blocking off one room from the other. Ranging from about 30 to 60 in. high, the doors are installed in pairs on opposite sides of an opening and roughly midway between the top and bottom. Installation is made with gravity pivot hinges which allow opening the doors in either direction and which close the doors automatically. The doors are available in both louvered and paneled designs.

MATERIALS. The great majority of doors are made of wood. Ponderosa pine is the first choice; fir is used in less expensive units. Hardwoods such as oak are also used but on a very limited scale.

Wood doors lend themselves to almost infinite designs. They can be sawed and planed to fit existing door openings or new openings which are not carefully

made. And they have good insulating value and are relatively soundproof. On the other hand, they must be refinished periodically. They often expand, contract, or warp. And they are combustible.

Steel doors are designed primarily for exterior use but are also used indoors. They are surfaced with steel sheets formed around a wood frame. Urethane foam is sandwiched into the center of exterior doors to provide outstanding protection against cold and heat.

The doors are usually produced in panel designs which are hard to distinguish from wood doors. A baked-on factory finish requires little maintenance. Warping and swelling problems are eliminated. Fire resistance is good, although unless a door is specifically made as a firestop, it does not prevent the penetration of heat. And it would take a burglar with a battering ram to break through. But unless a door is exactly sized to the opening, you must rebuild the entire doorway to install one.

Doors molded out of solid styrene and urethane are used indoors, primarily on closets. They are relatively inexpensive and never need refinishing. And although they feel flimsy, they have good dimensional stability. But they are not effective in stopping fire or noise, and they cannot be trimmed to fit an existing doorway.

Glass is used in doors primarily in small panes. In large sliding doors for exterior installation, it should be tempered so that if anyone crashes into it, it will break into tiny particles which cannot cause injury. Both single-thick and double-thick insulating glass are used.

Mirror doors are made of plate glass bonded to a rigid plywood backing.

Plywood is generally used to surface flush doors, but hardboard and laminated plastics may be substituted

Specially carved packaged doorway. Arabesque.

Double doors of steel. Full-length shutters used on exterior doors are for ornament only and need not be designed, like window shutters, to look as if they completely cover the door when closed. Steelcraft Manufacturing Co.

for it. The panels in panel doors are occasionally made of fiberboard. Ornamental ironwork or aluminum is used for some doors.

TYPES OF DOORS

HINGED DOORS. The majority of the doors in houses are hung on hinges. There are good reasons for this even though the doors take up more floor and wall space when opened than any other type. For one thing, they are easier to open and close than other doors, with the exception of swinging doors. When properly hung, they close tight and stop drafts, dirt, and insects from penetrating around the sides. Operation is noiseless except when doors are slammed. And unlike all other doors, they permit you to hang things on the front and back—a major advantage in closets.

When used in exterior doorways, hinged doors are hung so they swing in. As a general rule, interior doors should also swing into the rooms they are used to close off from halls; otherwise they interfere with passage through the halls. However, doors on hall closets must obviously swing into the halls, and it is often advisable to swing a kitchen door into a hall so it doesn't create problems with the kitchen layout.

Bathroom doors should, if possible, swing in; but if a bathroom is too cramped, the door should swing out. Doors between adjoining rooms other than bathrooms can be swung whichever way will cause less inconvenience. Doors at the head of stairways must swing away from the stairs.

Whether a door is hinged on the right or left depends on which position will interfere less with furniture placement and passage through the door. Ideally, room

doors should be placed close to a corner of the room so they can swing back into the corner.

Hanging a hinged door requires patience and care more than skill. Use two butt hinges with loose pins on interior doors; three on exterior doors. (If an exterior door swings out, use hinges with fixed pins.) Three-and-a-half-inch hinges are required for interior doors up to 32 in. wide; 4-in. hinges for wider doors. For exterior doors, use $4\frac{1}{2}$-in. and 5-in. hinges respectively.

A door should be $\frac{1}{8}$ in. narrower than the finish opening (between jambs) and $\frac{1}{8}$ in. shorter if there is a threshold. Delete another $\frac{1}{8}$ in. for an exterior door with weatherstripping. If there is no threshold, the door should clear the floor by $\frac{1}{2}$ in. or, if a rug is laid close to the door, it should just clear the rug. After measuring the opening, cut off the lugs at the top of the door; then trim down the bottom and the latch side as necessary with a plane. Clamp the door upright to make sure the edges are cut square. Then plane a $\frac{1}{8}$-in. bevel on the latch side of an exterior door so it will not bind against the jamb as it is swung open or shut. Finally, round the sharp corners along all edges slightly.

Stand the door in the opening and wedge it against the hinge jamb. Lay a $1\frac{1}{2}$-in. nail on the top edge and wedge the door up against the top jamb. Then mark the positions of the hinges on both the door and hinge jamb. The top hinge should be 7 in. below the top of the door; the bottom hinge, 11 in. above the floor; the middle hinge, midway between.

After removing the door from the opening, draw the outlines of the hinges on the edge and jamb. The leaves should be placed so they extend to within $\frac{1}{4}$ in. of the back of the door (thus the barrel in which the pin is inserted is set out from the face of the door $\frac{1}{4}$ in.). Cut the hinge mortises with a sharp chisel. The depth of the mortises should exactly equal the thickness of the leaves.

Screw the hinge leaves into the mortises and hang the door. If the door binds against the hinge jamb because you have cut the mortises too deep, you can correct the problem by inserting shims of cardboard under the leaves in the jamb.

Nail stops to the jambs after the door is hung. These are thin strips of wood which keep air from blowing around the sides and top of the door and which also prevent the door from swinging into the door opening farther than it should. On the hinge side, the stop is butted tight to the back of the door; on the latch side, allow $\frac{1}{16}$-in. clearance. Align the stop on the head jamb with those on the side jambs.

The last step in hanging a door is to install the lock or latch (see Chapter 26). The knob should be placed 38 in. above the floor.

Thresholds may be nailed across the bottom of interior doorways to keep air from blowing underneath or to conceal the junction of floorboards which are laid in

Packaged doorway with steel door and translucent colored glass sidelight. Steelcraft Manufacturing Co.

opposite directions on either side of the door. These are made of wood. To install them, cut off the bottom ends of the stops, slide the thresholds into place between the jambs, and nail them down with finishing nails.

Exterior door sills made of oak are installed with the door frames. If a door must be cut off well above the sill in order to clear a thick rug, install an aluminum threshold with a vinyl sealing strip either set into the top of the threshold or recessed in the bottom of the door.

SIDELIGHTS. An increasing number of manufacturers now sell so-called packaged doorways which include not only the door but also the frame, threshold, and weatherstripping. In addition, many packages come with one or two sidelights, and a few even have a transom.

The style of the sidelights is compatible with that of the door with which they are used. Some are glazed from top to bottom; others only partway down from the top. As a rule, the glass is fixed, but in larger sidelights it may be operable.

Standard width of sidelight panels is 1 ft. Wider units up to 3 ft. are available.

BIFOLD DOORS. Bifold doors are similar to those in telephone booths except that they open outward. They are used indoors only, because there is no way to seal the cracks around the edges. A door consists of two fairly narrow vertical panels which are hinged together. One panel is pivoted next to the door jamb; the other

glides in an overhead track. To open the door, you either give the track-mounted panel a shove toward the opposite door jamb or pull on knobs screwed to the panels at the hinged edges. This forces the panels to fold together back to back, at right angles to the door opening.

Single bifold doors are occasionally used instead of hinged doors to conserve floor and wall space when open. But they are normally installed in pairs to close wide openings in closets and between rooms. One door (two panels) is pivoted at the left jamb; the other door (also two panels) is pivoted at the right jamb. When both doors are open, you have an almost clear view through the doorway. Or you can have access to one-half of a closet without disturbing the door covering the other half.

Bifolds are available as stock units in a wide range of designs—paneled, louvered, and flush. The thickness of closet doors may be as little as $1\frac{1}{8}$ in. The smallest two-panel door is a nominal 18 in. wide; the largest four-panel door, a nominal 8 ft. wide. Doors of any width to a maximum of 24 ft. can be assembled by a carpenter out of individual doors up to 24 in. wide (instead of having only two panels, each unit is made up of six or eight panels).

Installation of a bifold door is a simple task if you buy a stock unit which is partially assembled at the factory. Screw the track to the top jamb, and screw the bracket on which the door pivots to the floor next to one of the side jambs. Then fit the door into the track and bracket and install the knobs. There is no lock or latch to worry about.

Hardware for non-stock bifolds is sold by lumber-yards and hardware stores.

SLIDING DOORS. Two types of sliding door are used in houses. Recess doors consist of one or two panels

Bifold doors. This is not a stock design although some stock units resemble it.

82

Bypass sliding mirror doors. Diston Industries, Inc.

which slide in a track screwed to the head jamb of the door opening. When a single-panel door is closed, it is simply pulled across the door opening until it meets the side jamb. When it is opened, it slides back into a pocket in the wall, where it is completely hidden. In a two-panel unit, the doors are hidden in pockets on both sides of the opening; and when they are closed, they come together edge to edge in the middle of the opening.

Bypass sliding doors made of one to four panels are always in view. Single doors, which are used only in cramped, low-cost houses, slide in a track that is mounted on the wall above the door opening. When closed, it overlaps the edges of the door opening; when open, it hangs against the wall to one side of the opening. By contrast, two-, three-, and four-panel doors are hung in two parallel tracks which are screwed to the head jamb of the door opening. Thus the doors are confined between the side jambs. In a two-panel unit, you can slide one door past the other from one side of the opening to the other; but no matter what you do, the opening is never open for more than half of its total width. When three- or four-door panels are used, the open space between doors is even more restricted.

Up to a few years ago, multi-panel bypass sliding doors were often used in extra-wide closets because they permit you to close enormous unobstructed openings and do not take up any space in the closets or adjoining rooms. But they lost favor when improved bifold and folding doors came along because they prevent you from seeing and reaching into more than half of a closet at one time. Furthermore, the doors tend to

warp. As a result, this type of door is today used primarily in exterior walls between indoor living areas and terraces.

Recess sliding doors, on the other hand, have never been very popular because the door openings and surrounding walls must be specially constructed. But they have two unique, closely related advantages: When open, they take up absolutely no floor or wall space, and they do not obstruct the door opening even a fraction of an inch. This makes them ideal for use between rooms when there is inadequate space for a hinged door. They are also good for closets but are rarely used in these because of cost and installation problems.

Any hinged door can be used to make a recess sliding door, though most are of flush design. The doors can also be cut out of ¾-in. plywood or particleboard. The total width of the door opening is limited to 3 ft. for a single door, 6 ft. for two doors. Maximum opening height is 6 ft. 8 in.

To install the doors you need a prefabricated steel pocketframe set. This is installed in an opening (framed with double studs and a header) which is a little more than twice the width of the doors to be hung. The pockets into which the doors slide are then covered on both sides with gypsum board or other wall-surfacing material.

Instead of door knobs, the doors are equipped with recessed pulls.

Bypass sliding doors for closets are also made of standard hinged doors or of plywood or particleboard. Prefabricated mirror doors with slender aluminum frames are available. The largest single door panel is 4 ft. wide. The height can be anything up to 8 ft. The

Steel pocketframe for a recessed sliding door.

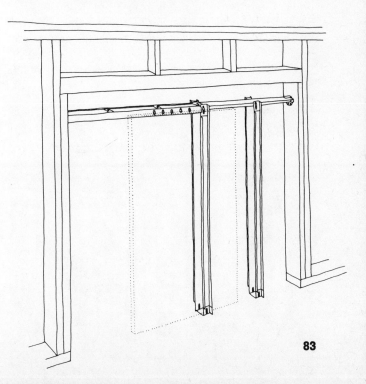

maximum width of door openings for two- and three-panel doors is 8 ft.; for four-panel doors, 12 ft.

Installation is extremely simple. The hardware required is sold separate from the doors by lumberyards and hardware stores. Screw the track in which the doors slide to the head jamb. Attach a pair of hangers, with wheels, to the back of each door panel at the upper corners. Fit the wheels into the tracks and adjust the hangers until the doors hang straight. Then screw a door guide to the floor to keep the doors from swaying.

FOLDING DOORS. Folding doors are made of thin, narrow, vertical strips which fold back to back into a compact bundle when the doors are pushed open. In the simplest doors, the strips are very small and are tied together with cords. Most, however, have wood slats about 4 in. wide which are hinged together with vinyl fabric or steel slats that are covered and hinged with vinyl. In all cases, the doors hang in a track and open and close between the side jambs. They are installed singly or in pairs.

The main use for folding doors is in closets and laundry niches. They are also used to divide large open spaces into two rooms. Unlike sliding doors, they do not seriously obstruct a door opening when they are open. For example, if a door opening is 8 ft. wide, the door when opened collapses into a bundle approximately 1 ft. wide.

The main objection to folding doors by people who think a door should look like a door is that they resemble stiff draperies. And like draperies, they have a tendency to wave in a strong draft. More important, they don't always operate as smoothly as they should, and they give scant protection against fire or noise.

The doors are available in heights to 14 ft. 1 in. Single doors range in width from 32 in. to 50 ft. 4 in. The maximum width of a pair of doors is thus 100 ft. 8 in. The tracks in which the doors slide are usually

Wood folding door which can be opened from either side. Panelfold.

Roller door. Wilmot Industries, Inc.

straight but can be curved as much as 90°.

You can hang the doors in a few minutes. Just screw the track to the head jamb of a closet door or the ceiling. Slip the hangers on which the doors glide into the track. Fasten one side of the door to the jamb, and install the simple latch which comes with the door to the other side. Locks for the doors are available.

ACCORDION DOORS. These are almost identical to folding doors. They are made, however, with a folding steel framework which is vinyl-covered on both sides. They open and close like an accordion, whereas a folding door has a serpentine movement.

Because they are more expensive than folding doors, accordion doors are rarely found in the house. They can be used in closets, but their main use is for dividing rooms. Those used as dividers in schools and other public buildings are frequently sound-insulated. Sizes up to 27 ft. high and 60 ft. wide are available.

ROLLER DOORS. This is a new kind of residential door, although similar units have been used for various purposes in stores for a long time. Installed only in closets, it operates like a window shade, rolling up above the door head and rolling down to the floor in tiny tracks on the side jambs. As a result, it permits unobstructed access through the door opening; and because of its thinness, it takes up even less floor space than a sliding door.

Made of Philippine-mahogany slats interwoven with vinyl, the door is operated either by an electric motor in the housing (when you touch a lighted button in the side jamb, the door rolls up or down in three and a half seconds) or by a hand crank (four turns open or close the door). The electric door is designed so that if the power fails, you can still operate it by hand; and if a descending door strikes a shoe or other obstruction on the floor, it instantly stops without any damage to the shoe or mechanism. A closet light automatically turns on and off as the door is raised or lowered.

The door is designed for finished openings measuring 48, 60, or 72 in. wide by 81 in. high. The rough opening must be constructed with a single 2×8-in. header. The housing is screwed to the back of the header.

SWINGING DOORS. Swinging doors—also called double-acting doors—are normally used only between the kitchen and dining room. You can push them open in either direction with your hand, shoulder, or hip; and unless you open them to an angle of 90°, they automatically swing shut after you.

Any standard hinged door is easily converted to swinging operation by shaving down the sides to provide clearance at both jambs. The door is held in place at the top by a pivot which is mortised into the head jamb and a corresponding socket mortised into the top edge of the door. A double-acting floor hinge controlled by a spring is notched into the bottom of the door and screwed to the floor. Pushplates are screwed to both sides to protect the finish against dirt and oil on the hands.

SLIDING GLASS DOORS. If sliding glass doors have not exactly revolutionized home design, they have at least brought about an enormous change. Whereas houses used to be pretty well walled off from the surrounding world, sliding glass doors have now made them part of the world. With them, the terrace and garden become, in effect, an extension of the house interior, for even though they are separated from each

Sliding glass doors with wood frames sheathed in vinyl. Andersen Corp.

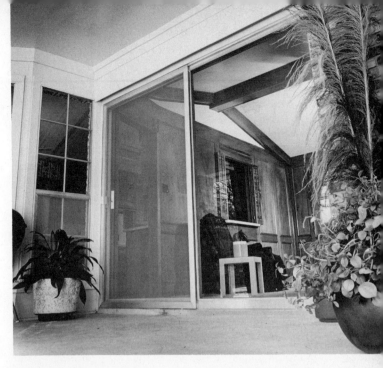

Reversible sliding glass door with aluminum frame. General Aluminum Corp.

other by a solid wall of glass, they appear to form a single large space.

Add to this achievement the fact that sliding glass doors provide an economical, convenient way to flood the house with light and air, and it's easy to see why most houses built today incorporate at least one and in many cases several doors.

Sliding glass doors are of the bypass type. The standard unit incorporates two panels, of which either one or both slides. Maximum width is 20 ft. In three-panel doors, one of the end panels is fixed and the other two slide, or only one panel (usually the center) slides. Maximum width is 30 ft. In four-panel doors, the two center panels slide in opposite directions over the fixed end panels or the two end panels slide to the center over the fixed center panels. Maximum width is 40 ft.

Beyond this, there are several variations in sliding arrangements, including six- and eight-panel doors. Many doors have so-called reversible panels, meaning that their slide direction can be reversed before or after installation. All doors have sliding screens.

The height of the doors ranges from 6 ft. 8 in. to as much as 14 ft.

The door frames, jambs, and sill are most commonly made of aluminum, which is natural, colored, painted, and/or anodized to give greater protection against corrosion. Recent improvements in design have separated the inner and outer faces so the frames do not transmit cold.

Wood frames, which are necessarily larger, are better insulators; but they also add to the cost of the doors. The frames are treated with wood preservative and can be painted or stained. Some have either a factory-applied polyurea finish or a rigid vinyl sheath that never needs refinishing.

All frames, jambs, and sills are fully weatherstripped to keep out air and moisture. Despite the weight of the doors, they move fairly easily on ball bearings. But to improve movement of very large doors and discourage jimmying, a new European door is designed so that when you turn the handle, it actually lifts off the bottom track and slides noiselessly to the side. By another turn of the handle, you then drop it back into the track. When closed in any position, the door presses so tightly against the bottom track that it is almost impossible to move.

Improved locking devices on all sliding doors give good protection against intruders. In addition to an interior latch, most doors can be locked and opened from outside with a key.

A special feature worth looking for is an easy method of leveling the doors yourself if they should get out of alignment because of settling of the house.

A wide choice of glazing is offered by all manufacturers. Tempered plate glass is a must and is now generally required by law. It is available in single-thick glass, insulating glass, and tinted heat-absorbing glass. For doors facing west or south, the ideal choice is insulating glass which is also tempered and tinted. If you dislike the effect of large, unbroken panes, you can buy from some manufacturers snap-in mullions which divide the panes into smaller rectangles. These can be removed when you wash the glass.

In spite of the size of sliding glass doors, they can be installed in almost any existing wall by knocking out the studs and replacing them with a large header. But this is a job for professionals. You can install the doors themselves, however.

TILTING SLIDING GLASS DOORS. These look like a conventional sliding glass door and work in the same way. The inner door, however, is designed so that when in closed position it can be disengaged from the top track and tilted into the room several inches to provide indirect ventilation while barring entry from outdoors. In this respect the door is similar to a hopper-casement window (see Chapter 6). It has a single handle.

SECURITY DOORS. A security door is installed on the outside of the regular house door like a storm door. It is built of structural aluminum with ornamental aluminum castings welded into the frame. Also set into the frame behind the castings is a large pane of tempered glass. The door is hinged to one side of the door frame and deadlocked. Thus when the doorbell rings, you can open the inner door and see and talk with the visitor before letting him in.

Because the door is completely weatherstripped, it also gives good protection against cold.

The manufacturer offers a selection of ornamental castings and builds the doors to fit any door opening.

GARAGE DOORS. The garage door is not only the largest piece of operating equipment in the house but also the most prominent. You should, therefore, give even more thought to it than to your other doors.

Two principal types of garage door are in use: the sectional, or roll-up, and the one-piece, or tilt-up. Both are popularly known as overhead doors because they swing up into the garage close to the ceiling. They are counterbalanced by massive springs which make them easy to raise and should prevent them from crashing down on you when you close them.

The sectional door is the more common, and it gives better protection against weather because it rests snugly against the stops and locks more securely. It is made up of several horizontal sections which are hinged together and guided by rollers in steel tracks on either side. The counterbalancing springs are placed above the door. In operation, the door glides straight up and bends around the curved corners of the tracks until it disappears behind the head jamb and lies parallel with the garage ceiling.

The one-piece door operates more quietly, but while it has fewer moving parts to get out of whack, it has a greater tendency to twist out of shape. It is a shade easier to open and close if you have a bad back. In operation, the entire door, which forms a large rigid panel, tilts back and up against the ceiling.

One-piece doors are controlled by three types of hardware system. The track system consists of a pair of horizontal tracks just below the ceiling and a pair of springs mounted vertically on the door jambs. When the door is opened and closed, the bottom edge moves in an almost straight up-and-down path. By contrast, doors using the jamb or pivot hardware system swing out at the bottom, thus making them more difficult to open if snow is piled against them. Furthermore, since neither system incorporates tracks, it is possible to twist the doors sideways so they bind against the jambs. The springs for a jamb-type door are mounted vertically behind the jambs just above the garage floor. Pivot-type doors swing on V-shaped arms which are attached to the side walls of the garage and are controlled by springs stretching from these arms to the ceiling.

For single-car garages, the recommended minimum door width is 8 ft.; and although there has been a recent trend to a 9-ft. width, this probably is unnecessary now that automobiles are getting smaller. Recommended minimum width for a single door on two-car garages is 15 ft.

Standard door widths are 8, 9, 10, 12, 14, 15, 16, 17, and 18 ft. Heights are 6 ft. 6 in., 7 ft., and 8 ft. In selecting a door, you must take into account the clearance required below the garage ceiling. Some doors fit within about 1 in. of the ceiling; others require 6 in. or more.

The choice of materials and designs is large. In addition to wood, you can buy doors of steel, aluminum, or fiberglass or hardboard bonded to a wood frame. Fiberglass doors are exceptionally lightweight, need no maintenance, and actually transmit a certain amount of light into the garage. But like wood and hardboard, they shatter if you back into them. Metal doors—especially those of steel—are the most damage-resistant, and as long as the baked-on finish isn't scratched, they need no painting. Hardboard is also factory-finished. Wood doors, however, must be refinished periodically, and unless the lowest panels and rails are treated with wood preservative, they are likely to rot out. On the other hand, they are more attractive than other doors and are the only kind which can be stained.

Paneled and flush doors are the standard designs. A ribbed effect is common on metal and fiberglass doors. Glass panes can be set into all doors except fiberglass doors. But this is a gross simplification of the wide array of designs you will be confronted with when the salesman asks, "Now how do you want your door to look?" Panels are of various sizes. Some are raised, some recessed. Glass insets can be of special shapes. Moldings and appliqués can be added to both flush and panel doors. You can even glue on ornamental strap hinges to give the effect of doors that swing open.

Once you have finally made up your mind about the door you want, leave the installation to the dealer or a carpenter.

Garage-door openers. With the rise in the crime rate new emphasis is being put on the automatic garage-door opener as a security device. For one thing, since an opener makes it easier to close the door when you leave home, you don't advertise to the world that the house is empty; and because the opener has an effective locking mechanism, it discourages intruders from trying to force the door. For another thing, the opener permits you to remain in your locked automobile while you open the door, turn on the garage light, drive in, and close the door. Thus it reduces chances of your being waylaid by a lurking criminal.

In addition to these advantages, an opener saves you from the strain of opening and closing the garage door, keeps you out of rain and snow, and improves the appearance of your house by encouraging you to close the door when you are away from home.

Openers are designed to operate all types of overhead doors up to 18 ft. wide and 7 ft. high. The heart of the device is an electric motor installed in a housing behind the door at ceiling level. This is connected to the door by a chain or screw-drive mechanism which automatically changes direction as the door is opened and closed. Operation is controlled by a small transmitter in the automobile and a receiver in the garage. Pushing the transmitter button as you drive up to your house opens the door as you roll into the driveway. Another

push closes it. The door can also be operated by a pushbutton on the garage wall and, in better models, by an outside key-operated switch. If the power fails, the door can be operated manually.

Step-by-step installation of a garage door opener. 1, attach wall mounting bracket over center of door.

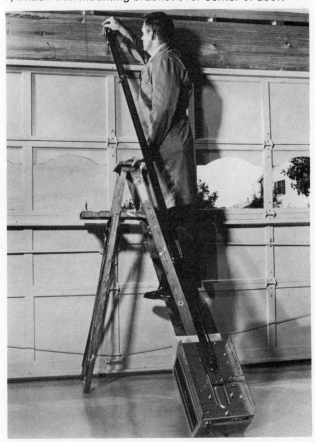

2, hang power unit from ceiling or joists.

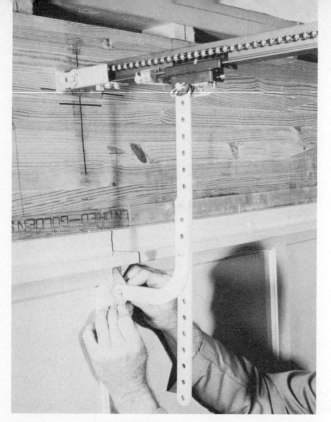

3, attach upper arm of actual operating mechanism to trolley; lower arm to door.

If the door meets an obstruction while opening or closing, it automatically stops or, in some cases, reverses.

Radio controls for a door opener should carry the approval of the Federal Communications Commission. To eliminate interference from other door openers in the neighborhood, the best openers employ two or three inaudible signals to activate the door. In the event that the interference continues, your transmitter and receiver can be recoded by a representative of the manufacturer.

4, hang radio receiver and attach to nearby power unit.

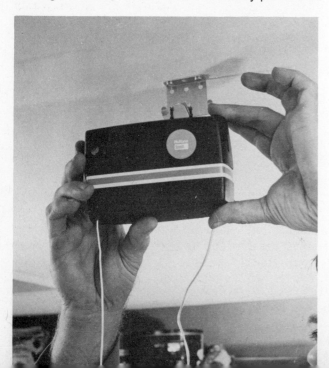

5, install pushbutton control near door from house and connect power unit to power source.

Despite their seeming complexity, all openers can be installed by the homeowner. Follow the maker's directions.

6, installation completed. NuTone—Scovill Manufacturing Co.

BASEMENT DOORS. One of the first things that rot and need attention on old houses is the bulkhead which covers the outside stairs to the basement. Instead of trying to rebuild it with wood, the sensible course is to tear it out and replace it with a new steel bulkhead.

The standard unit designed for installation on flat foundations has a pair of sloping doors and triangular sides. For slanting foundations, all you need is a pair of doors in a flat frame. Both types of door are made in sizes that fit most areaways; and if not long enough, they can be lengthened by attaching steel extensions.

Installation is easily made by following the manufacturer's directions. In essence, all you have to do is cut the siding on the house wall to fit the bulkhead and anchor the bulkhead to the foundations and wall.

SCREEN AND STORM DOORS. Screen doors are a necessity in almost all parts of the United States. Storm doors, though generally used only in the North, are equally valuable in the South if you hope to reduce the cost of air conditioning.

For northerners, a hinged combination door which is fitted with screens in the summer and glass in the winter is the simplest way to get protection against both insects and cold. Once the door is hung outside the primary door, it never needs to be removed. You just replace the lightweight, easily handled screen inserts with the glass or vice versa.

Combination doors are made in stock sizes to fit all standard exterior doors from 30 to 36 in. wide and 6 ft. 6 in. to 7 ft. high. Other sizes are fabricated to order. The frames are made of wood, natural aluminum, or prefinished aluminum. The inserts are usually framed in the same material as the door.

The standard door has either one or two openings with a solid panel at the bottom, but several variations are available. The basically simple, straightforward design of the doors can also be varied by substituting a cross-buck panel for a rectangular bottom panel, using inserts with scalloped-edged frames, or covering the lower of the two openings with a louvered insert or an insert made of closely spaced wood turnings.

Conventional screen and storm doors which are taken down and stored when not needed are rarely of such elaborate design. If you want to pretty them up, the easiest way is to screw an ornamental aluminum grille over the bottom opening. The grille also protects the screen or glass against damage.

The doors are made of either wood or aluminum.

The majority of states now require that all new combination doors and storm doors be equipped with unbreakable glazing material. Both tempered glass and acrylic are acceptable. Unfortunately, neither material can be easily installed in old storm doors. To correct this problem, one glass manufacturer now produces replacement panels of tempered safety glass which will fit about 70% of the 750-odd storm-door panel sizes currently in use. The new panels, available in nine sizes, have vinyl edges which are scored for easy cutting. Thus a 30×32-in. panel can be cut down, in ⅛-in. increments, to as little as 27×27 in.

DOOR ACCESSORIES

DOOR CLOSERS. The simplest form of door closer is a coiled spring, spring hinge, or spring pivot which is substituted for the pin in a convention hinge. Except for some of the very powerful new spring hinges, these are suitable only for screen doors and lightweight solid doors. They should not be used on doors with glass panes because they sometimes close with such force that the glass is shattered.

To close a door gently but firmly calls for a hydraulic or pneumatic closer. The former is made for light-duty installations (storm doors), medium-duty (standard-size exterior doors), and heavy-duty (extra-large or heavy exterior doors). Pneumatic closers are made for light-duty work only.

When shopping for a closer, note their limitations and requirements printed on the package. Some can be used indoors only. Incorrect placement of a closer on a door affects operation. A few units may be too large to fit in the space available.

DOOR BELLS AND CHIMES. The signal system which tells you somebody is at your door ranges from an inconspicuous buzzer costing about $12 to a handsome 4-ft.-long chime that sounds eight notes and costs about $150. Some chimes are housed in electric wall clocks.

Whatever the size and design of the signal-sounding device, all units are easily installed. The hardest part of the job is to snake the bell wires through the walls or, failing that, to semi-conceal them next to the trim and baseboards. The first step is to turn off the electricity and connect a small transformer into the house supply. Then, from the low-voltage side of the transformer, run one bell wire to the chime, and a second to the pushbutton at the front door. (If there is also a pushbutton at the back door, connect it to the wire leading to the front door.) Finally, run another wire from the pushbutton to the chime.

WEATHERSTRIPPING AND THRESHOLDS. If you're looking for something a little better and a little more attractive than the average weatherstrip, don't be disheartened by the very limited selection of materials offered in hardware stores and lumberyards. Ask the salesman to show you the catalogs of the larger weatherstripping and threshold manufacturers. The

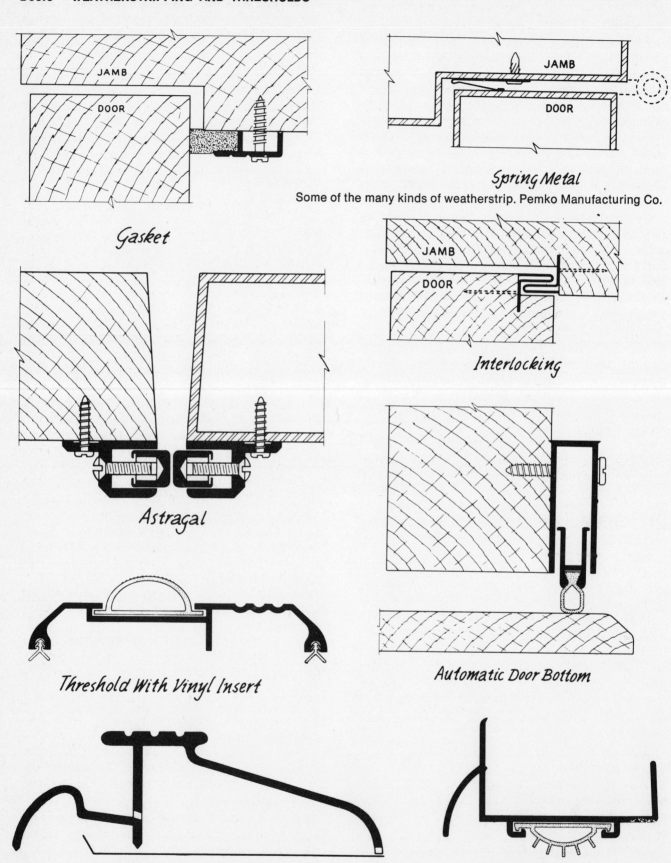

JAMB

DOOR

Gasket

JAMB

DOOR

Spring Metal

Some of the many kinds of weatherstrip. Pemko Manufacturing Co.

JAMB

DOOR

Interlocking

Astragal

Automatic Door Bottom

Threshold With Vinyl Insert

Interlocking Threshold

Door Shoe

chances are you will find the perfect answer to your problem. Because there is such a multiplicity of doors which require sealing against weather, dirt, sound, and light, weatherstripping is today available in many sizes and designs and, in certain cases, colors. One manufacturer alone requires a 36-page catalog to describe his offerings.

Prehung doors are sold with weatherstripping installed. For all others, it must be added after they are hung. In some cases, this calls for a carpenter or weatherstripping specialist. Other weatherstrips are simple enough to install yourself.

Weatherstripping of exterior doors requires perimeter strips which are attached to the side and head jambs; under-door strips or thresholds; and astragals to seal the vertical joint between double doors. Similar weatherstripping is sometimes required on interior doors to stop drafts and the transmission of sound.

Perimeter weatherstripping. Probably the most effective perimeter weatherstripping is the interlocking type consisting of two metal strips—one fastened to the door, the other to the jamb. Unfortunately, this must be installed by a professional. Furthermore, the weatherstripping can cause problems if it is not cleaned out regularly, if pebbles become lodged in it, if it freezes up because moisture collects in it, or if the door settles or warps.

Spring-metal weatherstrips are nailed to the jambs so that they bear tight against the edges of the closed door. The simplest is an almost flat strip which is tacked along the edge away from the stop. More reliable is a V-shaped strip tacked along the edge next to the stop (because of this arrangement, the nail heads are protected from the edge of the door and are not likely to be knocked loose by the door). A third metal strip is bow-shaped and has a right-angle flange which is fastened to the face of the jamb.

Spring-metal weatherstrips are less efficient than interlocking strips but are unaffected by dirt, pebbles, or freezing. On the other hand, they should not be used for doors which swell excessively in summer because they narrow the door opening a fraction of an inch (the bow-type strip requires a clearance of $\frac{1}{8}$ in. between the door and jamb). And they make a humming sound when the wind blows.

Gasket weatherstrips are least attractive because they are mounted on the face of the door or jamb. The cheapest type is nothing more than a strip of felt which won't take paint and which soon starts to fray. Better units are contained in an aluminum housing which can be painted to match the door.

Another serious drawback of many gasket strips is that they become brittle in cold weather, so if you live in a cold climate, you should make sure they are made of vinyl or neoprene, which will remain flexible even

when the temperature dips well below zero. An alternative if your door is made of steel is to use a magnetic strip.

On the plus side, gasket weatherstrips are easily and quickly installed. And if the screw holes in the aluminum housing are slotted, the strips can be readjusted if the door becomes warped or settling of the house throws it out of plumb. Feather-edged vinyl or rubber strips are available for use on doors with automatic closers to ensure that the closers shut the doors tight.

Astragal weatherstripping. Gasket weatherstrips are generally used to seal the joint between double doors. Some are recessed in the edge of one of the doors; others are screwed to the face of both doors. Spring-metal weatherstrips are also used but are less desirable because they may snag your clothing as you pass.

Under-door weatherstripping. On an existing door, if there is no need for changing the threshold. You can install spring-metal or interlocking weatherstrips like those used on the jambs, but neither is highly recommended. An easier-to-install alternative with fewer problems is a gasketed weatherstrip—called a door sweep—made of neoprene held in an aluminum channel. This is effective only on outswinging doors, however.

The best weatherstrips for existing doors are door shoes and automatic door bottoms. The former is a semi-circular vinyl strip held in an aluminum channel which is screwed to the bottom edge of the door so that it bears directly on the threshold. An automatic door bottom consists of a felt or neoprene strip in an aluminum channel which is recessed or rabbeted into the bottom of the door or fastened to the door face. Actuated by a slightly protruding rod, the strip automatically drops down onto the threshold when the door is closed, and retracts into the housing when the door is opened.

If you're putting in a new door or have some reason for replacing the threshold under an old door, an aluminum threshold can be used to take the place of an under-door weatherstrip.

Interlocking thresholds are designed with a projecting flange into which an L-shaped metal strip screwed to the back of the door hooks. This gives an excellent seal against the weather, but the hook can be damaged or forced out of alignment. In addition, the flange on the threshold can trip you up if you catch the sole of your shoe under it.

Some interlocking thresholds are designed with weepholes to catch and drain off water which is driven under the door by storms.

A more common type of weatherstripping threshold is a heavy aluminum saddle with a semicircular vinyl strip recessed in the top. These have been widely used since they were introduced about ten years ago, but they suffer from the fact that the gasket may eventually become worn out or deformed by traffic, and it is then not always easy to find a replacement strip of the same size.

Both interlocking and gasketed thresholds are available—despite what you may be told by your hardware dealer—in assorted heights to provide clearance over extra-thick rugs. Maximum height of interlocking thresholds is 2 in.; of gasketed thresholds, 1¼ in. You can gain further height by installing a board under a threshold.

Also available are non-weatherstopping thresholds of wood and aluminum in a variety of configurations and heights.

A useful device for deflecting water from doors which are badly exposed to storms and drips is a quarter-round aluminum drip cap. This is fastened to the face of a door just above the bottom.

SOUNDPROOFING FOR INTERIOR DOORS. As noted earlier, the best doors for stopping the transmission of noise between rooms are solid-core flush doors and raised-panel doors. Others have little value.

But to make a door completely soundproof, you must also seal the cracks around the edges. Gasket-type perimeter weatherstrips are the best for this purpose. At the bottom of the door, install either a threshold with a vinyl insert or a vinyl gasket on the edge of the door.

WHO MAKES IT

Acorn Building Components, Inc. · Sliding glass doors with thermalized aluminum frames. Two-panel doors reversible. Prehung exterior doors of aluminum with insulated core. Doors with or without sidelights. Sliding mirror doors in gold-anodized aluminum frames.

Afco, Inc. · Aluminum combination storm-screen doors.

Alcan Aluminum Corp. · Aluminum storm door with foam insulation.

Alsto Co. · Circular door with flexible plastic shutters to permit dogs and cats to go in and out by themselves.

Andersen Corp. · Sliding glass doors with wood frames finished in polyurea or covered with vinyl. Vinyl shutters for doors.

Arabesque. · Hand-carved doors of Philippine mahogany in great variety.

Bilco Co. · Steel basement doors.

Biltbest Corp. · Prefinished beige wood doors with snap-in wood grilles.

Julius Blum & Co. · Aluminum, bronze, and steel thresholds.

Boise Cascade Corp., Door Div. · Bifold doors. Interior and exterior hinged doors of flush-panel design. Fire doors. Doors available in several wood facings and with glass inserts and moldings applied.

Broan Manufacturing Co. · Door chimes.

E. L. Bruce Co. of Texas. · Interior and exterior flush hinged doors with plywood, hardboard, or plastic-laminate faces. Faces offered in different hardwoods, simulated hardwoods, or solid colors.

Cabanarama Industries, Inc. · Café doors. Interior wood shutters for doors.

Cannon Craft Co. · Wood bifold doors. Café doors. Interior shutters for sliding glass doors.

Celotex Corp., Jim Walter Doors Div. · Sectional garage doors of fiberglass, hardboard, particleboard with phenolic overlay.

Clopay Co. · Folding doors of wood or with vinyl covering in variety.

Como Plastics, Inc. Louvered plastic bifold doors.

Dalton Manufacturing Co. Hinge-type door closer.

Designware Industries, Inc. · Aluminum-framed sliding mirror doors.

Diston Industries. · Bifold and sliding mirrored closet doors with aluminum frames.

Eagle Electric Manufacturing Co. · Door bells, buzzers, and simple chimes.

Edwards Co. · Door chimes and bells.

Emco Specialties, Inc. · House numbers and letters of polystyrene.

Emerson Electric Co., Rittenhouse-Chromalox Div. · Door chimes.

Emhart Corp. · Russwin door closers.

Evans Products Co., Remington Aluminum Div. · Aluminum sliding glass doors with double locks. Steel bifold doors. Mirror bifold doors.

Ferum Co. · Hydraulic door closers.

Frantz Manufacturing Co. · Sectional garage doors of wood, fiberglass, aluminum. Insulated flush doors of hardboard. Garage door openers.

Gallatin Aluminum Products Co. · Reversible aluminum sliding glass doors. When insulating glass is used, rectangular or diamond-shaped mullions can be sealed between panes.

General Aluminum Corp. · Reversible sliding glass doors with aluminum frames.

General Electric Co., Wiring Device Dept. · Door bells.

General Products Co. · Prehung steel exterior doors with urethane-foam insulation. Steel bifold doors.

Gerber Industries, Inc. · Wood numbers and letters, 7 in. high.

Gordon Corp. · Steel basement doors.

Hager Hinge Co. · Door viewer. Hinge-pin door closer.

Ideal Co. · Prehung wood doors in prefabricated front entrances with and without sidelights. Wood exterior doors of conventional and unusual decorative designs. Dutch doors of wood. Wood bifold doors. Wood interior doors. French doors. Wood screen doors, many of decorative design. Louvered grilles for insertion in screen doors.

I.M.M.S., Inc., Roto International Div. · Lift-and-slide glass doors. Tilting-sliding glass doors.

International Window Corp. · Reversible aluminum sliding glass doors. Night lock allows door to be opened for ventilation. Sliding mirror doors in gold- or bronze-finished aluminum frames. Jalousie panels for insertion in wood doors.

Janus 2, Inc. · House numbers in raised design, three colors on steel.

Keller Industries, Inc. · Aluminum sliding glass doors, some reversible. Aluminum storm doors including one with a single full-length glass and self-storing combination storm-screen doors. Screen doors.

Kessler Enterprises. · Security doors in sculptured designs made of ⅜-in. cast aluminum.

Joseph C. Klein, Inc. · Wood sliding glass doors with snap-in wood grilles.

Larson Manufacturing Co. · Aluminum combination storm-screen doors, some self-storing. Aluminum decorative grilles to protect glass and screenwire.

Leigh Products, Inc. · White-finished aluminum louvered panels to install in doors for ventilation. From 8×8 in. to 24 × 18 in. Hydraulic door closers. Steel bifold doors, one model half-mirrored.

Louisiana-Pacific Corp. · Reversible wood and aluminum sliding glass doors. Exterior and interior hinged doors. Aluminum combination storm-screen doors, some of self-storing type.

Marvin Windows. · Wood sliding glass doors available with wood removable grilles.

Maywood, Inc. · Bifold doors of wood and plastic. Flush doors of hardboard are prefinished, except Philippine-mahogany doors are unfinished. Wood café doors. Wood shutters for interior doors.

Miami-Carey Co. · Door chimes and bells.

Milgard Manufacturing, Inc. · Reversible aluminum sliding glass doors.

Mon-Ray Windows, Inc. · Aluminum combination storm-screen doors, some of self-storing type.

Montgomery Ward & Co. · Aluminum combination storm-screen doors, one with decorative grille. Aluminum screen door with full-length glass. Sectional garage doors of wood, fiberglass, plywood, and steel. Garage-door opener. Café doors, one of decorative ironwork. Folding doors. Wood, plastic, and mirrored bifold doors.

Morgan Co. · Hinged wood exterior and interior doors. Wood entrance doors made to order with wide choice of panel designs. Dutch doors. Prefabricated front entrances of traditional design with and without sidelights. Front entrance trim of wood or acrylic-finished ABS plastic. Wood pediments. Wood and plastic bifold doors. Wood café doors. Wood door shutters.

Mortell Co. · Aluminum thresholds. Weatherstrips.

E. A. Nord Co. · Carved and paneled exterior doors of Douglas fir.

Northrop Architectural Systems. · Every possible type and size of aluminum sliding glass door.

Panelfold. · Folding doors and partitions.

S. Parker Hardware Manufacturing Corp. · Hinge-type door closer. Hydraulic closers of all sizes and varieties.

Peachtree Door. · Reversible sliding glass doors with clear or beige polyurea-finished wood frames. Aluminum sliding glass doors. Paneled, flush, and louvered bifold doors of steel. Wood-framed French doors with two or three panels, tempered glass, sliding screens. Prehung

exterior doors of steel with urethane insulating core.

Pease Co., Ever-Strait Div. · Prehung exterior steel doors with foam insulation; with and without decorative plastic moldings and tempered-glass lights. Complete entrance-ways with sidelights. Steel interior hinged doors.

Pemko Manufacturing Co. · Every type of weatherstrip you ever dreamed of. Aluminum thresholds. Garage-door weatherstripping.

PPG Industries. · Tempered safety glass replacement panels for storm doors, with snap-off edges to fit most doors.

Raynor Manufacturing Co. · Sectional garage doors of fiberglass, hardboard, wood (including ¾-in. redwood), steel. Garage-door opener.

Ridge Doors. · Sectional garage doors of wood (including ¾-in. redwood), plywood, plastic-coated hardboard, fiberglass, aluminum. Garage-door opener.

Rolleze, Inc. · Reversible aluminum sliding glass doors.

Rolscreen Co. · Sliding glass doors with removable wood grilles. Doors made of solid wood or with prefinished aluminum sheath on outside.

RSL Woodworking Products Co. · Glass inserts and louvers for wood, plastic, and metal doors. Wood and plastic moldings for doors.

Rusco Industries, Inc., Ador/Hilite Div. · Reversible aluminum sliding glass doors. Mirror sliding doors in aluminum frames finished in silver or gold.

F. E. Schumacher Co. · Aluminum and wood combination storm-screen doors. Some wood doors with louvered or balustered inserts. Wood screen doors. Aluminum sliding glass doors; two-panel doors are reversible. Wood café doors. Louvered wood bifold doors. Louvered wood hinge doors. Exterior wood doors. Prefabricated entrance-ways with insulated steel doors with and without side-lights. Hinged jalousie doors with wood frames. Aluminum thresholds.

Scovill Manufacturing Co., Caradco Window & Door Div. · Wood sliding doors.

Scovill Manufacturing Co., NuTone Housing Products Div. · Garage-door openers—three models. Door chimes and bells.

Seal Rite Windows, Inc. · Combination storm-screen doors with redwood frames.

Sears Roebuck & Co. · Wood bifold doors. Folding doors. Door chimes and bells. Sectional garage doors surfaced in hardboard. Garage-door opener. Molded urethane panels for application to doors. Aluminum sliding glass doors. Aluminum awninglike door canopies. Aluminum combination storm-screen doors. Aluminum thresholds. Plastic door shutters. Door viewer.

Season-All Industries, Inc. · Aluminum combination storm-screen doors. In one model with three vertical lights, the two narrow sidelights are glazed with mottled, colored plastic.

Simpson Timber Co. · Wood exterior doors of raised-panel design, many with carved panels. Sidelights available.

Stanley Works. · Hardware and pocketframes for recessed sliding doors. Heavy- and light-duty spring hinges.

Stanwood Corp. · Doors faced on one or both sides with sculptured hardwood panels. Custom-built to 1¾-in. thickness.

Steelcraft Manufacturing Co. · Exterior steel doors with urethane-foam insulating core; many designs, colors or wood grains. Prefabricated entranceways with single or double doors and sidelights. Steel interior doors. Steel or wood frames for all doors.

Tefco Doors. · Security doors. Storm doors.

Thermwell Products Co. · Weatherstripping and aluminum thresholds. Reflective house numbers.

3M Co. · Reflective house numbers and letters.

Three Rivers Aluminum Co. · Decorative aluminum combination storm-screen doors.

Unique Window Products Corp. · Gasket weatherstripping for exterior and garage doors.

U.S. Plywood. · Plastic door shutters.

Vemco Products, Inc. · Three models of garage-door opener.

Versa Products Co. · Ornamental wrought-iron café doors.

Vestal Manufacturing Co. · Steel doors 16 and 24 in. wide for installation in crawl space or basement walls.

Wal-Vac, Inc. · Two models of garage-door opener. Electronic pushbutton lock operates all makes of garage-door opener.

Whittlewood Corp. · Handmade ponderosa-pine exterior doors mostly in sculptured designs with sanded or weathered surfaces. Several unusual doors made up of small blocks of knotty wood.

Wilmot Industries, Inc. · Roller doors.

Woodcraft Millwork Specialties, Inc. · "Hewn" wood planking for use in paneling doors. Wood café doors. Wood and plastic bifold doors. Wood bifold door panels with top panel omitted so you can fill the space with fabric, plastics, etc. Wood bifold doors with open top panel filled with vertical turnings. Wood louvered shutters to flank exterior doors. Bifold mirror doors with aluminum frames. Decorative wood sliding doors without glass come in frame for installation inside aluminum sliding doors. Curtains are stretched across openings in doors behind frames.

Wood Specialty Products, Inc. · Folding doors of hemlock, Philippine mahogany, and veneers of birch, oak, ash, walnut, and teak. Solid-color finishes available.

8

Interior Walls

Except for painting, papering, and making necessary repairs, most homeowners leave the interior walls in their houses alone. There are several reasons for this. In most cases, nothing is wrong with the walls, so obviously it's pointless to tamper with them. But in many cases, inaction stems from some fear that, if the walls are touched, the house will collapse. Or perhaps the homeowner simply doesn't know what to do with his walls even though something is patently wrong with them.

Any such feelings you have are shortsighted or foolish. Interior walls are not sacrosanct. They can be torn out. They can be moved. They can be built anew. They can have holes cut in them. They can be resurfaced. They can be soundproofed. And in many cases, they need it.

These are often big jobs but they are rarely very difficult. Virtually all residential interior walls are frame walls built with 2×4-in. studs nailed at top and bottom to horizontal 2×4-in. plates. Although some of these walls—known as bearing walls—are designed to support the structure of the house, they can be treated exactly like nonbearing walls when you want to replace, say, a crumbling plaster surface with wood paneling. In other words, you can rip off the plaster and nail up the paneling without any worries about bringing the house down on your head. The only time you must call in a carpenter is when you remove an entire bearing wall—the framework as well as the facing material on both sides—or when you cut a hole in a bearing wall for a door.

PLASTER. Anyone can patch a plaster wall, but when it comes to replastering a wall or putting up a new plaster wall, that's a job for a plastering contractor. You can also leave the selection of plaster and method of application to him, although it's well to ask how many coats he plans to apply.

One-coat plaster work is not recommended, nor is it widely used. Two-coat and three-coat plastering are the rule. One is as good as the other. Aside from the number of coats applied, the basic difference is in the kind of lath used under the plaster. Three-coat plaster can be applied over either steel lath or gypsum lath; two-coat plaster must be applied over gypsum lath.

GYPSUM BOARD. Also known as Sheetrock or drywall, gypsum board is a strong, rigid panel of gypsum sandwiched between layers of paper. It has generally replaced plaster as the standard wall-covering material in homes because it is much cheaper to apply, doesn't crack (except possibly at the joints between panels), doesn't give off water vapor as plaster does when it dries, can be painted or papered within a day after completion of a wall, and can be put up by any strong, reasonably handy homeowner. The major disadvantages of the material are attributable entirely to faulty application. If the board selected is too thin, sound travels through it as if it were paper. And if the nails used to apply it are not of the annular-ring type, they are likely to pop through the gypsum surface, making unsightly pimples or holes.

Several types of gypsum board are on the market:

Standard gypsum board is the only kind you can count on finding in all lumberyards.

Superior fire-rated board is made of especially dense materials to give maximum protection against the spread of fire. Because of its density, it also has superior sound-stopping ability.

Foil-backed board is a standard board with aluminum foil laminated to one side. It is used only on the inside of exterior walls or top-floor ceilings. If the foil faces inward, it forms an excellent vapor barrier. If it faces outward and there is an open space at least 3/4 in. wide next to it, it helps to insulate the house.

Gypsum backer board is an inexpensive board used as the base layer in multi-ply construction. For example, if you want a wall with exceptional sound-stopping strength, backer board is applied to the studs and then covered with a top layer of standard board.

Moisture-resistant gypsum board is used primarily as the base for ceramic tile in bathrooms.

Vinyl-faced board is a standard board covered with a tough, decorative vinyl which takes the place of a conventional wall finish such as wallpaper or paint. Although more difficult to apply than ordinary gypsum board—because the joints take time to make—it is slightly less expensive than a wall made with standard board to which conventional vinyl wallcovering is applied. On the other hand, the choice of finish is limited.

All types of gypsum board are sold in 4×8-ft. panels but are available in other lengths ranging—in the case of standard gypsum board—from 6 to 16 ft. Available thicknesses (but not in all types of board) are $\frac{1}{4}$, $\frac{3}{8}$, $\frac{1}{2}$, and $\frac{5}{8}$ in. The $\frac{1}{4}$-in. board is applied only over existing wall surfaces. The $\frac{3}{8}$-in. board is used in multi-ply construction and in a single layer on top-story ceilings. It should not be used in a single layer on walls or ceilings between floors. The $\frac{1}{2}$-in. board is generally recommended for walls and ceilings between floors. The $\frac{5}{8}$-in. board is used on walls and ceilings to give better control of noise and fire.

The usual way to apply gypsum board is to nail it directly to the studs and joists. For ease in handling, install wall panels vertically after trimming the edges (if necessary) so they are centered on the studs and after cutting off the top or bottom so the panels are about $\frac{1}{4}$ in. shorter than the wall. Cutting is done by scoring the whitish paper on the face of the panels with a knife and bending the board backward along this line. For irregular or inside cuts, use a saw.

The annular-ring nails used should be $1\frac{3}{8}$ in. long for $\frac{1}{2}$-in. and $\frac{5}{8}$-in. board, and $1\frac{1}{4}$ in. long for $\frac{3}{8}$-in. board. Space them 6 to 8 in. apart around the four edges and over the intermediate studs. They should be placed at least $\frac{3}{8}$ to $\frac{1}{2}$ in. in from the edges. Drive them down about $\frac{1}{32}$ in. below the paper surface.

When two layers of gypsum board are applied, the first is nailed to the studs and the second is then fastened over it with nails or glue. Gluing is preferred since it produces a tighter, more durable bond and helps to reduce sound transmission slightly. Depending on the kind used, the adhesive is applied either in ribbons, daubs, or over the entire back of the face board. Press the board firmly to the subwall, secure it with several nails, and pound it down tight with a board and hammer.

Adhesive may also be used to apply $\frac{1}{4}$-in. gypsum board to an existing wall, provided the wall is smooth, sound, and level. Otherwise, use nails which are long enough to penetrate through the wall well into the studs (the vertical edges of the gypsum board must be centered on the studs).

Once you have covered a wall with gypsum board, fill the joints with gypsum-board joint compound and a paper tape made for the purpose. First spread a thin layer of compound over the joints, smooth the tape into this, and cover it with more compound. When this is dry, sand smooth and spread on more compound in a strip 6 to 8 in. wide. Feather the edges. Let it dry, sand it, then apply a third strip of compound 10 to 12 in. wide. Feather the edges. Sand as smooth as satin when dry. When painted, the joints should be completely invisible.

Inside corners are finished in the same way except that the tape must be bent lengthwise into a right angle before it is embedded in the cement. Outside corners are made with metal corner beads which are nailed over the corners and then covered with three layers of joint compound.

Nailheads are covered as the joints are taped simply by smearing joint compound over them. Two coats are usually enough.

To paint gypsum-board walls, whether with latex or oil-base paint, first apply a latex primer. Then apply a single finish coat. If you cover walls with wallpaper, vinyl, or other flexible material, always prime them first with an oil-base primer. If this is omitted, the paper cannot be stripped off the walls without damaging the paper surface of the gypsum board and thus weakening the walls.

Taping a joint in a gypsum-board wall. Bondex International, Inc.

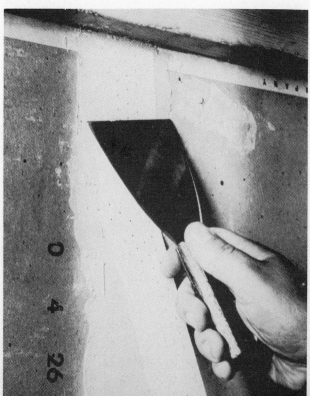

Saw-textured redwood board paneling with V joints. Georgia-Pacific Corp.

CEDAR SHINGLES. Shingles used to surface interior walls are the same as those used outdoors. Those with fancy butts are most popular. They are usually installed with a 9-in. exposure. To apply them over gypsum board, use adhesive; over plywood, nails or staples. Old plaster walls are covered by nailing up horizontal wood furring strips and nailing or stapling the shingles to these.

WOOD PANELING. Elaborate wood paneling of the type seen in so many ancient houses and more modern mansions is not for do-it-yourself installation. Simple vertical or sometimes horizontal or diagonal board paneling is another matter. You can put it up without hesitation.

V-jointed tongue-and-groove boards of nominal 1-in. thickness are most often used and are available in all lumberyards. Prefinished V-jointed hardwood boards are also sold in some yards. But you may prefer square-edged boards or boards milled to other patterns. Or if you don't want to use pine, you may have boards of oak, mahogany, etc. cut to order. Or if you look hard, you might be able to lay hands on paneling or siding boards taken from an old building which has been demolished. In all cases (except when using old lumber), give the faces and edges of the boards a coat of stain before installing them; or if you intend to paint the paneling, prime the boards with an oil-base primer. This is necessary to prevent the raw wood at the edges from showing up as white lines when the joints between boards later open up.

Board paneling can be applied over any existing wall which is furred out with horizontal 1×2-in. furring strips spaced approximately 33 in. apart, but this increases total wall thickness 1½ in. and means that the trim around doors and windows must also be furred out the same distance. It is therefore better to remove the old wall surface and build out from the studs. To do

this, you must nail two rows of 2×4-in. wood blocks between the studs to serve as a nailing base for vertical paneling (the blocking is not needed for horizontal or diagonal paneling). Place the blocks so they divide the space between the top and bottom plates roughly in thirds. (The alternative to using blocking is to nail furring strips to the studs, but this also increases the thickness of the wall and necessitates furring out of door and window trim.)

Use 2-in. finishing nails to apply the panels. To conceal the heads, drive the nails diagonally through the tongues into the crossblocks and plates. (If the paneling is to be painted, however, the boards can be face-nailed.)

Panel each wall from one corner to the other. The end boards should be scribed so the corner joints are tight. Before nailing, check each board with a carpenter's level to make sure it is straight up and down.

Baseboards at the foot of paneled walls are optional. If they are omitted, cover the joint between the panels and floor with a quarter-round shoe molding. If baseboards are used, they are usually made of 1¼-in. lumber and applied to the walls before the paneling. The paneling is then butted to the top edges of the baseboards and the ends of the boards are nailed to a third row of crossblocks installed between the studs just above the baseboards.

If the paneling is carefully scribed to the ceiling, no moldings are required at that point.

After a wall is completed, sand it lightly and apply another light coat of stain followed by white shellac, water-clear varnish, or penetrating wood sealer. On painted walls, use one or two coats of alkyd enamel.

PLYWOOD. Plywood has generally displaced solid wood for wall paneling because it costs less and is available in so many different woods and patterns. But it's a mistake to think that because it comes in 4-ft.-wide sheets measuring 7, 8, 9, or 10 ft. long that it is a great deal easier to install. On an unbroken wall it is; but if a wall is pierced with windows and doors, it isn't. And in all cases, the large sheets are more difficult to fit and install than boards.

Another drawback of plywood is that because the type specifically made for paneling is only $\frac{5}{32}$ in. or ¼ in. thick, it makes a very poor sound barrier. Consequently, it should be installed over an existing wall or over ½-in. gypsum backer board.

But the enormous choice of plywood paneling materials tends to obscure these problems. Pay a visit to a well-stocked lumberyard and you will find it hard to decide which panels to use. Yet what you see actually represents only a fraction of what is available.

Woods range from simple fir and pine to exotic rosewood and avodire. One manufacturer alone produces plywood paneling in more than 80 species of wood.

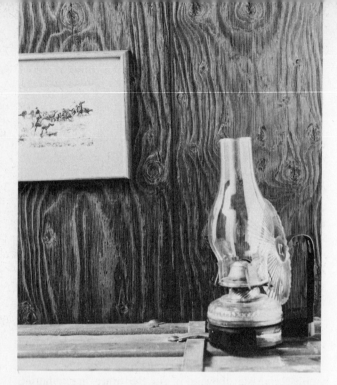

Prefinished rustic plywood paneling. Boise Cascade Corp.

Although most panels on display are vertically grooved to simulate a wall paneled in solid boards, some are textured to resemble driftwood, barn boards, etc., and still others are perfectly smooth. (The last are generally available only on special order. To see a full selection, you must visit a manufacturer's showroom.)

In some panels the surface ply is made of the wood it purports to be, such as oak or mahogany. In less expensive panels, the surface ply is a softwood which is printed or embossed or overlaid with vinyl to look like something more exotic.

Finally, to complicate the choice still further, some

Although plywood paneling grooved to resemble board paneling is usually installed vertically, it can also be used horizontally. Georgia-Pacific Corp.

panels are prefinished while others are not. The former are more expensive but eliminate the need for finishing the wall yourself, and the finish is presumably more durable. On the other hand, you must take greater care in building a wall of prefinished plywood because if you damage the finish, you can't touch it up so the spot is invisible (this is especially true if the plywood is printed or vinyl-covered).

Plywood paneling can be applied to studs (if you're not concerned about the noise it will transmit), to gypsum backer board, or to an existing wall. If applied to studs, no crossblocking or furring is necessary. Simply trim the panels so the edges are centered on the studs and fasten them in place with 1-in. brads or colored nails sold by the plywood manufacturer to

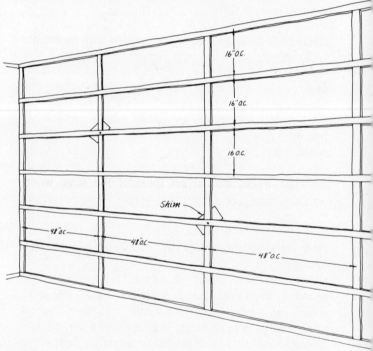

Proper arrangement of furring strips for a plywood or hardboard-paneled wall. Shims are used to level furring when old wall is uneven.

match the panels. Space the nails 6 in. apart along the four edges, and 1 ft. apart over intermediate studs. The alternative is to apply beads of panel adhesive to the studs and plates, and press the panels firmly into these.

If an existing wall is smooth, level, and sound, plywood can be applied directly to it, usually by gluing. Otherwise, it must be furred out with 1×2-in. wood strips nailed both horizontally and vertically. Nail the horizontal strips to the top and bottom plates and fill in the space between with strips spaced 16 in. from center to center. The vertical strips, which support the edges of the panels, are nailed to the wall between the horizontals on 48-in. centers. If the wall to which the strips are applied is uneven, the strips must be made plumb by placing shims under them in low spots and cutting channels in the wall through high spots. The panels are then nailed or glued to the furring strips.

Panels applied over newly installed gypsum backer board are usually glued directly to it—provided that the backer board is level.

Plywood panels which are vertically grooved to resemble boards are installed in sequence from one end of a wall to the other. Scribe the panels carefully to the corners and the ceiling. To facilitate positioning, cut the panels about ¼ to ½ in. shorter than the wall, butt them to the ceiling, and cover the open joint at the floor line with a baseboard or shoe molding. Butt the vertical edges of the panels. The joints are concealed by the grooves.

Ungrooved panels should be positioned so that those at each end of a wall are of equal width. The joints between panels can simply be butted tightly together, beveled and butted together, or covered with moldings.

If walls are paneled with prefinished plywood, use the special prefinished moldings, casings, and baseboards supplied by the manufacturer. It is almost impossible to match conventional moldings, casings, and baseboards to the paneling otherwise. It is equally difficult to achieve an exact match between conventional moldings, etc.—which are usually made of pine—and unfinished paneling unless they are made of the same wood, and to get them of the same wood means you must have them milled to order.

The choice of clear finishes for unfinished plywood depends in large part on the location of the paneling. In living areas where it will not be exposed to excessive soiling, the simplest finish is a penetrating oil or stain-wax which colors and protects the surface in one application. But in kitchens and bathrooms, as well as in other areas where the walls may be frequently touched by hands, a more durable, cleanable finish is recommended. Use an oil stain if you want to change the color of the plywood. Over this apply one or two coats of clear, penetrating wood sealer, white shellac, or water-clear varnish.

Textured fir plywood paneling which is to be painted should be primed with an alkyd primer and finished with alkyd enamel.

HARDBOARD. To the casual observer, most hardboard paneling is indistinguishable from plywood paneling. It comes in large sheets which are vertically grooved, colored, and textured to resemble solid board paneling. Close study, however, reveals several points of difference. Unlike plywood paneling with a face veneer made of real wood, the grain and color in hardboard paneling are entirely man-made (this doesn't detract from the effect of the paneling but may offend the purist who feels that if something looks like wood it

Traditional hardboard paneling. Masonite Corp.

should be made of wood). On the other hand, hardboard paneling has greater dimensional stability than plywood and is more resistant to moisture. Because it is extremely dense, it forms a better sound barrier. And it can be bent to conform to curving walls. Hardboard ⅛ in. thick, in fact, can be formed into a circle with a radius of only 7 in.

Other types of hardboard paneling boast the same advantages but bear no resemblance to plywood or solid wood. These simulate bricks, stones, marble, travertine, ceramic tiles, cork, leather, fabrics, wicker, etc. Some are painted solid colors. Some are covered with decorative vinyl fabrics. Some, made specially for installation around bathtubs, are given a thick plastic

V-jointed hardboard paneling. Masonite Corp.

Fiberboard paneling surfaced with light-brown cork veneer. Homasote Co.

finish in various designs. Some are filigreed for use in dividers. Some are perforated on 1-in. centers so you can hang things on them.

Hardboard paneling is installed like plywood. Use the ¼-in. thickness for most purposes. It can be applied directly to studs or, for best protection against noise, over ½-in. gypsum backer board. Hardboard ⅛ or 3/16 in. thick can be applied only to a smooth, level, solid subwall.

If you apply the panels with nails, use the small colored nails sold by the hardboard maker to match the panels, or 1¼-in. finishing nails. Space them 4 in. apart around the edges of each panel and 8 in. apart over intermediate studs. Gluing is preferable, however, since it does not mar the surface. Use the panel adhesive recommended by the manufacturer, apply it in thick beads, and press the panels into it firmly.

The butted joints between panels need not be filled or covered except in bathtub recesses, where special metal moldings are required to keep out moisture.

PARTICLEBOARD. Particleboard made specifically for wall paneling is either covered with vinyl to resemble plywood paneling or made with extra-large flakes and chips of wood which produce a unique mottled effect. The former is an inexpensive substitute for plywood or hardboard paneling and needs no finishing once it's installed. The latter, which is also relatively inexpensive, is particularly appropriate in contemporary homes in which natural wood is featured. It is finished on the job with shellac or varnish.

Both particleboards have exceptional dimensional stability combined with good strength, durability, and resistance to damage. Available only in ¼-in. thicknesses, they are installed like hardboard.

FIBERBOARD. Fiberboard has changed considerably since it was first used in houses many decades ago. Today, the cheap, drab, hard-to-finish material has been largely replaced by materials of much more attractive appearance. But like the earlier fiberboards, these are still made of compressed wood fibers and are rather easily damaged by hard blows.

One type is produced in 4×8-ft. panels approximately ½ in. thick. These come either with a primed surface ready for painting or an applied veneer of prefinished cork or burlap. They have an R value of 1.11. Installation is made directly to the framing or over a level wall surface with nails or glue. To accommodate expansion and contraction, joints are made with special plastic moldings available in several finishes.

The second type, which is used primarily to deaden sound within rooms, has a unique rough-textured surface composed of thousands of stringlike fibers which twist and swirl like a flattened mass of vermicelli. Made in 2-ft. or 4-ft. widths, 6-ft. to 12-ft. lengths, and 1-in. thickness, the panels are nailed directly to studs and crossblocks. They are sprayed, after installation, with latex paint.

ASBESTOS-CEMENT BOARD. See Chapter 2. Although rarely found inside homes, this extremely dense, tough, fireproof material might be just what you want in your furnace or utility room or to fireproof a wall between the house and garage. Because ⅛-in. sheets are very flexible, it can also be used to cover curving walls.

LAMINATED PLASTICS. The laminated plastic sheets used for surfacing walls are identical to those used in countertops except that they are only 1/32 in. thick. Their principal drawback is that they are rather difficult to install.

If standard sheets are used, they should first be glued to ½-in. particleboard or plywood with contact cement. The panels are then glued to the studs or furring strips like plywood paneling. Joints between panels are butted tight.

Installation is simplified by the use of prefabricated panels (consisting of the plastic sheet bonded to ⅜-in. particleboard) which come in 16-in. and 24-in. widths and 8-ft. and 10-ft. lengths. These are applied to furring strips which are nailed horizontally, on 16-in. centers, to the studs or an existing wall. The panels are held together and fastened to the furring with splines inserted in the grooved edges.

Panels designed for covering walls of shower stalls and bathtub recesses are made of laminated plastic bonded at the factory to a sheet of dense polystyrene foam which conforms to irregularities in the subwall. The panels can be glued to any sound, level existing wall or over a new wall of moisture-resistant gypsum

Fiberglass-reinforced brick paneling. Masonite Corp.

board or exterior-grade plywood. Special moldings are required to seal all joints against the entrance of water.

Detailed instructions for installing bathroom panels come with the panels; but even with these you won't find the work particularly easy. The resulting walls, however, are every bit as watertight as ceramic-tile walls and a little easier to keep clean, since they are completely smooth.

MORE PLASTICS. Because of the versatility of plastics, each passing month seems to bring a new type of plastic wall covering. Though made in different ways of different materials, all are notable for their attractive appearance, resistance to soiling, and easy cleanability.

Wall covered with 1×2-ft. self-sticking vinyl panels resembling woven cane strips framed in wood. Decro-Wall Corp.

But all have the disadvantage of being susceptible to damage by high heat and flame; consequently, they should not be used on fireplace breasts or behind ranges. The majority are also unsuited for installation in tub and shower enclosures. The following are currently available:

Plastic brick or stone paneling is most often made of fiberglass-reinforced plastic but is also made of styrene, urethane, or vinyl. The material is available in several sizes ranging from individual bricks to 4×8-ft. sheets. Installation is made by gluing to gypsum backer board or any kind of existing wall which is smooth, level, clean, and sound. Some bricks are self-sticking. The filler for sealing joints between individual bricks or entire sheets is supplied by the manufacturer.

Rectangular 1×2-ft. "tiles" of urethane or vinyl are applied in the same way. All are heavily textured to simulate wood, cork, carved wood, stucco, or cane.

Closely related to the tiles and applied in the same way is a 7½×48-in. plank which simulates the weathered wood on old barns.

Styrene tiles in 4½-in. squares are advertised as a low-cost substitute for the ceramic tiles they are made to resemble. They should not, however, be used in tubs and showers because the joints cannot be made sufficiently watertight. They are satisfactory only for other bathroom or kitchen walls, where they are not deluged with water.

On the other hand, large sheets of figerglass-reinforced plastic are made specifically for covering existing walls around recessed tubs. Sold in a kit, these include two panels which cover the end walls of the recess and extend partway around the corner to form part of the back wall, and a partial back wall panel with a molded-in soapdish. Because of this arrangement, the panels

Tub recess finished with methacrylate panels. Du Pont.

Large sculptured ceramic tiles on a fireplace wall. Design-Technics Ceramics, Inc.

can be glued to the subwall with a minimum amount of cutting and jointing.

Also suitable for use around bathtubs—as well as for application to other walls—are ½-in.-thick methacrylate panels. These are the most beautiful (and also the most costly) of all rigid plastic surfacing materials. They so closely resemble marble that until you touch them you can't be sure they are not the real thing. They are applied with special adhesive either directly to framing or to gypsum backer board.

CERAMIC TILE. Although once considered as a strictly utilitarian material suitable only for bathrooms, ceramic tile has blossomed to such an extent that it is now used to cover walls in practically all parts of the house. No other wall surfacing is available in so many colors and designs. Although catalogs portray these well, you should really spend a couple of days visiting the manufacturers' showrooms to appreciate them fully.

Yet for all their beauty, ceramic tiles are as practical today as they were when their principal color was white. They can withstand almost any punishment short of a hammer blow. They resist soiling and staining and are easy to clean. They repel water. And no matter how much they are scrubbed or exposed to the sun, they do not lose their brilliant color.

Although ceramic tiles are produced in many sizes and shapes, the standard wall tiles are 4¼-in. squares which are installed individually and 1-in.-square mosaics which are mounted on a backing and installed in 12×12-in. squares. The former are glazed; the latter, either glazed or unglazed.

The wall to which ceramic tiles are applied must be strong, free of cracks, level, smooth, and clean. Remove loose paint and all flexible wall coverings. In a

tub recess or shower stall, cover the wall with a skim coat of the adhesive used for applying the tiles, and let it dry overnight.

On prominent walls, individual large tiles should be installed from the center of the wall toward the corners so that the tiles in both corners are of equal width. On less prominent walls, you can start the installation at one corner and work across' the wall to the other. Because they are small, mosaic tiles are always installed from corner to corner.

In all cases, work from the foot of the wall up.

To apply tiles, use an organic adhesive recommended by the dealer. Spread this on the wall with a notched trowel. Cover no more than 3 sq. ft. at once. Press each tile into the adhesive with a slight twisting motion. Apply three or four tiles in a horizontal row, then three or four in a vertical row, then fill in between. Individual tiles have lugs on the edges which automatically control the spacing between units. The spacing of mosaics is fixed at the factory but the spacing between sheets must be established by eye. Make sure the joints are the same width as those between the tiles.

At inside corners, cut the tiles as necessary and butt them edge to side (but leave enough space for grouting). At outside corners, one tile is aligned with the corner and the adjacent tile—a so-called bullnose tile with one rounded edge—is lapped over it.

If the tiles extend only partway to the ceiling or to a wall, the border row is made with bullnose tiles or special border tiles.

To cut tiles, rent a tile cutter from the dealer or use a glass cutter. Irregular cuts are made with tile nippers or ordinary pliers by nibbling off bits until you reach the cutting line. Mosaic sheets are cut between tiles with sewing scissors.

When all walls have been tiled, fill the joints with a white cement grout mixed with water to a pastelike consistency. Spread this over the wall with a window washer's squeegee or rubber sponge and cram it into the joints. Then scrape off the excess and, after letting the grout set for about 15 minutes, tool the joints with the end of a rounded toothbrush handle. As soon as the

Use of pregrouted tiles in large sheets cuts installation time dramatically. American Olean Tile Co.

joints are firm, sponge off the wall repeatedly with clean water. During the next three or four days, mist the walls with water every 12 hours to hasten curing. Do not use the shower for two weeks.

Grouting is unnecessary if you use pregrouted tiles—the newest development of ceramic-tile manufacturers. Like ordinary mosaic tiles, these are bonded at the factory to a rectangular backing; in addition, the joints are filled with tough, pliable plastic. The edges around each sheet are also grouted. Thus the only joints you must fill—with a special filler matching the grout—are around the perimeter of the wall.

Because of the flexibility of plastic grout, a wall covered with pregrouted tiles rarely develops open joints or leaks even though there is movement in the subwall. The plastic grout is also much more resistant to soiling and easier to clean than cement grout, and it is available in colors as well as white. But the tiles themselves are available in only a few colors, designs, and sizes.

GLASS TILE. Tiles of vitrified glass are tough enough for use on floors as well as walls. They are made in glowing colors which extend all the way through the tiles, so if they are chipped by a hard blow, the damage is unnoticeable. The glass is opaque and has a slightly mottled look when examined closely.

The tiles are 1 or $1\frac{5}{8}$ in. across and come glued to 1-foot-square sheets of mesh ready for installation like ceramic mosaics. Three shapes are available: hexagonal, circular, and circular with half-moons cut out of two opposite sides.

The tiles are installed like ceramic tiles on the same kind of base. Latex-Portland cement mortar or epoxy mortar are recommended. Grouting is done only with gray cement.

METAL TILE. Like plastic tiles, tiles made in thin $4\frac{1}{4}$-in. squares of aluminum or steel are an inexpensive substitute for ceramic tiles, but they are suited for use only on walls which are not pelted with water. (Unlike plastic tiles, however, the metal units can be applied to walls around fireplaces or behind ranges.) Most are coated with colorful baked-on enamel; a few have a brushed or polished natural finish. All are glued to the subwall with special adhesive. The joints should not be grouted.

BRICK. Real bricks made for covering exterior as well as interior walls are only $\frac{1}{4}$ or $\frac{1}{2}$ in. thick. One type is installed by nailing; another more common type by gluing. Both are available in several standard-brick sizes and colors.

Nail-on bricks can be applied only to a plywood or wood subwall with $1\frac{1}{2}$-in. annular-ring nails driven through the flanges. The horizontal spacing between

Concrete bricks assembled in wire panels are embedded in concrete on masonry walls. Brock Co.

bricks is controlled by the flanges; vertical spacing is done by eye. Glue-on bricks are installed with adhesive like that used for ceramic tiles or with double-faced adhesive tape. They can be applied to any wall which is level and strong enough to support the weight. Spacing is automatically controlled by flanges on all four edges.

If tools for cutting the bricks cannot be rented from the dealer, use a cold chisel. Score the bricks on both sides and break them in two with a hammer. Smooth the edges with an old rasp or by rubbing them together.

Joints in a wall surfaced with nail-on brick are filled with mortar made of 1 part white masonry cement and 3 parts sand. Pack this solidly into the joints and strike it off with a mason's trowel or piece of pipe. Scrub off mortar stains on the bricks with a coarse wet rag. Joints in glue-on brick are filled with mastic applied from a squeeze bottle.

Concrete bricks in various true-brick colors and textures are assembled in 2×4-ft. panels backed with wire mesh to hold them together. The mesh is nailed to any nailable surface or embedded in concrete mortar on masonry walls. The ½-in. joints are filled with 1 part cement and 3 parts sand.

MARBLE. Large slabs of marble are too difficult and heavy for the amateur to work with, but you should have no trouble surfacing a wall with 8- and 12-in.-square marble tiles. These are available in about a

Lightweight manufactured stone can be used on inside and outside walls. Eldorado Stone Co.

dozen colors including whites, pinks, browns, greens, and black, and in either gloss or satin finishes. Unless used where they are subjected to abrasion, they should retain their cool, mellow beauty for many decades.

You can install the tiles on any strong, level wall with an adhesive recommended by the supplier. Space them ³⁄₃₂ in. apart and fill the joints, after wetting slightly, with white ceramic-tile grout. Cut the tiles with a glass cutter and tile nippers.

MANUFACTURED STONE. The same light manufactured stone used for exterior walls, as described in Chapter 2, can be used for interior walls. It can be attached with materials recommended by the supplier.

SLATE. Like marble, slate is available in large, heavy slabs and also in ¼-in.-thick tiles measuring 6, 9, or 12 in. square. The color is bluish black; the surface texture, slightly rough and irregular—just as it comes from the quarry after the huge blocks of slate are split. The backs of the tiles, however, are gauge-rubbed smooth so the tiles will lie in a flat, uniform plane when stuck to the wall with adhesive.

Install the tiles like marble, but either butt the joints tightly or make them ¼ or ½ in. wide and fill them with white masonry cement mixed with sand.

MIRRORS. One of the best, though certainly not the cheapest, ways to make a tiny area look much larger is to panel the walls with mirrors. You can do this either with enormous sheets of glass or acrylic mirror or with glass mirror tiles in 1-ft. or somewhat larger squares.

If you use glass sheets, you should aim for ¼-in. plate glass which is completely free of distortions; but if the cost is too prohibitive, you can settle for ¼-in. flat glass which is slightly less than perfect. Both types are available with a conventional silver backing or a black or figured backing. Installation should be made by professionals.

Acrylic mirror is safe and easy to handle yourself because it is unbreakable and is much lighter than glass. But it is not produced in such huge sizes (the largest panel measures 6×9 ft.), is not so completely free of distortions, and is combustible. It comes in silver and several other solid colors.

Acrylic mirror is readily cut with a special scribing tool available from the dealer. Installation is made to any smooth, level wall from which flaking paint and flexible wall coverings have been removed with double-faced foam adhesive tape or silicone adhesive; but if you ever take the mirror down, you cannot save it for further use because the reflective coating will be stripped off by the glue. You may therefore prefer to mount the mirrors with mirror clips or strips. In this case, there is no need to remove paint or wall coverings, but to achieve a secure anchorage, the screws used in the hangers must be driven into the studs.

Mirror tiles are available in thin sheet glass as well as float and plate glass; they come in silver, solid colors, and numerous figured patterns. Installation is made with double-faced adhesive tape. Tile a wall from the center out so that the corner rows are of equal width. Butt the edges of the tiles tightly together and leave the joints unfilled. The wall is not watertight.

GLASS BLOCK. See Chapter 6. Interior walls of glass block do not require a reinforcing framework if they are built up from a solid, level floor and are tied to the studs in adjacent walls and to the ceiling joists with metal anchors embedded in the mortar between blocks. But construction is best left to a mason.

OTHER LIGHT-TRANSMITTING MATERIALS. Numerous other materials besides glass block can be used to build light-transmitting room dividers. Made in panels ranging from roughly 2 ft. square to 6×10 ft., they are installed, as a rule, in a surrounding framework of smoothly finished 2×4-in. wood which is stained or painted. Some panels are not much thicker than heavy paper; others are as much as 4 in. thick. The materials include:

Perforated metal sheets stamped in simple or elaborate patterns. They are available in steel, aluminum, brass, and most other common metals.

Hardboard stamped in decorative patterns.

Solid wood panels pierced and carved so beautifully that they are widely used in churches.

Opaque plastics similarly pierced and sculptured.

Translucent plastics in thin textured and/or colored sheets. Other sheets are made with dried plant materials, butterflies, etc. embedded in the plastic.

Patterned and textured glass.

Two-way mirrors which you can see through from the back side.

LUMINOUS WALLS. Luminous walls are similar to luminous ceilings and built in much the same way with fluorescent lighting fixtures concealed behind the wall surface, which is made of diffusing glass or plastic panels. See Chapter 20.

SOUNDPROOFING WALLS. Many homeowners are under the impression that in order to stop sound from running wild through their houses they should stuff the walls with fibrous insulation. But since this is obviously a difficult thing to do, they don't do it. They're lucky they don't because they would be wasting their time. The only practical way to keep sound from passing through interior walls is to increase the density of the walls, and the easiest and least costly way to do this is to cover a wall—preferably on both sides—with an additional layer of ½-in. or ⅝-in. gypsum board. If the

Pierced panels of ½-in. particleboard. Angelus Consolidated Industries, Inc.

wall is already covered with gypsum board, simply nail or, better, glue new standard or superior fire-rated board over it. If the wall is covered with plywood or other decorative material, either leave well enough alone or remove the wall covering and install gypsum backer board or special sound-attenuating board underneath.

For severe noise problems, more elaborate construction methods may be required. Several major manufacturers of wall materials have pamphlets describing these.

BASEBOARDS. In the lumber industry, baseboards are classified as moldings if they are milled to special shapes. But you can also make baseboards out of ordinary boards. Sometimes these are left unadorned; in other cases, a slender, decorative base-cap molding is nailed along the top edge.

Vinyl cove base. Armstrong Cork Co.

Shoe moldings—which are usually quarter-round strips—may or may not be used with all types of wood baseboard. Their primary function is to conceal the joint between the baseboard and floor and to keep dirt out of it. They also help to simplify the job of installing resilient flooring because they are much easier to remove than baseboards so you can conceal the edges of the flooring.

Another kind of baseboard is a flexible vinyl or rubber strip which is most often used with resilient and seamless floors. One type, known as a straight base, suggests a large, fat ribbon; a second type, known as a cove base, is curved outward along the bottom edge so the joint between wall and floor is easier to clean. Both are made in various colors and in widths from 1½ to 7 in. They are glued to the walls with flooring adhesive. Corner joints are made either by slitting and bending the strips or by inserting preformed corners between straight strips.

MOLDINGS. Moldings are applied to walls (as well as to ceilings) to conceal objectionable joints, to provide ornamentation, or sometimes for both purposes. The majority are made of softwoods; some are made of plastic. The most commonly used types are base-cap moldings, applied to the top edges of baseboards; shoe moldings, which cover the joints at the bottoms of baseboards; cornice, or ceiling, moldings, which cover the joints between walls and ceilings; picture moldings, which are installed at the tops of walls and from which pictures are hung on long wires; cove moldings, used to conceal the joint in any inside corner, as in a corner between walls; corner guards, which are L-shaped moldings applied over outside corners; back bands, another type of L-shaped molding applied around the out-

Molding and ceiling medallion made of urethane. Focal Point, Inc.

Shell cap for niche made of urethane. Focal Point, Inc.

side edges of door and window casings to give an appearance of added depth to the casings; batts, which cover joints between wall panels; panel moldings, which are used to divide an unbroken wall surface into ornamental panels; and chair rails, which are nailed horizontally to walls to keep chair backs from damaging them.

Stock moldings are available in all lumberyards but usually in a very limited number of sizes and designs. Other sizes and designs are available on special order; but unless you can convince the yard that it will find other customers for the patterns you need, you will be required to purchase several hundred or even several thousand feet.

To obtain antique moldings and others which are no longer classified as stock designs, you must search in junkyards, have them milled to order, or buy by mail from the handful of companies that specialize in unusual woods and woodwork.

WHO MAKES IT

Abitibi Corp. · Vinyl- and plastic-covered hardboard panels. Decorative hardboard and plywood panels.

Agency Tile, Inc. · Ceramic tiles in unusual designs and shapes copied from foreign designs.

American Biltrite, Inc., Amtico Flooring Div. · Rubber and vinyl cove bases.

American Olean Tile Co. · Ceramic tiles in enormous variety. Pregrouted tiles.

Angelus Consolidated Industries, Inc. · Decorative pierced panels of ½-in. particleboard with prefabricated frames.

Anil Canada, Ltd. · Prefinished hardboard panels.

Bangkok Industries, Inc. · Unfinished and prefinished plywood panels of walnut, teak, rosewood, ebony. Sculptured teak panels.

Barclay Industries, Inc. · Cement brick and stone. Imitation weathered boards in 8-in. widths. Plastic-finished hardboard panels. Filigreed hardboard panels.

Wayne Boren Corp. · Panel moldings in straight and curved pieces.

John Brady Enterprises. · Naturally weathered barn boards in random widths.

Briare Co. · Vitrified glass tiles.

Brock Co. · 2×4-ft. panels of concrete bricks on wire mesh.

E. L. Bruce Co. · Solid prefinished pecan and elm paneling boards in random widths.

Burke Industries. · Rubber cove bases in many colors.

Cannon Craft Co. · Wood panel moldings.

Cavrok Corp. · 4×8-ft. or 5×8-ft. plastic panels in brick, stone, weathered-board, and Aztec-sculptured designs.

Celotex Corp. · Conventional gypsum board. Gypsum sound-deadening board. Sound-deadening fiberboard. Sound-attenuation blankets.

Columbia Moulding Co. · Vinyl moldings.

Dallas Ceramics Co. · Individual glazed tiles and unglazed mosaics. Glass mosaic tiles.

Decro-Wall Corp. · 1×2 ft. self-sticking vinyl panels in brick, stone, stucco, and cane-seat patterns.

Design-Technics Ceramics, Inc. · 1-ft.-square glazed and unglazed ceramic tiles with unusual sculptured faces. Some pierced for use in dividers.

Diamond K Co. · Weathered pine boards from old buildings up to 12 in. wide and 16 ft. long.

Dodge Cork Co. · 12-in.-square cork tiles in many patterns and shades, ⅛ to ½ in. thick.

Driwood Moulding Co. · Authentic reproductions of scores of antique moldings. Available in poplar wood (standard) or walnut and other woods on special order.

Du Pont. · Methacrylate panels.

Elon; Inc. · Handmade Mexican tiles in a fascinating array. Everything except mosaics.

Engineered Products Co. · Clips and channels for mounting mirrors on walls.

Flintkote Co. · Gypsum board—conventional and vinyl-covered.

Focal Point, Inc. · Traditional cornice moldings and niche caps.

GAF Corp. · Asbestos-cement panels.

General Electric Co., Silicone Products Dept. · Silicone tile grout for patching purposes.

Georgia-Pacific Corp. · Plywood paneling in tremendous variety. Conventional and vinyl-covered gypsum board. Sound-deadening gypsum board. Gypsum board with sand or stucco texture.

Grillion Corp. · Decorative pierced panels of plywood in several thicknesses with or without white translucent plastic sandwiched between the faces. Prefabricated frames. Shoji screens.

Hauserman, Inc. · Bulletin-board cork with colored vinyl finishes.

Homasote Co. · Unfinished and finished fiberboard panels. Fiberboard panels covered with burlap, cork in several colors and textures, and vinyl. Sound-deadening panels.

Homestead Mills, Ltd. · Fancy butt red-cedar shingles.

INRYCO, Inc. · Lightweight steel studs and plates. Studs telescope; can be adjusted to any height from 5 to 9½ ft.

Interpace Corp. · Individual glazed tiles in unusual colors.

Jarrow Products, Inc. · Vinyl moldings for use with plywood and hardboard paneling.

Johns-Manville Sales Corp. · Asbestos-cement panels.

H & R Johnson, Inc. · Individual glazed ceramic tiles. Self-sticking tiles.

Johnson Rubber Co. · Vinyl and rubber cove bases.

Lasco Industries. · Fiberglass panels in five pieces for surrounding recessed bathtubs.

Louisiana-Pacific Corp. · Fire-retardant particleboard.

Ludowici-Celadon Co. · Nail-on bricks.

MacMillan Bloedel, Ltd. · Sanded particleboard panels in natural color. Unsanded particleboard in natural and assorted stained colors.

Masonite Corp. · Hardboard paneling, unfinished and prefinished, in great variety. Also in plastic finishes.

Masonite Corp., Roxite Div. · Fiberglass-reinforced panels in brick and stone patterns.

Maybrik. · ¼-and ½-in.-thick bricks, glazed and unglazed.

Miracle Adhesives Corp. · Butyl rubber sound-control sealant to reduce noise transmission through holes in walls (around switch boxes, for example).

Montgomery Ward & Co. · Self-sticking cork tiles. Self-sticking plastic brick and stone panels. Cement bricks and stones. Individual and mosaic ceramic tiles. Plastic and plastic-finished hardboard panels for bathtub recesses. Translucent and filigreed plastic room dividers.

National Gypsum Co. · Asbestos-cement panels, solid and perforated on 1-in. centers. Conventional and vinyl-covered gypsum board.

Owens-Corning Fiberglas Corp. · Fiberglass acoustical batts.

Pioneer Plastics Corp. · 4×8-ft. panels of wood-grain laminated plastic sheets bonded to particleboard. Available in ⅜-in. and ¾-in. thicknesses.

Potlatch Corp. · Prefinished solid wood paneling in widths from 4 to 12 in., mainly ½ in. thick. Walnut, oak, ash, pecky cypress, butternut, cottonwood, pecan, cherry. Unfinished cedar boards sawn or rough-hewn.

Powers Regulator Co. · Acrylic wall panels for installation in bathtub recesses.

Rector Mineral & Trading Corp. · Bulletin-board cork in colors, with burlap backing. Cork panels from $\frac{1}{16}$ to 2 in. thick and in standard 2×3-ft. rectangles. Other sizes available.

SCM Corp., Macco Adhesive Div. · Acoustical sealant.

Sears Roebuck & Co. · Prestained rustic "barn" boards in random widths. Plastic and cement glue-on bricks. Enameled and metallic-finish aluminum tiles. Sculptured and rough-textured urethane tiles in 1-ft. squares. Wood-grain and colored vinyl-asbestos self-stick tiles. Individual and mosaic ceramic tiles, some pregrouted. Quarter-round ceramic tiles for sealing joints around bathtub rims. Plastic-finished hardboard panels for bathtub walls. Three-piece fiberglass panels for tub recesses. Mirror tiles.

Shakertown Corp. · Fancy butt red-cedar shingles.

Simpson Timber Co. · Redwood board paneling. Redwood plywood panels.

Stanwood Corp. · Sculptured panels of pine, oak, walnut, beech; pierced and solid in tremendous variety. Free-standing dividers.

Summitville Tiles, Inc. · Ceramic tiles in handsome array.

Swan Corp. · Fiberglass wall panels for installation in bathtub recesses.

United States Gypsum Co. · Conventional and vinyl-covered gypsum board. Sound-deadening board. Sound-attenuation blankets. Acoustical sealants. Prefinished hardboard panels.

U.S. Plywood. · Unfinished and prefinished plywood panels in countless woods and patterns.

Uvalde Rock Asphalt Co., Azrock Floor Products Div. · Vinyl and rubber cove bases.

Vermont Marble Co. · ¼-in. marble tiles in 8×8-in. and 12×12-in. sizes. Marble slabs to any dimension.

Vikon Tile Co. · Metal tiles of solid copper, aluminum, stainless steel, and aluminum with metallic glazes or colored enamel finishes. Suede leather for application to tiles. Cement bricks and stones applied with adhesive.

Ralph Wilson Plastics Co. · Wood-grain laminated plastic sheets bonded to $\frac{7}{16}$-in. particleboard in 4×8-ft. and 4×10-ft. panels.

Woodcraft Millwork Specialties, Inc. · Fancy moldings of wood and composition material. ½-in. cork tiles and rectangles. ⅜-in. self-stick cork rectangles 1×2 ft. "Hewn" boards for wall paneling.

Z-Brick. · Cement bricks and stones for adhesive application.

9

Paint

Almost everybody paints. If you want to get a job done right now—not "two weeks from now, if I'm free"—and cheaply, you must. And happily—thanks in part to the development of new finishes and new application tools—the work is easy enough for anyone.

But even people who have been painting for years find that there are always new things to learn. The paint industry's rather rapid switch from oil-base to water-base finishes, for instance, raises some problems while solving others. Similarly, paints which your friends espouse with enthusiasm don't necessarily work out well for you. So like the so-called experts (few painting contractors are as expert as they let on), we go on experimenting, discarding and picking up new ideas—learning as we work.

But one thing remains constant: Whatever the finishing or painting job—whether it be on the facade of your house or the top of a table—the general approach remains the same.

CHOOSE THE RIGHT FINISH. This is Step No. 1—and probably the most confusing of all. Paints—the general heading under which all types of liquid finish are included—are changing. For one thing, some of those extensively used in the past are disappearing (red lead primer is a good example), while others, such as old-fashioned milk paint, are coming back. For another thing, claims made by manufacturers for new paints are sometimes a little farfetched. The desirability of using latex paints on wood, for example, is a subject of hot debate among experienced painters.

The descriptions of available paints further on in this chapter should help to clarify not only what's presently available but also what you should use. Even so, before you start any painting job, it is essential to get clearly in mind what you want to accomplish and what problems must be overcome.

MAKE SURE CONDITIONS ARE RIGHT. Most amateur painters think they can undertake indoor painting jobs at any time. This is true to a considerable extent. Even so, there are times when it's better to wait. When the humidity is very high, for instance, paint dries much more slowly than it is supposed to. Or if there is an inordinate amount of dust in the air, you should let it settle. Or if the surface is the slightest bit damp, you should wait for it to dry, because no paint, not even latex, sticks securely to a damp base.

Outdoors, the timing of painting jobs is more critical. The temperature must be moderate (unless the label on a paint can says the paint can be applied at a specified low temperature, it is best never to begin a job unless the mercury stands above 40° or, better, 50° and you are sure it will not dip below freezing before the paint has dried). On the other hand, the surface to be painted should not be too warm, because if it is, the paint will dry too fast. The wind should be down so that dust isn't blown into the wet paint. Similarly, the smog level should be low so that large particles are not deposited in the paint. And the insect population should be quiet (one of the worst things you can do is to apply paint in the late afternoon to a house which is brightly lighted at night, because the insects, attracted to the light, will fly into the paint and get stuck).

As a rule, the best time to paint the exterior of a house is in the fall or spring.

PREPARE THE SURFACE CAREFULLY. Make certain it is dry. Clean it thoroughly. If it is already covered with a finish, use a solution of trisodium phosphate and rinse well. On bare wood, use a solvent-base cleaner made for the purpose. Take off wax with naphtha, paint thinner, or prepared wax remover.

Remove or thoroughly sand down old finish which is chipped, cracked, flaking, wrinkled, etc. On house walls and other large areas covered with old paint, use an electric paint remover to save time. Otherwise, use a prepared paint remover according to directions on the can. Use a thin liquid remover on horizontal surfaces and a paste-type remover on vertical surfaces and overhead horizontal surfaces.

Get rid of rust on iron and steel by sanding, scraping, filing, and/or scrubbing with a liquid or jellied rust remover. Also remove products of corrosion from aluminum and other metals.

Sand glossy finishes so the new paint will adhere better. So-called liquid sandpapers are effective but contain chemicals which are lethal if used in poorly ventilated rooms.

Repair the surface as necessary. Holes are best filled with interior-exterior spackle. High spots should be planed or sanded down, cut out and rebuilt, or minimized (if in a wall or ceiling) by covering with gypsumboard joint compound which is feathered well out to all sides. Prime the patched surfaces before applying the final finish.

Sand or steel-wool bare wood until it is satin-smooth and free of tiny fibers. After priming, sand the wood again lightly.

COVER NEARBY SURFACES. This is particularly important if you apply paint with a sprayer. But don't take chances when using a brush or roller. Use masking tape to mark the dividing line between painted and not-to-be-painted surfaces. If you are spraying, tape newspapers to every surface within about 4 ft. of the painted surface. Cover the floor with dropcloths (but not plastic dropcloths, which don't absorb paint).

Though you may think it wastes time, it will actually save time if you remove switch and outlet plates, door knobs and escutcheons, and other hardware so you don't have to paint around them or scrape paint off them later.

Move large furniture pieces into the center of the room and shroud them with old sheets or mattress pads. Pull shrubbery away from exterior walls. Take down vines if not of the clinging type (clingers may also be taken down but will not reattach themselves to the walls, so you might as well cut them to the ground and scrub the holdfasts off the wall with a wire brush).

APPLY A PRIMER. This is unnecessary if new paint is the same type and brand as the old. And no primer is used, as a rule, with clear finishes unless you want to seal the pores of wood. But when painting bare surfaces or surfaces coated with a dissimilar type or brand of paint, a primer is generally called for to seal the surface and form a compatible base to which the new paint will cling. Follow the directions of the finish paint manufacturer.

An alcohol-base primer—usually a stain-killer or shellac—is needed if you are painting a knotty softwood such as pine; otherwise, the resins exuded by the knots will bleed through the finish paint. This is used on bare wood as well as painted wood which already shows the telltale brown stains caused by bleeding.

Iron and steel surfaces must always be primed with a red-lead, red-oxide, or zinc-chromate primer.

SELECT YOUR PAINTING TOOLS. You may use a spray gun or aerosol spray paint, a brush, a roller, or a paint pad.

Few do-it-yourselfers bother with a spray gun, for although it speeds the actual application of paint, it takes a long time to mask and unmask the surfaces you don't want to cover. Furthermore, a spray gun with compressor is not a tool you use often; consequently, you usually wind up renting one from a tool-rental outlet, which adds to the total cost of the paint job and requires a trip downtown to pick up the sprayer and another to return it.

Aerosol sprays, on the other hand, are easy and convenient to use but cost more than conventional paints. As a result, they usually are chosen only for painting small areas or intricate surfaces such as wicker or when you need one of the several specialized paints which are packaged in this way.

For the great majority of paint projects, a brush is the best applicator. It can be used on all surfaces and worked into hard-to-reach places. It's easier to clean after your work is done than a roller or spray gun. It produces a smooth to almost satin-smooth surface with very little texture. And with it, you can work the finish into the pores of wood.

The size and kind of brush you need is dictated by the job. Use a 3-in. or wider wall brush on large flat surfaces, a 1-in. to 3-in. trim brush on woodwork and furniture, a 1-in. to 1½-in. sash brush on window muntins, and a 1-in. to 3-in. chisel-edged varnish brush for applying varnish. Whatever the brush, buy a good one. Cheap brushes are poor economy and give poor results.

A roller is the top choice for painting walls, ceilings, and flush doors because it covers so much area so rapidly. It is also a timesaver on bevel sidings and paneled doors, although you need a brush to get into the joints and to smooth out the rolled-on paint on doors. But it should be used to apply paint only—not stains or clear finishes.

Use a 7-in. to 9-in. roller for large areas, and a 3-in. roller on trim and woodwork. An edging roller can be used to paint into corners, although it is not as effective as a brush. The roller cover should be selected to suit the surface. Note the recommendations on the package. A short nap is used on smooth surfaces, a long nap on rough surfaces.

Other painting tools which may come in handy are

Paint pad. Shur-Line Manufacturing Co.

paint pads for flat surfaces which don't require a perfect finish, stripers for painting lines, and mitts for rough-painting surfaces you can't get at easily otherwise.

STIR THE PAINT WELL. If a skin or scum has formed on top, remove it carefully—preferably in a single piece. Then stir the paint around and around and up and down until the pigment and vehicle are completely combined. If the paint contains lumps, pour it through cheesecloth into a clean container, and don't return it to the original can until that is thoroughly cleaned, too.

NOW PAINT. Painting is neither an art nor a science. With a little practice you can be as proficient as anyone. The main things to watch are the following:

Don't overload a brush or roller. It makes for splatters and mess if you do. However, varnish and lacquer are applied with a rather full brush. Flow them on and then brush them out, but not excessively.

No matter in what direction you brush or roll on paint, always smooth it off with strokes in one direction.

Try not to paint in direct sunlight. It's uncomfortable. You can't tell where you have painted and where you haven't. And the heat may dry the paint too rapidly.

If working on a ladder, make sure it is firmly set. Don't reach more than a couple of feet to either side.

When working on walls and other large surfaces, apply the paint in 2-ft. to 3-ft. strips so you can start on a second strip before the first dries. This assures that the two strips will meld and you won't end up with distinct lines where the edges overlap. Similarly, if you must quit work on a wall before it is completely covered, stop at a window, door, or other break in the wall so that the dividing line between the two periods of work does not stand out.

CLEAN UP. Go back over the area where you've been working and wipe up all splatters and smears. Then clean your painting tools with paint thinner if you've been using oil-base paint, water for latex paint, alcohol for shellac and stain-killers, or lacquer thinner for lacquers.

Clean brushes by sloshing them up and down in the thinner; then wash them in a strong solution of trisodium phosphate, rinse and hang them up, or lay them on newspapers to dry. If you're going to use the brushes in oil paint the next day, you can simply leave them hanging—not standing on their bristles—in paint thinner.

To thoroughly clean old brushes in which paint has hardened, soak them in a paint-brush cleaner until the paint can be worked out with your fingers, a wire brush, or an old comb.

Clean rollers and roller pans used for latex paint simply by placing them in a sink and running water over them. Roll the rollers back and forth in the pans until few traces of pigment remain. Then hang them to dry. Rollers used for oil paint are too difficult to clean thoroughly to worry with. Use a cheap roller cover and toss it into the trash when your project is completed. But you can carry over a roller from day to day—until the job is done—by wrapping it tightly in plastic film or pouring paint thinner into the roller pan, rolling the roller up and down in it, and letting it stand in the thinner overnight. It does not have to be completely immersed.

EXTERIOR FINISHES

Oil-base house paint is the type traditionally used for painting exterior walls but is gradually losing favor because it is slow-drying, has a strong odor, and blisters if moisture gets behind it. It is most suitable for wood walls but can be applied to others. The variety known as chalking paint is designed to wash off very, very slowly under rain so that it never looks dirty; however, the "chalk" leaves a faint film on surfaces below.

Alkyd house paints, like oil-base paints, are thinned with turpentine or paint thinner; but they dry much faster, have little odor, and are easier to brush out—especially in cool weather. But because they produce a harder finish, they are not used on exterior walls so often. Some paints have a jellylike consistency to prevent dripping.

Latex house paints are water-thinned. Despite their name, they are made with acrylic or vinyl rather than rubber. They are almost odorless, dry so fast that you can apply two coats in a day, and can be applied to slightly damp (but not wet or permanently damp) surfaces. Because they breathe—meaning that they are permeable to moisture—they are not likely to blister when water condenses in a wall behind them.

Latex paints are especially good for use on masonry since they are not damaged by alkalis. As a rule, no primer is needed, but a clear penetrating sealer should be used on porous brick and concrete, stucco, or chalky paint surfaces. Latex paints are also widely used on wood and plywood, although many homeowners have reported problems with them. The wood should in all cases be given a prime coat. Some manufacturers call for a latex primer; others, an oil-base primer.

Metal to which latex paints are applied must be primed with a special metal primer.

Linseed-oil-emulsion house paints are made with linseed oil in a water solution and can therefore be thinned with water and applied to damp surfaces. They adhere well to old paint, but when used on wood, they must be applied over an oil-base primer.

One-coat house paints are heavily pigmented oil or latex paints which give complete coverage in one coat—but only if the wall is already painted or primed. They are more expensive than conventional paints.

Mildew-resistant house paints contain a mildew retardant that prevents growth of mildew but does not kill it if it is already present. Because mildewing is such a universal problem (except in arid regions), more and more house paints are being made with mildew retardants. However, any conventional paint can be made mildew-resistant by mixing in a small quantity of retardant.

Fume-resistant house paints are formulated especially to resist damage by polluted air. Many conventional house paints are semi-fume-resistant.

Trim paints, or enamels, are for the most part alkyd paints which dry to a high gloss. Semi-gloss latex paints are also used. The alkyds are extremely tough, durable, washable, and beautiful.

Barn paints were originally oil paints but are now also made with acrylic latex in a water vehicle. They are usually dark red but are sometimes available in other dark colors. They are economical and adhere well to poorly prepared and nonuniform surfaces. Oil-base paints fade rapidly; the latex types, a bit more slowly.

Portland-cement paints are used outdoors and indoors on concrete and masonry walls. Made of Portland cement and a pigment, they are mixed with water before application and are scrubbed into well-dampened walls with a stiff brush. They bond with masonry and help to seal out water. Durability is good.

But they are so tedious to apply that they have pretty well given way to latex paints.

Solvent-thinned rubber-base paints, also called chlorinated rubber paints, are applied to masonry and asbestos-cement materials. They are very resistant to moisture and abrasion.

Miracle coatings may be advertised under any number of names but somewhere in the description you are bound to come across the word "miracle" or "miraculous." They are, in truth, miraculously bad. Billed as the ideal cure-all for all exterior painting problems, they are also, as a rule, said to insulate houses and make them fireproof. They are sold only through advertising and door-to-door salesmen, and can be applied only by representatives of the manufacturer.

Any homeowner who buys a miracle coating treatment for his house is simply pouring money down a rat hole.

Stain-killers are alcohol-base, white-pigmented undercoaters used primarily to spot-prime knots to prevent them from bleeding. They can also be used for overall priming of wood when it is necessary to apply a protective finish in freezing weather.

Gutter paints are asphalt-base coatings, sometimes fortified with aluminum flakes, which protect metal gutters from rusting and wood gutters from cracking. Because of their heavy consistency, they also stop leaks at joints. They should be applied only in the gutter troughs—not on the outside.

Solid-color oil and latex stains give a finish closely resembling a paint finish and of no greater durability. The main difference is that stains do not form such a thick film as paint; therefore, they do not obscure the texture of wood so completely. For this reason, they are most commonly used on rough-sawn wood but are not limited to this. It makes no difference whether the wood is bare or painted.

Semi-transparent oil and latex stains are similar to the above but less heavily pigmented; consequently, they reveal a bit more of the texture of the wood to which they are applied. They are used on unfinished wood and wood that was previously coated with a semi-transparent or transparent stain.

Transparent oil stains are made with a penetrating oil which sinks deeply into the pores of wood and leaves no surface film. As a result, all the beauty of the natural wood is visible and the finish itself never cracks, peels, or blisters.

The stains—available in many colors—can be used on raw wood, wood previously treated with a similar stain, or water-repellent-treated wood. They last especially well on rough wood—up to eight or ten years—but only about five years on smooth wood. Two coats are needed on new wood, the second being applied within about 30 minutes of the first. On previously stained wood of the same color, only one coat is needed.

Creosote stains also penetrate wood but are a little less transparent than oil stains. Their main advantage is that they give long-lasting protection against rot and termites. They are, however, likely to bleed through paint which may be applied over them. A couple of dozen colors are available.

Similar stains but in fewer colors are made with pentachlorophenol instead of creosote. These do not bleed through paint.

Bleaching oils give new wood the weathered look of driftwood. They are composed of a penetrating oil, a bleaching agent, and a little gray pigment. The pigment is what gives the wood its instantaneous weathered effect. By the time it wears off after four or five years, the bleaching agent and sun have weathered the wood naturally, and from then on you don't have to do anything about it.

In some bleaching oils the pigment is omitted and the entire weathering process is left up to the bleaching ingredient and sun.

Water repellents are transparent, waterlike finishes designed to interfere with natural weathering so the original color of the wood is retained. They also minimize splintering and checking; and if they contain a mildew retardant—as most do—they prevent the growth of fungus. They are particularly popular on redwood but equally good on cedar, cypress, and other woods of unusually attractive appearance. Two coats are required at the start. An additional coat can be applied if and when the wood starts to darken.

If you want to color the wood slightly, water repellents can be mixed with a penetrating stain, or the stain can be applied over (but never under) the repellent.

Linseed oil was rather widely used to retain the natural character of wood before water repellents, bleaching oils, and improved stains came along. It is generally frowned on today because it darkens wood considerably and mildews badly.

Urethane and spar varnishes should be used outdoors only to protect doors and trim against soiling by hands. Both are more resistant to destruction by the sun's rays than other varnishes; even so, neither is very good. If using urethane, you should make sure it is specified for exterior use.

INTERIOR FINISHES

Latex interior paints have become the No. 1 choice because they go on very easily, are almost odorless, and

Textured paint conceals cracks in walls and ceilings. After it is brushed on, it can be textured with a broom, roller, or other devices. Bondex International, Inc.

can be recoated within several hours. They touch up so well that you can hardly tell where they were damaged. But they are not as washable as alkyd paints, and for this reason should not be used in kitchens or bathrooms. Flat, semi-gloss, and gloss finishes are available. Some paints are dripless.

Latex paints are most suitable for application to gypsum board and plaster. If you apply them to wood, plywood, or hardboard, prime the surface first with an alkyd primer. Never apply them directly to radiators and other iron and steel surfaces, because the water they contain rusts the metal, and then the rust bleeds through the paint.

Alkyd interior paints in flat, semi-gloss, and gloss finishes have largely replaced oil-base interior paints because of their superior durability, better appearance, and ease of application. They are almost odorless, and many new formulations dry within a few hours.

Alkyds are generally preferable to latex on wood as well as on all kitchen and bathroom surfaces. When they are applied to gypsum board, the board should first be covered with a latex primer (an alkyd primer raises the fibers on the paper surface).

Textured paints are thick-bodied oil or water-base paints which are used to produce a pronounced texture and/or to conceal imperfections in walls and ceilings. They are applied with a brush or roller and then textured with a sponge, whisk broom, comb, crumpled newspaper, or special texturing rollers. Unfortunately, they are extremely difficult to remove or smooth out if you tire of them.

Sanded paints are latex paints to which fine sand is added to produce a sandpaperlike effect and hide flaws in walls and ceilings. A similar effect can be achieved with any conventional paint simply by mixing sand or a gritty substitute into it.

Stippling paints are heavy-bodied alkyds used like textured and sanded paints to hide flaws in walls and ceilings and produce an attractive but subdued texture. They are stippled after application with a stippling brush or roller.

Glaze coatings are dense, paintlike epoxy, polyester, or acrylic materials which are about as hard, durable, and shiny as ceramic tiles when dry. Primarily used in public buildings, they are useful in the home wherever you need a childproof wall finish. Application can be made to concrete block and other masonry, plaster, gypsum board, wood, and plywood, but most manufacturers insist that the work be done by trained applicators. It is a two- or three-step process.

The coatings come in many finishes: transparent;

A glaze coating surfaced with stone chips which may then be overglazed as in left side of photo.

solid colors; colors with veiling, fleck, or splatter effects; textured. Some are surfaced with sand, pebbles, or marble chips.

Floor enamels, which usually can be used outdoors as well as in, are made with alkyd, latex, and epoxy. They are applied to wood or concrete but all of them wear off fairly rapidly. The toughest are the epoxies, which also happen to be the most slippery.

Epoxy paints are used not only on floors but also on any other surface requiring an exceptionally tough finish which is resistant to water, acids, alkalis, heat, fungus growth, and just about everything else that attacks paints. They are especially good for refinishing bathtubs and other porcelain-enameled fixtures and appliances.

The paints normally come in two parts which must be mixed together just prior to use. One-part epoxies are usually packaged as aerosol sprays. Application should be made to clean, paint-free surfaces over an epoxy primer.

Cementitious coatings—also called waterproof cement paints—are thicker than ordinary Portland-cement paints and used primarily to waterproof masonry interior and exterior walls (but not floors). The standard product is white, but a limited number of pastel colors are sold. The coatings should be applied only to bare masonry or masonry which has been previously coated with cement paint. You can apply as many coats as are needed to stop leaks.

Block fillers are heavy-bodied, white latex or epoxy coatings for filling the voids in concrete blocks and other masonry surfaces. Thus they reduce the number of finish coats required.

Fire-retardant paints are known as intumescent coatings because, upon exposure to heat, they intumesce (bubble up) and form an insulating barrier between the heat source and the painted material. Unfortunately, they produce only a flat, not very pretty finish.

Penetrating interior stains are generally oil-based but some are latex. Used to change the color of wood and plywood, they are overcoated when dry with a hard protective finish such as varnish. They are applied with a brush, allowed to sink in for a few minutes, and then wiped with a cloth to even out the color (this is why they are often called wiping stains). They are used on paneling and trim and sometimes on furniture.

Penetrating oil finishes are available with and without pigment. They penetrate deeply into wood and seal it so that no further finish, other than perhaps wax, is needed. One coat is usually enough but more can be applied.

Clear, colorless finishes are used when you want to maintain the true appearance of wood, but can be applied to stained wood. Pigmented finishes simultane-

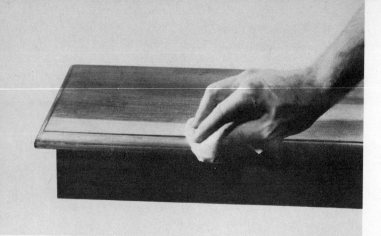

After penetrating oil finish is applied, excess is removed with rags. Minwax Co.

ously color and seal wood. Both types are used on paneling and trim as well as furniture.

Stain waxes go one step further by leaving a thin coating of wax on the surface. The wax protects walls satisfactorily but, despite claims to the contrary, is not durable on floors.

Sealers are colorless, transparent materials used simply to penetrate and seal the surfaces to which they are applied. Some are made for wood, others for masonry. Once a surface is sealed, it requires no further finishing. However, wood sealers are sometimes used as a primer under oil stains, varnish, or paint to minimize swelling and warping of wood and to make the topcoat spread further.

Penetrating floor sealers are generally rated by experts as the best of all clear wood-floor finishes because they work down into the wood and increase its wear and soil resistance and because they leave such a thin surface film that scratches in it barely show.

In addition, unless penetrating sealers are tinted, they do not change the color of wood materially. They are resistant to water and easy to maintain, and are not slippery. And of special importance, when you do have to touch up worn spots, the new finish blends into the old so well that you can't tell where the work has been done.

Concrete stains are oil stains used for changing the color of concrete floors, walls, etc., indoors and out. Before they are brushed on, the concrete must be thoroughly cleaned and etched with muriatic acid.

Varnish is a favorite material for protecting wood paneling, trim, doors, floors, furniture, etc. against soil and damage without concealing the grain or texture. It produces a tough, long-lasting, attractive finish, but when scratched, it cannot be touched up without showing lap marks between the new and old coatings. It also water-spots. Although there is no all-purpose varnish, the type which is simply labeled interior varnish is used for most purposes. Special formulations are required, however, for such things as floors and bars.

114

Until recently, all varnishes were oil or alkyd finishes producing a flat, semi-gloss, or gloss sheen. These tend to darken wood to a certain extent. New latex varnishes with a flat or semi-gloss sheen darken wood less and dry faster. Epoxy varnish is an extremely tough finish with a very high gloss. It tends to darken.

Urethane is often called urethane varnish because it looks like varnish and is used in the same way. Since it is the most wear- and damage-resistant of this group of finishes, it is the best for use on wood floors, and it can be used on any other surface which requires extra-good protection. But it also tends to darken wood and is impossible to touch up invisibly. Flat and gloss finishes are available.

Shellac is an alcohol-base finish which can be used instead of varnish for most of the same purposes. However, it is less durable and water-spots badly. On the other hand, when you apply new shellac over old, the two coats amalgamate and there are no lap marks.

Shellac is mainly valuable because it dries very rapidly. You can apply two coats in the same day. It also serves as an excellent base under other finishes. This means, for example, that you can apply a tough varnish finish to, say, a paneled wall in a single day by applying shellac first and overcoating it with varnish. By contrast, if you use varnish for both coats, the job will take two days to complete.

Water-base varnish can be applied to walls as well as furniture. It looks milky when wet but dries clear. PPG Industries, Inc.

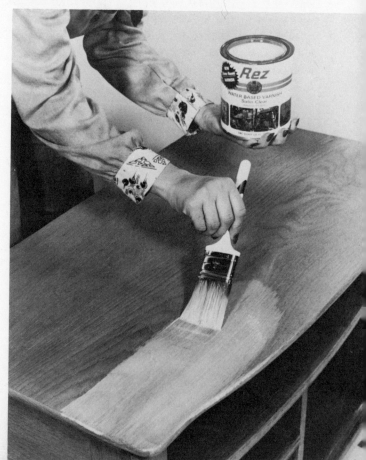

FURNITURE FINISHES

Many of the paints and clear finishes used for interior painting can also be used on furniture. Additional furniture finishes include the following:

Alkyd enamels are the first choice of most do-it-yourselfers when they want to apply a tough, beautiful, opaque, colored finish to indoor and outdoor wood and metal furniture. When used on unfinished furniture, they are brushed or sprayed on over an enamel undercoater or shellac. On previously painted furniture, you simply have to sand the old finish.

Milk paint, made of milk and pigment, is sold as a dry powder that is mixed with water to give either a dense finish or a thinner finish like that of a semi-transparent oil stain. It's used mainly to finish antique furniture as early colonists did, but can be used to paint exterior walls. It's best applied by brush. Once dry, it is almost impossible to remove except by sanding.

Lacquer is available as an opaque, colored finish and as a clear, colorless finish. It has good durability and is very attractive but is difficult for amateurs to handle because it drips about as freely as water and dries within minutes. Spraying is somewhat easier than brushing even when so-called brushing lacquers are employed.

Another problem with lacquer is that it takes off most finishes over which it's applied. The one exception is shellac, which is often used to undercoat lacquer.

Water and alcohol stains are substitutes for the penetrating interior oil stains described earlier, but they are generally used only on furniture. They bring out the full beauty of wood better than oil stains but are more difficult to work with.

In order to achieve a uniform color, water stains should be brushed on slightly damp wood in a very even coat. Speed is essential to prevent lap marks. After drying overnight, the wood must be sanded to take down the grain, which is raised by water.

Alcohol stains must also be applied rapidly and evenly to assure a uniform color, because they dry in a twinkling. You can use a brush or spray gun or simply wipe them on with a cloth. Final sanding is unnecessary.

After either type of stain is applied, the furniture is finished with varnish, shellac, or clear lacquer.

Varnish stains are pigmented varnishes used to color and protect wood in one or perhaps two coats. They have little penetrating power; they simply form a film which pretty well hides the texture of the wood. For this reason, they are not very attractive. Neither are they very durable. They are used principally to achieve a quick wood-toned effect.

Urethane stains are similar to varnish stains but are more durable.

Danish-oil finishes are the same as the penetrating oil finishes previously described.

Linseed oil is an old furniture finish which takes a long time to apply but is quite durable and easy to maintain. The oil is heated and brushed liberally on bare wood, then rubbed hard for about 20 minutes. This process is repeated several times—the more, the better—at weekly intervals.

Glazes are transparent or semi-transparent coatings made of finely ground pigments suspended in oil. They are used to produce antique effects or simply to impart depth and richness to a finish.

Glazes are applied to surfaces which have been previously coated with enamel or sometimes stain. They are brushed on, allowed to dry briefly, and wiped partially off. The effect achieved depends on the method of removal.

Wood fillers are clear or colored oil-base materials of pastelike consistency used on open-grain woods such as oak and walnut to fill the pores so you can achieve an even finish. Application is made after the wood has been stained by brushing into the pores and then wiping off the excess with rags.

OTHER FINISHES

Aluminum paint made with aluminum flakes in a varnish base is essentially an undercoater, although it may be used as a finish on metal. Applied to interior or exterior surfaces, it not only provides a smooth, even base for the final finish but also helps to seal knots against bleeding. It is also applied to the back of wood and plywood paneling to keep out moisture when the paneling is installed over slightly damp basement walls.

Gold, silver, bronze, and copper paints are sold in small bottles for decorating picture and mirror frames, furniture, etc.

Porcelain touch-up paints are tough, heatproof finishes in white and various colors. They are used to touch up ranges, sinks, and other fixtures and appliances finished in porcelain enamel.

Red lead primer is the outstanding undercoater for prevention of rust on steel and iron and for sealing in rusted surfaces on the same metals. It is, however, outlawed in some states.

Zinc-chromate primer has largely replaced red lead for rustproofing iron and steel and is the best primer for aluminum. It comes in several colors. Primers which are colored brownish red should not be mistaken for red lead primers.

Zinc-dust primers are used on galvanized steel.

Metal enamels are high-gloss oil-base or alkyd paints used for final finishing of all types of metal. They are hard and tough and have superior resistance to industrial fumes and salt air.

Fluorescent paints are latex and alkyd formulations with about four times the visibility of conventional paints. They glow in the dark when exposed to light. They are used outdoors and in to warn against possible danger—steps, low ceilings and low-hanging pipes, bad turns in driveways, etc. Available in orange and other bright colors, the paints are applied over a white primer recommended by the manufacturer. Since they fade fairly rapidly in sunlight, those used outdoors must be reapplied rather frequently.

Luminous paints, unlike fluorescent paints, are visible in pitch-black darkness because they are phosphorescent.

FILLERS

Although fillers have no direct connection with paints, they play a key role in many painting projects by filling holes, dents, and cracks before the finish is applied. Seven types of filler are used:

Spackle is a fairly slow-drying plasterlike material which is ideal for filling holes in gypsum board, plaster, wood, hardboard, and masonry whether the surfaces are painted or not. It is generally made for indoor use, but compounds which can be used outdoors as well as in are available.

The original spackle is a dry powder which is mixed with water as you need it. Most spackle today is a ready-mixed paste sold in cans. It is easier to use, smoother, and a little slower-drying.

Plaster of Paris is an extremely fast-drying plaster which can be used to repair plaster and gypsum-board walls. But it is difficult to work with.

Patching plaster is much like plaster of Paris but dries more slowly and is therefore used more often. Its principal value is in filling very deep holes. Spackle is better for shallow holes.

Putty is an oil-base material used for filling holes in wood—usually outside the house. It can also be used for setting window panes, but has been generally replaced for this purpose by glazing compound, a similar but more elastic material.

Putty sticks best when bare wood is lightly daubed with linseed oil. The oil is not used if the wood has been finished. The putty takes at least 24 hours to dry hard enough not to show bristle marks when you paint over it.

Wood putty—sometimes called water putty—comes as a dry, plasterlike, white powder which is mixed with water. It can be used indoors and out to fill holes in most materials. It is particularly desirable for repairing breaks in irregularly shaped surfaces because it can be molded as it dries, and can then be shaped further with files or other tools.

Wood plastic is a pungent, flammable filler made with finely ground wood particles. It is used for repairing wood inside and outside the house. It also sticks to most other materials.

Wood plastic is easy to spread and shape, but sets up rapidly. When dry, it has an ugly yellow color and a porous texture which has to be sanded hard before paint is applied. It will not take stain, so if you use it for repairing wood with a natural finish, buy one of the many colors which are available. Unfortunately, these are hard to find in most stores.

Shellac sticks are pencil-like pieces of shellac available in a wide range of colors for filling holes in wood. They are used by heating a knife blade on an electric burner or over an alcohol flame, touching this to the shellac stick, dripping the melted shellac into the hole, and smoothing it with the knife blade.

Wax sticks are large wood-colored crayons that are excellent for concealing scratches in finished wood paneling and furniture. But they cannot be used under paint or other hard finishes.

WHO MAKES IT

Absolute Coatings, Inc. · Last-n-Last urethane finishes of various types. Shellac. Stain-killer. Penetrating floor sealers. Interior varnish.

Authentic Products of Sheboygan. · Sat'n Oil penetrating oil finish.

Behr Process Corp. · Rawhide concrete stains. Transparent, semi-transparent, and solid-color exterior stains. Transparent interior stain. Urethane. Varnish. Interior stain-sealers. Wood sealers. Latex stains for use on plastics. Antiquing kits.

Bondex International, Inc. · Portland-cement paint. Latex exterior and interior paint. Latex floor paint. Texture paint. Wood putty.

Borden, Inc., Borden Chemical Div. · Krylon enamel. Fluorescent paint. Clear coating. Metal primer. Multicolor paint. All are aerosol products.

Samuel Cabot, Inc. · Transparent, semi-transparent, and solid-color exterior stains. Creosote stains. Stain-wax. Interior stains. Bleaching oil. Concrete stains. Oil-base house paint. Penetrating oil finish.

Cannon Craft Co. · Spray stains recommended especially for wood interior shutters.

Cook & Dunn. · Latex exterior and interior paints. Floor enamel. Masonry sealer.

Cook Paint & Varnish Co. · All kinds of oil-base and latex interior and exterior paints. Glaze coatings. Floor enamels. Oil stains. Semi-transparent exterior stains. Varnishes, including epoxies. Urethane. Lacquers. Aluminum paints. Fire-retardant latex paint. Alkyd stippling paint.

DAP, Inc. · Indothane urethane. Indolac stain-killer. Floor sealer. Shellac. Wood plastic. Wood putty.

Darworth Co. · Old Masters furniture finishes—enamels, oil stain, clear urethane, glaze, varnish. Wax sticks. Wood plastic.

Deft, Inc. · Clear penetrating oil finish. Transparent water stains. Urethanes. Aerosol lacquer-stain.

Du Pont. · Lucite latex and oil-base exterior and interior paints. Alkyd floor paint. Transparent stains. Urethane-stain. Urethane. Penetrating oil finish.

Dur-A-Flex, Inc. · Dur-A-Wall glaze coatings. White epoxy masonry paint.

Dynamic Development Corp. · Velvit Oil penetrating oil finishes, natural and in colors.

Fuller-O'Brien Corp. · All kinds of oil-base and latex exterior and interior Pen-Chrome paints. Semi-transparent and solid-color exterior stains. Epoxy paints. Urethanes. Floor paints. Interior stains. Aluminum paint. Masonry and wood sealers.

Georgia-Pacific Corp. · Wall and ceiling texturing compound which should be painted.

Gibson-Homans Co. · Aluminum paint. Wood plastic.

Minwax Co. · Penetrating oil finishes. Dura-Seal penetrating floor sealer. Urethanes.

Montgomery Ward & Co. · Exterior and interior latex paints. Barn paint. Sanded paint. Texture paints. Oil-base and latex floor paint. Urethane. Epoxy enamel. Semi-transparent exterior and interior stains. Aluminum paint. Antiquing kits.

Benjamin Moore & Co. Latex and alkyd interior paints. Latex and oil-base exterior paints. Solid, semi-solid, and semi-transparent exterior oil stains. Latex solid-color exterior stain. Rust-inhibitive primers. Masonry paint. Interior stains. Varnish. Urethane.

National Gypsum Co. · Stippling compound applied with roller; must be painted.

Old-Fashioned Milk Paint Co. · Milk paint in powder form for use inside and outside the house.

Peterson Chemical Corp. · Epoxy paint. Epoxy varnish. Epoxy aluminum paint. Epoxy-lead metal primers. Epoxy block filler. Epoxy coatings.

Pierce & Stevens Chemical Corp. · Fabulon clear floor and wood finishes in the lacquer family. Also urethane. Epoxy concrete sealer.

Plasti-Kote Co. · Easy-Way aerosol paints. Redwood stain. Epoxy paint. Fluorescent paint.

PPG Industries. · All kinds of oil-base interior and exterior paints. Rez solid-color, semi-transparent, and transparent exterior stains. Oil and latex interior stains. Varnishes. Urethanes. Masonry sealer. Red lead primer. Glaze coatings. Aluminum paint. Fire-retardant latex paint.

Red Devil, Inc. · Paint brushes, rollers, pads. Paint removers. Wood putty. Wood plastic. Brush cleaners.

Savogran. · Wood putty.

SCM Corp., Glidden-Durkee Div. · Spred oil-base and latex exterior and interior paints. Urethane and alkyd floor paint. Transparent, semi-transparent, and solid-color exterior stains. Varnishes. Oil interior stains. Aluminum paint.

Sears Roebuck & Co. · Latex exterior and interior paints. Epoxy, alkyd, and latex floor paint. Texture paint. Semi-transparent exterior stains. Latex furniture enamel. Antiquing kits.

Shakertown Corp. · Solid-color exterior oil stains. Semi-transparent exterior oil stains.

Sheffield Bronze Paint Corp. · Aluminum paint. Gold paint. Barn paint. Red lead primer. Spray enamels. All-purpose tinting colors. Aerosol epoxy paint. Wood plastic.

Shur-Line Manufacturing Co. · Paint pads and specialty painter's accessories.

Standard Dry Wall Products. · Portland-cement paint. Latex masonry paints. Clear masonry sealer.

E. A. Thompson Co. · Solid-color stains with a copolymer sealer for waterproofing.

United Gilsonite Laboratories. · Zar transparent interior stains. Redwood exterior stain. Urethanes. Masonry sealers. Portland-cement paint.

Watco-Dennis Corp. · Penetrating oil finishes. Interior wood stains. Penetrating floor sealer. Marble and terrazzo sealer. Masonry sealer.

Waterlox Chemical & Coatings Corp. · Penetrating sealer for wood and masonry. Oil interior stains. Urethanes. Tung-oil finish for interior wood. Clear and colored exterior wood sealers. Concrete stain.

Western Chemical Co. · Wesco penetrating floor finishes.

Wilson-Imperial Co. · Imperial penetrating floor sealers. Urethanes.

10

Flexible Wall Coverings

If all the parts of a house were measured in square feet, the interior walls would easily win honors as the largest. It is primarily for this reason that interior walls demand—and get—so much attention from homeowners. You bump into them everywhere you move, and unless your eyesight is failing, you can't help noticing that this one is cracked and this one is greasy and this one needs a major facelifting.

Paint is the first choice for redoing old walls; flexible wall coverings are the second. The former is cheaper and faster to apply. The latter are more beautiful; and in certain circumstances, you can redecorate with them a little more rapidly than with paint. (For instance, it takes less time to apply new wall covering over old than to strip off the old and then apply paint.)

Wall coverings are also far more varied than paint. They are made of many materials in infinite colors and patterns and in a wide range of textures. And for good measure, some of them have unusual characteristics which increase their desirability for specific installations.

WALLPAPER. Wallpaper is the most popular flexible wall covering—the first material the homeowner usually thinks of when he considers a possible alternative to paint. Ranging from roughly five cents to $1 a square foot, it costs a bit less than other wall coverings and is available in greater variety. Equally important, it long ago won recognition as a material which anyone can install without special training and with little practice.

Wallpapers are classified by several words and phrases:

Machine-printed describes a paper which is produced on a large printing press, whereas **hand-printed** means it was produced a roll at a time by the silk-screen process. Because about 1,000 times as much machine-printed paper is produced as hand-printed, machine-prints cost considerably less. They are also more dur-

able and uniform and are easier to hang. Hand-prints, on the other hand, are more luxurious and beautiful. Their use is normally restricted to the more formal areas of a house.

Pretrimmed means that the selvages have been removed from the wallpaper rolls at the factory. Most machine-printed papers are sold this way. Hand-prints, however, usually come untrimmed, and the selvages are cut off by the paperhanger after he has pasted each strip and just before he hangs it.

Prepasted papers eliminate the necessity for mixing and applying paste to each strip of wallpaper before hanging. The paste is factory-applied to the back of the paper. The paperhanger simply slathers water on the dried paste or runs the strip of wallpaper through a cardboard box filled with water, then smooths the strip on the wall. Many users, however, doubt whether prepasted paper actually saves work.

Washable wallpapers are plastic-coated papers which can be cleaned with a damp rag. Most are machine-prints; only a few are hand-prints. The degree of washability varies with the thickness of the plastic. To

No other kind of wall covering gives as much variety, color, and texture as wallpaper. Walls here are covered with two different patterns. ICI United States, Inc.

One of the newest types of wallpaper is made by bonding Mylar film to a paper backing and then printing the pattern on the Mylar to produce a soft glittering effect. James Seeman Studios, Inc.

test this, put a drop of water on the wallpapers you are considering. The more rapidly a paper absorbs the water, the less washable it is.

Strippable wallpapers are washable machine-prints which can be pulled off a wall in entire strips; consequently, they are used primarily in rooms which are redecorated every year or two because they save time and work in preparing walls for new paper. An additional advantage is their resistance to tearing during application, but this is largely negated by the fact that they have little stretch and are hard to hang on uneven walls.

Flocked wallpapers are hand-prints with a velvety fuzz—flock—applied in patterns to the surface. The papers are used for their ornamental and semi-three-dimensional effect and because they help to conceal imperfections in walls. On the other hand, they are difficult to hang, and soil badly.

Sand-finished papers are also hand-prints. They have a sandpaperlike finish which hides imperfections in walls but is hard to keep clean. Hanging is difficult.

Straight-pattern refers only to the way in which the pattern of a wallpaper is laid out. The paper may be a machine-print or hand-print; it may or may not be pre-trimmed, prepasted, washable, strippable, flocked, or sand-finished. On a paper of this type, the pattern at the left edge matches that at the right edge directly across the strip. By contrast, on wallpaper with a **drop pattern,** the pattern on opposite sides of the strip differs.

Generally there is less waste with a straight-pattern paper; and in the case of some papers—notably those with solid designs or stripes—there is no waste at all. But this is not a rule to be trusted.

Scenic wallpapers are hand-prints which form a picture like a mural. The parts of the picture are printed on separate strips which must be hung in the order specified by the manufacturer.

All wallpaper is sold in rolls 18 to 28 in. wide. Regardless of the width, a single roll contains 36 sq. ft.; but to allow for the inevitable waste in hanging, you should not expect it to cover more than about 30 sq. ft. of wall surface. (Most papers are actually put up in

Scenic wallpapers are applied in strips like ordinary wallpaper but must, of course, be in the proper sequence. James Seeman Studios, Inc.

double rolls, although they are always priced by the single roll.)

Hanging wallpaper is a time-consuming job, but one anyone can master. Preparation of the walls is the most onerous step but also one of the most important. Hanging paper around corners, doors, and windows requires the greatest care.

The walls must be sound, clean, and smooth. New plaster walls should be allowed to cure for at least two months before they are papered. New gypsum-board walls must be given a coat of alkyd primer. To assure a perfect job, old wallpaper should be completely removed; otherwise the paste holding it may be weakened by the paste on the new paper, thus causing irreparable blisters in the finished surface. (Many people, of course, have skipped this step without ill effects; but anyone who follows suit is simply taking a gamble.)

The final steps in preparing walls are to coat them with glue size and cover them with lining paper. Sizing is required to make wallpaper stick better, but it need not be applied in a separate step as long as the paste used to hang paper contains size. Lining paper is required only if you are hanging a hand-printed wallpaper or if the walls have a rough surface which is likely to mar the finish paper.

The paste used for all wallpaper is a dry powder made either of wheat or cellulose. This is mixed with water to the consistency of rich cream-of-tomato soup. Wheat paste is the more common; cellulose is usually used only on paper that is extremely subject to staining.

Prepasted papers, as noted, need only be soaked or sloshed with water. Manufacturer's directions to the contrary, they should then be folded paste side to paste side for about ten minutes to let the adhesive soften thoroughly and thus make the paper easier to position on walls.

Until you have gained experience, don't cut more than three strips of paper at a time. If you're using a plain straight-pattern paper, allow about 4 in. extra for lapping over onto the ceiling and baseboard. Most patterns, however, must be cut much longer than the height of the wall in order to match the strips on the wall. In this case, don't cut a second strip until you have matched it carefully with the first.

When applying paste to the back of a strip with a paste brush, be sure to cover every square inch. Take special pains to cover the edges. First apply paste to the top half of the strip, and fold the top quarter of the strip over onto the rest of the pasted surface. Then paste the bottom half of the strip and fold it up to meet the top edge.

The first strip is generally hung next to a door, window, or corner. Measure the width of the paper from the starting point, drop a plumb line, and draw a dotted line on the wall. Now take the upper corners of the strip in both hands and let it unfold slowly of its own

weight. Hold it along the ceiling line and dotted plumb line, press it to the wall, and smooth it down with your smoothing brush. Crease the paper into the corners at the top and bottom of the wall with the back of a scissors blade. Then cut along the creased lines with scissors or a single-edge razor blade.

Then proceed with the second strip of paper. Carefully match the pattern with the first, and butt the edge to it. Do not lap edges. If the strip isn't straight, has wrinkles or blisters, or doesn't match the pattern of the preceding strip at all points, peel it off the wall and start again. After hanging two or three strips, sponge them lightly with water to remove any paste left on the surface. Finally, roll the seams with a seam roller, using enough pressure to make the edges lie flat but not enough to make an indentation in the paper.

To hang wallpaper around a door or window, measure the space from the door frame to the edge of the preceding strip of paper. Add 1 in. Transfer the measurement to the strip to be hung, and cut the strip from end to end at this point. Paste the measured strip to the wall. Crease the edge into the corner of the door frame and cut it with a razor blade. At the top of the frame, fit the 1-in.-wide flap around the top of the frame. Then paste an appropriate length of the remaining portion of the original wallpaper strip above the door, or above and below the window.

When you reach a corner, measure the paper so it extends ½ in. onto the next wall. Cut the strip from end to end along this line. Paste the first part of the strip in the corner, and paste the other part of the strip on the other side of the corner. Make sure the latter is hung to a plumb line even though this may require the cut edge to overlap the cut edge of the first piece.

To paper around wall outlets and switches, remove the cover plates, paper right over the boxes, and then cut out around the boxes with a knife.

Vinyl wallcoverings are indistinguishable from wallpaper but more resistant to abrasion and easier to clean. Lennon Wall Paper Co.

VINYL. Vinyl wall coverings made for residential use so closely resemble wallpaper that they are difficult to distinguish; but unlike wallpaper, they are completely washable and a great deal more resistant to wear. They are available in machine-prints, hand-prints, and flocks. Most of the machine-prints are pretrimmed. Rolls are 20 to 27 in. wide and contain 36 sq. ft.

Vinyls are made with a paper or cloth backing in a wide range of weights. For home use, lightweight Type A vinyl is more than adequate. Types B and C, which are progressively heavier, are used in schools, hospitals, and other public buildings where they are exposed to hard wear and abuse.

Vinyl wall coverings are installed almost exactly like wallpaper. All old wall coverings are removed first; this is essential. If the walls are rough, sand them smooth (lining paper is never used). The alternative on concrete or concrete-block walls is to fill the pores with a block filler.

The adhesive used varies with the construction of the wall covering. Follow the manufacturer's directions, but don't use ordinary wheat or cellulose paste even though this may be suggested as a possibility.

Also note the manufacturer's directions about the method of hanging. In the case of more or less solid-patterned vinyls, every other strip may have to be hung upside down.

When smoothing vinyl on a wall, special pains must be taken to eliminate blisters, because the air trapped underneath cannot escape and the blisters never subside. If you can't remove them with an ordinary wallpaper smoothing brush, use a broad knife or a smooth piece of hardboard. Then, after the vinyl has been on the wall about 15 minutes, examine it once more for blisters you have missed. (This is especially important with cloth-backed vinyls.) To do this, hold a strong light close to the strip at one edge and then at the other.

Blisters which escape notice until after the adhesive has dried are punctured with a needle or razor blade. Then a few drops of water are injected underneath with a hypodermic needle or small oil can.

GRASSCLOTH. Grasscloth is used primarily for its attractive texture (and resultant ability to conceal imperfections in walls). The colors are subdued and tend to fade in a strong light. Patterned designs like those in wallpaper and vinyl are lacking.

True grasscloth is made of vegetable fibers laminated to a paper backing. Similar materials which are also called grasscloth are made of synthetics. All have a pronounced texture ranging from a rather open linen-like weave to a coarse strawlike weave.

Rolls are 3 ft. wide and 24 ft. long.

Installation is made over lining paper with wheat or cellulose paste. As soon as the paste is brushed on the

Four swatches of grasscloth give some idea of the range of textures available in this material.

back of a strip, the selvages are trimmed off with a razor blade. The strip is hung immediately, before it has soaked up too much paste and started to delaminate. Do not roll the seams, since that compresses the fibers.

A major drawback of grasscloth is that because of its texture, it collects dust and is almost impossible to clean. It is also easily damaged. It should therefore be used only in rooms which are little occupied.

BURLAP. Burlap is sturdier and more durable than grasscloth but equally susceptible to soiling and equally hard to clean. There are few houses in which it finds its perfect niche. Nevertheless, it contributes an attractive texture to any room in which it is used, serves as an excellent neutral background for furnishings and paintings, and not only hides imperfections in walls but, because of its strength, actually helps to keep imperfections from developing further.

As sold for wall covering, burlap is produced in a considerable range of colors and a few patterns. Some materials are vinyl-coated to make them resistant to water and soiling. The rolls are 36 or 45 in. wide and contain 36 sq. ft. Those incorporating a laminated paper backing are preferable to the unbacked type, because they are easier to hang.

Burlap is hung over lining paper with a water-mixed vinyl adhesive. The paste is applied with a short-napped paint roller in two successive coats. The selvages are then trimmed off and the strips smoothed on the wall with a broad knife. If solid colors are used, every other strip is hung upside down. Care must be taken not to distort or ravel the threads. Any that are broken along the edges should be stuck down with white wood glue or fabric glue.

FELT. Felt wall covering is a mothproofed, flameproofed, preshrunk wool felt which should always be laminated to a paper backing to simplify installation. It is put up in long rolls 54 in. wide, and is sold by the yard.

Although felt has some thermal-insulating and sound-absorbing characteristics, it is used mainly for its warm, rather simple beauty and vivid, solid colors. Textured felts are also available. However, the material seems to attract dirt and is reluctant to give it up.

Felt is hung over lining paper with wheat or cellulose paste. The actual work is no more difficult than that involved in hanging wallpaper, but such extreme care must be taken to keep paste off the surface that it is inadvisable for an amateur to attempt installation until he has watched experienced professionals (who are few and far between) in action.

MISCELLANEOUS FABRICS. Silks, linens, velvets, and other fine fabrics have been used to cover walls for generations, and interest in them is picking up once more. This is mainly attributable to the beauty of the materials, which is not equaled in other flexible wall-coverings.

Except for those which are specifically made for covering walls (the paper-laminated and self-glued types), most fabrics are put up in large bolts 45 in. wide and are sold by the yard. These are hung in three ways: with staples, with double-faced adhesive tape, or with water-mixed vinyl adhesive. The last is not recommended for amateurs, however, because of the problems involved in preventing the adhesive from staining the fabrics.

The staple method of installation is traditional. It involves fastening the fabric to a framework of wood lattice strips which are nailed to the wall. Because the fabric is thus separated from the wall by a ¼-in. air space, no preparation of the wall surface is required even though it may be pocked with holes and badly cracked. On the other hand, the fabric may be easily punctured and torn by anyone who strikes it or snags it in passing.

The lattice strips are nailed to the wall in continuous rows around the perimeter of the wall, around doors and windows, and around all electrical boxes. The fabric is then cut into strips the height of the walls, and the strips are sewn together into a piece that will cover the entire wall. This is stapled to the lattice strips first at the ceiling, then at the floor, then at the ends of the walls, and finally around the door, window, and outlet openings. The excess fabric is trimmed off, and the staples are covered with glued-on braid or wood moldings.

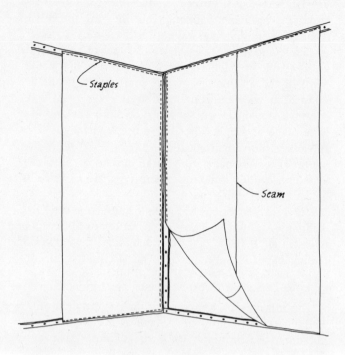

Traditional and still good method of covering walls with fabric is to staple the material to strips of lattice nailed around the perimeter of a wall.

When fabric is installed with double-faced adhesive tape, the walls must be sound, smooth, and clean, but the dangers of damaging the fabric are minimized because it is stretched skin-tight against the walls. Installation is made by sticking strips of adhesive tape around the edges of a wall and the openings in it. Additional vertical strips are positioned to hold the edges of the fabric strips. The fabric is then cut into wall-height strips and stretched over the adhesive tapes. The edges of adjacent tapes are butted.

Fabric which is laminated at the factory to a paper backing is hung on walls like wallpaper. The walls must first be covered with lining paper. The fabric strips are then hung with wheat or cellulose paste.

Fabric wall coverings are also available with contact adhesive applied to the back. These can be stuck directly to any smooth, clean wall after the protective paper backing has been peeled off.

CARPET. Carpet is sometimes used on walls to tie the walls to the floor (decoratively speaking) and vice versa. But the practical advantages of such an installation are often of equal value. The carpet protects the walls against even the most violent abuse, and it greatly improves the acoustics of the room by soaking up noises made in it.

Although any carpet can be used as a wall covering, tightly constructed commercial carpets with jute or synthetic backings are best. But if noise reduction is of paramount importance, use a carpet with a foam-rubber backing.

Carpet can be installed on any sound, clean wall with waterproof latex flooring adhesive, which is applied with a notched spreader. The carpet is rolled out across the wall from corner to corner in a single floor-to-ceiling-high strip. This is a two-man job. Until the adhesive dries, hold the carpet in place with double-headed tacks.

METAL FOIL. Metal-foil wall coverings are made by laminating thin sheets of metal to paper or cloth and printing or embossing a design on the metal. Some coverings have flocked designs.

The coverings are put up in standard wallpaper widths in single rolls containing 36 sq. ft. Cloth-backed foils are normally pretrimmed and hung like wallpaper directly over any clean, sound, smooth surface. Use the adhesive recommended by the manufacturer.

Foils backed with brown paper are trimmed on the job and hung over lining paper with vinyl adhesive. Before pasting, the paper must be moistened with water, rolled into a tube, and allowed to soak for about 20 minutes.

Foils with a white paper backing are also trimmed and hung over lining paper. But the vinyl adhesive is applied to the wall and the foil is smoothed into this.

Regardless of the type of foil, all those with solid or random patterns are hung with every other strip upside down.

CORK. This is an unusual, luxurious wall covering which is normally used only in the living room, dining room, or formal study. Although fragile and easily stained, it is not much harder to hang than wallpaper. Since it has no pattern, no effort is made to match the pattern of adjacent strips. Simply butt the edges and roll them down tight at once.

The material is made of thin slices of cork glued to a paper backing which is usually a black, gold, orange, or brilliant red. A hand-printed design is sometimes applied over the cork.

The coverings are produced in 30-in. and 36-in. widths and in lengths of 24, 36, and 45 ft.

SOLID CORK. Solid cork is used not only for covering walls but also on floors, bulletin boards, and other surfaces where you may need an attractive, thick, reasonably durable material which soaks up sounds. It is produced in three forms:

Bulletin-board cork comes in rolls up to 6 ft. wide and 90 ft. long. It is ¼ in. thick and has a fine texture. Cork which is dyed a color is laminated to a burlap backing; natural-colored cork is unbacked. Both are applied vertically or horizontally to any clean, reasonably level and sound wall surface with linoleum cement.

Patterned cork wall covering. Armstrong Cork Co.

Cork tiles, made primarily for flooring, are 1 ft. square and ³⁄₁₆ in. thick. They are finished at the factory with wax or urethane. Glued directly to walls with linoleum cement, they are generally applied in straight vertical and horizontal rows as on a floor. For best appearance, the vertical rows at both ends of the wall should be equal in width.

Cork slabs are made of rough-textured cork in sizes ranging from 12×12-in. squares to 24×36-in. rectangles. Thicknesses range from ½ to 2 in. As used by interior designers, the slabs are commonly applied in random sizes and thicknesses with linoleum cement.

LAMINATED WOOD VENEER. Laminated wood veneer is a flexible wall covering made of feather-thin sheets of real wood laminated to a fabric backing. The sheets are available in 10-in. to 24-in. widths and in lengths up to 12 ft. Although used primarily in commercial buildings, they may be installed in the home (1) when you want to panel a curved wall, (2) when you want perfectly matched wood paneling on a very large wall, (3) when you want to eliminate horizontal joints in a wall which is too high to be covered with conventional plywood paneling, or (4) whenever the fire code bans the use of conventional paneling because of its combustibility.

Laminated wood veneers are available in virtually all

Gypsum-coated wall fabric goes on like wallpaper but dries stiff enough to conceal joints in a concrete block wall. Wall & Floor Treatments, Inc.

native and exotic foreign woods ranging from afrormosia to zebrawood. Unmatched veneers are used to produce a random effect like that achieved with solid board paneling. Matched veneers, which are cut from the same slab of wood so that each strip matches the next almost exactly, are used to give a definite overall pattern effect like that you get with wallpaper. (For special orders, veneers can be end-matched as well as side-matched.)

Wood veneers can be hung on almost any smooth, hard, dry surface which is free of grease, dirt, and other wall coverings. The wall must first be primed with a thin coat of the adhesive recommended by the veneer manufacturer. When this is dry, the adhesive is applied to the back of the veneers, and they are smoothed on the wall with a broad knife. The edges must be butted perfectly; if they overlap because of irregularities in the wall, cut through both layers with a razor blade, remove the slivers, and smooth the layers down. Adhesive on the surface must be wiped off immediately with a damp cloth. After the installation has dried for 24 hours, examine it under a strong light for blisters, and press them down with a hot iron laid over a wet scrap of veneer.

When the installation is completed, sand it lightly with very fine sandpaper or steel wool, and apply a coat of water-white lacquer. Maintenance is generally limited to cleaning the walls now and then with a barely damp cloth. Most stains can be obliterated with white appliance wax; surface scratches can be removed by light sanding.

GYPSUM-COATED WALL FABRIC. This is a new material designed primarily for application to concrete block and other masonry walls because its $\frac{1}{16}$-in. thickness and rough texture completely hide the roughness of the walls. But it may also be used on other surfaces.

The fabric, which is sold in 4-ft.-wide rolls 30 yds. long, resembles a loosely woven burlap with color in the pores. (Several pastel shades are available.) After application, it hardens to a plasterlike consistency which is highly resistant to fire and damage.

Walls to be covered should be clean and free of other wall coverings but need not be carefully leveled as long as you do not smooth the fabric down too vigorously. (In other words, mortar joints need not be filled.) After coating the back of a strip with the adhesive supplied by the manufacturer, trim off the selvages and hang the strip like wallpaper. Butt the joints precisely and roll them down.

ROLL-ON FABRIC. Although roll-on fabric is new to the western hemisphere, it has been used in Japan for several decades. The material produces a delightful textured effect which—depending on the ingredients—resembles a nubby wool coat, rich brocade, unfinished marble, compressed straw mat, or white sand littered with tiny feathers. Colors range from the restrained to the garish.

Made of fabric fibers, bits of metal-like glitter, and glue, roll-on fabric comes from the factory as a dry, cereal-like material packaged in bags which cover 25 to 35 sq. ft. When mixed with a prescribed amount of water, the material forms a sticky dough that is pressed on the wall by the handful and spread to a thin coating with a short-napped paint roller.

Walls to be covered must be clean, free of loose paint and wall coverings, and coated with an oil-base

Roll-on fabric has a pronounced, soft texture. Dream Wall Sales, Ltd.

primer. But they need not be carefully smoothed or patched since the fabric fills and conceals all but the deepest depressions and cracks.

Roll-on fabric is maintained by frequent vacuuming. But once soiled, there isn't much you can do about it except pray that a damp sponge will remove the grime. (Adding an extra half-pint of glue to each bag of fabric at the time of mixing improves washability to some extent.) Repairs are easily made by mixing a little dry fabric with water and rolling it on.

WHO MAKES IT

Armstrong Cork Co. · Cork wall coverings.

Birge Co. · Wallpaper and vinyl wall coverings.

Borden, Inc., Columbus Coated Fabrics Div. · Vinyl wall coverings.

Central Shippee, Inc. · Tempora felt wall coverings.

Continental Felt Co. · Felt for wall covering.

Contract Vinyls, Inc. · Vinyl-coated wall coverings of burlap, silk, grasscloth, etc.

Dream Wall Sales, Ltd. · Roll-on fabric.

General Tire & Rubber Co. · Vinyl wall coverings.

B. F. Goodrich General Products Co. · Wallpaper and vinyl wall coverings.

ICI United States, Inc. · Vymura vinyl wall coverings.

Imperial Wallpaper Mill, Inc. · Wallpaper and vinyl wall coverings. Lining stock for covering concrete-block and cracked walls.

Lennon Wall Paper Co. · Wallpaper and vinyl wall coverings.

Mayflower Wallpaper Co. · Grasscloth. Cork wall covering.

McCordi Corp. · Vinyl-coated fabrics.

Montgomery Ward & Co. · Wallpaper and vinyl wall coverings.

Northeastern Wallpaper Co. · European foils.

Old Stone Mill Corp. · Handprinted wallpapers and vinyl wall coverings.

Peacock Papers, Ltd. · Handprinted wallpapers and fabrics.

Sears Roebuck & Co. · Wallpaper and vinyl wall coverings.

James Seeman Studios, Inc. · Mylar-surfaced wallpaper. Vinyl wall coverings. Foil wall coverings.

Shibui Wallcoverings. · Grasscloth in variety.

Standard Coated Products. · Vinyl wall coverings.

Standard Wallcovering Studio. · Handprinted wallpapers.

Thomas Strahan Co. · Wallpaper and vinyl wall coverings.

Richard E. Thibaut, Inc. · Wallpaper and vinyl wall coverings, including handprints. Foils.

United DeSoto, Inc. · Wallpaper and vinyl wall coverings.

U.S. Plywood. · Laminated wood veneers.

Wall & Floor Treatments, Inc., Flexi-Wall Systems Div. Gypsum-coated wall fabric.

Warner Co. · Burlaps. Grasscloths. Foils. Cork wall coverings.

11

Ceilings

The plaster and gypsum board used to cover ceilings are identical to those used on interior walls. The former should be applied professionally; the latter you can install yourself if you have strong arms and shoulders and an equally strong helper, because a 4×8-ft. panel of gypsum board is heavy and awkward to handle.

To make the job a little easier, use ⅜-in. gypsum board on ceilings under roofs and unoccupied areas. But to control the transmission of sound, you should use nothing less than ½-in. standard board under occupied areas.

As in walls, gypsum board can be applied directly to the joists, over an existing ceiling which is sound and level, or to 1×3-in. furring strips nailed at right angles to the joists. Furring strips are used, however, only if the old ceiling is in very bad shape or has a noticeable slope.

Install the gypsum-board panels perpendicular to the joists or furring strips with annular-ring nails. Use adhesive only for mounting panels on an absolutely smooth, level surface.

Wood paneling is most appropriate to sloping ceilings. The boards run either up and down the slope, in which case they are nailed to furring strips or 2×4-in. cross blocks nailed between the joists, or across the slope. You can use so-called ceiling boards—a tongue-and-groove board with small beads cut in the face along one edge and down the middle—or V-jointed or square-edged boards like those used for wall paneling.

DECK PLANKS. These are thick planks which serve not only as the roof sheathing but also as the ceilings for the rooms below. Used primarily in plank-and-beam construction, they are laid on top of the rafters or ceiling joists, which are exposed to view from inside the house. Two kinds of plank are available.

One is made of a solid wood, such as fir, cedar, or redwood, in thicknesses up to 5 in. The ceiling side of the planks has a smooth finish which can be stained or painted. The edges are usually chamfered, but may be square or milled in other ways.

The other type of plank is made of compressed wood fibers in 1½-in. to 3-in. thicknesses and 2-ft. to 4-ft. widths. The underside is textured slightly and must be painted.

Deck planks are rarely if ever used in simple remodelings. You might use them only if you were adding on a room in which the ceiling followed the roof line; and for this reason, you would probably have them installed by a builder. The choice of plank would depend primarily on the effect you desired, but you should also consider the insulating value. Composition planks are better in this respect, although even the thickest may be inadequate in cold climates. If wood planks are used, rigid insulation boards should be installed on top of them, under the roofing.

The underside of composition deck planks here serves as the finish ceiling. Homasote Co.

Ceiling tiles and panels come in a great variety of patterns and textures. Armstrong Cork Co.

CEILING TILES AND PANELS. Usually referred to as acoustical materials, ceiling tiles and panels made of compressed cellulose or mineral fibers are in some cases designed to soak up sound and in many other cases are not. But all are finished and textured to produce an attractive ceiling which even the most inept handyman can install.

Tiles come in 12-in. squares; panels, in assorted sizes up to 2×4 ft. as well as in pseudo-wood planks 5 to 8 in. wide and 4 ft. long. If your aim is simply to surface a ceiling, use whatever nonacoustical units strike your fancy. If you're trying to make a room quieter, however, you should select an acoustical unit with a noise reduction coefficient (NRC) which will give the proper results. As a rule, ceilings in kitchens, family rooms, and other very noisy rooms should have an NRC of .60 to .70. Elsewhere, an NRC of .40 to .50 is satisfactory. (Note that NRC ratings are based on the ability of a tile or panel to soak up the noise that is generated within the room in which it's installed. Noise made in other rooms will pass right through the tile or panel.)

Although ceiling tiles and panels are used to build ceilings where none exists (as in basements and unfinished attics), they are also frequently used to resurface existing ceilings and to lower high ceilings. No other kind of ceiling material is so well adapted for the latter two purposes.

Tiles are preferred for resurfacing ceilings which are sound and level because you can install them very rapidly. All you do is put several daubs of adhesive on the back of a tile, slip it into the interlocking edges of the previously laid tiles, and press it down. The tiles

should be laid out so that those on opposite sides of the room are of equal width and those at opposite ends are of equal width. (Ceiling panels should be arranged in the same way.) This means that you should install the first tile in the center of the ceiling and radiate out from it toward the walls. In the best installations, the border tiles are scribed to the walls so you don't have gaping joints which must be concealed with moldings. Cut the tiles (and panels) with a fine-toothed saw or sharp knife.

To cover an existing ceiling which is in poor condition or an unfinished ceiling in which the joists are exposed, use either tiles or panels. The first step after determining how the tiles should be arranged is to nail up 1×2-in. or 1×3-in. furring strips at right angles to the joists. Space the strips so they will be centered under the edges of the tiles or long edges of the panels. Then fasten the tiles or panels to them with 9/16-in. staples driven through the flanges.

To lower a ceiling in a high-ceilinged room, use panels and one of the easily assembled lightweight metal suspension systems sold by tile and panel makers. After establishing the height of the new ceiling, nail the L-shaped moldings that come with the framing system to the walls. Hang the long T-shaped main beams on wires looped through screweyes driven into the joists. Clip the short T-shaped cross beams between the main beams and wall moldings. And then simply slide the ceiling panels up through the openings in the frame-

Installing acoustical panels in a metal suspension system. Armstrong Cork Co.

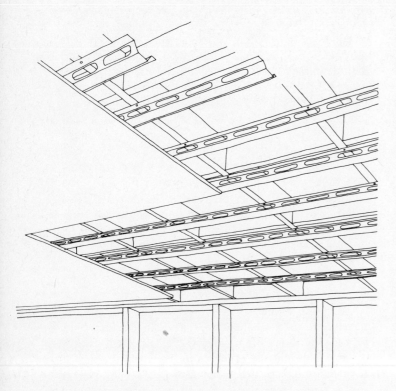

to 8-ft. lengths which can be pieced together to span the widest ceilings, they can be installed in a few minutes. No supports are needed. You just fasten them to any level surface with adhesive and a few finishing nails. They can also be applied to walls.

SOUNDPROOFING CEILINGS. Ceilings need to be soundproofed when people upstairs can hear talking downstairs and vice versa. But when people downstairs are annoyed only by the sounds of footsteps on the floors upstairs, ceiling soundproofing has little value; instead, the floors must be treated.

Methods for soundproofing ceilings are similar to those for interior walls. The simplest thing is to cover a new ceiling with ½-in. gypsum backer board and ½-in. or ⅝-in. standard or superior fire-rated gypsum board. Over an existing ceiling, nail or glue ½-in. or ⅝-in. standard or fire-rated gypsum board.

For maximum effect, screw resilient metal channels to the bottoms of the ceiling joists or old ceiling, and apply ⅝-in. fire-rated gypsum board to these.

The best way to soundproof a ceiling is to cover it with ⅝-in. gypsum board applied to resilient metal channels nailed to the joists.

work and drop them down. (The main beams and cross beams, of course, must be positioned so the panels rest in them squarely.)

Since ceiling tiles and panels are finished at the factory, no painting of a completed ceiling is required unless you want to change its color. However, paint can be applied at any time without affecting the texture or acoustical qualities of the ceiling. Use either latex or alkyd paint.

A completely different kind of ceiling panel—a throwback to Victorian times—is made of fancily embossed metal.

LUMINOUS CEILINGS. See Chapter 20.

CEILING BEAMS. Hand-hewn wood beams are not sold in lumberyards. You must either (1) buy sawn beams and hack them up with an ax; (2) find someone who can hew beams to order; or (3) buy old beams from small firms and individuals who have collected them from buildings which have been torn down.

Imitation wood beams of lightweight urethane foam are more readily available, and when you look up at them from the floor, the resemblance is amazing. But they have no structural strength and are therefore suitable only for dressing up existing ceilings. Made in 6-ft.

WHO MAKES IT

A. A. Abbingdon Ceiling Co. · Decorative metal panels for ceiling installation. Metal cornice moldings for use with panels.

Armstrong Cork Co. · Acoustical and nonacoustical tiles and panels and wood-grained planks. Metal framework for suspended ceilings. Fluorescent light fixtures for recessing in suspended ceilings.

Barclay Industries, Inc. · Urethane beams.

Celotex Corp. · Acoustical and nonacoustical tiles and panels. Metal framework for installation.

Certain-Teed Products Corp. · Acoustical and nonacoustical tiles and panels; metal frameworks for suspended ceilings.

Chicago Metallic Corp. · Metal frameworks for suspended ceilings.

Conwed Corp. · Acoustical and nonacoustical tiles and panels. Metal frameworks for suspended ceilings.

Diamond K Co. · Old, hand-hewn chestnut and pine beams up to 6×6 in. and in 30-ft. lengths. Old rough-cut weathered pine or spruce beams in smaller sizes.

Flangeklamp Industries, Inc. · Metal frameworks for suspended ceilings.

Flintkote Co. · Acoustical tiles and panels. Metal frameworks for suspended ceilings.

Focal Point, Inc. · Traditional ceiling medallions.

Homasote Co. · Compressed-fiber roof deck planks covered with white vinyl or polyetheylene on ceiling side.

Johns-Manville Sales Corp. · Acoustical and nonacoustical tiles and panels.

Leigh Products, Inc. · Mineral-fiber and plastic ceiling panels. Metal framework for suspended ceilings.

Leslie-Locke. · Metal frameworks for suspended ceilings.

Montgomery Ward & Co. · Acoustical and nonacoustical tiles and acoustical panels. Metal-framed suspension system. Fluorescent fixtures for installation in ceilings; translucent plastic light diffusers. Urethane beams.

National Gypsum Co. · Composition roof-deck planks with noise reduction coefficients ranging from .45 to .80.

Owens-Corning Fiberglas Corp. · Fiberglass acoustical tiles and panels and metal framework for installation. Recessed and surface-mounted light fixtures for suspended ceilings.

Potlatch Corp. · Wood deck planks in several textures and in natural or various semi-transparent colors.

Sears Roebuck & Co. · Urethane beams. Acoustical and nonacoustical tiles with metal framing for suspended ceilings.

United States Gypsum Co. · Weather-resistant gypsum board for extérior ceilings.

Woodcraft Millwork Specialties, Inc. · Urethane beams.

12

Floors

Although a great many homeowners make very conventional choices in flooring materials—they use resilient material in the kitchen, ceramic tile in bathrooms, and wood everywhere else because that is the traditional way of surfacing floors—the selection of materials should actually be given a great deal of thought. There are several obvious reasons why.

Because floors cover so much area, they must be closely tied in with the design and decoration of every room. No other part of a house receives so much wear and abuse. Cleaning and maintenance are constant and rather considerable chores. The physical and mental well-being of the house occupants is affected to some degree by the floors they walk on. And the cost of flooring is substantial.

In other words, when choosing flooring for the various rooms in your house, you should weigh the merits of the available materials from the following standpoints:
- Appearance.
- Durability.
- Ease of maintenance.
- Resistance to soil and stains and the ease with which these can be removed.
- Resistance to denting under static loads such as furniture and under live loads such as pounding under heels.
- Resistance to fading when exposed to sunlight.
- How comfortable the floor is to stand on.
- The amount of damage the floor can do to children's knees.
- The ability of the floor to muffle sound.
- The degree to which the floor reflects light (if it is very dark, for instance, it reduces room brightness and may accordingly raise your electric bill).
- Cost.

In addition, you must consider the subfloor on which the floor is laid and the position of the subfloor in relation to the ground.

The importance of a subfloor is obvious. You can't lay most types of wood floor on concrete because you can't fasten them down. Similarly, you can't lay most other types of flooring on a wood subfloor which is not sound, level, resistant to expansion and contraction, and tightly secured to the joists.

The position of the subfloor is of less obvious but equal importance because there are some flooring materials which will come up or disintegrate if exposed to moisture. Below-grade subfloors are the most difficult to deal with. Always made of concrete, they lie below the level of the ground surrounding the house; consequently, they are likely to be damp (though the dampness may not be visible) for a good part of the year. On-grade floors are also inclined to be damp unless they are built of 4 in. of concrete poured over a sheet of heavy polyethylene film which is, in turn, spread over a 6-in. layer of crushed rock or gravel. The only subfloors which are free of dampness are those suspended above the ground. These are almost always made of wood or plywood nailed to wood joists. Any finish flooring material can be laid directly on them provided the joists are large enough to support the weight.

TYPES OF FLOORING

WOOD STRIP FLOORING. Strip flooring is the most common type of wood flooring, not necessarily because homeowners prefer it to plank flooring but because manufacturers can turn it out in much larger quantities from relatively small trees. Nevertheless, it is attractive and practical. Although it is worn and sometimes damaged by traffic, it can be sanded down and refinished so it looks almost like new time and time again; consequently, it rarely needs to be replaced. But it can be used only on suspended floors and over on-grade concrete slabs which have been fully waterproofed.

The flooring is sold in bundles made up of strips of varying length. The width of the strips ranges from 1 to $3\frac{1}{2}$ in.; the most commonly used strips are $2\frac{1}{4}$ in. Thicknesses range from $\frac{5}{16}$ to $\frac{55}{32}$ in.; the most commonly used is $\frac{3}{4}$ in. As a rule, the strips are tongued and grooved along the edges as well as at the ends, but square-edged strips are available.

The woods used for strip flooring are:

Red oak. By far the most widely used wood, red oak is very tough, durable, and attractive. It has a slightly pinkish cast. The best—and most expensive—flooring is made of quarter-sawed lumber with a close, straight grain, and is available in only Clear and Select grades. Plain-sawed boards have an irregular grain and are available in five grades starting with Clear (meaning wood free of imperfections) and ranging downward through Select, No. 1 Common, No. 2 Common, and $1\frac{1}{2}$-ft. Shorts. (A bundle of the last grade is made up of an assortment of very short boards of the four higher grades.)

White oak. White oak is almost an exact duplicate of red oak except that it has a faint brownish cast. It is produced in the same grades.

As a rule, white-oak flooring is sold separately from red oak, but sometimes bundles of low-grade stock are mixed.

Maple. Cut from the sugar maple, this very durable flooring is most often used for floors in gymnasiums and public buildings. It varies in color from medium brown to nearly white, and has a rather fine grain. It is sold in First, Second, Third, and Fourth grades.

Beech. This is very similar to maple and is available in the same grades.

Birch. This is also like maple but has a slightly deeper color and more texture. The grades are the same.

Pecan. Pecan, a variety of hickory, is a handsome flooring with large pores. It is creamy white ranging to reddish brown. First Grade is the choice. This is followed by First Grade Red (cut from the dark heartwood); First Grade White (cut from the lighter sapwood); Second Grade; Second Grade Red; and Third Grade.

Ash, cherry, hickory, walnut. Flooring is made from these woods by so few manufacturers that no grading rules have been established. The flooring, however, is of excellent quality and durability, and that made from cherry and walnut is exceptionally beautiful.

Teak. A choice hardwood for many purposes, teak is used in floors only by those for whom money is no problem. It is one of the world's most durable woods, and is exceeded in beauty (among flooring woods) only by walnut and cherry. One top grade is sold.

Yellow pine. Yellow pine is used only when the homeowner is looking for low-cost flooring of good durability. The wood is not very pretty. Available grades are B and Better, C, C & Better, D, and No. 2. Unlike hardwood flooring, pine boards come in widths of 2, 3, 4, 5, and 6 in.

White fir. Because it's a softwood, white fir is less durable than other flooring woods but is useful as an economy flooring. It is light brown and has a close, straight grain. It's graded B & Better, C, D, and No. 2. The widths are 2, 3, 4, 5, and 6 in.

Cypress. Although rarely seen outside the deep South, cypress flooring is exceptionally resistant to decay and termites and wears well despite the fact that it's a softwood. It is generally a medium brownish red, but is often of a lighter hue. It is graded like the other softwoods and is produced in all widths except 2 in.

Although the standard strip floorings are unfinished, most of the hardwoods can be purchased with a factory-applied finish. This increases the cost and also calls for greater care in installation because it is hard to touch up areas that you may damage with your hammer or saw. However, the factory finishes are more uniform and durable than most do-it-yourself finishes, they save you a lengthy finishing job, and they permit you to refurnish the room and walk on the floor immediately.

In a new room or new house, strip flooring is laid either across or lengthwise of the room on a subfloor made of $\frac{1}{2}$-in. or $\frac{5}{8}$-in. structural plywood. In an old house, if you have torn up a worn-out finish floor and if the subfloor is made of boards, lay the new floor at right angles to the subfloor boards. This same arrangement should be followed when laying a new floor over an old finish floor; however, if the room is very narrow, it is permissible for the new boards to parallel the old as long as the joints do not line up exactly. In all cases, the old floor or subfloor should be covered with a layer of 15-lb. asphalt-coated building felt to protect the new floor and the house interior from dust, moisture, and cold air which might seep through the floor joints.

Ideally, in cases where the positioning of the flooring strips is not dictated by the subfloor, the strips should be laid in the same direction as those in the next room. However, if the room is isolated or if the adjoining floors are not made of boards, the strips look best if they run lengthwise of the room.

Remove the shoe moldings and baseboards. Allow a $\frac{1}{2}$-in. expansion gap between all edges of the new floor and the walls.

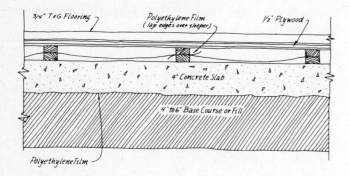

How to lay a wood floor over concrete.

Before nailing down any of the new flooring, lay three or four rows out on the subfloor and shift the strips until you get a pleasant arrangement of joints, colors, and grains. All end joints must be staggered at least 6 in. Use the longest strips at doorways and wherever they will be within view; the shortest strips in closets and in the middle of the floor under the rug.

Nail the first row of strips parallel to the wall from which you start your installation. The grooves should point toward the wall. Drive the nails through the face of the board close to the groove edge so they will be covered by the shoe moldings. In all other strips except the last, the nails are driven through the tongues at about a 45° angle. The last strip must be face-nailed like the first. Use 7d or 8d screw-type flooring nails for ¾-in. flooring and space them 10 to 12 in. apart (but if the subfloor is of ½-in. plywood, drive one nail into each joist and an extra nail midway between the joists). For ½-in. flooring use 5d nails; for ⅜-in., 4d nails spaced 8 in. apart.

Tap the grooves in each new row of flooring firmly over the tongues in the preceding row. Make sure the end joints are tight, too. Don't hit the flooring directly with your hammer; use a block of wood to protect it. (You can rent a floor-nailing tool that protects the floor and speeds your work.) Warped strips should be discarded or cut into short straight lengths.

To lay strip flooring over a concrete slab, it is necessary first to build up a base of 1×2-in. wood strips spaced 16 in. on centers. Saturate the strips with wood preservative, and glue them to the concrete with thick beads of panel adhesive. Lay a continuous sheet of 4-mil polyethylene film over the strips and lap it up on the four walls about 6 in. Then nail a second layer of 1×2-in. strips over the first, and nail a ½-in. or ⅝-in. plywood subfloor on top. Finally, put down the finish floor.

After you have completed laying a floor, it must be finished (if you haven't used prefinished flooring). The first step is to sand it with a rented drum sander and edging sander. Do the middle of the floor with the drum sander, then complete the perimeter with the edger. Three grades of sandpaper (also available from the rental outlet) are used with both machines: coarse, medium, and fine. If the flooring is very smooth and level, it may be possible to omit the coarse paper, but always finish the job with the fine paper even though it may seem unnecessary after using the medium paper.

To use a drum sander, start at one end of the floor and make a straight pass to the other end. Always work with the grain, never across it. Then back up over the same strip. Then move the machine and sand a new strip. The adjoining strips should overlap slightly. The edging sander, which has a flat revolving disk, can be moved from side to side or in one direction only. When using either sander, take care to keep it moving constantly; if you hold it in one place for just a few seconds, it will grind a hole in the floor.

(When refinishing an old floor, use the sanders in the same way. If the boards are badly cupped, however, you may find it necessary to make your first cut with the coarse sandpaper at a 45° angle to the boards. From then on, sand straight up and down the boards.)

After the entire floor is sanded, vacuum it thoroughly. Then, if you want to change the color of the wood, apply an oil stain. Brush this on in room-length strips about 24 to 30 in. wide. Rub each strip when completed with clean rags to remove excess stain and even out the color. Let the stain dry for 24 hours before applying the final finish.

Five types of clear finish are used:

Penetrating floor sealer is particularly recommended by flooring manufacturers because it penetrates the wood fibers and becomes part of them; thus it is highly resistant to wear and keeps dirt and stains from penetrating deeply into the wood. In addition, when worn, it can be touched up without showing laps.

The sealer is best applied with a brush, first across the boards and then with them. When the first coat is dry, buff it with medium steel wool; then apply a second coat, and buff this also.

Urethane is much like varnish but is more resistant to wear. It cannot be touched up without leaving lines of demarcation between the new and old coating. Two coats are required; three are better.

Varnish scratches more readily than urethane and tends to darken with age. Use only the kind that is made specifically for floors. Three coats are usually required, or you can use shellac for the first coat and follow with two coats of varnish.

Shellac is also used alone to finish floors. Its principal advantage is that it dries so fast you can apply two coats in one day. But it is easily scratched and is badly spotted by water and other liquids. On the other hand, when patched, new shellac blends into the old so the repair is invisible. Apply three coats. The first should be well thinned with denatured alcohol.

Lacquer dries so rapidly that the amateur should avoid it. But for the same reason, it allows you to use a floor within 24 hours. At least two coats are needed. The final finish has about the same resistance to wear as varnish but can be retouched without showing laps.

WOOD PLANK FLOORING. Planks were the first flooring materials used in American homes. For a period they lost popularity, but they are now enjoying a strong resurgence. They have the same characteristics as wood strips but are far more beautiful.

Planks are usually laid in random widths ¾ in. thick. The joints are slightly V-shaped, and each plank is pegged. But you can vary this arrangement by using planks of one or two widths or with square edges. You can substitute ornamental nails for the pegs, or you can omit surface fasteners entirely. You can also buy boards in several other thicknesses down to ⁵⁄₁₆ in.

Most lumberyards selling plank flooring carry only what is offered by national manufacturers. This is available in pretty much the same hardwoods that are used for strip flooring. Generally, the planks are pre-finished. Maximum width is 8 in.; maximum length, 8 ft. If you want longer or wider planks, you usually must have them milled to order. These are unfinished and in most cases have square rather than tongue-and-groove edges.

Extra-wide (to more than 20 in.) plank flooring can be purchased from salvage companies.

Planks made for installation directly on water-proofed on-grade concrete slabs and over old finished floors are also available. Although these resemble ordinary planks, they consist of a top layer of fine wood laminated to a bottom layer of less expensive wood.

Prefinished oak plank floor. E. L. Bruce Co.

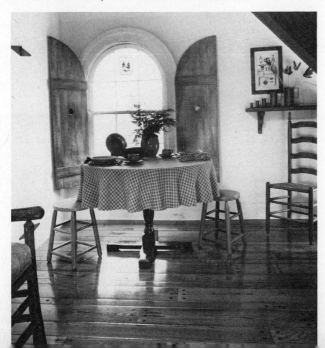

Total thickness is ⅜ in.; maximum length, 5 ft. The planks are laid with panel adhesive spread on the subfloor with a notched trowel.

A conventional plank floor is laid much like a strip floor over the same type of subfloor. If using random widths, arrange them to suit your fancy. Concentrate the short boards in the middle of the room and in closets.

Tongue-and-groove flooring is secured to the subfloor with screw nails driven through the tongues. It is then advisable, though not absolutely necessary except on the widest boards, to drive screws through the faces of the boards and cover them with wood plugs. (Prefinished planks are not screwed. The plugs are inserted at the factory.)

Square-edged flooring is fastened entirely with screws, which are covered with plugs. There are no rules for the number that should be used or where they should be placed, but the usual practice is to drive two screws through each board at both ends and to drive additional screws singly and in pairs at 24-in. to 30-in. intervals between the ends.

The most tedious job in installing a plank floor is to drill pilot holes for the screws and large holes for the plugs (which are ¾ in. across and about ¼ in. deep) and then to drive in the screws. This can be greatly simplified if you use an electric drill with a countersink-counterbore bit which drills the screw holes and plug holes simultaneously. Use a ratchet screwdriver or a screwdriver bit in a low-speed electric drill to drive the screws. When all the screws are in, tap the plugs into the holes. They do not have to be glued unless they fit loosely.

After a floor is laid, unfinished planks are sanded and finished like strip flooring.

PARQUET FLOORING. Although originally used only in mansions, parquet flooring is now widely used in more modest houses because it is relatively inexpensive, easily installed like resilient tile, and can be laid directly on on-grade concrete floors as well as on ¾-in. plywood or on any old wood or resilient floor which is first covered with ¼-in. hardboard or plywood underlayment.

Strictly speaking, a parquet floor is made of small pieces of wood which are installed piece by piece to form an attractive geometric pattern. But most parquet floors today are made of tilelike blocks consisting of small pieces which are preassembled at the factory. Generally, the small pieces are bonded to a fabric backing, but some are held together with paper which is stuck to the face and peeled off after the blocks are glued to the subfloor.

The variety to be found in parquet floorings is impossible to describe in condensed space.

Available woods include oak, maple, beech, birch,

133

Prefinished oak parquet floor. E. L. Bruce Co.

and a host of specialized designs with such names as Haddon Hall, Monticello, Canterbury, Saxony, Fontainebleau, and Louis Seize.

Block sizes range from approximately 6 to 39 in. square; thicknesses, from $\frac{5}{16}$ to $\frac{33}{32}$ in. (but $\frac{5}{16}$ is the most common).

Some flooring is prefinished. Some has chamfered edges.

And to add further to the variety, you can lay the flooring out in rows paralleling the walls or diagonally across the floor. You can cover the entire floor from wall to wall or use it in a field which is surrounded by a different type of border.

Even the installation varies to some extent, depending on whether the edges are tongued and grooved or squared and also on other minor differences in construction.

If parquet flooring is laid on a concrete slab on the ground (it should be installed below grade only by a professional—and even then the practice is questionable), the slab must be covered with a dampproofing membrane. Of the two methods used to apply this, the easiest is to coat the slab first with a primer specified by the flooring maker. When this dries, spread the adhe-

ash, pecan, cherry, walnut, mahogany, teak, cedar, and so-called ebonized wood (a dyed holly or white maple).

Patterns include simple strips, squares composed of strips, herringbone, basketweave, rhomboid, domino,

Just a few of the many parquet patterns available from flooring manufacturers.

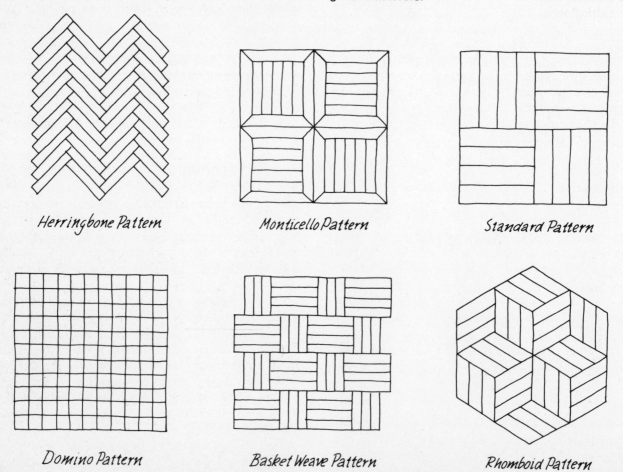

Herringbone Pattern Monticello Pattern Standard Pattern

Domino Pattern Basket Weave Pattern Rhomboid Pattern

sive used to install the flooring over it with the smooth edge of a flooring trowel. Then roll into the adhesive a 2-mil sheet of polyethylene film. Spread more adhesive on this with the notched edge of the trowel, and lay the flooring.

The blocks are arranged on the floor like resilient tiles. After you find the center of the floor and adjust the tiles so that the border units on opposite sides are of equal width, lay them from the center point toward the walls. Apply no more adhesive than you can cover in about 15 minutes. Set the tiles precisely, without sliding them, and butt the edges. Then press the tiles down firmly with your hand, a rubber mallet, a block of wood under a hammer, or a 150-lb. flooring roller. Remove the surface paper (if any) with water. At the perimeter of the floor, leave about a ½-in. gap for expansion, and conceal this with the baseboards.

Prefinished flooring is ready for service after the adhesive has dried 12 hours and all traces have been removed from the surface. To finish unfinished flooring, let the adhesive dry for 48 hours, then sand with a drum sander and edger with a 14-in. or larger disk. Sand the middle of the floor first with coarse and medium paper. Move the drum sander at a 45° angle to the pattern. Use the edger to sand along the walls. Then fine-sand the entire floor with the edger. Stain and finish like a strip floor.

WOOD TILES. This unusual flooring material is made of tongue-and-groove squares of particleboard which are factory-stained in seven colors and finished with acrylic that is specially hardened to resist wear. The effect is suggestive of a cork floor.

The tiles, which are 11⅜ in. square and ⅜ in. thick, are laid like parquet blocks on the same kinds of sub-floor.

RESILIENT TILES. Resilient tiles were the first flooring material recommended for do-it-yourself installation, and they are still the most popular for this purpose. But that is not the only reason why they are so widely used, especially in kitchens, bathrooms, and rooms built on concrete slabs. They are inexpensive; some tiles, in fact, cost less than any other flooring. They are colorful and attractive in their own right, and can be used in innumerable geometric patterns. They are water-resistant, resilient, and moderately easy to maintain. And although they show dents and ultimately wear out, few people hold these weaknesses against them.

Generally made in 12-in. squares (a few are smaller; a very few, larger), tiles are available in five materials:

Vinyl-asbestos. The first choice of the majority of homeowners, these tiles are low in cost but near the top in almost all performance characteristics, except

resiliency. They can be laid on grade, below grade, and above grade. An increasing number of those sold come with the adhesive already applied. You just tear off a protective covering and press them down. But unfortunately they are made of thinner material than conventional non-stick tiles and do not last as long.

Vinyl. In all-round performance, vinyl tiles are the best on the market. Their principal weakness is their poor resistance to burns. More important to the average buyer, they are not available in very many colors or patterns. They can be used at all grade levels.

Asphalt. These tiles are slowly disappearing from the market in spite of the fact that they are exceptionally durable, inexpensive, and resistant to dampness in below-grade and on-grade concrete slabs. But they have a drab appearance, are difficult to keep up, and are about as hard underfoot as masonry.

Rubber. Rubber tiles are sold in only a few stores. The color and pattern choice is limited, resistance to wear is fairly low, and they are not suitable for use below grade. But they are quieter and more resilient than any other composition material.

Cork. Unlike other resilient tiles, cork is not used in kitchens and bathrooms, but because of its color and texture, it is well suited to all living areas. Except for carpet, there is no quieter, softer, or warmer material to walk on. But it is not very durable and tends to stain and fade even though the majority of tiles are given a plastic finish at the factory. They should be used only on suspended floors and on well-waterproofed slabs on grade.

Although manufacturers say that, in certain circumstances, resilient tiles can be laid over old resilient

Vinyl-asbestos tiles are attractive, practical, durable. Azrock—Uvalde Rock Asphalt Co.

1

2

3

4

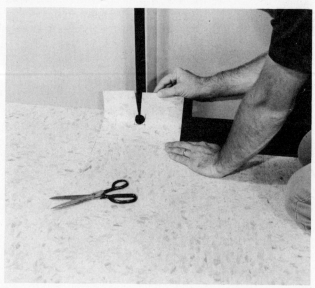

5

Key steps in laying a resilient tile floor. 1, cover old floor with underlayment panels. 2, after finding center of room, lay the tiles out along the chalk lines to one of the side walls and one of the end walls. 3, border tiles along opposite walls should be the same width. They should also be more than half the width of the tile. 4, spread adhesive on the floor and tile one-quarter of the floor at a time. 5, cut tiles, as here, to fit around pipes. Armstrong Cork Co.

flooring, the practice is questionable. Ripping up the old flooring and removing the adhesive (by washing or sanding) is much safer. As a general rule, you can lay the new tiles directly on the existing subfloor if made of hardboard or plywood.

Finish wood floors can be used as the base for tiles only if they are made of less than 3-in. strips which are well nailed to the subfloor. If they are not completely smooth, sand them well and seal the bare wood with shellac.

Floors which are laid on a subfloor and are made of boards more than 3 in. wide must be covered with 1/4-in. hardboard, plywood, or particleboard underlayment. Floors which do not have a subfloor must also be covered with underlayment. Use 1/4-in. material if the floorboards are tongued and grooved, 1/2-in. if they are not.

In all cases, underlayment panels are installed at right angles to the floor boards. Nail them with annular-ring nails spaced 4 in. apart around the edges and through the center.

In a new room, a subfloor made of 5/8-in. plywood laid over joists spaced 16 in. on centers can be tiled directly. The surface of the plywood, however, must be completely free of voids.

Concrete slabs to be tiled must be tested for dampness by spreading on them a strip of the adhesive used with the tiles and covering it for 72 hours with polyethylene film which is stuck down around the edges with masking tape. If the adhesive sticks tight, the slab is ready for tiling. But first you must remove all paint and grease. Scrub the slab with a dilute solution of muriatic acid to remove alkalis; grind down high spots, and level low spots with latex cement. In addition to these precautions, you must allow new slabs to cure for at least two months, and if they were made of concrete to which curing compounds or hardeners were added, you must also sand the entire surface with electric sanders.

Before tiling any floor, remove the shoe moldings or, if there aren't any, the baseboards. If possible, remove radiators, too. In bathrooms, if you don't choose to fit tiles around the toilet, take up the bowl and let the tiles extend underneath.

Cover all board floors with lining felt. Plywood, hardboard, and particleboard should also be covered, although they sometimes are not. Roll the felt into linoleum cement which is applied with a notched trowel, and smooth it down well with a rolling pin or flooring roller. Butt the edges.

In bathrooms, tiles are laid from the doorway wall toward the opposite wall. In all other rooms, they should be laid from the center of the floor toward the sides. The tile at the center point must be adjusted slightly so that the border tiles at the end walls are of equal width and those at the side walls are of equal width. In addition, the width of the end-wall tiles

should be approximately equal to that of the side-wall tiles.

Use an adhesive recommended by the tile dealer. Some are applied with a notched trowel, others with a paint brush. The area covered depends on how rapidly the adhesive sets.

Drop the tiles exactly in position, without sliding. Butt the edges as tightly as possible. Most patterned tiles are laid with the pattern at right angles in adjacent tiles. If the pattern is obscure, arrows are printed on the back to show which way it runs. After putting down 12 to 15 vinyl, rubber, or cork tiles, roll them into the adhesive with a rolling pin or rented flooring roller. Asphalt and vinyl-asbestos tiles should not be rolled because of their brittleness. If you can't press them down flat, play the flame of a propane torch over them briefly and smooth them down. Be careful not to hold the flame too close. A safer procedure is to heat the tiles slightly in a warm oven before laying them. (Oven heating is necessary to cut tiles on an irregular line.)

If tiles are laid to the edge of a step or if they project above the adjoining floor at a doorway, apply vinyl or metal edging strips along the edges to keep them from cracking as people walk across them.

RESILIENT SHEETS. The resilient sheet floorings are first cousins of resilient tiles. The major difference is that they are produced in long rolls 3, 6, or 12 ft. wide; consequently, when put down, there are few if any joints that can leak, and cleaning is that much easier. The patterns are prettier, the cost a bit higher, and some of the sheets have a cushioned backing which makes them much quieter and softer underfoot. The available materials are:

Vinyl. Conventional vinyl flooring is the most durable of all resilient materials—including those cut into tiles—partly because of the inherent toughness of vinyl and partly because it has a thicker wear layer than anything except linoleum. It is also the most stain-resistant, most resistant to denting, and easiest to maintain. It can be used at all grade levels.

Like other vinyl floorings, this so-called solid vinyl is made in two types—one that requires waxing, the other with a high-gloss finish that does not. As might be expected, homemakers have been attracted to the latter as bees go to honey. Before joining the parade, however, you should note that even though the shiny vinyls eliminate the irksome waxing and buffing chores, they are not completely perfect. If anything, you must sweep them more often than ordinary vinyls because scratches made by grit show up with unusual clarity. They need to be stripped with ammonia or a packaged wax remover when they become very dirty. And when they lose their gloss (which may happen a few months or a couple of years after installation, depending on the traffic over them), they must be reglazed.

Cushioned vinyl sheet flooring with a shiny no-wax finish. Mannington Mills, Inc.

Cushioned vinyl. This is far and away the most resilient and sound-absorbing of all flooring materials because it consists of a thin wear layer of vinyl bonded to a thick layer of vinyl foam. It is the ideal hard-surfaced flooring for installation in a children's playroom over the living room, dining room, or downstairs bedroom. If walking on hard surfaces gives you a backache, it's also excellent for use on concrete slabs on or below grade. But it is more expensive than conventional vinyls and less durable.

Rotovinyl. Rotovinyl is the poor man's vinyl. The colorful pattern is simply printed on top of felt or asbestos and then overlaid with a film of vinyl; consequently, the flooring doesn't last very long and is often used simply as a carpet which can be taken up at any time. Some rotovinyls have a cushioned back. Most can be used on all grade levels.

Do-it-yourself vinyl. This is a brand-new product which doesn't boast of much durability but atones for this shortcoming by being so easy to lay. Made in 12-ft. widths with a thin vinyl wear layer, a foam inner cushion, and a special backing, it's flexible enough to be folded like heavy fabric and elastic enough to lie flat even when the subfloor expands and contracts. It is used on suspended, on-grade, and below-grade floors.

Linoleum. This old standby is disappearing, along with that other old standby, asphalt tile. Many people will regret its passing, for although linoleum is not very colorful, isn't terribly easy to keep up, and can be used only on suspended floors, it wears well. A good many linoleum floors are still giving good service after 30 years and more.

Rubber. Rubber sheets are in as limited supply as rubber tiles. There is no difference between the materials except the size. Use the sheets only on suspended and on-grade floors. They come in 3-ft. widths.

The subfloor for a sheet material must, as a rule, be prepared like that for resilient tiles. However, conventional vinyl can be laid directly over an old resilient floor which is in good condition by Armstrong Cork

Co.'s Perimiflor installation system. Do-it-yourself vinyls can also be laid over old resilient coverings.

Regardless of the subfloor, all installations of conventional vinyl, cushioned vinyl, linoleum, and rubber should be made by a trained flooring mechanic. The job is too tricky for the amateur. The only sheets you should try to install yourself are those made specifically for the purpose and rotovinyls which are 12 ft. wide.

To install do-it-yourself vinyl, you simply roll it out on the subfloor after removing the shoe moldings or baseboards, and thorough-cleaning the edges of the subfloor. Butt one edge tight against a wall; lap the other edges up on the walls. Slit the lapped edges vertically at the corners. Then with a carpenter's square, force the flooring into the corners between the floor and walls and cut off the excess material. Finally, turn back the flooring slightly and glue the edges to the floor at doorways. Fasten all other edges with $9/16$-in. staples spaced 3 in. apart. The staples should be hidden by the shoe moldings or baseboards when these are replaced.

Rotovinyl is considerably more troublesome to install. Try it only in a room which is less than 12 ft. wide so you don't have to match and lay two sheets.

Make an accurate plan of the room in which the rotovinyl is to be laid and transfer this to the sheet (which is spread out in another room). Trim along the pencil lines. Then, with a helper, unroll the sheet in the room where it is to go and make sure it fits. Fold the sheet back on itself, spread adhesive on the exposed subfloor, and smooth the sheet into this. Take care when positioning the sheet under overhangs and around corners not to tear it. Repeat the process under the other half, and roll the entire floor with a rolling pin or flooring roller.

SEAMLESS FLOORING. Seamless flooring got its name from the fact that it is poured from a can and rolled out on the subfloor to form a continuous layer with joints only around the edges. It is, therefore, particularly suited to kitchens and bathrooms because moisture cannot get underneath. Furthermore, it

Do-it-yourself sheet vinyl is held down around the edges with staples. Armstrong Cork Co.

shouldn't be waxed; to clean it and maintain its appearance, you just go over it with a damp mop. It has good resistance to stains. And the material itself is fairly low in cost.

On the other side of the coin, installation takes several days and you can't use the room during this period; and unless the installation is very carefully made, the floor won't last too long. The surface must be reglazed from time to time, and when it is, you must stay off it for 24 hours. Finally, despite the fact that the flooring has a very pleasant texture, there are few patterns and colors to choose from.

Ideally, seamless flooring should be installed only by trained applicators, but if you take time and follow the manufacturer's directions to the letter, you can do the work yourself.

If the subfloor is concrete, remove all paint and either go over the surface with electric floor sanders or scrub it with muriatic acid to get it spotlessly clean. Level the concrete by grinding down high spots and filling holes and depressions with latex cement.

Wood floors must be surfaced with plywood or particleboard underlayment as they are for resilient tiles. In a new room, lay ½-in. or ⅝-in. plywood on joists spaced no more than 16 in. apart. In all cases, the plywood or particleboard should then be covered with a rubber-asbestos underlayment felt which is rolled into adhesive recommended by the underlayment maker. Butt the edges of the strips precisely.

The exact method of laying the seamless flooring varies with the brand and type. Generally, you cover the floor with a primer and sprinkle into this the granules or chips which give the floor its texture. Then you apply a topcoat followed by a sealer and glaze coat.

CERAMIC TILE. Always the favorite flooring material for bathrooms, because it is watertight and easy to clean, ceramic tile has in comparatively recent years branched out into many other rooms. The reason is easy to see if you visit a well-stocked manufacturer's showroom: tiles are now available in innumerable gorgeous colors, textures, patterns, shapes, and sizes. No other flooring offers such a tremendous choice.

Three basic types of tile are used:

Mosaics, which used to be called floor tiles, are little glazed or unglazed squares or rectangles bonded to a backing in large sheets. In a few cases, the joints between the tiles are filled with a flexible plastic grout.

Glazed tiles are larger and are installed individually. They are similar to the tiles most often used on walls but have a tougher, more scratch-resistant glaze. Standard sizes are 4¼×4¼ in. 4¼×6 in., and 6×6 in.; but there are many other shapes and sizes up to 1 ft. square. Standard thickness is ⁵⁄₁₆ in.

Ceramic tiles are so beautiful they should not be confined just to bathrooms. Interpace Corp.

Quarry tiles are heavy-duty units ½ or ¾ in. thick. The standard tiles are square ranging from 2¾ to 9 in.; but here again you have a choice of other shapes and sizes. Colors are fairly limited. Reds and browns are most common.

Ceramic tiles are today usually laid on floors with an organic adhesive recommended by the tile dealer. If the subfloor is concrete, make certain it is free of moisture and level. Remove all paint, grease, and dirt. Finish wood floors must be covered with exterior plywood or hardboard underlayment. Use ¼-in. thickness if the boards are less than 3 in. wide; ½-in. otherwise. Secure

Installing pregrouted mosaic tiles in 4-ft.-square sheets. American Olean Tile Co.

the underlayment panels with annular-ring nails spaced 4 in. apart throughout the panels.

If a new room is to be tiled, build the subfloor of ⅝-in. plywood and cover it with ⅜-in. exterior plywood.

Mosaic tiles are laid from one wall straight across the room. In bathrooms, individual glazed and quarry tiles are laid in the same way; but in all other rooms, they should be laid from the center toward the walls so that the border tiles along opposite walls are the same width.

Set ceramic tiles as you do on a wall (see Chapter 8). Fill the joints with the same kind of grout (however, gray is usually preferred to white since it does not show soil so readily). Joints between quarry tiles are ¼ to ⅜ in. wide; and instead of being tooled to a concave profile with a toothbrush, they are struck off flush with the surface of the tiles or recessed a fraction of an inch below the surface.

GLASS TILE. See Chapter 8.

BRICK. Bricks make a very attractive floor, especially in houses of contemporary design. But like all other masonry materials, they are unpleasant to stand on for long periods, and if not well sealed, they stain badly.

Although any kind of new or used brick can be used for flooring, the best choice is paving brick like that used on terraces because of its greater resistance to abrasion and staining. These are made in rectangles up to 11¾ in. long; squares from 4 to 16 in. across; and hexagons 6, 8, and 12 in. across. Standard thickness is 2¼ in., but units only ¼ or ½ in. thick are generally preferable indoors because you can install them level with other finish floors without making major changes in the subfloor. To install standard bricks level with other floors, you must drop the joists or make them of smaller lumber. In the latter case, you must also increase the number of joists to support the weight.

The simplest way to lay bricks is either to set them loosely on the subfloor or to stick them down with organic adhesive like that used for ceramic tiles. In either case, if you use rectangular bricks, the actual length of each brick should be exactly double the actual width. This will permit you to lay the bricks in any bond (pattern) you like. If the length is not twice the width (for example, a great many so-called 4×8-in. bricks actually measure somewhat less than this), you can use only a running bond or stack bond. (In a running bond, all the bricks are laid in one direction in parallel rows and the end joints are staggered. In a stack bond, all the bricks run in one direction and the end joints are aligned.)

Bricks to be laid dry (without any mortar or adhesive) should be at least ½ in. thick. The subfloor can be made of any material as long as it is level, sound,

and smooth. Cover it with two layers of 15-lb. asphalt-saturated building felt laid at right angles to each other. Gluing is unnecessary. Set the bricks directly on the felt as close together as possible. To keep the entire floor from shifting, the bricks must be laid tight to the walls or be surrounded by wood strips laid aginst the walls.

When the entire floor is laid, sweep fine sand into the joints and let it settle for about a week. Then, to prevent staining and make the floor easier to clean, apply two coats of transparent penetrating masonry sealer.

To set bricks in adhesive, omit the felt underlayment and spread tile cement directly on the subfloor with a notched spreader. Press the bricks into this. If you use ½-in. or thicker bricks, butt the edges and sweep sand into the joints. Quarter-inch bricks are made with flanges which separate the bricks ⅜ in. The joints are filled with a special grout sold by the brick company. In both cases, the completed floor should be coated with masonry sealer.

SLATE. This exceptionally durable material comes in an array of handsome blacks, grays, greens, purples, and reds. Clear stock is a uniform color; ribbon stock contains bands of color. The favorite finish for floors is a natural cleft finish, which is a little rough and irregular. Sand-rubbed finish gives a slight stippled effect.

You can buy slate in uniformly sized squares and rectangles ranging from 6 in. square to 18×24 in.; in random-sized squares and rectangles; and also in irregular shapes. Thicknesses range from ¼ to 1 in. If the slates you select are all of the same size, you will have no trouble laying them out on the floor in a running or stack bond. If you favor a random arrangement, however, it's advisable to let the dealer or manufacturer supply you with a numbered plan showing exactly where each slate should go. This saves you the trouble of working out the jigsaw puzzle yourself and of cutting —and probably wasting—a large number of stones. But you pay extra for this service. On the other hand, if you use irregular slates, the whole job of piecing them together and cutting them falls on your shoulders; and when placing your order, you should overestimate your requirements about 10%.

The subfloor for slate must be of sound, smooth, level concrete, plywood, or wood. If you lay the slates in ceramic-tile adhesive—the easiest procedure—use ¼-in. to ½-in. stock which is gauged to an even thickness. Spread the adhesive on the subfloor and press the slates into it. If all the slates are of the same size, butt the joints and don't bother to fill them. If the slates are of random size or irregular, leave ½-in. spaces between them and fill the joints with a mixture of 1 part white or gray Portland cement and 2 parts sand. Wipe off mortar stains on the floor surface with a damp rag. If any remain after the mortar has dried for ten days or

Blue-black slates with a natural cleft finish installed in random squares and rectangles. Buckingham-Virginia Slate Corp.

two weeks, scrub them off with dilute muriatic acid.

Normally it is unnecessary to seal a slate floor, but if it will be exposed to considerable staining, apply two coats of penetrating masonry sealer.

FLAGSTONE. Flagstone does not seem to have the distinctive air of slate—perhaps because we see it often on terraces. It is nevertheless a beautiful and generally excellent flooring material as long as it is protected against stains.

The most widely used flagstones are gray—pure gray, bluish gray, or brownish gray—but many other subdued colors are to be had if you hunt for them. The effect is best if these are not mixed. Even a mixture of grays is vaguely displeasing.

Unless you have stones cut to order, shapes are limited to squares, rectangles, and irregular pieces as they come from the quarry. Sizes are also variable. It's extremely difficult to find many stones of the same dimensions in any one supply yard, but you can order them from a quarry. In ½-in. thickness, standard squares and rectangles range from 11½×11½ in. up to 24×36 in. These are the easiest and most economical to use if you plan your floor layout yourself. If you prefer mixed squares and rectangles, have the floor laid out by the supplier or manufacturer.

Since flagstones are not gauged to a uniform thickness, they can be laid only on a 1-in.-thick concrete "cushion" spread over a concrete slab or heavily reinforced framing with ⅝-in. exterior plywood nailed on top. This complicates installation to such an extent that you probably would be wise to have the floor laid by a mason. If you're an optimist, however, proceed as follows:

Make the cushion of 1 part Portland cement and 3 parts sand, and put down only enough for one stone at a time. Press the stone firmly into the mortar and level it. Then lift out the stone without tilting or twisting and brush a pastelike slurry of cement and water on the back. Reset the stone immediately and tap it down lightly. When the floor is completed and the cushion has firmed, trowel a mixture of 1 part Portland cement and 2 parts sand into the joints—which should be ½ in. wide—and strike it off flush with the surface of the stones. Remove mortar stains promptly. To facilitate cleaning and prevent staining, brush on two coats of penetrating masonry sealer.

Irregular flagstones are installed in the same way after you have laid them out dry on the subfloor and cut them to size with a cold chisel. The width of the joints is bound to vary to some extent, but try to keep them between ½ and 1 in. wide.

MARBLE. The same 8-in. and 12-in. marble squares that are installed on walls are used on floors. In addition, you can buy enormous slabs, but these are likely to be out of all proportion to the average house and must be installed by professionals.

Lay the tiles either on a clean, dry concrete slab, on ⅝-in. plywood nailed to joists spaced 16 in. on centers, or on a finish floor which is covered with ¼-in. plywood or hardboard underlayment. The procedure is similar to that for installing ceramic tiles. Allow ³⁄₃₂-in. spaces between tiles and fill them with ceramic-tile grout. Apply two coats of transparent sealer made specifically for marble to minimize soiling and staining.

TERRAZZO. Though not often used in homes, terrazzo is a good flooring material for family rooms because it combines beauty with utility. Poured in large almost satin-smooth sheets, it can take the worst kind of punishment without showing wear. It is unaffected by spilled liquids and can be whisked clean with no effort. But of course, it is hard and cold.

True terrazzo is made of marble chips set in a Portland-cement matrix and ground smooth. It can be installed only on a concrete slab. Plastic terrazzo is a mixture of marble chips and epoxy or polyester. Put down in a layer only ¼ in. thick, it can be used on plywood and wood subfloors as well as concrete. Although it is less durable than cement terrazzo, it wears well enough to be used in many public buildings, feels a little warmer and more resilient, and is ready for service two days after installation starts.

Both terrazzos should be put down professionally.

TERRAZZO TILES. These look like sheet-type terrazzos but can be installed by anyone like resilient tiles over the same kind of subfloor. One type of tile has a cement matrix, another a plastic matrix. Both are available in 12-in. squares and several other shapes. Edges of plastic tiles are butted tight; those of cement tiles are slightly spaced and filled with ceramic tile grout.

CARPET. Wall-to-wall carpet is laid over any finish floor or directly over a plywood, wood, or on-grade or suspended concrete subfloor. Although the carpet industry does not encourage do-it-yourself installation, you don't have to be deterred by this. The first step—after leveling the floor, making sure all squeaks are silenced, and removing shoe moldings—is to nail so-called tackless strips around the edges of the floor at the foot of baseboards. These are thin wood strips studded with short sharp nails. Some are made for use on wood floors, others for use on concrete. Cut a rug cushion to fit inside the strips, and staple it down. Then cut the carpet about 2 in. longer and wider than the floor, position it carefully, and fasten it to the tackless strips, first along one wall, then along one of the adjacent walls, and finally along the opposite walls. Then return to the first two walls, stretch it tight, and refasten it.

The tool used for this operation is called a knee-kicker. You can rent it from the carpet dealer. Adjust the height of the teeth in the head so they don't dig into the carpet backing. Kneel on the floor facing the wall you're working on, press the teeth into the carpet near the edge, and hit the padded handle of the tool with your knee. After stretching the carpet tight, trim off the excess along the baseboards.

At doorways and open sides of the room, fasten the carpet to the floor with double-faced adhesive tape or large carpet tacks. Protect the edges with metal edger strips.

If strips of carpet must be joined, do it after the carpet is laid but before it is fastened down. Center thermoplastic carpet tape under the carefully trimmed and butted edges and stick the carpet to it with a rented seaming iron.

Cheap carpet made by a few firms especially for do-it-yourselfers is laid entirely with double-faced adhesive tape stuck under the edges.

Wall-to-wall carpets, like area rugs, are available in an enormous choice of colors, patterns, weaves, and fibers. What you buy is dictated largely by personal preference, decorating requirements, and cost; but, of course, you can never forget practicality and durability.

The following information about fibers is taken from a bulletin of the Connecticut Cooperative Extension Service:

Wool is the fiber against which all other fibers for carpets are compared. Carpet wool must be imported, because domestic wool is too soft. Good resilience, abrasion resistance, and soil resistance are found in medium- to high-priced carpets. The majority of wool carpets are permanently mothproofed.

Cotton, soft and comfortable underfoot, is subject to crushing except in very dense construction. Soiling occurs quickly, but cotton rugs are easily laundered. Low to medium in price.

Acrylics are considered excellent for carpeting. They are most like wool in handling and hand, compared with other man-made fibers. Resistance to abrasion and soiling and crush recovery are rated good to excellent. Medium- to high-priced.

Modacrylics have many of the characteristics of pure acrylics but pill (a fuzzing of the fibers into small balls caused by abrasion) more easily and lack resilience. They are often used in blends with pure acrylic fibers to increase the fire resistance of the fabric, and are also used to a lesser extent in area and accent rugs of 100% modacrylic. Medium- to high-priced.

Nylon is often rated as the strongest and longest-wearing of man-made fibers. Although staple nylon has a tendency to pill in loop pile, it has exceptional resistance to wear. In proper constructions, resilience is good and can be excellent. Soil resistance is good to excellent in delustered fibers, but falls off slightly in bright and semi-bright fibers. Textured-filament nylon provides better hand because of bulking of the yarn. It has the same basic properties as staple nylon, with these added qualities: no pilling, longer wear, and greater style versatility largely because of recent dye research. It has excellent resilience and is resistant to soil and abrasion. It is subject to static electricity. However, carpets and rugs are available with special finishes that reduce static. Mainly medium in price.

Polyesters have previously been limited to use in high-pile scatter rugs because of their good washability. Now a polyester fiber in a denier suitable for broadloom has been developed. Poor stain resistance and resilience are problems. High-medium price range.

Olefin (polypropylene) is used in all types of carpets and rugs, including those for outdoor use and kitchens and bathrooms. It is presently used in the carpet industry in filament form. Resistance to abrasion is rated good to excellent, resilience good, and resistance to soil good. Low to medium in price.

Rayon fibers are used in scatter, room-size rugs, and automotive carpeting. The key to rayon carpeting is in the construction. All properties, including resistance to abrasion, wear, and soiling and resilience, improve as the construction increases in density. Unless a high degree of density is obtained, the soil resistance is poor, abrasion resistance is poor to fair, and resilience is poor to fair. Low price range.

Saran is used in all types of carpet and rug. Some constructions are available for patio and poolside use. It has good soil and stain resistance, fair to good abrasion resistance. Color darkens over a period of time. It does not burn but has a low melting point. Medium price.

Unless you are an authority on carpets, price is generally your best guide to carpet durability. But you can tell something about durability by examining the carpet. The denser the pile, the longer life you can expect. To check density, bend back a corner: the less backing you see, the better the carpet. The resilience of the pile as you press it should also be considered. If the pile is too stiff, it wears down more rapidly. High twisted yarns and looped pile increase resilience. Check the backing of tufted carpets especially. The yarns must be securely anchored in a coating of latex or other resin.

CARPET TILE. Under the heading of carpet tile you will also find carpet strips. The tiles are 9-in., 12-in., and 18-in. squares. The strips measure 3×5 ft. Both are made of nylon or polypropylene and have an adhesive backing so you can stick them down quickly on any clean, dry, smooth surface. Surprisingly, they cost as much per square yard as full-size carpets, so the only things you gain by using them are easier installation and an ability to make instant replacement of damaged areas.

SOUNDPROOFING MATERIALS. The sound a floor gives off when someone walks across it can be annoying not only to people in the room but also to those in rooms below. The only way to make it less annoying is to cover it either with a soft material which doesn't make any noise under impact or with a resilient material which soaks up some of the noise.

Carpet laid over a top-grade, heavyweight rug cushion does both of these things better than any other flooring material. Cork and cushioned vinyl are its only competition.

To mute the sounds of footsteps on hard-surface flooring, the flooring should be laid over a resilient composition board made for the purpose. On an existing subfloor or finish floor, use ½-in. board; in a new room, nail 1½-in. or 1¾-in. board directly to the studs. Wood strip and plank flooring and carpet are laid directly on the composition board. Parquet, resilient flooring, and ceramic tile are laid on ⅜-in. plywood applied over the composition board.

Unfortunately, the use of resilient material does not substantially reduce the transmission through a floor of airborne sounds such as voices and music. To control these, you must increase the density either of the floor or of the ceiling below. Generally, it is easier to treat the ceiling. However, if you are laying a complete new floor as in an expansion attic, or if you tear up an old

finish floor, you may prefer to treat the floor. This is done by troweling a ¾-in. layer of a special gypsum compound on the subfloor and laying the finish floor on top. An additional advantage of the compound is that it is noncombustible and therefore controls the spread of fire up through a house. On the other hand, because it lacks resilience, it has little effect on impact sounds.

WHO MAKES IT

Agency Tile, Inc. · Glazed ceramic tile and pavers in browns, reds, blue-gray, off-white.

American Olean Tile Co. · Tremendous selection of all kinds of ceramic tile. Pre-grouted tiles.

ARCO Chemical Co. · Wood tiles in seven colors.

Armstrong Cork Co. · Vinyl, rotovinyl, cushioned vinyl, Tredway do-it-yourself vinyl flooring. Vinyl-asbestos tiles, including self-adhering and 9×9-in. tiles. Vinyl cove bases.

Bangkok Industries, Inc. · Parquet blocks and strips in teak and other exotic woods. Blocks in an enormous range of patterns.

Billy Penn Corp. · Steel bridging.

Boiardi Products Corp. · Seamless flooring. Polyester terrazzo. Cement terrazzo tiles in several shapes, ⅝ in. or ¾ in. thick.

Bondex International, Inc. · Fiberglass-reinforced cement for leveling floors.

E. L. Bruce Co. · Prefinished oak strip floors. Prefinished oak plank floors with and without pegs; one type installed with wrought-iron nails. Prefinished oak and teak parquet blocks.

Buckingham-Virginia Slate Corp. · Black slate tiles.

Burke Industries · Rubber tile and sheet flooring.

Connor Forest Industries. · Maple strip flooring.

Crown Mosaic-Parquet Flooring, Inc. · Unfinished and prefinished parquet blocks in oak, walnut, cherry, mahogany, ash, cedar, and maple. Oak and maple strip flooring.

Dallas Ceramics Co. · Individual glazed tiles, unglazed mosaics, and quarry tiles.

Diamond K Co. · Hard pine boards taken from old buildings; from 6 to 20 in. wide.

Dodge Cork Co. · Waxed or urethane-coated cork tiles in 1-ft. squares and 3/16-in. and 5/16-in. thicknesses.

Dur-A-Flex, Inc. · Seamless flooring specifically for do-it-yourself application.

Elon, Inc. · Individual tiles handmade in Mexico.

Erecto-Pat, Inc. · Wood decks in kits ready for erection range from 4×4 to 20×20 ft.

Fritz Chemical Co. · Square plastic terrazzo tiles ¼ in. and 3/16 in. thick.

H. B. Fuller Co. · Seamless flooring. Epoxy terrazzo.

Georgia Marble Co. · Marble chips in many blends for terrazzo floors.

Hanley Co. · Stain-resistant paving brick. Quarry tile.

Heckman Building Products, Inc. · Steel bridging.

Homasote Co. · Resilient fiberboard underlayment panels to deaden noise under wood floors, ceramic tile, resilient flooring, and carpet. Fiberboard subflooring panels for use under wall-to-wall carpet.

Horner Flooring Co. · Maple strip flooring.

Howmet Corp. · Steel bridging.

H & R Johnson, Inc. · Quarry tiles.

Interpace Corp. · Ceramic tiles in excellent colors and generally larger than average size.

Johnson Rubber Co. · Vinyl and rubber edging strips to protect carpets. Rubber pads for use under sleepers to improve resilience and sound-absorption qualities of wood floors built on concrete slabs.

Karnak Chemical Corp. · Mastic flooring underlayment for use on concrete slabs.

Mannington Mills, Inc. · Vinyl and cushioned vinyl sheet flooring.

Maybrik. · $\frac{1}{2}$-in.-thick glazed and unglazed paving bricks in several colors and shapes. $\frac{1}{4}$-in. bricks.

Montgomery Ward & Co. · Prefinished oak parquet blocks. Solid oak squares. $\frac{3}{8}$-in.-thick pegged oak planks. Vinyl-asbestos tiles. Vinyl, rotovinyl, and cushioned vinyl sheet flooring.

North Bangor Slate Co. · Black slate, cut and irregular.

Peace Flooring Co. · Finished and unfinished parquet blocks in red and white oak, walnut, and maple.

Peterson Chemical Corp. · Torginol and Placonite seamless flooring. Lexide rubber-asbestos underlayment for seamless floors.

R.C.A. Rubber Co. · Rubber flooring in sheets and tiles.

Rector Mineral & Trading Corp. · Cork floor tiles, plastic-finished, in 1-ft. squares and various thicknesses.

Rising & Nelson Slate Co. · Irregular and cut slate in assorted colors.

Robbins Flooring Co. · Maple strip flooring.

J. G. Robinson, Inc. · Quartzite-sandstone flagstones in grays and buffs. Irregular chunks or cut rectangles $\frac{3}{4}$ to 1 in. thick.

Savogran. · Water-mixed floor leveling compound.

Sears Roebuck & Co. · Self-adhering, prefinished oak parquet blocks in standard designs. Prefinished oak veneer planks with pegs.

Summitville Tiles, Inc. · Mosaic, glazed, and quarry tiles in many shapes and colors.

Teco. · Steel bridging.

Thermwell Products Co. · Aluminum carpet-edging strips.

United States Gypsum Co. · Gypsum acoustical underlayment board. Trowel-on gypsum compound for soundproofing and fireproofing floors.

Uvalde Rock Asphalt Co., Azrock Floor Products Div. · Vinyl-asbestos tiles, including self-stick tiles. Asphalt tiles in 9-in. squares.

Vermont Structural Slate Co. · Unfading green, purple, and purple-and-green slates in natural cleft or smooth rubbed finish. Cut and uncut.

Vestal Manufacturing Co. · Steel bridging.

Williams Lumber Co. · Cypress flooring.

13

Stairs

Unless a house is built on flat ground without a basement or attic, it almost certainly has at least one flight of stairs. Many houses have more: up to the front and back doors; from the first floor to the second and from the second to the third; up to the attic; down to the basement indoors and out. What's more, it is not unusual to add new flights of stairs when an addition is made to a house.

No matter what their purpose, all stairs have the potential of being tiring and hazardous. Some also have the potential of contributing considerable charm and beauty to the house. For these reasons, stair design and construction cannot be taken lightly.

To be sure, anyone can design a stair, and anyone can build a strictly utilitarian stair. But so many problems may arise in fitting a stair into a house (especially an existing house) and in designing a stair so it is attractive and isn't tiring or dangerous that expert help from an architect and/or skilled carpenter is usually called for. The only time you should go it alone is when you put in a simple exterior stair, basement stair, attic stair, or prefabricated circular stair.

STAIR DESIGN AND CONSTRUCTION. The principal parts of a stair are the stringers which support it, the treads on which you step, the risers (vertical boards) at the back of the treads, the railings, and the balusters and newel posts supporting the railings.

In designing a stair, the two most important points to consider are the rise and run of the stair and the headroom above it.

Rise and run can be defined as the angle of the stair, and this is determined by the depth of the treads and height of the risers.

Riser height is figured by measuring the distance from floor to floor in inches and dividing by eight. If the answer is a whole number, that is the number of risers required. If the answer contains a fraction, the next largest whole number is the number of risers required. You then divide the floor-to-floor height by the number of risers to find the exact height of the risers. For example, if floor-to-floor height is 108 in., dividing by 8 gives an answer of 13½. This means there should be 14 risers in the stair. So divide 14 into 108 to find the riser height—7⅝ in.

The depth of a tread is figured by subtracting riser height from 17 or 18 in. Thus, if riser height is 7⅝ in., tread depth should be 9⅜ or 10⅜ in. or any measurement in between—say, 10 in.

In a main stair, riser height should never exceed 8 in. It can be as much as 9 in. in a secondary stair, though this is not desirable.

Furthermore, riser height and tread depth must be uniform throughout the stair.

Headroom over a stair is measured vertically from the top of a tread at the front edge to the underside of the floor or stair above. On a main stair, the headroom should be between 7 ft. 4 in. and 7 ft. 7 in. high. The FHA minimum of 6 ft. 8 in. should be used only on a secondary stair—for example, an outside stair into a basement.

CONVENTIONAL FLOOR-TO-FLOOR STAIRS. The main stairs in a house can be straight; L-shaped with a landing at the turn; U-shaped with landings at each turn; narrow U-shaped (you might call it a double-back stair) with a single landing which is twice the width of the stairs; L-shaped with triangular-shaped treads called winders at the turn; U-shaped with winders at each turn; narrow U-shaped with winders at the turn; gracefully winding from top to bottom; or spiral.

All stairs with winders are dangerous because the treads are so narrow at the apex of the triangle.

Straight stairs are also dangerous because if you trip at the top you are likely to roll all the way down to the bottom. They are also tiring, because as a rule there's no wide space to stop and catch your breath. And they are not very attractive. But they cost least to build.

Winding stairs are also tiring and dangerous because the treads are not full depth at both sides and because you can fall a long way. But they are the most beautiful of all stairs.

L-shaped and U-shaped stairs are generally most satisfactory on all counts. Their one drawback is that they make it difficult to carry large articles up and down. This is especially true on narrow U-shaped stairs.

Regardless of their shape, stairs can be open on both sides, open on one side, or closed in by walls on both sides. Open strings, as they are called, are most attractive and decorative simply because they look and feel spacious (even though they may not be very wide) and also because of the balustrade on the open side.

Main stairs should be wide enough so two people can pass. Three feet is minimum; 40 to 42 in. is preferable —especially in L-shaped and U-shaped stairs which are closed for part of their length, because it is easier to maneuver large pieces of furniture on them.

Standard height of railings on the slanting portion of a stair is 30 in.; on landings, 34 in. All stairs should have one rail, and wide stairs should have two. Ideally, the railing should be continuous from floor to floor even if there are landings.

Since the design of main stairs varies to such an extent, you can't buy entire prefabricated flights from stock—only prefabricated parts (treads, balusters, newel posts, and rails). Today the normal way of building stairs is to have a local millwork shop assemble them in the shop according to blueprints or measurements made by the shop. Your carpenter, perhaps with the help of the shop, then makes the installation.

SPIRAL STAIRS.

Although they are dangerous and not particularly pleasant to ascend or descend (especially if you're not accustomed to them), spiral stairs are of value because they save space. You can install them where you cannot possibly fit in a conventional stair. They are rarely suitable as the only stair from floor to floor (although a few are large enough to fill the bill reasonably well). But if you need a second stair when space is limited, they are ideal. What's more, since they are rarely enclosed, they serve as an attractive decorative unit which becomes a focal point of the room in which they are used. They are also used outside to provide access to second-story balconies, decks, and rooms.

All spiral stairs are prefabricated in factories and shipped knocked down ready for assembly. If you follow the directions supplied by the maker, you will have little trouble making the installation.

Most units are made of steel with either steel or wood treads (risers are omitted). A few are all wood.

Prefabricated spiral stairs of simple but graceful design. Duvinage Corp.

The most common diameters are 42, 48, 54, 60, 66, and 72 in. Additional diameters, in 6-in. increments, are available to a maximum of 12 ft.

Every stair is made to the buyer's specifications regarding size, tread finish, and the design of the balusters and railing. When placing an order, you must specify the diameter of the stair, floor-to-floor height, location of the platform at the head of the stair, shape of the opening in the floor at the head of the stair, and the way in which you will descend the stair—clockwise or counterclockwise.

BASEMENT STAIRS.

Anyone can build a basement stair. The easiest approach is to buy a pair of ready-to-install wood or steel stringers from a lumberyard, set them in place, and nail on treads cut from 2×10-in. lumber.

The way in which the stringers are attached to the floor framing at the head of the stairs is illustrated.

OUTSIDE STAIRS.

Poured-concrete steps are built with 1 part Portland cement, $2\frac{1}{4}$ parts sand, and 3 parts coarse aggregate. In most parts of the country the concrete is poured on a 6-in. base of gravel or crushed stone. In cold areas, the steps should be further supported by digging a couple of 8-in. postholes below the first tread down to the frost line, and filling them with reinforced concrete. In both cases, the steps should be tied to the foundation walls of the house with steel

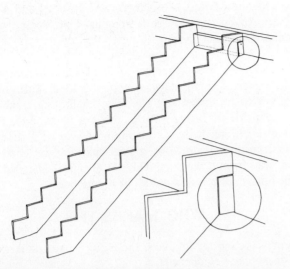

Basement and outside wood stairs are attached at the top by nailing a ledger strip (in circle) to the header, and notching the stringers to fit over it.

reinforcing rods anchored in the walls and extending 6 in. into the steps.

Pour the concrete in well-braced forms made of 2-in.-thick lumber. The treads can be surfaced with concrete or bricks.

Balustrades are prefabricated of iron or aluminum in a great many styles. They are anchored to the steps by

Stairs can spiral up clockwise or counterclockwise. American General Products, Inc.

A disappearing attic stair with rigid one-piece stringers. Bessler Disappearing Stairway Co.

setting the newel posts into the concrete or into metal flanges fastened to the tops of the treads.

Simple wood steps are built like basement stairs with precut stringers and 2×10-in. treads. The stringers should be treated with wood preservative, and the lower ends raised a couple of inches off the ground on concrete piers.

Stairs supported on steel stringers are considerably more attractive than those on wood. In fact, they're so attractive that they are often used inside modern and contemporary houses for main flights between floors. The stringers are available in several styles with and without landings. They are attached to the house according to the manufacturer's directions, and at the base are bolted to a concrete slab or piers.

The same manufacturers can also provide simple balusters to which wood railings are attached. You make your own treads from 2-in. lumber.

DISAPPEARING ATTIC STAIRS. These come completely assembled for installation in a prepared opening. They are attached to a trap door so that you just have to reach up and pull them down. There are two types. In one, the stair is a rigid unit which slides up and down parallel with the door. In the other, the stair is in three hinged sections which fold up into a compact bundle on top of the door. This is somewhat more wobbly and less safe than the rigid stair but requires much less room in the attic.

Folding stairs fit into homes with floor-to-ceiling

147

heights of 7 ft. 6 in. to 8 ft. 9 in. One model that is 16 in. wide requires a rough opening in the ceiling of approximately 23×54 in. An 18-in.-wide model requires a 26×54-in. opening.

Rigid stairs are available in many more sizes. They can be used with ceiling heights of 7 ft. 7 in. to 16 ft. 4 in. They are 17 or 19 in. wide and have treads from 4 to 8 in. deep. The smallest unit requires a ceiling opening of 2×4 ft. and headroom in the attic of 3 ft. Most units, however, require an opening of at least 2×5½ ft. and headroom of 3½ ft. or better.

ELEVATORS. If there's someone in your family who can't climb stairs, you must either build a bedroom on the first floor or put in an elevator. The latter is the less expensive course. You can even rent inclined-stair elevators, since they do not have to be built in. In fact, all you have to do is anchor them on the right or left side of the stair and plug into a 15-amp outlet.

Inclined elevators can be installed only on straight stairs. Rail length is sized to suit the stair, but cannot exceed 28 ft. The elevators are available with a foot platform and a flat seat that swivels, a seat that doesn't swivel, or a swivel seat with back and arm. When not in use, the seat and footrest fold up into a compact bundle against the wall. Two-seat units are available. The power unit can be placed at the head of the stairs, under the stairs, or in a basement.

Elevators are either completely enclosed in a shaft or simply set in a corner, in which case the opening in the upstairs floor is covered with a door that automatically closes when the car descends. The cars are built to

An inclined elevator can be installed on either side of straight stairs. Inclinator Co. of America.

various dimensions. The largest is 3 ft. deep and 4 ft. wide. An enclosed shaft is roughly 1 ft. deeper and wider than the car.

DUMBWAITERS. An electric dumbwaiter is nothing more than a small elevator enclosed in a shaft. It is fabricated to almost any size. The smallest cars, which are capable of lifting 100 lb., have a maximum floor area of 6¼ sq. ft. and a maximum height of 3 ft. The cars run up and down on a steel guide rail fastened to the wall behind the cars. The power unit is installed at the bottom or top of the shaft or to one side.

WHO MAKES IT

American General Products, Inc. · Steel spiral stairs with maximum 6-ft. diameter.

Bessler Disappearing Stairway Co. · One-piece and folding attic stairs.

Bilco Co. · Steel basement stair stringers.

Julius Blum & Co. · Balustrades, railings, balusters, newel posts primarily of metal (aluminum, bronze, steel) in infinite modern and traditional designs. Metal stair nosings.

Buckingham-Virginia Slate Corp. · Natural cleft unfading black slate treads.

Burke Industries. · Rubber stair treads and 7-in.-wide risers.

Flinchbaugh/Murray Corp. · Dumbwaiters.

Inclinator Co. of America. · Inclined elevators. Elevators. Dumbwaiters.

Johnson Rubber Co. · Rubber and vinyl stair treads and stair nosings.

Montgomery Ward & Co. · Ornamental iron and aluminum balustrades. Folding attic stairs.

Morgan Co. · Traditional wood balusters, rails, newel posts, treads, risers, sold separately or in packages ready for installation.

Mylen Industries. · Steel spiral stairs to maximum 12-ft. diameter. Steel stair stringers. Steel balusters. Steel brackets for supporting benches on porches and decks.

S. Parker Hardware Manufacturing Corp. · Handrail brackets.

R.C.A. Rubber Co. · Rubber and vinyl strips, 7 in. wide, to protect risers. Rubber and vinyl stair treads.

Sears Roebuck & Co. · Steel handrails. Ornamental aluminum and iron balustrades.

Stair-Pak Products Co. · All-wood spiral stairs to a maximum 6-ft. diameter.

Standard Equipment, Inc., Elite Products Div. · Wrought-iron balustrades.

Thermwell Products Co. · Metal step nosings.

Vermont Marble Co. · Marble stair treads and risers.

Versa Products Co. · Wrought-iron balustrades.

14

Bathrooms

Bathroom building or remodeling is a job of many parts and expensive to boot. Even though the room you're working on is small and utilitarian, you must buy fixtures (lavatory, toilet, and tub and/or shower), fittings (faucets, drains, etc.—they are sold separately from the fixtures to which they're attached), accessories such as towel rods and paperholders, a medicine cabinet, other storage facilities (because a bathroom without space in which to store towels, soap, etc. is just as inconvenient as a bedroom without a closet), wall coverings, flooring, lights, electrical outlets, heating units, and a ventilating fan.

By the time you get through adding up the cost of all these items plus their installation, you begin to wonder whether you really should go through with the project.

Let's face it—except for the kitchen, no room in the house costs more to install or redo than a bathroom. But to turn the coin, probably no other room—including the kitchen and family room—is more important to the convenience, comfort, and deep-down pleasure of the entire family.

And anyway, if money is tight, there are certain things you may be able to do to reduce the final bill:

1. Buy white fixtures instead of colored. True, modern colored fixtures are beautiful, but they cost more than white fixtures of the same quality.

2. Install the fixtures in the same locations as those you're tearing out. This reduces installation cost. After all, there's no point in changing fixture locations just for the sake of making a change. But of course, if the old fixture arrangement was bad, that's an entirely different matter.

3. Shop for faucets and other fittings. You don't have to take those that are normally sold with fixtures. You don't even have to use fittings made by the fixture manufacturer. Many others are on the market and they may be less expensive though just as good.

4. Try to place the fixtures so all are plumbed into the same wall. This is another way to reduce installation cost but applies only if you're building a new bathroom or must change the fixture layout in an old bathroom.

5. If building a new bathroom, place it as close as possible to another bathroom—preferably back to back or with the new bathroom directly over or under the old. Here again you cut the cost of piping.

6. Install an inside bathroom. If there's space in the center of the house, it will probably be cheaper to use it than to tear down and rebuild walls for the sake of having a window which you'll rarely look out of and which won't do any better ventilating job than a ceiling fan.

7. Leave the fixture installation to a plumber, but do the rest of the work (except extensive wiring) yourself. Here you can effect a really major saving, and if you turn to the interior-wall and flooring chapters, you'll find that the work isn't half as difficult as you may think.

LAVATORIES. If you prefer to call a lavatory a sink or basin, go ahead. "Lavatory" is the word the plumbing industry uses. It covers quite a range of basically similar yet different fixtures.

To begin with, lavatories are made of porcelain enamel on cast iron (very beautiful and durable), porcelain enamel on steel (less expensive, less durable, and not available in as many shapes and designs), vitreous china (much like ceramic tile and just as beautiful and tough), fiberglass with molded-in color (durable, lightweight, and therefore easier to install but a bit noisy), acrylic (much like fiberglass but more beautifully colored—often to resemble marble), and stainless steel (rarely used despite the popularity of stainless-steel kitchen sinks).

Lavatories are classified as wall-hung, pedestal, or countertop units. The first are space-savers because they are attached to the wall and because many are of very compact design. The pipes are exposed underneath.

Pedestal types are fastened to the wall, too, but are also mounted on large central pedestals which hide the piping. Some of the lavatories are of exotic design and look much like raised fountains.

Countertop lavatories are most popular because they are surrounded by counters above vanity cabinets which hide the pipes and increase bathroom storage space. These lavatories are, in turn, classified into four subcategories:

Flush-mounting bowls are suspended in a stainless-steel ring. Some people object to the ring because dirt lodges against the edges and is difficult to clean out. The faucets and spout come up either through a ledge built into the bowl or through the countertop.

Self-rimming lavatories have an integral rim which rests on the countertop. This reduces installation time and improves appearance, but the rim projects high enough above the counter to make it impossible to sweep splash water back into the bowl. Furthermore, the joint between the counter and rim is a dirt-catcher. The fittings are mounted on a ledge of the lavatory.

Under-counter lavatories are hung below an opening cut into marble or imitation-marble counters. The fittings are installed through the countertop.

Integral lavatories and countertops (with backsplashes) are molded out of one piece of acrylic or vitreous china and are installed in vanity cabinets. Because there are no joints (except at the base of the fittings, which come up through the top), cleaning is unusually easy.

Lavatory bowls more or less conform to the overall shape of the lavatory and are basically rectangular, semi-circular, circular, or oval. All are of about the same depth, but their horizontal measurements vary considerably. It's doubtful whether the manufacturers themselves know their actual capacities. So before making a purchase, you should inspect them and go through the motions of washing your hands in them.

Outside dimensions of under-counter lavatories are just a bit larger than the bowl dimensions.

Integral units made of acrylic are 19 or 22 in. deep (front to back). The 19-in. sizes are available only in widths of 25, 31, and 37 in. The 22-in. sizes range from 25 to 102 in. wide. In the larger sizes, the bowl may be centered in the counter or placed at either end. Widths above 60 in. sometimes incorporate two bowls.

Integral units of vitreous china are 20×18, 24×20, or 29×20 in.

Flush-mounting and self-rimming lavatories range from 14-in. circular models up to 30×20 in., but in most cases the size of the largest models is attributable to extra-wide rims. Only one model (measuring 29×19 in.) has an oversized bowl (23×14 in.).

Wall-hung lavatories of conventional design start at 15×12 in. and range to 24×21 in. There are also several enormous models (4 to 6 ft. long by 18 in. deep), which are known as wash sinks because they are usually installed in factory washrooms. They are not pretty, but for anyone with a lot of children, they might be ideal for installation in a mudroom or bathroom near the back door.

Wall-hung units for installation in corners are as small as 11×11 in. The largest is $18\frac{1}{2} \times 18\frac{1}{2}$ in.

Pedestal lavatories have a maximum size of $26\frac{3}{4} \times 22\frac{1}{2}$ in.

LAVATORY FITTINGS. One of the worst mistakes a homeowner can make is to try to save money on bathroom (and kitchen) faucets, pop-up drains, and other fittings. None of the many moving parts of a house can cause more trouble.

Unfortunately, there's no way the average person can distinguish a reliable, essentially maintenance-free fitting from one that will demand constant repairs. Your only guide is price: the higher it is—up to a point—the better the fitting. But watch out for fittings that are high-priced just because they are styled and finished exotically.

Most faucets and spouts have a bright chrome finish and are of basically utilitarian design. But if you want something more decorative (ornate is a better word), there's plenty to choose from: gold faucets, china faucets, and faucets made of all sorts of handsome plastics. Many of these are of rococo design.

Standard faucets fall into two basic groups—two-handle and single-handle. The former is a tried-and-true design which is easily fixed when it starts to leak—and since most new designs are made without washers, leaks don't occur very often. By contrast, faucets which are turned on and off by flipping a single lever or pushing and pulling on a single knob tend to develop more problems and are harder to fix; but they are much easier to operate since you turn them on and off and control the water temperature with one hand.

Both types of faucet have a single spout which extends only a couple of inches out over the lavatory bowl; as a result, women often complain that it does a poor job of rinsing out a dirty bowl and complicates hair-washing. One answer to these problems is a long spout which swivels. A second is a short upward-angled spout which delivers water in a fountainlike stream.

Another improvement available in double- and single-handle faucets is a watersaver device which reduces flow to 2 or 3 gal. a minute.

A third type of faucet is a revolutionary system in which water for the lavatories as well as the sinks, tubs, and showers throughout the house is mixed at a console of solenoid valves located near the water heater. From the console, a single small pipe carries water to each

Pedestal lavatory. American-Standard, Inc.

Integral lavatory and countertop of acrylic. Du Pont.

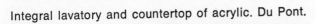

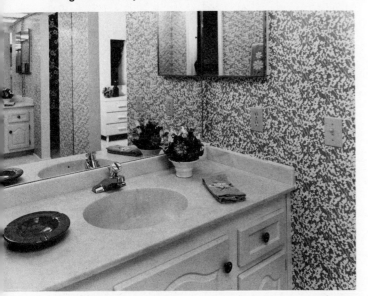

Water from this faucet arches upward. American-Standard, Inc.

Self-rimming lavatories. Above, Universal-Rundle Corp.; below, unusually large model with built-in spray attachment and swivel faucet spout. Kohler Co.

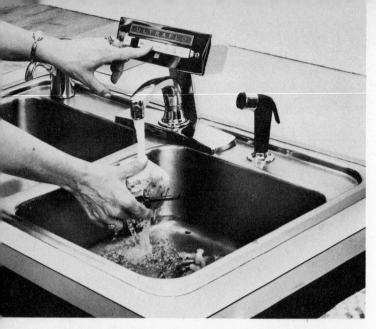

Pushbutton faucet is made for kitchen sinks and lavatories. Water temperature is set at a bank of solenoid valves installed near water heater. Ultraflo Corp.

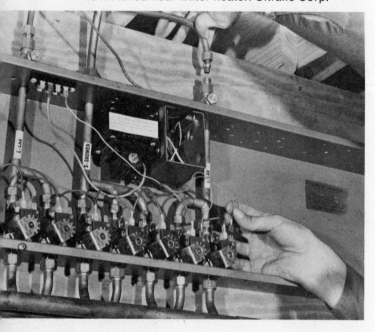

faucet. When you push a button at the faucet, a low-voltage electrical circuit signals the faucet to deliver water of the selected temperature to the spout.

At the sink there are eight buttons marked hot, warm, cold, drink (the water is bypassed around a water softener), disposer, high flow, low flow, and off. At the lavatories four buttons provide hot, warm, cold, and off. At tubs and showers, four buttons provide three warm temperatures and off. The temperature of the water as well as the rate of flow for each button is set when the system is installed (it can be readjusted later if you wish).

The system not only saves fiddling with your faucets but also saves water because you don't have to let it run until it's the right temperature and because the flow is controlled. Water-heating and installation costs are also

reduced. And you don't have any faucet washers to replace.

TOILETS. The most important thing to consider in buying a toilet, or water closet, which is always made of vitreous china (sometimes with an ABS plastic tank), is its flushing action. There are four choices:

The washdown toilet, which is now outlawed by some building codes and is no longer made by most major manufacturers, is the noisiest of all toilets and the least effective in removing wastes. It's easily identified by the very small water surface and a protruding liplike bulge below the front rim.

The reverse-trap toilet is quieter and more sanitary than the washdown but has a smaller water area and trapway than the siphon-jet. It's a good buy for the economy-minded.

The siphon-jet is an improvement in every way over the reverse-trap design. It has the best cleaning action of all residential toilets and is very quiet.

The siphon flush toilet is like the siphon-jet but has an almost silent action. Water covers most of the bowl interior. It is the most expensive toilet you can buy.

In addition to flushing action, toilets differ in a number of other ways.

In the better models, the tank and bowl are made in one piece, thus giving the toilet a low silhouette. The tank top is only about 19 in. above the floor whereas the standard top is 28 in. In other models, the tank is bolted to the top of the bowl. (There are no more toilets with the tank hung on the wall and connected to the bowl by a short L-shaped pipe.)

While the standard toilet has a more or less round bowl (as seen from the top), many models have elongated bowls. The latter are required by law in some communities.

To save water, some toilets have a smaller tank and

A low-profile one-piece toilet and matching bidet. Kohler Co.

Wall-hung toilet. Kohler Co.

with hot water so that the water in the tank is a little warmer than the air.

To remove odors more effectively, several toilets have a self-ventilating action which creates a vacuum that draws odors back through holes in the flushing rim and then into the discharge outlet.

As an aid to the elderly and infirm, some toilets are made with 18-in.-high (rather than the customary 15-in.-high) bowls.

Wall-hung toilets are suspended above the floor to simplify mopping underneath. The toilets also make it possible to adjust seat height to suit the users.

Toilets with triangular tanks fit into corners to save space in tiny bathrooms and powder rooms.

Toilets with outlets above floor level discharge wastes into the wall rather than the floor. Thus they simplify and reduce the cost of installation in houses built on concrete slabs.

Finally, there are toilets made for use in basements below the sewer line. When flushed, wastes are pumped up into the house drain, from which they flow by gravity into the sewer.

Toilet sizes vary only slightly. The most compact design (with reverse-trap flushing action) is 17 in. wide by 21 in. deep. The largest is $22\frac{3}{8} \times 30$ in. An average size is 20×27 in. With few exceptions, all toilets are installed $\frac{1}{2}$ to 1 in. out from the back wall.

New flushing mechanism operates on hydraulic pressure, eliminating need for float ball. JH Industries, Inc.

Thermostatic valve behind the round plate mixes warm water with cold so toilet tank won't sweat. C. & L. Pegg.

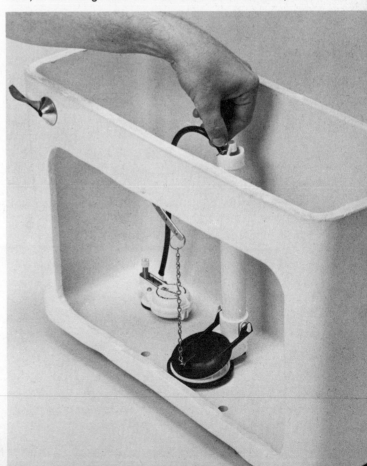

use no more than $3\frac{1}{2}$ gal. per flush—about $1\frac{1}{2}$ gal. less than a conventional tank.

To stop condensation from forming on tanks in hot weather, some tanks come with a built-in polystyrene liner. For others there are optional liners of urethane foam. All others—including the millions of toilets now in use—can be equipped with an easily installed thermostatic valve which mixes the incoming cold water

Small plastic toilet tank stores air under compression; uses less water for flushing than conventional toilets. Water Control Products/N.A., Inc.

Toilet fittings. Flushing mechanisms in new toilets have been improved to the point where you don't have to fiddle with them frequently to make them operate properly, but most still depend on a float ball to control the water level.

If you have to replace the flushing mechanism in an old toilet, look for a unit which does away with the float ball entirely. These are turned on and off by hydraulic pressure rather than by the action of the ball floating on the water in the tank. Thus you put an end to the problems which arise when a float ball becomes waterlogged or the washers in the ballcock wear out. In addition, you can adjust the water level in the tank just by turning a knob on the fill valves.

Another solution to the problem of the old flushing mechanism which doesn't work is a unique tank which contains only one simple moving part and holds only about 2½ gal. of water. The tank works much like the pressure tank in a private water system. It is completely enclosed so that air is held under compression. When the toilet is flushed, the air forces the stored water to flow rapidly into the bowl. Then as fresh water flows into the tank from the supply line, the air is once again compressed and ready to discharge the water when the toilet is flushed a second time. The tank is made of plastic and is much more compact than the standard tank. It can be quickly installed on any toilet in which the tank is bolted to the back rim of the bowl.

BATHTUBS. Bathtubs have changed more than any other fixture in the bathroom. To the traditional porcelain-enamel-on-cast-iron and porcelain-enamel-on-steel tubs have been added lightweight, easy-to-install fiberglass and acrylic tubs. And the advent of these plastic tubs has brought a brand-new kind of tub with end and back walls which extend above the showerhead (approximately 6 ft. above the floor). In one case, the ceiling over the tub is made part of the package. Result: No more dirt-catching, hard-to-caulk cracks around the tub rim. No more cracks in the walls at the corners of the tub. Since the walls are seamless, they're easier to clean. And for good measure, the soapdish is molded into the back wall.

The new wall-surround tubs, which are also used for shower bathing, are designed for recessing; and because of their light weight, one man can handle the entire installation job. There are two sizes: 48×36 in. and 60×36 in. (or thereabouts).

If you don't like the design of the one-piece tubs, you can achieve the same effect by putting in a plastic tub which is specifically designed for the addition of matching wall panels. But as noted in Chapter 8, similar panels are available for installation over any recessed tub.

But this is only one of the new kinds of tub. Another is the tub recessed in the floor.

In times past, about the only way anyone could have a sunken tub was to build it of concrete and line it with tile. This is still done by people who want tubs the size of miniature swimming pools. Then a few fixture manufacturers began to turn out cast-iron and steel tubs which could be built in so they looked more or less like sunken tubs. But these lacked appeal because they were the same size and shape as ordinary tubs; and while it was easy to build them into the floor of a stage, it was considerably more difficult to drop them below the level of the main floor.

But then came plastic tubs and suddenly the whole problem of how to build a tub which can be sunk into the floor or into a raised platform above the floor was solved.

The new tubs are like a cupcake pan made for one cake. They have rather wide flat rims with a bowl in the center. But unlike a cupcake pan, the bowl is only occasionally round. Usually it is oval. Sometimes it is almost rectangular.

Generally it is big. The smallest sunken tub measures 40×40 in., which doesn't sound like much but actually has an area only a little less than that of a standard tub. And what it lacks in area it makes up in extra depth. The drain is 32 in. below the rim so that when you're perching on the seat molded into one side, you are almost totally immersed.

Other sunken tubs measure 60×36×20 in. (4 in. deeper than normal); 66×42×16; 72×36×16. Some of these are pretty straightforward tubs; others have armrests or seats. But the biggest of all is a Roman bath

opposite
New bathtub designs. 1, a throwback to the past, Kohler Co. 2, deep 36-in.-diameter dunking tub, American-Standard, Inc. 3, more or less conventional sunken tub, Kohler Co. 4, enormous two-person tub, Kohler Co. 5, another two-person tub in clover-leaf shape, Adamsez Baths, Inc. 6, one-piece acrylic tub with integral walls and ceiling and unframed sliding doors of safety glass, Powers Regulator Co.

1

2

3

4

5

6

Fiberglass tub with integral walls and grab bar, Universal-Rundel Corp.

measuring 84×66×16¼ in.—almost the equivalent of three standard-size conventional tubs. The oval bowl is so big, in fact, that the manufacturer has punched holes through the rim for two complete sets of faucets.

Another new kind of bathtub is a glorified throwback to the past. It's a freestanding enameled cast-iron unit on gold- or chrome-plated ball-and-claw feet. The antique faucets are separate and finished to match the feet. The tub is available in white, red, or black enamel and painted to match on the outside. The size is 72×37½ in.

Standard recessed tubs are approximately 30 in. wide and 12, 14, 15, or 16 in. deep. They are made in 4,

Simple attachment for creating a whirlpool bath in any tub. Kohler Co.

4½, 5, 5½, and 6-ft. lengths. Other recessed tubs are 48×42, 42×36, 42×30, and 39×38 in. And there is one oversized 72×54-in. tub with a built-in seat.

Tubs for installation in a corner with either the right or left end exposed measure 60×30 and 48×44 in.

WHIRLPOOL BATHS. Any tub can be converted into a whirlpool bath. The oldest of the mechanisms used is a powerful electric pump which is hung over the side of the tub whenever you want to take the ache out of your muscles in hot, pulsating, bubbly water. A newer and simpler mechanism is little more than a pipe which is permanently connected to the underside of a special spout that can be installed in place of most conventional spouts. It operates by mixing water flowing into the tub with air.

If you would prefer a real whirlpool bath, several tubs are made specifically for the purpose (most of them can also be used as a conventional tub). They include:

A conventional recessed, 5-ft., enamel-on-steel tub with four jet inlets.

A 6×3-ft. fiberglass tub with three inlets. It can be recessed or sunk in the floor.

A 4×5-ft. fiberglass tub with four inlets. It is 2 ft. deep. Since it is skirted on all four sides, it can be freestanding in the center of a large bathroom. It can also be recessed in the space normally occupied by a standard 5-ft. tub or sunk partially or wholly in the floor.

A 53×30-in. fiberglass tub with two inlets. It is 34 in. deep. Made without exterior walls, it is generally recessed in the floor but can be set on the floor and enclosed with any kind of skirting you like.

All the above tubs are permanently plumbed in. The largest baths are not: you plug them into any 240-volt outlet, and fill and drain them like an aboveground swimming pool. The smaller unit is 8×5×2 ft. and has three inlets. The larger is 8×7×2 ft. and has six inlets. Both are made of fiberglass and are skirted on all sides. A combination filter and heater is available as an optional accessory.

All whirlpool baths come completely factory-assembled with pump, jets, piping, drain, and overflow.

Bathtub fittings. The simplest tub drain, which is rarely used any longer, is closed with a rubber stopper on the end of a chain. In another kind of simple drain, the plug is opened by pulling it up with your hand, and closed by pushing down. For cleaning, it can be pulled all the way out.

The most popular drain plugs are controlled by a lever in the overflow outlet in the end wall of the tub. In one case, the lever controls a pop-up drain like that in lavatories. In another case, the plug is concealed below the drain opening, which is covered with a strainer.

Flow-regulating shower heads. Trigger on left valve allows you to cut off water while soaping. Merwin Manufacturing, Inc.

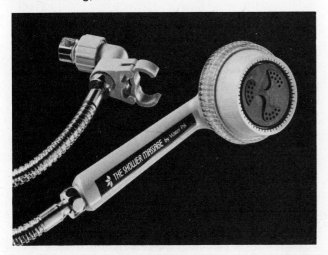

Spray from this personal shower head can be adjusted from fine to coarse. Teledyne Aquatec.

Faucets are installed in the wall above the end of the tub. Some have two handles, others a single handle. The same faucets control the water for both the tub spout and shower head. Normally when you turn the water on, water flows from the tub spout. To make it flow from the shower head, you press a button in the top of the spout. When the faucets are turned off after you have taken a shower, the diverter in the tub spout automatically returns to its normal position. In some tubshower controls, however, diversion of water from the tub spout to the shower head is done with a handle mounted on the wall with the hot- and cold-water faucets.

The safest and best type of faucet for a tub that is used for shower bathing is a mixing valve which balances the water pressure. Once you set it for the desired water temperature, you don't have to worry about being scalded or frozen because of changes in the pressure in the hot- and cold-water supply lines.

It takes just one hand to operate a mixing valve. In addition to adjusting the water temperature, the valve turns the water on and off.

Shower heads which can be adjusted from a fine to a coarse spray by turning a handle on the head are now standard for quality installations. But flow-regulating heads are available in only a few models and from about only half the manufacturers of bathroom fittings. These are designed to cut the rate of water flow and thus reduce water usage by as much as 60% without reducing the cleansing effects of the shower. Once you install such a shower head, however, you can't switch back and forth at will between partial flow and full flow. The change can be made only by removing the head and pulling out the regulator inside.

Personal showers are the newest idea in shower bathing, although they have been used in Europe for years. They are small hand-held shower heads which let bathers direct the stream of water to any part of the body and particularly let women shower without wetting their hair. But the main appeal stressed in advertising is the "massaging," "stroking," "pulsating," etc. effect of the water on the body. (Each manufacturer claims to have a different water action. Some heads can be adjusted to provide several actions.)

The shower heads come with a long hose which is connected to the shower arm in place of the built-in head, to the built-in shower head, or to the tub spout. (There are also personal showers which are snapped onto a kitchen or bathroom faucet.) The head itself can be mounted in a fixed position anywhere on the walls

Personal shower can be raised or lowered on the wall-mounted bar; removed and used by hand. Interbath, Inc.

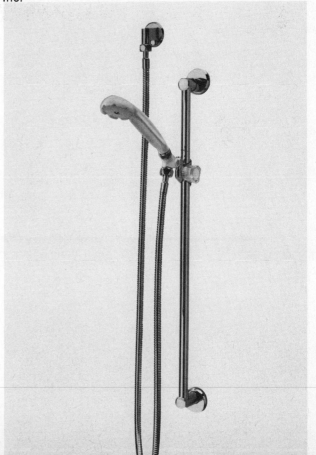

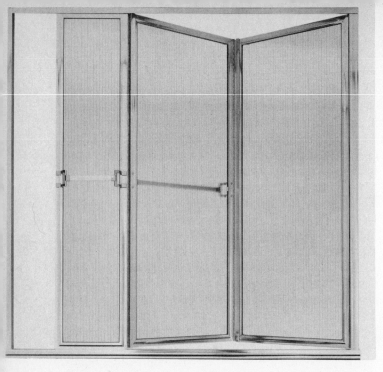

Bifold plastic-glazed shower door gives almost full access to all parts of bathtub. Midland Manufacturing Corp.

surrounding the tub, clamped to a chrome-plated rod mounted vertically on the wall so it can be raised and lowered to suit the bather, or hung in a wall holder from which it is removed when in use.

One-piece fiberglass shower stall. Kohler Co.

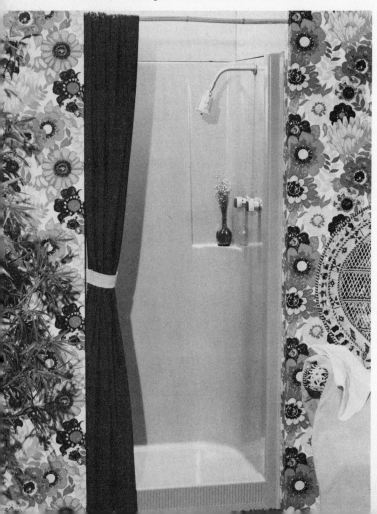

Shower doors for tubs. Doors used in place of shower curtains are available to fit all standard recessed and corner tubs. To prevent serious accidents, they should always be glazed with safety glass or plastic. The aluminum or chrome-plated brass frames are quickly installed by screwing to the surrounding walls.

Shower doors are usually bypass sliding doors (see Chapter 7) which provide access to only one-half of the tub at one time. But other designs are available. In one, the door consists of a fixed panel at one end of the tub and a hinged panel at the other end. In another, there are two doors, each pivoted at its center. Neither of these doors, however, is any better than a sliding door in providing access to a tub.

The only doors which let you reach into all parts of the tub are folding units. One is a glass bifold which swings back into the recess like a telephone-booth door. The other, made of styrene, pushes back from one end of the tub to the other like a folding closet door. It is made in stock sizes to fit all recessed tubs and can be custom-made to fit corner tubs and tubs with raised seats at the back end. Closely related is a folding door made in two panels which can be slid back and forth like bypass sliding doors or which can be folded back to the opposite ends of the tub in accordion fashion.

SHOWER STALLS. The least expensive shower stall you can put into your home is a prefab. It is also the easiest to install.

The smallest sizes have enamel-covered steel walls which are anchored to a precast imitation-stone receptor (floor) made of fiberglass and plastic resins mixed with stone. The stalls measure 30×30, 32×32, and 36×36 in. The best models are 81 in. high—about 6 in. more than cheaper models. They can be freestanding, or placed in a corner or in a niche. In one 36×36-in. corner model, the door is set at a 45° angle across the front corner of the stall.

Steel shower stalls, however, have generally given way to those made of fiberglass or acrylic. These not only come in larger sizes but also have a variety of special features such as molded-in soapdishes and seats. Conventional rectangular stalls which are usually meant to be built into a wall come in the same heights as steel stalls and in the following sizes: 32×32, 34×32, 36×32, 36×36, 48×36, and 60×36 in. In almost all cases, the floor and walls are molded together so there is no chance of leaking except around the drain. Several models come with a built-in plastic ceiling or can be equipped with a ceiling.

Two unique fiberglass shower stalls are round instead of rectangular. The 36-in.-diameter model has a semicircular door which slides back into the stall when opened. The other model is shaped something like a snail and occupies a space 56 in. wide by 40 in. deep. The stall is entered through a narrow opening at one side; the bathing area is contained in the other side so that water cannot splash out through the open door.

Semi-prefabricated fiberglass shower stalls are essentially the same as complete prefabs except that they are in four parts—three wall panels and a receptor—which are assembled on the job.

Despite the advantages of factory-built shower stalls, many homeowners prefer stalls built to order—if for no other reason, because these can be built to any size and shape.

Ceramic or glass tile is usually used for the walls, but laminated plastics similar to those used for covering walls above tubs (see Chapter 8) are gaining popularity. Receptors are made either of imitation stone or ceramic tile. The stone receptors are less likely to leak and easier to clean but are made in only the most popular shower-stall sizes and shapes (square, rectangular, and five-sided corner type). Ceramic floors are more attractive and can, of course, be made to any design. To prevent leaking, the tiles must be laid in cement or a waterproof organic adhesive over a carefully formed one-piece sheet of lead, copper, or heavyweight composition material.

Shower-stall doors and fittings. Like tub-shower recesses, shower stalls can be curtained or equipped with shatterproof glass or plastic doors. The latter are made like tub doors with hinged, sliding, bifold, or folding panels. Some door manufacturers also supply fixed glass or plastic wall panels for stalls built into a corner or projected out from a back wall.

Shower-stall controls and heads are like those in recessed tubs. Drains are unstoppered and covered with a grille.

STEAM BATHS. Steam-generating appliances for converting recessed tubs and shower stalls into steam baths are small suitcase-size units built into a vanity, closet, basement, or attic up to about 20 ft. away from the bath. The generators are equipped with electronic controls and timers so there is little chance of the bather being scalded. Unit size depends on the cubic-foot capacity of the bath.

Any tub or shower stall can be used for steam bathing provided the walls and ceiling are surfaced with tile or plastic which is not damaged by steam. The opening to the tub or stall must be tightly closed with glass or plastic doors which extend all the way to the ceiling (if they don't extend to the ceiling, the space above existing doors must be filled). A 240-volt electrical circuit brings power to the generator. Water is introduced to the generator through a ¼-in. copper tube connected into an existing supply line, and steam is carried from the generator to the bath through a ½-in. tube.

BIDETS. Bidets are 15-in.-high washbowls which the user sits astride to wash the pelvic and anal areas of the body. They are also used for washing and soaking aching feet.

Made of vitreous enamel, the fixture is approximately 15 in. wide and 22 in. from front to back. Water enters either in a fountainlike spray from an inlet in the bottom of the bowl or through a flushing rim which washes down the sides of the bowl. A pop-up drain holds water in the bowl.

PACKAGED BATHROOMS. If you want to build a complete bathroom into a small space at minimum cost, consider the packaged bathroom. It comes preplumbed, prewired, and equipped with walls, floor, ceiling, fixtures, fittings, accessories, and lights; consequently, it can be installed and ready for use a couple of hours after the piping connecting the unit into the house plumbing is roughed in.

The principal parts of the bathroom—walls, floor, ceiling, tub, lavatory, and medicine cabinet—are molded out of fiberglass. These are shipped from the factory in three or four large sections which will pass through a 30-in. door. The sections are bolted together and fastened to the house framing to form a rigid, virtually seamless module. Holes for heating and ventilating ducts are cut through the walls as necessary. Finally, a conventional vitreous-china toilet is set in place and all fittings and accessories are installed.

Since the bathrooms don't have windows, they are normally installed in the center of a house, although it is possible to cut a window opening above the tub. The minimum space required for the smaller of the two available bathrooms is 62 in. wide, 56 in. deep, and 88 in. high. The larger unit requires a space 70 in. wide, 69 in. deep, and 89 in. high.

PIPING. A census taken of the piping materials used in residential plumbing systems in the United States would bring to light an interesting cast of characters. In thousands of old houses the supply pipes are made of galvanized steel. In a few, they are made of brass. The drain lines are made of a mixture of galvanized steel and cast iron.

In houses built since World War II, copper tubing has almost completely replaced steel and brass in the supply lines; and in still more recent houses, it has also taken the place of steel and iron in the drain lines.

And in a few very new houses, plastic has come in in place of copper in both the supply and drainage systems.

Piping, in brief, has changed and continues to change. Steel and brass lost out to copper for supply lines because they are, in many parts of the country, either eaten out by corrosive water or clogged by hard water. Copper is little affected by either problem. In addition, because it has a smoother surface, it can usually be used in smaller sizes to carry the same volume of water. It takes up less space in the walls, and it goes in much more easily and quickly.

As a drainage material, copper took a longer time to become popular and is still unacceptable in some communities. But here again it has generally displaced iron and steel because, despite its high cost, it is so much easier to install that labor cost is cut drastically. Furthermore, it takes up much less space than cast iron, and because of its smoother bore, it can often be used in smaller sizes.

Copper is the standard piping material today. Three types are used:

Type L has relatively thick walls so it can carry hot and cold water under high pressures. So-called hard tube comes in straight, rigid lengths up to 20 ft. Soft tube, which is easily bent, comes in coils up to 60 ft. long. In new construction, hard tubes are generally used throughout the house. Soft tubes are mainly used in existing houses because of the ease with which they can be run through the walls. However, they should be used only in vertical pipe runs (risers). In horizontal runs they may sag, collect water at the low points, and burst in freezing weather.

(Type K copper tube is very similar to Type L but is normally used only for carrying water underground to the house.)

Type M has thinner walls than Type L and can be used only in drain lines. It's a rigid tube made in 20-ft. lengths and diameters of no less than 2 in.

DWV has such thin walls that many building codes do not accept it for use in drain lines, even though it has proved more than adequate for this purpose in many other areas. It is also a rigid tube available in 20-ft. lengths and large diameters.

Copper tubing is today almost always installed with sweated (soldered) joints. Once in, it usually causes no serious problems and is forgotten. It may, however, react to certain corrosive waters and make greenish-blue stains in plumbing fixtures. This can be prevented by installing a water conditioner (see Chapter 17). In drainage systems, copper tubes are also sometimes annoying because when a second-floor toilet is flushed, the water pouring down through the tubes in the walls sounds like Niagara Falls. This, too, can be prevented, but only by opening the walls and encasing the pipe in a special insulation made for such purposes or in countless layers of tightly wrapped asphalt-saturated building felt.

In the long run, copper tube will undoubtedly be displaced by plastic pipe. The change is already starting, because plastic is cheaper than copper and seems to be totally immune to problems caused by water. However, no one type of plastic has yet demonstrated that it is the best for use in all piping. As a result, the pipes used inside the house are made of three different materials:

PVC pipe is suitable only for carrying cold water in supply lines. It is a rigid pipe sold in 10-ft. lengths.

CPVC pipe can be used in both hot- and cold-water supply lines. It also is rigid and comes in 10-ft. lengths.

ABS pipe is made in rigid, 10-ft. lengths and in large diameters for use in drainage systems only.

MEDICINE CABINETS. There are two ways of installing medicine cabinets: in the wall between the studs and on the wall surface. The majority of cabinets are made for one installation or the other, but a few can be used either way, and some manufacturers offer a kit to adapt a recessed cabinet to wall mounting.

Generally it is better to recess than to surface-mount a cabinet because the cabinet doesn't protrude so far and therefore looks better. But cabinet capacities are limited, since the cabinets are supposed to fit within standard stud openings; for this reason, most are approximately 14 or 30 in. wide (although a few measure 12, 18, or 24 in.). The cabinets can be centered over lavatories only if the lavatories are centered on a stud space. And the noise of people rummaging in the cabinets may be clearly audible and objectionable to people sleeping on the other side of the wall.

By contrast, the placement of surface-mounted cabinets is not affected by the stud spacing or by pipes and wiring concealed in the walls. They create no noise problem. They are easier to install. And they come in more sizes and designs.

Surface-mounted cabinets range from 14 to 61 in. wide and project from the wall 4 to 8 in. Standard models are 15 to 36 in. high (roughly the same as recessed cabinets). In addition, there are long, flower-box-like cabinets only 7 to 9 in. high which are usually installed under mirrors mounted flat against the walls. And there are tall, narrow, wedge-shaped cabinets which are installed in corners adjacent to wall-mounted mirrors so you can see both sides of your face at once.

Doors on both recessed and surface-mounted cabinets are, with few exceptions, mirrored. (One nonmirrored type is meant to be covered with wall-

Surface-mounted medicine cabinet with drawers and a shelf. Allibert, Inc.

Bathroom vanity, Westinghouse Electric Corp.

paper so the cabinets are more or less concealed.) On narrow cabinets the doors are hinged; on wide units, they slide. In some cases, mirrors are hinged to both sides of the cabinet to form a triptych. In the deepest cabinets, shelves are mounted on the backs of doors.

Many cabinets have built-in fluorescent lights, either across the top of the cabinet or on the sides. Some have locks. And some have an open shelf below the door.

Installation of surface-mounted cabinets is a simple job of driving four long screws through the backs into the studs. Recessed cabinets which fit between an adjacent pair of studs are screwed through the sides into the studs. It is not necessary to install cross blocks between the studs above and below the cabinet, although in new construction these are normally used. When a large cabinet filling two stud spaces is installed, however, 2×4-in. headers must be nailed horizontally between the studs. The lower header supports the cabinet; the upper supports the intermediate stud in the wall above.

VANITIES. Built-in under-lavatory cabinets—normally made of wood—are available for the most part from manufacturers of kitchen cabinets but are also sold by manufacturers of bathroom fixtures or medicine

Vanity with extra cabinets, International Paper Co.

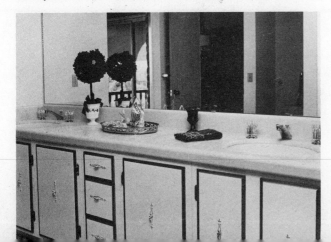

cabinets. If you cannot find the size you want in a stock design, you can have it made by a local cabinet or millwork shop.

Since the cabinets generally are not a great deal wider than the lavatories, they have doors on the front. Much wider cabinets are made, however. In these, the space not directly beneath the lavatory may have doors with shelves behind, drawers, or a combination of drawers and shelves.

The standard depth of vanities is 21 in.; height, 29½ in. Units as shallow as 16 in. are made for very small lavatories. Standard widths are 24, 30, 36, 42, 48, and 60 in. If a longer row of cabinets is needed, you just

A useful addition to a vanity is a soiled-clothes hamper. H. J. Scheirich Co.

buy additional 12-, 15-, or 18-in. cabinets and bolt them to the sides of the vanity.

In addition to conventional cabinets, some vanity makers offer a cabinet with a tilt-out soiled-clothes hamper, and vanity fronts which can be used in place of under-lavatory cabinets. The latter, like kitchen-sink fronts, are nothing more than a frame with doors. The frame is fastened between the cabinets on either side. The bathroom floor serves as the bottom of the space enclosed.

Vanity countertops are made of the same materials and in the same way as kitchen countertops. The alter-

Mirror with built-in lights makes shaving and make-up easier. Allibert, Inc.

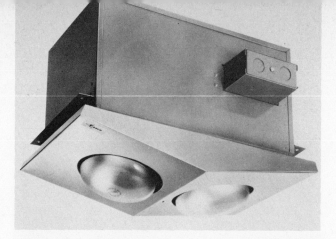

Bathroom ceiling heater wtih infrared heat lamps. Fasco Industries, Inc.

native is to install a lavatory which is molded into a top (see lavatories above).

OTHER BATHROOM CABINETS. Two other types of cabinet are sold by manufacturers of vanities.

Utility cabinets are approximately 7 ft. high, 18 in. wide, and 21 in. deep. The cabinets have two doors, one above the other. The space at the top is equipped with adjustable shelves; that below is an open compartment used for cleaning tools, etc.

Wall cabinets are 30 or 36 in. high, 15 or 18 in. wide, and 6 in. deep.

ACCESSORIES. Accessories include soapdishes, paperholders, toothbrush and tumbler holders, shower rods, towel bars, towel rings, towel ladders, towel hooks, coat hooks, solid shelves, rod shelves from which towels can be hung, shelves with drawers underneath, grab bars, facial-tissue dispensers, soap dispensers, and mirrors. No one manufacturer offers all these items. Mirrors are normally available from medicine-cabinet rather than accessories manufacturers.

Accessories are made of ceramic tile, metal (brass is best), plastics, or wood in ultramodern or rococo styling.

Paper, soap, and tumbler holders can be recessed or surface-mounted. They are approximately 6 in. square. In one unusual recessed paperholder, the ready-for-use roll of paper projects from the wall and a spare roll is

Combination ventilating fan-heater-light. Broan Manufacturing Co.

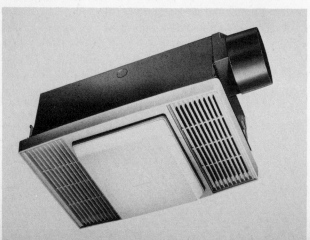

concealed behind it. Another recessed accessory contains a tumbler, toothbrushes, and bar of soap behind a hinged door.

Towel bars are 18, 24, 30, and 36 in. long.

Straight grab bars are 9, 16, 24, and 32 in. long. L-shaped bars, which are installed in tub-shower combinations, have a 16-in. leg and a 32-in. leg.

VENTILATING FANS. To carry off odors and humid air, a ventilating fan is essential in all inside bathrooms and recommended for outside bathrooms. Select a fan which can move approximately 100 cu. ft. of air per minute.

In an inside bathroom, the fan is centered in the ceiling and connected to a duct which extends up through the roof or the nearest exterior wall. Ideally, the fan should turn on automatically when you flip the light switch. In an outside bathroom, you can use the same kind of fan or install a through-wall unit in the exterior wall.

Inside a sauna, Viking Sauna Co.

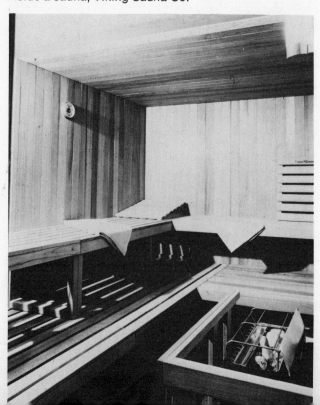

Saunas are small enough to fit into most basements. Fasco Industries, Inc.

Some ceiling fans incorporate a light, some an electric heater, and some both a light and a heater. (Also available are heater-light combinations without fans.)

SAUNAS. A sauna is a dry-heat bath in which temperatures range from 170° to 230° while humidity is held to a desertlike 7 to 20%. The room is constructed entirely of redwood or western red cedar. Heat is supplied by a 240-volt electric heater filled with igneous rocks which retain heat and help to even out the temperature in the sauna. The heater is controlled from inside the sauna.

Completely prebuilt saunas or precut saunas which you assemble yourself are made in sizes ranging from 36×40×80 in. high (adequate for one person) to 8×12 ft. They can be installed anywhere in the house but should be close to a bathroom, since you take a shower before and after soaking up the heat.

WHO MAKES IT

Acorn Building Components, Inc. · Vanity tops with integral single or double lavatories made of a blend of marble dust and polyester. Same material used in prefabricated wall panels for bathtub recesses.

Adamsez Baths, Inc. · Acrylic bathtubs, including 60-in.-diameter round tub with cloverleaf-shaped bowl 19 in. deep and corner model with rounded front and 19-in.-deep heart-shaped bowl.

Air King Corp. · Ceiling and wall bathroom fans, some with resistance heater, some with heater and light, some with one or two heat lamps.

Allibert, Inc. · Surface-mounted medicine cabinets of modern design, some with shelves on backs of doors, some with small drawers under cabinets. Modern clear and solid acrylic accessories of all kinds, including facial-tissue dispenser and grab bars. Circular, oval, and rectangular framed mirrors with concealed lighting. Clear acrylic toilet seats.

American-Standard, Inc. · Enameled cast-iron tubs, one model without sides for building in. Fiberglass tubs, including 40-in. circular sunken model, 84×45-in. tub which may be sunk, floor-mounted 72×54-in. model. Fiberglass tub with integral wall surround and ceiling.

Fiberglass shower stalls. Vitreous china, enameled cast-iron, and fiberglass countertop, wall-hung and pedestal lavatories, one model with colored designs. Toilets, including wall-hung and self-ventilating models. Toilet seats in variety. Bidet. Complete line of fittings, including gold-plated faucet that arches water into lavatory bowl.

Amtrol, Inc. · Pressurized ball attaches to inlet lines under bathroom fixtures to stop water hammer.

Baths International, Inc. · Steam generators for steam baths. Custom-built saunas.

Boise Cascade Corp., Kitchen Cabinet Div. · Wood vanity cabinets finished in natural wood color or enamel. Utility cabinets.

Borg-Warner Corp., Plumbing Products Div. · Fiberglass tub with built-in grab bar. Fiberglass tub with integral wall surround; another fiberglass tub with separate three-piece surround. Vitreous-china countertop and wall-hung lavatories. Single or double round lavatories molded into countertops of imitation marble. Pedestal and wall-hung toilets, some with watersaver tanks. Shower-stall receptors of molded nylon.

Bradley Corp. · Vanity tops with integral single or double lavatories in imitation marble made of acrylic or marble dust mixed with polyester. Faucets, mixing valves, shower heads in a wide range of styles and finishes. Vitreous-china bathroom accessories.

Brammer Manufacturing Co. · Wood vanities with natural and enameled finish.

Brearley Co. · Towel bars, towel rings, paperholders, shelves of oil-rubbed oak.

Briggs Manufacturing Co. · Enameled steel tubs, one with four jets for whirlpool baths. Vitreous-china countertop lavatories. Enameled steel countertop and wall-hung lavatories. Toilets, including wall-hung model and watersaver model. Bidet.

Broan Manufacturing Co. · Bathroom ventilating fans for ceiling or wall, some with resistance heater, some with heater and light, some with one or two heat lamps.

Chicago Faucet Co. · All kinds of lavatory and bathtub faucets, including pressure-balancing mixing valves. Personal showers. Foot and knee valve controls for lavatories. Other fittings.

Composite Shower Pan. · Laminated asphalt-polyethylene-fiberglass sheets used as a waterproofing membrane under ceramic-tile shower-stall receptors.

Crane Co. · Vitreous-china and enameled steel lavatories, including self-rimmed countertop model with built-in hose spray, swinging spout, and concealed soapdish. Others with colored floral designs. Enameled steel and fiberglass tubs. Fiberglass tubs with integral wall surround. One-piece fiberglass shower stalls. Toilets, including self-ventilating unit and wall-hung model. Insulated tanks available. Bidets. Packaged bathrooms. Fittings in variety for all fixtures.

J. C. DeJong & Co. · Ornate towel bars and rings, paperholders, soapdishes, toothbrush and tumbler holders, coat hooks.

Delta Faucet Co. · Faucets, shower heads, mixing valves (including pressure-balancing type) in many styles. Built-in soap and hand-lotion dispenser.

Designware Industries, Inc. · Sliding glass tub doors with aluminum frames. Hinged shower-stall doors. Medicine cabinets. Metal frames for wall-mounted mirrors. Adjustable tilt-frame mirror.

Diston Industries, Inc. · Sliding aluminum-framed tub and shower stall doors with tempered glass available to fit all shapes of tub and stall.

Du Pont. Methacrylate vanity tops with single or double lavatories molded in.

Elkay Manufacturing Co. · Oval, round, and rectangular stainless-steel lavatories.

Elon, Inc. · Large and small, round and oval ceramic lavatories in various colors and decorated with flowers, birds, etc. Decorated ceramic bathroom accessories.

Emerson Electric Co., Rittenhouse-Chromalox Div. · Pryne bathroom wall and ceiling ventilating fans. Recessed models with lights, resistance heaters, or both. Also recessed fans with one and two heat lamps.

Engineered Products Co. · Stainless-steel or aluminum-framed mirrors with and without shelves. Triple-view mirrors. Bypass sliding mirrors up to 72×72 in. in metal frames for installation over completely recessed medicine cabinets without doors.

Fasco Industries, Inc. · Saunas from 4×4 ft. to 8×12 ft. shipped knocked down. Recessed ceiling fans, some with resistance heaters and light, one model with two heat lamps, some models with lights alone.

Fluidmaster, Inc. · Hydraulic-pressure-controlled toilet flushing mechanism.

Genova, Inc. · CPVC and PVC pipe and fittings. Polybutylene riser tubes for connecting bathroom fixtures and sinks to supply lines.

P. E. Guerin, Inc. · Lavatory, tub, and shower faucets and accessories in a great range of unusual, mostly rococo designs (acanthus leaf, bamboo, swans, dolphins, etc.) and in polished brass, gold plate, bronze plate, silver plate, pewter plate, etc. Decorated round vitreous-china lavatories for countertop installation. Medicine cabinet with reeded metal frame around mirror.

Haas Cabinet Co. · Wood vanities with natural and enameled finish.

Hastings Tile. · Imported Italian toilets, bidets, and shell-shaped pedestal lavatories of vitreous china. Circular fiberglass shower stall.

Ideal Co. · Recessed medicine cabinets with louvered wood doors.

Interbath, Inc. · Personal shower with adjustable spray. Hose connects to a shower arm or tub spout. Shower head can be hooked to a wall holder or vertical bar.

International Paper Co., Long-Bell Div. · Wood vanity cabinets finished in natural wood colors or enamel.

International Window Corp. · Sliding glass doors for tubs; pivoted glass doors for shower stalls.

ITT Corp., Lawler Div. · Thermostatic and pressure-controlled mixing valve for showers. Thermostatically controlled mixing valve.

Jacuzzi Research, Inc. · Whirlpool baths described in text. Motor-driven whirlpool pump for use in existing tubs.

JH Industries, Inc., Exelon Div. · Toilet flushing mechanism which operates by water pressure.

H & R Johnson, Inc. · Ceramic-tile bathroom accessories.

Keller Industries. · Glass and plastic sliding doors in aluminum frames for tubs. Hinged doors for shower stalls.

Kirkhill, Inc. · Repair parts for just about every make of faucet as well as countless other plumbing fittings. Replacement toilet-tank mechanism. Towel bars, paperholders, and other bathroom accessories in several styles.

Kirsch Co. · Decorative antique accessories including towel bars and rings, soapdishes, toothbrush holder, paperholders, switch and outlet plates, shower-curtain rods.

Kohler Co. · Enameled cast-iron bathtubs, including old-style tub on legs and 20-in.-deep model without sides for building in or sinking into floor. Also model that drains directly into wall. 84×66-in. sunken fiberglass tub. Fiberglass tub with integral wall surround. Fiberglass shower stalls. Vitreous china and enameled cast-iron wall-hung and countertop lavatories, including 28×19-in. countertop model with swinging spout and pull-out spray. Lavatories molded into imitation-marble acrylic countertops. Toilets, including wall-hung and self-ventilating models, watersaving models, and models with insulated tank. Bidet. Complete line of fittings, including watersaver faucets and shower heads, pressure-balanced mixing valves. Personal showers. Air-actuated jet attachment for whirlpool baths. Thermostatic valve to stop toilet-tank sweating.

Lasco Industries. · Fiberglass tub with high ledge around three sides and seat on the outside of front rim, measures 60×49 in. Fiberglass tub with integral wall surround. Fiberglass shower stalls, including two corner models.

F. H. Lawson Co. · All kinds of medicine cabinet. Stainless-steel framed mirrors with and without shelves.

Merwin Manufacturing, Inc. · Flow-regulating shower heads.

Miami-Carey Co. · Medicine cabinets in great variety, including theater-style models surrounded by exposed light strips. Painted and natural-finish wood vanity cabinets and matching utility cabinets. Bathroom accessories in several finishes, including grab bars, concealed paperholder, and soap-toothbrush holder, towel ladders. Ceiling ventilating fans, some with heater and/or light. Wall fans.

Midland Manufacturing Corp. · Steam generators for steam baths. Glass and plastic sliding and bifold doors for tubs. Hinged and bifold doors for shower stalls. Glass and plastic panels to enclose corner tubs and stalls.

Midwest Victorian Marble Co. · Imitation marble vanity tops with molded-in lavatories made of marble dust and polyester. Painted or stained wood vanity cabinets.

Montgomery Ward & Co. · 4×4-ft. and 4×6-ft. saunas. Enameled cast-iron and steel bathtubs. Toilets. Vitreous-china wall-hung lavatories. Enameled cast-iron and steel countertop lavatories. Vitreous-china and imitation-marble lavatories molded into countertops. Painted and natural-finish vanity cabinets. Surface-mounted and recessed medicine cabinets. Glass and plastic sliding tub doors. Chrome-plated accessories including L-shaped grab bars up to 16×32 in. Polypropylene and steel shower stalls. Imitation-stone receptors. Hinged glass shower-stall doors. Personal shower. Fittings of all kinds.

Recessed ceiling and wall ventilating fans, one with fan and heater, another with two heat lamps. Galvanized steel, copper, PVC, and ABS pipe.

Owens-Corning Fiberglas Corp. · Fiberglass tubs and shower-stall receptors with three-piece fiberglass wall-surround panels.

Charles Parker. · Utilitarian medicine cabinets, chrome-plated accessories, including concealed tumbler and toothbrush holder. Best available line of grab bars for invalids and the elderly—not pretty but in all sizes.

C & L Pegg. · Mixing valve to stop toilet-tank sweating.

Powers Regulator Co., Powers-Fiat Div. · Enameled steel and fiberglass shower stalls with imitation-stone receptors. Plastic doors optional. One-piece acrylic shower stalls with molded-in ceiling available with optional doors of unframed safety glass. Acrylic tubs with integral wall surround and ceiling available with optional sliding doors of unframed safety glass. Pressure-balancing mixing valve.

Price Pfister. · Full line of fittings for all bathroom fixtures.

Pyramid Industries, Inc. · PVC pipe.

Rusco Industries, Inc., Ador/Hilite Div. · Sliding glass aluminum-framed tub doors. Hinged shower-stall doors.

H. J. Scheirich Co. · Vanity cabinets made of wood, two lines enameled, one vinyl covered.

Scovill Manufacturing Co., NuTone Housing Products Div. · Medicine cabinets in great variety. Sleeve to convert recessed cabinets to surface mounting. Clear-finished or enameled wood vanity cabinets with tilt-out hampers. Matching utility and wall cabinets. Bathroom accessories of modern and decorative designs. Recessed wall and ceiling fans. Fans with lights, heaters, or both. Fans with one or two heat lamps. Brass or chrome bathroom accessories.

Sears Roebuck & Co. · Toilets. Vitreous-china wall-hung lavatories. Vitreous-china and imitation-marble lavatories molded into countertop. Enameled steel and fiberglass tubs. Fiberglass shower stalls. Sliding glass and folding plastic tub doors. Bifold, sliding, and hinged glass shower-stall doors. Personal showers. Recessed and surface-mounted medicine cabinets. Vanity and wall cabinets. Towel rods, paperholders, soapdishes, tumbler and toothbrush holders made of ceramic tile or die-cast aluminum with enameled or antiqued brass or silver finishes. 4×6-ft. sauna. Wall and ceiling vent fans, one model with light, one with light and heater. Fittings. CPVC, ABS, and RS pipe.

Shower Door Co. · Tub and shower doors of several types built of safety glass with aluminum or chrome-plated brass frames. Tub doors slide, pivot, or bifold; shower-stall doors are hinged, sliding, or bifolding. Glass panels to enclose ends and sides of corner tubs and stalls. Four-sided all-glass shower stalls.

Speakman Co. · Personal showers, one with adjustable spray, attach to shower arm, shower head, or tub spout. Head at end of flexible hose hooks to wall bracket or vertical bar. Pressure-balancing mixing valves. Shower heads, some with flow regulators to save water. Faucets.

Stanadyne Corp., Moen Div. · Single-control faucets. Pressure-balancing mixing valves for showers and tub-showers. Shower heads.

Swan Corp. · Circular fiberglass shower stall with ceiling. Snail-shaped stall with ceiling.

Symmons Industries, Inc. · Pressure-balancing valves for showers and tub-showers. Lavatory faucets. Personal showers.

Teledyne Aquatec. · Personal showers which adjust the spray. One model with flexible steel hose is attached to shower arm and is hand held; other model is permanently attached to shower arm.

ThermaSol, Ltd. · Steam generators for steam baths.

Tocomc of Atlanta. · Acrylic bathtubs with integral wall surround and ceiling. Acrylic shower stalls with integral ceiling.

Tub-Master Corp. · Folding plastic doors push back to side of shower stalls or end of tubs. Doors for tubs are also designed so they fold back to ends of tub or slide past each other in rigid panels. Personal showers which attach to shower arm.

Ultraflo Corp. · Pushbutton system for supplying water at preselected temperatures to bathroom fixtures and kitchen sink.

United Cabinet Corp. · Vanity cabinets in six natural-finish styles and two painted styles.

Universal-Rundle Corp. · Fiberglass tubs with integral wall and ceiling surrounds. Fiberglass or enameled cast-iron tubs, some with separate three-piece acrylic wall panels and ceilings. Fiberglass shower stalls with integral ceilings. Countertop and wall-hung vitreous-china lavatories, one model with colored designs. Fiberglass countertop lavatories. Vitreous-china bowls molded into countertops up to 30 in. wide. Toilets, including wall-hung and self-ventilating models. Bidet. Complete line of fittings. Bifold fiberglass tub doors. Vanity cabinets up to 30 in. wide. Wall cabinets.

Vermont Marble Co. · Marble vanity tops built to order.

Viking Sauna Co. · Prefabricated saunas from 36×40 in. to 78×150 in.

Wallace-Murray Corp., Eljer Plumbingware Div. · Enameled cast-iron and enameled steel tubs, some with raised outlets so they can be drained directly into the wall rather than a slab floor. Fiberglass tubs with integral wall surrounds; optional ceiling. Fiberglass shower stalls. Vitreous-china pedestal lavatory; vitreous-china and enameled cast-iron wall-hung lavatories; vitreous-china, enameled cast-iron, and enameled steel countertop lavatories. Cast-iron wash sinks. Toilets, including wall-hung models. Insulated tanks available for some models. Bidet. Personal showers. Complete line of fittings. Vanity cabinets up to 24 in. wide.

Water Control Products/N.A., Inc. · Pressure-type toilet tank to eliminate flushing mechanism problems.

Westinghouse Electric Corp., IXL Div. · Natural-finish and painted wood vanity cabinets.

Wrightway Manufacturing Co. · Shower heads, one with watersaver control. Flapper valves for toilets.

15

Kitchens and Appliances

For most homeowners, kitchen remodeling is more than just a straightforward replacement project. It also involves the replanning and redesigning of the entire room. This is by far the most difficult part of the job, and any homemaker who turns it over to a so-called kitchen-planning expert is simply asking for disappointment.

In a sense, a kitchen is as personal a thing as a dress. There is only one person it must please; if that person does not take an active part in designing and fitting it to herself, the odds are strongly against its working out to her complete satisfaction.

The planning process involves five important steps.

1. Make sure you know exactly how you use a kitchen. Take time to analyze this, because even though you may think you can alter your habits to suit a new kitchen, you will find it very hard to do. Ask yourself such questions as these: How do I actually go about cooking and cleaning up? Do I tolerate distractions when working in the kitchen? How do my physical characteristics and weaknesses affect my kitchen work? To what extent do entertaining and outdoor eating affect kitchen work? How much do other members of the family occupy or actually work in the kitchen? What must be stored in the kitchen?

2. Draw up a list of the important things you want to incorporate in the kitchen. An eating area. Laundry. Television and study area. Food freezer. Planning desk. Barbecue. Overflow storage space. A second sink. A second range.

3. Draw a plan of your present kitchen as it would look if all cabinets and appliances were removed. Or if you are making an addition which will incorporate the kitchen, draw a plan of this.

This takes time and requires extreme accuracy. Use a 6-ft. rule and make all horizontal measurements above the baseboards.

First measure the total length of each wall and out-line a plan of the room on graph paper to these measurements.

Then measure each segment of each wall—from a corner to a door, the width of the door, from the door to a window, the width of the window, etc. Fill in the doors, windows, etc. on the plan and indicate all measurements. Then total the segment measurements for each wall and make sure they equal the total length of the wall.

Remeasure the room to determine the location of radiators, registers, electric switches and outlets, lights, drains, thermostats, etc. Mark these on the plan.

Measure the height of the ceiling and note it on a margin of the plan.

Measure the heights of door and window openings, ventilating fans, electric outlets and switches, registers, etc. and note them in the margin of the plan.

4. Draw your new kitchen plan on tracing paper laid over the basic floor plan. Locate the range, refrigerator, sink, and dishwasher first. Then draw in the counters and wall cabinets (use dotted lines for the latter). Don't worry about making your lines straight, but indicate appliance sizes as accurately as possible.

After analyzing the good and bad points of the plan, set it aside and draw a new one. Repeat this process as often as necessary—always on a clean sheet of tracing paper—until you have finally arrived at the ideal arrangement. Then redraw that plan on a clean piece of paper with a ruler.

5. Now ask the cabinet or appliance dealer from whom you will buy your equipment to go over the plan. If he has any worthwhile changes to suggest, by all means consider them. But remember that you are the one who knows what you need, so don't give in too easily unless he can prove that what you have drawn is wrong. He may, however, suggest a number of minor changes which must be made in order to fit equipment in properly.

Wood cabinets are available in an infinite number of styles. Above, Westinghouse Electric Corp.; right, Leigh Products, Inc.; right below, United Cabinet Corp.

The complete remodeling of a kitchen is best done by experts who are familiar with the many intricacies of the job and can get the room into working order in three or four days. To save money, however, you can lay the floor and do the decorating yourself.

But if you're making only piecemeal changes in a kitchen, there is no reason why you shouldn't be able to handle all the work except the plumbing and wiring. The directions are given below.

CABINETS. Kitchen cabinets are made of wood (usually plywood) with a clear or paint finish, steel with a paint finish, or particleboard or plywood surfaced with laminated plastics. Also available are steel cabinets with wood fronts. Each material has its advantages. Wood has innate natural beauty; steel is exceptionally strong; plastic is most wear-resistant. But aside from this, there is little to choose between them provided all are of the same quality (that is, you can't make a fair comparison between a cheap steel cabinet, a medium-cost plastic cabinet, and an expensive wood cabinet).

When shopping for cabinets, look for the following: Straight-hanging, solid-sounding doors which open easily and close with little noise. Drawers that roll in

Cabinets covered with laminated plastic. Contemporary Systems, Inc.

and out smoothly and quietly and can be lifted out easily for thorough cleaning. Rigid, easy-to-clean shelves which can be adjusted up and down (adjustability is especially important in wall cabinets; less so in base cabinets).

Wall cabinets are approximately 12½ in. deep (measured from the face of the door to the back of the cabinet). Standard widths are 9, 12, 15, 18, 21, 24, 27, 30, 33, 36, 39, 42, 45, and 48 in., and some manufacturers offer additional widths up to 60 in. Standard heights (which are not available in all widths) are 12, 15, 18, 21, 24, 27, 30, 33, 36, and 42 in. The cabinets are equipped with shelves (the most commonly used 30-in.-high cabinet has three). Cabinets up to 21 or sometimes 24 in. wide have a single door which can be hinged on either side, depending on the homeowner's

Steel cabinets raised off the floor on legs. St. Charles Manufacturing Co.

Most wall cabinets have hinged doors. In these the doors lift up. Contemporary Systems, Inc.

needs. Larger cabinets—up to 48 in. wide—have two doors, and still larger sizes have three.

Base cabinets are 24 in. deep and 34½ in. high (so that with countertop added, they are 36 in. high). Widths start at 12 in. and go upward in 3-in. increments to 48 in. and, in some cases, 60 in. Standard cabinets have three shelves, or three drawers, or a single drawer at the top and two shelves below. Cabinets with two, four, or five drawers are available.

Special cabinets, of which there are many, include:

Corner wall and base cabinets. The most popular —and most expensive—type has revolving shelves which swing out when the door on either side of the corner is pushed. Another type has a door set at a 45° angle across the corner. The shelves are either fixed or rotating. Both cabinets are essentially square.

A third type of corner base cabinet forms a long

When closed, the doors on the revolving-shelf base cabinet above form a 90° corner. Revolving-shelf wall cabinets are designed in the same way or have the door set at a 45° angle to corner, as below. International Paper Co.

In this corner base cabinet the half-moon shelves swing back into the corner. St. Charles Manufacturing Co.

rectangle which tucks halfway into the corner. When you open the door on the exposed half, the semicircular shelves attached to the back swing out.

Sink and range bases. Designed for installation under a sink or built-in cooktop, these are shelf cabinets with a fixed panel across the top (in place of a drawer). Widths range from 24 to 48 in. In addition, sink bases up to 84 in. wide are made for use in small apartment-house kitchens.

Sink fronts. Many kitchen planners prefer sink fronts to sink bases since they save money. They are nothing more than a flat frame with doors. The frame is bolted between the base cabinets on either side of the sink. The space behind the doors is open to the floor and has no shelves.

Oven cabinets. Standard oven cabinets are 84 in. high, 24 in. deep, and 24, 27, or 30 in. wide. They are made with openings of several sizes to house single built-in ovens or stacked double ovens (double ovens which are placed side by side require a special cabinet). The enclosed shelf space above the oven is used for miscellaneous storage. A similar storage space with shelves or sometimes drawers is usually available below the oven.

Utility cabinets. These are also 84 in. high, and 15, 18, 21, 24, 27, 30, and 36 in. wide. They are available either in standard wall-cabinet or base-cabinet depth. The cabinets normally have two doors, one above the other, or four doors (on cabinets over 24 in. wide), two over two. The space behind is shelved.

In utility cabinets made for cleaning equipment, the bottom door is approximately 65 in. high and shelves are omitted from the space behind it.

Pantry cabinets. Pantry cabinets, which are also known by other names, are nonstandard units measuring 84 in. wide, 24 in. deep, and about 18 to 33 in.

wide. They are designed primarily for storage of canned and other packaged foods and contain a variety of narrow swinging or revolving shelves to permit easy access to small items stored in the back.

Similar under-counter cabinets are made.

Peninsula cabinets. These are wall or base units with doors on front and back. They are used in peninsulas or islands—primarily between the kitchen and eating area—so you can remove and store dishes from either side.

Sliding-door cabinets. In these, the standard hinged doors are replaced with sliding doors. The cabinets are used mainly when space in a kitchen is limited. Both wall and base cabinets and also peninsula cabinets are available.

Tray cabinets. Narrow base units with vertical dividers.

Waste-receptacle cabinets. Base cabinets with a wastebasket which rolls or tilts out.

Utensil cabinets. These narrow base cabinets are equipped with a vertical panel of perforated hardboard on which pots and pans are hung. The panel is attached to the door, which pulls completely out of the cabinet.

Mixer cabinets. In these base cabinets, a large stand-type food mixer is stored on a shelf which swings out and up like a typewriter shelf in a desk.

Serving-cart cabinets. Base cabinets used to garage a serving cart. In some cases, the cart is concealed behind doors. In other cases, the door forms a part of the cart.

Intermediate cabinets. Also called space-saver cabinets, these are small units which are installed against the wall directly under wall cabinets. They usually have sliding doors; they measure 6 to 8 in. deep and about 10 in. high and 24 in. long.

Pantry cabinet with revolving shelves as well as shelves on back of door. International Paper Co.

Peninsula cabinets open from both sides. International Paper Co.

1

2

3

4

5

6

7

8

Useful special cabinets and accessories: 1 and 2, Contemporary Systems, Inc. 3, 4, and 5, St. Charles Manufacturing Co. 6, International Paper Co. 7, Towel rod slides out automatically when cabinet door is opened, International Paper Co. 8, Slide-out chopping block, International Paper Co. 9, Entire table pulls out, Contemporary Systems, Inc. 10, Sliding utensil tray in top of drawer, Contemporary Systems, Inc. 11, St. Charles Manufacturing Co.

10   11

In addition to these special cabinets, manufacturers produce a large number of accessories designed to increase the usefulness of standard base and wall cabinets. These include sliding cutting boards, sliding wire baskets, sliding towel racks, drawer dividers, roll-out shelves, bread boxes, wine racks, etc.

Also available are open-shelf units for installation between wall cabinets, in corners, and at the ends of peninsulas; ventilating fan hoods in designs and materials matching the cabinets; and refrigerator enclosures.

If you're not satisfied with the design of standard cabinet doors, you can buy doors with special inserts such as louvers, metal grilles, decorative plastics, glass, and fancily turned spindles.

Since the sides of cabinets are normally made of inexpensive, unfinished material, you must order finished side panels for cabinets installed next to windows or doors, in islands, or in peninsulas. Similarly, finished back panels must be ordered for base and wall cabinets which are not installed against a wall.

Front panels which match cabinets are available to make dishwashers and refrigerators look built-in. Side panels must be ordered for dishwashers which are not built in between cabinets.

Fillers are an essential element of almost all cabinet installations. They are strips 1 in. to 3 in. wide which are finished to match the cabinets and are used (1) to piece out a row of wall or base cabinets so it exactly fills a wall space; (2) to fill a gap between the end of a row of cabinets and a slanting or crooked wall; or (3) to wedge cabinets in U-shaped or L-shaped kitchens out from the corners so the drawers or doors on either side of a corner can be opened all the way.

Fillers of different contour are made for base cabinets and wall cabinets. They are fastened to the sides of the cabinets with screws or bolts. In some cases, however, the strips—called extended stiles—are integral parts of the cabinets.

To install a row of base cabinets, place them in position against the wall. Level the cabinet at the highest point in the floor from side to side and front to back and fasten it to the wall with screws driven into the studs. Then shim up the other cabinets with wood shingles so the tops align and the entire row is level. Screw each cabinet to the wall. Then fasten the cabinets together with bolts driven through the sides.

Lay the countertop on the cabinets and attach it with long screws driven up from the cabinet frames.

Installation of wall cabinets requires two persons. First draw a level line on the wall to mark the bottom of the cabinets. Then mark the positions of each cabinet and the studs behind it. Hold the cabinets against the wall, flush with the level line, and fasten them with 4-in. round-head screws driven into the studs. Use four screws for each average-size cabinet; a couple more for very large cabinets. After the cabinets are hung, bolt them together side to side.

The space above wall cabinets can be left open but is generally closed to improve the appearance of the installation and eliminate the need for cleaning dust and grease off the tops of the cabinets. Use $1/4$-in. hardboard, particleboard, plywood, or $3/8$-in. gypsum board. After cutting this to fit the space between the cabinets and ceiling, nail it to furring strips fastened to the tops of the cabinets and the ceiling. The face of the panels should be flush with the face of the cabinet frames. Cover the joints along the horizontal edges of the panels with moldings.

COUNTERTOPS. The ideal kitchen counter is attractive, nonglary, very easy to clean, durable, waterproof, and resistant to scratching, heat, acids, grease, and alkalis. It also makes relatively little noise when things

171

Most popular countertop materials are laminated plastic, above, Westinghouse Electric Corp.; and ceramic tile, below, Interpace Corp.

are dropped on it and does not chip china and glass when they are set down carelessly.

No one countertop material satisfies all requirements. But with the exception of wood, all come close enough.

Laminated plastic is the most widely used material. It consists of several layers of phenol-impregnated paper and a surface layer of melamine-saturated paper bonded together under pressure and heat to form tough, rigid, durable sheets $\frac{1}{16}$ in. thick. Counters made of the material are exceptionally easy to keep clean, in part because the sheets are very smooth even when textured and in part because they are so large that there are few if any joints in the counters. Although the surface is hard, it does not chip things which are dropped on it, and resistance to most kinds of damage is high. You can, however, scratch counters by cutting on them with a sharp knife and scorch them if you let an overheated cast-iron frying pan or laundry iron stand on them for more than a few seconds.

The plastics are made in every color of the rainbow. There are solid colors, patterns, wood grains, and numerous finishes resembling stone, leather, fabrics, stucco, etc.

Countertops are made by gluing the laminated plastic to a base of particleboard or, in some instances, plywood. The process is tricky because the contact adhesive used forms an instant bond which cannot be broken and because joints must be perfectly made to prevent leaks; consequently, instead of trying to fabricate counters yourself, you should let a local countertop maker do it for you. The finished tops are $1\frac{1}{2}$ in. thick and normally incorporate a backsplash which is either 4 in. high or extends up the walls to the bottoms of the wall cabinets. The edges of the counters are normally square and self-edged (covered with the same plastic used on the horizontal surfaces). Stainless-steel edging strips are rarely used any longer. The edges and joints between the tops and backsplashes can also be rounded if so-called postforming plastic sheets are used instead of general-purpose sheets.

Methacrylate is a relatively new countertop material with virtually the same characteristics as laminated plastics. Unlike the laminates, however, the material is $\frac{3}{4}$ in. thick and requires no backing or special edging (when installed, the tops are $\frac{3}{4}$ in. lower than a range surface). If scratched or burned, the damage can be removed with 400-grit waterproof sandpaper.

The panels are available in only three colors. One is solid white; the other two—a pale green and a beige—have such an amazing resemblance to marble that you would be hard put to distinguish them from true marble. Because of the nature of methacrylate (a type of acrylic) and the thickness of the panels, counters have a rich opalescence.

Methacrylate countertops should be fabricated by shops accustomed to working with the material.

Ceramic-tile counters are even more durable than the plastics and impervious to damage. You can carve on them and set down hot utensils without fazing them in the slightest; for this reason, they are ideal for installation next to ranges. But they are noisy and hard on fragile china and glass. And the numerous joints between tiles are difficult to clean, although this drawback can be corrected to some extent if they are filled with epoxy rather than cement grout.

Tiles for counters are like those used on walls and floors. Your choice of colors, patterns, and textures is almost limitless. You can install the tiles yourself on a base of waterproof plywood. Follow the directions for tiling interior walls, and cover the edges of the counters with bullnose tiles. The joints between countertops and backsplashes are made with cove tiles.

Wood countertops are made of narrow strips of $1\frac{1}{2}$-in.-thick hard maple glued together side by side. Because the wood is readily stained, scarred, and burned, the tops are usually only 24 in. wide and set between larger areas of plastic. You can, however, buy prefabricated counters in lengths of 3, 4, 5, 6, 8, and 10 ft. Prefabricated backsplashes are also available but must be attached to the counters at the site.

Stainless-steel countertops, despite their exceptional durability and resistance to heat, are rare. They are readily scratched, have a splotchy, uneven appearance (although they may be completely clean and sanitary), and are noisy. Furthermore, they look too clinical for most homemakers' tastes and are very expensive. Fabrication should be handled by a firm experienced in making restaurant-kitchen counters.

Glass-ceramic is a strong, durable, glasslike material which performs like ceramic tile. It is available in small (up to 24×24-in.) pieces which are inset in plastic countertops to serve as cutting boards and hot mats.

SINKS. Of the five materials used in sinks, stainless steel is today most widely used mainly because it is generally thought to be easier to keep in pristine condition than enameled sinks. Actually this is only partly true. Since stainless-steel sinks have no surface finish, they do not craze, chip, or discolor, but they do show fingerprints and tiny scratches and are not as easy to keep looking clean as enameled sinks.

They are also noisy, especially if made of 20-gauge metal. For this reason, you should buy sinks made of heavier and more expensive 18-gauge metal. Make sure they are covered with an undercoating comparable to that used on automobiles.

These disadvantages, however, are outweighed by the advantages of stainless-steel sinks. For one thing, because they are relatively easy to form, they are available in an unusual variety of designs. They are impervious to hard wear and last forever. Because of their resilience, they rarely chip china and glassware. Their neutral color is compatible with any kitchen color scheme. And they are easy to install because they are lightweight and self-rimmed (the almost flat rims rest on the countertop instead of being hung below it).

Porcelain-enamel-on-steel sinks are a close runner-up in popularity to stainless-steel sinks. Their main appeal is their low cost. They are also available in a good many colors to match or contrast with cabinets and appliances. But they suffer from the fact that the enamel is rather weak.

Porcelain-enamel-on-cast-iron sinks are preferable because, despite their high cost, the enamel is extremely attractive, tough, and cleanable. The sinks weigh so much, however, that plumbers don't like to handle them. Furthermore, installation is fairly difficult because they must be hung below the countertop in stainless-steel rings. To correct this problem, many new sinks are self-rimmed, but the rim is usually so high that it's impossible to sweep water from the counter into the sink.

Cast-iron sinks are also responsible for more breakage of china and glass than any other type of sink.

Fiberglass sinks are a new development and not widely available. They are colorful, easy to clean, rea-

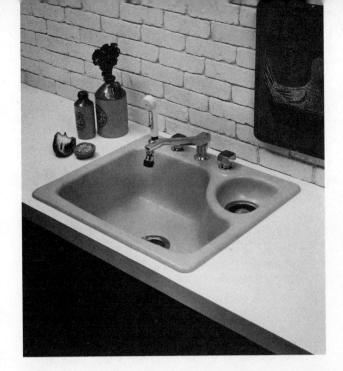

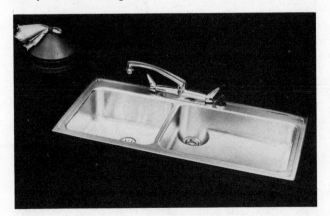

New shapes in kitchen sinks. Top, porcelain-on-cast-iron sinks, Kohler Co.; bottom, stainless-steel sinks, Elkay Manufacturing Co.

sonably durable, and cause little breakage, but because of the thinness of the material, they are rather noisy.

Acrylic sinks, another new development, are made only in small sizes for bars. The bright color extends all the way through the plastic, which, like fiberglass, is fairly noisy but resilient enough to prevent chipping of glassware. Cleaning is easy. Scratches, however, are difficult to eradicate.

Sinks are made in so many sizes and designs that if you have any doubts about what you need, you'll have a hard time selecting one.

In considering sizes, it's important to note that the dimensions given in catalogs are outside measurements. For example, in a 33×22-in. sink, the exposed rim of the sink is 33 in. wide and 22 in. deep. You might conclude from this that the sink cannot be dropped into a cabinet that measures 33 in. wide. But the fact is that the bowl or bowls are several inches less than 33 in. wide so the sink should fit into the cabinet if its framework does not interfere (this point should be checked).

Another point to note about sink dimensions is that whereas the faucet in most sinks is mounted on the sink rim, it is placed on the countertop—behind the rim—in other sinks. This obviously means that the overall measurements of sinks with rim-mounted faucets (called ledge-back sinks) are the greater. Actual bowl dimensions, however, may be similar or even less.

The smallest kitchen sink—with a single bowl—measures 15×15 in. (the smallest bar sink is 13×13 in.). The largest—with two bowls and drainboards on both sides—is 66×22 in. The most commonly used single-bowl sink is 24×22 in.; the most commonly used double-bowl model, 33×22 in.

Normal sink-bowl depth is 7½ in., but 6-in. depth is not uncommon. In many double-bowl sinks, the bowls are of different depth. Some bar sinks are 9 in. deep. Laundry sinks are generally 10 or 12 in. deep.

Whether you need a single-, double-, or triple-bowl sink depends entirely on the way you like to work in your kitchen. If you have a dishwasher, one large bowl is usually adequate. (For maximum convenience, you might put in two single-bowl sinks—one in the working center of the kitchen, the other at some other point in the kitchen.) A great many homemakers, however, still favor double-bowl sinks just as they did in pre-dishwasher days. But the trend is away from sinks with two bowls of equal size. In a growing number of homes, the sink has one large bowl of standard 7½-in. depth and a smaller, shallower bowl which feeds into a garbage disposer. This arrangement not only makes it less likely that you will drop silver into the disposer but also permits you to keep waste food and dirty water away from utensils and foods being washed in the large bowl.

Triple-bowl sinks are much less popular. The most common design has two large bowls flanking a small bowl in which the disposer is installed. Some models,

however, have three bowls of equal size. One unique model meant for use in a peninsula or island has two medium-size bowls side by side, and behind these a very large, 4-in.-deep bowl for washing vegetables and oversize equipment such as oven racks.

Regardless of the number of bowls, the majority of sinks are designed for installation in straight counters—usually under a kitchen window. The notable exception is the corner sink. This is a double-bowl unit (the bowls are the same size) which fits around an inside corner in a counter so you have one bowl to the left and the other to the right of the corner.

Along with changes in design, modern sinks—like

Sink faucet can be aimed in any direction and water flow can be adjusted from solid stream to a spray. Delta Faucet Co.

Hot-water dispenser can be added to most sinks. Emerson Electric Co.

Acrylic bar sink. Kohler Co.

Dishwasher door can be covered with any material—in this case to match the wallpaper. Maytag Co.

Special sinks are often used in other rooms as well as the garage. In many cases, these same sinks are installed in kitchens to supplement the primary sink.

Laundry sinks, as noted, are deep units made of the same materials as kitchen sinks. They have one or two bowls. The largest single-bowl unit measures 25×22 in.; the largest double-bowl, 43×22 in.

Bar sinks are also available in one- and two-bowl conventional models as well as in two-bowl corner models. Most are equipped with high gooseneck faucets.

Floor sinks resemble small tubs with very low sides. They are designed for washing wet mops, filling buckets, draining rain-soaked clothing, washing dogs, and potting plants. The faucets are mounted on the wall above them.

DISHWASHERS. Dishwashers are available in four similar designs: the built-in, convertible, portable, and dishwasher-sink combination. Built-ins are designed for installation in any 24-in.-wide space under a standard kitchen counter. Convertibles are identical to built-ins except that they come on casters and have an integral top. They are made for families who do not presently have space for a built-in dishwasher but who hope to incorporate one in their kitchens at a later date. When the casters and top are removed, convertible dishwashers fit into a 24-in. space under a counter.

In the dishwasher-sink combination, the dishwasher is an ordinary built-in model which is combined with a 24-in. base cabinet under a stainless-steel countertop incorporating a single-bowl sink.

Portable dishwashers differ from the others in that they either open at the top rather than in front and/or have a slightly larger cabinet; consequently, they are not adapted to permanent undercounter installation.

Building in a dishwasher calls for a plumber and electrician, although the work is not too complicated for a handyman who understands the two trades. If the dishwasher is located next to the sink (the best position), all you have to do is connect the dishwasher inlet into the hot-water supply line and the dishwasher drain into the sink drain. Flexible tubing is used. You must also bring in a 120-volt, 20-amp wiring circuit which serves no other outlets or appliances except a disposer.

Since all dishwasher tubs are of approximately the same size, they should theoretically hold approximately the same number of dishes, glasses, utensils, etc. Because of differences in the design of the upper and lower racks, however, some are more capacious than others. This is difficult to determine without actually watching a salesman load them.

The only other major difference between dishwashers is in the number of cycles they offer. The least expensive models provide only a single 50- to 60-minute "normal" cycle consisting of one or two wash periods,

kitchen appliances—have been embellished with new features. Of these, the most desirable is a pop-up drain which lets you empty the bowl without reaching into hot, dirty dishwater. A common feature is a retractable hose spray for rinsing operations. Less common is a built-in soap dispenser which pumps out a measured amount of liquid soap when you push the handle.

Another useful feature is a faucet equipped with a water-flow regulator that reduces water consumption to as much as 2 gal. per minute.

Two more elaborate optional accessories are an instantaneous hot-water dispenser and ice-water dispenser. The former supplies up to $\frac{1}{2}$ gal. of 190° water per hour. The latter is installed when the water is of such poor quality that a separate source of filtered or unsoftened water is desired for drinking.

Both dispensers consist of a small faucet which is installed on the sink rim or nearby counter, and a small heater or chiller in the cabinet under the sink.

OTHER SINKS. Sinks are not restricted to kitchens.

175

three or four rinses, and a drying period. Top models, by contrast, provide not only a long wash cycle but also a variety of short cycles for washing special loads, rinsing, and warming plates.

Other desirable features to look for include:

An energy-saver device which permits you to turn off the electricity during the drying cycle.

Forced-air drying which dries the dishes by circulating air through the tub.

A wetting-agent dispenser which automatically adds a water conditioner to the final rinse so that dishes will dry without spotting.

An insulated door panel to muffle the sound of the washing operation.

GARBAGE DISPOSERS. Despite the fact that garbage disposers were invented before World War II and are considered indispensable by almost all families who own them, they are still prohibited in a handful of cities in the U.S. In other communities, by contrast, their installation in new and remodeled houses is mandatory.

When used in homes with septic systems, building codes generally require that the size of the septic tank be increased approximately 250 gal. Disposers cannot, however, be used in homes with cesspools.

Disposers can be installed by a plumber directly below the drain opening in any modern sink. They can also be installed in very old sinks if the plumber has cutting tools to enlarge the drain opening. A 120-volt, 20-amp circuit is required to supply power to the disposer. This circuit may also be used to run a dishwasher but should not serve any other outlets.

Two types of disposer are made. Batch-feed models grind up one load of waste at a time. After loading the waste into the grinding chamber, you turn on the cold

Trash compactor fits into 15-in. space under counter. Gaffers & Sattler, Inc.

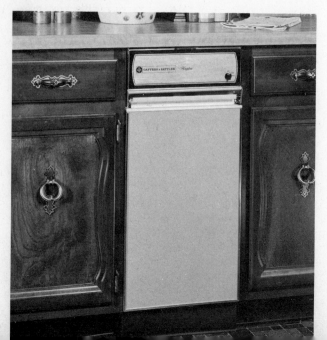

water and set a special cover which serves as the switch into the sink opening. The disposer starts when you turn the cover in one direction, stops when you turn the cover back.

Continuous-feed disposers grind up waste as long as you keep on pushing it into the grinding chamber. The operation is controlled by a switch mounted on the wall near the sink.

Both disposers perform the same function. Batch-feed models are safer because you cannot reach into them or accidentally drop in a piece of silver while they are operating. If you have a great deal of waste to get rid of, however, you must turn them on and off several times before the job is done.

For many years, the major drawback of most disposers was a tendency to jam when bits of bone or, more likely, corn silk and similar fibrous materials caught in the grinding wheel. This is largely corrected in current models by an automatic reversing switch or by an impeller which swivels backward when it encounters an obstacle that might stall the motor.

Other features to look for include:

Stainless-steel parts which resist the corrosive action of water, acids, and alkalis.

A heavily insulated housing to contain noise.

COMPACTORS. Unlike a garbage disposer, which completely eliminates food wastes by flushing them down the sewer, a compactor compresses them into a polyethylene bag which must be dumped into a garbage can for subsequent removal to the town dump. Thus it does not eliminate flies and rats as a disposer does.

On the other hand, a compactor is used to dispose not only of food but also of all other kinds of small household trash—paper, cardboard, cans, bottles, wood, fabrics, etc. You simply toss the wastes into the mouth of the appliance, close the door, and push a switch. A powerful ram mashes the wastes into a wad about one-quarter of their original size, and drops them into a collection bag. Odors are controlled by a built-in deodorant dispenser or by air circulating through an activated-charcoal filter. When the bag is full, you lift it out and put it outdoors for collection. One bag holds about a week's trash.

Compactors look like a small dishwasher and are installed under a counter in the same way. They occupy a space 15 or 18 in. wide. A separate 120-volt, 15-amp circuit is required for operation.

RANGES. Despite the resurgence of interest in old-fashioned wood and coal stoves, the odds are that when you buy a new range it will operate on electricity, natural gas, or LP gas. But it's possible that even you don't know which type of range you will choose. As much depends on the layout of the kitchen as on your personal preference.

Freestanding ranges are the standard type. They are 36 in. high (to the cooking surface; the backsplash extends above this); stand on the floor; and are finished on the sides so they can be installed between counters, placed at either end of a counter, or located by themselves (a poor practice).

The smallest gas and electric models are 20, 21, or 24 in. wide and have three or four burners. Models 30 in. and 36 in. wide have four burners; models 40 in. wide have four or, in a few cases, six burners and one or two ovens.

Two-oven, eye-level ranges are freestanding 30-in. units with a large oven and broiler below the four-burner cooktop and a smaller oven projecting out over the cooktop. The upper oven can be used only for baking in some models, for both baking and broiling in others. Microwave ovens are available.

Stack-on ranges resemble a two-oven, eye-level range without the large lower oven. The four-burner cooktop rests on a 30-in.-high base cabinet, and the oven and broiler project out from the backsplash above it. The ranges are 30 in. wide.

One manufacturer produces a stack-on range which is combined with a dishwasher. The latter is placed below the cooktop.

Drop-in ranges are compact, four-burner units, 27 or 30 in. wide, with unfinished sides which are built into a niche between cabinets. The cooking surface is level with the countertop; the bottom of the oven is approximately 10 in. above the floor. The cabinet manufacturer should provide a fixed panel to close off the space below the oven, or he can install a drawer.

Drop-ins with backsplashes are designed for placement against a wall. Those without backsplashes are

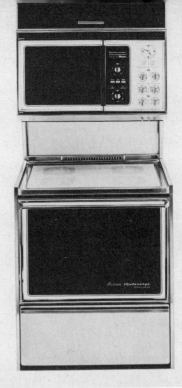

Two-oven, eye-level range with microwave oven at the top. Amana Refrigeration, Inc.

installed in peninsulas or islands. The unfinished back of the range is covered with a panel matching the adjacent base cabinets.

Built-in ranges consist of a cooking top and a totally separate oven. They permit greater flexibility in planning a kitchen than conventional one-piece ranges because you can place the cooktop in the center of the kitchen where most activity takes place, the oven elsewhere. Another advantage of built-ins is that you can install the oven at waist height or whatever height is most convenient for you. Similarly, you are not restricted to the usual 36-in.-height for the cooktop.

Cooktops are made with two to seven burners, and vary from 14 to 45 in. long. They are dropped into a hole cut in a countertop. Single built-in ovens, including microwave units, are 24 in. wide and are installed in 24-in.-deep oven cabinets. Double ovens with one unit above the other are the same width. Side-by-side double ovens—relatively uncommon—are 48 in. wide.

Countertop ovens are rather small boxy ovens which are set on a counter under a wall cabinet. They are approximately 15 in. high, 17 or 23 in. deep, and 18 or 23 in. wide. All countertop ovens today are microwave units which cook in about one-fourth the time of conventional ovens, and reduce energy consumption accordingly. A 5-lb. roast, for instance, takes 35 minutes; a hamburger, just one minute. Cooking can be done in the serving dish, since the food alone gets hot. Because the oven itself stays cool, splatters don't bake onto it and can be wiped off with a sponge. All cooking operations are automatically controlled.

Modern ranges are far more elaborate and complex than those of the past. This is, unfortunately, best illu-

Freestanding 30-in. electric range with seamless glass-ceramic top and electronic control panel. Frigidaire—General Motors Corp.

Unusual drop-in cooktop has a broiler below central panel. Chambers Corp.

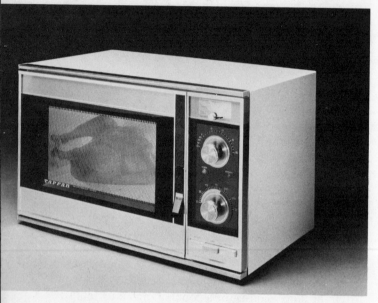

Microwave oven for use on top of counter. Tappan Co.

strated by the fact that whereas ranges used to require little servicing, they are now responsible for a high percentage of all calls that come into appliance-service companies. On the other hand, they make cooking a great deal easier. Among the many excellent features they offer are the following:

1. Conventional cooking surfaces with exposed burners are replaced in many electric ranges with solid, flat panels of high-strength glass-ceramic. Thus you can clean the cooking surface with a quick wipe of a sponge or paper towel. There's no need to remove grease, crumbs, and spills from the burners themselves.

In glass-ceramic tops, the heating elements are concealed beneath the translucent panels. When the burners are on, sunburst designs embedded in the glass-ceramic glow yellow but the areas between burners remain cool. However, in order to transfer heat rapidly and with minimum loss from the burners to cooking foods, the pots and pans used should have perfectly flat bottoms. This means you might have to replace your old utensils if you put in a range or built-in cooktop with this kind of cooking surface. Even with the proper utensils, many homemakers complain that this type of range is much slower and more wasteful of energy than conventional ranges.

2. Ovens that clean themselves are of two types. The so-called self-cleaning, or pyrolitic, oven is available in

electric ranges only. The cleaning is roughly a two-hour operation during which the door of the heavily insulated oven is locked and the inside temperature soars to about 1000°. At the end of the cleaning period, only a powdery ash remains. This can be removed with a cloth.

In the less effective continuous-cleaning, or catalytic, oven, the oven interior is finished with a porcelain enamel containing a catalyst. This causes a chemical reaction which oxidizes food soils whenever the oven is being used for baking. Such ovens are incorporated in gas as well as some electric ranges.

3. Thermostatically controlled surface burners bring foods to the correct cooking temperature and automatically hold them at this temperature. Thus you don't have to worry about pots boiling over.

4. Infinite heat control permits you to adjust electric burners like gas burners to any temperature—not just to the high, medium, and low points set by the manufacturer.

5. Automatic oven timers allow you to set the times when the oven will turn on and off before you leave home for the day. In cook-and-hold ovens, the oven goes on at the hour selected, cooks for the predetermined length of time, and then turns itself down and holds at a low warming temperature until you're ready to serve.

6. Pilot lights on gas ranges are replaced with electric ignition switches. This reduces fuel consumption by 10% or more.

7. Electronic controls allow you to program cooking operations just as you program an electronic calculator—by touching a few buttons on the backsplash of the range.

8. Electric broiling elements above and below the food cook steaks in half the usual time.

Conventional gas pilot light is here replaced by an electric ignition switch. Caloric Corp.

This drop-in electric range has a built-in ventilating system which obviates the need for the conventional exhaust fan. Jenn-Air Corp.

One unique electric range—available as a freestanding, drop-in, or built-in unit—contains in the cooking surface an exhaust fan which draws smoke, grease, and moisture down into the body of the range and then vents it outdoors through a duct. The manufacturer's built-in ovens have a similar exhaust system. In the ranges, the exhaust opening is centered between the burners, which are placed two on the left side of the cooktop and two on the right side. One or both burner panels can be removed at any time and temporarily replaced by barbecue grills with 2,800-watt elements.

Except for countertop microwave ovens, which are plugged into a 120-volt, 20-amp circuit, all electric ranges require 230-volt, 40-amp or 50-amp circuits. Gas ranges require, in addition to a gas line, a 120-volt, 15-amp circuit which they can share with other outlets.

BARBECUE GRILLS. A barbecue is simply a heavy metal box with grids in the top and, if you buy it as an accessory, a motorized rotisserie. Some units use charcoal, others gas, still others electricity. They can be built into solid masonry, as in a fireplace, or into a kitchen counter with cabinets on both sides and underneath. In the latter case, the grill must have an insulated shell which separates it from adjacent combustible or easily damaged surfaces.

Most barbecues are roughly 31 in. wide, 23 in. deep, and 15 in. high. The smallest—an electric model—is 18 in. wide and 22 in. deep. Like the ranges described above, it has a built-in ventilating fan which sucks smoke and odors down into the space below the grid and out through a vent.

Except for the latter, all barbecues require a hooded vent fan separate from the fan over the range. Because of the heavy smoke, grease, and carbon monoxide given off by grilling, the fan should be the most powerful available.

FOOD WARMERS. Various kinds of small portable food-warming appliances have been available for a number of years. Now there is a built-in warmer which is installed either in a base cabinet or built-in oven cabinet. The device, which measures about 23 in. deep, 22 in. high, and 24 in. wide, has two warming drawers, each holding a complete meal for a family of four for as much as six hours.

REFRIGERATORS. Relatively few conventional refrigerators with a single door and small 10° ice-cube compartment are sold today. Of these, a high percentage have a capacity of less than 5 cu. ft. and are used in family rooms, recreation rooms, bars, offices, and outdoors. Large sizes—up to a maximum of approximately 13 cu. ft.—are used in kitchens.

Two-door refrigerator-freezers with a large fresh-food compartment and smaller zero-degree freezing compartment have become standard for kitchen use. Three types are made:

Refrigerators with top-mounted freezers have from 12 to 23-cu.-ft. capacity. The freezing compartment accounts for roughly one-fourth of the storage space in smaller models and one-third in larger models. Exterior dimensions are: depth, 27 to 31 in.; width, 30 to 34 in.; height, 60 to 68 in.

Food warmer built into a kitchen base cabinet. Modern Maid—McGraw-Edison Co.

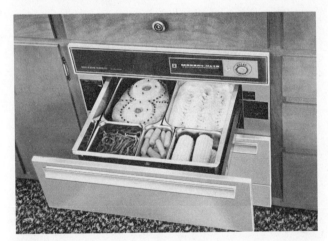

Glass-ceramic countertop warming unit. Corning Glass Works.

Refrigerators with bottom-mounted freezers, after a period of great popularity, have almost disappeared. The few still produced have a total capacity in the neighborhood of 20 cu. ft. The freezer space is about 6 cu. ft.

Refrigerator-freezers with side-mounted freezers—usually called side-by-side models—are divided vertically, with the freezer on the left side. Capacities range from about 17 to 25 cu. ft., with 6 to 9 cu. ft. of the total given over to freezing space. Dimensions are: depth, 28 to 30 in.; width, 30 to 36 in.; height, 60 to 67 in.

In some side-by-side refrigerators, the freezing-compartment door is divided horizontally so that the refrigerator has a total of three doors. The small upper cabinet houses an icemaker.

The newest feature in refrigerators is an automatic ice and ice-water dispenser installed in the door front so you can help yourself without opening the door. In some makes, the door also incorporates dispensers for orange juice and other drinks. Despite the appeal of such devices, however, their importance is secondary to a pair of older features:

Frost-free designs eliminate the need for defrosting ice-cube compartments. But while this saves work, it adds materially to the amount of electricity consumed.

Automatic icemakers eliminate another annoyance by producing a continuous supply of ice cubes without any attention. A ¼-in. tube connected to a cold-water supply line fills the icemaker automatically as cubes are deposited into a storage bin underneath. But this also is a feature which increases current consumption. Perhaps worse, icemakers sometimes require a long breaking-in period with numerous service calls before they operate reliably.

Other important features to look for in refrigerators are:

Super-cooled meat drawers keep meat fresh, without freezing, for up to seven days.

Cantilevered shelves can be adjusted up and down in 1-in. increments to increase storage flexibility.

Energy savers reduce fuel consumption in frost-free models.

Reversible doors on top- and bottom-mounted refrigerator-freezers allow you to change the swing from right to left or left to right when you remodel your kitchen or move to a new home. (All manufacturers produce refrigerators with right- or left-hand doors. But ordinarily, after you make your original choice, you cannot change it.)

Except for single-door models, all refrigerators require separate 120-volt, 20-amp circuits. If a refrigerator has a condenser on its back, a 1½-in. to 2-in. space must be provided between the top of the refrigerator and an overhead cabinet in order to allow the heat given off by the condenser to escape. However, if the

refrigerator exhausts heat from a grille under the door, a space above the refrigerator is unnecessary.

FREEZERS. Upright freezers resemble single-door refrigerators. Frozen foods are stored on shelves, in baskets, and in door racks. In low, top-opening chest freezers, foods are stored in the bottom of the chest and in lift-out baskets.

Uprights have surpassed chests in popularity because food is somewhat more accessible, the cabinets take up less floor space, and some models never form frost. On the other hand, cold air doesn't spill out of chests to such an extent when they are opened. You can fill them more solidly with food. And because you lift a lid instead of swinging open a door, you don't need as much floor space in front to load and unload them.

Upright capacities range from about 8 to 31 cu. ft. Dimensions are: depth, 27 to 34 in.; width, 23 to 32 in.; height, 59 to 70 in. Chest freezer capacities start at 5 cu. ft. and rise to 28 cu. ft. The freezers are 23 to 30 in. deep, 22 to 70 in. wide, and 35 to 37 in. high.

Most upright freezers have right-hand doors, but left-hand models are available. Since the condenser is on the back of the cabinet, space is needed above the freezer so the heat it gives off can escape freely.

A separate 120-volt, 20-amp circuit should be provided for all freezers of more than 12-cu.-ft. capacity. Smaller freezers can be plugged into 15-amp. lighting circuits.

ICEMAKERS. These are home-size versions of the large freestanding icemakers found in motel corridors. They turn out, on average, about 20 lbs. of ice cubes a day and store up to 700 cubes at one time. Measuring approximately 15 in. wide, 17 in. deep, and 26 in. high, they can be built into kitchens, pantries, and bars or used as freestanding appliances anywhere.

Icemakers are plugged into a 120-volt, 15-amp lighting circuit. They are connected by a ¼-in. tube to a cold-water supply line. Some models require a drain; others dispose of melt water by evaporation.

COMPACT KITCHENS. The compact kitchen is an all-in-one unit which is built specifically for small apartments and condominiums but which is sometimes used in homes as an auxiliary to the main kitchen. It incorporates a small, single-door, under-counter refrigerator; a sink; and a two-burner or four-burner gas or electric cooktop. Larger kitchens also have an oven and broiler which are usually built in under the cooktop but in a few cases are above the cooktop. All units except the last are 36 in. high and 25 in. deep. The smallest are only 30 in. wide; the largest, 72 in.

The kitchens have stainless-steel or porcelain-enamel-on-steel work surfaces and sinks. They are available with left- or right-hand refrigerator doors. A disposer

Compact kitchens. The larger unit contains a complete range. King Refrigerator Corp.

can be installed in some of the larger kitchens. Electric models with ovens require a 240-volt service. Small models with only two surface units are available for either 120-volt or 240-volt service. Gas models require a 120-volt, 15-amp circuit.

FOOD CENTERS. A food center is a small built-in appliance which is used with various attachments to mix, beat, or blend foods; grind, shred, or slice foods; extract juice; crush ice; sharpen knives. It consists of an electric motor suspended in a base cabinet just beneath a countertop, and a stainless-steel top exposed in the counter. To operate it, plug the mixer or blender attachment, etc., into the top and turn a control. The attachments are stored in the cabinet with the motor.

BUILT-IN TOASTER. This is a one-of-a-kind appliance which is built into a standard wall between studs. When you pull on the door, a four-slice automatic toaster slides out behind it. A disconnect switch makes it impossible to operate the toaster except when it is fully extended from the housing. The appliance

should be connected to a 120-volt, 20-amp appliance circuit.

VENTILATING FANS. Because of the smoke, grease, odors, and moisture given off by cooking operations, a ventilating fan should be installed as close as possible to the range in all kitchens. As a rule of thumb, the capacity of the fan as measured in cubic feet per minute should be great enough to give a complete air change in the kitchen once every four minutes. This means that if a kitchen measures $10 \times 10 \times 8$ ft. (800 cu. ft.), the fan must deliver at least 200 cfm. For maximum comfort, however, you should buy the largest fan available.

Five basic types of fan are used.

Ducted-hood fans are considered the most efficient because the fan is installed in a metal hood that overhangs the range top. Smoke, grease, etc. rise straight up into the hood and are exhausted outdoors through a 4-in. duct.

Most two-oven, eye-level ranges and stack-on ranges can be equipped with hood fans which look like an integral part of the upper oven. The fronts of the fans

This toaster is designed for building into a wall. Modern Maid—McGraw-Edison Co.

Kitchen exhaust fan installed on outside wall reduces noise in kitchen. NuTone—Scovill Manufacturing Co.

open out to form hoods when the fans are on, and lie flush with the fronts of the ovens when the fans are off.

Non-ducted-hood fans also consist of a fan installed in a hood over the range. But since there is no duct leading to the outdoors, the fans are incapable of removing any of the moisture which fogs windows and may cause severe condensation problems. Smoke and odors are absorbed in a charcoal filter. Grease is trapped in a fibrous-steel filter which must be washed periodically in detergent solution.

Wall fans are installed in the wall above the range backsplash. If the range is placed against an outside wall, the fan exhausts directly to the outdoors. A small exterior door keeps out air when the fan is not running. For ranges located on inside walls, another variety of wall fan is used. It is connected to a duct which carries the kitchen air up through the wall and then to the outdoors through the roof or exterior wall.

Ceiling fans are the least efficient type of ducted fan because they are necessarily installed farther from the range. But they are often essential when ranges are located in islands or peninsulas, and they are often used when a range is placed against an inside wall.

Exterior-mounted fans are the quietest type simply because they are installed outdoors and pull the inside air to them. For maximum efficiency, they should be connected directly to the kitchen; air should not reach them via a duct. The fans are designed for installation either in walls or on the roof.

A hood fan should be installed with the lower edges of the hood just high enough above the range surface so the homemaker can see into tall pots on the back burners. Maximum height is 30 in. The hood should be slightly wider than the range, and ideally, it should also be slightly deeper.

A wall fan should be centered behind and 18 to 24 in. above the burners. A ceiling fan should be centered on the burners.

If a duct is required, it should be straight and not over 10 ft. long. If an elbow is unavoidable, duct length should be reduced. A weatherhead with a gate which swings closed when the fan is not in use is installed at the outer end of the duct to keep out wind.

Power for a fan is supplied by a 120-volt, 15-amp circuit which also serves the lights in the kitchen.

WASHERS. Although wringer and spinner washers are still produced, they have been largely supplanted by fully automatic machines which wash, rinse, and damp-dry up to about 20 lbs. of clothes at one time. In the conventional washer, clothes are loaded through a door in the top and washing is done by an agitator. In front-opening models, washing is done in a perforated drum revolving around a horizontal axis. Both types are 36 in. high (not counting the backsplash), 25 to 28 in.

deep, and 26 to 29 in. wide. (Top-opening models are also made in small sizes. Depending on the manufacturer, these measure 24 in. wide by 15 in. deep by 30 in. high, or $21 \times 24 \times 36$ in.) Installation requires a 120-volt, 20-amp circuit which serves no other outlets; and hot- and cold-water supply lines. Water is drained from the washer through a rubber hose into a laundry tub or a standpipe connected into the house drain.

The major advantage of front-opening washers is that they use less water and therefore less detergent and bleach than top-opening models. Home economists feel, however, that they do not clean as thoroughly. In addition, they do not afford as great flexibility of operation.

The best of the top-opening washers are designed to wash all kinds of fabrics completely automatically. They have several agitator and spin speeds, three wash-water temperatures, and two rinse-water temperatures. Simply by pushing buttons or turning controls, you can vary the wash-rinse-spin-dry cycles by changing water temperatures, speeds, and wash times. You can also program the washers to provide a variety of partial cycles such as a long soak, an extra wash, an extra rinse, etc.

Other important features include:

Watersaver controls permit you to fill the wash basket to several different levels. (All washers provide two water levels.)

Special permanent-press and knitwear cycles prevent wrinkling of clothes.

Automatic bleach and fabric-softener dispensers.

Suds-savers let you save and reuse hot, sudsy water.

Unbalance controls prevent the wash basket from banging against the sides of the washer if a load gets out of balance, or automatically stop the washer until the load is adjusted.

DRYERS. Automatic gas and electric dryers are made by all laundry-appliance manufacturers to match their automatic washers in appearance and more or less in size (the dryers are often 3 or 4 in. wider than the washers). Ordinarily the two appliances are installed side by side, but if you have a front-opening washer, you can place the dryer above it.

All dryers are loaded through a door in the front. As the drum turns, warm air circulates through the tumbling clothes so rapidly that the average load is fully dried in about 30 minutes. The dried clothes are softer and fluffier and have fewer wrinkles than clothes dried on a line.

All dryers have a timed drying cycle which permits the homemaker to control the drying time from a few minutes to an hour or more. The best machines also have a number of automatic cycles which are controlled by pushing a button corresponding to the type of load to be dried. These cycles include a normal cycle for use with most fabrics; a heavy-fabric cycle; a permanent-press cycle; a "delicate" cycle for woolens, nylons, etc.; a damp-dry cycle which dries clothes ready for ironing; and a fluff cycle, without heat, which is used for pillows and heat-sensitive draperies and fabrics.

The majority of electric dryers operate on 240 volts and require a circuit fused at 30 amps. Some operate on 120 volts. This doubles the drying time. Gas dryers need a 120-volt, 20-amp circuit to turn the drum.

Dryers should be vented to the outdoors through a 4-in. duct which can be connected to the side, back, or bottom of the dryer. The duct should be as straight as possible. If it has one elbow, it should not exceed 20 ft. in length. Duct kits are sold by all appliance dealers.

COMBINATION WASHER-DRYERS. Not long ago several manufacturers offered a combination washer-dryer which looked like and took up no more space than a conventional front-opening automatic washer. This has disappeared from the market. Today if you need a washer and dryer in very small space, you must stack one appliance on top of the other.

Several manufacturers have washer and dryer models which are designed for this kind of arrangement. One company actually puts them together in a single unit. This consists of a top-opening washer in the base of the cabinet and a front-opening electric dryer in the top. The combination appliance measures 28 in. deep, 24 in. wide, and 66 in. high. Depending on the model, it operates on either a 120-volt, 20-amp circuit or a 240-volt, 30-amp circuit.

CENTRAL VACUUM CLEANERS. Built-in vacuum-

Combination washer-dryer in a single 24-in.-wide unit. Frigidaire—General Motors Corp.

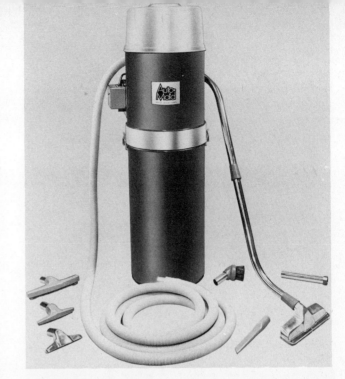

Except for the plastic tubes and wires which are concealed within the walls and floors, here are the basic components of a central vacuum-cleaning system. Colt Industries.

cleaning systems have one major drawback: They are expensive. But they have a number of pluses: You can clean several rooms—even an entire floor in a small house—without stopping to pull out the plug and push it into another outlet. They are almost completely noiseless. None of the dust they pick up is recirculated into the air as it is with a conventional vacuum cleaner. And the dust bag is so large that it does not have to be emptied more than once every couple of months.

Whether the cleaner cleans more thoroughly than an upright, canister, or tank cleaner is debatable. Because of the large size of the motor, it has greater suction power, but some of this is dissipated in the long run from the cleaning nozzle to the collection tank. Furthermore, since most built-in cleaners depend on suction alone, they do not beat the dust out of carpets as an upright cleaner or canister with brush attachment does. However, they do an excellent job.

The cleaning system consists of a central motor and dirt tank installed in the garage, basement, or other out-of-the-way place. From the tank, 2-in. plastic tubes run through the walls and floors to strategically located wall outlets in the living area. The cleaning tools are attached to a 20-ft. to 36-ft. flexible hose. Plugging the hose into an outlet automatically turns the cleaner on.

Central systems are easily installed in new houses before the walls are closed in. In an existing house, the job is obviously more difficult but perfectly feasible. The extent of the work depends on the construction and layout of the house as well as on the number of outlets required. Ordinarily only three or four outlets are needed in the average small house.

Central station of an intercom system. NuTone—Scovill Manufacturing Co.

Stereo system from which music is piped throughout house. NuTone—Scovill Manufacturing Co.

INTERCOMS. An intercom system is, in effect, a small-scale telephone system restricted to your home. With it, you can converse between rooms without raising your voice, find out who is at the front door without moving from wherever you are, keep an ear open for a baby or sick person, watch over children playing in the basement, check on suspicious sounds from your bedside, or pipe music throughout the entire house.

One type of system is installed by the telephone company and operates through the telephones and telephone wiring in the house. The other system is installed by an electrical contractor and operates through its own network of low-voltage wires, transmitters, and receivers.

In the latter, which is the more common, a master station is installed in a wall or under a built-in wall cabinet at some central location. Small substations are recessed in walls in as many other rooms as you like, and also at the outside entrances and on the terrace. (You can tailor the system to your own requirements; add to it later.) From the master station you can speak to all other stations and listen in to all stations. From the substations, you can communicate with the master station and also with other substations. Power for the system is supplied by a power unit which can be concealed in any remote location. One type plugs into a 120-volt, 15-amp general-purpose wiring circuit; another is battery-operated.

WHO MAKES IT

Acme-National Refrigeration Co. · Compact kitchens 30 to 72 in. wide, gas and electric. One model with sink, refrigerator, and two electric burners contained in a 40-in. wood-finished cabinet for use in family rooms, etc. 24-in. and 30-in. undercounter refrigerators, one in wood-finished cabinet. Freestanding icemaker.

Air King Corp. · Wall and ceiling exhaust fans. Largest (a ceiling unit) rated at 340 cfm.

Allibert, Inc. · Clear acrylic swinging towel bars, soapdishes, towel ring, shelves, and facial-tissue dispenser.

Amana Refrigeration, Inc. · 30-in. two-oven eye-level electric ranges with microwave ovens at eye level. Countertop microwave ovens. 20-cu.-ft. bottom-mounted refrigerator-freezer. Top-mounted refrigerator-freezers, some with doors which can be converted from right- to left-hand opening. Side-by-side refrigerator-freezers, several with water and ice dispensers in door. Upright and chest freezers. 18-in. trash compactor.

American-Standard, Inc. · Enameled cast-iron and stainless-steel sinks with single, double, and triple bowls. Corner sink in stainless steel. Bar and laundry sinks.

Bangkok Industries, Inc. · 2-ft. to 8-ft. countertops laminated of solid teak. 1 ¼ in. thick.

Boise Cascade Corp., Kitchen Cabinet Div. · Kitchen cabinets in four styles, three made of natural-finish oak, the fourth of wood sheathed with rigid wood-grained vinyl.

Bradley Corp. · Chrome-plated and colored plastic sink faucets.

Battery-operated electronic unit built into the door of a three-door refrigerator can record messages and also incorporates a radio and tape recorder and player. Frigidaire—General Motors Corp.

Brammer Manufacturing Co. · Six styles of oak and pine kitchen cabinets.

Briggs Manufacturing Co. · One- and two-bowl enameled steel sinks.

Broan Manufacturing Co. · Central vacuum-cleaning systems. Small-capacity model has dirt-collection tank built into a cabinet that recesses between studs. Hose is plugged directly into tank. Wall and ceiling ventilating fans. Largest (a wall unit) is rated at 550 cfm.

Brown Stove Works. · 20-in., 24-in., 30-in., and 36-in. gas and electric freestanding ranges.

Caloric Corp. · 30-in. electric and 30-in. and 36-in. gas freestanding ranges. 30-in. electric and gas two-oven eye-level ranges. Electric and gas built-in cooktops. 24-in. built-in gas oven and broiler. 24-in. single and double built-in electric ovens. Undercounter and convertible dishwashers. Continuous-feed disposers. 18-in. trash compactor. Single- and double-bowl stainless-steel and enameled steel sinks. Ducted and ductless range hoods. Splash plates to protect wall between range and hood fan.

Central Vac International. · Central vacuum-cleaning systems.

Chambers Corp. · Unusual stack-on electric or gas cooktop is 42 in. wide, 8 in. high; rests on a 28-in.-high base cabinet. Made of stainless steel; has four burners and a broiler beneath a tilt-back panel in the top. The broiler unit can also be used as a griddle. 24-in. single and double electric built-in ovens. 24-in. built-in gas oven and broiler. Built-in electric and gas cooktops. 30-in. electric and gas drop-in ranges. Ducted and ductless range hoods. Compact chest freezers.

Chicago Faucet Co. · Many kinds of sink faucet.

Colt Industries. · Central vacuum-cleaning system.

Consoweld Corp. · DuraBeauty laminated plastics in solid colors, wood grains, distressed wood grains, marbles, abstract designs. Flexible edging trim in all patterns.

Consoweld Distributors. · Glass ceramic inserts for counters.

Contemporary Systems, Inc. · Tielsa cabinets from West Germany in sleek modern design. Cabinet bodies made of particleboard with plastic finish; doors of laminated plastic, solid wood, or wood veneer in many colors or natural finishes. Many wall cabinets with hydraulic lift-up doors. Great range of standard and special cabinets, including cabinets for installation of ducted ventilating fans. Stainless-steel sinks. Stainless-steel countertops incorporating sink and electric cooktop. Electric towel dryer.

Corning Glass Works. · 30-in. freestanding and drop-in electric ranges. Built-in electric cooktops. 24-in. single and double built-in electric ovens. Glass-ceramic warming unit which also serves as cutting board builds into countertops and measures 17×21×2 in.

Crane Co. · Two single-bowl and one double-bowl sinks with fittings.

Delta Faucet Co. · Chrome-plated sink faucets. Wall-mounted models, one with hose and spray.

Diller Corp. · Metallic laminated plastics.

Du Pont. · Corian methacrylate panels for countertops.

Dwyer Products Corp. · Gas and electric compact kitchens, 39 to 87 in. wide, all with steel wall cabinets and back-splash panels. 48-in. electric kitchen contained in sand- or ebony-colored cabinets for use in family rooms, etc. 39-in. unit with sink and undercounter refrigerator only. 15-in. and 21-in. utility cabinets.

Elkay Manufacturing Co. · Every type of stainless-steel sink you can think of—single, double, and triple bowls; corner sinks; sinks with drainboards; sinks with electric food centers concealed beneath a drainboard; sinks with drinking fountains; bar sinks. Hot- and cold-water dispensers. Complete line of sink fittings.

Emerson Electric Co., In-Sink-Erator Div. · Continuous and batch-feed disposers. Built-in hot-water dispensers for installation at sink.

Emerson Electric Co., Rittenhouse-Chromalox Div. · Pryne wall and ceiling ventilating fans. Largest models (ceiling units) have a rated capacity of 280 cfm. Intercoms.

Exxon Chemical Co. · Nevamar laminated plastics in solid colors, wood grains, leathers, marbles, abstracts, unusual dimensional finishes such as blue denim, cordoba leather, woven cane, slate.

Fasco Industries, Inc. · Central vacuum-cleaning systems. Wall and ceiling ventilating fans. Ducted-hood and ductless-hood fans. Largest unit (a wall unit) has rated capacity of 480 cfm; however, utility fans up to 3,800 cfm are available.

Fedders Corp., Norge Div. · Undercounter and convertible dishwashers. Automatic washers and gas and electric dryers. 21-in.-wide washer and dryer can be installed with the dryer above the washer.

Gaffers & Sattler, Inc. · 20-in., 30-in., and 36-in. gas freestanding ranges. 30-in. electric freestanding ranges. 30-in. gas and electric drop-in ranges. 30-in. gas and electric two-oven eye-level ranges. Gas and electric built-in cooktops. 24-in. electric single and double built-in ovens. 24-in. gas built-in oven with broiler. Countertop microwave ovens. Ducted-hood and ductless-hood fans. Undercounter and portable dishwashers. Continuous and batch-feed disposers. 15-in. trash compactor.

General Electric Co., Hotpoint Div. · 30-in. and 40-in. freestanding electric ranges. One 30-in. model has an oven that cooks conventionally and with microwave. 21-in. and 30-in. slide-in electric ranges. 30-in. drop-in electric ranges. 30-in. two-oven eye-level electric ranges. Built-in electric cooktops. 24-in. and 27-in. built-in single and double ovens. Countertop microwave ovens. Top-mounted and side-by-side refrigerator-freezers. Single-door refrigerators. Chest and upright freezers. Undercounter and convertible dishwashers. Continuous and batch-feed disposers. 15-in. trash compactors. Automatic washers and gas and electric dryers. Ducted and ductless range hoods.

General Electric Co., Major Appliance Div. · 21-in. and 30-in. freestanding electric ranges. 30-in. two-oven eye-level electric ranges, one model with a microwave oven that can be used as a conventional oven below the cooking surface. 27-in. electric drop-in ranges. Electric built-in cooktops, one with remote controls. 24-in. and 27-in. single and double built-in electric ovens. Microwave oven can be built in or used on countertop. Ducted and ductless range hoods. Top-mounted and side-by-side refrigerator-freezers, several with water and ice dispensers in door. Single-door refrigerators. Undercounter dishwashers. Continuous and batch-feed disposers. 15-in. trash compactors. Automatic washers and gas and electric dryers.

General Motors Corp., Frigidaire Div. · 30-in. and 40-in. freestanding electric ranges. 30-in. two-oven eye-level ranges. Built-in electric cooktops. 24-in. built-in single and double electric ovens. 30-in. drop-in ranges. Microwave oven can be built in or placed on counter. Top range models have electronic controls. Top-mounted and side-by-side refrigerator-freezers, some with water, ice, and soft-drink dispensers in door. Single-door refrigerators. Chest and upright freezers. Undercounter and convertible dishwashers. Continuous and batch-feed disposers. 15-in. trash compactor. Automatic washers and gas and electric dryers. Combination washer-dryer.

Goodwin of California, Inc. · Rectangular fan hoods of steel finished in baked-on enamel. Hoods are designed to hang from ceiling either over an island or peninsula range or over a range installed against a wall. Charcoal barbecues in wide range of sizes that drop into the middle of a counter or slide into the front. Smoking compartment to fit over barbecues. Rotisserie.

Haas Cabinet Co. · Three styles of wood kitchen cabinets.

Hardwick Stove Co. · 30-in. freestanding and two-oven, eye-level electric and gas ranges. 20-inch freestanding gas and electric ranges.

Hobart Corp. · KitchenAid undercounter and convertible dishwashers. Dishwasher-sink combinations. Batch-feed and continuous-feed disposers. 18-in. trash compactors. Built-in hot-water dispenser.

International Paper Co., Long-Bell Div. · Four styles of natural-finish wood cabinets. Several special cabinets including 84-in.-high pantry cabinet and serving-cart cabinet.

Jenn-Air Corp. · Electric ranges, ovens, cooktops, and barbecues with built-in ventilating system. 30-in. freestanding and drop-in ranges. 30-in. built-in single oven; 24-in. built-in double ovens. Built-in cooktops. In all models the burners can be replaced with barbecue grills, griddles, French fryers. Barbecue grills can be built into countertops. Power-driven rotisseries and shish-kebabs available for use on grills.

Just Manufacturing Co. · Stainless-steel sinks of every conceivable type. Bar sinks.

Keller Industries, Keller Columbus Div. · 20-in., 30-in., and 36-in. freestanding electric and gas ranges. 30-in. two-oven eye-level electric and gas ranges. 30-in. electric and gas stack-on ranges. Built-in electric cooktops. 21-in. built-in electric ovens. Undercounter dishwasher. Continuous-feed disposers. Ducted-hood and ductless-hood fans. Wood kitchen cabinets with wood-grained rigid vinyl bonded to the fronts. Three cabinet styles in three colors.

King Refrigerator Corp. · Gas and electric compact kitchens 30 to 72 in. wide. One 30-in. model with eye-level oven. 33-in. and 48-in. models enclosed in colored or wood-grained steel cabinets for installation outside the kitchen.

Kirkhill, Inc. · Repair parts for most makes of sink faucet.

Kohler Co. · Single-, double-, and triple-bowl enameled cast-iron sinks. Acrylic bar sinks. Cast-iron laundry sink. Faucets with watersaver controls.

Kristia Associates. · Cast-iron Norwegian wood stove with oven and two hot plates. $22\frac{1}{2} \times 16 \times 27\frac{1}{2}$ in. high.

Leigh Products, Inc. · Dryer-vent kits.

Leigh Products, Inc., Rutt Custom Kitchens Div. · Solid cherry, oak, and birch cabinets in eight styles and numerous natural, antique-glazed, or enameled finishes. Many special cabinets including 84-in.-high and undercounter pantry units, peninsula cabinets, serving-cart cabinets, angular cabinets, refrigerator cabinets.

Magic Chef. · 20-in., 30-in., and 36-in. freestanding gas and electric ranges. 30-in. gas and electric two-oven eye-level ranges. 30-in. electric drop-in and slide-in ranges. Electric built-in cooktops. Electric single and double built-in ovens 24 or 26 in. wide. Microwave ovens for built-in and countertop installation.

Martin Industries, Inc., King Products Div. · Old-fashioned cast-iron coal or wood stove with six cover plates, oven, and two eye-level warming ovens. Modern white-enameled wood or coal stove with five cover plates, oven, water tank.

Maytag Co. · Automatic washers and gas and electric dryers, including 115-volt portable models 24 in. wide, 15 in. deep, and 30 in. high. Dryer can be hung on wall over washer. Undercounter and convertible dishwashers. Batch-feed and continuous-feed disposers.

McGraw-Edison Co., Modern Maid Div. · 30-in. stack-on electric and gas range with dishwasher built into cabinet below the cooktop. 30-in. gas freestanding and slide-in ranges. Gas built-in cooktops. Gas built-in oven and broiler. Built-in gas oven with a microwave oven underneath. Built-in electric food warmer. Built-in toaster. Undercounter and freestanding dishwashers. Continuous-feed disposers. 15-in. trash compactor.

McGraw-Edison Co., Speed Queen Div. · Automatic washers with stainless-steel tub. Automatic gas and electric dryers with stainless-steel drum. Wringer washers.

Medford Corp., Diamond Industries Div. · Three styles of wood cabinet. One style of laminated-plastic cabinet.

Miami-Carey Co. · Wall and ceiling ventilating fans. Hooded ducted and ductless fans. Largest fan (a hooded model) has rated capacity of 310 cfm. Colored splash plates to protect wall between fan hood and range top.

Michigan Maple Block Co. · Laminated maple blocks and countertops up to 10 ft. long and $1\frac{1}{2}$ or $1\frac{3}{16}$ in. thick. With and without backsplashes.

Montgomery Ward & Co. · Two styles of wood cabinet. Three lines of semi-assembled cabinets that you put together yourself: unfinished birch and fir; wood with pecan finish. Limited line of steel cabinets. Laminated plastic countertops with rounded edges. Ducted-hood fans. Two-bowl enameled cast-iron sinks. One- and two-bowl stainless-steel and enameled steel sinks. Continuous-feed disposers. Built-in, convertible, and portable dishwashers. 12-in. trash compactors. 30-in. gas and electric freestanding ranges, one model with warming shelf. 24-in. and 40-in. electric and 20-in. and 36-in. gas freestanding ranges. 30-in. gas and electric two-oven eye-level ranges; an electric model with microwave oven above the work surface. Built-in gas and electric cooktops. Single and double 24-in. built-in electric ovens. 24-in. built-in gas oven and broiler. Countertop microwave ovens. Top-mounted and side-by-side refrigerator-freezers. Single-door refrigerators. Upright and chest freezers. Ceiling and wall ventilating fans. Ducted-hood and ductless-hood fans. Capacity of largest fan (wall model) is 300 cfm.

Morgan Co. · Built-in ironing board cabinets.

Murray Equipment Co. · Two-level lazy-susan corner "cabinet" in a frame for building into a 36×36-in. space with any type of base cabinet. Doors must be added.

Billy Penn Corp. · Automatic-dryer vent kits.

Pioneer Plastics Corp. · Pionite laminated plastics in solid colors, wood grains, marbles, abstract designs.

Powers Regulator Co., Powers-Fiat Div. · Fiberglass laundry sinks are wall-hung, floor-mounted, or enclosed in white metal cabinet. Fiberglass floor sinks.

Price Pfister. · Faucets and fittings for kitchen sinks.

Ronson Corp. · Electric food center built into counter.

Roper Sales Co. · Microwave ovens for countertop installation, or built into wall with a conventional oven below, or as a top oven in a 30-in. double-oven eye-level range. 30-in. electric and 30-in. and 36-in. gas freestanding ranges. 30-in. electric and gas two-oven eye-level ranges. 30-in. electric and gas slide-in and drop-in ranges. Electric and gas built-in cooktops. 24-in. electric single and double built-in ovens. 24-in. gas built-in oven with broiler. Undercounter and convertible dishwashers. Continuous-feed disposers. 15-in. trash compactor. Ducted and ductless range hoods.

St. Charles Manufacturing Co. · Eight styles of cabinet, including one line which is raised off the floor. The cabinet bodies are made of steel; fronts may be of steel in an array of unusual colors, natural-finished wood, or wood-grained plastic laminates. An additional line of cabinets is laminated plastic throughout. Special cabinets of almost every conceivable type. One-piece countertops of laminated plastic, stainless steel, or maple.

H. J. Scheirich Co. · Ten lines of wood kitchen cabinets and three lines of particleboard cabinets covered with vinyl in wood colors and textures.

Scotsman. · Freestanding icemaker.

Scovill Manufacturing Co., NuTone Housing Products Div. · Food centers. Central vacuum cleaners with motor-driven brush attachment. Intercoms of every kind imaginable. All kinds of wall and ceiling ventilating fans, exterior-mounted fans, ducted and ductless hood fans. Fans for building into large custom-designed hoods. Largest fan (a roof-mounted model) has a rated capacity of 1,000 cfm.

Sears Roebuck & Co. · 21-in., 30-in., and 40-in. electric freestanding ranges. 21-in., 30-in., and 36-in. freestanding gas ranges. 30-in. electric and gas drop-in ranges. 30-in. two-oven eye-level gas and electric ranges. Gas and electric built-in cooktops. 24-in. electric single and double built-in ovens. 24-in. gas built-in oven and broiler. Countertop microwave ovens. Ducted-hood and ductless-hood fans. Wall and ceiling fans. Largest fan (ducted hood) has a capacity of 420 cfm. Top-mounted and

side-by-side refrigerator-freezers. Upright and chest freezers. Built-in, convertible, and portable dishwashers. Continuous-feed disposers. 15-in. trash compactor. Enameled steel and stainless-steel single- and double-bowl sinks. Bar sink. Plastic laundry sink. Four styles of wood cabinet with numerous special cabinets. One style available only partially assembled. One style of plastic cabinet. Steel cabinets. Laminated-plastic countertops with rounded edges. Central vacuum-cleaning systems with optional motor-driven brush attachment.

A. O. Smith Corp. · Continuous and batch-feed disposers.

Speakman Co. · Chrome-plated sink faucets.

Stanwood Corp. · 2-ft. to 12-ft. countertops, table tops, etc. laminated of solid teak, walnut, oak, maple, beech. Built to order in thicknesses up to 4 in.

Superior Fireplace Co. · Charcoal and gas barbecues.

Symmons Industries, Inc. · Kitchen faucets.

Talk-A-Phone Co. · Intercoms.

Tappan Co. · 30-in. electric and gas freestanding ranges, one model with a warming shelf which incorporates the controls for the entire range raised above the cooking surface. 36-in. gas freestanding ranges. 30-in. drop-in electric ranges. 30-in. two-oven eye-level electric and gas ranges, one electric model with a microwave oven at eye level. Electric and gas built-in cooktops. Single and double built-in electric ovens. Built-in gas oven with separate broiling compartment. Countertop microwave ovens. Ducted and ductless range hoods. Top-mounted and side-by-side refrigerator-freezers, one of the latter with water and ice-cube dispensers in door. Single-door refrigerators. Undercounter and convertible dishwashers. Continuous-feed disposers. 15-in. trash compactors.

Triangle Pacific Cabinet Corp. · Nine styles of natural-finish wood cabinets.

U-Line Corp. · Freestanding icemaker in three models.

United Cabinet Corp. · AristOKraft cabinets, including 84-in.-high pantry cabinet and peninsula cabinets. Ten natural-wood-finish designs. Some cabinets of wood, some faced with plastic laminates.

Universal-Rundle Corp. · Single- and double-bowl enameled cast-iron sinks.

Wallace-Murray Corp., Eljer Plumbingware Div. · Enameled cast-iron and enameled steel single- and double-bowl sinks. Cast-iron wall-hung sinks. Laundry and floor sinks.

Wal-Vac, Inc. · Central vacuum-cleaning systems. Small-capacity model has dirt tank built into a cabinet that recesses in a wall between studs. Hose is plugged directly into tank. Power-driven brush optional.

Westinghouse Electric Corp., Decorative Micarta Div. · Micarta laminated plastic in solid colors, wood grains, leathers, marbles, fabric weaves, abstract designs.

Westinghouse Electric Corp., IXL Div. · Kitchen cabinets in three designs made of natural-finish oak, pecan, or pine.

Whirlpool Corp. · 30-in. freestanding and drop-in electric ranges. Built-in electric cooktops. 24-in. and 30-in. single and double built-in electric ovens. Top-mounted refrigerator-freezers. Undercounter dishwashers. Continuous and batch-feed disposers. 15-in. trash compactor. Automatic washers and gas and electric dryers. Ducted and ductless exhaust hoods.

White-Westinghouse Appliance Co. · 30-in. and 40-in. free-standing electric ranges. 30-in. electric slide-in ranges. 30-in. two-oven eye-level electric ranges. Built-in electric cooktops. 25-in. built-in electric single and double ovens. Countertop microwave oven. Undercounter and convertible dishwashers. Top-mounted and side-by-side refrigerator-freezers. Single-door refrigerators. Upright and chest freezers. Top-opening and front-opening automatic washers. Gas and electric dryers. Dryers can be stacked on top of front-opening washers in a 27-in.-wide floor space.

Ralph Wilson Plastics Co. · Wilson Art laminated plastics in solid colors, wood grains, leathers, metallics, and abstract designs.

Wood-Mode Cabinetry. · Five basic styles of wood cabinet available in an infinite range of natural and paint finishes and hardware. Numerous special cabinets including 84-in.-high and undercounter pantry units, utility cabinets with lazy-susan shelves and pull-out trays, serving-cart cabinet.

Wrightway Manufacturing Co. · Replacement faucet handles. Faucet aerators. Replacement hoses and spray assemblies for sinks.

16
Storage

If you were to measure up the space which is devoted to storage in your home, you would find that most of it was built by a carpenter out of ordinary lumber, plywood, and gypsum board. This is surprising in view of the lengths to which manufacturers have gone to prefabricate all other parts of the house, but there is a simple explanation. For one thing, closets—which account for the largest proportion of storage volume—are not readily standardized. They are built in where there is room for them, and so they are of many shapes and sizes. For another thing, manufacturers are understandably loath to ship a product—in this case, a closet—which is composed about 90% of air.

If industry has largely failed to simplify closet construction, however, it has more than made up for it by providing a wealth of easy-to-use storage units and equipment. The following descriptions include only those items which can be or normally are permanently attached to a house.

PREFABRICATED CLOSETS. The only ceiling-high closet on the market is a knocked-down unit of particleboard measuring 30 in. deep and 3 or 4 ft. wide. The height is adjustable from 7 ft. 10 in. to 8 ft. 2 in. The closet comes with two sides and a front, including a bifold door, and is designed for erection against a wall or in a corner.

Most prefab closets are only 5½ to 6 ft. high, 15 or approximately 22 in. deep, and 24 to 72 in. wide. Made of plywood, hardboard, or steel, they are completely enclosed and have sliding doors. They are not meant to be built in, but if you anchor them in a corner and fill in the space above them, they look as if they were.

CEDAR CLOSETS. Cedar closets are built like conventional closets until it comes to finishing the interior. The same finishing process is followed in converting an existing closet into a cedar closet.

The cedar boards used are sold by lumberyards in bundles covering 30 sq. ft. The boards are ⅜ in. thick, 2 to 4 in. wide, 2 to 8 ft. long, and tongued and grooved on both the edges and the ends. You can nail the boards directly to studs or to any flat existing wall.

Work on one wall at a time from the floor up. Install the boards horizontally and scribe the ends to fit the adjacent walls so there are no gaps at the corners of the closet. Nail the first boards along the floor line with two 1½-in. finishing nails in each stud. All succeeding boards require only one nail per stud. Interlock the edges and ends of the boards tightly. The end joints need not be centered on the studs since the tongue-and-groove joints hold them securely.

After the walls are covered, it's a good idea to cover the floor, ceiling, and back of the door with cedar to intensify the odor. Weatherstrip the door, which must be of the hinged variety. The cedar is not finished in

Constructing a cedar closet with tongue-and-groove boards.

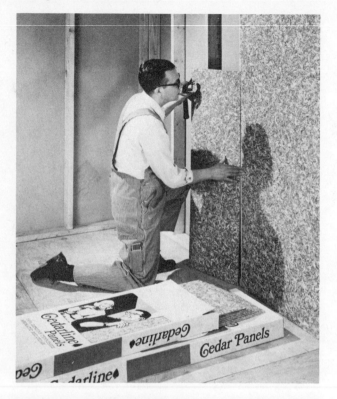

Particleboard made of cedar can also be used to build cedar closets. Giles & Kendall Co.

any way. If it begins to lose its aroma later on, sand it.

CABINETS. See Chapters 14 and 15. Most kitchen and bathroom cabinets are so well designed and finished that they can be built in anywhere.

Louvered and raised-panel doors for home-built cabinets or for replacement of doors on old kitchen and other cabinets are available in a few stock sizes.

SHELF UNITS. Preassembled shelf units suitable for installation in your living room are furniture pieces of such simple design that, with very little work, you can build them in so they look as much a part of the house as shelves built by a carpenter. They are 72 to 76 in. high, 12 to 14 in. deep, and 24 to 36 in. wide. Some units contain shelves from top to bottom; others have shelves and cabinets; still others have shelves, cabinets, and a fold-down panel serving as a desk. In many cases, the depth of the cabinets in the base of the units is increased to 15 in.

The units are made of particleboard with a surface veneer of beautiful wood or vinyl.

Back-of-door shelves and cabinets, which are most often used in bathrooms and closets, are 4 in. deep, 14 to 24 in. wide, and up to 60 in. high. On panel doors, screw the units to the stiles or rails; on hollow-core flush doors, use nylon anchors. Although the shelves themselves are not heavy enough to warp a door or

loosen the hinge screws, you should not overload them with heavy bottles and the like.

CORNER CUPBOARDS. Cupboards of authentic Colonial design have enclosed cupboards in the base, shelves with glass doors (which don't have to be used) above. They are 7 ft. high or slightly higher and have an overall width (measured diagonally to the walls) ranging from 32 to 42 in.

Made of pine, the cupboards are shipped knocked down and require a modicum of skill to build in. The existing walls serve as the backs.

DRAWERS. If you don't feel up to building your own drawers, have them made by a local millwork shop. A possible alternative—but only if you're building drawers into a closet—is to buy a molded plastic drawer measuring approximately 11 in. wide, 6 in. high, and 16 in. deep. The latter is most easily installed in a light metal rack made by the drawer manufacturer.

If you want to build in a chest of drawers, buy a drawer case. This consists of a frame with three, four, or five drawers. The frame has no back, sides, top, or bottom so it can be built into a wall.

Drawer cases come in various sizes. Those most suitable for the home are made of wood. Steel cases are primarily for factory use, but if you apply a couple of coats of enamel to the plain, unadorned fronts, they will look fine.

DRAWER SLIDES. Drawer slides take the place of the wood framework on which drawers in furniture pieces rest. Made of steel with ball bearings, they are installed in pairs—usually one on either side of a drawer. Half of each slide is screwed to the drawer case, the other half to the drawer. A drawer so equipped slides in and out as easily as a drawer in a modern kitchen base cabinet (which is also equipped with slides).

The slides are designed in so many ways and so many sizes that the only way you can make an intelligent selection is to ask a hardware dealer to show you a catalog and then order the slides you need. Some slides are mounted along the top edges of the drawer, some along the bottom edges, and some are installed underneath. There are slides which are used to suspend a drawer under a countertop, which allow you to pull a drawer all the way out of the frame without its falling to the floor, which close the drawer automatically, and so on.

SHELF STANDARDS. Slotted metal standards are designed for cantilevering shelves from a wall or building shelved room dividers. Those used for cantilevering are slender, U-shaped, 1-ft. to 12-ft. aluminum strips with a row of vertical slots spaced 1 in. apart from end to

Cantilevered shelves built with slotted metal standards and brackets. Stanley Works.

end. The strips are mounted vertically on the face of a wall and screwed to the studs. The shelves (any number can be used) are supported on wedge-shaped aluminum brackets which are clipped into the standards at any height. The brackets range from 4 to 24 in. long. Although most are designed to support shelves at right angles to the wall, some are slanted downward.

The standards are normally spaced 16 to 32 in. apart, depending on the weight to be carried by the shelves. For exceptionally heavy loads, standards are made with two rows of slots to hold double brackets.

Standards used for freestanding shelves are hollow, square tubes wedged between the floor and ceiling. They are made in three sizes to fit 7½-ft. to 9-ft. ceilings, 9-ft. to 10½-ft. ceilings, and 10½-ft. to 12-ft. ceilings. Each strip is slotted on two opposite sides so that shelves can be cantilevered on brackets from either or both sides.

BOOKSHELF SUPPORTS. The simplest way to install adjustable shelves in built-in bookcases is to drill two rows of ¼-in. holes in each end of the bookcase, and set the shelves on small L-shaped metal or plastic supports that are pushed into the holes. The alternative is to screw slotted metal strips into the ends of the bookcase and set the shelves on metal clips which slip into the slots. The strips, which are made in 1-ft. to 12-ft. lengths, differ from slotted metal standards in that they are much thinner and the slots are horizontal rather than vertical.

SHELF HANGERS. The original bracket used to support a single shelf on a wall was a steel right angle. It is still used for utility shelves. Some brackets are hinged so the shelf can be folded down against the wall when not in use. Others used to support closet shelves have a hook in the front end to support the closet rod as well.

Other kinds of utility shelf brackets include (1) a wall bracket with a deep slot into which the shelf slides—it is almost invisible when installed; (2) a two-piece bracket for hanging a shelf on a slanting ceiling, as under a stairway; (3) a U-shaped heavy wire bracket used to hang a shelf from the ceiling joists in the basement.

Decorative brackets of wood or metal are essentially triangular and are made for hanging individual shelves or two or three shelves one above the other.

Adjustable shelf hangers consist of a pair of heavy vinyl straps separated by metal strips on which the shelves are placed.

Slotted strip and clip used for building adjustable bookshelves. Knape & Vogt Manufacturing Co.

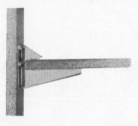

New kind of wall shelf bracket. William Shine Design, Inc.

Bracket for hanging shelves under stairs and sloping ceilings. William Shine Design, Inc.

Shelves hung from vinyl straps. Vikon Tile Corp.

SHELVING. If you're too lazy to cut and finish your own shelves, you can buy prefinished shelving. It is sold in various designs, finishes, widths, and lengths.

CLOSET SHELVES AND RODS. Steel shelves and rods save you the trouble of cutting and painting wood. The shelves are finished with baked enamel and come in an assortment of lengths, each of which can be extended a foot or more beyond its basic length. Thus an 18-in. shelf can be installed in a closet up to 30 in. wide; a 96-in. length can be extended to 144 in. Installation is made with special brackets which can be screwed either into a stud or a nylon anchor inserted through a hole in gypsum board.

Closet rods of stainless steel are extendable, too.

There are also revolving closet rods; nonextendable shelves made of heavy wire sheathed in white vinyl.

Closet shelf bracket with holder for the closet rod. Knape & Vogt Manufacturing Co.

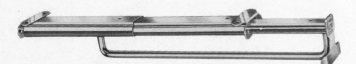

Clothing carrier is fastened to back wall of closet, left; pulls out through closet door, right. Knape & Vogt Manufacturing Co.

CLOTHING CARRIERS. A clothing carrier is the only solution for a closet which is so deep and narrow that, if you fill it to capacity, you can't get at the clothes hung in the back.

The carrier is a sturdy steel device screwed to the front and back wall of a closet squarely behind the door. Clothing hangs from a rod which slides out from the closet when you pull the handle. Carriers are made in nine sizes from 10 to 48 in. long. All except the shortest can be extended to fit a closet of somewhat greater depth.

Extendable hang rod. Knape & Vogt Manufacturing Co.

CLOSET ACCESSORIES. These include hooks of many shapes and sizes, broom clips, swinging trouser and skirt hangers, compact serpentine trouser and skirt hangers, shoe racks, hat racks, tie racks, extendable hang rods, and sawtoothed garment brackets to hold coat hangers.

PERFORATED HARDBOARD. Perforated hardboard is a wall-surfacing material ⅛ or ¼ in. thick with small holes spaced 1 in. apart in horizontal and vertical lines. The holes hold an assortment of specially designed hooks, brackets, tool holders, etc.

Vinyl-clad wire shelves. Shelfmaster Corp.

The hardboard is sold in standard 4×8-ft. unfinished or decorative panels which can be nailed directly to the studs in a wall or furred out from an existing wall with

1-in. wood strips. Use ⅛-in. panels for hanging light loads; ¼-in. panels will support such things as lawnmowers and wheelbarrows.

WHO MAKES IT

All Enterprises. · Circular steel closet rods are suspended from the ceiling of 4×4-ft. closets and revolved by hand or electric motor.

Barclay Industries, Inc. · Decorative shelf-brackets. Slotted metal standards and shelf brackets. Wood shelving. Wood-grain particleboard shelving.

Cannon Craft Manufacturing Co. · Louvered wood cabinet doors.

Contemporary Systems, Inc. · Room dividers assembled from Tielsa kitchen cabinets and finished with wood veneers and/or lacquer.

Dalton Manufacturing Co. · U-shaped steel utility brackets for hanging ladders and other heavy equipment.

Designware Industries, Inc. · Three-panel, folding dressing mirrors 60 and 66 in. high.

Dorfile Shelving Systems Co. · Metal standards, brackets, and prefinished shelves in variety. Storage cabinets for use with shelves.

Ferum Co. · Wrought-iron decorative shelf brackets. Hanger brackets for tools and equipment up to 1,000 lbs.

Flair-Fold, Inc. · Walnut-stained, rough-hewn shelf brackets, shelf standards, and shelves, including corner shelves.

Giles & Kendall Co. · Particleboard made of red cedar in 4×8-ft. and 16×48-in. panels for building cedar closets.

Grant Pulley & Hardware Corp. · Drawer slides for every type of installation. Slotted bookshelf strips and clip supports.

Hager Hinge Co. · Adjustable closet rods. Decorative iron shelf brackets. Utilitarian shelf brackets, including folding type.

Kirsch Co. · Decorative oak shelf brackets.

Knape & Vogt Manufacturing Co. · All kinds of slotted shelf standards and slotted bookshelf strips. Hangers for use in perforated hardboard. Clothing carriers. Closet accessories. Adjustable closet rods. Closet shelf brackets. Drawer slides in great variety. Particleboard shelving in printed and vinyl wood grains as well as colored vinyl.

Leigh Products, Inc. · Steel closet shelves and rods. Steel recessed shoe rack.

Leslie-Locke. · Hanging shelf brackets.

Montgomery Ward & Co. · Steel wardrobes, some with wood doors, 24, 30, 36, and 42 in. wide and up to 66 in. high. Shelves and cabinets hung between a pair of chrome-plated steel poles that clamp between floor and ceiling. Slotted metal standards and shelf brackets.

Morgan Co. · Traditional corner cupboards of wood.

S. Parker Hardware Manufacturing Corp. · Slotted standards and clip supports for bookshelves.

Peachtree Door. · Steel closet shelves and rods. Kit of five adjustable steel shelves with two pairs of shelf standards for linen-closet installation.

Sears Roebuck & Co. · Wood corner cupboard. Prefab closet of plywood for building into a corner measures 51½ in. wide, 24 in. deep, and 8 ft. high, with louvered bifold doors and flush sliding doors above. Decorative wood shelf brackets and shelving to 5 ft. long. Slotted metal standards, shelf brackets, and vinyl-finished particleboard shelves. Wood drawer cases. Steel wardrobes 36 and 42 in. wide and 66 or 72 in. high. Preassembled shelf units. Shelves and cabinets mounted on steel poles that clamp between floor and ceiling.

Shelfmaster Corp. · Vinyl-clad wire shelves for clothes and linen closets. One type with a right-angle lip available in widths of 9, 12, 16, and 20 in. and 10-ft. lengths. Another type, without lip, has a clothes rod under front edge; comes in 1-ft. widths and 10-ft. lengths.

William Shine Design, Inc. · Almost invisible slotted shelf brackets. Brackets for hanging shelves on sloping ceilings.

Standard Equipment, Inc., Elite Products Div. · Hanging shelf brackets.

Stanley Works. · Slotted shelf standards and brackets. Slotted shelf bookcase strips. Shelving in laminated wood grains, Philippine mahogany. Adjustable steel shelves and rods. Shelf brackets.

Teco. · Steel closet shelves and rods.

Vikon Tile Corp. · Vinyl-strap adjustable shelf hangers.

Wessel Hardware Corp. · Adjustable closet rods.

Woodcraft Millwork Specialties, Inc. · Paneled wood cabinet doors.

Wood-Mode Cabinetry. · Wood kitchen cabinets custom-designed to special storage purposes; for example, wardrobes, shoe cabinets, storage walls.

17

Water Supply

Since water is essential to life, every person in the United States is vitally concerned about his water supply. Is there enough water to supply his needs? Does it flow from the outlets at adequate pressure? Does it damage the pipes, fittings, fixtures, and appliances with which it comes in contact? Is it fit for drinking, suitable for washing?

To the homeowner served by a public water supply, the adequacy and pressure of the supply are somewhat less important than they are to the homeowner with his own well—but only because he has less, if any, control over them. Families with wells put all questions about water supply ahead of everything else, because if the supply fails, normal life in the home stops. Water quality, however, is of equal concern to everyone. True, water from a public supply is likely to be more unpleasant to drink than that from a well. But well water is more likely to be seriously contaminated. And as for the effect that water has on pipes and appliances and the washing of bodies, dishes, clothes and walls, the source of supply makes little difference.

Happily, we today have answers to almost every water problem that arises. But since most of these are somewhat technical, it's generally best to find a highly regarded local authority on well drilling, water systems, or water conditioning and trust in his recommendations. This is not to say that you cannot install much of the equipment yourself—especially now that most piping is done with copper or plastics. But when it comes to deciding what type of, say, pump or which size water softener you need, talk to an expert.

PRIVATE WATER SYSTEMS. A private water system consists of a well, pump, pressure tank, and the pipe carrying water to the house. There are several types of each of these four components.

All wells are classified either as shallow (less than 25 ft. in depth) or deep. They should be located at least 50 ft. from all septic tanks, 100 ft. from all disposal fields, and 10 ft. from property lines. They should never be within the foundation walls of a building except, possibly, in the coldest parts of Alaska.

Dug wells are shallow wells up to about 8 ft. in diameter. They are dug by hand and lined with boulders or concrete blocks. In remote areas where there is relatively little chance of contamination, they are usually an excellent source of water, although they are more likely to run dry in periods of drought than deep wells.

Driven wells are usually shallow but may be as much as 100 ft. deep. They are constructed by driving a series of tightly coupled pipes with a well point at the bottom end into soil which is free of rock; and as long as they tap a bountiful vein of water, they are pretty reliable. But because of the small size of the pipe, they hold little water; you are entirely dependent on the speed with which water flows into them. And since the pipe is made of steel, it will in time corrode.

Bored wells are made with a huge auger up to 3 ft. wide. A large pipe, perforated at the bottom, is centered in the hole and surrounded with crushed rock so that you are assured of a good supply of water even though the vein tapped may not run full. The wells can be either shallow or deep.

Drilled wells are the type most often put in today, when it is so often necessary to go to great depths for an ample supply of pure water. This doesn't mean, of course, that they never run dry or never become contaminated. But generally they are reliable and safe.

The wells are put down with either a rotary drill or a cable-tool drill which slowly punches a hole in the ground. Once water has been struck (ideally, it should have a sustained flow of at least 5 gal. a minute), a large (usually 4-in.) pipe called the casing is slipped into it down to the first impervious rock strata to prevent the walls from caving in and to keep out polluted

Jet pump. Jacuzzi Bros., Inc.

Submersible pumps are centrifugal pumps contained in long, slender cylinders which are dropped down inside deep wells far removed from the pressure tanks. Though a comparatively recent development, they are now the most widely used pumps in deep wells because they can push water up from greater depths than jet pumps. They are very efficient, reliable, and maintenance-free, but are frequently knocked out by lightning; consequently, you should insist on a model which has built-in lightning protection or take other steps to protect them.

The capacity of the jet or submersible pump you install is related to the amount of water you normally use during the periods of peak consumption from 6:00 to 8:00 in the morning and 5:00 to 8:00 in the evening. To determine the size you require, multiply the number of outlets which are turned on during these peak periods by 3 gal. per minute; and then multiply the answer by 60. For example, if there are four persons in a house with two bathrooms, peak water usage probably occurs in the morning when they are using the lavatory, tub, and toilet in each bathroom as well as the kitchen sink. Therefore the home requires a pump which can deliver $7 \times 3 \times 60$—a total of approximately 1200 gal. per hour. This, however, does not allow very much for fighting a fire (you might add another 500 gal. for that purpose), for increased usage in the future, or for a possible drop in the level of water in the well. So it's always advisable to buy a somewhat larger pump

water. A so-called pitless adapter is attached to the top of the casing and extends above ground to keep ground water out of the well.

Regardless of the type of well, the pumping system which draws out water and supplies it to the house may be installed either in a wellhouse or in the house itself. In the past, below-ground well pits were commonly built directly over wells; but today this practice is frowned upon because it may lead to contamination of the well. The type of pump used depends primarily on the well depth, its capacity (calculated in gallons per hour), and the water usage of the household.

Reciprocating pumps are rarely used today, although they are extremely dependable and smooth-running. They are suitable only for shallow wells. Operating on a piston principle, they have a plunger which draws water into the pump and forces it into the discharge line as it moves back and forth.

Jet pumps are basically centrifugal pumps with an impeller wheel attached to the motor shaft. As this turns at high speed, it draws in water and sends it out of the discharge by centrifugal force. A venturi, or jet, added to the pump or in the well increases the velocity of the water and thus creates additional suction which can pull water from greater depths. The pumps are designed either for shallow or deep wells. Many models are convertible from shallow-well to deep-well operation in case the water level in the well drops.

Jet pumps are normally installed close to the pressure tank, and in packaged systems, they are mounted directly on the tank. But a few jets are designed for use without a tank. These are suitable only for small homes—especially vacation homes—where the demand for water is spasmodic.

Submersible pump. Weil-McLain Co.

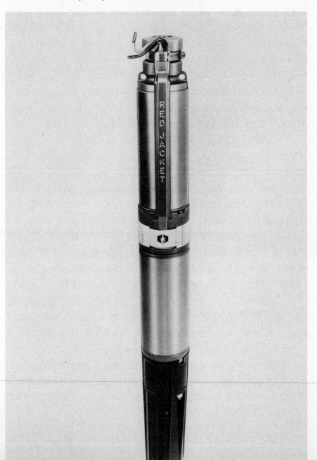

than peak usage calculations call for. A larger pump costs more initially but it costs little more to operate, since it doesn't take as long as a small pump to deliver any given amount of water.

The pressure tank into which a pump discharges the water it draws from a well serves two purposes: It supplies water to the outlets at a fairly uniform pressure, and it keeps the pump from turning on and off frequently as it would if there were no tank (frequent starting and stopping wears out a pump faster than continuous pumping). And it provides water—at least for a while—if the pump quits or the power fails.

When a water system is in service, a pressure tank is filled partly with water and partly with air. The air forms a cushion above the water, and as water is drawn out of the tank, the cushion expands and loses pressure. When the pressure drops to a predetermined point, the pressure switch turns on the pump and water flows into the tank from the well until the air cushion is compressed and the pressure rises to another predetermined point at which the pump is turned off.

Until recently, pressure tanks were nothing more than large cylinders in which water and air were stored together. As a result, the water gradually absorbed the air and the air cushion grew smaller until finally the tank became "waterlogged." This caused the pump to turn on and off every few seconds whenever a faucet was opened; and the best way you could correct the situation was to pump more air into the tank through a snifter valve in the side—a tiring, tedious process, especially if you had to use an automobile tire pump.

This same kind of tank is still in wide use. It is made of galvanized steel, enameled steel, or fiberglass. Standard sizes range from 6 to 1,000 gal. The closest thing to a standard size for homes is a 42-gal. or 82-gal. tank.

But a brand-new type of tank is rapidly changing the picture. In this, the air and water are completely separated so that no air is lost and the tank never becomes waterlogged.

Tanks of this type are made of galvanized steel or fiberglass. The interior design varies. In some, the air is contained in a plastic bag. In others, the water is in a plastic bag. And in still others, a plastic disk floating on the water serves as the barrier between water and air.

Unlike conventional tanks, the size of air-contained tanks is stated in terms not of their capacity but of their drawdown (the number of gallons a tank will deliver between the time the pump shuts off and the time it starts again). This makes them somewhat confusing to buy. But if you tell a dealer that you want to replace, say, a 42-gal. conventional tank with an air-contained tank of equivalent size, he will know what you mean. Don't be shocked, however, when you discover that the new tank is considerably smaller than the old. That's the way air-contained tanks are; they actually hold

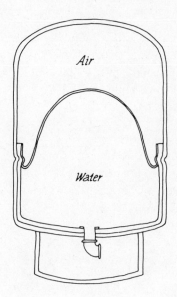

An air-contained pressure tank.

much less water than conventional tanks—which means that if the power fails, you can't count on them to give you very much water for a very long time. But in day-to-day operation, they will keep you just as well supplied as a conventional tank.

The fourth part of a private water system is the pipe which carries the water from well to house. In older homes, this was usually made of galvanized steel or of copper. Today, most installers use plastic because it's low-cost, easy to install, durable, and corrosion-proof.

Flexible polyethylene pipe in long coils is the first choice. It comes in several grades, but for anything as important and hard to get at as your water-supply line, you should use the best. To join lengths of pipe or to connect the pipe to the pressure tank or a metal pipe, you simply insert a special fitting made of hard plastic and fasten it with a worm-drive screw clamp slipped over the outside of the pipe.

PVC (polyvinyl choride) and CPVC (chlorinated polyvinyl chloride) pipe are also used. The former is made specifically for outdoor cold-water lines. The latter is also suitable for this purpose but is primarily used for hot and cold lines indoors. Both are rigid pipes in 10-ft. lengths. The pipes are easily joined by daubing them on the inside with a special solvent, applying additional solvent to the fittings, which are also made of PVC or CPVC, and immediately pushing a fitting into the pipe and giving it a quarter turn.

WATER CONDITIONING. None of the water consumed in American homes is 100% pure. Most of it is hard—containing calcium and magnesium dissolved from rock. It may also be turbid, colored, nasty-tasting, smelly, corrosive, or full of harmful bacteria. Except for the fact that it is safe to drink, even water supplied by utilities contains imperfections.

Many families, of course, live with their water problems without complaint. But it is silly to put up with severe problems, and thanks to the development of new kinds of water-conditioning equipment, there is no reason why anyone should. Such equipment may not be able to make objectionable water perfect, but it can improve it to a remarkable degree at relatively low cost. All you have to do is ask a local water-conditioning equipment dealer with an established reputation to test your water and make recommendations.

In doing this, be warned of three things:

1. Not all water-conditioning specialists (as they like to call themselves) are as expert as they let on. After all, water chemistry is a complex subject and you can't expect a man or woman who has been in the business for only a few years to know all the answers. Most specialists who represent national water-conditioning-equipment manufacturers, however, can call on their home offices for help if they're in a quandary.

2. Some water-conditioning specialists are high-powered salesmen who are more interested in selling merchandise than in helping the homeowner. But if you suspect the man who first calls on you of this failing, it's easy enough to call in one of his competitors for a second opinion. There are plenty of firms that make and sell water-conditioning equipment.

3. No single type of water-conditioning appliance will cure all water problems, so watch out for the fellow who claims otherwise.

Water softeners. According to the U.S. Geological Survey, more than half the homes in the U.S. have moderately hard to hard water. As a result, soap used by the family doesn't lather and wash well. Scummy deposits form in bathroom fixtures and appliances as well as on pitchers, bowls, hair, and clothing. Worst of all, a rocklike scale forms in water heaters, pipes, and shower heads, thus gradually reducing their ability to supply water in normal volume and at adequate pressure.

Water hardness is measured in grains per gallon or parts per million. Water with less than 1 grain of hardness per gallon is soft; with 1 to 3.5 grains, slightly hard; with 3.5 to 7 grains, moderately hard; with 7 to 10.5 grains, hard; and with more than 10.5 grains, very hard.

Water softeners used to remove hardness from water are water-heater-size tank appliances which are connected into the cold-water line where it enters the house. Many people have the softener set up so that only water which is to be heated is softened. This is done on the theory (which is correct) that heated water clogs pipes faster than cold, so by bypassing the cold water, they can reduce the cost of operating their softeners. The practice, however, is shortsighted because eventually cold-water pipes will clog, too—and you are

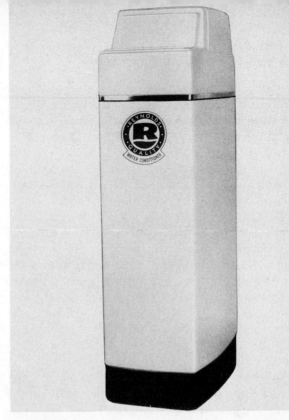

Water softener in a streamlined housing. Reynolds Water Conditioning Co.

no better off with an inadequate cold-water supply than an inadequate hot-water supply. On the other hand, relatively little harm is done and some money can be saved if water to outside faucets is not softened.

A water softener removes hardness by the process of ion exchange. (In the process, the softener also removes sediment and small amounts of iron. Special softeners which remove other undesirable elements are available.) The tank contains a permanent bed of small granules or beads which are initially charged with sodium ions. As the water passes through the bed, the calcium and magnesium which cause hardness are attracted to the granules and held. At the same time, sodium is released into the water. This exchange occurs countless times during the softening process until eventually so much of the sodium has been replaced by calcium and magnesium that the softener must be "regenerated."

This is done by flushing a strong solution of common salt (sodium chloride) through the softening bed, and pouring the brine with the hardness it has picked up down the drain. The bed of granules is then ready once again to remove hardness from water. Since the process can be repeated almost indefinitely, new granules need never be added to the softener. Your only expense is the cost of the salt.

Water softeners are available in manual and automatic models. With the former, the homeowner must be on hand to initiate and complete regeneration about once a week. The automatic softeners have a separate brine tank which holds salt for many regenerations and dissolves it for use as needed. Thus the homeowner need only add salt occasionally to the brine tank. Some automatic softeners recharge themselves on a pre-determined schedule governed by a timer. The newest units have an electronic sensor which determines when the water is becoming too hard and initiates the regeneration. This kind of softener reduces salt demand substantially. It is particularly useful in cities where water hardness varies.

The capacity of the water softener required in a home depends on the number of persons in the family, their daily water consumption, how much water is used during peak periods, the hardness of the water, and how often the softener needs to be regenerated (as a rule, the softener should have enough capacity to last at least three days between regenerations). Since the computation requires a graph to establish the flow rate in peak periods, it is best to let a water-softener dealer do the figuring for you.

Most water-conditioning-equipment dealers offer water softeners either on a sale or rental basis. In the long run, buying saves money but you have to operate and maintain the softener yourself. If you rent, the dealer assumes this responsibility.

Removing iron and manganese from water.
Water containing iron and manganese deposits brown to black stains on plumbing fixtures and may affect the taste of coffee, tea, and food. As noted earlier, water softeners are capable of removing some of the chemicals, but if the concentration is high or if you don't need a water softener, other steps must be taken.

One possibility is to install a special filter capable of oxidizing dissolved iron or manganese to the insoluble state. The filter must be flushed out periodically and then regenerated with potassium permanganate.

Another device used is a clinical feeder or feed pump which injects polyphosphate compounds into the water. These react chemically with the iron and manganese to keep them in solution so they cannot cause stains or build up deposits in the plumbing system.

A third device—also a feed pump—is used to oxidize iron and manganese by introducing chlorine into the water. This system, which also disinfects water, is required for exceptionally high concentrations of iron or manganese or in cases where iron or manganese are bound into organic matter or where iron and manganese bacteria are present.

Controlling corrosive water.
Corrosive water eats out pipes and deposits red stains (if the pipes are steel) or blue-green stains (if the pipes are copper or brass) on plumbing fixtures. The corrosive action of the water is caused by acids, dissolved oxygen, or galvanic action resulting from the use of dissimilar metals in the plumbing system or by high concentrations of minerals in the water itself.

Large water filters used for removing undesirable elements from the water supply for an entire house. Model at left is fully automatic; two at right, semi-automatic; small unit, manually operated. Universal Water Systems, Inc.

If the prime cause of corrosion is acidity, you can control it either by passing the water through a neutralizing filter containing calcium carbonate, magnesium oxide, or similar materials or by feeding a solution of soda ash into the water with a feed pump. The latter system is recommended if the water also contains high concentrations of iron or needs to be disinfected (in which case the feed pump is used to inject chlorine along with the soda ash).

If the prime cause of corrosion is dissolved oxygen or electrical conductivity, control is more difficult. However, you can reduce the corrosive action of the water by feeding in several types of polyphosphate or silicate compounds. These form a thin film on all metal surfaces in contact with the water, thus protecting them to some extent.

Removing turbidity, color, odor, and taste.
Removal of the impurities which cause these problems in water is accomplished by several methods.

Sand filters or filters containing synthetic granular materials are large tanks used to filter the entire household water supply when the water is overloaded with relatively large or gelatinous particles. Like swimming-pool filters, they must be backwashed periodically to remove the accumulated matter.

Cartridge filters are usually smaller than sand filters and are often used to treat the water only in a single supply line. The filtering media are more or less cartridge-shaped and are available with pores of different size, depending on the size of the particles to be removed. When the cartridges become clogged, they usually must be replaced. Some, however, can be cleaned for reuse.

Activated-carbon filters are used to remove soluble organic compounds as well as gases such as chlorine and hydrogen sulfide, both of which are noted for the unpleasant effect they have on water. The filters are available in the form of big tanks which are filled with granular activated carbon and in the form of small cartridges filled with fine powder. The latter are usually installed under the sink and attached to the cold-water line, but hot-water filters are available also.

Granular filters must be backwashed from time to time, and when used to remove hydrogen sulfide, the activated carbon must eventually be replaced. If used to remove chlorine, small amounts of carbon are added to replace the material consumed.

Cartridge filters, similarly, must be cleaned or replaced periodically.

Chemical feed pumps are used occasionally to treat

Activated-carbon filter installed at kitchen sink removes odor and chlorine taste from water. Morton Salt Co.

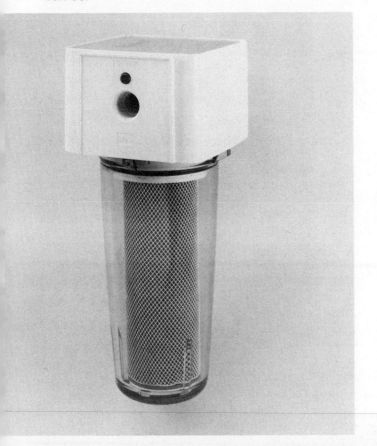

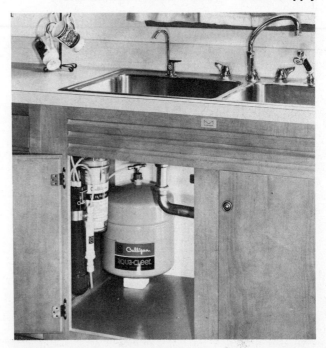

Reverse-osmosis water conditioner. Culligan International Co.

color, taste, and odor problems in water by injecting chlorine into the water.

Reverse-osmosis water conditioners are a recent development which has proved to be highly effective in removing many impurities from water. They are the most economical means for making brackish water fresh.

The conditioners contain a semi-permeable membrane which filters out most of the impurities while allowing most of the water to pass on through. A small amount of the water containing the rejected impurities flows down the drain.

The conditioners, which may be purchased or rented, are available in small units capable of treating only the water to be used for cooking and drinking. They operate continuously on water pressure alone, and contain a reservoir for the treated water. No regeneration or backwashing is required; but in some cases, to prevent clogging of the membrane, it is necessary to filter the water before it enters the conditioner.

DISINFECTING WELL WATER. Although ultraviolet rays, ozone, silver, and iodine are used to make water bacteriologically safe for drinking and cooking, chlorination is the standard practice.

The chlorine is introduced into the water by a feed pump installed between the well pump and pressure tank and wired to operate with the well pump. Should the taste of the chlorinated water be objectionable, it is passed through an activated-carbon filter after leaving the pressure tank.

If the well water is generally free of organic matter,

this system is all that is needed to make water potable. If, on the other hand, the water contains a great deal of organic matter which is broken down slowly by chlorine, additional tanks or coils of tubing should be installed to give the chlorine more time to work.

WHO MAKES IT

Alron Industries. · Automatic water conditioners pass ozone through water to remove harmful bacteria, odors, tastes, color, iron, manganese. Small model installed near sink. Large model treating up to 360 gal. per hour installed on main supply line.

Amtrol, Inc. · Air-contained steel water tanks with water contained in polypropylene liner separated from air by butyl diaphragm.

Carbon-Pure. · Small filter with granular activated carbon coated with silver removes pathogenic organisms, tastes, odors, discoloration. Attaches at sink for storage of water in bottles.

Culligan International Co. · Reverse-osmosis water conditioner processes 150 gal. per month for drinking and cooking. Automatic water softeners, some with automatic sensors.

Franklin Electric. · Submersible pumps with built-in lightning arresters.

Genova, Inc. · Automatic water softeners.

Goulds Pumps, Inc. · Tankless jet pump for shallow wells. Jet pumps for shallow and deep wells operate to depth of 150 ft. Standard submersible pumps for 4-in. wells operate to depth of 660 ft.

Jacuzzi Bros., Inc. · Shallow-well and deep-well jet pumps operate to depth of 260 ft. Submersible pumps with stainless-steel case operate to depth of 1,240 ft.

Montgomery Ward & Co. · Manual and automatic water softeners. Filters. Submersible pumps for 4-in. wells operate to depth of 450 ft. Shallow-well and deep-well jet pumps operate to 140 ft. Air-contained glass-lined-steel pressure tanks with floating disk. Conventional glass-lined steel tanks to 27-gal capacity. Polyethylene pipe.

Morton Salt Co. · Small activated-carbon filter removes odor, tastes, discoloration. Installed below sink.

P. E. Myers & Bro. Co. · Shallow-well and deep-well jet pumps operate to depth of 320 ft. Submersible pumps with stainless-steel housing for 4-in. wells operate to

800 ft. Self-priming centrifugal pumps. Galvanized and epoxy-coated pressure tanks. Galvanized air-contained pressure tank with disklike float separating air and water. Manual and automatic water softeners. Filters to neutralize acidity, remove odors and tastes, iron, and turbidity.

Peabody Barnes. · Reciprocating pumps for shallow wells. Shallow-well and deep-well jet pumps operate to 180-ft. depth. Submersible pumps with stainless-steel housing for 4-in. wells operate to 800 ft. Glass-lined pressure tanks to 82-gal. capacity.

Precision Control Products Corp. · Metered chemical feed pump.

Pyramid Industries, Inc. · Polyethylene pipe and fittings.

Reda Pump Co. · Standard submersible pumps for 3-in. and 4-in. wells operate to a maximum depth of 2,400 ft. Fiberglass housings on pumps.

Reynolds Water Conditioning Co. · Automatic water softeners are clock-controlled but can be equipped with electronic sensors.

Sears Roebuck & Co. · Manual and automatic water softeners. Filters. Chemical feed pumps. Submersible pumps for 4-in. wells operate to 450-ft. depth. Shallow-well and deep-well jet pumps operate to 280-ft. depth. Air-contained pressure tank with water contained in vinyl bag. Conventional steel pressure tanks to 120-gal. capacity. Polyethylene and PVC pipe.

Structural Fibers, Inc. · Air-contained fiberglass water tank with replaceable vinyl air bag.

Universal Water Systems, Inc. · Manual and automatic water softeners. Manual softeners can be equipped with timers for semi-automatic operation. Large manual, semi-automatic, and automatic filters using activated carbon, calcium carbonate, sand, or manganese greensand to remove tastes and odors, acidity, sediment, and iron respectively. Small and large cartridge filters. Chemical feed pumps.

Weil-McLain Co., Red Jacket Div. · Shallow-well and deep-well jet pumps operate to 300 ft. Submersible pumps with stainless-steel or thermoplastic housings for 4-in. wells operate to 960-ft. depth. Some models have lightning arresters in control box. Automatic water softeners. Large activated-charcoal, calcite, sand, and manganese filters. Some backwash automatically. Chemical feed pumps.

Wrightway Manufacturing Co. · Activated-charcoal filter mounts on wall, has diverter which attaches to faucet, pushbutton control.

18

Waste-Treatment Systems

Whether he is building a new house or occupying an old one, every homeowner who lives beyond the community sewer lines is faced with the problem of how to dispose of household wastes. And as each year goes by, the magnitude of the problem increases because of population growth and growing concern about the ecology.

The roots of the problem are both old and new:

Even at their best, private waste-treatment systems require regular and ever more expensive maintenance.

Because lots are growing smaller and once-open land is being built up, the space required for safe disposal of wastes is dwindling and in some tightly jammed neighborhoods is nonexistent.

Because of the pressures to make use of every foot of land in suburban communities, houses are being put up on rocky, marshy, or other sites which are unsuitable for the now prevalent type of waste-treatment system consisting of a septic tank and disposal field.

Laws regulating the type, design, and placement of waste-treatment systems are becoming increasingly restrictive. For example, cesspools have been generally outlawed. The sizes of septic tanks and disposal fields have been enlarged. And in at least one state, laws prohibit installation of any new septic system unless there is sufficient space to build a separate second system when the first one fails.

In short, home treatment of household wastes must no longer be regarded as a relatively simple matter which can be turned over to a local septic-tank service for routine handling. If you're planning to build a new house or vacation cottage, you may find yourself enmeshed in hours of discussion with your builder and local building and health officials. If you live in an old house, you will sooner or later come hard up against a waste-treatment problem which will at best call for installation of a larger septic tank and at worst require an entirely new system.

SEPTIC SYSTEMS. The standard way to dispose of household wastes if you live beyond the sewer lines is to put in a septic system. This consists of a large watertight tank into which the house drain empties and a network of underground drains which disperse the liquid portion of the wastes flowing out of the tank. In the tank, bacterial action breaks the waste matter down into sludge, liquid, scum, and gases. The sludge settles to the bottom, where it decomposes until it reaches such depth that it must be pumped out—about every 18 months—by a septic-tank-cleaning service. The liquid lies on top of the sludge and is itself covered with scum. Excess liquid, called the effluent, flows out of the tank into the drain lines, which are perforated, and settles into the ground. Gases from the decomposition process escape back through the house drain and up the vent stack into the open air.

Septic systems must be built by qualified contractors in accordance with local or state building and health codes. As a rule, the tank must be located at least 5 ft. from the house and 50 ft. from any water source. The disposal field must be 10 ft. from all dwellings and property lines, 25 ft. from any stream, and 100 ft. from a well.

The capacity of the tank and disposal field is based on the number of bedrooms in the house. Minimum tank size specified by the FHA is as follows:

	Gallon capacity without garbage disposer	Gallon capacity with garbage disposer
2 bedrooms or less	750	1,025
3 bedrooms	900	1,350
4 bedrooms	1,000	1,500
Each additional bedroom	250	375

The size of the disposal field depends not only on the number of bedrooms and whether you have a disposer but also on the time it takes for the soil to absorb water. This is determined by a percolation test. The actual area of the field is figured by multiplying the width of the trenches in which the drainpipes are laid (usually 2 ft.) by the total length of the trenches. Thus if your code calls for 100 sq. ft. of absorption area per bedroom in soils having a percolation rate of three minutes, and if you have three bedrooms in your house, you would have to dig 150 ft. of 2-ft.-wide trenches.

Most septic tanks are prefabricated of reinforced concrete; some are steel. Most are rectangular, some cylindrical. One performs as well as another. Tanks with two compartments, however, are somewhat more efficient than those with a single compartment. If it's necessary to increase the capacity of an existing tank, the usual practice is to connect a new tank on either the inlet or discharge side of the old. The size of the new tank should be at least one-third and preferably one-half that of the existing tank.

The tank, as a rule, should be buried deep enough so that wastes flow into it readily from the house. But some houses are so situated that there is no space lower than the house for the tank and disposal field. In these cases, the tank must be located above the house drain and the wastes are carried up into it by a powerful pump in the basement. The newest pump grinds the wastes into small particles so they can be lifted into the tank through 2-in. rather than 4-in. to 6-in. pipes.

Wherever the tank is located, the top ideally should be only 1 ft. below ground so that a septic-tank cleaner can easily dig down and remove the hatches for cleaning out sludge. If the tank is much deeper than this, manholes should be built around the hatches.

From the tank a solid pipe leads to a small distribution box from which the effluent flows out into the disposal field. The latter usually consists of two or more trenches 6 to 9 ft. apart and 18 to 30 in. deep. Perforated 4-in. drainpipes are laid in the bottom. The trenches are partially filled with gravel or crushed rock which is covered with building paper before the soil is finally filled in.

The area in which the field is constructed should be free of trees. The ground can be flat or sloping, but the trench bottoms must always be level so that the effluent will trickle out through the pipes over their entire length.

Seepage pits. On lots which are too small or otherwise unsuited for disposal fields, seepage pits may be used to disperse the septic-tank effluent. The pits are large, deep, cylindrical wells with concrete blocks laid up around the sides with a minimum of mortar so the liquid can trickle out through the sides. The space between the blocks and surrounding soil is filled with coarse gravel or crushed rock.

The bottom of the seepage pit must be at least 2 ft. above the water table. The size of the pit depends on

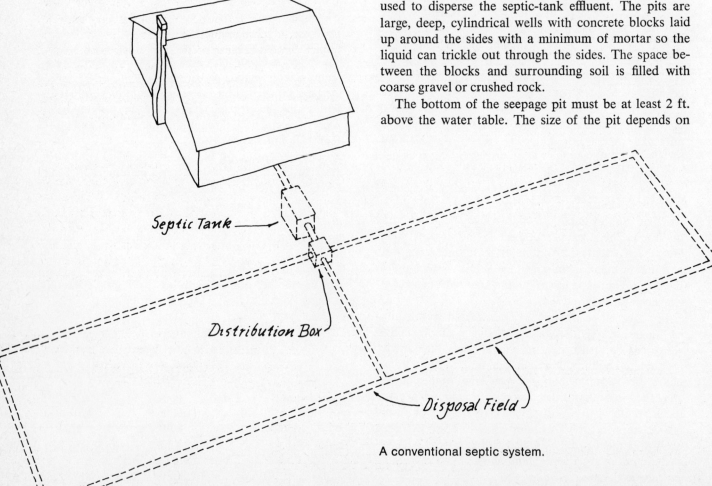

Septic Tank

Distribution Box

Disposal Field

A conventional septic system.

the amount of absorption area required for the septic system. Some homes have two or even three pits.

A seepage pit can also be used as an adjunct to a disposal field where there is not enough space on a lot for a full-size field.

Galleries. These are an alternate solution in situations where it is impossible to build a disposal field. The galleries are constructed like an enormous hallway in a house, but are, of course, completely buried. The walls are built of concrete blocks, and each gallery is divided into compartments by additional walls of block.

EVAPOTRANSPIRATION SYSTEMS. Evapotranspiration is a process by which water escapes from the ground by a combination of direct evaporation and transpiration through the leaves of plants. New waste-treatment systems which are based on the principle of evapotranspiration have been developed to solve the problem of how to get rid of the liquid portion of household wastes when there isn't space on the lot for a septic system, or when the ground is incapable of absorbing effluent, or when the effluent might run into and pollute a well, lake, or stream.

The heart of these systems is a pair of fiberglass tanks, one inside the other, with a combined capacity of 1,500 gal. The tanks are installed in an underground pit surrounded by an enormous dish-shaped dispersion reservoir which is enclosed in a continuous sheet of thick polyvinyl chloride, filled with gravel and sand, and covered with soil and small moisture-loving plants.

Wastes flow from the house through a pipe into the central tank where the solid matter settles and decomposes. The effluent overflows into the outer tank and then trickles out through holes into the dispersion reservoir, where it is gradually drawn to the surface by capillary action and finally disappears into the atmosphere through evaporation and transpiration of the plants covering the reservoir. In some installations—particularly in areas with heavy precipitation or where space for the system is limited—a thermostatically controlled electric heater is installed in the outer tank to raise the temperature of the effluent and thus hasten its evaporation.

Because the system is surrounded by plastic film, contamination of the surrounding soil and water is impossible. For this reason, the location of the system is not of such critical importance as the location of a septic system. By the same token, it makes no difference whether your soil has a good percolation rate or is solid rock or clay. Nevertheless, the system should be in a fairly open area to facilitate evaporation. The ground should be level; otherwise it is necessary to regrade it so that the gravel layer in the reservoir is level (the sand layer on top of the gravel is sloping) and so that surface water cannot flow into the reservoir. The area should also be large enough to accommodate the reservoir.

Although the reservoir is only 1 to 2 ft. deep (except at the center, where the tanks are installed), it covers an area of several thousand square feet. The exact size, which depends on the number of bedrooms in the house and the climatic conditions of the region, is calculated by the manufacturer for each installation. For example, a three-bedroom house in Denver, where the evaporative rate is .193 gal. per square foot per day, requires a reservoir of 2,500 sq. ft. The reservoir can, however, be laid out in any shape—a circle, square, narrow rectangle, etc.

Installation should be made by a contractor under the supervision of a representative of the manufacturer. The cost is considerably higher than that of a septic system, largely because of the huge quantities of sand and gravel required to fill the reservoir (the tanks themselves cost about $800). Maintenance cost, on the other hand, is very low, since the sludge in the central tank need not be pumped out more than once every 10 to 15 years.

MULTRUM SYSTEM. The multrum system is a Swedish invention designed to dispose of toilet wastes and kitchen garbage—the solids which account for most pollution in residential areas. It does not handle the liquid wastes from other plumbing fixtures, but since these contain few contaminants, little harm is done by letting them flow into drywells and then into the ground. Like evapotranspiration systems, the multrum

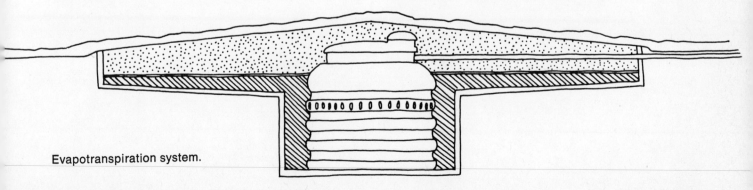

Evapotranspiration system.

Tank of a multrum system installed in basement. Clivus Multrum USA, Inc.

system is used primarily on properties which for one reason or another cannot incorporate a septic disposal field.

The system consists of a large fiberglass tank set in the basement directly below a toilet chute in the bathroom and garbage chute in the kitchen. Wastes from the two sources drop directly into the tank through wide (12 in. for garbage; 16 in. for the toilet) plastic tubes. No water is used. Once in the tank, the wastes slide down the tank, which is set at a 30° angle, at a rate slow enough to ensure that they are completely decomposed by the time they reach the storage chamber. The resulting humus is so reduced in volume that it can be left in the tank for several years. When it is finally shoveled out, it is almost free of pathogenic organisms and can be used in the garden.

The system is entirely free of odors because gases released by the process are carried by natural draft up through a 6-in. vent which extends through the roof to a point about 20 ft. above the top of the garbage chute.

An additional advantage of the system is that it reduces household water consumption by roughly 100 gal. a day (the amount which a family of four normally uses to flush toilets).

On the other hand, the system is presently suitable for installation only in one-story houses with a single toilet; and even here it can be used only if the toilet and garbage chute are placed back to back and the toilet chute is connected to the open end of the tank ahead of the garbage chute. Furthermore, in very cold climates, the tank may have to be insulated or heated to maintain a constant rate of decomposition. And you need a special toilet which is not very attractive.

The cost of the system is comparable to that of a septic system. Two tank sizes are available. The larger, which is approximately 9½ ft. long, 7½ ft. high when set at the required angle, and 4 ft. wide, serves a family of four to six persons, and with the addition of a midsection, it will serve four more persons. Installation is simple enough for the homeowner to handle himself.

WHO MAKES IT

Bio Systems, Inc. · Evapotranspiration system.
Clivus Multrum USA, Inc. · Multrum system.
Genova, Inc. · Sewage ejector pumps.
Peabody Barnes. · Sewage ejector grinder-pump.

19

Wiring

Wiring or rewiring houses is a risky occupation recommended only for people who have a pretty good idea of what it is all about. True, Sears Roebuck has a publication that enables anyone who can follow directions to do the work. But just one slip can cause a possibly fatal accident or burn your house to the ground. So why take chances?

This doesn't mean, of course, that you can't do a number of simple wiring jobs yourself. Neither does it mean that you should not be familiar with the many devices and materials that go into a residential wiring system, because if you're building a new house or making extensive changes in an old one, you ought to be able to talk intelligently with your wiring contractor about what you want and don't want.

Electricity enters your house through a service drop consisting of three wires running from the utility's pole to the side of the house. From the connection point on the house, a large three-wire cable extends down the wall to the meter and then into the house to the main disconnect switch, or master switch, and circuit-breaker panel or fuse box. Most electrical codes require that the cable, main switch, and circuit-breaker panel or fuse box be rated for 100-amp service. Houses with electric heating generally require 200-amp service.

From the circuit-breaker panel or fuse box, branch circuits fan out to carry electricity to the points at which it is used. The number of circuits required varies from house to house, depending on the size of the house and how much electrical equipment is used, but the rules regarding them are standard.

General-purpose 120-volt circuits are required to serve lights, clocks, radios, and other small appliances throughout the house. If No. 14 wire is used, the circuits are fused at 15 amps and have a maximum capacity of 1,800 watts. One such circuit is needed for each 375 sq. ft. of floor area. If larger No. 12 wire is used, the circuits are fused at 20 amps and have a

maximum capacity of 2,400 watts; consequently, one circuit will serve an area of 500 sq. ft.

Two two-wire 20-amp, 120-volt appliance circuits should be installed to serve kitchen, laundry, and dining room convenience outlets into which you plug small appliances such as coffee makers, toasters, and irons. The alternative is to install a single three-wire 20-amp "split" circuit.

An individual 20-amp, 120-volt circuit is required for each refrigerator-freezer combination, freezer, automatic washer, dishwasher, and disposer (one circuit will serve either or both of these appliances), and the workshop.

One 15-amp, 120-volt circuit is required for the furnace.

One 20-amp, 120- or 240-volt circuit is required for each room air conditioner, bathroom heater, and a water pump.

One 30-amp, 240-volt circuit is required for an electric dryer.

One 40-amp, 240-volt circuit is required for an electric range. A separate circuit of the same size serves a central air conditioner.

One 20-amp or higher, 240-volt circuit is required for an electric water heater.

CIRCUIT BREAKERS AND FUSE BOXES. From the safety standpoint there is no choice between a circuit breaker and fuse box; if a circuit is overloaded or develops a short, one gives as good protection as the other. In new homes, however, circuit breakers have generally supplanted fuse boxes because, when the power suddenly fails in part of the house, you can restore it simply by flipping the trigger of the breaker controlling that particular circuit. With a fuse box, on the other hand, you must first identify the fuse that has blown, then take it out and put in a replacement.

A second advantage of a circuit breaker is that, once

installed, no one can accidentally or purposely change the amperage of a circuit. That is, a 15-amp circuit is always a 15-amp circuit. By contrast, if you have a fuse box, you can easily put a 20-amp or 30-amp fuse into the socket in place of a 15-amp fuse; consequently, the circuit may become overloaded and so hot that it starts a fire.

BRANCH-CIRCUIT WIRING. Wiring is run through the walls and floors of houses in four ways: with nonmetallic sheathed cable, plastic-sheathed cable, armored cable, or conduit.

Nonmetallic sheathed cable (designated Type NM or NMC) consists of two or three insulated conductors covered with a tough, braided jacket. Because it is inexpensive, lightweight, and easy to handle, it is very widely used throughout the country, although it is not permitted in all communities. Type NM cable can be installed indoors only in locations that are permanently dry. Type NMC is also restricted to indoor applications but may be exposed to dampness.

Plastic-sheathed cable (Types UF or USE) consists of two or three insulated conductors in a plastic jacket. Like nonmetallic cable, it is not permitted in all communities. But it can be used outdoors as well as in and can even be buried in the ground (U stands for underground). The plastic jacket is extremely tough and highly resistant to fire, rodents, and mechanical abuse.

Armored cable is commonly known as BX cable. It consists of a spirally wound steel sheath enclosing two or three insulated wires, and because of this construction, it is accepted throughout the country for all dry interior installations. But it cannot be used outdoors or in damp areas indoors. Although it cannot be bent around sharp corners like the preceding cables, it is flexible enough to be run through walls and floors without great difficulty. Even so, it is not so easy to work with.

Conduit is a steel pipe through which two or three insulated conductors are pulled after it is in place. Because of its rigidity, it is normally used only in new construction, but it is accepted everywhere for indoor and outdoor installation. It is available in two types: rigid conduit, which is more like a steel water pipe, and thin-wall conduit, made of lighter metal.

SURFACE WIRING. It's not very attractive to run electric wires along the tops of baseboards, around doors, and across bare walls and ceilings, but sometimes—especially when walls are made of masonry—it can't be avoided. When this happens you have three types of wiring to choose from: nonmetallic sheathed cable, plastic-sheathed cable, and metal raceways.

The two cables are installed in the same way but the plastic is preferable simply because it is smooth and white. If you use the cheaper nonmetallic cable, ask for

Type NMC, which is more neatly sheathed than Type NM. Special surface-mounted wiring devices used with the two cables include switches, outlets, and lampholders. To install the wiring, splice the cable to that in an existing outlet or junction box and run it along the

Outlet and lampholder used in surface wiring which is done with exposed cables. Pass & Seymour, Inc.

wall to, say, a surface-mounted switch. Insert the wire in one end of the switch and connect it to the terminals. Then insert a new length of wire into the other end of the switch and connect it, and continue it across the wall to an outlet, where it is inserted and connected in the same way. From the outlet you can go on to another outlet or a lampholder, and so on. You can have as many outlets and/or lampholders as the wire is capable of serving. Use either No. 14 or No. 12 wire.

Raceways are slender, enclosed metal channels—larger than cables but of neater appearance. In the one-piece type of raceway, insulated wires are pulled through the channel after it is fastened to the wall or ceiling. In the two-piece type, which is bigger than is generally needed in the home, the base of the raceway is fastened in place, the wires are laid into it, and a cover is snapped on.

Raceways come in various sizes and with fittings to

go around corners, loop around pipes, form branches, etc. There are also outlets, switches, etc. that are inserted in the raceways. Installation is made in about the same way that cables are installed.

BOXES. When wiring is run through the walls and ceilings, all splices must be made within boxes and all outlets, switches, and lights are installed in boxes. The boxes are made of galvanized steel (plastic boxes are rarely used, and only with nonmetallic or plastic-sheathed cables).

Outlet boxes are rectangular, square, octagonal, or round. The National Electrical Code requires that, except in unusual circumstances, they must be at least 1½ in. deep. Despite their name, the boxes are used not only for outlets and light fixtures but also as junction boxes and, occasionally, as switch boxes. When used as a junction box, a metal cover must be screwed on top and the cover must be exposed (you can't bury it under plaster or gypsum board, in other words).

Switch boxes are rectangular and range from 1½ to 3½ in. deep. The 2½-in. depth is standard. Each box

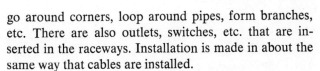

Raceways, above, with special type of outlet, below, which is used with them. Wiremold Co.

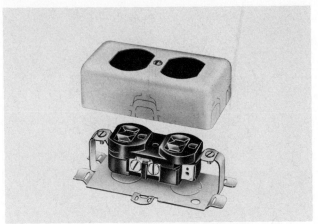
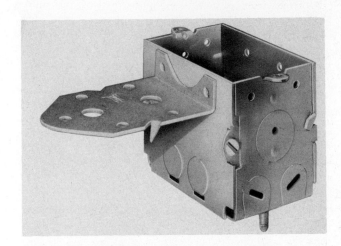
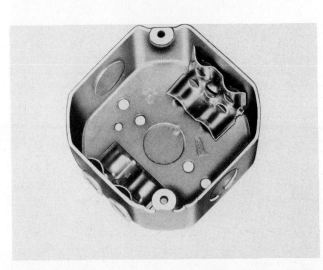
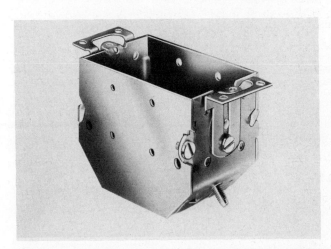

Above, octagonal junction box with built-in cable clamps; above right, switch box with flange for fast attachment to studs in new construction; above, switch box with cutoff corners simplifies installation in rewiring work. General Electric Co.

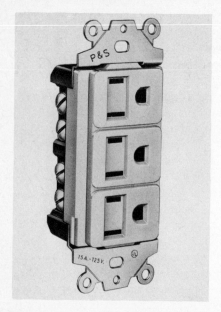  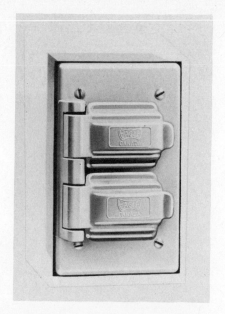

Left, a three-plug grounded outlet, Pass & Seymour, Inc.; center, a four-plug ungrounded outlet, General Electric Co.; right, a weatherproof outlet, Eagle Electric Manufacturing Co.

is large enough for a single switch, but since the sides can be removed, it is possible to gang two or more boxes together to hold additional switches.

Switch boxes come with a variety of brackets attached to the sides to simplify mounting in walls—usually next to studs. Outlet boxes are normally held in place with special hangers. Some hangers are made for new work (installation in a new building), others for old work. In remodeling, when for one reason or another it's impossible to use standard box hangers or brackets, you can mount a box within a stud or joist space with a pair of metal hanger strips which fold around the sides of the box.

Most boxes are equipped with built-in clamps so cables can be connected with a minimum of work. In a box without clamps, a separate connector is used to attach BX cable and another kind of connector is used for nonmetallic and plastic-sheathed cable.

All boxes installed outdoors must be of weatherproof design that is resistant to corrosion and keeps out moisture.

OUTLETS. Outlets into which lamps, appliances, etc. are plugged are known to the electrical industry as receptacles. Most of those now in use are grounded outlets with three slots for each plug. You can plug an ordinary two-prong plug into a grounded outlet but obviously you cannot plug a three-prong plug into a nongrounded outlet. For this purpose you need a grounding adapter.

Conventional outlets are made to hold one, two, three, or four plugs. After the wires are attached, the outlets are screwed into the boxes and covered with protective metal or plastic cover plates. In some cases,

however, the outlet is made with the cover plate already attached.

Special outlets are available for wall clocks, ranges, and dryers. There are also weatherproof outlets for outdoor installation, outlets in which a receptacle is combined with a switch, and outlets combined with porcelain lampholders. To keep children from poking

Outlet with oversize plate for concealing cords that are too long. James R. Bell Co.

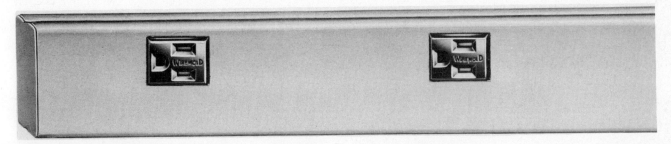

Plug-in strip. Wiremold Co.

things into the holes of a receptacle, there are safety outlets with spring-action covers which automatically close when the plugs are withdrawn. Another kind of safety outlet prevents current flow until the prongs of an electric plug are inserted in both holes. There are also outlet plates in which you can wrap up extension cords which are too long.

To replace an outlet, turn off the currrent, remove the cover plate, remove the screws holding the outlet to the box, pull the outlet from the box, and unscrew the wires. Most new outlets are made so you can either attach the wires to terminal screws or insert them in holes in the back of the outlets. In either case, make sure that black wires are connected to gold-colored screws or inserted in the holes next to the gold screws, and that the white wires are connected to the silver screws. Attach one end of a short wire to the green grounding screw and the other end to a screw driven into one of the holes in the box.

Plug-in strips. If you need a lot of closely spaced outlets, as in a kitchen, the plug-in strip is the best solution. The conventional strip resembles a large metal raceway with outlets inserted in the front. It comes in 1-ft. to 6-ft. lengths which can be joined together into longer lengths. The most convenient type is prewired so that all you have to do is connect it at one end to a cable in the wall or to the cable at an existing outlet box.

A newer type of strip is flexible and comes in 25-ft. and longer coils. After it is fastened to a wall, you can insert the outlets wherever you want them and move them to another location whenever you wish.

SWITCHES. Electric switches that snap like a gunshot when you flick them are pretty much a thing of the past. Most standard switches now make little noise, and mercury switches, which are guaranteed for up to 50 years, are completely silent. If you live in a house with paper-thin walls and old-fashioned switches, one of the biggest improvements you can make is to install a whole new set of switches.

Switches are designed in several ways. Most are installed singly in a box which is then covered with a plate. Some come fastened in the cover plate. There are switches combined with pilot lights or outlets, weather-proof switches, dimmer switches (see Chapter 20),

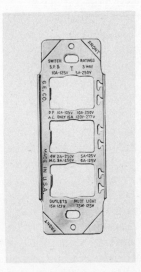

Interchangeable pilot light and outlet with the three-hole strap in which they are mounted in an outlet box. There is also an interchangeable switch. General Electric Co.

grounded switches, automatic closet switches which are mounted in the door jamb so that they turn the closet light on when the door is opened and turn it off when the door is closed, and switches with pushbuttons instead of toggles.

The principal difference between switches, however, is in the way they control lights and outlets. Single-pole switches have two terminals and are used in two-wire circuits to control a light from one location. Three-way switches have three terminals and are used in three-wire circuits so you can control a light from two locations—say, at the inside door to the kitchen and also at the back door into the yard. Four-way switches have four terminals and are used in four-wire circuits to control a light from three locations, but they are very expensive and rarely found in homes.

To replace a single-pole switch, shut off the current and remove the switch from the box. Attach either wire to either terminal on the new switch, and screw the switch into the box. If the switch is a mercury unit, make sure it is installed with the "top" side up. A conventional switch can be installed with either end up.

On a three-way switch, one terminal is marked "common" and/or has a screw that is a different color from the other two terminals. When taking out the old switch, mark or tag the wire that has been attached to the common terminal; then be sure to connect it to the common terminal in the new switch. The other two wires can be attached to either of the two remaining terminals.

INTERCHANGEABLE WIRING DEVICES. These switches, outlets, and pilot lights are so small that you can install three of them in one standard 2×3-in. switch box. You can use one of each in a box, two of one and one of another, or all three of one. Later you can change the arrangement as you wish. Thus you save space and money. The devices are held in a special steel strap beneath the cover plate.

You can also install one device to a box or two to a box and later add one or two additional devices. The three-hole strap is used for all installations, but the cover plate must be changed.

GROUND FAULT CIRCUIT INTERRUPTERS. A ground fault circuit interrupter is a new safety device designed to protect against shock when a faulty electrical appliance allows current to leak to the ground. They are considered so important that the National Electrical Code now requires that they be installed in new houses to protect all bathroom and outdoor outlets as well as all equipment, lighting fixtures, and outlets near swimming pools. You are not required to install

A ground fault circuit interrupter that is installed at the circuit-breaker panel, General Electric Co.

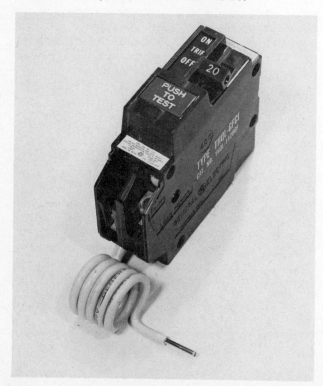

A GFCI that takes the place of a conventional outlet in a wall, 3M Co.

them in an existing home unless you remodel a bathroom or put in a pool, but it's a good idea to do so anyway.

The GFCIs, as they are usually called, are available in two types. One is installed at the circuit-breaker panel to protect an entire branch circuit (or circuits). The other fits into a rectangular outlet box and provides protection for the outlet itself or for all other outlets beyond the GFCI on the same circuit. Obviously, if you have a lot of outlets to protect, the former is the more economical even though it should be installed by an electrical contractor.

You can install the outlet type of GFCI yourself, however. Instructions are included in the package.

LIGHTNING ARRESTERS. If your electrical system is properly grounded, you don't have to worry very much about lightning. Even so, if you live in the country, there is always the possibility that your appliances, water pump, etc. will be damaged by lightning striking the wires or coming close to the wires.

You can get almost complete protection against this eventuality by having a small, inexpensive lightning arrester installed on your service entrance panel.

LOW-VOLTAGE WIRING. This is a system for controlling lights and outlets with switches operating at 24 volts. The wire used is the same size as that used for doorbells. As the system is installed, the lights and outlets are connected to 120-volt circuits in the conventional manner. A 24-volt transformer supplies power to the switches, which are controlled by pushbuttons rather than toggles. When you press a switch to turn a light on or off, it activates a relay which in turn activates the light.

The main advantage of the system is that it permits much greater flexibility in controlling lights and outlets than conventional 120-volt wiring, but costs little if any more. Because the components of the system are inexpensive, you can install more switches. You don't need expensive three-way and four-way switches. And you can put in a master switch which allows you to control up to 25 different lights throughout the house from one point.

In addition, switching is much safer.

WHO MAKES IT

Baldwin Hardware Manufacturing Corp. · Enameled and decorated switch plates. Decorative brass switch and outlet plates.

James R. Bell Co. · Outlet plate for storing excess lengths of lamp cord.

Cutler-Hammer. · Circuit-breaker panels. Ground fault circuit interrupters for installation at circuit-breaker panels.

J. C. DeJong & Co. · Sculptured switch and outlet plates of heavy brass in many finishes.

Eagle Electric Manufacturing Co. · All kinds of outlets, switches, interchangeable wiring devices, switch plates, weatherproof boxes with outlets and switches, simple lampholders, one-fuse outlets. Transformers.

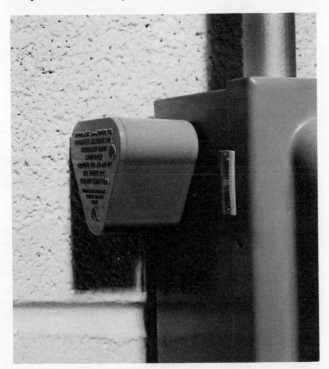

Lightning arrester installed at service entrance panel. Joslyn Manufacturing & Supply Co.

Elon, Inc. · Decorated ceramic-tile switch and outlet plates.

General Electric Co., Circuit Protective Devices Product Dept. · Ground fault circuit interrupters for installation in outlet boxes and circuit breakers.

General Electric Co., Transformer and Distribution Equipment Business Div. · Lightning arrester.

General Electric Co., Wiring Device Dept. · Outlets, including four-plug and safety units. Switches. Simple lampholders. Surface wiring devices. Switch and outlet plates. Interchangeable wiring devices. Weatherproof switch and outlet plates. Boxes.

P. E. Guerin, Inc. · Heavy brass sculptured switch and outlet plates, polished or in almost any plated finish.

Homelite Manufacturing Co. · Gasoline-driven standby generators in wide range of capacities.

I-T-E Imperial Corp. · Flexible plug-in strip and necessary fittings.

Joslyn Manufacturing & Supply Co. · Lightning arrester.

Montgomery Ward & Co. · Ground fault circuit interrupters for installation in outlets and circuit breaker panels. Circuit breakers and fuse boxes. Outlets. Switches. Boxes. Interchangeable wiring devices. Surface-mounted wiring devices. Plug-in strips. Weatherproof outlets and switches. Standby generators.

Onan Corp. · Standby generators driven by gasoline, diesel fuel, or LP gas in capacities ranging from 1,000 to 6,500 watts.

Pass & Seymour, Inc. · Ground fault circuit interrupters for installation in outlet boxes. Switches including closet-door units and pushbutton switches that glow when off. Conventional and special outlets, including safety unit. Interchangeable wiring devices. Surface wiring devices. Switch and outlet plates. Weatherproof outlets and switches. Simple lampholders.

Perfect-Line Manufacturing Corp. · Weatherproof outlets. Clock hanger outlets. Automatic closet light switch. One-fuse outlets with receptacle or switch. Weatherproof boxes. Switch plates including red plates for furnace switches.

Sears Roebuck & Co. · Ground fault circuit interrupters for installation in outlets and circuit-breaker panels. Plug-in strips. Switches. Outlets. Simple lampholders. Weatherproof outlets. Plain and decorative switch plates. Circuit breakers and fuse boxes. Standby generators.

3M Co. · Ground fault circuit interrupters for outlet-box installation.

Westinghouse Electric Corp., Bryant Div. · Switches, including models without any switch handle: you just touch the cover plate. Closet light switches. Outlets, including covered floor outlets. Interchangeable wiring devices. Simple lampholders. Switch and outlet plates. Outdoor plates. Circuit breakers. Ground fault circuit interrupters for installation at circuit-breaker panels.

Wiremold Co. · Metal raceways and the boxes, switches, outlets, fittings used with them. Plug-in strips of every description with fittings. Lampholders that plug into plug-in strips so you can make your own track lights.

20

Lighting

Good lighting is supposed to be decorative, but more than anything else, it must produce a high level of illumination so you can see what you're doing without eyestrain. Many people, in their zeal to achieve unusual effects, overlook this vital point.

To be fully effective, the lighting in your home should fulfill five requirements:

1. It must give enough light not only for you to see but also to eliminate sharp, eyestraining contrasts between bright and dark areas.

2. It must be free of glare—the glare caused by light bouncing off bright surfaces and by the lights themselves. Some sort of diffusing or shielding should be provided so you can't see the bulbs and tubes from which the light emanates.

3. There must be enough fixtures and lamps so you can adjust the room lighting to your needs and moods.

4. The surfaces in each room should be finished in colors that contribute to the brightness of the room. Ceilings should be white or some other very light color; walls, a medium tone; floors, only slightly darker. This not only contributes to your comfort and convenience but also helps significantly to reduce the actual amount of light the fixtures must produce. Thus it cuts operating cost.

5. Light must be provided for general illumination of the entire room as well as for specific visual tasks such as reading and sewing. Lighting used for the latter purpose is called local lighting and is done primarily with portable lamps but also with built-in fixtures.

One of the first things to be decided in lighting a room is whether to use incandescent or fluorescent bulbs.

Fluorescents in straight, circular, and U-shaped tubes give about four times as much light per watt as incandescents, produce much less heat, and last seven to ten times longer. Their principal disadvantage, in many minds, is their unnatural color, but light from

Warm White and Deluxe Warm White tubes is actually very close in color to incandescent light. A more valid objection is that the fixtures in which the tubes are used are large and, because of the weight of the ballasts, heavy. This means that they cannot be as easily placed as incandescents and must be very well anchored to walls and ceilings.

Incandescents are made in more types, shapes, and wattages than fluorescents. Because of their size, they are easier to handle; and because most bulbs have a medium screw-base, you can change the light output of a lamp or fixture simply by taking out the old bulb and putting in a new one. But their relatively short life and low light output are objectionable, particularly at this time when the cost of electricity is high. This problem can be ameliorated to some extent by the following measures. First, when buying bulbs, note the information printed on the jackets about lumen, wattages, and average hours of life. If you're looking for efficiency— the most light per watt—buy the bulbs with the highest

U-shaped fluorescent tube. General Electric Co.

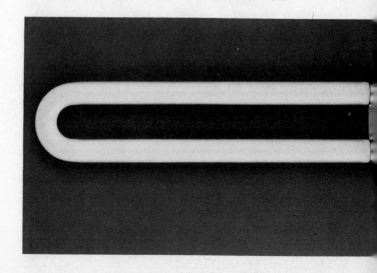

lumen output. For instance, given a choice between a 60-watt bulb with an output of, say, 860 lumens and another 60-watt bulb with an output of 760 lumens, take the former. Bulbs with unusually long life—over 900 hours—have a much lower lumen output than those with a shorter life and should, as a rule, be used only where light output is of secondary importance (as in a back hall or storeroom) or where the fixture is so located that it's difficult to reach (as on a 16-ft. ceiling). Second, use a single high-wattage bulb instead of several low-wattage bulbs. One 100-watt incandescent gives about 50% more light than four 25-watters, although it uses no more electricity.

The next step in planning the lighting for a room is to decide, first, how you will provide general illumination and then what local lighting is required. For kitchens, bathrooms, halls, and perhaps other rooms, built-in fixtures will serve both purposes. For all other rooms, you will probably need both built-ins and portable lamps, although either can be used alone. In both cases, you must also determine where the outlets into which the lights are connected will be located, which types of switch are needed (single-pole, three-way, and four-way), and where the switches will be located.

General Electric has a good pamphlet on this somewhat complex subject. Or send to the Illuminating Engineering Society, 345 E. 47th St., New York, N.Y. 10017 for its 48-page booklet "Design Criteria for Lighting Interior Living Spaces" ($4.50).

READY-MADE FIXTURES. Although fixtures which come from the factory ready for installation are made in relatively few basic types, they are available in so many styles, shapes, and sizes that you must spend hours wandering through showrooms or poring over

Pendant ceiling fixture of traditional design. Sturdy Lantern Manufacturing Co.

catalogs to make a good selection. When trying to settle on shapes and sizes, your best source of help is a salesman in a wholesale outlet which sells primarily to decorators, builders, and electrical contractors. Lamp and fixture dealers, as a rule, know little more than you do yourself. Fixture styling, which ranges from the sublime to the ridiculous, is a matter you must decide yourself.

Basic fixture types are as follows:

Surface-mounted ceiling fixtures are incandescent or fluorescent fixtures which are mounted directly on a ceiling with the bulbs just an inch or two below the ceiling and shielded from view. When the shielding is translucent (as it most often is), light is distributed up, down, and to the sides; as a result, a single fixture with bulbs of adequate wattage can be used to light a room of as much as 250 sq. ft. On the other hand, if the shielding is opaque, all light is directed upward and has comparatively little value in relieving the darkness of the room. If the shielding is transparent, the wattage of the bulbs must be so reduced in order to relieve the glare that the light is also of little value.

Pendant ceiling fixtures include chandeliers and other less elaborate incandescent fixtures hung well below the ceiling on a chain or rod. Because they are directly in the line of sight, either the shielding around the bulbs must be quite dense or the wattage must be low; consequently, they do not illuminate the room as well as a surface-mounted fixture. Their principal value is decorative.

Pulley fixtures are pendants which can be raised or lowered as you wish.

Each of these surface-mounted ceiling fixtures incorporates two U-shaped fluorescent tubes. Wellmade Metal Products Co.

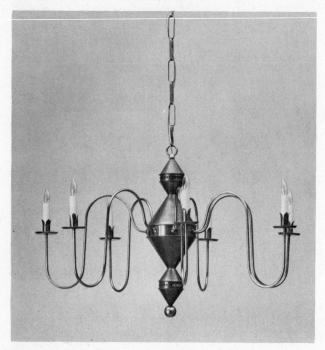

Modern reproduction of a Colonial chandelier. Village Lantern.

Surface-mounted downlights are cylindrical incandescent fixtures which direct all light downward. Their lighting effect is similar to that of a recessed ceiling fixture.

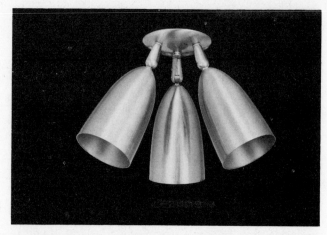

Surface-mounted downlights. The position of the lights can be adjusted. Majestic Metal Spinning & Stamping Co.

Pendant downlights are like the above except that they hang below the ceiling.

Recessed ceiling fixtures using incandescent or fluorescent bulbs distribute 90 to 100% of their light downward. Because of this, you may need three or four fixtures to light the room as well as you could light it with a single surface-mounted fixture, and this adds to the initial cost as well as operating cost. But many people prefer to pay this price in exchange for an unbroken expanse of ceiling.

Wall-washer type of recessed ceiling fixture. Westinghouse photo.

Track lights are the current rage in lighting. Halo—McGraw-Edison Co.

Most recessed residential fixtures (which are called troffers if they incorporate fluorescent tubes) are non-directional: light spreads out below them in all directions. Directional fixtures, by contrast, focus light on specific areas. Using incandescent bulbs only, the latter are of value for accent lighting of pictures, art objects, flower arrangements on the dining table, etc.; for functional local lighting of restricted work areas, card tables, pianos, etc.; and for lighting draperies and walls so they will reflect light into the room.

Specific varieties of directional light include high-hats with apertures 3 to 6 in. in diameter in the face. Pinhole lights with 1-in. to 2½-in. apertures are used for pinpointing small decorative objects. In some of the fixtures the shape of the aperture can be adjusted to control the shape of the light beam. Wall-washers direct light sideways so you can flood a wall with light or feature pictures on a wall. Eyeball lights have an adjustable bulb housing which permits you to rotate the lights in almost a full circle and also change the angle up and down.

In order to fit recessed lights within the joist space above a ceiling, you must determine the depth of the space and order fixtures accordingly. Some can fit within a 6-in.-deep space; others require 10 or even 12 in. A few fixtures are adjustable in height.

Semi-recessed ceiling fixtures are housed within the joist spaces like recessed fixtures, but the diffusers project slightly below the ceiling so that light is distributed down and to the sides. They give more light than recessed fixtures but not as much as surface-mounted units.

Track lights are incandescent fixtures which are surface-mounted on ceilings and sometimes on walls. They consist of a wired track into which several lights can be inserted wherever you like. You can change their positions at any time. The lights may be pointed straight down or at any downward angle. The bulbs are normally concealed in metal canisters of various shapes. The tracks can be almost any length and laid out in a straight line, L shape, cross shape, or rectangle.

Wall brackets are any kind of wall-mounted fixture. Since they are installed within the line of sight, the bulbs should be shielded with fairly dense translucent glass or plastic or with opaque material. If the shielding is clear, the bulbs should be of low wattage.

Because of their positioning around the sides of a room, brackets do not illuminate the room as well as surface-mounted ceiling fixtures.

Sconces and wall torches are varieties of wall brackets, so named because of their appearance. Functionally they are like any other wall bracket.

Track lights can be arranged in straight lines, L shapes, cross shapes, or rectangles. Halo–McGraw-Edison Co.

Lighting strips normally consist of a straight strip into which low-wattage incandescent bulbs are screwed. The unshielded bulbs are spaced about every 4 to 6 in. apart. The strips are used primarily for framing wall-mounted mirrors above dressing tables and bathroom counters.

Also available is a flexible strip light incorporating miniature 6-volt bulbs. It is made in lengths up to 4 ft. and is so small that it can be hidden behind moldings. It is used for such things as lighting cabinets and shelves containing art objects, shell collections, etc.; outlining arches and niches; and even for concealing under handrails to light flights of stairs.

Undercabinet lights are fluorescent fixtures mounted on the bottom of kitchen wall cabinets or

Indoor (Village Lantern) and outdoor (MarLe Co.) wall brackets of traditional design.

Large fluorescent wall bracket lights both the mirror and the person standing at the lavatory exceptionally well. Wilson Research Corp.

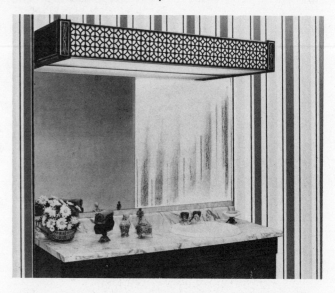

Lighting strips surrounding mirror used for make-up. LCA Corp.

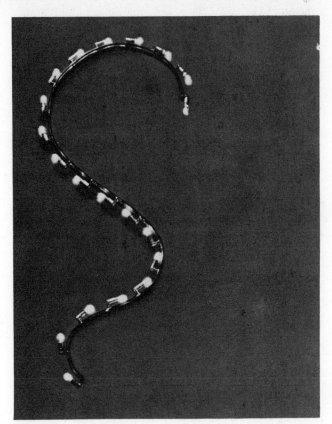

Flexible lighting strip with tiny 6-volt bulbs (shown at left) is used to illuminate cabinets such as this. William Wirtz Associates.

These undercabinet lights are completely recessed in the wall cabinets. St. Charles Manufacturing Co.

Slim fluorescent fixture designed for installation under cabinets and shelves. Alkco Manufacturing Co.

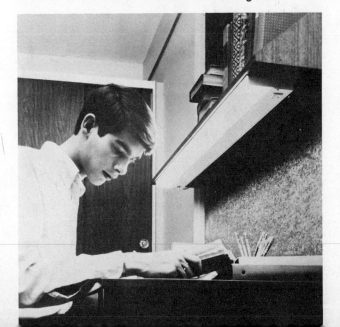

shelves to provide a high level of light on the work surfaces below. They are normally so thin that they are almost completely hidden behind the aprons of the cabinets. Even so, the fixtures are equipped with plastic shields to hide the tubes and diffuse their light. Fixture lengths range from 12 to 42 in.

A few undercabinet lights use incandescent bulbs, usually of the slim tubular variety.

Post lights are exterior incandescent lights placed beside a front walk or driveway.

SITE-ASSEMBLED FIXTURES.

SITE-ASSEMBLED FIXTURES. You can construct these fixtures yourself. All are built around inexpensive fluorescent fixtures, called channels, which are available from any store selling wiring and lighting supplies.

The channels are long metal boxes with lampholders protruding from the front. The heavy ballasts required for all fluorescent tubes and the wiring are enclosed in the boxes. The channels are designed for either preheat tubes which take several seconds to go on after the switch is flipped or for rapid-start or trigger-start tubes which light almost instantly. Channels for preheat tubes contain small metal canisters called starters.

Valance lights consist of a long row of fluorescent channels mounted on the wall above a window and concealed from view by a board at least 5 in. wide. Light is normally directed down on the draperies and up on the ceiling. However, if the channels are placed less than 10 in. below the ceiling, the top of the valance should be closed so that all light is directed down.

The principal purpose of valance lights is to provide general illumination throughout the room; but to be effective, the draperies must be a light color. The lights also bring out the beauty of the draperies.

Cornice lights are essentially similar to valances ex-

Valance lights direct light up and down, are excellent for general illumination. General Electric photo.

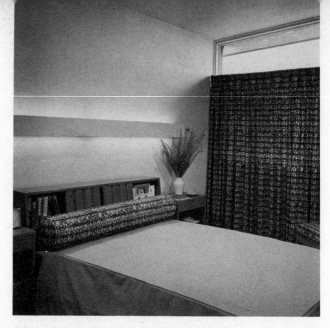

A homemade fluorescent wall bracket.

cept that they are installed directly below the ceiling above a blank wall. They are used for general illumination, but since all light is distributed downward, the level of illumination is somewhat reduced.

The fluorescent channels are mounted on the ceiling immediately behind a 6-in. or wider shielding board so the tubes are hidden from view unless you're standing almost directly below them.

Wall brackets are built like valance lights but are hung on blank walls closer to the floor. Since they

Cornice lights direct light entirely downward. General Electric photo.

direct light up as well as down, they serve as a source of general illumination, but they are used mainly for local lighting over a desk, the head of a bed, etc. The width of the shielding boards depends on the height at which the brackets are installed. The top of a fixture is often covered with a sheet of diffusing plastic to shield the tube from people standing and also to serve as a shelf on which plants, ornaments, etc. are displayed.

Soffit lights are ceiling fixtures commonly used over kitchen sinks and dressing tables to provide a high level of illumination on the surfaces below. They consist of two or three short, parallel rows of fluorescents mounted on the ceiling behind an 8- to 12-in.-wide shielding board. A sheet of diffusing glass or plastic or a grille of metal, wood, or plastic is placed below the fluorescents to conceal them and diffuse their light.

Cove lights are used for decorative purposes only. Because all light is directed up on the ceiling, they have little functional value. The tubes are strung out in a single row along a wall and at least 12 in. below the ceiling. They are concealed from below by a wide board and from the front by a 5-in. or wider board nailed vertically or at an outward-slanting angle to the edge of the bottom board.

Luminous ceilings are gigantic fixtures which cover an entire ceiling or form a recessed panel in the middle of a ceiling. No other type of fixture produces such a high level of glarefree, virtually shadowless illumination; and for this reason, the ceilings are most often used in kitchens and bathrooms. They are so decora-

Soffit lights are used to provide a high level of illumination on counters and other surfaces directly below. Westinghouse photo.

Cove lights direct all light upward. General Electric photo.

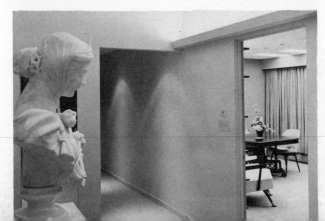

No other kind of lighting fixture gives such a high level of shadowless, glarefree illumination as a luminous ceiling. General Electric photo.

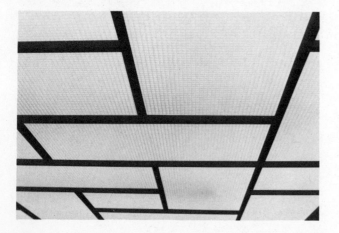

Metal frameworks in which diffusers for luminous ceilings are hung are designed to blend into the ceiling or to form a strong pattern on the ceiling. Wilson Research Co.

tive, however, that they are often installed in other rooms where a better-than-average light level is called for.

The fixtures are constructed by mounting rows of fluorescent channels end to end on a ceiling or within the joist spaces, and suspending diffusing panels or grilles below them in a metal framework like that used for hanging acoustical ceiling tiles and panels (see Chapter 11). In order to achieve a uniform intensity of light across the entire ceiling and prevent bright streaks on the ceiling surface, the diffusers should be hung 10 to 12 in. below the centerlines of the fluorescent tubes, and the rows of tubes should be spaced 15 to 18 in. apart. The surface to which the channels are fastened must be painted flat white.

Luminous walls are like luminous ceilings, but because of their position, they do not light a room as evenly. They are useful, however, for balancing the light in deep rooms with windows in only one wall, giving the effect of natural light filtering through a thinly curtained window, emphasizing structural features, and silhouetting art objects displayed in front of them. But they are difficult to construct so that the diffusing panels are of uniform brightness.

In one type of luminous wall, the lights are installed in the cavities between 6-in.-wide studs, and the diffusing panels are fastened to the faces of the studs on one or both sides of the wall. But because the tubes are so close to the diffusers, they show through as bright streaks. To eliminate this problem, the best type of luminous wall is built with the lights mounted on gypsum board nailed to conventional 2×4-in. studs. The diffusing panels are installed in a separate framework 8 to 12 in. in front of the lights.

INSTALLING LIGHT FIXTURES. The average homeowner should leave the installation of new light fixtures to an electrical contractor. But it takes no skill or knowledge and only a couple of minutes to replace old fixtures.

First, shut off the current at the fuse box or circuit breaker. Remove the fixture from the ceiling or wall and separate the wires behind it. Then twist the bare end of the black wire in the new fixture around the end of the black cable in the outlet box; twist the white wire around the white cable. Screw wire nuts—thimble-shaped plastic devices also called solderless connectors—over the spliced wires. The bare copper should be completely enclosed. Then attach the fixture to the outlet box.

A fluorescent fixture is installed in the same way, but to get at the wires, you must unscrew the cover on the channel. To mount the channel on a wall or ceiling, pry out one of the circular knockout tabs in the channel back. The channel is then attached to the box with several small gadgets called a stud, hickey, nipple, and locknut. To secure the channel further, a couple of screws should be driven through the back into the wall. If the wall is surfaced with combustible material, a piece of asbestos-cement board should be inserted between it and the channel. The alternative is to fur the channel out from the wall at least ½ in.

PORTABLE LAMPS. Lamps which are purely decorative should not be used to provide light for important seeing tasks, although there is no reason to exclude them from your home. Wherever you need a lamp really to see what you are doing, you should select one which is both attractive and functional. The size and design of the lamp depends on what it is used for and where it is to be placed.

Lamp size is measured from the bottom of the lamp base to the bottom edge of the shade. Floor lamps should be 47 to 49 in. high. Wall lamps should be hung so they are also 47 to 49 in. high.

Table-lamp height depends on the height of the table on which the lamp is placed and the eye height of a person seated in a chair alongside—usually 40 in. above the floor. The height of the lamp plus that of the table should equal eye height. For example, if the table is 18 in. high, the lamp should be 22 in. high. If the table is 25 in., the lamp should be 15 in.

In lamps holding a single bulb, the top of the socket should be level with the bottom of the shade. Bulb placement in lamps with several bulbs is variable, but the bulbs should always be close to the bottom of the shade and completely hidden from sideways view.

Lamps used primarily to distribute light downward on books, games, etc. should incorporate within the shade a bowl or dish-shaped diffuser of translucent glass or plastic. This should either encircle the bulb or be set below it.

Lampshades should be at least 16 in. in diameter at the bottom. For wall lamps used in pairs, however, the diameter can be reduced to 12 in.; and for bureau and dressing-table lamps, it can be further reduced to 9 in. The shades should be deep enough so you cannot look into the top when standing; if not, a diffusing or perforated disk should cover the top.

Shades on lamps used for downlighting should be translucent enough to transmit light but dense enough not to reveal the exact location of the bulbs. The inner surfaces should be nearly white; the outer surfaces, white or a light neutral color. Dense or opaque shades are used only in rooms with very dark walls.

DIMMERS. With a dimmer switch you can not only turn one or more lights on and off but also raise and lower their intensity. It must not be used to control an outlet into which a motor-driven appliance such as a vacuum cleaner may be plugged. The type of dimmer used depends on whether the light you're controlling is incandescent or fluorescent. The size must be coordinated with the wattage of the light.

Most incandescent dimmers used in homes are small enough to replace a conventional switch in a standard 2½-in.-deep switch box. Just remove the old switch and connect the black wire in the box to the gold screw on the dimmer, the white wire to the silver screw.

Fluorescent dimmers should be installed by a contractor.

A modified type of incandescent dimmer is a high-low switch which provides either full light or approximately half light.

TIMERS. An automatic timer which turns lights on and off at the same or different times every night provides a measure of protection against burglars breaking into your house while you're away.

Most homeowners are content with a timer with an extension cord that plugs into any outlet. Built-in timers, like all built-in devices, are a little neater, and are capable of controlling many more lights (or motors

Dimmer switches are designed to control one or more lights with a definite total maximum wattage. This is a large unit. Superior Electric Co.

up to 1 hp. if you want a timer for some purpose other than burglarproofing). The built-ins are connected into the cable running from the switch to the lights.

AUTOMATIC SWITCHES. These serve the same purpose as timers but use a photoelectric cell to control the lights. Installed near a window (but not in direct sunlight), they turn lights on when darkness falls and turn them back off when day breaks. Both built-in and cord-connected units are available.

WHO MAKES IT

Alkco Manufacturing Co. · Under-cabinet and under-shelf fluorescent fixtures. Fluorescent wall brackets. Surface-mounted fluorescent ceiling fixtures. Narrow troffers.

Authentic Designs. · Handcrafted chandeliers and sconces taken from early New England designs.

Baldwin Hardware Manufacturing Corp. · Sconces of Colonial design.

Ball & Ball. · Accurate reproductions of 18th-century lighting fixtures.

Camer Glass, Inc. · Chandeliers of hand-blown glass.

Design-Technics Ceramics, Inc. · Pendant fixtures with handcrafted glazed ceramic shielding.

Eagle Electric Manufacturing Co. · Photoelectric switches.

General Electric Co., Housewares Business Div. · Automatic timers. One model can be set to turn lights on and off at different times.

General Electric Co., Wiring Device Dept. · Dimmer switches.

F. H. Lawson Co. · Fluorescent fixtures for surface-mounting on bathroom ceilings or over bathroom mirrors.

LCA Corp., Progress Lighting Div. · Track lights with 17 types of lampholder including a wall-washer. Two types of track system, one containing a single circuit, the other three individually controlled circuits. Also a complete array of all other types of exterior and interior fixtures ranging from modern architectural designs to Colonial and rococo. Crystal chandeliers. Strip lights.

Leslie-Locke, Lighting Div. · Exterior wall brackets and post lanterns. Photoelectric switches.

Lighting Products, Inc. · Surface-mounted ceiling fixture using two U-shaped fluorescent tubes.

Lighting Services, Inc. · Track lights—six types of lampholder.

Majestic Metal Spinning & Stamping Co. · Mainly decorative fixtures including pendants, surface-mounts, surface-mounted downlights, wall brackets, strips. Many chandeliers of different types.

MarLe Co. · Reproductions of early lighting fixtures, especially exterior wall brackets.

McGraw-Edison Co., Halo Lighting Div. · Track lights with five types of lampholder in several finishes. One type uses exposed spherical G-type bulbs.

Miami-Carey Co. · Decorative wall brackets and pendants for bathrooms. Strip lights.

Montgomery Ward & Co. · Pendant ceiling fixtures and chandeliers. Surface-mounted ceiling fixtures. Recessed incandescent and fluorescent downlights. Eyeballs. Wall brackets. Exterior wall brackets and post lights. Automatic timers.

Gates Moore. · Authentic handcrafted early Colonial chandeliers and exterior wall brackets.

Pass & Seymour, Inc. · Dimmer switches.

Perfect-Line Manufacturing Corp. · Weatherproof adjustable lampholders. Photoelectric control to convert existing exterior lights to automatic operation.

Scovill Manufacturing Co., Lightcraft of California Div. · Ornate pendant fixtures and chandeliers. Surface-mounted ceiling fixtures. Wall brackets. Post lanterns. Exterior wall brackets.

Scovill Manufacturing Co., NuTone Housing Products Div. Decorative wall brackets and pendant fixtures for bathrooms. Fluorescent and incandescent fixtures for installation over mirrors and medicine cabinets.

Scovill Manufacturing Co., Sterling Lighting Div. · Sleek modern recessed ceiling downlights, including eyeballs, high-hats, pinholes, fluorescents. Semi-recessed ceiling fixtures. Wall-washers. Wall brackets, incandescent and fluorescent. Surface-mounted ceiling downlights. Under-cabinet fluorescents. Track lights.

Sears Roebuck & Co. · Surface-mounted ceiling fixtures. Dimmer switches.

Sturdy Lantern Manufacturing Co. · Primarily exterior wall brackets, pendant ceiling fixtures, and post lights of stagecoach-days design. A few brass interior wall brackets and front-hall pendants of the same era.

Superior Electric Co. · Dimmer controls for every purpose.

Swivelier Co. · Track lights with 20 types of lampholder including one with exposed G-type bulbs, two pendant fixtures, and a projector fixture with adjustable shutters for casting a sharp-edged beam on paintings, etc.

Village Lantern. · Authentic reproductions of early Colonial chandeliers and sconces.

Wellmade Metal Products Co. · Surface-mounted ceiling fixtures incorporating U-shaped fluorescent tubes.

Westinghouse Electric Corp., Bryant Div. · Photoelectric switches.

Wilson Research Corp. · Luminous ceiling systems including framework and plastic diffusers or grilles. Fluorescent wall brackets for use over bathroom lavatories.

William Wirtz Associates. · Flexible low-voltage lighting strips.

21

Fireplaces and Chimneys

Fireplaces have always been built to unusual as well as usual designs. In ancient times, a fireplace was nothing but a hearth and a hole in the roof. Later, even after the design became more or less standardized as we know it today, homeowners never hesitated to branch out in new directions if they thought it would yield a better source of heat. That's how Ben Franklin came up with a new stove which, in somewhat modified form, is going strong today.

With this background, it's not surprising that our modern fireplaces come in myriad shapes and sizes. Most, it is true, are still the tried-and-true rectangular hole in a wall. But as the pictures on these pages show, there are also fireplaces that are open on two or three sides, fireplaces that hang from the ceiling, fireplaces that look like Indian teepees, and so on. This would seem to indicate that fireplace design and construction are complicated. And to some extent that's true: if you want to create a fireplace from scratch, you can't—or at least you shouldn't—do it yourself. You need an architect or mason with long experience in fireplace building. On the other hand, if you don't feel bound to traditional designs, there is a host of excellent prefabricated fireplaces that almost anyone can install in a short time and at low cost.

FIREPLACE BASICS. Whatever its appearance, a fireplace should do four things: (1) Permit complete combustion of fuel. (2) Exhaust the by-products of combustion from the house. (3) Deliver as much heat as possible into the room. (4) Be safe.

In addition, it should be located so that people sitting in all areas of the room can enjoy it. In a long, narrow room, for example, it's better to place the fireplace on one of the long side walls than in a short end wall, because people always feel compelled to cluster around a fireplace, and when it's in the latter location the opposite end of the room is totally unpopulated.

There should be ample room around the fireplace for furniture. But the furniture should not interfere with traffic in and through the room, and it should not be so close to the fireplace that the occupants are baked. A space of at least 6 ft. should be allowed between a fireplace and chairs or sofas directly in front of it.

Finally, the fireplace should be more or less in scale with the room. As a rule of thumb, there should be 5 sq. in. of fireplace opening for every square foot of floor area. This does not mean, however, that if you have an enormous living room you are obligated to put in an enormous fireplace. The practical problem of using the fireplace must also be considered. Huge fireplaces throw proportionally less heat into the room than smaller fireplaces unless you feed outsize logs into the fire. Furthermore, large fireplaces require more air to operate properly, and in a well-insulated and weather-stripped home adequate air for combustion is not always available unless the windows are left open or, in extreme situations, there is a duct which brings in outside air to an ash dump installed in the hearth in front of the fireplace.

MASONRY FIREPLACES. The principal value of conventional masonry fireplaces is that they can be built to designs and sizes which are not available in prefabricated fireplaces. On the other hand, they are much more expensive than prefabs. There is always the possibility—especially with an unusual design—that the designer or builder will make some mistake that causes the fireplace to operate badly. And unless you're building a new house, it is almost a necessity to build the fireplace on an outside wall (if built within the house, major changes must be made in the framing in order to accommodate the fireplace and chimney).

The essential elements of a masonry fireplace are:

Foundations. Because of the size and weight of the fireplace and chimney, they must stand unsupported on

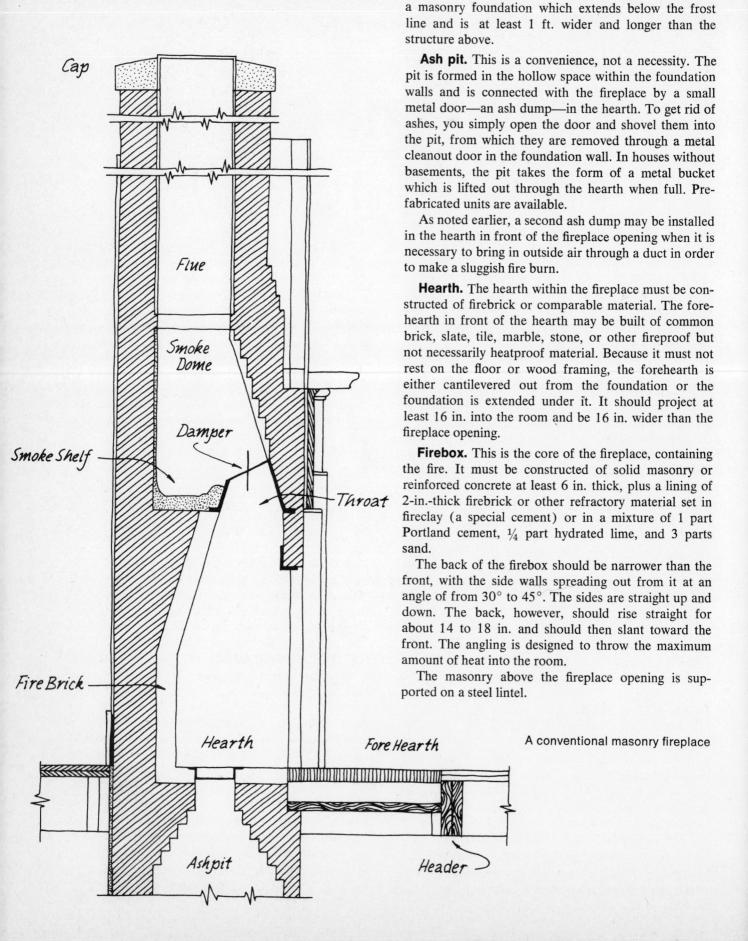

a masonry foundation which extends below the frost line and is at least 1 ft. wider and longer than the structure above.

Ash pit. This is a convenience, not a necessity. The pit is formed in the hollow space within the foundation walls and is connected with the fireplace by a small metal door—an ash dump—in the hearth. To get rid of ashes, you simply open the door and shovel them into the pit, from which they are removed through a metal cleanout door in the foundation wall. In houses without basements, the pit takes the form of a metal bucket which is lifted out through the hearth when full. Prefabricated units are available.

As noted earlier, a second ash dump may be installed in the hearth in front of the fireplace opening when it is necessary to bring in outside air through a duct in order to make a sluggish fire burn.

Hearth. The hearth within the fireplace must be constructed of firebrick or comparable material. The fore-hearth in front of the hearth may be built of common brick, slate, tile, marble, stone, or other fireproof but not necessarily heatproof material. Because it must not rest on the floor or wood framing, the forehearth is either cantilevered out from the foundation or the foundation is extended under it. It should project at least 16 in. into the room and be 16 in. wider than the fireplace opening.

Firebox. This is the core of the fireplace, containing the fire. It must be constructed of solid masonry or reinforced concrete at least 6 in. thick, plus a lining of 2-in.-thick firebrick or other refractory material set in fireclay (a special cement) or in a mixture of 1 part Portland cement, $\frac{1}{4}$ part hydrated lime, and 3 parts sand.

The back of the firebox should be narrower than the front, with the side walls spreading out from it at an angle of from 30° to 45°. The sides are straight up and down. The back, however, should rise straight for about 14 to 18 in. and should then slant toward the front. The angling is designed to throw the maximum amount of heat into the room.

The masonry above the fireplace opening is supported on a steel lintel.

A conventional masonry fireplace

Throat. The throat is the upper part of the firebox. It is the same width as the firebox and about 5 in. deep. (In cross-sectional area, it should be at least 15% of the fireplace opening.) The bottom of the throat should be about 4 in. above the lintel. At the top of the throat—well above the lintel so that smoke cannot be deflected back into the room—is the damper. This is generally hinged at the back, and when open should permit almost completely unrestricted passage of smoke up the chimney.

Smoke shelf. One of the most important parts of the fireplace, the smoke shelf serves the purpose of deflecting air that blows down the chimney away from the fire. It should be as wide as the throat and not less than 8 in. deep (the depth varies to suit the dimensions of the firebox). Although most shelves are flat, a slightly concave design is considered more efficient.

Smoke dome. Known also as a smoke chamber, this is the roughly triangular space above the smoke shelf which funnels smoke into the flue. The back wall should be vertical and flush with the flue. The other walls should be built at an angle of at least 60° to the horizontal.

Chimney. Chimney height depends on the shape of the roof as well as on surrounding trees, buildings, hills, etc. Generally, a chimney should project at least 2 ft. above the peak of a sloping roof, 3 ft. above a flat roof. Additional height may be necessary if there are other nearby obstructions such as trees or buildings.

The chimney and fireplace must not touch any wood in the house structure. A 2-in. space is required at all points except behind the firebox, where it must be increased to 4 in. The space between the chimney and floor members should be firestopped with incombustible material.

Although a chimney may be lined with brick, there is less likelihood of soot building up inside the flue if a clay-tile lining at least 5/8 in. thick is used. The joints between the tiles must be completely filled with mortar and smooth on the inside. The lining is surrounded with at least one course of 4-in. common brick, stone, or concrete block.

Each fireplace should have its own flue, and it is not a good idea to vent any other heating unit, such as a furnace, into the flue.

To protect the masonry and direct air currents upward, the chimney is capped with a slab of concrete or brick sloped upward toward the flue (which should extend about 2 in. above the cap). The cap must also project a couple of inches beyond the sides of the chimney to prevent water from dripping down the brick and working into the joints.

Whether a flue needs to be covered with a hood, or hat, to keep out rain and strong winds is usually difficult to determine when a fireplace is built. For a

Chimney-top draft inducer. Conco.

very large flue, it is probably advisable; but for most flues it is unnecessary. If a hood is needed, it is generally made of a slab of stone supported at the four corners on bricks. The area of the openings under the hood must be at least equal to the area of the flue.

Other kinds of hood are prefabricated of steel, and although not attractive, they are particularly useful for solving serious draft problems. One resembles a medieval knight's helmet with several visors in front and back. The other is a conical device with a built-in electric fan which is used to induce draft even during storms. Both devices also help to keep birds and squirrels out of chimneys.

Fireplace facing. A facing covering the exposed edges of the firebox is optional. In many cases, the bricks or stones of which the firebox is built are left exposed. In other cases, the edges are faced with marble, ceramic tile, glass, metal, or plaster—almost any attractive, incombustible material.

Fireplace dimensions. Fireplace dimensions vary tremendously, but as a general rule, the height of the opening should be two-thirds to three-quarters of the width, and the depth of the firebox should be one-half to two-thirds of the opening height. For openings up to 6 ft. wide, the height should usually not exceed 3½ ft.; 4 ft. is a good maximum for fireplaces over 6 ft. wide.

The average fireplace has an opening 30 to 40 in. wide and 30 in. high. The depth is between 16 and 18 in.

The size of the fireplace opening determines the flue area. If the chimney is under 15 ft. high, measured from the throat to the top, the area of the flue should equal one-eighth the area of the opening. If the chimney is over 15 ft. high, the flue area should be one-tenth of the opening area.

Multiple-opening fireplaces. Fireplaces with openings on more than one side are more difficult to keep from smoking than conventional fireplaces and therefore trickier to build. Since special dampers are ordinarily required, you should follow the damper manufacturer's directions about sizing the fireplace. Typical dimensions recommended by the FHA are as follows:

Fireplaces opening at one side and one end

Width of front opening	Height	Depth	Flue
30 in.	36 in.	30 in.	16 × 16 in.
34	30	20	12 × 16
42	42	24	16 × 20

Fireplaces opening on two opposite sides

30	42	24	16 × 20
34	30	28	16 × 16
38	36	28	16 × 20

Fireplaces opening on two sides and one end

34	24	24	16 × 16
38	30	28	16 × 20
38	36	28	20 × 24

A major problem with all multiple-opening fireplaces is to provide enough fresh air to support combustion and draft. In extreme cases, it may be necessary to install a small ventilating fan in the flue.

CIRCULATING FIREPLACES.

The circulating fireplace is a prefabricated steel shell incorporating the firebox, smoke dome, smoke shelf, and damper. It greatly simplifies construction because all the mason has to do is to build the foundation and hearth, set the shell on the hearth, and lay up bricks around the shell. The shape and dimensions of the fireplace are determined for him.

But the real advantage of a circulating fireplace stems from the fact that it heats not only by radiation (as a conventional fireplace does) but also by circulating heated air directly into the room or even into adjoining rooms. As a result, it has almost twice the heat output of a conventional fireplace.

The walls of the circulator are two layers of steel separated by an air space. Cold air enters this air space through grilles installed at the floor line next to the fireplace. As it passes through the space, it is heated and then exhausted through grilles near the top of the firebox or high in the wall. To speed the movement of air, circulator manufacturers offer air inlets containing electric fans. Fans should also be used in warm-air outlets placed in adjoining rooms.

The chimney may be of conventional masonry construction or prefabricated of steel.

Circulating fireplaces are made with one, two, or three openings. Those with one opening can sometimes be installed in existing fireplaces to improve heating performance. Opening widths range from 28 to 71 in.

PREFABRICATED BUILT-IN FIREPLACES.

This type of fireplace not only reduces construction costs still further but makes it possible to install a fireplace of

Prefabricated built-in fireplace during installation. Temco, Inc.

traditional design almost anywhere in an existing house. The fireplaces consist of a steel firebox complete with hearth, damper, smoke dome and shelf, and prefabricated chimney. They are made with one opening in the front or with one front and one side opening. They are 24 to 26 in. deep and 38, 46, 52, or 58 in. wide (outside dimensions).

Most prefab built-ins are designed with zero clearance, which means that they can actually touch any building or framing material around the bottom, sides, and back. Because of this, you can build them right into a wall at floor level or above, or let them project out from the walls. In either case, you can almost completely surround them with wood paneling or any other wall-surfacing material. The only place you can't use wood is in the facing.

Another advantage of the prefabs is that they weigh relatively little; consequently, there is no need to place them on a masonry foundation. You can, instead, set them directly on the subfloor or finish floor and build whatever kind of fire-resistant forehearth you like out over the floor in front of them.

The entire installation can be made in a weekend. The hardest part of the job is to install the flue through

This prefabricated built-in fireplace is open in the front and at one end. Preway, Inc.

holes you cut in the roof and ceiling. Once this is in and the fireplace is connected to it, the job consists of building the stud framing to which the wall surfacing materials are nailed.

PREFABRICATED CIRCULATING FIREPLACES.

These are like other prefabricated built-ins except that they are designed to heat air circulating through the shell. The air enters through a slot under the slightly raised hearth, passes up around the sides and back of the firebox where it is heated, and then returns to the room through a register just above the fireplace opening. A circulating fan can be installed on one side of the fireplace to speed the air flow.

FREESTANDING FIREPLACES.

These are the least expensive fireplaces and the easiest of all to install because all you have to do is set them in place and run a flue through the roof or the nearest exterior wall. The fireplaces are made of steel or sometimes cast iron in a variety of designs and are finished with porcelain enamel in red, green, yellow, black, white, and other colors. Some units stand on the floor, others hang on the face of a wall, and still others can be suspended from the ceiling on chains. They're all very modern-looking but give off plenty of good old-fashioned warmth (this is especially true of cast-iron models).

Installation varies somewhat, so note the requirements before you make a purchase. Generally, the fireplaces can be placed right against unpainted masonry walls, but if a wall is built of or surfaced with combustible material, a clearance of several inches is required behind them and even greater clearance is required on the sides.

All fireplaces should be placed on or above a fire-resistant surface which extends far enough beyond the hearth to catch whatever sparks escape.

Freestanding fireplaces come in many shapes and sizes. 1, 2, and 3, Martin Industries, Inc. 4 and 5, A. R. Wood Manufacturing Co. 6, Malm Fireplaces, Inc.

1   2   3

4   5   6

Two more freestanding fireplaces, Malm Fireplaces, Inc.

Prefabricated wall-hung electric fireplace. Fasco Industries, Inc.

GAS AND ELECTRIC FIREPLACES. Fireplaces with gas logs are available in prefabricated built-in and freestanding models. All burn natural gas or, with slight modification, LP gas.

Electric fireplaces are made in freestanding models and models that you can build into a wall and finish to resemble a conventional fireplace of any design. They come with realistic logs which glow red when turned on. Heat from a concealed element is forced into the room by a hidden fan. The units operate on 120 to 240 volts.

There are also gas and electric logs which can be installed in any conventional fireplace.

STOVES. If you are looking for heat more than glamour, a wood- or coal-burning stove is your best choice. And the choice is wide, ranging from the reli-

able old Franklin stove measuring about 32 in. across the front and the superefficient Ashley stove measuring as much as 35 in. across by 21 in. deep (or vice versa) down to a quaint Norwegian model that takes up just a shade more than 1 sq. ft. of floor space. They're made of cast iron or steel, and some models, such as the Ashley, have a thermostat.

Except for the Franklin stove, which fits into any not-too-formal home, the imports tend to be more attractive than our domestic models. Many of them are finished with colorful porcelain enamel. Even so, they are really suited only to contemporary houses and vacation homes.

Like freestanding fireplaces, stoves must be set out from combustible walls, and although most of them stand on legs, they should usually be centered on a noncombustible "pad" of some sort. They are vented

Ashley stove. Martin Industries, Inc.

228

Prefabricated French Provincial mantel made of heat-resistant urethane. Focal Point, Inc.

through a metal flue into an existing chimney or prefabricated chimney. Because they need less air for full combustion than fireplaces, several stoves can be hooked into the same chimney provided they are at different levels.

PREFABRICATED CHIMNEYS.

If it weren't for prefabricated chimneys, the tremendous current demand for fireplaces to be added to existing homes could never have occurred. It's one thing to build a masonry chimney; quite another to put in a prefab. Because the latter is constructed with 1 in. of highly efficient insulation sandwiched between two layers of steel, there is no need to surround it with bulky bricks. The outer shell can be placed within 2 in. of wood framing members, sheathing, and floors. As a result, a small 6-in. flue takes up a space only 1 ft. square; a large 14-in. flue requires only 20×20 in.

Another advantage of the chimneys is that the pipes are lightweight, made in lengths up to 30 in., and come with every kind of fitting you need to put them together. So once he has cut the necessary openings through the roof, ceilings, and floors, one un-handyman can assemble an entire chimney in about an hour.

And if you worry about how your house will look with a metal stovepipe sticking out through the roof, don't give it another thought. The chimney manufacturers can also provide a metal housing which, from the ground, looks exactly like brick.

One thing to note when buying a chimney is that there are several models even though they all look alike. Some are made only for venting gas-fired appliances, furnaces, and water heaters. The type needed for a fireplace (unless it's a gas-burner) is an all-fuel model made of stainless steel. This is capable of con-

tinuous operation at 1,000° F flue-gas temperature and up to one-hour operation at as much as 1,400°.

MANTELS.

There is no rule which says that every built-in fireplace must have a mantel. Many do not; they are made an integral part of the surrounding wall by carrying the wall-surfacing material—usually brick or stone—right up to the edges of the fireplace opening. Generally, however, the fireplaces which people call beautiful have a mantel, and it is the mantel which is chiefly responsible for the beauty.

This doesn't mean, of course, that all mantels are attractive. Many are hideous because the persons who designed them didn't know what they were doing. Mantel design is an art which is best left to an architect if you want something a little unusual. But if you are perfectly content with a tried-and-proven mantel design, there is no need to go further than your nearest lumberyard to find one.

Precut mantels of excellent traditional design are stock items available in sizes to fit the most popular sizes of fireplace, and most of them can be trimmed to fit smaller fireplaces. Some designs consist only of the pieces which surround the fireplace opening; others include a mantel shelf.

Also available as stock items are semi-rustic mantel shelves which are installed alone—without the fireplace surround.

All wood mantels must be set back from the edges of fireplace openings to keep them from catching fire. The FHA requires a minimum clearance of 3½ in., but most fireplaces look better if this is increased to 7 or 8 in. Mantel shelves and any other wood projecting more than 1½ in. beyond the fireplace breast must always be installed at least 12 in. above the opening.

FIRESCREENS.

For maximum protection against fly-

Glass firescreen. Bennett-Ireland, Inc.

Heat booster with blower added. The warmed air emerges through the holes in the metal hood. Stites Manufacturing Co.

into a rough C with the ends of the tubes facing into the room. When a fire is built in the grate, cold air enters the tubes at the bottom, is warmed as it passes through, and flows back into the room at the top. For maximum effectiveness, a fan installed outside the fireplace may be used to force air through the tubes.

The grate is normally used for a wood fire but can be equipped with a coal grate which rests on the tubes.

A somewhat similar booster consists of a long rectangular box placed on the hearth across the front of the fireplace opening and a flat box on which the fire is built. A fan in the first box draws in air at one end and funnels it through a large tube into the second box, where it is warmed. The air then flows out through a second tube into the front box, from which it issues into the room through slots.

ing sparks, a firescreen should fit snugly within the fireplace opening or against the face of the firebox. Flexible metal screens which draw like draperies are the kind most often used. One variety hangs from a track which is screwed to the inside edges of the opening; the other hangs from a track—which is often enclosed in a brass hood—that is screwed to the face of the firebox. In both cases, the andirons are usually placed behind the screen.

A freestanding version of the overlapping built-in draw screen is available. In this, the draw screens are hung in a rigid frame which overlaps the face of the firebox. The bottom member of the frame is about 6 in. high and serves as a fender. The andirons are usually placed in front of the screen, with the shanks on which logs rest extending into the fireplace through slots in the fender. Some screens, however, are designed to have the andirons placed behind them.

Glass screens provide even greater protection against sparks. In addition, they allow less air to enter the room when the fireplace is not in use. They are particularly valuable on multiple-opening fireplaces when it's necessary to reduce the amount of incoming air to make a fire burn properly.

The screens are made with tempered-glass doors enclosed in a frame which is attached to the face of the fireplace. A built-in fender at the bottom of the frame has a draft control so you can adjust the amount of air flowing into the fireplace from the room. An optional metal draw screen which installs behind the doors is available to contain sparks in case you want to open the doors to enjoy the sound and smell of the fire.

HEAT BOOSTERS. A heat booster is designed to transform a fireplace from a source of radiant heat only to a source of both radiant and convected heat.

One type of unit is a grate made of steel tubes bent

WHO MAKES IT

Acorn Building Components, Inc. · Fireplace facings made of blend of marble dust and polyester.

Atlanta Stove Works, Inc. · Freestanding fireplaces—two rectangular, two others more or less elliptical.

Barclay Industries, Inc. · Rustic mantel shelves.

Bennett-Ireland, Inc. · Every type of flexible, glass, and freestanding firescreen.

Buckingham-Virginia Slate Corp. · Honed-finish and natural cleft unfading black slate for hearths and facings.

Cavrok Corp. · Fiberglass-reinforced plastic fireplaces in stone or brick patterns up to 59 in. wide. Electric logs included.

Conco, Field Control Div. · Chimney top draft inducer.

Fasco Industries, Inc. · Floor-mounted and wall-hung electric fireplaces. Electric fire logs. Electric heater built like a grate for use in a conventional fireplace with real logs piled on top.

Flair-Fold, Inc. · Walnut-finished rustic mantel shelves.

Focal Point, Inc. · Georgian and French-provincial mantels. Former is 59½ in. wide; latter, 64 in.

General Products Co. · Prefabricated all-fuel and gas-venting chimneys. Heat-circulating fireplaces, front-opening only.

Goodwin of California, Inc. · Custom-built freestanding fireplaces open on all sides for placement in center of a room.

Gordon Corp. · Freestanding rectangular fireplace.

Hart & Cooley Manufacturing Co. · Prefabricated all-fuel and gas venting chimneys.

A. C. Hathorne Co. · Copper fireplace hoods in curved or straight design for 36-in., 42-in., and 48-in. fireplace openings. Also custom-made hoods to any size, design, application.

Hayes-te Equipment Corp. · Boxlike stove on legs is placed on fireplace hearth and vents through a metal plate which covers fireplace opening.

Kristia Associates. · Norwegian enameled cast-iron fireplaces and stoves in a dozen-odd designs. A foot-square stove burns coal as well as wood. One design suitable for building into existing fireplace.

Leigh Products, Inc. · Electric fireplaces mount on walls or in corner. Multi-visored chimney-flue caps.

Majestic Co. · Prefabricated built-in fireplaces—front opening and opening in front and at one end. Front-opening prefab built-in gas-burning fireplaces. Freestanding fireplaces in great variety, including round hanging model open on all sides. Freestanding electric fireplaces. Heat-circulating fireplaces. Prefab chimneys. Conventional dampers and dampers for multiple-opening masonry fireplaces.

Malm Fireplaces, Inc. · Freestanding fireplaces in variety, including round hanging model and Franklin-stove design.

Martin Industries, Inc. · Prefabricated built-in fireplaces, one burning gas. Freestanding round and rectangular fireplaces, one round model burning gas, another electric. Electric wall-hung fireplaces. Gas fire logs. Prefabricated chimneys.

Martin Industries, Inc., King Products Div. · Wood or coal stoves in old and new designs, two with built-in thermostats. Thermostatically controlled Ashley stoves—two models in modern cabinets. Gas Fire logs.

Metal Concepts, Inc. · Heat booster with blower discharges heated air through box on hearth.

Miami-Carey Co. · Freestanding and wall-hung electric fireplaces. Electric fire logs. Two freestanding rectangular wood-burning fireplaces. Flexible-draw firescreens in frames.

Montgomery Ward & Co. · Prefabricated built-in fireplaces. Electric fireplaces and logs. Semi-circular and rectangular freestanding wood-burning fireplaces including cast-iron Franklin stove. Stoves, including models that heat several rooms. Flexible and glass firescreens.

Morgan Co. · Traditional wood mantels. Rustic mantel shelves.

Philips Industries, Inc. · Freestanding rectangular fireplace.

Preway, Inc. · Elliptical and long-octagonal freestanding fireplaces. Prefabricated built-in fireplaces, one burning gas, one with glass doors, one open at front and at either end. Prefab chimneys. Electric fire logs.

Sears Roebuck & Co. · Dark-stained pine mantel shelf.

Stites Manufacturing Co. · Heat booster with blower and U-shaped tubes in grate discharges air through hood.

Superior Fireplace Co. · Heat-circulating fireplaces that open in front, front and back, front and side. Ash dumps. Clean-out doors. Conventional dampers and dampers for multiple-opening masonry fireplaces. Chimney spark arresters.

Tel-o-Post Co. · Heat booster with U-shaped tubes in grate. Blower available.

Temco, Inc. · Freestanding round fireplaces for installation in a corner. Wall models with built-in 35,000-Btu gas heater for supplementary use. Prefabricated built-in fireplace.

Thermograte Enterprises, Inc. · Heat booster with U-shaped tubes in grate. Blower available. Coal grate available.

Vega Industries, Inc., Heatilator Div. · Heat-circulating fireplaces, front-opening. Prefabricated built-in fireplaces open in front and front and one side. Heat-circulating built-in prefab fireplace. Freestanding round and rectangular fireplaces. Prefab chimneys. Ash dumps. Clean-out doors. Dampers for multiple-opening fireplaces.

Vermont Marble Co. · Fireplace facings.

Vestal Manufacturing Co. · Front-opening heat-circulating fireplaces. Dampers. Clean-out doors. Ash dumps. Dutch-oven doors. Incinerator doors.

Victor Oolitic Stone Co. · Indiana limestone (Bedford stone) cut and finished for hearths and mantel shelves. Ashlar and rubble veneer stone for building fireplaces.

Wallace-Murray Corp. · Prefabricated all-fuel and gas-venting chimneys.

Washington Stove Works. · Cast-iron Franklin stoves.

A. R. Wood Manufacturing Co. · Freestanding fireplaces including circular model open on all sides and corner model which can be installed against any wall material. Built-in prefabricated heat-circulating fireplace.

22

Heating

Once a heating system is installed in a house, major changes are usually expensive to make. That is why heating systems should always be designed by a competent heating contractor or, if there is any doubt about which type of system is best, by a heating engineer. (Engineers are experts in the design of all types of systems, whereas contractors specialize in the type they sell.)

But although many changes may appear difficult to the homeowner, they may be perfectly feasible. For example, there is no great problem about:

· Switching from oil to gas heat or vice versa.
· Installing a new furnace or boiler.
· Heating an addition.
· Adding new heating outlets.
· Cleaning up a dirty warm-air heating system.
· Improving the efficiency of a heating system.
· Relocating heating outlets.
· Zoning a heating system.

FUELS. To all intents and purposes, natural gas, LP gas, oil, and electricity—the most widely used fuels—are equally good for heating purposes. All are dependable, safe, clean. The main difference is their cost, which varies from one part of the country to another. Bear in mind, also, that it changes from year to year, and although one may be much cheaper than another right now, there is no assurance that this will be true next year.

Another less important difference is that gas and oil heating systems must be connected into a chimney which carries off the products of combustion. With electric heat, no chimney is needed.

Coal and wood are also used as fuel in heating plants with chimneys, but they lag far behind the other fuels in popularity because of the labor involved in feeding and cleaning out the furnace. Even so, the energy crisis is becoming so severe that we may reasonably expect both fuels to come into wider use.

Wood-burning heating systems, in fact, are already winning a fair number of converts. Furnaces that burn wood alone are on the market; and there are also furnaces and boilers (used for hot-water or steam heating) that burn wood in one chamber and oil, gas, or electricity in the other chamber so you can switch from automatic to hand-fired operation as you wish.

On the other hand, anyone shopping for a coal-fired furnace or boiler must make a very aggressive search to find one. And stokers that automatically feed the coal into the fire are nonexistent.

FORCED-WARM-AIR HEATING SYSTEMS. Forced-warm-air heating is the most popular system for homes. Any fuel can be used. The system is inexpensive to install, delivers heat rapidly when called for and distributes it fairly evenly throughout each room, and can be used for summer cooling and humidifying. On the other hand, the system can be noisy. If not properly put in, problems may be difficult to correct. And the system is inherently dirty, although it can be as clean as any other system—indeed, cleaner—if equipped with filters.

A forced-warm-air heating system is built around a central furnace from which heated air is blown throughout the house in supply ducts. The air enters the rooms through registers which, in cold climates, should be under windows in outside walls. As a result of this placement, the ducts help to warm the floors (an especially important consideration in houses built on concrete slabs) and the registers blanket the windows and surrounding walls with warm air which counteracts the cold air seeping through them. As the air loses heat, it enters return registers placed high in the inside walls and flows back to the furnace through return ducts. At

Electric furnace for a forced-warm-air heating system. Fasco Industries, Inc.

the furnace it is filtered, humidified and reheated, and circulated back through the house once again. The blower and filters are located on the return side of the furnace; the humidifier on the supply side.

In warm climates where air conditioning is more important than heating, the system works in the same way. But the supply registers should be located high in the interior walls or ceilings.

Operation of the heating system is controlled by a thermostat. In most systems, the burner and electrically powered blower which forces the air through the ducts turn on together at the command of the thermostat and turn off within a minute or two of each other. In superior heating systems, however, the blower operates all the time to give continuous air circulation. Blowers in old systems can be easily adjusted to operate in the same way. This helps to even out conditions in the house, and by so doing helps to save a little fuel since you are not so tempted to push up the thermostat.

Since it's difficult for the average person to distinguish between good and poor furnaces, selection should be made on the basis of rated efficiency and guarantee. The higher the efficiency (which is stated in a percentage) and the longer the guarantee (ten years is average for top-notch furnaces), the better the furnace. The actual design of the furnace depends on where it is located. In most houses, the furnace is in the basement and the ducts fan out across the ceiling. In basementless houses, the furnace can be placed anywhere (but usually in a utility room) and warm air leaves through the bottom and returns through the top. Horizontal furnaces can be hung from the joists in crawl spaces or installed on attic floors.

Ducts are normally made of galvanized steel. To reduce noise made by the heated air passing through them, the best ductwork is made of metal which has been stamped in a pattern to increase its rigidity. Metal stiffeners can be added to the sides of ordinary ducts. The supply ducts should also be connected to the furnace with flexible connectors.

Since all ducts passing through unheated spaces should be insulated, ducts in new houses are sometimes made of fiberglass covered with a vapor barrier. These not only contain the heat but are also quieter than metal ducts.

When ducts are so long or tortuous that air moves through them sluggishly, efficiency can be greatly increased by building into them small electric fans known as duct boosters.

Registers are made in countless sizes, shapes, and designs for installation in walls and ceilings. They are also made for installation in floors at the foot of floor-to-ceiling windows and glass doors, in place of baseboards, or in the corner between a wall and floor. For most effective distribution of heat, the supply registers should be equipped with adjustable deflectors so you can direct the air up and down. Some also are designed so air can be directed to the sides. Further to control heat flow and prevent draperies from waving, clear plastic deflectors can be fastened to the fronts of the registers. Return registers should have a damper so they can be closed.

GRAVITY WARM-AIR HEATING SYSTEMS. Gravity warm air is an obsolete system but still found in old houses. It is built around an enormous furnace in the basement. Warm air rises naturally through huge ducts and registers in the floor or baseboards near the center of the house. To replace the system, you must rip most, if not all, of it out.

FORCED-HOT-WATER SYSTEMS. This type of system is most popular in the Northeast but is suitable in any home that is not centrally air conditioned (because the system can't be used for air conditioning). It is reliable, fast, and heats by radiation as well as convection. Though more expensive to install than a warm-air system, it is easier to install properly and takes up less space in the basement as well as in the house walls. In addition, the boiler can be used for heating the water you use for cooking and bathing. But on the negative side, the system cannot be used to filter or humidify air

Oil-fired hot-water boiler contains a coil for heating domestic water as well. H. B. Smith Co.

in the house, and if the house is unoccupied in winter, the system must be drained to keep it from freezing.

The heart of the system is a cast-iron or steel boiler (the former is better) which uses either gas, oil, or electricity. When the thermostat calls for heat, hot water is circulated by a small pump from the boiler to radiators or convectors placed under windows and along the exterior walls. The water then returns to the boiler, where it is reheated and recirculated. As in a warm-air system, the water can be continuously circulated through the system, even when the boiler is not operating, to provide more even heat. An expansion tank and pressure-relief valve protect the system against abnormal changes in the water pressure.

The piping for a forced-hot-water system is almost always made of copper. In small houses a single line of pipe is used to carry the hot water and the returning cold water. The piping can be laid out so it runs directly from one radiator to another and then back to the boiler, or so each radiator is served by a separate branch from the main pipe. The latter arrangement is the more expensive but permits you to turn off any radiator without affecting the others. In the series-loop arrangement, shutting off one radiator shuts off all the others after it.

Large houses usually have a two-pipe system in which one pipe delivers hot water and the other returns the cold water to the boiler.

Radiators are made of cast iron or of nonferrous metal (aluminum and/or copper). In the latter, fins of metal are clipped around a pipe through which the water circulates. The whole unit is contained in a steel shell. Because of its light weight, it is easier to install than a cast-iron radiator, but it loses heat more rapidly when the boiler and circulating pump turn off.

Both types of radiator are much smaller than those of yesteryear. They can be placed in front of a wall or recessed in it. Where possible, however, it is usually better to install baseboard radiators. These are only 7 to 9 in. high and about 3 in. thick. They are made in many lengths; you can even stretch them out across an entire wall and around a corner onto an adjacent wall. Thus they blanket a large expanse of wall with warm air without spoiling the appearance of a room or complicating the furniture arrangement. Rooms in which they are used are more evenly heated than those with conventional radiators, and some of the heat goes into the floors. Because of this, baseboard radiators are especially suitable for use in slab houses.

All radiators are controlled by a valve which regulates the flow of water. More precise control is possible by installing a thermostatic valve which allows you to adjust the heat in each room to your requirements.

RADIANT HEATING SYSTEMS. A radiant heating system is a hot-water system in which the water is circulated through pipes embedded in a concrete floor and also in walls and ceilings. This results in very uniform

Gas-fired cast-iron hot-water boiler. Utica Radiator Corp.

Thermostatic valve for hot-water and steam radiators. Honeywell, Inc.

temperatures throughout the house. The floors feel delightfully warm. And there are no visible heating outlets. But while the heated surfaces are slow to cool off after the boiler stops running, they are also slow to heat up. And if a pipe ever starts to leak, repairs are difficult and costly to make. For these reasons, the system is no longer widely used even though it was quite popular only 20 years ago.

GRAVITY HOT-WATER HEATING SYSTEMS. This was the earliest type of hot-water heating system, but like gravity warm-air systems, it is no longer installed. It worked pretty well in small, compact houses. However, water took a long time to heat to a point where it rose naturally from the boiler into the radiators, so house temperatures fluctuated badly.

STEAM HEATING SYSTEMS. Steam heating systems have also largely disappeared, although many old houses in the East still have them. Water is heated by gas, oil, or electricity in the boiler until it forms steam, which circulates naturally through pipes to the radiators. When the steam condenses, it flows back to the boiler. Some systems use a single pipe to carry both the steam and the condensate; others have two pipes.

Steam systems respond rapidly when the thermostat calls for heat. But the radiators are dangerously hot, and when the thermostat switches off, they quickly become cold. Furthermore, if the vent valves on the radiators don't work properly, some of the steam escapes into the rooms and condenses on the windows. And the entire system of pipes and radiators gives off a variety of banging, gurgling, and whistling sounds.

Radiators used in steam systems are cast-iron units usually somewhat larger than those in hot-water systems. Baseboard radiators, however, do not perform very well. For maximum control, each radiator should be equipped with an adjustable vent valve. The same type of thermostatic valve used on hot-water radiators can be installed in the supply line to a steam radiator.

VALANCE HEATING. This is a brand-new system which is also used for cooling, but it is so expensive that it has not been installed in many homes. The system is completely silent and draft-free, produces very uniform temperatures throughout each room (even when you sit right in front of a large window, you feel warm), lowers humidity and filters the air in summer (even though it has no filtering apparatus), and does not interfere with furniture placement.

The system gets its name from the fact that the elements which heat and cool the air are concealed in a large, troughlike valance suspended just below the ceiling near an outside wall and extending for the entire length of the wall. Water is heated in a gas, oil, or electric boiler, and cooled in a separate electric chiller. From the central plant, the water is pumped up through pipes in a slender, boxlike chase installed against the wall at one end of each valance. From the chase, it flows into finned pipes in the valance, where it conditions the air surrounding it. In winter, warmed air floats up out of the valance and across the ceiling, where it radiates heat down into the room. At the same time, it warms the ceiling, which also radiates heat down into the room. In summer, cooled air flows down from the valance to the floor, where it spreads out and rises up the walls.

In a four-pipe valance system, two pipes are used for heating and two for cooling. Since every room has its

Valance heater can also be used for air conditioning. Edwards Engineering Corp.

Single-package air-to-air heat pump. Lennox Industries, Inc.

own thermostat, you can heat one room while cooling another. In a less expensive two-pipe system, the same pipes are used for both hot and cold water; consequently, all rooms in the house are at the same temperature.

CENTRAL ELECTRIC HEATING SYSTEMS. There are four types of central electric heating systems. One is a conventional forced-hot-water system with a boiler in which the water is heated by electricity. Another is a conventional forced-warm-air system with a furnace heated by electricity. The third is a forced-warm-air system in which small electric heating elements are installed in the ducts and filtered air is circulated throughout the entire system by a central blower. The fourth is a forced-warm-air system built around a heat pump.

The heat pump is a remarkable all-in-one appliance from which conditioned air flows through ducts and registers laid out like those for a forced-warm-air heating system. In winter, the heat pump supplies heat; in summer, it automatically reverses itself and supplies cooling. One setting of the thermostat maintains a year-round comfort level.

Heat pumps work like an air conditioner in reverse, which is why they are sometimes called reverse-cycle air conditioners. Instead of manufacturing heat out of fuel, they extract it from air or water.

The water-to-air heat pump, relatively rare, is used most widely in Florida. In winter, it extracts heat from well water and uses this to heat the house air circulating through it. In summer, it takes the heat out of the inside air and discharges it down the well.

The more common air-to-air heat pump works in the same way but draws its heat in winter from the outdoor air. In summer, working like a conventional air conditioner, it extracts heat from the indoor air and dissipates it outdoors.

Such is the efficiency of an air-to-air heat pump that

it produces about twice as much energy as it needs to operate. For example, when the outdoor temperature is 45°, a 5-ton heat pump delivers approximately 60,000 Btu of heat for every 23,500 Btu of electricity it consumes. Of course, as the temperature drops, the heat pump is able to extract less heat from the air, but at the same time it uses less electricity. Eventually, however, it reaches a point where, in order to keep the house warm, it must turn on a resistance heater to supplement the heat taken from the air. This raises its consumption of electricity. Even in the coldest climates, however, a heat pump does not use more electricity or cost any more to run than ordinary resistance heating systems. In mild climates, you can heat your home for less than is possible with any other form of heating system, regardless of the fuel used.

The cost of cooling a house with a heat pump is identical to the cost of using a conventional air conditioner.

Heat pumps are sold in sizes suitable for most homes in every climate (although they are recommended especially for warm and temperate climates). They are designed for installation in basements, utility rooms, crawl spaces, attics, outdoors on a slab, or on the roof. Like conventional air conditioners, they are available in single-package systems as well as in split systems (see Chapter 23). Some models can be added to an existing heating plant, which then serves as the supplementary heat source when the temperature drops below freezing. In all cases, the principal installation requirements are a source of outdoor air and a 240-volt electrical circuit.

ELECTRIC ROOM HEATERS. Despite the efficiency of the heat pump, most electric heating to date has been done with individual heaters installed in each room. The principal advantage of this system is that each room has its own thermostat and can therefore be heated to whatever temperature the occupant likes regardless of how the other rooms are heated. You can, in other words, heat your living room to 72° while your bedrooms are set at 68°. Or you can turn off the heat in

Baseboard electric heater. Robbins & Myers, Inc.

Electric floor heater. Emerson Electric Co.

Electric unit heater. Fasco Industries, Inc.

unoccupied rooms without affecting conditions in occupied rooms. This cuts the cost of operation.

The other advantage of room heaters is that they have no moving parts so they require little if any service to keep them in operating condition. All operate at 240 volts.

The heaters are available in several forms—almost all of such tidy, compact design that you are hardly aware of them. They can be used in any combination you like—baseboard heaters here, wall heaters there, ceiling heaters somewhere else, and so on.

Baseboard heaters are long, slender units installed at the base of outside walls. They are made in lengths of 2 to 12 ft.; they can be placed end to end to make longer lengths. Depending on the wattage, they put out roughly 600 to 800 Btu per hour per lineal foot.

Baseboards are the most commonly used type of room heater and are particularly suited to large and medium-size rooms. Their one drawback is that you must cut off floor-length draperies just above them; otherwise the draperies will interfere with heating performance and become scorched (but they won't burn).

Recessed floor heaters are for the most part similar to baseboards but are installed in the floor—usually at the base of sliding glass doors and floor-to-ceiling windows. More compact, boxlike heaters which recess between floor joists are also available. Some of these contain fans.

Valance heaters are also long strip heaters. Surface-mounted on walls just below the ceiling, they are used in large rooms where there is no space for baseboards or floor heaters. They're particularly suited to kitchens.

Wall heaters are rather compact, rectangular units which are recessed in or sometimes surface-mounted on a wall. They are most often installed in bathrooms, entries, and other small rooms but can be used in large rooms which don't accommodate strip heaters. Many of the heaters incorporate fans to circulate the heated air.

Ceiling heaters are small recessed or surface-

Electric undercabinet heater. Fasco Industries, Inc.

Electric wall heater. Fasco Industries, Inc.

mounted heaters used primarily in bathrooms. Those with coiled heating elements usually have a circulating fan; those with heat lamps do not. The heaters are sometimes combined with a ventilating fan and/or a light.

Under-cabinet heaters are ideal for kitchens and bathrooms because they are made to fit under 24-in.-wide base cabinets within the dimensions of a standard kick space. They have an output of 5,000 to 7,000 Btu per hour. A small fan forces the heat into the room.

Utility heaters are small units designed for installation on walls or ceilings of pump houses, utility rooms, etc. They have a built-in thermostat.

Unit heaters are larger fan-forced utility heaters with high output. They are generally used in commercial garages, shops, etc. but might be used in a home workshop or basement in which you want a lot of heat from a single source and don't care what the source looks like.

Through-wall heaters and air conditioners are made specifically for motels, hotels, and apartments but are equally useful in homes—especially in new additions which cannot be heated or cooled by existing central systems. They are installed in openings made through outside walls so the heat taken out of the inside air by the cooling mechanism can be exhausted directly outdoors.

Radiant ceiling panels are 2×4-ft. panels about 1 in. thick which are mounted on ceilings or sometimes walls and painted to blend into the background. They can be installed individually wherever you especially need warmth or grouped in the center of the ceiling to warm the entire room. Their Btu output ranges from about 1,700 to 2,600.

Radiant ceiling cables are completely concealed heaters used to bathe entire rooms in gentle, even warmth. The cables are looped across a gypsum board or plaster ceiling in parallel rows, anchored in place, and covered with another layer of gypsum board or plaster.

Electric fireplaces are also made. See Chapter 21.

WALL FURNACES. Gas-fired wall furnaces are most often used to heat very small, compact homes in mild climates but are equally good for heating one or two rooms in new additions. Designed for installation against a wall or partially recessed within a wall, they are 14 to 24 in. wide, 8 to 12 in. deep, and 68 to 87 in. high. Some units are designed for direct venting (placed against an exterior wall, they vent directly through the wall to the outdoors); others, for up-venting through a prefabricated, insulated flue to the rooftop. The latter can be installed anywhere within a house.

Most furnaces are of counterflow design, meaning that they draw in room air at the top and fan-force the heated air out through the bottom so that the heat is

Gas-fired wall furnace. Temco, Inc.

evenly distributed throughout the room and not layered at the ceiling. Gravity units (without fans) and some fan-forced models operate in the opposite way.

Although the furnaces have a substantial heat output (to as much as 64,000 Btu per hour), they are normally used to heat only the room in which they are placed or, in the case of up-vented models which are recessed in a wall, the rooms on both sides of the wall. To heat an entire house with a wall furnace, you should use an upflow model and install openings in the walls of adjacent rooms and ducts into rooms beyond these. Duct length should not exceed 18 ft. from the furnace to the center of any room.

FLOOR FURNACES. Gas- and oil-fired floor furnaces are used in small, compact houses of one or two stories as well as in individual rooms in additions. Installed in a basement or crawl space under a grilled opening in the floor, they heat entirely by gravity. In a two-story house, the heat rises through a grilled opening in the second floor above the heater. Although the furnaces put out a lot of heat (up to 45,000 Btu per hour), distribution of the heat is uneven. Dust and dirt which fall through the grille are circulated far and wide.

Furnace sizes range from about 14×30 in. to 22×40 in. Depth is approximately 26 in.

SPACE HEATERS. This undescriptive heading encompasses a variety of gas- and oil-fired heaters which generally look something like large, neatly enclosed radiators. A few models resemble short, oversized baseboards. Used for heating individual rooms, they stand on the floor either against a wall or set out several inches from it. Some are hung on a wall.

The majority are vented through the wall to the outdoors. Some do not require venting, but before using these, check to make sure your building code allows them. Heat is radiated directly into the room or circulated by a fan. In one offbeat fan model, the heat is also ducted into the room or into nearby rooms through a metal baseboard with louvers in the front panel. The baseboard is available in 4-ft. sections which can be pieced together to a maximum length of about 40 ft.

HEAT RECLAIMERS. A substantial amount of the heat produced in a furnace or boiler escapes up the chimney. Much of this can, however, be captured and used in the house. The devices designed for this purpose are small enough to be easily mounted on the flue between the heating plant and chimney.

A typical heat reclaimer consists of several pipes enclosed in a housing with an electric fan. The housing is fastened to the side of the flue. The pipes extend into the flue, where they are heated by the high-temperature flue gas. The fan draws in fresh air from outside the reclaimer, passes it over or through the pipes, and returns it to the furnace room, where it helps indirectly to

Heat reclaimer. Chimney Heat-Reclaimer Corp.

warm the rest of the house. None of the flue gas is allowed to escape. If you wish, the heated fresh air can be ducted into the return-air duct of a warm-air furnace or carried by ducts for up to 20 ft. into other parts of the house.

As a rule, heat reclaimers can be installed on any warm-air, hot-water, or steam system fired by gas, oil, or coal. Tests indicate that they can recover as much as 10,000 Btu per hour of the heat that is normally wasted. This is enough to maintain comfortable conditions in an otherwise unheated room of moderate size. Fuel savings of as much as 14% are possible.

THERMOSTATS. The thermostat is the nerve center of your heating system. It turns the furnace or boiler on when your house begins to get cold, and turns it off when the temperature climbs to the setting you have selected.

The simplest type of thermostat has open metal contacts which react to changes in temperature and open or close the electrical circuit controlling furnace operation. Some thermostats work on 120 volts, others on 24 volts. The low-voltage units are generally more reliable; in addition, they incorporate an anticipator which shuts off the burner shortly before the desired temperature is attained. The furnace blower or circulating pump, however, continues to operate until the residual heat in the furnace is circulated into the house, bringing it up to the proper temperature. (On a 120-volt thermostat without an anticipator, the thermostat turns off the burner at the preset temperature, but since the blower keeps on going, house temperature continues to rise.)

Although open-contact thermostats are widely used—mainly because of their low cost—they tend to give more trouble than other types because dirt settling on the contacts interferes with their operation.

Sealed-contact thermostats are unaffected by dirt and

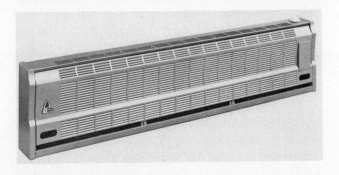

Gas-fired space heaters. Above, wall-mounted unit, Dearborn Stove Co.; center, baseboard unit, and bottom, unusual type of baseboard unit, both Empire Stove Co.

are therefore considered slightly superior. But like open-contact thermostats, they sometimes cause problems when the contacts become pitted.

Mercury thermostats are best and also most expensive. In these, a small vial of mercury is attached to a sensitive spring. When house temperature drops, the spring tilts the vial to a point where a circuit is completed and the heat is turned on. Later, as the temperature rises, the mercury vial tilts in the opposite direction and shuts the heat off.

Since there are no contacts which can be coated with dust or become pitted, mercury thermostats operate without problems almost forever. They perform badly only if they are installed on a slight slant or are accidentally knocked off level.

Most mercury thermostats are set by hand, but some are clock-controlled. Those with manual spring-wound timers are used primarily by families who want to save fuel while they are absent from the house during the day. When you leave home, you can turn the thermostat down for periods of up to about 10 hours. The thermostat automatically turns up the heat before you return home.

Automatic clock controls, on the other hand, need to be set only at the beginning of the heating season. There is one temperature setting for days, another for nights. Once these have been selected, the thermostat automatically turns your house temperature down to the nighttime setting when you go to bed, and turns it back up to the daytime setting shortly before you arise.

Relatively inexpensive timers that can be added to standard thermostats to convert them to automatic operation have recently been introduced.

The installation of a new thermostat can be made by any homeowner who follows the directions supplied by the manufacturer. To control the temperature properly, however, the thermostat must be located about 4 ft. above the floor on a wall where air circulates (but doesn't actually blow) around it freely. The best location is on an inside wall in a room which is frequently occupied. Do not install a thermostat in a kitchen, bedroom, or interior hall; in a room with a much-used fireplace; near an exterior door or sunny window; above a television set or large lamp; in a room above the furnace; or on a wall which is warmed by ducts or pipes hidden within the stud spaces.

SOLAR HEATING. Solar heating proves the old adage that you can't get something for nothing. Homebuilders and owners who have installed it have found it is amazingly expensive initially and does not produce the pure savings they expected. But this does not mean it's a flop.

Although there have been solar-heated houses for a good many years, the system is still in its infancy. But the idea behind it is sound. And despite the fact that many solar-heated houses have disappointed their owners, they have nevertheless proved that free energy from the sun can be used successfully to heat houses and domestic water supplies in most parts of the United States, and that it can cut heating costs drastically in the process.

Although solar-heating systems differ in many ways, they are all basically the same. The sun's heat is trapped in a large, flat, heavily insulated box with a glass top and a steel, aluminum, or copper bottom which is painted black. Water or air is circulated through the box to absorb the heat and is then pumped into a storage unit, from which it is circulated through the house as needed.

All of which sounds a great deal simpler than the system actually is.

To begin with, any house which is solar-heated must be insulated to a fare-thee-well. Roof insulation should be the equivalent of about 18 in. of mineral wool; wall and floor insulation should be 3½ in. thick. All doors and windows should be covered with storm sash.

The collectors must be installed facing south at an angle of about 60°. In a new house, they can be incorporated in the roof. But in most old houses, they can be located on the roof only if the framing is adequate to support them and if steps are taken to prevent them from being blown off by high winds. Placement on the ground may be more feasible but is possible only if there is enough unshaded space in the yard.

The size of the collectors depends on their efficiency. Most manufacturers recommend that they be one-third to one-half as large as the floor area of the house. A few companies claim that because of their more efficient designs, the collector area can be a great deal less than this.

The heat-transfer medium may be either water or air. Most solar-equipment manufacturers use the former. This is stored in a huge, well-insulated tank which is normally installed in the basement or in the ground under or outside the basement. Heated air, by contrast, is stored in a large tank filled with small stones.

There is violent disagreement within the fledgling industry about the merits of water and air collectors. These boil down to this: With a water system you can both heat and cool a house and also heat domestic water. On the other hand, an air system does a more efficient house-heating job but is not well adapted to cooling or water heating.

The pipes used to carry heated water take up less space and are less expensive to install than the ducts required in an air system. The circulating pumps are also smaller and use less electricity. But a water system must be filled with gallons of antifreeze to keep it from freezing in winter. There are problems with corrosion and scaling in a water system, and leaks are more likely to develop and are harder to fix when they do.

Solar-heating collectors installed on a new house. Edmund Scientific Co. photo.

Solar water heater. Fred Rice Productions, Inc.

Heat-exchange surfaces in a water system are smaller. But the rock used to store heat in an air system retains it longer than the water in a water system.

At this stage in the development of solar heating the argument cannot be settled. The only thing that is established is that there are few, if any, places in the country where the homeowner can rely on a solar system to provide adequate heat every day of the year. A small standby unit burning gas, oil, or electricity is re-quired to take up the slack during long spells of very cloudy, rainy, or snowy weather. (You should note, however, that even on overcast days, the sun provides some energy to heat the water or air in collectors. This explains why Harry Thomason, a Washington, D.C., patent attorney who put in one of the earliest solar systems, spent only $18.45 during the first three years of operation for auxiliary fuel.)

The majority of solar-heating manufacturers today sell collectors only. Relatively few firms sell complete systems.

Some companies sell solar water-heating systems. These are miniature versions of whole-house heating systems, and also require standby power to assure a steady supply of hot water.

Solar cooling systems are not sufficiently developed to be marketed.

AIR CLEANERS. One of the advantages of forced-warm-air heating systems is that, unlike other systems, they filter dust and dirt from the house air. The devices generally used for the purpose (all new furnaces are equipped with them) are lightweight metal frames filled, as a rule, with fiber pads. These are installed in the return-air duct at the furnace so that all air entering the furnace from the house must pass through them. As it does so, the dirt is trapped in the fibers and held until eventually it becomes so thick that air circulation is retarded. The homeowner must then remove the filters and either replace them or clean them according to the manufacturer's directions. In many houses, this must be

Partially disassembled electronic air cleaner. Lennox Industries, Inc.

blood pressure.) Air enters a cleaner through a mechanical filter which removes large dirt particles. It then passes through a charging section where the small particles receive an electrical charge. From there it enters the collection chamber in which the charged particles are attracted to and held by a series of oppositely charged metal electrical plates. Finally, the clean air enters the furnace, where it is heated and returned to the house.

The operation of the cleaner is entirely automatic. The only thing you must do is to clean the mechanical filter and collection plates occasionally. A few models are plumbed in so they can wash themselves.

Portable cleaners operate in the same way but incorporate a fan to circulate the air. The slower the fan runs, the more dirt the cleaner removes. For best results, a cleaner should be placed as close as possible to the ceiling.

done at least once a month during both the heating and air-conditioning seasons.

Unfortunately, while the filters—classified as mechanical filters—do a very good job of trapping large dirt particles, they are not effective against small particles. Tests made by the National Bureau of Standard's dust-spot method—the only accurate way of rating a filter's efficiency—show that only about 10% of the particles passing through are actually removed from the air.

In order to remove both visible and invisible particles, you need an electronic air cleaner with a 70 to 90% efficiency rating. This will remove dust particles as small as .03 microns (there are 25,400 microns in one inch) as well as pollen. It does not remove gases and odors (although some cleaners are equipped with charcoal filters which trap some of these). Neither does it remove large particles which settle out of the air on rugs, furniture, and other house surfaces. (In other words, an air cleaner can filter out of a house only the particles which are actually in the air.)

Electronic air cleaners are rather large appliances costing several hundred dollars, and are adapted to old as well as new warm-air heating systems and central air-conditioning systems. Portable cleaners are used with any other kind of heating system.

The built-in cleaners are installed in the return-air duct just ahead of the furnace and wired into a 120-volt circuit so they will operate only when the furnace blower is running. (For maximum efficiency, the blower should be set for continuous air circulation; otherwise, dust in the house will have time to settle when the blower is off. On the other hand, the more an air cleaner runs, the more ozone it produces, and if the ozone level in a house gets too high, it can cause eye, nose, and throat irritation as well as cramps and low

Electronic air cleaner designed to fit between wall studs. It takes the place of the usual return-air grille. Trion, Inc.

A portable cleaner can be effectively used to clean only the room in which it is located. A built-in cleaner cleans the whole house except for those areas without heating or cooling ducts. In both cases, the size of the unit is based on the cubic footage of the room or rooms to be cleaned. The cfm rating of a built-in cleaner must match the cfm rating of the furnace blower.

HUMIDIFIERS. In many houses, especially those built in the past 20 to 30 years, the air is so humid that condensation on windows and within the outside walls becomes a serious problem (see Chapter 4). In many others, however, the air is so dry that the occupants feel parched, house plants wilt, furniture cracks at the joints, and static electricity is a constant nuisance. If your house falls into the second category, you need a humidifier. With a warm-air heating system, the humidifier should be installed at the furnace so the ducts can

Portable electronic air cleaners. Philips Industries, Inc.

carry humidified air throughout the house. With a non-ducted heating system of any kind, you can use either a portable humidifier or a model which is built into a wall or closet near the center of the house.

The two best types of humidifier in current use are high-output electrical appliances which plug into a 120-volt circuit. In the evaporative type, a moving belt or drum that is kept constantly damp releases moisture into the air blown over it by a fan. In the atomizing

An evaporative humidifier installed at the furnace. Philips Industries, Inc.

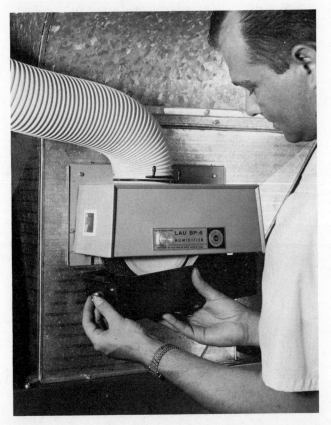

type, an almost invisible spray of water is blown directly into the air. Which of these you use depends on the mineral content of your water supply. If the water is hard, the evaporative humidifier is the better choice because the minerals are retained in the humidifier and can be easily removed from time to time. By contrast, an atomizing humidifier spews the minerals into the house in the form of a fine white dust which settles everywhere. The minerals also tend to clog the nozzle of the humidifier.

In a house with soft water, on the other hand, an atomizing humidifier is generally preferable because it

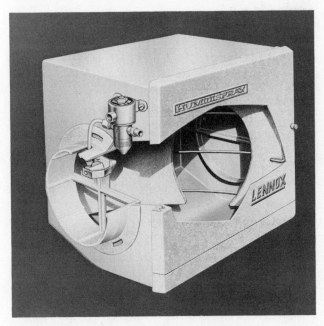

Atomizing humidifier. Lennox Industries, Inc.

puts out a great deal of moisture and usually requires less attention.

A third type of humidifier is a pan-evaporator unit containing plates which suck up water from a tray and release it into the moving air. No electricity is used. The cost of the device is low, but so is the efficiency. Furthermore, in hard-water areas, the plates become clogged fairly quickly and must be cleaned frequently.

Humidifiers are rated according to the amount of water they can deliver per day. The size of the unit required depends on the size and construction of the house, the number of occupants, and the temperature and humidity levels preferred. To arrive at a precise answer, let the humidifier dealer figure it for you from tables supplied by the manufacturer. As a rule of thumb, however, you should install a humidifier which delivers at least 1 gal. per room per day.

Installation of a humidifier in a warm-air heating system is relatively easy if you follow the manufacturer's directions. The unit is placed next to the furnace either in the return duct or supply duct, depending on the design. Water is piped in through a ¼-in. copper or plastic tube tapped into a cold-water supply line. The humidifier is wired into the furnace-blower circuit so it will operate only when the blower is running. A low-voltage humidistat which automatically controls the humidifier is installed either at the furnace or elsewhere in the house.

Atomizing humidifiers are built into a wall and are connected into a cold-water supply line and any 120-volt electrical circuit. They can be used with or without a humidistat.

Portable humidifiers plug in anywhere. Most have a water reservoir which must be filled by hand; a few can be connected to a cold-water line. Some have built-in humidistats for automatic operation.

ODOR CONTROLLERS. The odor controller is a new electrical device that counteracts odors automatically throughout the house by introducing a tiny amount of fragrant neutralizer into the air circulating through the ducts of a forced-warm-air heating system and/or air-conditioning system. It can also be mounted on a wall in the house but is effective only in its general vicinity. It consists of a compact dispenser with a two-speed fan which is mounted on the return duct at the furnace, and a control switch installed in the kitchen, front hall, or wherever. If the control is set at the normal low-speed dispersal position, a 4-oz. bottle of air freshener should last about three months.

WATER HEATERS. Standard water heaters fall into two categories: storage heaters and tankless indirect heaters. There are also solar heaters, described above.

The tankless heaters—which are less common—are small units which can be used only if you have an automatic gas- or oil-fired hot-water or steam boiler, because they contain no heating mechanism of their own. In essence, they are just a long coil of copper tubing through which water circulates on its way to the faucets. The water is heated by the boiler water surrounding the coil.

Modern tankless heaters are almost always made of copper, but a few cast-iron heaters similar to those of earlier years can be found. The heaters are installed either outside the boiler or—especially in new boilers—inside.

The principal appeal of this type of water heater is that it costs almost nothing to operate in winter, because every time the boiler turns on to heat the house, the water in the water heater is heated, too. In summer, however, the water heater uses somewhat more fuel than storage water heaters.

Tankless heaters are also generally free of problems. They contain no moving parts, and since the coils are made of copper, they are resistant to corrosion and last a long time. But they may become clogged by hard water, in which case they must be purged with acid.

Water temperature is controlled by an aquastat on the boiler. When a faucet is turned on, hot water is delivered to it rapidly, and continues to flow at the same temperature for about as long as you want it.

Storage water heaters are completely independent of the house heating system. They are large tanks in which water is heated by gas, oil, or electricity. Gas and oil heaters must be vented into a flue, and must therefore be installed fairly close to a chimney. Electric heaters do not require venting and can be placed anywhere—in the basement, crawl space, utility room, attic, or a closet.

The main difference between storage heaters is in the speed with which they bring cold water up to the desired temperature after the stored supply has been drawn down. Oil-fired heaters have the fastest recovery rate. Gas heaters are somewhat slower but are still rated as "fast-recovery" units. Electric water heaters are even slower and are called "slow-recovery" heaters.

The recovery rate of a heater varies inversely to the size of the storage tank. For example, a family of four with two bathrooms needs only a 50-gal. gas or oil heater but an 82-gal. electric heater. The actual tank size required depends on how much hot water you use at peak periods of consumption in the morning and evening. This is readily determined from the chart below. To determine the size of a gas or oil heater, add the heater's recovery rate to its capacity. Thus if there are five persons in your family and you have two bathrooms, an automatic dishwasher and a clothes washer, you need a 40-gal. heater with a recovery rate of 40 gal. or more per hour. To determine the size of an electric heater, multiply the kilowatt capacity by 4.1 to determine its recovery rate; then add this figure to the capacity of the heater.

Number of people in family	Wringer-type clothes washer						Automatic clothes washer					
	Wash dishes by hand			Automatic dishwasher			Wash dishes by hand			Automatic dishwasher		
	1 bath	2 baths	3 baths	1 bath	2 baths	3 baths	1 bath	2 baths	3 baths	1 bath	2 baths	3 baths
2	40	50	60	50	60	70	45	55	65	55	65	75
3	45	55	65	55	65	75	50	60	70	60	70	80
4	50	60	70	60	70	80	55	65	75	65	75	85
5	55	65	75	65	75	85	60	70	80	70	80	90
6	60	70	80	70	80	90	65	75	85	75	85	95
7	65	75	85	75	85	95	70	80	90	80	90	100
8	70	80	90	80	90	100	75	85	95	85	95	105
9	75	85	95	85	95	105	80	90	100	90	100	110
10 or more	80	90	100	90	100	110	85	95	105	95	105	115

Whatever the size of an electric water heater, it must be insulated better than a gas or oil heater to keep the water warm over long periods of time. The best models have a rated heat loss of no more than 4 watts per square foot.

The construction of a water-heater tank is just about as important as the capacity, because the life of the heater depends largely on how well it can withstand the corrosive effects of the hot water.

Most tanks are glass-lined—made of steel coated with porcelain enamel. By and large, these have good resistance to corrosion; but as an extra precaution, many tanks are equipped with a magnesium rod which, in effect, draws the attention of the corrosive elements away from the tank walls. The best tanks are guaranteed for ten years.

Tanks are also made of fiberglass, copper, and galvanized steel. The first is relatively new, so its life expectancy has not been fully established, but results to date have been excellent. If a tank fails, it is not because of corrosion.

Copper tanks also have outstanding resistance to corrosive water but are so expensive that they are rarely used in homes. Galvanized tanks, on the other hand, have a very short life expectancy in most parts of the country; consequently, they, too, are becoming rare.

CABLES AND MATS TO THWART COLD AND SNOW. Sooner or later almost everyone living in the north wishes there were some easy way to stop Old Man Winter from getting the upper hand. The answer lies in several varieties of electric heating cable.

Roof-heating cables which are strung along the eaves are used to prevent the formation of ice dams which back meltwater up under the roofing and then down into the house. Cables operating at 120 volts come in 20-ft. to 100-ft. lengths; 240-volt cables, in 40-ft. to 160-ft. lengths. Installation is made according to the drawing. The distance between the base points of the triangles, marked X, depends on how much snowfall you normally have. Allow 12 in. for heavy snow, 18 in. for medium snow, 24 in. for light snow. When the entire roof has been covered, the cable is looped back through the gutter and dropped down through the leader. To turn it on, simply plug it into a nearby outlet.

Roof heating cable keeps ice dams open so water will not back up inside the house.

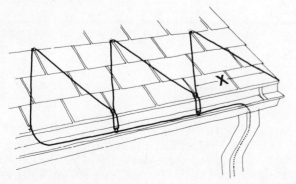

Pipe-heating cable is used to protect pipes exposed to below-freezing temperatures. It is either wrapped around the pipe in a spiral or laid in a straight line along the pipe and then covered with insulating tape. The cables are sold in 6-ft. to 100-ft. lengths for operation at 120 or 240 volts. They are available with or without built-in thermostats.

Snow-melting cable is used to melt snow off masonry porches, steps, walks, and driveways. It is also used in asphalt driveways. To simplify installation, the cable is normally made up into loosely woven 240-volt mats which are 18 or 36 in. wide and from 4 to 60 ft. long. These are embedded 2 in. below the surface and are turned on and off with a manually operated switch. Automatic control is available.

WHO MAKES IT

Air King Corp. · Bathroom ceiling heaters: surface-mounted with resistance heater or heater and fan; recessed with resistance heater and fan; surface-mounted with light; recessed with ventilating fan, with one or two heat lamps, or with heat lamps and exhaust fan.

Broan Manufacturing Co. · Bathroom ceiling heaters: surface-mounted resistance heater with fan; recessed with one or two heat lamps; recessed with resistance heater and lamp and ventilating fan; recessed with heat lamps and ventilating fan. Recessed fan-forced bathroom wall heaters.

C & C Solarthermics, Inc. · International Solarthermics Corporation's complete solar-heating system with air-circulating collector, storage structure, fans, motors, and controls.

Chimney Heat Reclaimer Corp. · Heat reclaimer.

Coleman Co. · Combination gas-heating and electric-cooling units. Electric furnaces.

Columbia Boiler Co. of Pottstown. · Cast-iron and steel gas- and oil-fired boilers with and without tankless water heaters. Nonferrous baseboard radiator-convectors. Glass-lined oil-fired storage water heaters. Most boilers are for hot-water heating systems; several oil-fired units for steam systems.

Conco, Field Control Div. · Duct boosters. Barometric draft controls.

CSI, Solar Systems Div. · Collector for solar water heater.

Dearborn Stove Co. · Gas wall furnaces and space heaters.

E & K Service Co. · Collectors for water-circulating solar heating systems.

Edwards Engineering Corp. · Valance heating and cooling systems.

Emerson Electric Co., Emerson-Chromalox Div. · Electric room heaters: baseboard, compact floor, wall, under-cabinet, unit. Radiant ceiling panels. Thermostats. Electric boilers. Electric duct heaters for systems with central blowers. Roof and pipe heating cables. Snow-melting mats.

Emerson Electric Co., Rittenhouse-Chromalox Div. · Surface-mounted electric ceiling resistance heaters with fans. Recessed ceiling heaters with one, two, or three heat lamps. Surface-mounted spotlight-shaped ceiling heater with heat lamp. Recessed ceiling heaters with fans or fans and lights. Fan-forced recessed wall heater.

Emerson Electric Co., White-Rodgers Div. · Automatic thermostats.

Empire Stove Co. · Gas wall furnaces, floor furnaces, space heaters, including baseboard model. Space heater which distributes air through metal baseboards installed on either side.

Fasco Industries, Inc. · Electric wall, ceiling, under-cabinet unit, and baseboard heaters. Bathroom ceiling heaters with two heat lamps. Radiant ceiling cables. Electric furnaces.

Fedders Corp. · Gas, oil, and electric furnaces. Combination gas or electric heating and electric cooling units. Split-system and package heat pumps. Electronic air cleaners and evaporative humidifiers.

Fuel Sentry Corp. · Controls to automate existing heating/cooling thermostats.

Gaffers & Sattler, Inc. · Gas and electric furnaces. Combination gas-heating and electric-cooling units for outdoor installation.

General Electric Co., Wiring Device Dept. · Roof and pipe heating cables.

General Fittings Co. · Tankless water heaters for all types of automatically fired boilers.

General Machine Corp., Electric Furnace-Man Div. · Oil furnaces. Oil-fired boilers for hot-water heating systems —with tankless water heaters. Electric boilers for hot-water heating systems.

Golden Investments, Ltd. · ISC complete solar heating system.

Hamilton Humidity, Inc. · Humid-Aire evaporative humidifiers. Atomizing humidifiers for installation in heating ducts.

Hart & Cooley Manufacturing Co. · All kinds of aluminum registers, diffusers, and grilles. One diffuser automatically adjusts the air pattern.

Heat Controller, Inc. · Comfort-Aire gas, oil, and electric furnaces. Split-system and package heat pumps. Built-in and portable electronic air cleaners and evaporative humidifiers. Built-in atomizing humidifiers. Electric through-wall heating-cooling units. Combination gas-heating and electric-cooling units.

Honeywell. · Thermostats, including manually controlled clock thermostats, automatic clock thermostats, and multi-stage thermostats. Built-in and portable electronic air cleaners. Odor controller. Thermostatic radiator valves.

Isothermics, Inc. · Heat reclaimer.

ITT Corp., Bell & Gosset Div. · Circulating pumps for hot-water heating systems. Relief valves.

Johns-Manville Sales Corp. · Insulating jackets for tank water heaters.

Leigh Products, Inc. · All kinds of steel registers, grilles, and diffusers. Pan-evaporator humidifiers.

Lennox Industries, Inc. · Gas, oil, and electric furnaces. Combination gas- or oil-heating and electric-cooling units. Single-package and split-system heat pumps. Heat pumps for use with new or existing gas, oil, and electric

furnaces. Through-wall all-electric heaters-air conditioners. Built-in electronic air cleaners. Evaporative and atomizing humidifiers.

Longwood Furnace Co. · Furnaces burning wood and oil or gas.

Martin Industries, Inc. · Gas wall furnaces, floor furnaces, space heaters. Electric baseboard, wall, ceiling, under-cabinet, and utility heaters. Radiant ceiling cables. Electric furnaces. Through-wall electric heating-cooling units.

Martin Industries, Inc., King Products Div. · Gas wall furnaces, floor furnaces, space heaters. Small coal heaters capable of heating several rooms.

Melnor Industries, Inc., Walton Laboratory Div. · Built-in and portable power evaporators. Atomizing-type power evaporator for installation in warm-air heating system and in houses without ductwork. Table-top atomizing evaporators.

Metro Marketing, Inc. · Control to automate existing heating/cooling thermostats.

Miami-Carey Co. · Fan-forced electric ceiling and wall heaters for bathrooms. Conventional wall heaters. Heat-lamp ceiling heater. Resistance heater or heat lamps in combination with recessed bathroom ceiling fans.

Montgomery Ward & Co. · Gas and electric storage water heaters. Cast-iron gas- and oil-fired boilers. Gas, oil, and electric furnaces. Combination gas-heating and electric-cooling units. Gas wall furnaces and space heaters. Oil space heaters. Nonferrous baseboard radiator-convectors. Built-in and portable electronic air cleaners. Electric baseboard, wall, and ceiling heaters. Thermostats. Registers. Ductwork.

Mortell Co. · Vinyl foam pipe-insulating tape. Paintlike plastic coating to stop tanks, pipes, etc. from sweating.

National Gypsum Co. · $5/8$-in.-thick radiant electric heating panels measuring 4 ft. wide by 6, 8, 10, or 12 ft. long.

Northland Boiler Co. · Boilers burning wood and gas, oil, or electricity.

Owens-Corning Fiberglas Corp. · Fiberglass ducts.

Philips Industries, Lau Industries Div. · Evaporator and pan-evaporator humidifiers. Portable electronic air cleaners.

Prill Manufacturing Co. · Coal-fired boilers.

Reynolds Metals Co. · Collector for water-circulating solar heating systems.

M. R. Rhodes, Inc. · Controls to automate existing heating thermostats.

Fred Rice Productions, Inc. · Collector for solar water heaters.

Riteway Manufacturing Co. · Furnaces burning wood alone. Furnaces and boilers burning wood and oil.

Scovill Manufacturing Co., NuTone Housing Products Div. · Surface-mounted and recessed resistance heaters for bathrooms. Recessed heaters with one, two, or three heat lamps. Heaters in combination with lights, ventilating fans, or both. Fan-forced and radiant wall heaters.

Sears Roebuck & Co. · Electric radiant ceiling panels. Electric baseboards and wall heaters. Gas wall furnaces. Oil and gas space heaters. Oil, gas, and electric furnaces. Electronic air cleaners. Evaporative humidifiers. Gas and electric storage water heaters. Clear plastic deflectors which are added to conventional registers to direct air flow.

Singer Co., Climate Control Div. · Gas and oil furnaces. Combination gas-heating and electric-cooling units. Combination electric heating-cooling units. Electronic air cleaners. Evaporative humidifiers. Electric baseboard, wall, floor, unit, and utility heaters. Radiant ceiling panels and cables.

A. O. Smith Corp. · Gas and electric glass-lined storage water heaters. Gas-fired boilers.

H. B. Smith Co. · Cast-iron oil-fired boilers with tankless water heaters. Another model with provision for addition of water heater. Cast-iron gas-fired boilers.

Solar Energy Co. · Air-circulating collector, heat exchanger, filter, blowers, dampers, controls for solar heating systems.

Solar Energy Digest. · Collector for solar water heater.

Solar Manufacturing Co. · ISC complete solar heating system.

Solaron Corp. · Complete solar heating system including collector, air handlers, automatic controls, and optional domestic water heating and cooling systems. Air used as heat-transfer medium.

Solar Power, Inc. · ISC complete solar heating system.

Solarsystems, Inc. · Collector for water-circulating solar heating systems.

Solar-Thermics Enterprises, Ltd. · ISC complete solar heating system.

Sol-Therm Corp. · Complete solar domestic hot-water systems with two collectors, storage tank, fittings.

Sun Glow, Inc. · ISC complete solar heating system.

Sun-Saver, Inc. · ISC complete solar heating system.

Sunworks, Inc. · Liquid-heating and air-heating collectors for solar systems available in flush-mounted models which become part of the house exterior and surface-mounted models for addition to house.

Taco, Inc. · Circulating pumps for hot-water heating systems. Relief valves. Steam vent valves. Valves for controlling zoned hot-water systems. Tempering valves to prevent excessively hot water at faucets.

Tappan Co., Air Conditioning Div. · Combination gas- or electric-heating and electric-cooling units. Gas, oil, and electric furnaces. Split-system and package heat pumps. Built-in electronic air cleaner. Built-in evaporative humidifiers, one model designed for houses without ductwork.

Temco, Inc. · Through-wall gas-fired heater and air conditioner. Gas wall furnaces. Gas space heaters, including model with gas logs. Gas floor furnaces.

Thermotrol Corp. · Controls to automate existing heating/cooling thermostats.

Thermwell Products Co. · Asbestos, fiberglass, vinyl-foam, and cork-filled pipe insulation. Electric heating cables for roofs and pipes.

Trion, Inc. · Built-in and portable electronic air cleaners in variety.

United States Register Co. · Steel and aluminum registers, diffusers, and grilles. Grilles with built-in filters.

Utica Radiator Corp. · Cast-iron oil-fired boilers for hot-water or steam heating systems. Replacement boilers when burner and controls of old unit are available. Cast-iron gas-fired boilers for hot-water heating systems. Some units with tankless water heaters.

Vulcan Radiator Co. · Nonferrous baseboard radiator-convectors.

Weil-McLain Co., Hydronic Div. · Cast-iron oil, gas, and electric boilers. Cast-iron baseboard radiators. Nonferrous baseboard radiator-convectors. Recessed floor convectors. Recessed cast-iron radiators.

Westinghouse Electric Corp., Central Residential Air Conditioning Div. · Package and split-system heat pumps. Electric duct heaters. Combination gas-heating and electric-cooling units. Gas, oil, and electric furnaces. Built-in electronic cleaners. Built-in evaporative and atomizing humidifiers.

White-Westinghouse Appliance Co. · Portable humidifiers.

Williamson Co. · Gas, oil, and electric furnaces. Gas, oil, and electric year-round heating-cooling units. Single-package heat pumps. Thermostats. Gas and oil conversion burners. Electronic air cleaners. Evaporative and pan-evaporator humidifiers.

23

Cooling

Just as there are a lot of ways to heat a house, there are also a lot of ways to cool it. You can install:

· A central air conditioner which cools by extracting the heat from the air in the house.

· A central heat pump which cools in the same way and automatically reverses itself and heats the house in winter by extracting heat from the outdoor air.

· A central hydronic system which cools by circulating chilled water through the house and which heats by circulating hot water.

· One or more room air conditioners which work like a central air conditioner.

· One or more room-size heat pumps which work like a central heat pump.

· An evaporative cooler which cools by blowing outdoor air into the house through a pad wet with water.

· An attic fan which sucks heat from the house and discharges it outdoors.

Some of these systems are obviously more effective than others. But if properly used, all reduce indoor temperatures so you don't dry up like a roast in an overheated oven or melt into a pool of water.

CENTRAL AIR CONDITIONERS. A central air conditioner is a large electrically powered refrigerating mechanism which not only lowers temperatures in the house but also dehumidifies, filters, and circulates the air. It is usually installed in houses with forced-warm-air heating systems, but it can also be installed in houses with any other type of heating.

The manner in which a central air conditioner works helps to explain how it's installed. It has two principal parts: an indoor section containing an evaporator, and an outdoor section with a compressor and condenser. When house air flowing through the return-air ducts enters the evaporator section, it is cooled and dehumidified by a refrigerant circulating through the evapo-

rator coils. The conditioned air is then blown back through the supply ducts into the house. Meanwhile, the refrigerant, which is now hot, passes into the compressor and condenser, where its heat is dissipated into the outdoor air. The cold liquid then returns to the evaporator and the entire cycle is repeated.

The evaporator, compressor, and condenser are built into a central air conditioner in two ways. In a package system, all three parts—together with the blower which moves the chilled air into and through the supply ducts—are contained in one cabinet. In a split system, the evaporator and blower are combined in one unit while the compressor and condenser are in another unit some distance away. Both systems are identical in operation, however, and one is as effective as the other. Technical and economic considerations determine which is to be used.

A package air conditioner can be located deep inside a basement or utility room and vented to the outdoors by a duct which carries off the heat from the refrigerant. It can be installed through an exterior wall with the evaporator section inside and the compressor-condenser section outside. Or it can be installed in a weatherproof housing entirely outside the house—on a concrete slab laid on the ground or on the top of the roof.

Packaged air conditioner. Fasco Industries, Inc.

In a split system, the outdoor section is installed on a slab or through the basement wall while the indoor section is installed at the furnace or in a crawl space, attic, or closet.

When either of these systems is used in a home with forced-warm-air heating, the conditioner is either combined in the cabinet with the furnace or added to the furnace, and the heated and cooled air is circulated through the house in the same ductwork.

On the other hand, in a house which is heated by hot water, steam, gravity warm air, electric room heaters, or gas- or oil-fired space heaters, the air-conditioning system must be completely separate from the heating plant. For this reason, owners of such homes tend to believe that it's impossible to have central air conditioning. This is not true. Though the system costs more to install (because of the new ductwork required), it may well do a better and more efficient cooling job than a combined heating-cooling system. Furthermore, the installation is in most cases relatively easy to make. In a one-story house with an attic, the air conditioner is located in the attic and cooled air is delivered to the rooms below through a simple arrangement of ducts and ceiling registers. In a house without an attic, the air conditioner is installed high in an outside wall and delivers air through ducts built in just below the ceiling and registers installed high in the interior walls. In a two-story house, the second story is cooled from the attic or from a conditioner installed in an outside wall above the second story; the first floor is cooled by a separate conditioner in an outside wall at the first-story level or by a conditioner in the basement or crawl space which feeds air up into the room through floor registers.

By and large, all central air conditioners are very much alike. So in buying one, you should look for solid performance and quality rather than features. Make sure the conditioner is sturdily constructed and well finished if it is to be installed outside. Mechanical filters must be readily accessible for cleaning. The entire unit must be quiet. And if you live in a part of the country where you use the air conditioner throughout the summer or where electric rates are unusually high, the conditioner should have a high energy efficiency ratio, or EER—which means it should produce at least 7 and preferably 8, 9, 10, or 11 Btu of cooling per watt.

Installation of a central air conditioner is best made by a qualified air-conditioning contractor with a local reputation for reliability. Get two or three bids from different contractors before you sign a contract. Don't be surprised if you find upon examination of the contractors' proposals that one recommends a package system while another recommends a split system. After all, there are several ways to install central air conditioning and one may be just as good as another. But you should beware of a contractor who estimates your cooling re-

In a split-system air conditioner, the compressor-condenser section is installed outdoors or through an exterior wall. Carrier Corp.

quirements—expressed in Btu per hour—much lower or much higher than others do. Some slight discrepancies are inevitable; but a major difference means that someone has deliberately or accidentally figured wrong.

As a rule of thumb, 12,000 Btu of cooling will take care of 500 sq. ft. of floor area. However, the capacity of an air conditioner must be closely related to the cooling requirements of the house. If it is undersized, it doesn't cool adequately; if it is oversized, it will be inefficient and expensive to run and will not reduce the house humidity as it should. Consequently, in order to figure the exact size of a central air-conditioning system, a careful survey of the house must be made to determine the heat gain of the entire house as well as of each room. The contractor must determine the size of the house and all rooms; the size, number, and orientation of the windows; and the construction (including insulation) of the exterior walls and roof. He must also take into consideration the number of persons in the family, how much entertaining the family does, the planting around the house, and the proximity of other buildings and hills.

In a new house, if the air conditioner is combined with a furnace, the ductwork should be sized to meet cooling rather than heating requirements, because cooling ducts must be somewhat larger than heating ducts in order to move the air efficiently. In an old house in which an air conditioner is being added to an existing warm-air heating system, however, the small heating ducts can be used if the capacity of the blower is increased.

As noted in the heating chapter, air-conditioning registers are placed high in the walls or in the ceilings of houses in warm climates; returns are near the floor. But in cold climates, where heating is more essential than cooling, the registers are installed low in the walls or floors and the returns are high in the walls. These should be equipped with double-deflection grilles so that warm air can be directed down, cool air up.

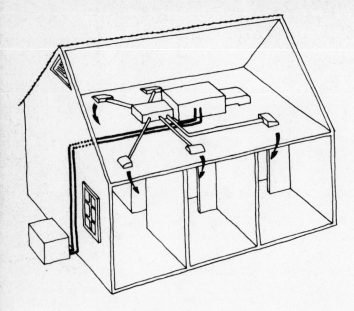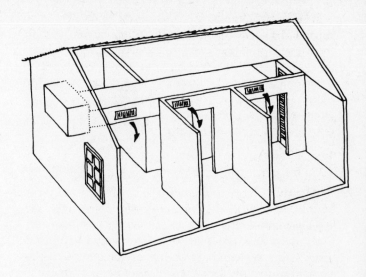

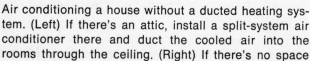

Air conditioning a house without a ducted heating system. (Left) If there's an attic, install a split-system air conditioner there and duct the cooled air into the rooms through the ceiling. (Right) If there's no space in the attic, install a packaged unit in an outside wall and deliver the air into the rooms through a large central duct installed just below the ceiling.

Other things which contribute to a first-class ductwork installation are discussed in the heating chapter.

Power to operate a central air conditioner is supplied by a 240-volt circuit. If your house has 100-amp service, there is almost certainly adequate capacity.

The thermostat used is like that for a heating system. In most homes, one thermostat controls the furnace, a second the air conditioner. But you can use a single multistage thermostat to control both operations. This kind of thermostat is designed to change over automatically from heating to cooling and back again.

CENTRAL HEAT PUMPS. See Chapter 22.

CENTRAL HYDRONIC SYSTEMS. In a hydronic system, icy water circulating through pipes supplies the cooling. The water is cooled in a chiller which may either be separate from the heater or combined with it so the same unit provides both heat and cooling. From the chiller, the cold water is piped to an air handler in which air is blown over the pipe and delivered into the house.

Although they have been available for a good many years, hydronic cooling systems have not caught on among homeowners, largely because of their cost. But they are widely used in public and commercial buildings.

Hydronic systems are designed in various ways. In a house with forced-warm-air heating, for example, the chilled water can be piped into a coil at the furnace. From there cold air is circulated through the house in the existing ductwork. In a house without ductwork, the chilled water can go into an air handler installed in the attic, crawl space, closet—any convenient point—and

from there new ductwork carries the chilled air into the house. An alternative in a house with forced-hot-water heat is to pipe the chilled water into special convectors installed in each room. The convectors are also used for heating the rooms in winter. Still another system circulates chilled water in summer and hot water in winter through a valance in each room (see Chapter 22).

The chiller at the heart of a hydronic system operates on either electricity or gas. Electric chillers are nothing more than giant refrigerators. Gas chillers operate on an absorption principle, using heat as the catalyst. They have no compressor and relatively few moving parts. They are similar to the gas refrigerators which were once rather widely used in homes. Since both types of chiller give off large quantities of heat (like air, water is chilled by extracting heat from it), they are commonly installed outdoors but may be installed indoors if a duct is provided to carry away the heat.

ROOM AIR CONDITIONERS. A room air conditioner is a miniature central electric system without ductwork. Placed in a window, in an opening through an exterior wall, or on an exterior wall, they draw in air from the room; cool, dehumidify, and filter it; and circulate it back into the room. The heat extracted from the air is exhausted outdoors.

Room conditioners currently on the market have capacities of approximately 4,000 to 35,000 Btu per hour. The smaller units can be used to cool only the rooms in which they are installed, but by putting in several of them, you can do a pretty good job of cooling an entire house. Unlike a central system, they allow you to cool only those rooms which you are occupying. This reduces operating costs.

In compact houses of up to about 1,500 sq. ft., a single large room conditioner can often be used to cool the whole house, provided it is heated by a forced-warm-air system. To do this, the conditioner must be installed in a room that has a return duct to the furnace, and the blower in the furnace must be set for continuous air circulation. The register in the return duct is kept open, but the supply registers in the room are closed. Return registers in other rooms are closed, and their supply registers are left open. In this way, the cool air in the conditioned room is circulated throughout the house.

Also available are air conditioners which heat as well as cool. In some of these the heating is done by electric resistance coils, in others by a gas heater.

A room conditioner must be carefully sized to the space it is used to cool. As with central systems, it can be neither too small nor too large. The following factors should be taken into consideration in sizing a unit: the direction the room faces and its sun load, the number of windows and their location, whether the room is upstairs or down, how many people and electrical appliances are normally in the room, and the R value of the insulation in the walls and roof. The dealer from whom you buy the conditioner should inspect the room before he advises on the capacity you need.

The house wiring system should also be checked. Conditioners which operate on 120 volts and at less than 7.5 amps can be plugged into an existing 120-volt, 15-amp circuit provided lamps and appliances plugged into the circuit don't have a combined wattage in excess of 860. All other 120-volt conditioners must be installed on individual 120-volt, 20-amp circuits. All 240-volt conditioners require individual 240-volt circuits. These are usually fused at 20 amps.

Features worth looking for when buying a room air conditioner include:

· Fans with several speeds so you can adjust the rate of air circulation in the room.

· Fully adjustable louvers so you can direct air up, down, or to the sides.

· Quiet operation.

· Electronic air cleaners which remove a high percentage of the dust and pollen circulated through the conditioners. These are usually sold as optional accessories.

· A chassis which can be slid out of the cabinet for servicing. This is particularly desirable on large conditioners.

· High efficiency with an EER of 7 or better.

· Most room conditioners are designed for installation either in double- or single-hung windows, casements, or sliding windows. If an air conditioner is not too heavy, you can quickly put one in yourself according to the manufacturer's directions.

Through-wall conditioners are installed in an opening cut in an exterior wall below or above a window,

Room air conditioner made for installation in casement windows. Fedders Corp.

above a door, over a kitchen counter—anywhere you like. The opening must be framed like a window opening with 2×4s. The main advantage of this kind of installation is that it doesn't block the view from a window or make the window useless for ventilation on mild days. Furthermore, the conditioner can be placed where it doesn't spoil the appearance of the room or interfere with furniture placement. But unfortunately, the efficiency of through-wall conditioners is generally below that of window units because air circulation over condenser coils is restricted.

A third kind of room conditioner is made in two parts so the evaporator section can be hung anywhere on the inner surface of an exterior wall. The compressor-condenser section is installed on the ground outside or mounted on brackets on the outside of the wall. The two sections are connected by three flexible tubes carrying the wiring, refrigerant, and condensate.

Room air conditioner with compressor-condenser section outdoors. Evaporator section is hung on wall indoors. Heat Controller, Inc.

ROOM HEAT PUMPS. A room heat pump is just like the central heat pump described in Chapter 22 except that it is contained in a room air-conditioner cabinet which is installed in a window or through an exterior wall.

EVAPORATIVE COOLERS. Evaporative coolers are not in the same league with air conditioners. At best they can lower the temperature in a house only about 10 degrees. And they are fully effective only in the Southwest; in humid climates they are worthless. Nevertheless, they do increase comfort at modest cost.

Evaporative coolers are electrical appliances incorporating a motor, blower, pump, and absorbent pad. They are placed in front of a window or through a hole in an exterior wall and either filled with water or connected to a cold-water supply line. When a cooler is turned on, the pump distributes the water over the absorbent pad, keeping it constantly wet. The blower pulls in outdoor air through louvered openings in the back of the cooler, blows it through the wet pad, and on into the room.

Large coolers are made for permanent installation outside a house on a concrete slab or wall brackets. There are also models, used mainly in commercial establishments, which are installed on roofs and deliver the cooled air through the ceiling. Smaller coolers are mounted in windows or can be set on a table indoors.

ATTIC FANS. Like evaporative coolers, these big fans have been largely supplanted by air conditioners, but many are still sold to homeowners in regions where cooling is required only a few days in the year.

When an attic fan is turned on in the early evening, it pulls the hot air out of the house in a matter of minutes and lowers indoor temperature to within a few degrees of the outdoor temperature. It is also used off and on during the day to exhaust superheated attic air and thus maintain more comfortable temperatures in the living areas, to maintain a pleasant movement of air throughout the house, and to flush out smoke and odors.

To install an attic fan, it is necessary first to cut an intake opening in the attic floor over a central hall and to install louvered exhaust openings in the attic walls or in a small dormer or penthouse on the roof. The size of the openings depends on the size of the fan. The floor opening is equipped with shutters which open and close automatically when the fan is turned on and off by a switch located in the living area.

One type of attic fan is installed horizontally directly over the opening in the floor. A second type is installed vertically in front of one of the exhaust openings. Manufacturers of both types also sell the shutters for the intake opening.

The size of the fan used is determined by calculating the cubic footage of the house (closets, pantries, and other dead air spaces are excluded) and dividing the answer by 1.5. For example, if the volume of your house is 12,000 cu. ft., you need a fan with a cfm rating of 8,000. A fan of this size will completely change the air in the house once every 90 seconds.

The fan is served by a 120-volt, 15-amp or 20-amp general-purpose circuit.

POWER ATTIC VENTILATORS. Power attic ventilators are designed not to cool houses, but to help keep them from becoming overheated. They do this indirectly by removed overheated air from the attic before the heat can penetrate to the rooms below. Thus they not only contribute to the comfort of the occupants but also lessen the load on air conditioners and lower air-conditioning costs.

In addition, the fans are used in winter to remove moisture from attics before it impairs the effectiveness of insulation or rots the rafters and roof sheathing. Humidistats which control this operation are sold by some ventilator manufacturers.

Ventilators are small electric fans controlled automatically by a thermostat. The thermostat turns a fan on when attic temperature rises to 100°, then turns it off when the hot air is removed from the attic and the temperature drops to 85°. In the deep South, ventilators are set to turn on at 105° and turn off at 90°.

One type of ventilator is installed in the attic roof, another in one of the attic walls, a third in a cupola (see Chapter 3). The first is generally preferred because it can be easily and inexpensively installed near the center of the attic for maximum efficiency. Whichever you use, be sure to select a model with .7 cfm capacity for each square foot of floor space. Allow an extra 15% if the roof is a dark color.

To replace the air removed from the attic, screened and louvered intake openings must be provided in the roof overhangs or gable ends of the attic. One sq. ft. of net-free opening (the area of the opening after subtracting the space occupied by louvers and wires) is required for every 300 sq. ft. of floor space, provided that half the opening area is installed under the eaves. If under-eaves vents are not used, the free area of the openings in the gables must be doubled.

Installation of a ventilator is largely a matter of cutting holes in the roof, eave soffits, and/or gables. Slip the power ventilator into the roof hole with the flashing flange under the up-slope shingles, and nail it in place. Screw the louvered soffit ventilators and gable-end ventilator into place. Then cut into a live electric line running through the attic, install a junction box, and connect the power-ventilator wiring to the cables as directed by the manufacturer.

NATURAL VENTILATION SYSTEMS. Even though you may not need a power ventilator, you definitely

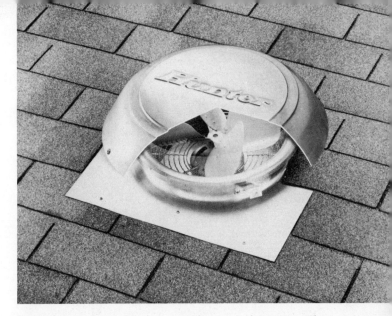

Attic fan designed for horizontal installation above louvered opening in attic floor. Philips Industries.

Partially cutaway view of a roof-mounted power attic ventilator. Robbins & Myers, Inc.

need ventilated openings of some sort in your attic to remove the worst of the heat in summer and carry off any humid air which penetrates through your ceiling vapor barrier in winter. The units used are called fixed ventilators, and if the floor of your attic is properly insulated, they should be kept open the year round.

There are several types: gable-end ventilators, which may be triangular or rectangular; under-eaves ventilators; and roof and ridge ventilators.

A combination of ridge and under-eaves ventilators

generally does the best ventilating job. The former provides a continuous opening along the ridge line of a pitched roof, but is easily installed only when a roof is being built. Under-eaves vents can be installed at any time through holes cut in the eave soffits—provided the soffits are wide enough. The vents are flat metal plates with small louvered openings. The alternative is a continuous soffit strip made of metal, vinyl, hardboard, or asbestos-cement board (see Chapter 3).

Gable ventilators are larger devices. The triangular

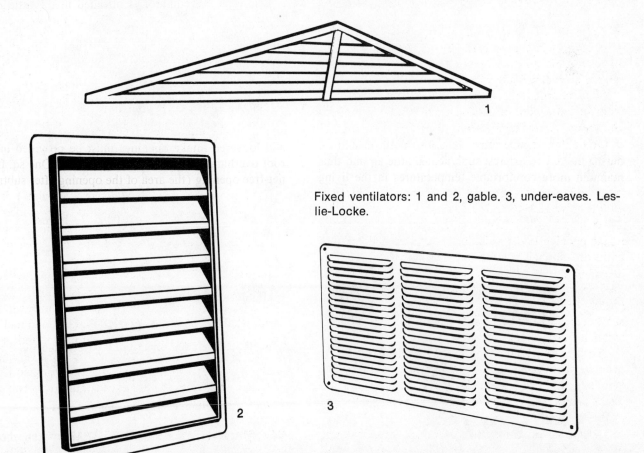

Fixed ventilators: 1 and 2, gable. 3, under-eaves. Leslie-Locke.

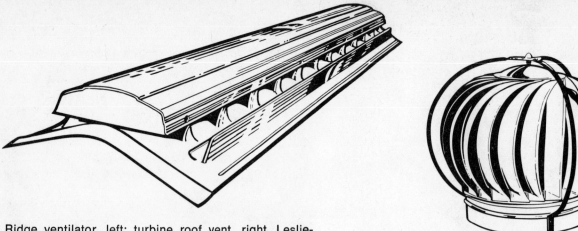

Ridge ventilator, left; turbine roof vent, right. Leslie-Locke.

units are installed directly under the roof peak; the rectangular type is installed a little farther down in the gable walls. Wherever possible, a ventilator should be installed at both ends of the roof. For best air circulation, they are used in conjunction with under-eaves vents.

Standard roof vents are similar in appearance to power vents but do not have fans. Since they are small, they must be used with under-eaves vents.

Another type of roof vent which was widely used before the power vent came along is a mushroom-shaped turbine vent which is driven by the wind. It is made of metal or fiberglass, and in especially windy locations should have external bracing.

Whichever type of ventilator is used, it should provide a net-free area of at least 1 sq. ft. for each 300 sq. ft. of floor space.

MIDGET LOUVERS. Midget louvers are small ventilators used not only for ventilating attics but also for carrying off humid air which penetrates exterior walls. They are round screened and louvered metal gadgets which are simply pushed into holes drilled with an expansive bit or hole saw. Some of the louvers have covers which can be rotated to adjust the air flow.

Larger sizes (up to 6 in. in diameter) are installed in the soffits under eaves and sometimes in gable ends to carry off heat and moisture from attics and other roof spaces. Small 1-in. louvers are installed in stud spaces

Miniature louver being installed in an exterior wall. Midget Louver Co.

in exterior walls to prevent blistering of paint caused by condensation within the walls.

FANS. Even though fans don't do much actual cooling, they are about as popular as ever. And somewhat surprisingly, the old-fashioned slow-moving ceiling fan—the most expensive of all—has enjoyed one of the sharpest sales increases. It's especially suitable for use on porches, where other cooling devices are useless.

Ceiling fans are made in two-speed models: a 36-in. fan rated at 4,000 cfm, and a 52-in. fan rated at 7,000 cfm. Both operate on a 120-volt, 15-amp circuit and are controlled by pull switches. (A wall switch can be substituted.) Because of their weight, they must be hung directly below a joist.

Other built-in ceiling and wall fans are high-speed units enclosed in safety grilles. Because of their appearance, they are more often used in commercial establishments than homes.

DEHUMIDIFIERS. If your house is air-conditioned, it is automatically dehumidified as it is cooled. Without an air conditioner, you may need a portable dehumidifier which plugs into any 120-volt outlet. Though not a very glamorous appliance, it's highly effective. A model with a 14-pt. capacity (meaning that it will extract 14 pts. of moisture from the air in 24 hours) dehumidifies an area of up to 1,500 sq. ft. A 23-pt. model (maximum size) serves an area of about 2,500 sq. ft.

To use a dehumidifier, just plug it in and turn it on. Water vapor sucked in by a built-in fan is condensed and drips into a pan or a hose which is stuck into a plumbing drain.

WHO MAKES IT

Amana Refrigeration, Inc. · Window-mounted and through-wall room air conditioners with capacities from 5,000 to 29,000 Btu per hour. Dehumidifiers.

Arkla Industries, Inc. · Central hydronic cooling systems and year-round cooling-heating systems with gas-fired chillers.

Borg-Warner Corp., York Div. · Split-system air conditioners.

The old-fashioned ceiling fan is enjoying a comeback in popularity. Robbins & Myers, Inc.

Carrier Corp. · Split-system and package air conditioners and heat pumps. Room air conditioners for window mounting or through-wall installation in capacities from 5,000 to 33,500 Btu per hour.

Coleman Co. · Split-system air conditioners. Combination gas-heating and electric-cooling units.

Dearborn Stove Co. · Window-mounted and through-wall room air conditioners from 6,000 to 35,000 Btu per hour. Evaporative coolers.

Emerson Electric Co., Emerson-Chromalox Div. · Attic fans. Ceiling fans. High-speed fans mounted on wall brackets or suspended from ceiling.

Energy Conservation Unlimited, Inc. · Energy conservation unit installed in conjunction with central air conditioner or heat pump increases air-conditioning efficiency and reduces cooling costs; also uses heat given off by air conditioner to help heat water for bathing, laundry, etc.

Fasco Industries, Inc. · Split-system and package air conditioners. Attic fans. Power attic ventilators.

Fedders Corp. · Window-mounted and through-wall room air conditioners with capacities from 5,000 to 34,000 Btu per hour. Electronic air cleaners optional in some models. Split-system and package air conditioners and heat pumps. Some package conditioners available with electric heating. Year-round air conditioners with gas or electric heating.

Gaffers & Sattler, Inc. · Combination gas-heating and electric-cooling units for outdoor installation. Split-system and package air conditioners.

General Electric Co., Hotpoint Div. · Window-mounted and through-wall room air conditioners ranging from 4,000 to 27,000 Btu per hour.

General Motors Corp., Frigidaire Div. · Window-mounted and through-wall room air conditioners with capacities ranging from 5,000 to 30,000 Btu per hour.

Kool-O-Matic Corp. · Power attic ventilators with optional humidistat. Cupola with ventilating fan.

Leigh Products, Inc. · Power attic ventilators with optional humidistat. Under-eaves, gable, roof, and foundation ventilators. Miniature louvers.

Lennox Industries, Inc. · Single-package and split-system air conditioners and heat pumps. Year-round cooling-heating systems with gas or oil heat. Heat pumps to be used with existing as well as new heating plants.

Leslie-Locke, Lighting Div. · Power attic ventilators with optional humidistat. Roof, gable, under-eaves, ridge, and foundation ventilators. Steel turbine ventilators. Miniature louvers.

McGraw-Edison Co., Air Comfort Div. · Split-system air conditioners for do-it-yourself installation.

Midget Louver Co. · Miniature louvers of every type and size.

Montgomery Ward & Co. · Year-round air conditioners with gas heating. Window-mounted room air conditioners with 6,000 to 19,000 Btu per hour capacity. Attic fans. Power attic ventilators. Steel turbine ventilators. Roof and under-eaves ventilators. Package and split-system air conditioners. Dehumidifiers.

Morgan Co. · Wood gable ventilators—round, half-round, quarter-round, rectangular, and triangular.

Philips Industries, Inc., Lau Industries Div. · Attic fans.

Phil Rich Fan Manufacturing Co. · Windmaker attic fans. Power attic ventilators. Ceiling fans.

Robbins & Myers, Inc., Hunter Div. · Ceiling fans.

F. E. Schumacher Co. · Rectangular gable ventilators of wood.

Scovill Manufacturing Co., NuTone Housing Products Div. · Power attic ventilators.

Sears Roebuck & Co. · Window-mounted and through-wall room air conditioners with 4,500 to 29,000 Btu per hour capacity. Package and split-system air conditioners. Attic fans. Roof, ridge, and under-eaves ventilators. 1-in. miniature louvers. Dehumidifiers.

Shur-Line Manufacturing Co. · Miniature louvers of plastic.

Singer Co., Climate Control Div. · Split-system air conditioners. Combination gas-electric and all-electric heating-cooling systems.

Tappan Co., Air Conditioning Div. · Split-system and package air conditioners, some of the latter with optional electric heating. Split-system and package heat pumps. Year-round air conditioners with gas or electric heating.

Thermwell Products Co. · Fiberglass, aluminum, and foam air-conditioner filters.

Vestal Manufacturing Co. · Under-eaves ventilators. Foundation ventilators.

Webb Manufacturing, Inc. · Wood gable ventilators—round, half-round, quarter-round, rectangular, triangular, octagonal, and inverted-U-shaped.

Westinghouse Electric Corp., Central Residential Air Conditioning Div. · Package and split-system heat pumps and air conditioners. Combination gas-heating and electric-cooling units.

White-Westinghouse Appliance Co. · Window-mounted and through-wall room air conditioners ranging from 5,000 to 27,000 Btu per hour capacity. Combination cooling-heating room air conditioners. Dehumidifiers.

Williamson Co. · Split-system and package air conditioners. Gas, oil, and electric year-round heating-cooling units. Single-package heat pumps.

Wind-Wonder, Inc. · Power attic ventilators, some with a thermostat which turns the fan off if a fire starts in the house. Fiberglass turbine roof ventilators.

24

Fire Alarms

The importance of installing some kind of fire detection and alarm system in your home is indicated by studies made by the National Fire Protection Assn. These show that approximately 75% of all dwelling fires break out between 9:00 p.m. and 6:00 a.m., when few people are awake, and that in approximately 68% of dwelling fires that result in deaths, "delayed discovery contributed significantly to the loss of life."

Although the meaning of these and similar statistics does not seem to have made a great impression on most American homeowners, they have inspired government agencies to take steps to make new homes safer against fire. The FHA now requires installation of one or more smoke alarms in all new dwellings covered by FHA-insured mortgages. In addition, four regional building codes, many states, and several dozen major cities have adopted similar rules.

If you haven't already done so, you would be wise to protect your home at least to the same extent, because while fire detectors do not prevent fires or put them out, they will, if properly installed and maintained, give warning when a fire is starting and thus enable you to get out of the house and summon help before it's too late.

Two basic types of detection-warning systems are employed—the multi-station system and single-station detector. Before investing in either type, make certain that it is approved either by Underwriters' Laboratories (UL) or Factory Mutual System (FM).

MULTI-STATION SYSTEMS. Multi-station systems are complete housewide systems composed of several smoke and heat detectors connected to an alarm. The exact number and type of detectors depends on the size and layout of the house. For maximum protection, the NFPA recommends that smoke detectors be installed in each separate sleeping area (usually in the hall outside the bedrooms) and at the head of each basement stair, and that heat or smoke detectors be installed in the living room, dining room, kitchen, front hall, bedrooms, furnace room, basement, attic, and attached garage.

All the detectors must be connected to a central alarm which is loud enough to wake you and your family. In addition, you can put in an outdoor alarm to alert your neighbors in case you're away from home. And for maximum protection, the system can be set up so it sounds an alarm in the nearest fire station.

Power for the system should be supplied by the house electrical system as well as by batteries in the event the power fails.

The system must be designed so it can be tested once a week without damage to the detectors.

(An additional feature of some multi-station systems is that they can be combined with a burglar-alarm system.)

The cost of a multi-station detection system starts at about $400. Although the installation can be made by any reasonably adept handyman, it is best made by an experienced professional because no matter how reliable the components of the system, they may fail to perform as they should if not located and wired in properly. Your fire department may be willing to recommend installers. In some communities, the department reserves the right to inspect all new systems before it will permit them to be linked to the fire station by a telephone line.

Single-station fire detectors can be just as reliable as multi-station systems but obviously do not give as complete protection unless placed at every point where a multi-station detector would be installed. On the other hand, they cost considerably less (about $40 up) and do not require professional installation.

SMOKE DETECTORS. Of the two kinds of single-station fire detectors, those which respond to the pres-

Smoke detectors are installed high on walls or ceilings. First location to be equipped should be in the central hall off the sleeping area. Westinghouse Electric Corp.

ence of smoke are slightly better for home use because they detect relatively low-temperature smoldering fires which might go unnoted by heat detectors. Furthermore, when installed in a bedroom area, they give earlier warning of a fire breaking out in a distant part of the house because smoke is likely to reach the bedroom area before the heat in the area builds up appreciably.

On the other hand, smoke detectors are not as good as heat detectors for installation in kitchens and garages—where most fires start—because they may be actuated by smoke and fumes given off by cooking and automobiles. And they are obviously less responsive to fires which develop rapidly with little smoke production. It is for these reasons that you need both kinds of detector for maximum protection in all parts of the house.

Smoke detectors are classified either as ionization or optical units.

The ionization devices contain a tiny amount of radioactive material which ionizes the air in the sensing chamber and indirectly produces an electric current. Smoke entering the sensing chamber interrupts the current flow and causes the alarm to sound. Unfortunately, the device is so sensitive that it can be set off by dust as well as relatively small amounts of smoke. But by the same token, it is preferable to the optical detector when there's a hot fire with little smoke.

The optical detector is operated by a light directed at a photoelectric cell. It sounds an alarm when the light beam is obscured by smoke. Reaction to smoky, smoldering fires is extremely fast.

HEAT DETECTORS. These are classified in three ways: fixed-temperature, rate-of-rise, and combination.

Fixed-temperature detectors incorporate either a bimetallic element or a fusible link. When the tempera-

ture of the surrounding air reaches a certain point— usually 135°—the element or link sets off the alarm. By contrast, rate-of-rise detectors are designed to sound the alarm not when a predetermined temperature is reached, but when the temperature rises faster than usual. For this reason, they are especially suitable for use in attics, where summer temperatures often climb gradually to well over 100°.

Combination detectors respond both to a fixed temperature and to a rapid increase in temperature.

WIRED-IN VS. BATTERY-OPERATED DETECTORS. All smoke detectors are electrical devices. Some are wired into the house electrical system or plugged into an outlet; others operate on batteries.

Most modern heat detectors operate in the same way, but there are also units in which the alarm is set off by a spring or cylinder of gas connected to the fusible element.

By and large, wired-in and plugged-in smoke and heat detectors are preferred to battery-operated units because they are less likely to fail in an emergency. However, since their placement is restricted to some extent by the design of the house wiring, they cannot always be located in the ideal spots for detecting fire. And if the power should go off at the time a fire starts, they are useless.

Battery-operated detectors can be placed more strategically. But whether they will sound an alarm when fire breaks out depends entirely on how faithful you are about changing the batteries every six months or so. To help you remember, most detectors are designed automatically to sound a signal and, in some cases, hang out a red flag when the batteries are running low. Even this will fail, however, if you don't

Battery-operated ionization smoke detector. General Electric Co.

notice the signal or if you put in new batteries which have no more life in them than the old.

INSTALLATION. It is just about as easy to wire in a single-station detector as to plug it into an outlet. All you do is run cable from the detector into the nearest junction box or an outlet box which is not controlled by a switch, and attach the black wire in the cable to the black wires in the box and the white wire in the cable to the white wires in the box.

Finding the ideal spot to install the detector is more difficult. If you're putting in a smoke detector, you might build a small smoky fire in a metal wastebasket placed where you believe a fire is most likely to start, and adjust the position of the detector on the ceiling above. But a safer procedure (essential with a heat detector) is to seek the advice of a local fire official.

WHO MAKES IT

Alarm Device Manufacturing Co. · Multi-station fire-alarm system combined with burglar-alarm system. See Chapter 25.

American General Products, Inc. · Recessed fire-hose cabinet fits between studs, contains hose and fire extinguisher. Hose is connected directly to water line.

Edwards Co. · Multi-station system with two fixed-temperature heat detectors to which additional detectors can be

Built-in hose and extinguisher allow you to respond positively and quickly if a fire breaks out. American General Products, Inc.

connected. Rate-of-rise heat detectors. AC-operated optical heat detectors. One model can be used in tandem with additional smoke detectors so all sound alarm simultaneously.

Emerson Electric Co., Emerson-Chromalox Div. · Optical smoke detectors for AC operation.

Emerson Electric Co., Rittenhouse-Chromalox Div. · AC-operated optical smoke detector. Multi-station detection system with fixed-temperature heat detectors and ionization smoke detectors.

Emhart Corp. · Battery-operated ionization smoke detectors.

Evergard Co. · Temperature-actuated fire alarm uses aerosol gas to sound alarm.

Fenwal, Inc. · AC-operated ionization smoke detectors.

Fire-Lite Alarms, Inc. · AC-operated optical smoke detectors available with fixed-temperature heat detectors. Combination fire- and burglar-alarm systems with optical smoke detectors which may incorporate fixed-temperature heat detectors; fixed-temperature or rate-of-rise heat detectors; magnetic burglar sensors; garage-door sensors; floor mats.

General Electric Co., Housewares Business Div. · Ionization smoke detectors, battery- and AC-operated.

Honeywell, Inc. · Ionization smoke detector, AC-operated.

Montgomery Ward & Co. · AC- or battery-operated ionization smoke detectors, one with fixed-temperature heat detector.

Pittway Corp., BRK Electronics Div. · Ionization smoke detectors for battery or AC operation. Battery-operated detector which may be connected to other smoke detectors or sensors to give better coverage of entire house. The latter can also activate a remote horn or trigger a telephone dialer.

PLC Electronics, Inc. · Ionization smoke detector, AC-operated. Multi-station detection systems combined with burglar alarms. See Chapter 25.

Pyrotector, Inc. · AC-operated optical smoke detectors. Some models also serve as fixed-temperature heat detectors.

Pyrotonics. · Ionization smoke detectors for AC operation. One model may be teamed up with additional detectors which sound alarm simultaneously. Multi-station system with ionization smoke detectors and fixed-temperature or rate-of-rise heat detectors. Multi-station system can be combined with burglar-alarm system using magnetic sensors and floor mats with optional telephone dialer.

Scovill Manufacturing Co., NuTone Housing Products Div. · Multi-station fire-alarm system with optical smoke detectors and fixed-temperature heat detectors. Single-station optical smoke detectors for AC operation. Combination fire- and burglar-alarm systems (see Chapter 25).

Sears Roebuck & Co. · AC- or battery-operated optical smoke detectors.

Statitrol Corp. · Ionization smoke detectors operated by AC or battery.

Wal-Vac, Inc. · AC-operated optical smoke detector, mounts on wall.

Westinghouse Security Systems, Inc. · AC-operated optical smoke detector mounts on wall. Multi-station system combined with burglar-alarm system (see Chapter 25).

25

Burglar Protection

The rising crime rate has forced homeowners to take a new look at their home defenses. All too often these are sadly wanting. The exterior doors can be easily forced. Windows can be jimmied or raised simply by breaking a pane of glass and turning the latch. And once he's inside, a burglar, given time, can have a field day.

Few people can afford a security system which will foil the skilled professional burglar. But few burglars fit this description. The great majority are common thieves who lose interest in breaking into a house if they can't do it quickly. To cope with these, you have a wide and growing assortment of simple and ingenious protection devices to choose from.

The first and most important, of course, is a good door lock like those discussed in the next chapter. If you add locks on your downstairs windows, you may need nothing more. However, families who have unusually valuable possessions or live in high-crime-rate areas often feel it necessary to go further.

PERIMETER ELECTRONIC ALARM SYSTEMS.

Although they cost hundreds or even thousands of dollars, the demand for electronic alarm systems which summon help when an intruder tries to enter a house has soared in the past five years. Not all have proved to be as effective as they should be, however. And many have caused acute embarrassment for homeowners either because they malfunction or because the family makes a habit of forgetting to turn them off when they are home and awake.

There's nothing you can do to correct the latter problem except to develop a memory. But you need not be saddled with an ineffective or malfunctioning system if you take four simple steps before you buy one:

1. Select a system which other homeowners you know have found satisfactory.

2. Select a system approved by Underwriters' Laboratories.

3. Buy from a firm which has established a local reputation for reliability and honesty.

4. Check local laws concerning alarm systems. Some systems may not be permitted.

Perimeter alarm systems are designed to keep intruders entirely out of the house. They are like the skin on the body: nothing of any size can break through it without alerting you.

The normal system consists of small, more or less concealed sensory devices installed in all doors, windows, and other openings providing ready access to the house. These are connected in a continuous closed-circuit loop to a central control box which triggers an alarm when someone tries to get in through one of the doors, etc.

In most systems, the alarm is a loud clanging bell or shrill siren located at some point in the house where a burglar is not likely to find it and tamper with it. For added protection, another bell or siren can be installed outside the house to alert neighbors when you are away from home.

Other systems are designed to turn on lights inside and outside the house. Or if you prefer, you can have a system that turns on lights as well as sounding an alarm.

The alternative to a local alarm system is a silent system which sounds an alarm at a point remote from the house. Known as a central reporting system, this takes two forms. In one system a signal is transmitted over leased wires either to the police department or to a central station manned by the company which manufactures and/or installs the alarm system. The advantage of this setup is that instead of simply frightening off the criminal, it brings help (or at least it is supposed to bring help—there is no guarantee of this) who will catch the criminal. However, the system is more expensive to install than the conventional system, and you must also pay a monthly fee for the monitoring service.

Basic ingredients of a perimeter burglar alarm system. PLC Electronics, Inc.

The other type of central reporting system incorporates an automatic dialer which sends a prerecorded message or coded signal over regular telephone lines to the alarm-company office, a telephone-answering service, the police (if laws permit), or a friend. However, this, too, adds substantially to the original cost of the system. And if the dialer cannot bypass incoming telephone calls (you must check this before you invest in such a system), it's possible for a burglar to circumvent the dialer simply by telephoning your home and leaving the receiver off the hook.

In the most elaborate perimeter systems, the alarm not only is sounded inside and outside your home but is also transmitted to the police department or alarm company's monitoring station.

For good measure, you can have a fire-protection system installed along with any house-wide burglar-alarm system.

All perimeter systems must, of course, be designed so that you can deactivate them when you return home without setting off the alarm. In some cases, this is done by inserting a key in a switch outside the door. In other cases, the alarm circuit incorporates a 15- or 20-second delay feature so you can open the door and turn off the system by an indoor switch.

Another difference between systems is that in some the signal from the sensors to the control box is carried by low-voltage wires while in wireless systems the sensors are connected to tiny radio transmitters which broadcast signals to the control box. The latter simplify installation of the system since it is not necessary to run wires throughout the house. But you must remember to change batteries in the transmitters.

The sensors used in the alarm systems are of several types. The most widely used is a magnetic contact made in two parts. One part is mounted on a door, window, or transom, the other on the adjacent frame. When the door, etc. is opened, the alarm sounds.

Another type of sensor is a recessed contact button which is installed in a door or window jamb. This is rapidly gaining popularity since it is completely concealed from the burglar and cannot be deactivated as easily as a magnetic contact.

A sensor which is designed to sound an alarm when a burglar, trying to outwit a magnetic or recessed contact, breaks a window pane is a magnetic tape that is glued around the edges of the glass.

A fourth kind of sensor is a special window screen with a built-in alarm wire.

Also available are emergency signaling devices which allow the homeowner himself to set off the alarm when he hears someone creeping around the house. The simplest are built-in pushbuttons wired to the control box. Others are tiny transmitters you can carry in your bathrobe or pajama pocket.

INTERNAL ALARM SYSTEMS. Internal alarm systems give less protection than perimeter systems because they don't stop a burglar outside the house. Instead, they sound an alarm only when the burglar, having entered the house through a door or window, makes contact with them indoors. But they are relatively easy for a skilled burglar to avoid, and if they do sound an alarm, it is heard only within the house. On the other side of the coin, the systems are much less expensive than perimeter setups. They include the following devices:

Photoelectric detectors sound an alarm when a person interrupts a beam by walking through it. These are easily built into a wall and are effective in halls and stairways through which a burglar must pass to reach the various rooms of the house. They can also be used in individual rooms which require special protection.

Infrared detectors work in the same way, but while a photoelectric device has a transmitter and separate receiver, these incorporate the transmitter and receiver in one unit.

Ultrasonic detectors trigger an alarm when there is any movement in the protected area. Since the high-frequency sound waves generated by these devices blanket a sizable area, only one of them is needed in a room, whereas several photoelectric detectors would be necessary to give equivalent protection. But they can be upset by wind, loud external noises, and vibrations. And unless they are carefully positioned, someone in the family may accidentally set them off.

Combination burglar- and fire-alarm system not only sounds an alarm but also flashes the cause of trouble. At the same time, it alerts a manned communications center downtown. Westinghouse Electric Corp.

BURGLARY

A chain door guard which sounds an alarm when the door is forced. Wessel Hardware Corp.

Noise-monitoring detectors designed to detect minute sounds are also good for large-area protection. But they, too, are easily set off. In fact, if you don't live in a very quiet area, they can be a constant source of annoyance.

SIMPLE ALARMS. Some of these can be used for internal protection only; others can be installed at doors and windows for external protection. Their main disadvantage is that you need a lot of them to give good protection. And since most of them are battery-operated, you must remember to replace the batteries regularly. The devices include the following:

· Pressure mats which sound an alarm when a burglar walks across them. But they also go off when a cat or dog who likes to roam around the house at night steps on them.

· Deadbolt locks which sound an alarm if the lock is forced.

· Chain door guards, sliding door locks, and window locks which do the same thing.

· Magnetic contact switches which are installed in doors and wired to a remote horn. These are similar to a full-scale perimeter system but can be used only to warn against unauthorized entry through one door. A time-delay feature allows you to activate the alarm before leaving home, and deactivate it after opening the door upon your return.

DOOR SENTRIES. Door sentries are designed not to scare away burglars or warn you when they have broken in, but to tell you who's at the door before you open it.

The simplest of all such devices is a tiny door viewer —like those in apartment houses—which is installed in a hole drilled through a solid door. With it, you can see the person on the outside from head to foot even though he is not standing directly in front of the lens.

Conventional intercoms allow you to talk with whom-

ever is at the door from deep within the house (see Chapter 15). Even without a complete intercom system, however, you can do the same thing with a pair of outdoor and indoor speaker-receivers. These can be easily added to any house that already has or will have a 16-volt doorbell system.

Closed-circuit television is the ultimate in door sentries, although it is no more effective than less costly devices. The TV camera is placed so that the homeowner has a clear view of whomever is at the front door. The monitor can be a vacant channel on an existing television set or a special CCTV monitor. But the system will work only if the area around the front door is well lighted.

LIGHTING. Lighting plays a double role in home protection. Indoors it makes your house look occupied even when it is not. Outdoors it is used to flood the yard with light so that anyone sneaking across it can be seen.

Automatic control of interior as well as exterior lights is easily achieved with an automatic timer (see Chapter 20). Floodlighting a yard requires only that you install one or more lights under the eaves at the corners of your house. Use 75- or 150-watt PAR floodlamps in weatherproof lampholders. The number of lights needed depends on the size and shape of the yard and house. Four may be adequate.

WINDOW AND DOOR GUARDS. The most dependable of the window and door guards is made of ½-in. steel bars welded into a frame which is fastened to the outside of the window or door frame with large screws. Guards for windows are available to fit most standard-size windows; those for doors must be made to order. The one serious drawback of window guards is that they bar escape during a fire unless they are locked into place—and even then you must remember to look for the key before you can get out. Since door guards take the place of door screens or storm doors, they are less

A fire safe. Meilink Steel Safe Co.

dangerous—though here again, you must have a key to unlock them before you can get out.

Other guards are designed simply to prevent easy entry through windows and doors in which the glass has been broken. One kind is a thick screen of welded construction. The other is an open grille which does not interfere with the view or block the incoming light to any appreciable extent. Both types are fastened to the window sash and doors themselves.

SAFES. If you want to protect valuables and papers against fire, you need a fire, or record, safe. Made in sizes as small as $13 \times 10 \times 10$ in. (inside measurements), these are designed to insulate their contents against fire for at least one hour. Safes carrying the Class C label established by Underwriters' Laboratories can go through a 1,700° fire for one hour with contents unscathed. The Underwriters' B label provides similar protection for two hours at 1,850°, and the A label is for four hours at 2,000°.

Fire safes, however, afford little protection against a professional burglar (although they might discourage an amateur who didn't feel up to making off with a roughly 75-lb. weight). You need a burglar safe instead. The smallest units are designed for installation in a concrete floor or wall (if thick enough). Larger units which are too heavy to be stolen except by a burglar with a hand truck are simply hidden in closets or, for extra security, equipped with flanges for bolting to studs in a wall.

Burglar safes have some resistance to fire but not a great deal. For maximum protection against both burglary and fire, you need a burglar safe welded or bolted inside a fire safe.

WHO MAKES IT

Alarm Device Manufacturing Co. · Combination burglar- and fire-alarm system with magnetic sensors, ultrasonic detectors, vibration sensors, automatic telephone dialer, panic buttons, floor mats, photoelectric detectors, magnetic tapes; ionization smoke detectors and fixed-temperature or rate-of-rise heat detectors.

AMF, Inc. · Combination burglar and fire alarm system with fixed-temperature heat detectors, ionization smoke detectors, recessed door and window sensors and other optional devices. Single-station ionization smoke detectors are AC or battery operated.

John D. Brush Co. · Fire and burglary safes.

Nelson Cross Co. · Door viewer. Deadlock bolt with built-in alarm. Magnetic switch with remote alarm for individual doors. Window-lock alarm. Chain door-guard alarm. Sliding-door-lock alarm. Pressure-mat alarm.

Detection Systems, Inc. · Infrared, photoelectric, and ultrasonic detectors.

Emerson Electric Co., Rittenhouse-Chromalox Div. · Perimeter systems with magnetic sensors, pressure mats, panic alarm. Door sentries which allow conversation with person at front door.

Fire-Lite Alarms, Inc. · Perimeter system combined with fire-alarm system. See Chapter 24.

Kwikset Sales & Service Co. · Perimeter system with magnetic and recessed sensors.

Leigh Products, Inc. · Door viewers.

Meilink Steel Safe Co · Fire and burglary safes

Montgomery Ward & Co. · Fire safes. Ultrasonic detectors.

Mosler Safe Co. · Fire and burglary safes.

S. Parker Hardware Manufacturing Corp. · Door viewers, one with built-in nonelectric door chime. Mechanical door alarm which sounds when door is opened.

Perfect-Line Manufacturing Corp. · Two-bulb weatherproof lampholder with built-in photoelectric cell that automatically turns on at dusk, off at dawn.

PLC Electronics, Inc. · Ultrasonic detector. Wired and wireless perimeter systems, some of which are combined with multi-station fire-alarm systems. Systems employ several kinds of sensor; fixed-temperature heat detectors; ionization smoke detectors. Automatic telephone dialers.

Pyrotonics. · Perimeter system combined with fire-alarm system (see Chapter 24).

Scovill Manufacturing Co., NuTone Housing Products Div. Perimeter burglar- and fire-alarm systems with magnetic sensors, recessed sensors, floor mats, panic buttons; optical smoke detectors, fixed-temperature heat detectors. One system incorporates an intercom with an AM/FM radio, tape player, and fire-warning system.

Sears Roebuck & Co. · Perimeter system with table-top control, magnetic sensors, and panic alarm. Smoke alarm can be connected into system. Door viewer. Steel door and window guards and grilles.

Standard Equipment, Inc., Elite Products Div. · Window guards.

Tefco Doors. · Aluminum ornamental window guards.

3M Co. · Ultrasonic detectors and alarm horns.

Versa Products Co. · Door and window guards.

Wessel Hardware Corp. · Chain door-guard alarm.

Westinghouse Security Systems, Inc. · Combination burglar- and fire-alarm system which also reports special emergencies such as air-conditioner failures. When activated, system sounds an alarm, spells out the type of problem on the control panel, and simultaneously sends a coded message to a communication center over the telephone lines. The system employs magnetic and recessed sensors, fixed temperature and rate-of-rise heat detectors, optical smoke detectors.

26

Hardware

No homeowner doubts the importance of the locks, latches, hinges, pulls, catches, door stops, sliding-door tracks, and other pieces of hardware which are built into his house. Why, then, do homeowners everywhere make the mistake of buying hardware on the basis of price rather than quality—only to find, a year or two later, that the hardware doesn't work or has lost its finish and needs to be replaced?

The answer is that most homeowners take the hardware in their homes for granted. A hinge is a hinge, a lock is a lock—or so they think.

Furthermore, relatively few of the hardware stores and building-supplies outlets from which homeowners buy hardware carry anything but the cheapest lines.

From now on, whenever you are in the market for a hardware item, remember that there are three basic grades of hardware: (1) The "builder's," "lightweight," or "budget" grade. This is the type sold in most outlets patronized by homeowners. (2) The "light-commercial" or "medium" grade. And (3) the "commercial" grade.

Of these, the first is the cheapest and poorest quality—to be avoided whenever possible, especially when you're buying locks and latches. The third is the most expensive and best quality, but it is made for the extra-hard usage hardware gets in commercial buildings and is therefore rarely used—or needed—in homes.

The medium grade, in short, is your best buy. It is well finished and sturdily built. Barring unusual abuse, it should last just about forever without giving trouble.

Where do you find it? In hardware stores which make a specialty of hardware—not housewares. Also in outlets which are listed in the Yellow Pages under "Hardware—Builder's" or "Hardware—Architectural."

Decorative hardware of unusual styling is available in some hardware stores, but the choice is limited. For a wide selection you must search out the few stores in metropolitan areas that specialize in selling hardware to interior decorators. An example is Kraft Cabinet & Hardware, Inc., 300 E. 64th St., New York, N.Y. The alternative is to order by mail from the manufacturers.

LOCKSETS. "Lockset" is an industry term for door locks with knobs. It covers locks which actually lock and interior door locks which only latch. The latter are known as "passage sets."

Locksets used on the permanent hinged doors in a house are classified as mortise locks, cylindrical locks, and tubular locks. In a mortise lock, the locking mechanism is contained in a rectangular box which is set into the edge of a door. In a cylindrical lock, the locking mechanism is a big cylinder which is inserted through one of the door faces. It has a single bolt which is locked into the strike in the door jamb by a key inserted in one of the knobs. A tubular lock works in the same way and is installed in the same way but is of somewhat different construction. It is much less common than the cylindrical lock because it is usable only for interior use in passageways, bedrooms, and closets.

Since cylindrical locks are easier to install than mortise locks, the great majority of homes built since World War II have been equipped with them, and on interior doors they have served well. On exterior doors, however, the average lock left a great deal to be desired because burglars could open it with ease either by picking or "loiding" (pushing against the beveled lock bolt with a piece of celluloid or other thin, rigid plastic).

Mortise locks could also be picked, but because the lock bolt—which is separate from the latch bolt—had a square end, loiding was almost impossible.

Today, thanks to the public demand for more burglar-resistant locks, the situation is much improved. Although the same kind of pickable cylindrical lock—without a locking mechanism or with a locking mechanism controlled by a pushbutton in one of the knobs—is still used indoors, the best exterior locks are being

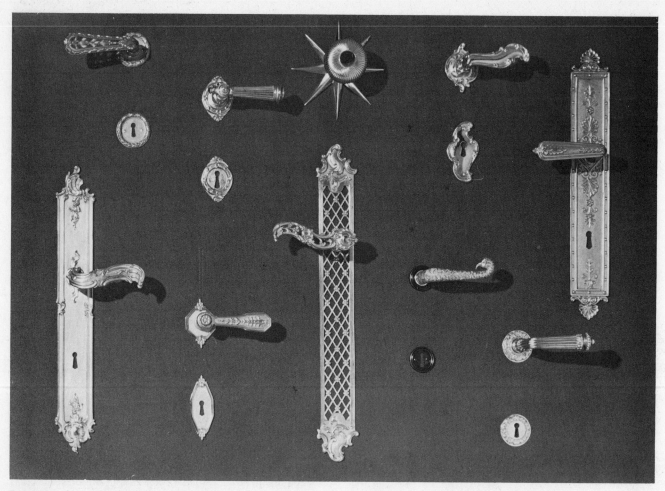

Beautiful decorative hardware is available but you have to know where to look for it. J. C. DeJong & Co.

made with a deadlatch or deadbolt and the locking mechanism is more pickproof.

A deadlatch (found only in key-in-knob locks and auxiliary locks) is a stout metal pin behind the flat side of the latch bolt. This jams the pin into the strike so that no matter how hard a burglar tries, he can't push the bolt back.

A deadbolt is a square, rectangular, or round lock bolt—without a beveled end—which can be opened only by a key from outside and in or by a key from outside and a thumbpiece from inside. It is completely independent of the latch bolt.

Any lock with a deadlatch or deadbolt—especially one with a 1-in. throw (meaning that it projects 1 in. from the door edge when in locked position)—provides more security than the usual cylindrical lock. Even so, a burglar who is expert at picking locks can open it. Hence the current emphasis by lockmakers on developing pickproof locking mechanisms.

These new maximum-security locks work in various ways, most of which are difficult for the layman to understand.

In one new cylindrical lock, the tumbler pins which control the movement of the lock bolt are interlocked in one unit rather than installed in two sections as in a conventional lock. Before the lock will open, you must insert a special key which not only raises the tumblers but also rotates them to the proper angle.

Another cylindrical lock has interlocking pins operated by a key which cannot be duplicated on ordinary corner-store key-copying machines.

A third cylindrical lock incorporates a deadlatch controlled by a thumb button in the knob and a separate deadbolt controlled by a key. When the thumb button is turned, the outside knob spins freely. If you are caught inside the house by fire, both the deadbolt and deadlatch open simultaneously when you turn the knob or the thumb-turn controlling the deadbolt from inside the house.

Complete easy-to-follow directions for installing new cylindrical or tubular locks are in the carton. To install a mortise lock, drill a series of deep, closely spaced holes in the edge of the door and chisel the hole into a smooth rectangle to receive the lock box. Drill small holes through both sides of the door for the knobs and lock cylinder. Screw the lock into the edge of the door so the face is flush with the door edge, and attach the knobs and lock cylinder.

escape through the door unless you happen to have the key handy.

Auxiliary locks are installed either on the door with

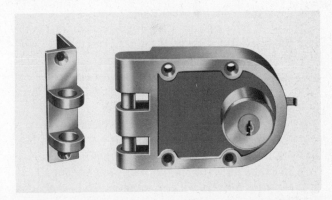

Jimmyproof rim lock. New England Lock & Hardware Co.

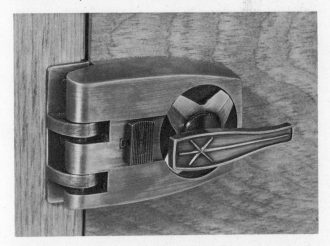

Modern drop-bolt lock. Ideal Security Hardware Corp.

Pushbutton lock with deadbolt. Simplex Security Systems, Inc.

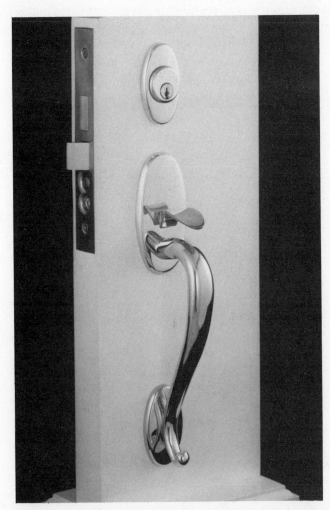

Mortise lockset for a front door. Baldwin Hardware Manufacturing Corp.

To replace an old tubular lock with a cylindrical lock, you must simply enlarge the hole through the door face. On the other hand, the only sure way to replace a cylindrical lock is with a new cylindrical lock of the same size or larger. Occasionally, however, you can replace it with a mortise lock which has an escutcheon large enough to conceal the big hole made originally for the cylinder.

Replacing a mortise lock with any kind of key-in-knob lock is troublesome because you must glue a tight-fitting block of wood into the mortise before you can bore the holes for the new lock.

AUXILIARY LOCKS. As opposed to a lockset, which has knobs for latching and unlatching doors, a lock is strictly a lock—equipped either with a deadbolt or, occasionally, a deadlatch. It is normally operated by a key outside and thumb-turn inside. Some locks, however, are keyed from both sides. This arrangement is recommended for doors with glass insets, because if a burglar breaks the glass he still cannot open the lock. On the other hand, if your house is on fire, you can't the bolt projecting from the edge, or on the inside face of the door. The latter are called rim locks.

In-door cylinder locks are installed like key-in-knob locksets. You bore a hole through the face of the door for the lock body, and drill a second hole into the edge for the bolt. Rim locks are even easier to install since you just screw them to the door face.

The most jimmyproof lock is a 50-year-old invention resembling a hand with three fingers. The fingers interlock with a surface-mounted strike which has two projecting teeth with holes. When the key or thumb-turn is turned, the drop bolts hidden in the fingers slide vertically down through the holes in the teeth.

Deadlocks of this type which incorporate only a thumb-turn can be operated only from inside the house. Keyed locks can be opened from inside or outside.

A much newer type of rim lock with a deadbolt is opened from outside with pushbuttons rather than a key. There are five buttons, which can be set in hundreds of different combinations. The lock will open only when the correct buttons are pushed in the correct sequence. The combination can be changed whenever you wish with a special tool. From inside, the lock is controlled by a lever.

Another unique kind of auxiliary lock which can be installed on the face of the door or in the edge is an electronic device opened by a tiny pocket transmitter that automatically sends a coded signal when you come within 12 ft. of the door. Then when you walk away from the door, the transmitter locks the door again.

In addition to the lock and transmitter, the equipment required includes a small antenna installed near the door and a receiver-decoder which can be located anywhere in the house.

OTHER LOCKING DEVICES. Chain guards let you open a door a few inches to see who's there, and can themselves be opened only from the inside by removing the chain from the slide screwed to the door face. However, some incorporate a keyed lock in the chain holder screwed to the door trim. This allows you to attach and detach the chain from outside the door.

Hasps are unattractive devices usually consisting of a metal strap with a slot which fits over a staple and is held secure by a padlock or peg slipped through the staple. But they are easy to install and use. In a more elaborate type, the strap contains a keyed lock. And in still another type, the strap incorporates a sliding bolt to which a padlock is permanently attached.

All hasps are particularly suitable for locking or double-locking garage doors.

Pivot locks look much like hinges and are even simpler to install. You just screw the rectangular leaf of the lock to the door jamb so the knuckle is flush with the door. Then, when the rounded leaf is folded over

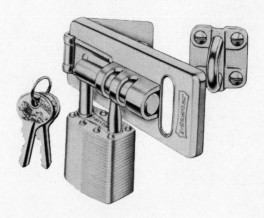

Keyed hasp lock. Master Lock Co.

Chain guard with sliding bolt. New England Lock & Hardware Co.

the face of the door, the door is held firmly shut. Flipping the door leaf back over the trim allows you to open the door.

Hooks and eyes are available in lengths from 1 to 12 in. They are made of steel and brass. One type has a strip of metal which slides under the eye to lock the hook into it.

Cabin-door hooks are hooks and eyes made in solid brass with brass mounting plates.

Turnbuttons are short, shaped strips of metal which pivot on a screw. They are used to hold doors shut and also to hold together porch screens which are put up in sections.

SLIDING-DOOR LOCKS. All exterior sliding doors come equipped with locks, but unfortunately those on old doors are not very reliable. The best way to lock such doors securely is with a lock which attaches to the

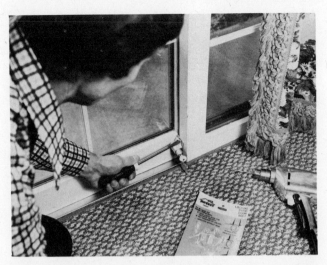

This sliding-door lock locks together the two door panels. Stanley Works.

track so the doors cannot be pried up out of the frame. The lock bolt projects into the side of the door frame.

Locks for recess sliding doors are mortised into the edges of the doors. The bolt is a vertical sliding hook which engages securely with the strike. Passage locks of similar design are available.

WINDOW LOCKS AND CATCHES. The familiar window catch is of no value if a burglar chooses to break the pane behind it. However, catches of similar design are available with locks which can be opened only with a key.

Another type of lock is fastened to one of the side rails of the top sash. It secures the window in closed or partially open position, depending on where you place it.

Yet another lock for single-hung windows is bolted to one end of the top rail on the lower sash. The deadbolt latches into a strike mounted on the window frame. By installing several strikes at different heights, you can also lock the window when it is partially open for ventilation.

A similar idea is a spring bolt inserted in a hole in the side rails of wood double-hung or single-hung windows. The bolt slips into holes drilled in the pulley stiles. Like a conventional window catch, however, it can be opened by breaking a nearby window pane. On the other hand, unlike a keyed lock, it does not keep you from escaping out the window in an emergency.

LOCKING BOLTS.

Barrel bolts are the most common type of bolt. They consist of a metal plate with a pair of protruding U-shaped straps in the center. A cylindrical or sometimes square steel bolt with a handle is held in the straps and slides into a U-shaped strike. Both pieces are surface-mounted, but in cases where the door is set in behind

the jamb, a flat strike like that used on a hinged door may be screwed to the jamb face.

Spring bolts are similar to barrel bolts except that the bolt is square and is equipped with a heavy spring which holds it in position.

Cane bolts, used on doors and gates to supplement locks, are long L-shaped bolts which are fastened vertically to the door face. The bolt slips down into a hole drilled in the threshold or floor.

Surface bolts are similar in operation to a cane bolt but are smaller and straight and are installed at the top as well as at the bottom of French doors and casement windows.

Cremone bolts, also used on French doors and casements, simultaneously lock a door at both top and bottom when you turn a thumb-piece on the central control mechanism. The bolt is available in lengths to fit almost any door.

Foot bolts are spring-action bolts which are screwed to the door face. When you step on the top end of the bolt, it drops into the strike in the floor. When you step

Barrel bolt, above; cane bolt, below. Stanley Works.

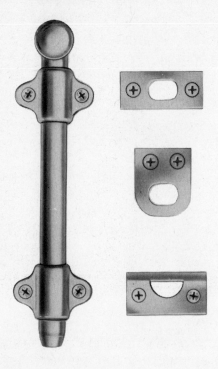

Above, surface bolt. Right, chain bolt. Below, foot bolt.
Stanley Works.

on the side-mounted trigger, the bolt releases automatically.

Chain bolts are essentially similar to foot bolts except that they are installed at the top of doors and hopper windows placed high in walls. The bolt is opened by pulling a chain hanging from the lower end. Transom catches are identical but may have a pull ring instead of a chain.

Mortise bolts have a round bolt in a housing which is inserted in a hole drilled into the edge of a door. The

bolt is opened and closed by a thumb-turn mounted on the door face.

Flush bolts are concealed in the door edge at the top or bottom. A lever or sliding handle recessed in the face of the mechanism controls a hidden bolt which slides up (or down) into the strike in the jamb.

LATCHES. There is considerable confusion between latches and catches. For clarity, a latch is here defined as a device which holds a door shut until the handle is turned or lifted. By contrast, a catch has no handle and is opened simply by pulling on the door itself. Neither has a locking mechanism. Both are used on windows as well as doors of all types.

Thumb latches are a very old type of latch usually made of black iron. On one side of the door, the handle has a thumb depressor; on the other side, it is an L-shaped lift. The latch tongue is pivoted on the face of the door and falls into a notch cut in the strike.

Surface latches consist of a tongue with a small knob for a handle. This is loosely screwed to the door face and raises up and down in a strike screwed to the door frame. The latch opens the door only from the pull side and is used primarily on closet doors.

A new kind of surface latch has a bow-shaped handle with a thumb button in the top. Pressing the button opens the tongue on the other side of the door.

Cupboard latches resemble simple kinds of rim lock. The bolt, however, has a beveled end so that it

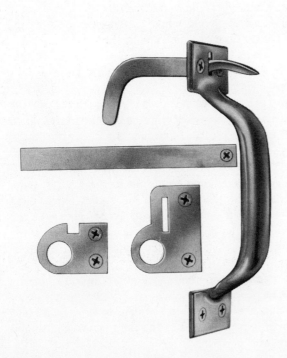

Thumb latch. Stanley Works.

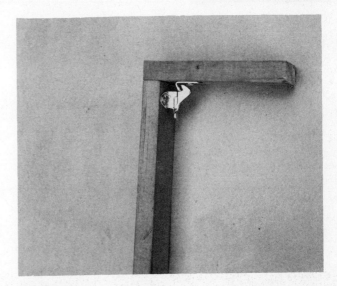

Elbow latch.

automatically engages the strike when the door is pushed closed. To open the door, you slide or turn a thumb piece.

Elbow latches are installed on the back of one of a pair of French-type cabinet doors. They consist of a hook which engages an L-shaped strike in the top of the cabinet. To open the door, you must first open the other door and then pull down the hook.

Storm- and screen-door latches installed on new aluminum doors normally are operated by a pushbutton in the top of the outside handle and by a push-type thumb lever on the inside. The latch tongue is spring-actuated. Latches on wood doors have bow-shaped horizontal handles on both sides.

Casement latches are similar to old-style surface latches but the tongue is fastened to the handle to form a double reverse L. When the handle is turned to horizontal position, the tongue slips into a groove in the strike.

Ring latches are used mainly on cabinet doors in cases where you don't want the latch to protrude from the door face. The main body of the latch is mortised into the door and has a ring-shaped handle. Pulling the ring disengages the latch tongue from the strike.

Quadrants are used to hold the two halves of Dutch doors together. One part screwed to the face of the upper door has a pivoted, roughly triangular arm which slides over a small knob in the center of the second part, which is screwed to the face of the lower door.

CATCHES.

Roller catches are spring-actuated devices with one or two rollers which grip the strike when closed.

Adjustable spring catches are used on casement windows and large doors. The spring section screwed to the jamb has an outswinging arm which engages a hook on the window and pulls the window firmly shut.

Screen-door catches, also spring-actuated, are one-piece, L-shaped devices mounted on the door frame. As it swings closed, the door strikes an inner roller which releases the spring. This, in turn, causes the arm, with a roller in the end, to fold around the edge of the door and pull it shut.

Magnetic catches have a magnet mounted on the jamb which attracts and holds a metal plate on the back of the door.

Friction catches are used on small cabinet doors. A spring-actuated button recessed in the door edge engages a saucerlike strike in the jamb.

Touch catches are similar to roller catches but release automatically when the closed door is given a slight push.

Adjustable spring catch.

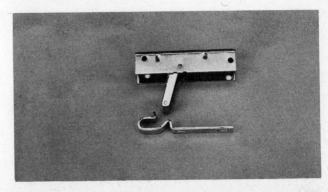

Bullet catch. Knape & Vogt Manufacturing Co.

Magnetic catch and screen door catch. Stanley Works.

HINGES. The selection of the correct hinge for a given purpose is dictated by many things:

· The width and thickness of the door (see Chapter 7).

· Frequency of door operation. This is rarely a crucial point in homes, but some manufacturers recommend use of anti-friction hinges on front and back doors.

· The construction of the door.

· The desired appearance of the door when hung.

· How much work you're willing to put into the hinge installation.

· Whether the door is hinged on the right or left. But this is a matter for consideration only if you're using loose-pin or loose-joint butt, paumelle, or olive-knuckle hinges, which should be specified for right- or left-hand doors.

· Whether the hinge is to be installed indoors or out.

· The hinge finish.

Hinges—but not all types—are made of wrought brass, bronze, steel, stainless steel, and aluminum. Brass, bronze, stainless steel, and aluminum hinges have a polished or satin finish but are not covered with a coating. Steel hinges are either plated, painted, or prime-coated for painting. Even so, they should not be used outdoors or in damp locations indoors.

To Determine the Hand of a Hinge

The hand of a butt hinge is determined from the outside of the door to which it is applied.

The outside of a cupboard, bookcase, or closet door is the room side. For other doors, the outside is usually the "push" or jamb side.

If you are standing outside a door which opens *from* you to the right, it takes right-hand butt hinges. If to the left, it takes left-hand butt hinges.

If you are standing outside a door which opens toward you to the right, it takes left-hand butt hinges. If to the left, it takes right-hand butt hinges.

To determine the hand of a loose-joint hinge, open the hinge with its face toward you. If the knuckle on the right leaf is at the bottom, it is a right-hand hinge. If the knuckle of the left leaf is at the bottom, it is a left-hand hinge.

The hand of casement windows is taken from the room side.

Opening in—if the window opens to the left, it takes right-hand butt hinges; if to the right, it takes left-hand butt hinges.

Opening out—if the window opens to the left, it takes left-hand butt hinges; if to the right, it takes right-hand butt hinges.

© The Stanley Works 1973

Another difference between hinges—but again not all types—is the manner in which the leaves are constructed. In a standard hinge, the leaves are not swaged and there is a fairly wide gap between them when they are closed. In a swaged hinge, one or both leaves are slightly offset at the barrel, or knuckle, so that when they are closed, there is only a $\frac{1}{16}$-in. gap between them; as a result, there is a smaller gap between the edge of the door and the jamb than with unswaged hinges.

In the standard swaged hinge, both leaves are swaged. In some swaged hinges, however, only one leaf is swaged. The latter are used when a door is set back from the edge of the jamb and the unswaged leaf is surface-mounted on the jamb. If you prefer to mortise the hinge into the jamb, use a raised-barrel hinge in which both leaves are swaged in the same direction.

Butt hinges, which are often known simply as butts, are the most commonly used type of hinge. When opened flat, they are square or rectangular—sometimes with rounded corners.

Large butt hinges normally have a loose pin so you can take down a door without unscrewing the leaves from the door or jamb. Small hinges commonly have fixed pins. In a third type of butt, known as a loose-joint hinge, one leaf has a fixed pin and the other has a barrel which slips over the pin. Hinges with removable pins or loose joints must be installed right side up.

The standard hinge for hanging doors in homes has leaves of equal size, and both are mortised. This is called a full-mortise hinge. In a half-mortise hinge, the jamb leaf, which is narrower than the door leaf, is screwed to the face of the jamb and the door leaf is mortised.

Full-surface hinges have leaves of equal size and both are surface-mounted. In a half-surface hinge, the narrower jamb leaf is mortised and the door leaf is surface-mounted.

Wrap-around hinges are a form of butt hinge in which one or both leaves are bent so that when the door is opened 90° it will swing clear of the jamb. Although it has little applicability to homes (its principal use is in hospitals), it is useful on doors which swing into narrow halls because you don't have to take the door down in order to squeeze a bulky piece of furniture through the opening.

Another type of wrap-around hinge in which the door leaf is bent into a right angle is used to hang doors made of plywood, because the door leaf can be screwed into both the edge and back of the doors. This is necessary because screws do not hold securely in the edges of plywood; consequently, a plywood door may pull away from a conventional butt hinge.

Parliament hinges are like butt hinges but are wider and H-shaped. They provide extra clearance between the door and jamb when the door is opened.

Wide-throw hinges are used for the same purpose as parliament hinges but are rectangular.

Paumelle hinges are decorative butt-type hinges with small barrel-shaped knuckles.

Olive-knuckle hinges are similar to paumelle hinges but have small olive-shaped knuckles.

Non-mortise hinges are designed for quick mounting on the jamb and door edge but are suitable only for lightweight doors. When closed, the leaves interlock and lie in a single plane so there is only a tiny gap between jamb and door.

Strap hinges are used outdoors more than in. The more common and less attractive type has two long, narrow triangular leaves which are surface-mounted horizontally on the door and frame. A decorative type consists of a very long, slender, arrow-shaped leaf that is surface-mounted on the door and a small rectangular leaf that is either surface-mounted on the door frame or mortised into the jamb.

T hinges are T-shaped utility hinges with a long triangular leaf which is surface-mounted on the door and a rectangular leaf (the crossbar of the T) which is surface-mounted on the door frame.

H and H-L hinges are surface-mounted decorative hinges usually of black steel with a hammered finish. They are used mainly on cabinets. The H hinge is H-shaped. The H-L hinge is like an H and L combined.

Invisible hinges are mortised into a door edge and jamb so that nothing shows on the surface when the door is closed.

Pivot hinges are used mainly in the home for cabinet doors which are difficult to hang with conventional hinges. They are made in various ways but are always installed at the top and bottom corners of the door. Only a small portion of a hinge shows when the door is closed.

Gravity pivot hinges are designed so they automatically close the door (some, however, will hold a door open at 90°). They are used mainly on café doors.

Cabinet hinges are made in many shapes and styles for conventionally hung doors as well as flush, lipped, and overlay doors. There are butt hinges, olive-knuckle hinges, wrap-around hinges, pivot hinges, ornamental surface-mounted hinges. One type used for lipped doors consists of a rectangular leaf which is screwed to the back of the door and a very slender vertical leaf—often roughly halfmoon-shaped—which is surface-mounted on the door frame.

Piano hinges, or continuous hinges, are a form of slender butt hinge made in 24-in. to 72-in. lengths. They are used on cabinets and furniture to impart extra strength and prevent warping of doors.

Spring hinges close a door automatically as soon as you let go of it. Old types used on screen doors have a coiled spring wrapped around the pin and are surface-mounted. On the new type, which is so powerful that a single hinge used in conjunction with a pair of butt hinges will close a heavy exterior door, the spring is concealed in a barrel. These hinges are mortised into the door edge and jamb.

Double-acting spring hinges are used on swinging doors. The most frequently used type is concealed behind metal plates in the bottom corner of the door and is connected to a floor plate on which it pivots. A simple pivot is installed in the top edge of the door. A second kind of double-acting hinge is installed on the door edge and jamb like a butt hinge. It is quite unattractive since a big knuckle is exposed on either side of the door.

Screw-hook-and-eye hinges are used for hanging shutters and gates, especially when the jamb is made of masonry. A long straplike hinge leaf is screwed to the face of the shutter or gate, and its knuckle slips over a pin attached at right angles to a screw anchored in the window frame or jamb. (The pin piece is called a pintle or screw hook.) Thus the shutter or gate can be re-

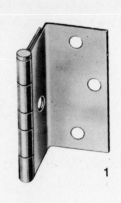

1

2

3

4

5

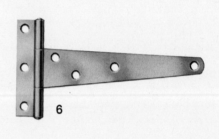

6

1, wrap-around hinge for hanging plywood doors. 2, paumelle hinge. 3, olive-knuckle hinge. 4, strap hinge. 5, invisible hinge. 6, T hinge. 7, pivot hinge. 8, cabinet hinge for lipped doors. 9, screw-hook-and-eye hinge. Stanley Works.

7

8

9

Not Swaged

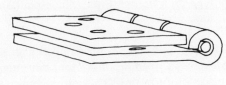

Swaged

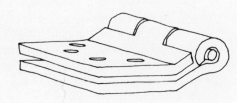

Raised Barrel Hinge

Swaged, unswaged, and raised-barrel hinges.

moved simply by lifting it off the pin. In some cases, the screw end of the pintle is a bolt. In other cases, the hinge leaf is replaced by a screw with an eye.

SLIDING-DOOR HARDWARE. Hardware for bypass sliding doors consists primarily of the track which is screwed to the top jamb. It is made in standard lengths of 4, 5, 6, and 8 ft. The doors are suspended from the track by hangers with wheels. The hangers should be designed to permit raising, lowering, and leveling the doors. A guide is screwed to the floor to keep the doors from swaying.

Recess-sliding-door hardware consists of a track fastened to the bottom of a steel pocketframe set (see Chapter 7), and the door hangers.

Tracks for sliding garage and barn doors are large, heavy, U-shaped steel channels. The hangers are similar to those for interior sliding doors but bigger and sturdier.

FOLDING-DOOR HARDWARE. This consists of a single track mounted on the head jamb, door hangers, pivots for the fixed-end of the door panel, and an aligner to hold the other end door in place when closed. The tracks are available in 4-ft. to 12-ft. lengths.

BIFOLD-DOOR HARDWARE. The elements are the same as those for folding doors. Tracks are 2 to 8 ft. long.

KNOBS. Door knobs on cylindrical and tubular locksets are interchangeable only if made by the same manufacturer, and even then you should take the old knob to the hardware store to make sure you can find its counterpart in another design. This means that when you buy a lockset of this type, you should take a look at the many styles of knob most manufacturers offer, because you may not be able to change it if you decide you don't like it.

Knobs on mortise locksets, on the other hand, are screwed to a spindle so you can quickly take off one and install another whenever you like. The choice of designs is enormous. Materials used in the knobs include brass, steel, aluminum, glass, plastic, and ceramics. Since plated and painted finishes on metal knobs tend to wear off, solid brass and aluminum are preferable but need occasional polishing.

Fixed knobs used as pulls on doors are often available in the same designs and materials as operating knobs. Small knobs for cabinets and drawers are also available in many designs.

DOOR HANDLES. Lever handles can be substituted for knobs on mortise locksets. Styles and materials vary widely from the severely modern to ornate.

PULLS. Pulls take the place of knobs on doors and drawers. They are normally U-shaped and project

There's no need to settle for ordinary knobs if you want something better looking. J. C. DeJong & Co.

horizontally. In some, the U-shaped or ring-shaped handle is loose and falls against the escutcheon when not in use. Recessed pulls—either round or oval—are used on sliding doors. They have no handle as such; you simply poke a finger into them.

LIFTS. Lifts are used on double- and single-hung windows. The surface-mounted type is identical to many U-shaped pulls, and the two can be used pretty much interchangeably. Recessed lifts have larger openings than the average recessed pull so you can use three or four fingers for leverage.

ROSES. These are the small, simple to ornate plates which cover keyholes. They are made of metal only.

PUSHPLATES. A pushplate is a rather large (roughly 3×10 in.) plate mounted on the face of a swinging door at a height of about 4 ft. to protect the finish. It is made of brass, bronze, stainless steel, aluminum, glass, or plastic. Some plates incorporate a U-shaped pull to permit opening a door in either direction from one side.

KICKPLATES. These are like pushplates but are always of simple design and never made of glass. They are screwed horizontally to the bottom rail of a swinging door.

DOOR HOLDERS. The simplest door holder is a spring-steel clip (like that used for hanging brooms) which is screwed to the door face. This engages a prong screwed to the wall or floor.

A more positive holder is a wall- or floor-mounted rubber-tipped door bumper with a hook which is lifted by hand into an eye screwed to the door.

Recessed door holders are set into the floor so they are out of the way when not in use. They contain a lever which folds up and back against the door.

Door holders which can be used to hold a door open at any angle are one-piece devices screwed to the door face. One type contains a rubber-tipped plunger which holds the door firmly when you step on it. To open it, you step on a trigger. A roller door holder, suitable only for uncarpeted floors, automatically maintains pressure on the floor in all positions. A lever-type holder has an arm which swings up against the door when not in use, and swings down against the floor when you nudge it with your toe.

Overhead door holders contain a long rod which slides in a pivot device attached to the head jamb. They hold the door open only at a 90° angle. A coiled spring around the end of the rod serves as a shock absorber. The hold-open feature can be disengaged to convert the holder into a door stop.

Left, lever-type door holder. Right, hinge-pin door stop. Stanley Works.

DOOR STOPS. These are rubber-tipped gadgets used only to prevent an opening door from crashing into a wall or piece of furniture. They are screwed to the baseboard or door face. An L-shaped bumper is screwed to the floor.

Hinge-pin door stops slip under the pin of a door hinge. The shank of the bumper is threaded so the door can be stopped at any desired angle.

Chain door stops are used primarily to keep the wind from ripping storm doors out of their frames when they are opened. They incorporate a spring which cushions the door against a sudden jerk as it swings open.

DOOR KNOCKERS. Door knockers are made of brass or black wrought iron. Those of conventional design are in one piece. More unusual knockers frequently have a separate button against which the knocker falls.

DOOR GUARDS. Used in screen doors to protect the screening, door guards are available as straight rods and ornamental grilles.

LETTER SLOTS. For installation in the front door, a letter slot consists of a front plate with a flap, a matching back plate, and a sleeve to cover the edges of the cut-out wood. The slots are made of brass or aluminum and have openings from 1½ to 2½ in. high and 7½ to 12¼ in. wide. A vertical slot with a spring-actuated flap is made for glass doors.

SCREEN- AND STORM-WINDOW HARDWARE. This hardware is required only for screens and storm windows that you put up and take down. Two-piece hangers are used to hold the screens and windows in the window opening at the top; hooks and eyes secure them at the bottom. Adjustable arms screwed to the sides of the window frame permit opening storm windows to any position and holding them secure against wind.

Screen couplings are used to tie together porch screens which are put up in sections to fill a wide opening between columns. They are flat metal strips with two slots which slip down over screws set in adjacent screen frames.

SHUTTER HOLDBACKS.

SHUTTER HOLDBACKS. You can hold shutters open with hooks and eyes or with spring-steel door stops which clip around prongs screwed to the wall. Both devices are concealed behind the shutters. The alternative is to install an ornamental S-shaped holdback in front of the shutters.

WHO MAKES IT

Acme General Corp. · Bifold- and sliding-door hardware.

Baldwin Hardware Manufacturing Corp. · Authentic reproductions in brass and iron of Colonial rim locks and door knockers. Also in modern design—door knockers, mortise locks, knobs, door holders and bumpers, pushplates and bars, spring latches, chain door guards, letterbox plates, etc.

Ball & Ball. · Beautiful, painstaking reproductions of every piece of brass or iron hardware used in early America—from pulls and hinges to locks and wolf's-head door knockers.

Julius Blum & Co. · Iron, steel, aluminum, and bronze ornaments such as rosettes, cups, leaves, candle pans, spear heads, moldings in great variety.

Albert Constantine & Son. · Cabinet hinges. Cabinet locks. Elbow latches. Magnetic, spring, and touch catches.

J. C. DeJong & Co. · Incredible collection of decorative hardware in mainly traditional designs from Europe—door knobs, levers, pulls, door knockers, pushplates, letter-slot covers, hinges, door stops, locksets, passage sets, cabinet knobs and pulls, coat hooks, cremone bolts. Unlimited choice of finishes. Knobs available in decorated porcelain, stoneware, pottery, wood, and crystal as well as metal.

Eaton Corp., Lock & Hardware Div. · Yale cylindrical locksets with deadlatches; one with a deadbolt. Rim locks with deadbolts or deadlatches. Jimmyproof rim locks with drop bolts. Tubular dead locks. Mortise locks. Passage and closet latches. Bathroom locks. Privacy lock with turn button on inside can be opened from outside with emergency key.

Elon, Inc. · Ceramic-tile door pulls.

Emhart Corp. · Russwin cylindrical and mortise locksets. Maximum-security locks with interlocking pins, a special key, hardened-steel anchor rods, and drill-resistant shield.

Engineered Products Co. · Magnetic catches for doors of every weight. Aluminum pulls and aluminum or brass knobs in modern designs. Tracks for cabinet doors from $\frac{1}{8}$ to $\frac{3}{4}$ in. thick.

Ferum Co. · Hinges of most types. Barrel bolts. Magnetic, spring, and roll catches. Window and touch latches. Pulls, knobs, and lifts. Door stops. Hasps. S-shaped shutter holdbacks. Quadrants. Keyed hasp locks. Keyed chain door guard. Hingelike pivot lock.

Grant Pulley & Hardware Corp. · Hardware for bypass and recessed sliding doors.

Gries Reproducer Co. · Perforated hardboard hooks that can't pull out. Sculptured surface-mounted cabinet hinges.

P. E. Guerin, Inc. · Decorative metal hardware in many designs: mortise locks, rim locks. Door knobs, pulls, and levers. Push plates and escutcheon plates. Cremone bolts. Hinges. Door knockers. Small knobs and pulls. Made of solid brass, gold plate, silver plate, pewter plate, etc.

Hager Hinge Co. · All kinds of hinges.

Ideal Security Hardware Corp. · Drop-bolt deadlock keyed from outside; locked by lever inside. Locks automatically when door is closed; has nighttime lock button. When lock is not engaged, door is held shut by spring-loaded catch. Outside handle bolted through door.

Knape & Vogt Manufacturing Co. · Sliding-door hardware. Tracks for cabinet doors of glass and other thin materials. Recessed door pulls. Aluminum drawer pulls. Magnetic and bullet catches.

Kwikset Sales & Service Co. · Double-locked security locksets with 1-in.-throw deadbolts and $\frac{1}{2}$-in.-throw deadlatches. Cylindrical locksets with deadbolts. Many designs and finishes.

Leigh Products, Inc. · Brass door knockers.

Master Lock Co. · Padlocked hasp. Conventional hasps. Cabinet locks.

Montgomery Ward & Co. · Deadlatched cylinder locks. Rim locks with drop bolts. Keyed chain door guard.

New England Lock & Hardware Co. · Jimmyproof rim deadlocks including famous Segal interlocking deadlocks with drop bolt. Rim-mounted night latch. Chain door guard with slide bolt. Conventional chain guard with bicycle-type chain attached into steel pins.

Old Guilford Forge. · Black-iron reproductions of Colonial latches, Dutch-door latches, slide bolts, quadrants, ring door pulls, strap hinges, H and H-L hinges.

S. Parker Hardware Manufacturing Corp. · Rim lock with drop bolt. Mortise locksets. Cylindrical locksets with deadlatches. Passage locksets. Keyed window lock. Hasp lock. Quadrants. Cabin-door hooks. Butt, piano, wraparound, paumelle, spring, invisible hinges. All kinds of door stops and holders. Mail box plates. Locking bolts. Catches. Recessed pulls. Kick and pushplates. Door pulls. Window latches.

Pulse Dynamics Manufacturing Corp. · Electronic lock.

Sargent & Co. · Cylindrical lockset with deadlatch has key that cannot be duplicated on ordinary machines.

Schlage Lock Co. · Double-locked security locksets with 1-in.-throw deadbolts and $\frac{1}{2}$-in.-throw deadlatches. Keyed and nonkeyed cylindrical locksets, include closet locks, passage latches, and privacy locks which can be opened from outside with screwdriver. Auxiliary deadlocks operated by key and/or thumb piece. Grip-handle front door locksets with deadbolts or deadlatches. Wide range of designs and finishes.

F. E. Schumacher Co. · Push bars and grilles for screen and storm doors.

Sears Roebuck & Co. · Window locks. Keyed chain door guard. Sliding glass door locks. Double-locked security lockset. Rim locks, including unit with drop bolt. Keyed and nonkeyed cylindrical locksets. Decorative locks, and hinges with enameled finish.

Simplex Security Systems, Inc. · Pushbutton lock.

Stanley Works. · Everything—and then some—except locks. Hardware for all types of sliding door including recess and heavy garage or barn doors.

Tremont Nail Co. · Hand-forged iron strap hinges, tulip and butterfly hinges, door knockers, latches in early Colonial design.

Wessel Hardware Corp. · Keyed and conventional chain door guards.

27

Fasteners

Fastening is the most important step in any kind of building operation. Without proper fastening, shingles fly off the roof in high winds, floors squeak, nailheads blister and pop through gypsum-board walls, doors hang at a slant, knobs and latches fall off, draperies pull from windows, stair rails give uncertain support—it's theoretically possible that the entire house may shift off its foundations.

Fastening is done with many devices as well as the adhesives discussed in the next chapter. In many cases, there are several kinds of fastener you can use; in other cases, only one will work. In making a choice, you must decide not only which will hold best but also whether you can readily use it (you can't, for example, drive a nail if there is no space to wield a hammer). But this is only the beginning. You must also ask yourself what if any effect the fastener will have on the material. Will it split the wood, for instance? Will its appearance be objectionable? Will it allow you to take apart whatever you have put together in case you someday want to do this? How will it affect the final finishing of the material? How many fasteners will be necessary?

Fastening, in other words, is not a job you can just toss off.

NAILS. The good old nail is still and probably always will be the most important fastener used in the home—and for the very simple reason that it does an excellent job and is easy to use.

Nails are made of aluminum, copper, and, most of all, steel. Ordinary bright steel nails are used inside the house in dry locations but should never be used outdoors or in wet locations because they rust rapidly, gradually disintegrating and staining the surrounding surface. Even if you apply putty over them, you can't be sure they won't rust. For outdoor use, galvanized nails should always be used (you might also use aluminum, although they are more expensive). Steel nails

also come with a so-called cement (actually a resin) coating which makes them hold better for a short time. So-called blued nails have a bluish-black finish which gives slight protection against rust in damp indoor locations (they are unsuitable for outdoor use).

In addition to all these modern nails, you can also buy wrought-iron nails which are hand-forged to resemble the nails our Colonial forebears used. If you can't find these in stores, order them by mail.

The standard method of sizing nails is by the penny system. In speaking of a 2-in. nail, for example, carpenters call it a 6-penny nail. In writing, penny is abbreviated by the letter d. Thus a 6-penny nail is a 6d nail. There is no requirement, however, that you must refer to nails in this way. If you find it easier to ask for a 2-in. nail, the hardware dealer will have no trouble interpreting your needs. Some kinds of nail, in fact, are always specified by their actual inch length.

The table shows the sizes of all standard nails:

4d	1½ in.	12d	3¼
5d	1¾	16d	3½
6d	2	20d	4
7d	2¼	30d	4½
8d	2½	40d	5
9d	2¾	50d	5½
10d	3	60d	6

Nails are available in numerous configurations. The most important for use around the house are the following:

Common nails. As the name suggests, this is the most commonly used kind of nail. Its thick shank gives it greater strength than is found in most nails, so it's used primarily for basic structural purposes. But because it has a large, flat, circular head which is hard to conceal, it is used where it will not be seen—within the walls of the house, for example.

Common nails are available in all sizes.

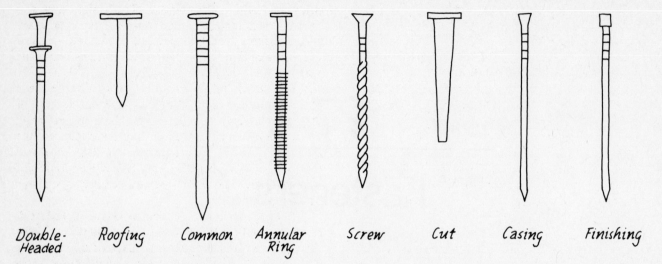

Double-Headed Roofing Common Annular Ring Screw Cut Casing Finishing

Basic types of nail you're likely to use.

Spikes. Spikes are common nails over 6 in. long. They are sold by the inch rather than the penny.

Box nails. Box nails are similar to common nails but have very thin shanks so you can drive them into wood which common nails might split. They come in 3d, 4d, 5d, 6d, 7d, 8d, 10d, 16d, and 20d sizes.

Finishing nails. Again as its name suggests, the finishing nail is used for finishing work, and is the second most common type of nail. It has a thin shank and a very small head which is more or less globular. Thus the head is easily countersunk beneath a wood surface so it can be concealed with a filler such as spackle.

Finishing nails come in 3d, 4d, 6d, 8d, and 10d sizes.

Casing nails. These nails are also used in finishing work such as applying casings around doors. They have slightly thicker shanks and cone-shaped heads for easy countersinking. For most purposes, you can use them interchangeably with finishing nails. Available sizes are 4d, 6d, 8d, 10d, and 16d.

Brads. Brads are tiny finishing nails used to apply thin pieces of wood. They run from ½ to 1½ in. long.

Wire nails. These are used for the same purposes as brads, but since they are miniature common nails, the heads are not so easily concealed. They range from ⅝ to 1½ in. long.

Shingle nails. Shingle nails are used for applying wood shingles and are always made of galvanized steel. They are shaped like common nails but come only in 3d, 3½d, and 4d sizes.

Roofing nails. Nails for applying asphalt roofing have very large-diameter, flat, circular heads and are made of galvanized steel. Sizes are 3d, 4d, and 5d.

Annular-ring nails. In this type of nail most of the shank is covered with deep, closely spaced grooves to increase the nail's holding power. The head is flat, wide, and circular. It is also called a ring-grooved or ringed-shank nail.

The most common use for annular-ring nails is in applying gypsum-board panels to walls and ceilings. Lengths are 1¼, 1⅜, and 1½ in. Larger annular ring nails are substituted for common nails when greater holding power is required.

Screw nails. Screw-nail shanks are spirally grooved to give them greater holding power. They are used for various purposes. Those with cone-shaped heads are the favorite type of nail for putting down wood floors. They come in 6d, 7d, and 8d sizes. Nails with small, flat heads are used for installing asbestos-cement shingles. Nails with larger heads are used in aluminum siding and sometimes in redwood siding.

Wood siding nails. Unless you tell them otherwise, carpenters usually use galvanized common nails to install clapboards and other forms of wood siding. But there are several types of nail made specifically for the purpose. The best has a head which is flat and circular on top and beveled underneath. This is called a sinker head, because it's easier to sink flush with the wood surface than the head of a common nail. It's made in 6d, 7d, 8d, and 10d sizes.

Cut nails. Cut nails are similar in shape to early-day handmade nails. The shank is rectangular in cross section and tapers from the point back to the head, which is similarly shaped and just a little larger.

Cut nails are used mainly for putting down wood floors. They come in sizes ranging from 6 to 20d.

Masonry nails. These are thick-shanked nails with diamond points for easily penetrating hard surfaces. One type has a square shank; the other, a round, fluted (semi-screw-threaded) shank. Lengths range from ½ to 3 in.

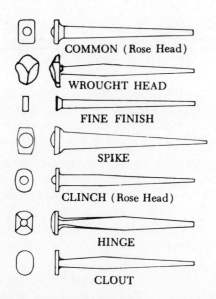

COMMON (Rose Head)

WROUGHT HEAD

FINE FINISH

SPIKE

CLINCH (Rose Head)

HINGE

CLOUT

Cut nails like those used by our forefathers are still being made. Tremont Nail Co.

Double-headed nails. These are common nails with two heads, one about ¼ in. above the other. They are used only for temporary fastening of such things as scaffolds. Because the upper head projects well above the surface of the wood, you can slip the claw of a hammer under it in an instant and yank it out. Sizes are 6d, 8d, 10d, 16d, and 20d.

SCREWS

Wood screws. Wood screws are the second most

commonly used type of fastener. They are called wood screws to differentiate them from other types of screw and, obviously, because they are used in wood. But they are also frequently used to fasten other materials, such as metals and plastic, to wood.

Wood screws take more time to install than nails because you have to drill a hole for them (except in very soft lumber) and then twist them in gradually. Even with a ratchet screwdriver, this takes time. On the other hand, screws hold more securely than nails, and they hold even in very thin wood. They are also easier to install and remove without any damage to the surrounding surface.

The screws are made of bright steel, galvanized steel, cadmium- and chromium-coated steel, blued steel, aluminum, brass, and bronze. And they come in so many sizes that it is likely that only the manufacturers know all of them. Lengths range from $\frac{3}{16}$ to 6 in. The diameter of the shank, measured just below the head, ranges from $\frac{5}{64}$ to $\frac{3}{8}$ in. (Diameters are expressed in gauge numbers which start at 0, the smallest, and run up to 24, the largest.) Screws of the same length may be available in several gauges. But no one type of screw is made in every length and in every gauge.

The principal difference between wood screws is in the shape of the heads. Flat-head screws are flat on top and conical underneath so they can be countersunk flush with or even below the surface of wood. Round-head screws are round on top and flat underneath and cannot be countersunk. Oval-head screws are oval on top and conical underneath so they can be partially countersunk. Filister-head screws, which are less com-

Screws and screwheads.

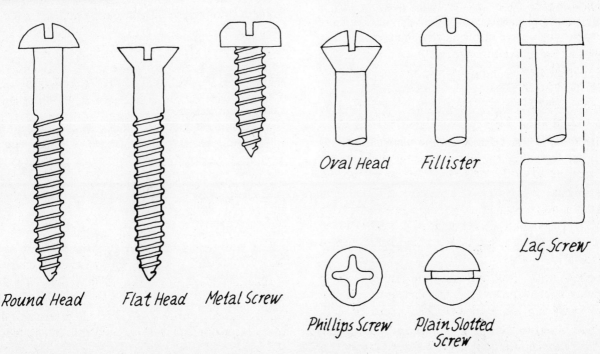

Round Head   Flat Head   Metal Screw

Oval Head   Fillister   Lag Screw

Phillips Screw   Plain Slotted Screw

mon than the preceding types, are U-shaped on top and flat underneath. They cannot be countersunk.

Most wood-screw heads have a straight slot to receive the blade of a conventional screwdriver. In the Phillips-head screw, however, the slots form a small cross and can be driven only with a Phillips screwdriver. Slots of still different shapes are used in other screws, but you rarely run into these in the home. The purpose of the Phillips-head screw is to make it easier to drive. Once the screwdriver tip is set in the cross slots, it cannot slip out.

Lag screws. The lag screw is a thick-shanked screw which is used only in heavy construction. It comes in 1-in. to 6-in. lengths and ¼-in. to ⁹⁄₁₆-in. diameters, and has a square unslotted head which is turned with a wrench.

Sheet-metal screws. You run into this kind of screw most often in appliances and heating plants, where it is used to fasten thin sheets of metal. It is also called a self-tapping screw because you don't have to cut a threaded hole to receive it.

The most common kind of sheet-metal screw has a large flat or oval head. The thick shank is threaded from the point all the way up to the head. The screws are ⅛ to 2 in. long.

Machine screws. You will rarely have any use for a machine screw but will encounter it in some of the thicker metals used in appliances. It looks like a bolt rather than a screw, but unlike a bolt, it is driven into a threaded hole instead of being drawn tight with a nut.

BOLTS. The holding power of bolts far exceeds that of nails and screws because there is no possible way of pulling them out except by removing the nuts. Bolts of four types are made of steel, aluminum, brass, and bronze.

Most common types of bolt.

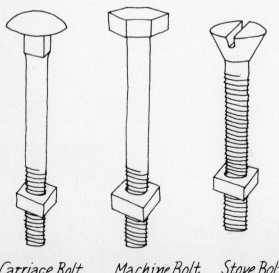

Carriage Bolt   Machine Bolt   Stove Bolt

Stove bolts have heads like wood screws. The shanks range from ⁵⁄₃₂ to ½ in. in diameter and ⅜ to 6 in. long. The bolts are installed with a screwdriver and wrench.

Machine bolts have square or hexagonal heads which are turned with a wrench and cannot be countersunk. The shanks are threaded only partway. The bolts are ¾ to 39 in. long, ³⁄₁₆ to 1¼ in. in diameter.

Carriage bolts have unslotted, oval heads with square collars underneath to keep the bolts from turning when installed. The shanks are threaded for only part of their length and are ¾ to 20 in. long and ³⁄₁₆ to ¾ in. across.

Continuous-threaded bolts are nothing but rods which are threaded from end to end. They come in 3-ft. lengths and in ¼-in to ¾-in. diameters. To use them, you cut them to the desired length and screw nuts on both ends. The bolts can be bent to any angle or curved into a U.

Bolts are generally installed with washers between the nuts and the surface against which the nuts bear. Smooth flat washers are used to keep the nuts from turning into the wood. You may also use them under both the nut and the bolt head when you insert a small bolt in a hole which is larger than the nut and head.

Lock washers are used under nuts to hold them secure against a metal surface or flat washer. The conventional washer is a split, slightly twisted ring. Other lock washers are made of very thin metal and are saucer-shaped or have teeth on the edges.

TACKS. Tacks of steel, copper, or aluminum are classified by various specific names, none of which means a great deal to the user. The ordinary tack has a flat head and tapered shank. Others have oval heads and straight shanks. They come in lengths from ³⁄₁₆ to ⅞ in.

STAPLES. Insulated staples are used for tacking down wires. Large electrician's staples with square corners hold electric cables.

The handiest kind of staple resembles the ordinary office staple but is made of heavier wire and comes in lengths of ¼ to ⁹⁄₁₆ in. The staples are fabricated in strips of 100 and are driven by a hand-held stapler. They are ideal for installing faced insulation batts and blankets, building paper, polyethylene vapor barriers, and screenwire.

SPECIAL WOOD FASTENERS

Corrugated fasteners, also called wiggle nails, are straight or circular strips of corrugated steel with teeth along one edge. They are used to join a pair of boards side by side or end to end. The resulting joint does not have a great deal of strength but is adequate in such things as picture frames and closet shelves which are

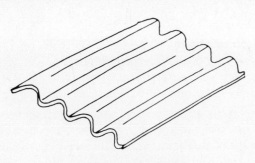

Corrugated Fastener

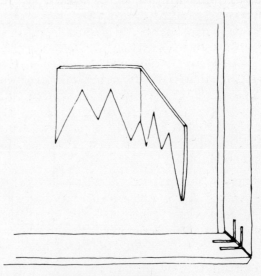

Chevron Fastener

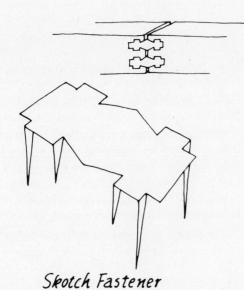

Skotch Fastener

Connector Plate

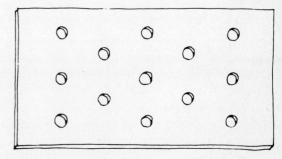

Strap Nail

Tie Plate

Special wood fasteners.

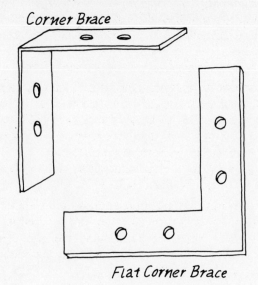

Corner Brace

Flat Corner Brace

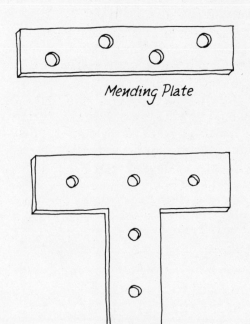

Mending Plate

T Plate

Metal plates used for making and reinforcing joints.

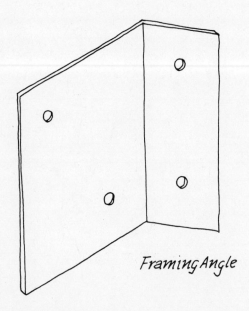

Framing Angle

not expected to bear a heavy weight. The fasteners come in lengths up to ¾ in. and in several widths.

To use the fastener, you simply hold it across the joint and tap it down flush with the surface. Care must be taken not to split the wood.

Skotch fasteners are used for the same purpose as corrugated fasteners. They have four sharp prongs projecting from the underside of a flat steel strip.

Chevron fasteners are another substitute for corrugated fasteners. They are L-shaped and have diamond-pointed teeth along the bottom edge.

Strap nails are stronger than any of the above because, as the points are driven into wood, they curve downward and inward more or less like the points of a gun-driven staple. The nails, which look like a rectangular spider, have from two to 24 teeth. A special

type is designed for fastening pipes and cables to a wall.

Connector plates are rectangular plates up to about 3 in. long with several dozen sharp prongs on the underside. Because of their size, they are suitable for joining heavier lumber than the above fasteners; nevertheless, if you exert very much pressure against the plates, unsupported timbers will come apart.

Tie plates are known also as connector plates. They are flat steel plates punctured with many holes through which nails are driven to hold timbers together. They are most often used in building trusses. The plates range in size from $1¾ \times 5$ in. to $2¼ \times 15$ in. They are also made in $1⅜$-in.-wide straps from 4 to 36 in. long; but in these, the nail holes are clustered at the ends of the straps.

Flat corner braces. Like most people, you probably call these angle irons. They are L-shaped metal straps which are laid over the faces of two boards forming a corner, and are held with screws or sometimes bolts driven through the holes in each arm. This results in a strong but unattractive joint.

Steel and corrugated-steel corners measure 2 to 8 in. along each arm. Brass corners are smaller.

Corner braces, also called angle irons, differ from the flat corner braces in that the strips are bent across the face into an L which is installed inside a corner formed by two boards. For this reason, the joint has a neater appearance.

Steel and corrugated-steel braces measure 1 to 10 in. along each arm. Brass braces are smaller.

T plates are steel or brass braces formed into a flat T with three screw holes in each arm. They are used when one piece of wood is butted to the middle of another piece. The arms are 3 to 6 in. long.

Mending plates are close relatives of the corner braces and T plates but are straight straps of steel or brass. Steel and galvanized-steel plates are 2 to 10 in. long; brass plates only 2 or 3 in. long.

Joist and beam hangers are sometimes called stirrups because of their shape (they are actually U-shaped with square corners). They are used to join joists or beams to the sides of other joists or beams. A hanger is

first nailed to the side of the supporting beam. The end of the meeting joist is then set into the stirrup and nailed.

The hangers are available in many sizes.

Framing angles. Imagine an extra-wide corner brace with one arm longer than the other, and you have a framing angle. It's made of steel and held in place with nails. You can use it either for making right-angle joints in timbers or for reinforcing such joints.

The angles are made in widths of 3, 5, 7, and 9 in. The longer arm is 2½ in. long.

All-purpose framing anchors are wide steel plates bent into a right angle. They can be used in place of framing angles, or by bending the two legs at the bottom, you can anchor a timber to the bottom of another timber.

Special fasteners.

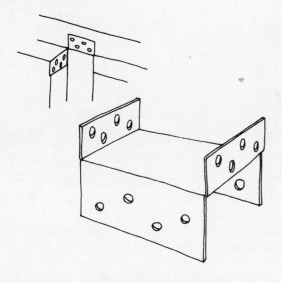

Post Cap

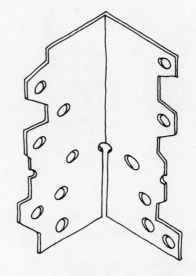

All Purpose Anchor

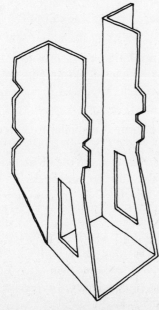

Joist and Beam Hanger

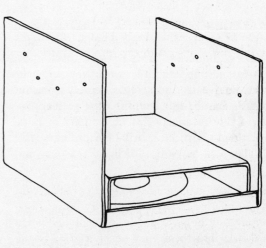

Post Anchor

283

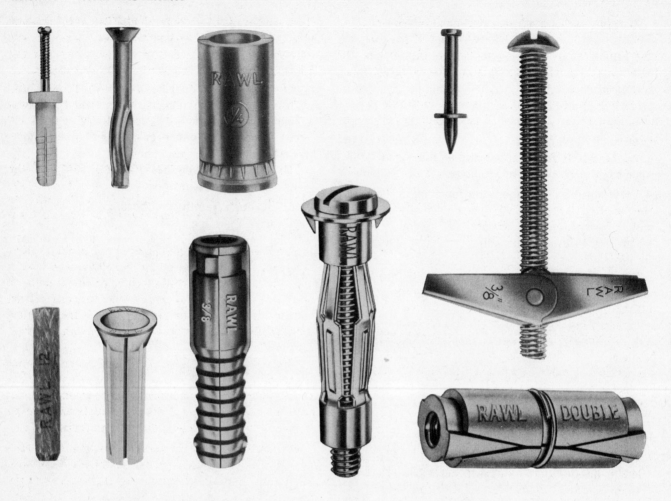

Bottom, left to right: Rawl plug, lead anchor, lag shield, hollow-wall screw anchor, machine-bolt anchor. Top: nylon anchor, expansion bolt, machine-screw anchor, stud, toggle bolt. Rawlplug Co.

Post anchors are used to tie a 4×4-in. wood post to a concrete or wood porch floor or concrete pier. They are U-shaped. Some anchors have a double bottom so the post is raised off the base and won't stand in water.

Post caps form a double, reverse U so you can tie the top of a 4×4-in. wood post to the bottom of a beam.

WALL FASTENERS. One of the commonest and meanest little jobs homeowners face is to fasten things—pictures, draperies, furring strips, towel rods, gates, etc.—to masonry and tile walls and to walls which do not hold nails and screws securely (plaster, gypsum board, hardboard, thin plywood). Happily, there are a number of anchors which simplify matters. For most of them you need a drill—an ordinary drill for "soft" walls; a carbide-tipped drill for masonry and tile.

Rawl plugs are small jute-fiber cylinders lined with lead which can be used in any masonry or tile wall. The plugs are inserted in holes drilled in the wall, and when screws are driven into them, they expand and grip the sides of the holes.

The important thing to remember in using Rawl plugs—as well as similar types of anchor—is that the hole you make must be the same size as the plug, and the screw must be sized to fit the plug. The plugs are made in sizes to hold screws of No. 6 to No. 22 gauges as well as lag screws up to $\frac{5}{8}$ in. in diameter.

Plastic anchors are similar to Rawl plugs except that they are made of plastic and are used in smaller sizes. They do not provide as positive an anchor as Rawl plugs.

Lead anchors, also similar to Rawl plugs, are made of solid lead. They're a little stronger than the plugs but should not be used where the object you hang is subject to considerable vibration or shocks.

Most lead anchors are used with screws. A few are designed for nails.

Lag shields are overgrown lead anchors made of a soft alloy. They are used in thick masonry walls to anchor heavier objects than any of the preceding anchors can support. They will receive lag screws of $\frac{1}{4}$ to $\frac{3}{4}$ in. in diameter.

Machine-screw anchors are even stronger than lag shields because a machine screw is used to anchor the object being hung. As the screw enters the threads in the end of the anchor, the anchor expands against the sides of the hole.

The hole drilled for a machine-screw anchor must be not only the same diameter as the anchor but also the same depth.

Machine-bolt anchors are used with machine bolts rather than machine screws in masonry walls of doubtful strength. The anchor is a complex little metal device with opposing wedges in the ends. When the anchor is set in a hole and the bolt is screwed into the end, the wedges are drawn up tightly into the anchor, forcing the sides to expand against the hole.

Expansion bolts have enormous holding power in hard masonry walls (they are not good in soft masonry) and are easily installed in a drilled hole with a hammer. Made of high-strength spring steel, the bolts look something like an old-fashioned clothespin. When pounded into a hole, the bowed legs grip so hard against the sides of the hole that you almost can't pull the anchor out.

The bolts are made with several kinds of head, three of which are useful in the home. One is conical like a flat-head screw, one is oval, and the other is threaded to receive a nut.

Nylon anchors can be used in thick masonry walls as well as in hollow walls surfaced with ¼-in. or ⁵⁄₁₆-in. plywood which is too thin for other types of fastener. Like Rawl plugs, they are inserted through a hole in the wall. Then a screw or special screwlike nail is driven in. This forces the anchor to expand so it cannot be withdrawn.

A anchors derive their name from the fact that they are short plastic sleeves which expand to an A shape when screws are driven into them. They are used for fastening things to hollow walls with very shallow hollows—for example, a wall surfaced with hardboard nailed to furring strips. They support moderate weights.

Hollow-wall screw anchors, also called Molly screws, are designed for use only in hollow walls and are capable of supporting surprisingly heavy weights. The anchors consist of a cylindrical sleeve into which a slender bolt is driven. As the bolt enters the cylinder, it causes the sides of the cylinder to buckle outward and grip the back of the wall. Once the cylinder is set, the bolt can be removed whenever necessary.

Hollow-wall screw anchors are made in many sizes for use in walls from ⅛ to 1¾ in. thick. A special type of anchor available in only a few sizes can be hammered through a wall.

Toggle bolts can be substituted for hollow-wall screw anchors in hollow walls, and are also available in sizes to fit walls up to 5 in. thick. The most common kind, known as a spring-wing toggle bolt, consists of a long bolt with a flat, oval, or round head and a unique nut with two spring-actuated wings. To use the device, a hole large enough to pass the nut (when its wings are folded) is drilled through the wall. The bolt with nut attached is then pushed through the hole; and as the bolt is tightened, it pulls the opened wings of the nut against the back of the wall.

Toggle bolts can support heavier weights than hollow-wall screw anchors, but if the bolt is removed, the spring-wing nut falls down and is lost in the wall. In addition, the hole made for the nut is so large that it is sometimes hard to conceal.

Studs are entirely different from any of the anchors described above. They are used in solid masonry walls when there are so many things to be anchored that you don't have time or energy to drill holes for conventional anchors. In homes, their principal use is for fastening furring strips to walls prior to paneling with plywood, hardboard, etc.

The studs, or drive pins, have a general resemblance to a common nail and are made of specially heat-treated steel. They are driven into the masonry either with a tool called a stud driver which is actuated by hammer blows or with gunpowder in a special pistol.

Pronged anchors are another unique type of fastener. They consist of a large, flat, perforated metal plate with a nail, bolt, or flat metal strip projecting from the middle. The anchors are secured to the wall by embedding the plates in dabs of silicone adhesive. The object to be hung is then slipped over the prong and held in place by bending the end of the nail or strip or by screwing a nut on the bolt.

The anchors are used singly to fasten individual objects and in groups to fasten furring strips or rigid insulation boards. The prongs are made in lengths up to 7 in.

FASTENERS FOR NEW MASONRY WALLS. Since these are rarely needed by homeowners, they are not described here. However, it's well to bear in mind that many kinds of anchors designed to be embedded in masonry walls during construction are available from masonry-supplies dealers.

WHO MAKES IT

Heckman Building Products, Inc. · Expansion bolts. Joist hangers. All-purpose framing anchors. Post anchors. Post caps. Many other special fasteners.
Miracle Adhesives Corp. · Pronged anchors.

Billy Penn Corp. · Joist and beam hangers. Framing anchors.

Rawlplug Co. · Rawl plugs. Lead anchors. Plastic anchors. Lag shields. Machine-screw anchors. Machine-bolt anchors. Expansion bolts. Toggle bolts. Hollow-wall screw anchors. Hollow-wall drive anchors. Nylon anchors. Drive pins and studs. Other masonry fasteners.

Star Expansion Industries Corp. · Lead anchors. Plastic anchors. Jute-fiber anchors. Nylon anchors. Drive pins and studs. Toggle bolts. Hollow-wall screw anchors. Hollow-wall drive anchors.

Teco. · Joist and beam hangers. Strap nails. Tie plates and straps. Framing angles. All-purpose framing anchors. Post anchors. Post caps. Other special fasteners.

Tremont Nail Co. · Old-fashioned cut nails of many types from 2d to 40d.

USM Corp. · Plastic anchors. Hollow-wall screw anchors. Stud driver.

Vermont Weatherboard, Inc. Imitation hand-forged nails, 4, 6, 8, and 10d.

Vestal Manufacturing Co. · Joist hangers.

28

Adhesives

Adhesives have been used to put things together for several hundred years, but up until World War II no one thought very much about using them for anything except wood, paper, fabrics, and rubber. Today, however, the situation has changed drastically. There are adhesives for just about every material we use, and they're so strong that they are frequently used instead of nails and screws. Glue has, in fact, been improved to such an extent that the large timbers which go into the framing of houses are now sometimes made out of glued wood strips.

HOUSEHOLD GLUES. Many of the strongest adhesives are used only by manufacturers, either because they are stronger than the homeowner needs or because they can be handled only under controlled factory conditions. Even so, the adhesives now available to you through local hardware stores and building-supplies outlets make up an arsenal of highly useful fasteners.

PVA glue is also known simply as white glue because it comes out of the squeeze bottle like buttermilk, but it dries clear. It is excellent for bonding wood, and many expert cabinetmakers use nothing else. It also glues fabrics and paper. Because it is only moderately moisture-resistant, it should not be used outdoors.

Animal glue is the oldest kind of wood glue. Animal, or hide, glue is sometimes prepared by melting hard sheets of it in hot water, but prepared mixtures are easier to use. The glue is strong but becomes brittle with age. It is not water-resistant.

Casein glue, another old wood glue, is prepared by mixing a powder with water. It is strong and fairly moisture-resistant.

Urea glue also comes as a powder which is mixed with water. It has good resistance to heat but poor resistance to moisture; it is very strong. It's used on wood.

Resorcinol glue is the best adhesive for wood used outdoors—strong and resistant to water, most solvents, and mold. It comes in two parts—a purplish liquid and a powder—which are mixed together before use. When dry, the glue leaves a dark-red stain which can be removed by sanding.

Epoxy glue is the strongest of all adhesives. You can use it to bond metal, glass, ceramics, stone, leather, and some plastics. It is also useful for gluing wood, especially when the pieces don't fit together very well, but some craftsmen feel that since it does not penetrate the pores as well as other wood glues, it is not ideal for this purpose.

Epoxy is available in a variety of formulations. Some are faster-setting than others; some are more flexible than others and therefore preferable for bonding dissimilar materials. It comes either in one tube or two. The latter type is better and not as troublesome as the novice might think. You simply squeeze a ribbon from one tube (the resin) out on a piece of glass, metal, or similar smooth surface; squeeze a ribbon of the same size from the second tube (the hardener) alongside; mix them together with a knife; and spread them on the articles you want to fasten together. The edges of the articles do not have to fit perfectly because the glue is effective even when spread rather thick. Don't use clamps.

In addition to its great strength, epoxy is waterproof and heatproof.

Epoxy menders are thick, one-tube epoxy adhesives which are made for filling holes in metal and other materials but which can also be used to stick things together if necessary. The adhesives generally come mixed with powdered steel or aluminum.

Heavy rubber cements are also made for general patching purposes. But the epoxies are generally preferred since they can be filed and sanded smooth to blend into the patched material. They can then b painted.

Plastic glue is often called "clear glue" because it is transparent and colorless. It also has a fairly pungent but pleasant odor. Used on wood, glass, ceramics, and a few plastics, it has good strength and is water-resistant enough so you can mend a broken shower-stall tile with every expectation that it will stay mended.

Plastic-mending glue is also a plastic glue and closely related to the above. But its principal use is for mending plastics. It works on most of these but not on polyethylene or styrene.

Vinyl glue, another plastic glue, is particularly good for repairing articles made of vinyl and leather.

Urethane glue is much like epoxy but comes in one tube so no mixing is called for. But it is not quite as strong as epoxy; requires a thin glue line and clamping.

Rubber cement of the kind you use for mounting photos and many other purposes is not reliably strong enough for major joining operations. For these, you need a cement which is specifically labeled for use on rubber, leather, and fabrics that are bonded together or to rigid surfaces.

For the strongest bond, the cement should be applied to both surfaces and allowed to set for about five minutes before the surfaces are placed together.

Silicone adhesive can be used for many jobs that defy other adhesives because it can fill a gap ½ in. wide or more. For this reason, it is the favorite material for caulking rims of bathtubs (despite its name, bathtub caulk is silicone glue). It's also good for such jobs as stopping leaks in pipes, gluing masonry, seating drain pipes in sinks, etc. It sticks to almost everything.

The adhesive smells like vinegar; it is available in clear, white, gray, and black. As a rule, paint does not stick to it, though a few brands are paintable.

Hot-melt glue is a synthetic-resin adhesive which is put up in sticks that must be used in an electric glue gun. Because of this gadget, the glue is easy to apply but sets too rapidly to permit adjustment of surfaces which are not properly positioned in the first place. Hot-melt is used on wood, metal, leather, and some plastics.

Cyanoacrylate glue is being billed in advertising as the super glue. It is nothing of the sort. It's true that if you don't handle it with care, you may stick your fingers together, and you can also stick other materials such as glass and ceramics and wood together. But don't expect miracles.

The most interesting thing about the glue is that you need only a few drops. These are spread in such a thin layer that no glue line is visible in the articles you have joined. The only visible line is the joint itself. This makes the glue ideal for mending objects which are used for display but are not subjected to a great deal of handling.

USING HOUSEHOLD GLUES. Although almost all Americans start using glue at an early age, they don't inevitably grow into expert gluers. Gluing takes practice. But it also calls for a certain amount of direction and a lot of attention to small details.

The steps in the gluing procedure are as follows (although not always in this exact sequence):

1. Select the right adhesive. You may or may not have a choice. The type you use must be compatible with the materials being bonded. It must be able to perform in the wet or dry, hot or cold, etc. atmosphere to which the glued object will be exposed. It must produce the kind of glue line demanded by the situation; that is, if the edges of the materials cannot be perfectly joined when dry, you will need an adhesive such as epoxy that is strong even when thickly spread. On the other hand, if the edges can be perfectly joined, use an adhesive such as resorcinol that requires a thin glue line.

2. Clean the surfaces to be glued down to the base material. Remove dirt, old glue, paint, rust, etc. True enough, glue often sticks very well to paint and other materials which should be removed; but the paint, etc. may not stick to the surface underneath.

3. If gluing wood, try to shape the two pieces so they fit together perfectly. This is necessary since the best wood glues require a thin glue line.

4. Roughen the glued surfaces lightly with sandpaper or steel wool so the adhesive will grip better.

5. Apply the glue to one or both surfaces as the package directions indicate. Generally, the glue coating should be thin and even. A thick coating is permissible only when you're using epoxy or silicone glue.

6. Clamp the glued objects together (but only if a thin glue line is required) until the glue has dried for the time indicated on the package. (Allow 12 hours if no directions are given.)

Clamping can be done in several ways: (1) With clamps of the type described in the next chapter. (2) By wrapping string or wire tightly around the object. For example, when gluing rungs into chair legs, tie a heavy cord around the legs, stick a screwdriver or piece of wood between the loops, and twist the cord windlass-fashion. (3) By weighting the objects down under books, bricks, bags of sand, etc.

CONSTRUCTION ADHESIVES. Construction adhesives differ from ordinary adhesives in that they are, as a rule, thick synthetic-rubber substances which do not require a tight fit between the surfaces being glued. Most of them are water-resistant. And most come in large cans ready for application with a brush, putty knife, notched trowel, or caulking gun.

Contact cement is an extremely tenacious adhesive used most often to bond laminated plastics to plywood or particleboard to make countertops, but also used to mount plywood and hardboard panels on walls. It is also effective with metal, canvas, and leather.

The cement is difficult to use. It must be applied in a uniform coat to both surfaces and allowed to set. Then the two surfaces are pressed together and rolled. If they are not positioned perfectly, you are out of luck, because once the glue bond is made it cannot be changed.

Resilient flooring adhesives make up a variable group that includes old-fashioned linoleum cement. All the adhesives can be used with several types of flooring, but none can be used successfully with all flooring. Some dry rapidly, so you can put down only a few floor tiles at a time; some must be allowed to set for 30 minutes or so before you can lay flooring. Generally, it's best to use the type recommended by the dealer who sells the flooring.

Ceramic-tile adhesives are another variable group; you should follow the advice of the tile dealer. All the adhesives are waterproof and applied with a notched trowel. The same adhesives can usually be used to glue bricks, slates, marble, and the like to floors and walls.

Drywall adhesive is used to install gypsum board directly to studs or to a base layer of gypsum board. It is normally applied with a caulking gun.

Panel adhesive is used for applying plywood, hardboard, and particleboard panels to studs and furring strips, and for attaching panels and furring strips to masonry and gypsum-board walls. It is also used to install plywood subflooring to joists. It is applied with a tube or caulking gun.

Foamboard adhesive sticks styrene and urethane insulating boards to basement walls indoors and out. The adhesive for styrene is slightly different from that for urethane.

Ceiling-tile adhesive is a quick-setting adhesive which you can rely on to stick tiles to the ceiling as soon as they are applied and for a long time afterward.

Carpet adhesives are designed for putting down certain types of carpet and carpet tile (read the label carefully to make sure the type you buy will work on the carpet you're laying). Some, unfortunately, stick so tight that you cannot take up the carpet without ruining it; it's best to look for a "releasable" adhesive.

ADHESIVE TAPES. For years there were only a few kinds of sticky tape. Now there are super tapes for every imaginable job. A number are of special interest to the homeowner:

Electrical tape is made of black plastic for insulating wires.

Double-faced carpet tape with adhesive on both sides is used for anchoring carpets. It can also be used for temporary fastening of loose tiles, etc.

Duct tape is made of a sturdy fabric for sealing joints in heating and air-conditioning ducts.

Aluminum tape is made of thin aluminum backed with adhesive. It is used for patching holes in gutters, leaders, ducts, etc.

Neoprene-foam tape is used for emergency weatherstripping and also to cushion one surface against another and to hang acrylic mirrors.

WHO MAKES IT

Borden, Inc., Borden Chemical Div. · Elmer's PVA glue. Plastic glue. Contact cement. Fabric glue. Epoxy glue. Casein glue. Resorcinol glue. Panel adhesive. Aerosol pressure-sensitive glue. Mystik electrical tape. Double-faced carpet tape. Duct tape. Aluminum tape.

Contech, Inc. · Panel adhesive.

DAP, Inc. · Duratite PVA glue. Contact cement. Panel adhesive.

Darworth Co. · Panel adhesive.

Dow Corning Corp. · Urethane glue.

H. B. Fuller Co. · Contact cement. Panel adhesive. Drywall adhesive. Foamboard adhesive. Hardboard adhesive. Carpet adhesives.

General Electric Co., Silicone Products Dept. · Silicone glue.

Georgia-Pacific Corp. · Drywall adhesive.

Gibson-Homans Co. · Panel adhesive.

Miracle Adhesives Corp. · Epoxy glues. Plastic glue. Contact cement. Silicone rubber mastic adhesives for general-purpose gluing. Panel adhesive. Foamboard adhesive. Carpet adhesive. Drywall adhesive.

National Gypsum Co. · Drywall adhesive.

Pierce & Stevens Chemical Corp. · Hybond panel adhesive. Contact cement.

W. J. Ruscoe Co. · Pliobond rubber cement. Contact cement. Aerosol rubber adhesive. Epoxy glue. Panel adhesive.

SCM Corp., Macco Adhesive Div. · Panel adhesive. Foamboard adhesive. Acoustical-tile adhesive. Contact cement.

Thermwell Products Co. · Duct tape. Electrical tape. Stainless-steel adhesive tape.

3M Co. · Scotch epoxy glue. Contact cement. Aerosol general-purpose glue. Panel adhesive. Duct tape. General-purpose cloth tape. Electrical tape. Double-faced carpet tape.

United States Gypsum Co. · Drywall adhesive.

USM Corp. · Hot-melt electric glue gun.

U.S. Plywood. · Panel adhesive.

Woodcraft Supply Corp. · Animal glue. PVA glue. Electric glue pot.

Woodhill Chemical Sales Corp. · Cyanoacrylate glue.

29

Tools

Tools make the handyman. You can't build, repair, or maintain your home without them. Only a few tools are essential, however. Reduced to a bare minimum, these include a claw hammer, nailset, screwdriver, crosscut saw, wood chisel, cold chisel, block plane, pocket knife, razor blades, sharpening stone, file, electric drill, awl, slip-joint pliers, needle-nose pliers, wire snips, crescent wrench, putty knife, C clamps, combination square, and rule.

All others can be added as the need arises. Some are so rarely used or so expensive that it makes better sense in the long run to rent them.

Here, then, is the first rule to follow in acquiring tools: Don't overstock.

The second rule is to buy quality tools. To be sure, tiptop quality is not essential in some basically simple, low-cost tools such as screwdrivers and putty knives. But in the more complex, high-cost tools, it is. Top-quality tools not only last for years—often a lifetime—but they are also much easier to work with and actually do a better job than cheap tools.

Although the tools described below are primarily used by carpenters, some of the special forms are also used—or used exclusively—by other trades.

GENERAL-PURPOSE TOOLS

AWLS. You can use an icepick for an awl. The true awl is somewhat shorter and thicker. It is used for making holes for screws and marking lines on wood.

BEVELS. Used for marking angles, a bevel consists of an adjustable blade screwed to a handle.

BIT BRACES. There is relatively little need for a bit brace if you have an electric drill, but you will find yourself reaching for it from time to time—especially when boring large-diameter holes or long holes through the house framing, etc. A brace has a large chuck in which the drill bit is clamped, and a U-shaped sweep handle for turning the bit. A good brace should also have a ratchet so you can drive the bit into wood even when working in a tight place where you cannot turn the handle in a complete circle.

BIT GAUGES. A bit gauge is an adjustable device which clamps onto an auger bit to control the depth of the hole being drilled.

BITS. Bits are the actual drilling tip of a bit brace or electric drill. There are many types.

Auger bits have a small, sharp screw centered in the tip between two cutting spurs. The end of the shank is four-sided and tapered so it is held firmly in the chuck of the brace. The bits are made in diameters from $\frac{1}{4}$ to $1\frac{1}{2}$ in. The size is stamped in the tapered end and is stated in 16ths of an inch. Thus a drill stamped with the number 8 is $\frac{8}{16}$ or $\frac{1}{2}$ in. in diameter; one stamped with 20 is $\frac{20}{16}$ or $1\frac{1}{4}$ in. in diameter.

The overall length of standard auger bits ranges from $7\frac{1}{2}$ to $9\frac{1}{2}$ in., depending on the diameter. Longer bits are made for electricians and other trades. Very long bits are used in electric drills.

Expansive bits are used in bit braces to drill holes beyond the size range of regular auger bits. The cutting head is adjusted with a screwdriver. Each bit comes with two adjustable cutters. With a small bit you can drill holes from $\frac{5}{8}$ to $1\frac{3}{4}$ in. in diameter; with a large bit, you can drill holes from $\frac{7}{8}$ to 3 in. in diameter.

Electric-drill bits of the type most often used are called twist drills. They are short and rod-shaped, available for drilling holes from $\frac{1}{16}$ to 1 in. in diameter. All sizes can be used in drills with $\frac{1}{2}$-in. chucks, but the maximum diameter of the bits suitable for $\frac{1}{4}$-

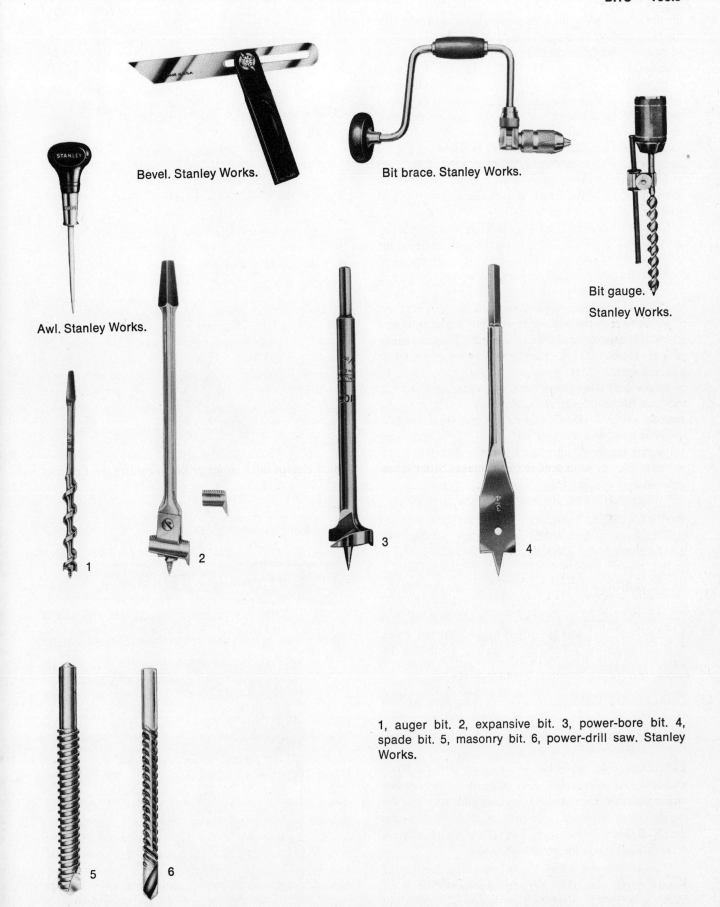

Bevel. Stanley Works.

Bit brace. Stanley Works.

Bit gauge.
Stanley Works.

Awl. Stanley Works.

1

2

3

4

1, auger bit. 2, expansive bit. 3, power-bore bit. 4,
spade bit. 5, masonry bit. 6, power-drill saw. Stanley
Works.

5

6

in. drills is only ½ in. (see power tools, below). Bits made of carbon steel can be used in wood only. Those of heat-treated high-speed steel are used in both wood and metal.

Power-bore bits used in ¼-in. electric drills bore holes ⅜ to 1½ in. in diameter. They have a flat, horizontal cutting head with a sharp point, and are designed especially for precision work.

Spade bits also allow you to drill holes up to 1½ in. in diameter with an electric drill. At the cutting end, the bits are shaped like a spade with a sharp point. They are suitable only for rough work because they tend to splinter wood if not used carefully.

Countersinks are electric-drill bits which simultaneously drill a pilot hole for a screw shank and a larger hole for the screw head. Countersink-counterbores go one step further and drill a hole for a wood plug as well as a screw. They are most often used for putting down pegged wood floors.

Masonry bits used in electric drills have carbide tips for fast boring into concrete, brick, etc. They are made in sizes from ³⁄₁₆ to ¾ in. The largest sizes fit only in ½-in. chucks.

Power-drill saws are electric-drill bits used to drill, cut, and shape holes in wood and plastics. There is only one size.

Bit extensions are straight 12-in. or 18-in. rods used to extend the length of bits so you can drill into hard-to-reach places. One kind fits a bit brace, another an electric drill.

BUTT GAUGES. These are used to mark the position and thickness of butt hinges on doors and jambs. They can be used with hinges of any size.

BUTT MARKERS. Butt markers are inexpensive devices for marking and actually cutting the outline of a mortise for a door hinge. They are made in three sizes for 3-in., 3½-in., and 4-in. butt hinges. To use them, you just lay them on the door edge or jamb and hit them with a hammer.

CHALK-LINE REELS. Used for marking long straight lines, chalk-line reels contain a cord which is automatically coated with blue chalk when it is pulled out.

CHISELS. Wood chisels have a sharp beveled blade attached to a wood, plastic, or sometimes steel handle. They are used for cutting holes and mortises and for paring off wood when there isn't space to work with a plane. Blades are from ⅛ to 2 in. wide. A chisel with a ¾-in. blade is good for general purposes.

Cold chisels are made of hardened steel for cutting masonry and metal. The blade is beveled on both sides, and is available in ¼-in. to 1-in. widths. A number of

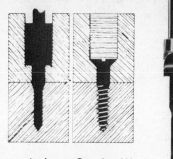

Countersink-counterbore. Stanley Works.

Butt marker. Stanley Works.

Chalk-line reel. Stanley Works.

Wood chisel, above; cold chisel, below. Stanley Works.

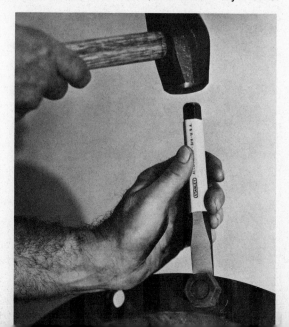

C clamps with unusually deep throats.

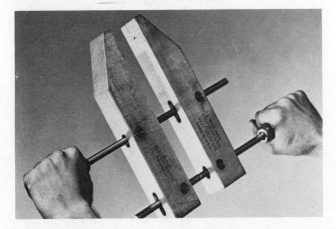
Hand screw.

Bar clamps.

Web clamp. Adjustable Clamp Co.

cold chisels with specially shaped blades are also made. One for which a do-it-yourselfer has some need is a brick chisel with a 3-in. to 4-in. cutting edge.

CLAMPS. Clamps are essential to most gluing operations and are also used for holding pieces of material together while you work on them. The most common type is called a C clamp because of its shape. It contains a threaded bolt with a handle to bring the glued pieces together and exert pressure on them until the glue dries. The clamps are available in several sizes.

Spring clamps resemble pliers with the jaws held closed by a spring in the joint. They are useful for clamping objects together quickly because they can be used with one hand, but they do not exert as much pressure as a C clamp.

Hand screws are large clamps with two parallel jaws of hardwood which are screwed together by a pair of bolts. Because the bolts are adjusted separately, the clamps can be used on nonparallel as well as parallel surfaces.

Bar clamps are large devices used to glue boards edge to edge. One jaw is secured to the end of a 6-ft. bar of steel; the other jaw, with an adjustable screw, slides along the bar.

Web clamps are used to hold round and irregular shapes under even pressure. They consist of a 12-ft. belt of nylon which is looped through a steel "buckle" with a ratchet for tightening the belt.

Band clamps are similar to web clamps but incorporate a steel strap rather than nylon webbing and are tightened with a screwdriver. They are suitable for clamping round and oval work only.

Corner clamps are right-angle devices used for clamping the corners of furniture frames, picture frames, chests, and the like.

DIVIDERS. The usual pair of dividers has two pointed legs which are pivoted below the handle and adjusted by a bow-shaped arm. They are used for making measurements and scribing. Angle dividers have two folding, adjustable arms attached to a center piece. They are used to bisect angles.

DOWELING JIGS. One of the neatest ways to fasten things together securely is with dowels, but if both ends of a dowel are concealed, it is virtually impossible to make the holes in the two pieces being joined line up precisely unless you have a doweling jig. The jig not only positions the holes but serves as the guide for the auger bit when you drill the holes.

DRAWKNIVES. The drawknife is used for taking a board down to a rough line when you don't want to use a rip saw. It has a long sturdy blade with handles set at right angles to both ends. The knife is pulled toward you.

DRILL GUIDES. These are used for holding drill bits when you're boring holes up to ¼-in. in diameter. They prevent the bit from straying off the mark and hold it straight while it turns.

FILES. Files are used primarily for sharpening tools and shaping metal but are also used for shaping wood. Made in 4-in. to 14-in. lengths, they are flat, half-round, round, triangular, or square. In single-cut files, the cutting teeth are arranged diagonally to the sides of the file in closely spaced parallel lines. Double-cut files have two sets of teeth which cross.

The speed with which a file cuts depends on the coarseness of the teeth. A coarse file has the coarsest teeth; a smooth file, the finest. A bastard file is moderately coarse; a second file, moderately smooth.

Files come without handles but have slender tangs for insertion in wood handles.

HAMMERS. In a carpenter's hammer—the only type most homeowners need—the head has a more or less flat, round face for driving nails and a claw for pulling nails. The handle is made of wood, steel, or fiberglass.

There are four points to consider when buying a hammer:

The composition of the handle is least important. One material is as easy to work with as another. Wood handles, however, may split.

For inexperienced handymen, the hammer head should be bell-faced—slightly convex so you can drive a nail flush without denting the surrounding surface. Plain-faced hammers have a flat striking surface and should be used for rough work only. Grooved faces (called checker faces) should be avoided, for although they do not slip off a nail as easily as a polished face, they leave cross-hatched marks in wood.

Claws are either curved or straight. The curved design is better for pulling nails. A straight claw also pulls nails but is meant primarily for ripping things apart.

A hammer should weigh between 12 and 16 oz. Lighter hammers are of little value for driving most nails. Hammers weighing 20 oz. or more are too heavy for most people to wield.

Ball-peen hammers used in metalworking have a conventional flat face and a round face instead of a claw.

Other special hammers are made for bricklayers, riveters, tinners, blacksmiths, etc.

HAND DRILLS. You probably will not use a hand drill often if you have an electric drill. This is especially true of the conventional hand drill in which the bit is turned by rotating a cogged wheel. A push drill is more useful because it can be worked in places into which you cannot get an electric drill and is operated by one hand. It's a handy tool to have when you install hinges

Doweling jig. Stanley Works.

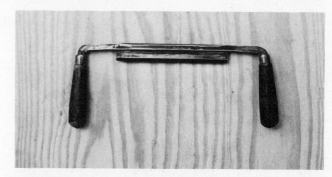

Drawknife.

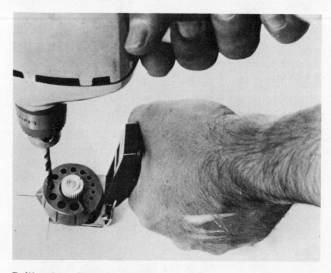

Drill guide. Stanley Works.

Single-cut file, top, and double-cut file, center, are both flat files. The half-round tool at the bottom is not a true file but a rasp, used only on wood.

on a door. The bit is turned by pumping the handle up and down.

HATCHETS. A hatchet is a hammer with a more or less triangular or rectangular cutting blade in place of a claw. In many cases, the blade has a slot for pulling nails.

Hatchets are used primarily for laying wood shingles. They are also useful for rough-shaping wood and cutting stakes if you don't have an ax.

JOINT KNIVES. Also called broad knives, these are oversized wall scrapers or putty knives with flexible blades. They're made for applying gypsum-board joint compound to newly taped gypsum-board walls, but are excellent for large wall-patching jobs as well. Professionals use knives of various widths up to 12 in. The do-it-yourselfer can get by well enough with a 4-in. and 6-in. knife.

LEVELS. A level is used to determine whether a surface is absolutely level or plumb. It is a rectangular wood or aluminum tool measuring 9, 12, 18, 24, 28, 48, 72, or 78 in. long. In the simplest levels, a glass vial filled with alcohol is set in the middle of one of the long edges, and a second vial is set in a round hole at one end. Larger levels have several vials. A bubble in the alcohol indicates when a surface is level or plumb.

Small pocket levels are available for determining horizontals only. A similar level with hooks in the end is hung on a cord to establish a level line between two widely separated points. This is called a line level.

MARKING GAUGES. The marking gauge is a form of rule used for marking lumber for cutting. For example, if you want to rip a wide board to a 5-in. width, you set the sliding head on the inch-marked arm, lay the gauge across the board, and draw it along the edge of the board from end to end. As you do so, a prong in the end of the arm scratches a line into the board.

MITER BOXES. Cutting wood to a precise angle calls for a miter box which holds the saw at the desired angle and straight up and down. An elaborate box can be set at any angle from 0° to 90°. Less expensive boxes—which are satisfactory for most purposes—can be set only at 90° and 45° and perhaps also at 30° and 60°.

NAILSETS. A nailset is like a short steel pencil with a tiny cup in the point. It is used for countersinking nails. Tip sizes range from 1/32 to 5/32 in. in diameter.

A self-centering nailset is used for setting nails without marring the surface. The set consists of a cylinder with a spring-actuated pin which is struck with a hammer.

Steel-handled hammer with curved claw, above.

Fiberglass-handled ripping hammer with straight claw, center; ball-peen hammer with fiberglass handle, below. Stanley Works.

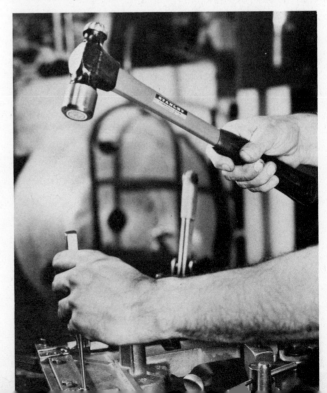

Push drill. Stanley Works.

Marking gauge. Stanley Works.

A simple miter box. Stanley Works.

Joint knife with 10-in. blade. The knives are available in widths down to 4 in. Red Devil, Inc.

A small level. Stanley Works.

Nailset. Stanley Works.

PLANES. Conventional planes are used for taking down and smoothing wood; special types are used for rabbeting, routing, and other shaping.

Block planes are the most useful type for the handyman, since they can be used in one hand to smooth wood with as well as across the grain and can be worked into tight spots. They are 6 or 7 in. long and have a cutting edge, known as the plane iron, 1⅝ in. wide.

Trimming planes are simplified block planes only 3 in. long and 1 in. wide. They are useful mainly for rounding edges.

Jack planes are the best type for cutting wood with the grain because they ride over uneven spots instead of

Block plane, above; smooth plane, below. Stanley Works.

Slip-joint pliers. Stanley Works.

following the surface. Two hands are usually required for operation. The planes are 14 to 15 in. long and have a 2-in. plane iron.

Other varieties of jack plane are the junior jack ($11\frac{1}{2}$ in. long with $1\frac{3}{4}$-in. plane iron), smooth plane (8 or 9 in. long with $1\frac{3}{4}$-in. plane iron), fore plane (18 in. long with $2\frac{3}{8}$-in. plane iron), and jointer plane (22 in. long with $2\frac{3}{8}$-in. plane iron).

Rabbet planes are constructed in several ways and used for cutting rabbets in the edges of boards. Blade width ranges from $\frac{1}{2}$ to $1\frac{1}{2}$ in.

Router planes remove the wood from dadoes and grooves after the sides have been cut with a saw. There are two types. The larger comes with three interchangeable blades.

Plow planes are used for making grooves in uncut wood. They hold blades of several widths.

Circular planes are designed for shaping wood to convex or concave contours. The bottom of the plane is made of flexible steel so it can be precisely adjusted to the desired contour. The cutter is $1\frac{3}{4}$ in. wide.

PLIERS. The jaws of this gripping and turning tool are shaped in various ways. Some open straight ahead like scissors, others to the side. Some are short and oval-shaped, others have long needle noses that reach into tight spots. Some can open so wide and no more; the most useful have a slip joint so they will fit around a nut or pipe 2 in. across.

Combination pliers, or plier-wrenches, can be used as pliers or locked onto an object like a pipe wrench.

PLUMB BOBS. The easiest way to establish a precise vertical line is to drop a line with a plumb bob tied to the end. This is a heavy, round arrowhead with a hole through which the line is threaded so the bob always hangs straight.

PRY BARS. Pry bars used for prying and wedging wood are straight or, more commonly, bent lengths of forged steel. One or both ends are chisel-shaped. The ends may also incorporate a slotted claw for pulling nails. In addition, flat bars contain a tear-drop slot for pulling nails.

PUNCHES. Punches are used to make small holes in the surface of wood, metal, and other materials. They are made either of one piece of steel with a long tapered tip or of two pieces with a straight tip.

Self-centering punches consisting of a loose pin held in a cylinder are used to make pilot holes for screws exactly in the center of the screw holes in hinges, strikes, etc. The cylinder centers the pin in the screw holes.

PUTTY KNIVES. This simple tool with a thin $1\frac{1}{4}$- or $1\frac{1}{2}$-in.-wide blade is a must in every tool box. You'll need it not only for setting window panes but also for

Plumb bobs. Stanley Works.

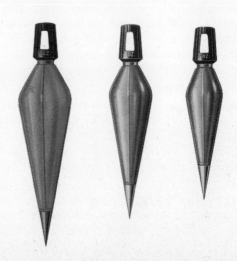

Three kinds of punch. Stanley Works.

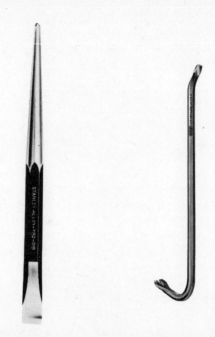

Pry bar, left. Ripping bar, right. Stanley Works.

Tape rule, top; folding rule, center; caliper rule, bottom. Stanley Works.

filling holes and scraping loose paint, glue, etc. The knife blade should be flexible but not so flexible that it bows like cardboard when pressure is exerted on it, and it should be riveted into the handle.

RASPS. A rasp is a file made specifically for shaping wood. It has coarse, triangular teeth in closely spaced rows; it is usually flat on one side, oval on the other.

RIPPING BARS. A ripping bar is used mainly to tear things apart but comes in handy for wedging boards and timbers into place. It is a one-piece tool of forged steel with a slightly bent chisel blade in one end, a gooseneck with a claw for pulling spikes in the other end. Lengths range from 12 to 36 in.

RULES. For making measurements, you can use a folding wood rule, a steel tape rule, or both. Folding rules come in 6-ft. and 8-ft. lengths, and because of their relative rigidity, do not have to be laid on something when you make horizontal measurements. Some rules have a small extension rule which slides out of one end to permit making accurate measurements inside doorways, windows, boxes, etc.

Tape rules are 6 to 25 ft. long and roll up into a compact case. Unlike wood rules, they're unbreakable, but they must be supported for horizontal measurements.

Bench rules are one-piece wood or metal rules 1 or 2 ft. long.

Caliper rules are 4-in. rules with clamplike jaws which are placed around pipes and other cylindrical or irregular objects to measure their outside diameter.

Prongs on the ends of the jaws are used to make inside measurements.

SAWS. A beginning do-it-yourselfer with a limited budget should start out with a crosscut saw, which is used for cutting lumber across the grain and, in a pinch, with the grain. This kind of saw is made in 20-in. to 28-in. lengths (a 26-incher is best for general purposes) and with 8, 10, or 11 teeth to the inch (the first is best for general purposes). Some models are Teflon-coated to reduce binding and maintenance, but it is more important to select a saw which (1) is slightly thicker along the smooth top edge than at the toothed edge and (2) snaps back into a straight line when bent double.

Rip saws for cutting lumber with the grain have 5½ teeth to the inch and are 26 in. long.

A back saw has a rectangular blade which is reinforced along the back edge so it cannot bend. Used with a miter box to cut angles, it has 11 to 14 teeth per inch and comes in 12-in. and 28-in. lengths.

Dovetail saws are miniature back saws with very thin blades for cutting smooth narrow kerfs.

Compass, or keyhole, saws have narrow, wedge-shaped blades so they can be inserted through a hole drilled in a surface and used to make an inside cutout. Wallboard saws are similar but have a straight rather than a hooked handle. The tip of the blade is sharpened so it can be jabbed through gypsum or insulating board to start a cut. Both saws have coarse teeth. The blades are 10 to 14 in. long.

A coping saw consists of a slender, U-shaped frame into which a tiny, fine-toothed blade is clamped to cut wood into round or intricate shapes. The frames are either 4¾ or 6¾ in. deep.

Hacksaws used for cutting metal also have a U-shaped frame holding a ribbonlike blade. The frames can be extended to hold 8-in., 10-in., or 12-in. blades.

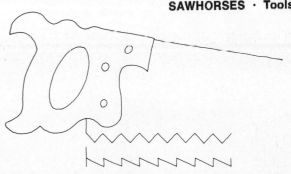

Teeth of a crosscut saw (top); ripsaw (bottom).

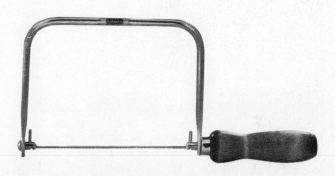

Coping saw, above; hacksaw, below. Stanley Works.

Back saw, above; compass saw, below. Stanley Works.

SAWHORSES. Building a sawhorse takes but a few minutes if you use steel sawhorse brackets. Just cut the legs and rail to the desired lengths, slip them into the brackets, and fasten with nails. Some brackets fold so you can quickly dismantle a sawhorse for storage in a small space.

Sawhorse brackets. Dalton Manufacturing Co.

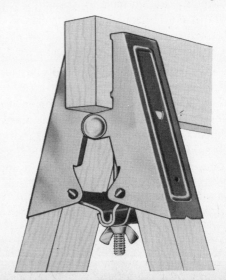

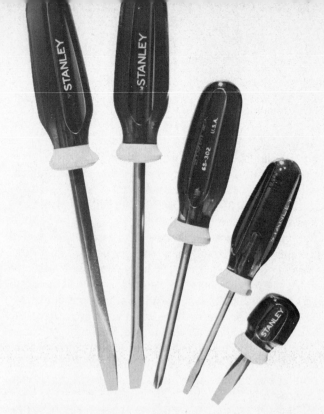

Hand scraper. Red Devil, Inc.

SCRAPERS. Unless you go in for cabinetmaking, you need only two kinds of scraper. A hand scraper is a pull tool with a sharp blade in the end for taking down wood and scraping off paint. In the most common design, the blade is clamped in the end of the handle. In another design, a triangular blade with three cutting edges is permanently fixed to the handle.

Wall scrapers are shaped like triangular putty knives. The stiff blade is designed to remove paint and wallpaper.

A cabinet scraper has two earlike handles on either side of a clamp into which a big, rectangular blade is inserted. It is used for smoothing wood.

SCREWDRIVERS. There are screwdrivers and screwdrivers, and with only two exceptions all are alike. The basic differences are in their overall length and width and shape of blade.

In the standard screwdriver, the blade flares out just above the tip. The tips range from $7/32$ to $3/8$ in. in width. In cabinet-tipped screwdrivers, the blade is the same diameter from end to end so it can be worked into tight spots. The narrowest tip is only .06 in. wide; the widest, $3/16$ in.

Screwdrivers with cabinet tips have long blades, as do the majority of standard screwdrivers. Some standard screwdrivers, however, are stubby tools measuring less than 4 in. from end to end.

Phillips screwdrivers have star-shaped points to fit Phillips-head screws. The blades are the same diameter throughout their length. Stubby as well as normal-length models are available.

In offset screwdrivers the blade tip is at right angles to the handle so you can turn a screw in the side of an electric outlet box or in other confined situations.

Ratchet screwdrivers with interchangeable screw-

Two standard screwdrivers, left; Phillips screwdriver, center; cabinet-tipped screwdriver, second from right; stubby screwdriver, right. Stanley Works.

driver bits are time- and labor-savers when a great many screws are to be driven. They can be adjusted for right- or left-hand drive. In standard models, the handle is returned manually to its driving position. Quick-return models incorporate a spring which returns the handle automatically.

SHARPENING STONES. A tool chest without a sharpening stone is about as useless as a rake without a handle. Buy a 2×7-in. stone with a coarse grit on one

Ratchet screwdriver, left; offset screwdriver, right. Stanley Works.

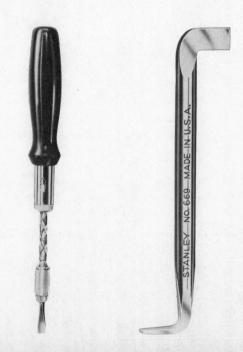

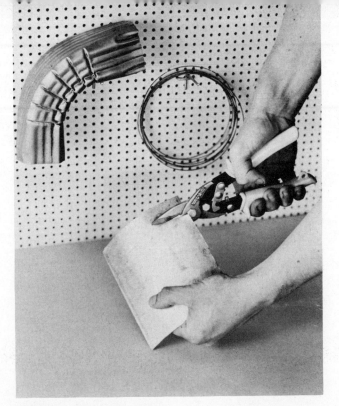

Snips. J. Wiss & Sons Co.

side, fine grit on the other. Coat both sides with No. 30 engine oil before using.

SNIPS. Snips are metal-cutting scissors. Those with duckbill cutting edges are used to make inside, circular, and irregular cuts. Straight-pattern snips make straight cuts. Aviation snips with compound leverage are designed for straight cuts, right-hand curves, or left-hand curves.

Wire snips have small jaws and are used only for cutting wires.

SPOKESHAVES. Resembling a bird in flight, a spokeshave is used for planing wood, primarily to special shapes. The wood is clamped in a vise and the spokeshave is either pulled toward the worker or pushed away from him.

SQUARES. Next to a rule, a square is the most important tool for measuring and is necessary for marking materials to be cut at 90° angles. For major construction jobs, the carpenter's framing square is almost essential. It is a large, flat, L-shaped steel or aluminum device with a 16-in. blade, called the tongue, and a 24-

Spokeshave. Stanley Works.

in. blade, called the body. The blades are not only marked off in fractions of an inch but are also stamped with tables which tell the professional carpenter at a glance how to mark angles, cut rafters, measure lumber, etc. Smaller squares without tables are also made.

A second extremely useful square is a combination square with a handle which slides along the blade. With it you can mark 45° as well as 90° angles, and gauge the depth of holes. Some models incorporate a spirit level for checking horizontals and verticals.

Try squares have 6-in. to 12-in. blades and thick handles. The tool saves time in measuring and marking boards because when the edge of the handle is pressed against the edge of a board, the board is instantly ready for marking to a 90° angle. There is no need to line the handle up with the edge of the board as with a framing square. The square is also used for rapidly checking the squareness of lumber.

Top, framing square. Center, combination square. Bottom, try square. Stanley Works.

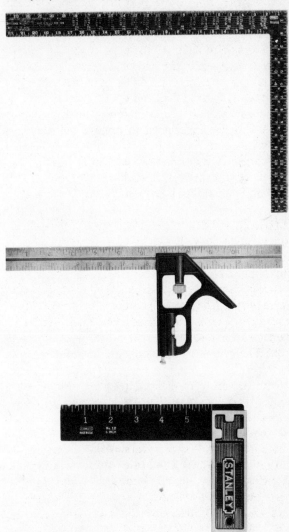

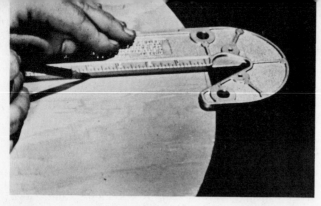
Center square. Stanley Works.

Hook-shaped center squares are used to locate the center of a circle and to find any angle.

STAPLERS. The handyman's stapler is used for fastening thin materials such as vapor barriers to wood. It works like an office stapler and drives similar staples of heavier gauge. To use the tool, hold it flat against the surface and squeeze the handle.

Stapler. Arrow Fastener Co.

Surform tools are made in several forms but all have a cheese-grater-like cutting blade that is excellent for taking down, smoothing and shaping wood and other materials. Stanley Works.

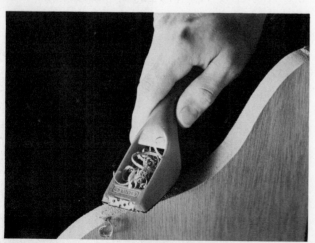

SURFORM TOOLS. This new kind of tool has a cutting blade with hundreds of tiny, sharp cutting edges like those in a kitchen grater. It is excellent for shaving down and shaping wood and plastic. Thus it takes the place of a rasp or plane.

The tools are shaped in several ways. Some have a general resemblance to a plane and are used with one or two hands in much the same fashion. Another is like a rasp with a slightly offset handle. A third is a round rasp. A fourth, resembling a cheese scoop, works on a pull stroke. A 2-in.-diameter drum-type tool is made for use in an electric drill.

Except for the drum tool, the cutting blades for all Surform tools are replaceable.

TRAMMEL POINTS. Trammel points solve the problem of how to draw circles which are too large for an ordinary compass. The points are attached in pairs to the side of a straight stick or metal bar. One point is placed at the center of a circle; the other is swung around to mark the circle edges.

UTILITY KNIVES. A utility knife contains a stout, replaceable triangular razor blade in the end of a light-weight aluminum handle. In most knives, the blade projects about an inch and withdraws into the handle when not being used. The knives are used principally for cutting soft materials such as gypsum board and carpets.

VISES. A vise is used to hold a board or other piece of material firmly while you work on it. If you have a workbench, buy a large woodworker's vise which is fastened under the bench with the top edges of the jaws level with the work surface. The jaws can be opened as much as 12 in.

Other vises are clamped or permanently screwed to the top of a workbench. Those made specifically for

Trammel points. Stanley Works.

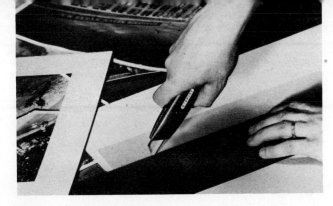

Utility knife. Stanley Works.

Adjustable angle wrench, above; set of open-end wrenches, below. Stanley Works.

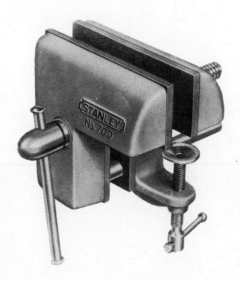

This woodworker's vise clamps to top of workbench. Stanley Works.

woodworking have oversized jaw faces so they grip wood tightly without marring the surface. Vises with small jaw faces are best for metal work.

WRENCHES. Wrenches made for grasping and turning nuts and bolts, pipe fittings, etc.—the most common type—have U-shaped heads with smooth jaws. In a monkey wrench, the jaws are at right angles to the handle and, depending on the size of the wrench, can be opened to a width of 6 in. The wrench is used mainly in plumbing work. In an adjustable angle wrench the jaws are set at about a 15° angle to the handle and have a maximum opening of 1 in. Rigid open-end wrenches are one-piece tools with jaws set at a slight angle to both ends of the handle. Made in graduated sizes for turning nuts up to 1 in. wide, the wrenches do not slip off a nut as readily as an adjustable wrench, but you need a set of five or six to turn nuts of different sizes.

Pipe wrenches—also called Stillson wrenches—have serrated jaws which firmly grip plumbing and heating pipes. They are essential in the installation and repair of piping systems made of brass or steel but are not

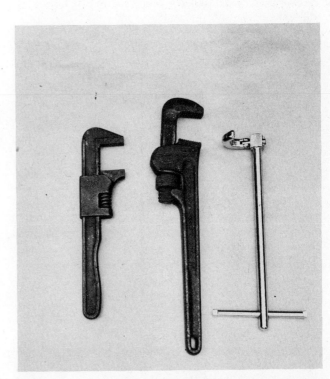

Monkey wrench, pipe wrench, and basin wrench, left to right.

needed for copper pipes. For home use, a wrench with jaws which open to a width of 3 in. is more than adequate, but much larger wrenches are made.

Basin wrenches are needed for installing kitchen sinks and lavatories because they reach up into the confined space behind the bowl so you can turn the nuts tying the faucets to the supply lines. The jaws are toothed and can be adjusted for right- and left-hand turns.

Allen wrenches are small, one-piece, L-shaped, hexagonal rods. (They are also called hex wrenches.) Without them, you are powerless to remove the tiny set screws with hexagonal openings that are used in door

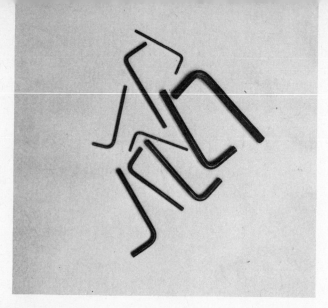

Allen wrenches.

knobs, plumbing fittings, etc. Buy a set of wrenches of different sizes.

SPECIAL-PURPOSE TOOLS

Unless you get into some extraordinarily extensive, complicated projects, you probably will never need any more special-purpose tools than those described below. There are, however, a great many more.

PROPANE TORCHES. Propane torches have generally replaced blowtorches because they are much less troublesome. The torch consists of a nozzle with a thumb screw for adjusting the flame. This is screwed into the end of a replaceable fuel canister. For most purposes, a cylindrical nozzle with a ½-in. opening is all you need. Special nozzles are available. Use the torch for soldering and burning off paint.

Propane torch.

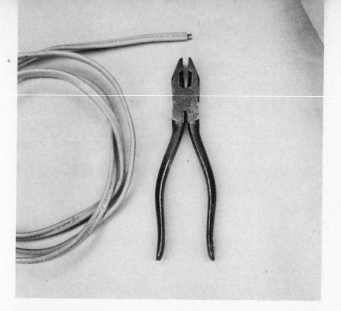

Lineman's pliers.

LINEMAN'S PLIERS. These are heavy-duty pliers for cutting wires (especially large wires) and for many twisting and turning operations; but because the jaws do not open very wide, they don't completely replace the slip-joint pliers described above.

MASON'S TROWELS. A flat more or less diamond-shaped mason's trowel is required for almost all masonry work, such as buttering bricks with concrete, slushing joints, and smoothing concrete.

POINTING TROWELS. The pointing trowel is a small mason's trowel made specifically for filling masonry joints. It's easier to use for this purpose than a large trowel because it has a thinner, slightly flexible blade.

ADHESIVE SPREADERS. An adhesive spreader is a flat, 12-in.-wide steel tool with a handle. The edge of the blade is notched for applying flooring, wallboard, and ceramic-tile adhesive in evenly spaced beads across a large surface. The most useful type of spreader is a rectangle with L-shaped handle. One side and end are notched; the other side and end are smooth. The

Mason's trowel.

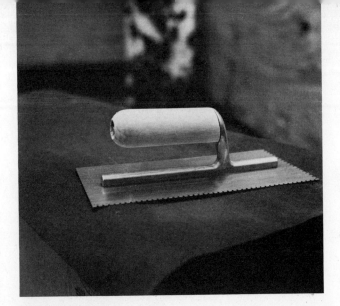

Adhesive spreader.

smooth edges are used for applying skim coats of adhesive, gypsum-board joint compound, and plaster.

GLASS CUTTERS. These are pencil-size steel tools with a tiny revolving cutting wheel in one end and notches in the side. They are used for cutting ceramic tiles as well as glass. With the notches you can grasp a strip of glass and break it off from the main piece.

WINDOW-WASHER'S SQUEEGEES. The best tool for washing windows, the squeegee is also used for grouting ceramic-tile walls.

LINOLEUM KNIVES. The linoleum knife has a semi-hook-shaped blade with a sharp point which simplifies cutting resilient flooring, asphalt roofing, and insulation board.

WALLPAPER SCRAPERS. No other tool removes

Glass cutter. Red Devil, Inc.

Wallpaper scraper. Red Devil, Inc.

wallpaper as easily as this tool. All you have to do is work it under an edge of the paper and push. The paper comes off in long strips. Since there is usually no need for wetting the paper, there is relatively little mess.

The scraper has a long rigid handle with a head set at an angle. A stout, razor-sharp, replaceable blade is clamped in the head.

WALLPAPERING BRUSHES. You need two types: a 10-in. or 12-in. paste brush with a long handle for applying paste to wallpaper and a 12-in. smoothing brush with short bristles for smoothing the paper on the wall.

SEAM ROLLERS. These are used for pressing down the edges of wallpaper strips. They're made of wood or plastic. A 1¼-in. width is adequate.

PAINT BRUSHES AND ROLLERS. See Chapter 7.

RAZOR BLADES. Single-edge razor blades purchased in boxes of 100 from paint and wallpaper stores are among the most useful tools in any chest. Use them for cutting wallpaper, scraping paint off windows, etc.

POWER TOOLS

Of the many electric tools made, only the portable hand tools are of real value for work around the house. And of these, the electric drill is the only one that ranks with hammers, saws, and screwdrivers as essential.

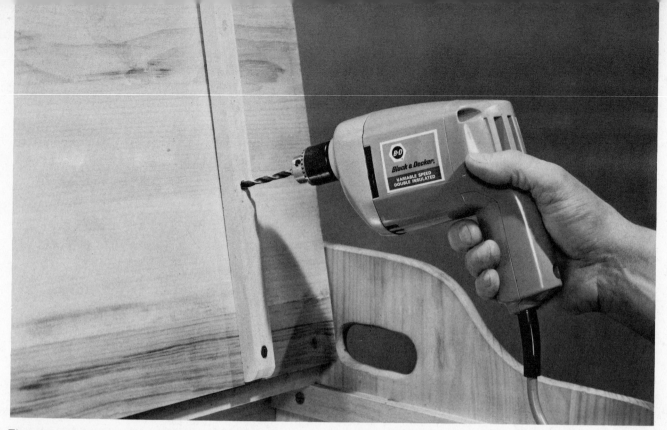

Electric drill. Black & Decker Manufacturing Co.

ELECTRIC DRILLS. Drills are categorized by the size of the chuck in which the bits are clamped. The ¼-in. drill is the most common and is more than adequate for most handyman purposes, but the bits you can use in it are limited to those with ¼-in. or smaller shanks. The largest conventional bit bores a ½-in. hole. The drills operate at high speeds.

The ⅜-in. drill accepts bits up to ⅜ in. in diameter. The largest bores a 1 in. hole. The drills run at approximately half the speed of ¼-in. drills and therefore have more power and can be used for longer periods in metals and masonry.

The ½-in drill operates at still slower speeds and is used almost entirely by professionals for extensive heavy-duty work. The ½-in. chucks accept bits with shanks up to ½ in. in diameter and can therefore be used for making holes as small as those made with a ¼-in. drill up to a maximum of 1 in.

A ¼-in. drill costing as little as $12 not only is likely to perform extremely well but will also last for many years if not given prolonged hard use. More expensive drills, however, are more durable as well as more versatile. Most of these are designed to operate at two speeds or variable speeds from barely turning to full speed. Some drills also have a reversing switch for removing bits that are jammed in wood, metal, etc. and backing off screws.

Hammer drills with ¼-in. or ½-in. chucks can be used like a conventional drill for rotary drilling into wood, plywood, etc., and can also be used to hammer holes in concrete, brick and stone. When set for masonry work, the bit rotates at the same time that it pounds up and down. Thus you can drill a hole in a matter of seconds.

Cordless drills are ¼-in. models powered by a self-contained power pack which is recharged by plugging into an electric outlet. The drills not only can be used anywhere but also permit safe drilling in locations where a conventional drill might cause a shock.

All drills including cordless models can be used with an assortment of attachments for rough-sanding, polishing, and wire-brushing. In addition, variable-speed drills can be used for driving screws and making holes up to 2½ in. across with a cylindrical hole saw.

SANDERS. Four types of electric sander are made: orbital, dual-action, disk, and belt. The last two are of interest to professional craftsmen only.

Orbital and dual-action sanders are identical in appearance. They have a rectangular sanding pad measuring about 4×11 in. The motor is more or less centrally mounted above the pad and has handles at both ends so you can operate the sander with one hand or, for better sanding action, two. In the orbital sander the sandpaper clamped to the pad moves in an elliptical pattern at more than 4,000 orbits a minute. It is ideal for fine-sanding and moderate rough-sanding of all flat surfaces.

The dual-action sander can be operated in either an orbital pattern or straight back-and-forth pattern that produces the same effect as hand-sanding.

CIRCULAR SAWS. A circular saw is an extremely dangerous tool but a tremendous work-saver when you undertake extensive building projects. With it you can rip timbers and boards in a fraction of the time it takes with a hand saw, and cut large plywood panels where

Dual-action sander. Black & Decker Manufacturing Co.

you need them rather than wrestling them into the workshop. You can also, of course, save energy—if not much time—cutting lumber across the grain.

In a circular saw, the blade projects down through a flat plate called the shoe. The blade can be adjusted up and down for cutting lumber up to 2⅜ in. thick. The shoe can be tilted from side to side for angle or bevel cuts. The best models have a shoe which wraps completely around the blade so the saw is well supported and is hard to tip accidentally.

Most saws take a 7¼-in.-diameter blade. Blades are designed for general-purpose cutting or for such special jobs as cutting plywood, metal, masonry, or ceramic tile.

JIG SAWS. The electric jig saw is used to cut wood in

Circular saw. Black & Decker Manufacturing Co.

Electric jig saw. Black & Decker Manufacturing Co.

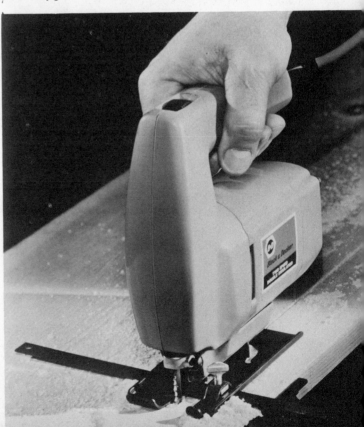

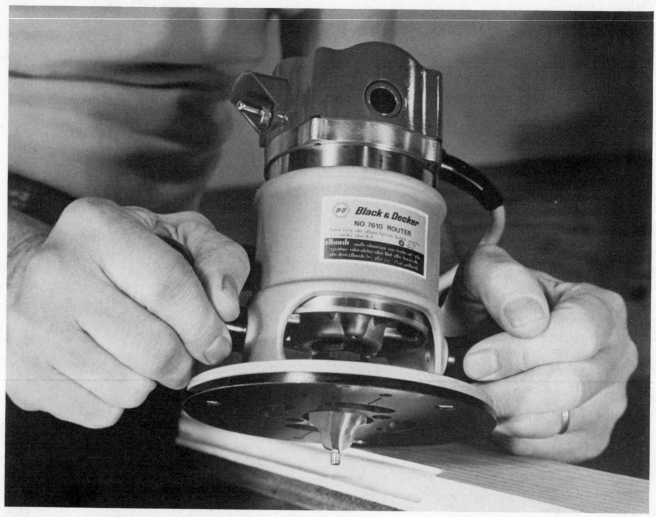

Router. Black & Decker Manufacturing Co.

a circular or irregular pattern or to make large holes in the middle of a surface. In the latter operation it will cut its own starting hole. The small blade clamped into the head of the tool and projecting through the flat metal shoe works up and down in short high-speed strokes. It cuts softwood as much as 2 in. thick.

For heavy-duty or continuous use, select a model with a ⅓-hp. motor. The best models operate at variable speeds and have a tilting shoe.

ROUTERS. A router is the only power tool available for cutting intricate contours in wood. With it you can cut multi-curved moldings, make rabbet and dovetail joints, mortise wood for hinges and other recessed objects, plane edges, cut tiny grooves, and trim laminated plastics.

The tool has a powerful motor contained in a cylindrical housing which is placed flat on the surface and guided by both hands. The motor turns an assortment of special bits at speeds of up to 25,000 rpm. The most commonly used types and sizes of bit are sold in sets, and to these you can add dozens more.

BENCH GRINDERS. Bench grinders make short work of all tool-sharpening operations; can also be used for wire-brushing and buffing. The grinders come with two grinding wheels with different grits or, in a few cases, with a grinding wheel and a buffing wheel. Wheel diameters range from 5½ to 10 in.

PAINT REMOVERS. Removing paint from large surfaces is not easy under any circumstances, but you can get the job over with faster with an electric paint remover than with any other type of remover. All you have to do is hold the 3×6-in. heating element against the wall or floor until the paint blisters; then zip it off with a scraper. If the paint is not too thick, you can push the remover across it in a steady motion and remove the paint as you go with the sharp scraping edge built into the tool. Despite the intense heat, there is less chance of igniting the paint or underlying wood than with a torch.

PAINT SPRAYERS. If you feel you must have a paint sprayer of your own, don't settle for a so-called airless sprayer which works without a compressor, because it isn't a great deal better than the sprayer attachment which is sometimes sold with vacuum cleaners. For good distribution of paint, reliable operation, and long life, put your money into a complete outfit with an electrically driven compressor, hose, and spray gun.

Three types of gun are used for residential painting: suction-feed guns which are best suited only for small jobs and application of thin finishes; pressure-feed guns for large jobs and all kinds of paint; and all-purpose guns which convert from suction- to pressure-feed. The last is obviously the best choice for the handyman.

Most guns come with a 1-qt. paint canister. If you make a habit of using a sprayer for large jobs requiring gallons of paint, you may also want to invest in a pressurized tank that holds up to 3 gal. of paint.

Electric paint remover. Red Devil, Inc.

Bench grinder. Black & Decker Manufacturing Co.

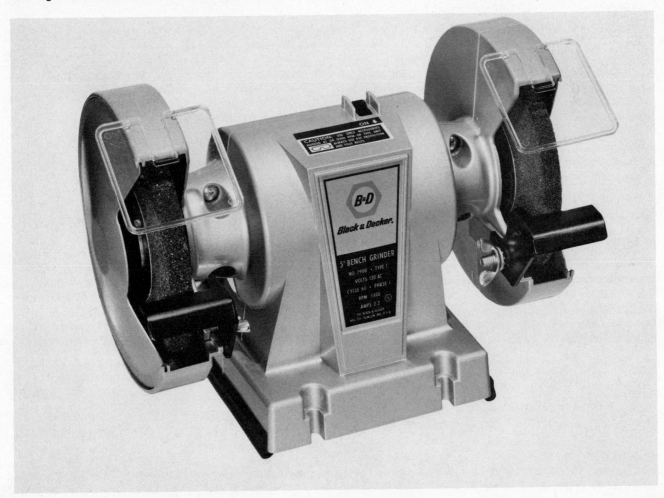

Paint sprayer. Black & Decker Manufacturing Co.

Abrasive wheel. Merit Abrasive Products, Inc.

WHO MAKES IT

Adjustable Clamp Co. · Every conceivable type of clamp.

Arco Products Corp. · Surform tools. Countersink-counter-bores. Router bits. Electric drill accessories. Grinding wheels. Hole saws. Circular saw blades. Sharpening stones.

Arrow Fastener Co. · Staplers.

Black & Decker Manufacturing Co. · Electric drills and bits. Electric jig saws. Circular saws. Routers. Bench grinders. Sanders of all types.

Channellock, Inc. · Plier-wrenches.

Cooper Industries. · Crescent wrenches. Pliers. Screw-drivers.

Dalton Manufacturing Co. · Sawhorse brackets; brackets with legs.

Estwing Manufacturing Co. · All kinds of hammers and hatchets. Hacksaws. Pry bars.

Hager Hinge Co. · Collapsible sawhorse brackets.

Hyde Manufacturing Co. · Putty knives. Wall scrapers. Wood scrapers. Electric paint removers. Linoleum knives. Utility knives. Wallpaper seam rollers. Wallpaper scrapers. Paperhanger's brushes.

Irwin Auger Bit Co. · Auger bits, expansive bits, and spade bits in profusion. Bit extensions. Chalk-line reels. Screw-drivers.

Kirkhill, Inc. · Pipe wrenches. Basin wrenches. Chain wrenches. Slip-joint pliers. Plumber's friends. Toilet augers. Drain augers. Snakes.

Lufkin, Inc. · Tapes and rules.

McDonough Co. · Plumb hammers.

Merit Abrasive Products, Inc. · Abrasive wheels made of flexible strips of sandpaper for use in electric drills and bench grinders. Other abrasives.

Montgomery Ward & Co. · Just about everything.

Rawlplug Co. · Carbide-tipped electric-drill bits in all sizes and lengths.

Red Devil, Inc. · Putty knives. Scrapers. Taping knives. Glass cutters. Utility knives. Cement and plasterer's trowels. Notched trowels. Linoleum knives. Masonry tools. Caulking guns. Tilesetter's tools.

Sears Roebuck & Co. · Just about everything.

Skil Corp. · Electric drills. Electric jig saws. Circular saws.

Stanley Works. · Everything in the general-purpose-tool category.

Star Expansion Industries Corp. · Carbide-tipped drills in all sizes and lengths.

Swingline, Inc. · Staplers.

USM Corp. · Staplers.

J. Wiss & Sons Co. · Snips and more snips.

Woodcraft Supply Corp. · Most common carpenter's tools as well as a great many special tools for woodworking.

Addresses of Manufacturers and Suppliers

A. A. Abbingdon Ceiling Co., 2149 Utica Ave., Brooklyn, N.Y. 11234

Abitibi Corp., Birmingham, Mich. 48011

Absolute Coatings, Inc., 34 Industrial St., Bronx, N.Y. 10461

Acme General Corp., Box 300, San Dimas, Cal. 91773

Acme-National Refrigeration Co., 19–26 Hazen St., Astoria, N.Y. 11105

Acorn Building Components, Inc., 12620 Westwood, Detroit, Mich. 48223

Adamsez Baths, Inc., 14001 Goldmark Dr., Dallas, Tex. 75240

Adjustable Clamp Co., 417 N. Ashland Ave., Chicago, Ill. 60622

Afco, Inc., 906 E. 6th St., Hobart, Ind. 46342

Agency Tile, Inc., 499 Old Nyack Turnpike, Spring Valley, N.Y. 10977

Air King Corp., 3057 N. Rockwell St., Chicago, Ill. 60618

Alarm Device Manufacturing Co., 165 Eileen Way, Syosset, N.Y. 11791

Alcan Aluminum Corp., Box 511, Warren, Ohio 44482

Alcoa Building Products, Inc., 2 Allegheny Center, Pittsburgh, Pa. 15212

Alfol, Inc., 9839 York Rd., Charlotte, N.C. 28217

Alkco Manufacturing Co., 4224 N. Lincoln Ave., Chicago, Ill. 60618

All Enterprises, Box 729, Petoskey, Mich. 49770

Allegheny Natural Stone Co., 1237 Belmont Ave., North Haledon, Paterson, N.J. 07508

Allibert, Inc., 315 E. 62nd St., New York, N.Y. 10021

Alron Industries, 4800 Dewey Ave., Rochester, N.Y. 14612

Alsto Co., 11052 Pearl Rd., Cleveland, Ohio 44136

Amana Refrigeration, Inc., Amana, Iowa 52203

AMF, Inc., 1025 N. Royal St., Alexandria, Va. 22314

American Biltrite, Inc., Amtico Flooring Div., Trenton, N.J. 08607

American General Products, Inc., 1735 Holmes Rd., Ypsilanti, Mich. 48197

American Olean Tile Co., Lansdale, Pa. 19446

American-Standard, Inc., Box 2003, New Brunswick, N.J. 08903

Amtrol, Inc., West Warwick, R.I. 02893

Andersen Corp., Bayport, Minn. 55003

Angelus Consolidated Industries, Inc., 2911 Whittier Blvd., Los Angeles, Cal. 90023

Anil Canada, Ltd., East River, Nova Scotia, Canada

Anti-Hydro Waterproofing Co., 265–277 Badger Ave., Newark, N.J. 07108

APC Corp., Hawthorne, N.J. 07506

Arabesque, 2322 Myrtle Ave., El Paso, Tex. 79901

Architectural Engineering Products Co., Box 81664, San Diego, Cal. 92138

ARCO Chemical Co., Centre Square, 1500 Market St., Philadelphia, Pa. 19101

Arco Products Corp., 110 W. Sheffield Ave., Englewood, N.J. 07631

Arctic Roofings, Inc., Wilmington, Del. 19809

Arkla Industries, Inc., 400 E. Capitol, Little Rock, Ark. 72203

Armstrong Cork Co., Lancaster, Pa. 17604

Arrow Fastener Co., 271 Mayhill St., Saddle Brook, N.J. 07663

Atlanta Stove Works, Inc., Box 5254, Atlanta, Ga. 30307

Atlantic Asphalt & Asbestos, Inc., Stratford, Conn. 06497

Authentic Designs, 139 E. 61st St., New York, N.Y. 10021

Authentic Products of Sheboygan, Box 742, Sheboygan, Wis. 53081

Baker Drapery Corp., 1116 Pioneer Pkwy., Peoria, Ill. 61614

Baldwin Hardware Manufacturing Corp., 841 Wyomissing Blvd., Reading, Pa. 19603

Ball & Ball, 463 W. Lincoln Hwy., Exton, Pa. 19341

Bangkok Industries, Inc., 1900 S. 20th St., Philadelphia, Pa. 19145

Barclay Industries, Inc., 65 Industrial Rd., Lodi, N.J. 07644

Baths International, Inc., 101 Park Ave., New York, N.Y. 10017

Behr Process Corp., 1603 Walton St., Santa Ana, Cal. 92702

James R. Bell Co., 707 San Fernando Rd., San Fernando, Cal. 91340

Addresses of Manufacturers and Suppliers

Bennett-Ireland, Inc., Norwich, N.Y. 13815

Bessler Disappearing Stairway Co., Conneaut, Ohio 44030

Bilco Co., New Haven, Conn. 06505

Biltbest Corp., 175 Coyne St., Ste. Genevieve, Mo. 63670

Bio Systems, Inc., 1280 28th St., Boulder, Colo., 80302

Bird & Son, Inc., Washington St., East Walpole, Mass. 02032

Birge Co., 390 Niagara St., Buffalo, N.Y. 14240

Black & Decker Manufacturing Co., Towson, Md. 21204

Julius Blum & Co., Carlstadt, N.J. 07072

Boiardi Products Corp., 1525 Fairfield Ave., Cleveland, Ohio 44113

Boise Cascade Corp., Door Div., 875 Sherman Ave., Pennsauken, N.J. 08110

Boise Cascade Corp., Kitchen Cabinet Div., Box 514, Berryville, Va. 22611

Bondex International, Inc., Brunswick, Ohio 44212

Borden, Inc., Borden Chemical Div., 50 E. Broad St., Columbus, Ohio 43215

Borden, Inc., Columbus Coated Fabrics Div., 1280 N. Grant Ave., Columbus, Ohio 43216

Wayne Boren Corp., 4960 Cranswick, Houston, Tex., 77040

Borg-Warner Corp., Plumbing Products Div., Mansfield, Ohio 44901

Borg-Warner Corp., York Div., Box 1592, York, Pa. 17405

Bradley Corp., Box 348, Menomonee Falls, Wis. 53051

John Brady Enterprises, 215 N. Jean St., Ramsey, N.J. 07446

Brammer Manufacturing Co., Davenport, Iowa 52808

Brearley Co., 2107 Kishwaukee St., Rockford, Ill. 61101

Briare Co., 964 Third Ave., New York, N.Y. 10022

Briggs Manufacturing Co., 5200 W. Kennedy Blvd., Tampa, Fla. 33609

Broan Manufacturing Co., Hartford, Wis. 53027

Brock Co., 1042 Olive Hill Lane, Napa, Cal. 94558

Brown Stove Works, Cleveland, Tenn. 37311

E. L. Bruce Co., 1648 Thomas St., Memphis, Tenn. 38101

E. L. Bruce Co. of Texas, Box 826, Center, Tex. 75935

John D. Brush Co., 900 Linden Ave., Rochester, N.Y. 14625

Buckingham-Virginia Slate Corp., 4110 Fitzhugh Ave., Richmond, Va. 23230

Burke Industries, 2250 S. 10th St., San Jose, Cal. 95112

Burns & Russell Co., Box 6063, Baltimore, Md. 21231

Cabanarama Industries, Inc., Box 470945, Miami, Fla. 33147

Samuel Cabot, Inc., 1 Union St., Boston, Mass. 02108

Caloric Corp., Topton, Pa. 19562

Camer Glass, Inc., 979 Third Ave., New York, N.Y. 10022

C & C Solarthermics, Inc., Box 144, Smithsburg, Md., 21783

Cannon Craft Manufacturing Co., Box 558, Sulphur Springs, Tex. 75482

Carbon-Pure, 340 E. Madison, Phoenix, Ariz. 85004

Carrier Corp., Carrier Tower, Syracuse, N.Y. 13201

Cavrok Corp., Industrial Park Ave., Vernon, Conn. 06066

Celotex Corp., Tampa, Fla. 33622

Celotex Corp., Jim Walter Doors Div., 3825 Henderson Blvd., Tampa, Fla. 33609

Central Shippee, Inc., Bloomingdale, N.J. 07403

Central Vac International, 3008 E. Olympic Blvd., Los Angeles, Cal. 90023

Certain-Teed Products Corp., Box 860, Valley Forge, Pa. 19482

CGM, Inc., 1463 Ford Rd., Cornwells Heights, Pa. 19020

Chambers Corp., Box 927, Oxford, Miss. 38655

Channellock, Inc., Meadville, Pa., 16335

Chicago Faucet Co., 2100 S. Nuclear Dr., Des Plaines, Ill. 60018

Chicago Metallic Corp., 4849 S. Austin St., Chicago, Ill. 60638

Chimney Heat Reclaimer Corp., 53 Railroad Ave., Southington, Conn. 06489

Clivus Multrum USA, Inc., 14A Eliot St., Cambridge, Mass. 02138

Clopay Co., Clopay Square, Cincinnati, Ohio 45214

Coleman Co., Wichita, Kans. 67201

Colt Industries, 3601 Kansas Ave., Kansas City, Kans. 66110

Colonial Hand Split Shingles, Inc., Box 565, Chatham, N.Y. 07928

Columbia Boiler Co. of Pottstown, Pottstown, Pa. 19464

Columbia Moulding Co., 4747 Hollins Ferry Rd., Baltimore, Md. 21227

Columbus Coated Fabrics, 1280 N. Grant Ave., Columbus, Ohio 43216

Como Plastics, Inc., subsidiary of PPG Industries, 1 Gateway Center, Pittsburgh, Pa. 15222

Composite Shower Pan, Box 26188, Los Angeles, Cal. 90026

Conco, Field Control Div., Mendota, Ill. 61342

Connor Forest Industries, Wausau, Wis. 54401

Consoweld Corp., Wisconsin Rapids, Wis. 54494

Consoweld Distributors, Wisconsin Rapids, Wis. 54494

Albert Constantine & Son, 2056 Eastchester Rd., Bronx, N.Y. 10461

Contech, Inc., 7711 Computer Ave., Minneapolis, Minn. 55435

Contemporary Systems, Inc., 10 Kearney Rd., Needham, Mass. 02194

Continental Felt Co., 22 W. 15th St., New York, N.Y. 10011

Contract Vinyls, Inc., North Bellmore, N.Y. 11710

Conwed Corp., 332 Minnesota St., St. Paul, Minn. 55101

Cook & Dunn, Box 117, Newark, N.J. 07101

Cook Paint & Varnish Co., Box 389, Kansas City, Mo. 64141

Cooper Industries, 200 Harrison St., Jamestown, N.Y. 14701

Corning Glass Works, Corning, N.Y. 14830

C. P. Chemical Co., 25 Home St., White Plains, N.Y. 10606

Crane Co., 300 Park Ave., New York, N.Y. 10022

Nelson Cross Co., 2131 Larkdale Dr., Glenview, Ill. 60025

Crown Mosaic-Parquet Flooring, Inc., Box 272, Sevierville, Tenn. 37862

CSI, Solar Systems Div., 12400 49th St., N., St. Petersburg, Fla. 33732

Culligan International Co., Northbrook, Ill. 60062

Cutler-Hammer, 4201 N. 27th St., Milwaukee, Wis. 53216

Dallas Ceramics Co., 7834 C. F. Hawn Freeway, Dallas, Tex. 75217

Dalton Manufacturing Co., 130 S. Bemiston Ave., St. Louis, Mo. 63105

DAP, Inc., Box 999, Dayton, Ohio 45401

Darworth Co., Avon, Conn. 06001

Dearborn Stove Co., Box 28426, Dallas, Tex. 75228

Decro-Wall Corp., 375 Executive Blvd., Elmsford, N.Y. 10523

Deft, Inc., 612 Maple Ave., Torrance, Cal. 90503

J. C. DeJong & Co., 130–15 91st Ave., Richmond Hill, N.Y. 11418

Delta Faucet Co., Greensburg, Ind. 47240

Design-Technics Ceramics, Inc., 160 E. 56th St., New York, N.Y. 10022

Designware Industries, Inc., Box 32008, Minneapolis, Minn. 55432

Detection Systems, Inc., 400 Mason Rd., Fairport, N.Y. 14450

Diamond-Brite, 2042 Jericho Turnpike, East Northport, N.Y. 11731

Diamond K Co., 130 Buckland Rd., South Windsor, Conn. 06074

Diller Corp., 6126 Madison Court, Morton Grove, Ill. 60053

Diston Industries, Inc., 3293 E. 11th Ave., Hialeah, Fla. 33013

Ditrek Corp. 11 S. Fullerton Ave., Montclair, N.J. 07042

Diversified Insulation, Inc., Box 188, Hamel, Minn. 53340

Dodge Cork Co., Lancaster, Pa. 17604

Dorfile Shelving Systems Co., Freeport, Ill. 61032

Dow Corning Corp., Midland, Mich. 48640

Dream Wall Sales, Ltd., 1397 Commercial Dr., Vancouver, B.C., Canada

Driwood Moulding Co., Box 1369, Florence, S.C. 29501

E. I. du Pont de Nemours & Co., Wilmington, Del. 19898

Dur-A-Flex, Inc., 100 Meadow St., Hartford, Conn. 06114

Duvinage Corp., Box 828, Hagerstown, Md. 21740

Dwyer Products Corp., Michigan City, Ind. 46360

Dynamic Development Corp., Box 164, Appleton, Wis. 54911

Dyrelite Corp., 63 David St., New Bedford, Mass. 02744

Eagle Electric Manufacturing Co., 45–31 Court Square, Long Island City, N.Y. 11101

E & K Service Co., 16824 74th NE, Bothell, Wash. 98011

Eaton Corp., Lock & Hardware Div., Box 25288, Charlotte, N.C. 28212

Edmund Scientific Co., 555 Edscorp Bldg., Barrington, N.J. 08007

Edwards Co., Norwalk, Conn. 06856

Edwards Engineering Corp., 101 Alexander Ave., Pompton Plains, N.J. 07444

Eldorado Stone Co., Box 125, Kirkland, Wash., 98033

Elkay Manufacturing Co., 2700 S. 17th Ave., Broadview, Ill. 60153

Elon, Inc., 964 Third Ave., New York, N.Y. 10022

Emco Specialties, Inc., 2121 E. Walnut St., Des Moines, Iowa 50317

Emerson Electric Co., Emerson-Chromalox Div., 8100 W. Florissant Ave., St. Louis, Mo. 63136

Emerson Electric Co., In-Sink-Erator Div., 4700 21st St., Racine, Wis. 53406

Emerson Electric Co., Rittenhouse-Chromalox Div., Honeoye Falls, N.Y. 14472

Emerson Electric Co., White-Rodgers Div., 9797 Reavis Rd., St. Louis, Mo. 63123

Emhart Corp., Berlin, Conn. 06037

Empire Stove Co., Belleville, Ill. 62222

Energy Conservation Unlimited, Inc., 811 S. Wilma St., Longwood, Fla. 32750

Engineered Products Co., Box 108, Flint, Mich. 48501

Erecto-Pat, Inc., 32295 Stephenson, Madison Heights, Mich. 48071

Estwing Manufacturing Co., 2647 Eighth St., Rockford, Ill. 61101

Evans Products Co., Remington Aluminum Div., 100 Andrews Rd., Hicksville, N.Y. 11801

Evergard Co., 19th St. and Indiana Ave., Philadelphia, Pa. 19132

Evode, Inc., 403 Kennedy Blvd., Somerdale, N.J. 08083

Exxon Chemical Co., Odenton, Md. 21113

Fasco Industries, Inc., Fayetteville, N.C. 28302

Fedders Corp., Edison, N.J. 08817

Fedders Corp., Norge Div., Edison N.J. 18817

Fenwal, Inc., Box 309, Ashland, Mass. 01721

Ferum Co., 815 E. 136th St., New York, N.Y. 10454

Fire-Lite Alarms, Inc., 40 Albert St., New Haven, Conn. 06504

Fisher Skylights, Inc., 186 15th St., Brooklyn, N.Y. 11215

Flair-Fold, Inc. East Farmingdale, N.Y. 11735

Flangeklamp Industries, Inc., 1971 Abbott Rd., Buffalo, N.Y. 14218

Flinchbaugh/Murray Corp. 390 Eberts Lane, York, Pa. 17403

Flintkote Co., Building Materials Div., 480 Central Ave., East Rutherford, N.J. 07073

Flotec, Inc., 14510 S. Carmenita Rd., Norwalk, Cal. 90650

Fluidmaster, Inc., 1800 Via Burton, Anaheim, Cal. 92805

Focal Point, Inc., 3760 Lower Roswell Rd., Marietta, Ga. 30060

Follansbee Steel Corp., Follansbee, W. Va. 26037

Fomo Products, Inc., 3250 W. Market, Akron, Ohio 44313

Franklin Electric, Bluffton, Ind. 46714

Frantz Manufacturing Co., 301 W. Third St., Sterling, Ill. 61081

Fritz Chemical Co., Box 17087, Dallas, Tex. 75217

Fuel Sentry Corp., 79 Putnam St., Mt. Vernon, N.Y. 10550

H. B. Fuller Co., 315 S. Hicks Rd., Palatine, Ill. 60067

Fuller-O'Brien Corp., 450 E. Grand Ave., South San Francisco, Cal. 94080

GAF Corp., 140 W. 51st St., New York, N.Y. 10020

Gaffers & Sattler, Inc., 4851 S. Alameda St., Los Angeles, Cal. 90058

Gallatin Aluminum Products Co., Gallatin, Tenn. 37066

General Aluminum Corp., Box 34221, Dallas, Tex. 75234

General Electric Co., Circuit Protective Devices Product Dept., Plainville, Conn. 16062

General Electric Co., Hotpoint Div., Appliance Park, Louisville, Ky. 40225

General Electric Co., Housewares Business Div., Bridgeport, Conn. 06602

General Electric Co., Major Appliance Div., Appliance Park, Louisville, Ky. 40225

General Electric Co., Plastics Business Div., 1 Plastics Ave., Pittsfield, Mass. 01201

General Electric Co., Silicone Products Dept., Waterford, N.Y. 12188

General Electric Co., Transformer and Distribution Equipment Business Div., Box 2188, Hickory, N.C. 28601

General Electric Co., Wiring Device Dept., Providence, R.I. 02940

General Fittings Co., East Greenwich, R.I. 02818

General Machine Corp., Electric Furnace-Man Div., Emmaus, Pa. 18049

General Motors Corp., Frigidaire Div., Dayton, Ohio 45401

General Products Co., Box 887, Fredericksburg, Va. 22401

General Tire & Rubber Co., 377 Rte. 17, Hasbrouck Heights, N.J. 07604

Genova, Inc., 300 Rising St., Davison, Mich. 48423

Georgia Marble Co., 3460 Cumberland Pkwy. NW, Atlanta, Ga. 30339

Georgia-Pacific Corp., 900 SW Fifth Ave., Portland, Ore. 97204

Gerber Industries, Inc., 1510 Fairview Ave., St. Louis, Mo. 63132

Gibson-Homans Co., 2366 Woodhill Rd., Cleveland, Ohio 44106

Giles & Kendall Co., Box 188, Huntsville, Ala. 35804

Glasteel, 1727 Buena Vista, Duarte, Cal. 91010

Globe Industries, Inc. 2638 E. 126th St., Chicago, Ill. 60633

Golden Investments, Ltd., 7701 Whitepine Rd., Chesterfield, Va. 23832

B. F. Goodrich General Products Co., 500 S. Main St., Akron, Ohio 44318

Goodwin of California, Inc., 1075 Second St., Berkeley, Cal. 94710

Gordon Corp., 504 Main St., Farmington, Conn. 06032

Goulds Pumps, Inc., Seneca Falls, N.Y. 13148

W. R. Grace & Co., Construction Products Div., 62 Whittemore Ave., Cambridge, Mass. 02140

Grant Pulley & Hardware Corp., High St., West Nyack, N.Y. 10994

Gries Reproducer Co., 125 Beechwood Ave., New Rochelle, N.Y. 10802

Grillion Corp., 189 First St., Brooklyn, N.Y. 11215

P. E. Guerin, Inc., 21–25 Jane St., New York, N.Y. 10014

Haas Cabinet Co., 615 W. Utica St., Sellesburg, Ind. 47172

Hager Hinge Co., 139 Victor St., St. Louis, Mo. 63104

Hamilton Humidity, Inc., 3757 W. Touhy Ave., Chicago, Ill. 60645

Hanley Co., Summerville, Pa. 15864

Hardwick Stove Co., Cleveland, Tenn. 37311

Hart & Cooley Manufacturing Co., Box 903A, Holland, Mich. 49423

Hastings Tile, 964 Third Ave., New York, N.Y. 10022

A. C. Hathorne Co., 55 San Remo Dr., South Burlington, Vt. 05401

Hauserman, Inc., Gotham Div., 131 Larchmont Ave., Larchmont, N.Y. 10538

Hayes-te Equipment Corp. Unionville, Conn. 06085

HC Products Co., Box 68, Princeville, Ill. 61559

Heat Controller, Inc., Jackson, Mich. 49203

Heckman Building Products, Inc. 4015 W. Carroll Ave., Chicago, Ill. 60624

Hobart Corp., Troy, Ohio 45374

Homasote Co., West Trenton, N.J. 08628

Homecraft Veneer, Box 3, Latrobe, Pa. 15650

Homelite Manufacturing Corp., Port Chester, N.Y. 10573

Homestead Mills, Ltd., 3247 63rd SW, Seattle, Wash. 98116

Honeywell, Inc., 2701 Fourth Ave. S, Minneapolis, Minn. 55408

Horner Flooring Co., Dollar Bay, Mich. 49922

Howmet Corp., Box 1786, Lancaster, Pa. 17604

Hyde Manufacturing Co., Southbridge, Mass. 01550

ICI United States, Inc., Wilmington, Del. 19897

Ideal Co., Box 889, Waco, Tex. 76703

Ideal Security Hardware Corp., 215 E. Ninth St., St. Paul, Minn. 55101

I.M.M.S., Inc., Roto International Div., Hitchcock Corner, Essex, Conn. 06426

Imperial Wallpaper Mill, Inc., 23645 Mercantile Rd., Cleveland, Ohio 44122

INCA Distributing Co., Stanton & Empire Sts., Wilkes-Barre, Pa. 18702

Inclinator Co. of America, 2200 Paxton St., Harrisburg, Pa. 17105

INRYCO, Inc., Box 393, Milwaukee, Wis. 53201

Interbath, Inc., 3231 N. Durfee Ave., El Monte, Cal. 91732

International Paper Co., Long-Bell Div., Box 579, Longview, Wash. 98632

International Window Corp., 5625 E. Firestone Blvd., South Gate, Cal. 90280

Interpace Corp., 2901 Los Feliz Blvd., Los Angeles, Cal. 90039

Irwin Auger Bit Co., Wilmington, Ohio 45177

Isothermics, Inc., Box 86, Augusta, N.J. 07822

I-T-E Imperial Corp., Spring House, Pa. 19477

ITT Corp., Bell & Gossett Div., 8200 N. Austin Ave., Morton Grove, Ill. 60053

ITT Corp. Lawler Div., Mt. Vernon, N.Y. 10552

Jacuzzi Bros., Inc., 11511 New Benton Hwy., Little Rock, Ark. 72203

Jacuzzi Research, Inc., 1440 San Pablo Ave., Berkeley, Cal. 94702

Janus 2, Inc., 117 S. Chester Rd., Swarthmore, Pa. 19081

Jarrow Products, Inc., 2000 N. Southport Ave., Chicago, Ill. 60614

Jenn-Air Corp., 3035 Shadeland, Indianapolis, Ind. 46226

JH Industries, Inc., Exelon Div., 1712-F Newport Circle, Santa Ana, Cal. 92705

Johns-Manville Sales Corp., Greenwood Plaza, Denver, Colo. 80217

H & R Johnson, Inc., State Highway 35, Keyport, N.J. 07735

Johnson Rubber Co., 16025 Johnson St., Middlefield, Ohio 44062

Joslyn Manufacturing & Supply Co., 155 N. Wacker Dr., Chicago, Ill. 60606

Just Manufacturing Co., 9233 King St., Franklin Park, Ill. 60131

Karnak Chemical Corp., 330 Central Ave., Clark, N.J. 07066

Keller Industries, Inc., 18000 State Road Nine, Miami, Fla. 33162

Keller Industries, Keller Columbus Div., 2999 Silver Dr., Columbus, Ohio 43224

Kessler Enterprises, 8600 Gateway East, El Paso, Tex. 79900

King Refrigerator Corp., 76–02 Woodhaven Blvd., Glendale, N.Y. 11227

Kirkhill, Inc., 12021 Woodruff Ave., Downey, Cal. 90241

Kirsch Co., Sturgis, Mich. 49091

Joseph C. Klein, Inc., Northeast Industrial Park, Schenectady, N.Y. 12306

Knape & Vogt Manufacturing Co., 2700 Oak Industrial Drive NE, Grand Rapids, Mich. 49505

Kohler Co., Kohler, Wis. 53044

Kool-O-Matic Corp., 1831 Terminal Rd., Niles, Mich. 49120

Koppers Co., Pittsburgh, Pa. 15219

Kristia Associates, 449 Forest Ave., Portland, Me. 04104

Kwikset Sales & Service Co., Box 3579, Anaheim, Cal. 92803

Larson Manufacturing Co., Brookings, S. Dak. 57006

Lasco Industries, 3261 E. Miraloma Ave., Anaheim, Cal. 92806

F. H. Lawson Co., Cincinnati, Ohio 45204

LCA Corp., Progress Lighting Div., Box 12701, Philadelphia, Pa. 19134

Leigh Products, Inc., Coopersville, Mich. 49404

Leigh Products, Inc., Rutt Custom Kitchen Div., Rte. 23, Goodville, Pa. 17528

Lennon Wall Paper Co., Box 8, Joliet, Ill. 60434

Lennox Industries, Inc., Box 250, Marshalltown, Iowa 50158

Leslie-Locke, 11550 W. King St., Franklin Park, Ill. 60131

Leslie-Locke, Lighting Div., Ohio St., Lodi, Ohio 44254

Lighting Products, Inc., 1549 Park Ave., W., Highland Park, Ill. 60035

Lighting Services, Inc., 801 Second Ave., New York, N.Y. 10017

Liken, Inc., Del Mar Div., 7130 Fenwick Lane, Westminster, Cal. 92683

Logan-Long Co., 6600 S. Central Ave., Chicago, Ill. 60638

Longwood Furnace Co., Gallatin, Mo. 64640

Louisiana-Pacific Corp., 324 Wooster Rd. N., Barberton, Ohio 44203

Ludowici-Celadon Co., 111 E. Wacker Dr., Chicago, Ill. 60601

Lufkin, Inc., Box 728, Apex, N.C. 27502

Lumaside, Inc., 7300 W. Bradley Rd., Milwaukee, Wis. 53223

MacMillan Bloedel, Ltd., 1075 W. Georgia St., Vancouver, B.C., Canada

Magic Chef, Cleveland, Tenn. 37311

Majestic Co., Huntington, Ind. 46750

Majestic Metal Spinning & Stamping Co., 537 Sackett St., Brooklyn, N.Y. 11217

Malm Fireplaces, Inc., 368 Yolanda Ave., Santa Rosa, Cal. 95404

Mannington Mills, Inc., Salem, N.J. 08079

MarLe Co., 170 Summer St., Stamford, Conn. 06901

Martin Industries, Inc., Box 1527, Huntsville, Ala. 35807

Martin Industries, Inc., King Products Div., Box 730, Sheffield, Ala. 35660

Marvin Windows, Warroad, Minn. 56763

Masonite Corp., 29 N. Wacker Dr., Chicago, Ill. 60606

Masonite Corp., Atlas Roofing Div., Box 5777, Meridian, Miss. 39301

Masonite Corp., Roxite Div., Rock Falls, Ill. 61071

Master Lock Co., 2600 N. 32nd St., Milwaukee, Wis. 53210

Maybrik, 4545 Brazil St., Los Angeles, Cal. 90039

Mayflower Wallpaper Co., 363 Mamaroneck Ave., White Plains, N.Y. 10605

Maytag Co., Newton, Iowa 50208

Maywood, Inc., 900 E. Second Ave., Amarillo, Tex. 79105

McCordi Corp., 707 Fenimore Rd., Mamaroneck, N.Y. 10543

McDonough Co., Box 1774, Parkersburg, W. Va. 26101

McGraw-Edison Co., Air Comfort Div., 704 N. Clark St., Albion, Mich. 49224

McGraw-Edison Co., Halo Lighting Div., 400 Busse Rd., Elk Grove Village, Ill. 60007

McGraw-Edison Co., Modern Maid Div., Box 1111, Chattanooga, Tenn. 37401

McGraw-Edison Co., Speed Queen Div., Ripon, Wis. 54971

Medford Corp., Diamond Industries Div., Box 1008, Grants Pass, Ore. 97526

Meilink Steel Safe Co., Box 2847, Toledo, Ohio 43606

Melnor Industries, Inc., Walton Laboratory Div., Moonachie, N.J. 07074

Merit Abrasive Products, Inc., 201 W. Manville, Compton, Cal. 90224

Merwin Manufacturing, Inc., 136 E. Fourth St., Dunkirk, N.Y. 14048

Metal Concepts, Inc., Box 25596, Seattle, Wash. 98125

Metro Marketing, Inc., 2083 E. Jericho Tpk., East Northport, N.Y. 11731

Miami-Carey Co., 203 Garver Rd., Monroe, Ohio, 45050

Michigan Maple Block Co., Box 245, Petoskey, Mich. 49770

Midget Louver Co., 800 Main Ave., Norwalk, Conn. 06852

Midland Manufacturing Corp., 162 E. Industry Court, Deer Park, N.Y. 11729

Midwest Victorian Marble Co., 13900 Antioch Rd., Overland Park, Kans. 66223

Milgard Manufacturing, Inc., 2202 Port of Tacoma Rd., Tacoma, Wash. 98421

Minwax Co., 72 Oak St., Clifton, N.J. 07014

Miracle Adhesives Corp., 250 Pettit Ave., Bellmore, N.Y. 11710

Mon-Ray Windows, Inc., 6118 Wayzata Blvd., Minneapolis, Minn. 55416

Montgomery Ward & Co. (see your local store)

Benjamin Moore & Co., Chestnut Ridge Rd., Montvale, N.J. 07645

Gates Moore, River Rd., Silvermine, Norwalk, Conn. 06854

Morgan Co., Oshkosh, Wis. 54901

Morgan Veneers, 915 E. Kentucky St., Louisville, Ky. 40204

Mortell Co., Kankakee, Ill. 60901

Morton Salt Co., 110 N. Wacker Dr., Chicago, Ill. 60606

Mosler Safe Co., 1561 Grand Blvd., Hamilton, Ohio 45012

Murray Equipment Co., 1228 E. Philadelphia St., York, Pa. 17405

F. E. Myers & Bro. Co., 400 Orange St., Ashland, Ohio 44805

Mylen Industries, 650 Washington St., Peekskill, N.Y. 10566

National Gypsum Co., Buffalo, N.Y. 14202

Naturalite, Inc., Box 1547, Garland, Tex. 75040

NCI, Inc., Box 284, Des Moines, Iowa 50301

New England Lock & Hardware Co., 46 Chestnut St., South Norwalk, Conn. 06856

E. A. Nord Co., Everett, Wash. 98206

North Bangor Slate Co., Bangor, Pa. 18013

Northeastern Wallpaper Co., 292 Summer St., Boston, Mass. 02210

Northland Boiler Co., East Haddam, Conn. 06423

Northrop Architectural Systems, 999 S. Hatcher Ave., City of Industry, Cal. 91749

Old-Fashioned Milk Paint Co., Box 222, Groton, Mass. 01450

Old Guilford Forge, Guilford, Conn. 06437

Old Stone Mill Corp., Old Stone Mill, Adams, Mass. 01220

Onan Corp., 1400 73rd Ave. NE, Minneapolis, Minn. 55432

Owens-Corning Fiberglas Corp., Fiberglas Tower, Toledo, Ohio 43659

Panelfold, 10700 NW 36th Ave., Miami, Fla. 33167

Charles Parker, 290 Pratt St., Meriden, Conn. 06450

S. Parker Hardware Manufacturing Corp., 27 Ludlow St., New York, N.Y. 10002

Pass & Seymour, Inc., Syracuse, N.Y. 13209

Peabody Barnes, 651 N. Main St., Mansfield, Ohio 44902

Peace Flooring Co., Box 87, Magnolia, Ark. 71753

Peachtree Door, Box 700, Norcross, Ga. 30071

Peacock Papers, Ltd., 979 Third Ave., New York, N.Y. 10022

Pease Co., Ever-Strait Div., 7100 Dixie Hwy., Fairfield, Ohio 45023

C & L Pegg, 149 Grant St., Wabash, Ind. 46992

Pemko Manufacturing Co., 5755 Landregan St., Emeryville, Cal. 94662

Perfect-Line Manufacturing Corp., 80 E. Gates Ave., Lindenhurst, N.Y. 11757

Billy Penn Corp., 1831 N. Fifth St., Philadelphia, Pa. 19122

Peterson Chemical Corp., 704 S. River, Sheboygan, Wis. 53081

Phifer Wire Products, Inc., Box 1700, Tuscaloosa, Ala. 35401

Philips Industries, Inc., 4801 Springfield St., Dayton, Ohio 45401

Philips Industries, Inc., Lau Industries Div., 2027 Home Ave., Dayton, Ohio 45407

Pierce & Stevens Chemical Corp., 710 Ohio St., Buffalo, N.Y. 14240

Pioneer Plastics Corp., Pionite Rd., Auburn, Me. 04210

Pittsburgh Corning Corp., 800 Presque Isle Dr., Pittsburgh, Pa. 15239

Pittway Corp., BRK Electronics Div., 780 McClure Ave., Aurora, Ill. 60507

Plasti-Kote Co., 1000 Lake Rd., Medina, Ohio 44256

PLC Electronics, Inc., 39–50 Crescent St., Long Island City, N.Y. 11101

W. H. Porter, Inc., 4240 N. 136th Ave., Holland, Mich. 49423

Porter-Hadley Co., 255 Cottage Grove SE, Grand Rapids, Mich. 49502

Potlatch Corp., Box 3591, San Francisco, Cal. 94119

Powers Regulator Co., Powers-Fiat Div., 3400 Oakton St., Skokie, Ill. 60076

PPG Industries, 1 Gateway Center, Pittsburgh, Pa. 15222

Precision Control Products Corp., 1396 Main St., Waltham, Mass. 02154

Preway, Inc., Wisconsin Rapids, Wis. 54494

Price Pfister, 13500 Paxton St., Pacoima, Cal. 91331

Prill Manufacturing Co., Sheridan, Wyo. 82801

Pulse Dynamics Manufacturing Corp., Fulton & Depot Sts., Colchester, Ill. 62326

Pyramid Industries, Inc., 1422 Irwin Dr., Erie, Pa. 16505

Pyrotector, Inc., 333 Lincoln St., Hingham, Mass. 02043

Pyrotonics, 8 Ridgedale Ave., Cedar Knolls, N.J. 07927

Quaker City Manufacturing Co., Sharon Hill, Pa. 19079

Rapperswill Corp., 305 E. 40th St., New York, N.Y. 10016

Rawlplug Co., 200 Petersville Rd., New Rochelle, N.Y. 10801

Raynor Manufacturing Co., Dixon, Ill. 61021

R.C.A. Rubber Co., 1833 E. Market St., Akron, Ohio 44305

Rector Mineral & Trading Corp., 9 W. Prospect Ave., Mt. Vernon, N.Y. 10551

Reda Pump Co., Bartlesville, Okla. 74003

Red Devil, Inc., 2400 Vauxhall Rd., Union, N.J. 07083

Fred Reuten, Inc., Closter, N.J. 07624

Revere Aluminum Building Products, Inc., 11440 W. Addison St., Franklin Park, Ill. 60131

Reynolds Metals Co., Box 27003, Richmond, Va. 23261

Reynolds Water Conditioning Co., 12100 Cloverdale Ave., Detroit, Mich. 48204

M. R. Rhodes, Inc., 99 Thompson Rd., Avon, Conn. 06001

Fred Rice Productions, Inc., 6313 Peach Ave., Van Nuys, Cal. 91401

Phil Rich Fan Manufacturing Co., 1001 West Loop North, Houston, Tex. 77055

Ridge Doors, New Rd., Monmouth Junction, N.J. 08852

Rising & Nelson Slate Co., West Pawlet, Vt. 05775

Riteway Manufacturing Co., Box 6, Harrisonburg, Va. 22801

Robbins & Myers, Inc., Hunter Div., 2500 Frisco Ave., Memphis, Tenn. 38114

Robbins Flooring Co., Box 16902, Memphis, Tenn. 38116

J. G. Robinson, Inc., Box 208, Fort Washington, Pa. 19034

Rockwood Industries, Inc., 9725 E. Hampden, Denver, Colorado 80231

Rodman Industries, Inc., Rimco Div., Box 97, Rock Island, Ill. 61201

Rolleze, Inc., 12177 Montague St., Pacoima, Cal. 91331

Rolscreen Co., Pella, Iowa 50219

Ronson Corp., 1 Ronson Rd., Woodbridge, N.J. 07095

Roper Sales Co., 1905 W. Court St., Kankakee, Ill. 60901

RSL Woodworking Products Co., RD 1, Box 560, Fernwood Ave., Cardiff, N.J. 08232

Rusco Industries, Inc., 1100 Glendon Ave., Los Angeles, Cal. 90024

Rusco Industries, Inc., Ador/Hilite Div., 2401 W. Commonwealth Ave., Fullerton, Cal. 92633

W. J. Ruscoe Co., 483 Kenmore Blvd., Akron, Ohio 44301

St. Charles Manufacturing Co., St. Charles, Ill. 60174

Sargent & Co., 100 Sargent Dr., New Haven, Conn. 06509

Savogran, Box 130, Norwood, Mass. 02062

H. J. Scheirich Co., Box 21037, Louisville, Ky. 40221

Schlage Lock Co., Box 3324, San Francisco, Cal. 94119

F. E. Schumacher Co., Hartville, Ohio 44632

A. F. Schwerd Manufacturing Co., 3215 McClure Ave., Pittsburgh, Pa. 15212

SCM Corp., Glidden-Durkee Div., 900 Union Commerce Bldg., Cleveland, Ohio 44115

SCM Corp., Macco Adhesive Div., Wickliffe, Ohio 44092

Scotsman, 6251 Front St., Albert Lea, Minn. 56007

Scovill Manufacturing Co., Caradco Window & Door Div., Dubuque, Iowa 52001

Scovill Manufacturing Co., Lightcraft of California Div., 1600 W. Slauson Ave., Los Angeles, Cal. 90047

Scovill Manufacturing Co., NuTone Housing Products Div., Madison & Red Bank Rds., Cincinnati, Ohio 45227

Scovill Manufacturing Co., Sterling Lighting Div., 5691 Rising Sun Ave., Philadelphia, Pa. 19120

Seal Rite Windows, Inc., 3500 N. 44th St., Lincoln, Nebr. 68504

Sears Roebuck & Co. (see your local store)

Season-All Industries, Inc., Indiana, Pa. 15701

James Seeman Studios, Inc., 50 Rose Place, Garden City Park, N.Y. 11040

Semling-Menke Co., Box 378, Merrill, Wis., 54452

Shakertown Corp., Box 400, Winlock, Wash. 98596

Sheffield Bronze Paint Corp., 17814 Waterloo Rd., Cleveland, Ohio 44119

Shelfmaster Corp., 3171 E 11th Ave., Hialeah, Fla. 33013

Shibui Wallcoverings, Box 1268, Santa Rosa, Cal. 95403

William Shine Design, Inc., 31 E. Dale Dr., Monroe, Conn. 06468

Shower Door Co., Southampton, Pa. 18966

Shur-Line Manufacturing Co., 80 W. Drullard Ave., Lancaster, N.Y. 14086

Simplex Security Systems, Inc., 10 Front St., Collinsville, Conn. 06022

Simpson Timber Co., 900 Fourth Ave., Seattle, Wash. 98164

Singer Co., Climate Control Div., Finderne Ave., Somerville, N.J. 08876

Skil Corp., 5033 Elston Ave., Chicago, Ill. 60630

A. O. Smith Corp., Box 28, Kankakee, Ill. 60901

H. B. Smith Co., Westfield, Mass. 01085

Solar Energy Co., Box 614, Marlboro, Mass. 01752

Solar Energy Digest, Box 17776, San Diego, Cal. 92117

Solar Manufacturing Co., 40 Conneaut Lake Rd., Greenville, Pa. 16125

Solaron Corp., Stapleton Field Industrial Park, 4850 Olive St., Denver, Colo. 80022

Solar Power, Inc., 75 Snyder St., Sharon, Pa. 16149

Solarsystems, Inc., 1802 Dennis Dr., Tyler, Tex. 75701

Solar-Thermics Enterprises, Ltd., Box 238, Creston, Iowa 50801

Sol-Therm Corp., 7 W. 14th St., New York, N.Y. 10011

Sonoco Products Co., Hartsville, S.C. 29550

Speakman Co., Wilmington, Del. 19899

Stair-Pak Products Co., Rte 22, Union, N.J. 07083

Stanadyne Corp., Moen Div., Elyria, Ohio 44035

Standard Coated Products, 120 E. Fourth St., Cincinnati, Ohio 45202

Standard Dry Wall Products, 7800 NW 38th St., Miami, Fla. 33166

Standard Equipment, Inc., Elite Products Div., Bel Air, Md. 21014

Standard Wallcovering Studio, 26106 Greenfield, Oak Park, Mich. 48237

Stanley Works, 195 Lake St., New Britain, Conn. 06050

Stanley Works, Drapery Hardware Div., Wallingford, Conn. 06492

Stanwood Corp., Stanley, Wis. 54768

Star Expansion Industries Corp., Mountainville, N.Y. 10953

Statitrol Corp., 140 S. Union Blvd., Lakewood, Colo. 80228

Steelcraft Manufacturing Co., 9017 Blue Ash Rd., Cincinnati, Ohio 45242

Stephenson Co., Conneaut, Ohio 44030

Stites Manufacturing Co., 615 Hunter Lane, Santa Rosa, Cal. 95404

Thomas Strahan Co., 150 Heard St., Chelsea, Mass. 02150

Structural Fibers, Inc., Elite Products Div., Bel Air, Md. 21014

Sturdy Lantern Manufacturing Co., 41 P St., South Boston, Mass. 02127

Summitville Tiles, Inc., Summitville, Ohio 43962

Sun Glow, Inc., 12500 W. Cedar, Lakewood, Colo. 80215

Sun-Saver, Inc., 1565 Ninth St., White Bear Lake, Minn. 55110

Suntint of New York, Inc., 6 Bryant Crescent, White Plains, N.Y. 10605

Sunworks, Inc., 669 Boston Post Rd., Guilford, Conn. 06437

Superior Electric Co., Bristol, Conn. 06010

Superior Fireplace Co., 4325 Artesia Ave., Fullerton, Cal. 92633

Swan Corp., 721 Olive St., St. Louis, Mo. 63101

Swedlow, Inc., 7350 Empire Dr., Florence, Ky. 41042

Swingline, Inc., 32–00 Skillman Ave., Long Island City, N.Y. 11101

Swivelier Co., Nanuet, N.Y. 10954

Symmons Industries, Inc., 31 Brooks Dr., Braintree, Mass. 02184

Taco, Inc., 1160 Cranston St., Cranston, R.I. 02920

Talk-A-Phone Co., 5013 N. Kedzie Ave., Chicago, Ill. 60625

Tappan Co., Tappan Park, Mansfield, Ohio 44901

Tappan Co., Air Conditioning Div., 206 Woodford Ave., Elyria, Ohio 44035

Teco, 5530 Wisconsin Ave., Washington, D.C. 20015

Tefco Doors, 2368 Prospect St., Memphis, Tenn. 38106

Teledyne Aquatec, 1730 E. Prospect St., Fort Collins, Colo. 80521

Tel-o-Post Co., Box 217, Linesville, Pa. 16424

Temco, Inc., 4101 Charlotte Ave., Nashville, Tenn. 37202

Thermal-Barrier Products, Inc., 7230 Northfield Rd., Bedford, Ohio 44146

ThermaSol, Ltd., 101 Park Ave., New York, N.Y. 10017

Thermo/Foam, Inc., 1425 Bancroft Ave., San Francisco, Cal. 94124

Thermograte Enterprises, Inc., 51 Iona Lane, St. Paul, Minn. 55117

Thermotrol Corp., 29400 Stephenson Hwy., Madison Heights, Mich. 48071

Thermwell Products Co., 150 E. Seventh St., Paterson, N.J. 07524

Richard E. Thibaut, Inc., 315 Fifth Ave., New York, N.Y. 10016

E. A. Thompson Co., 1333 Gough St., San Francisco, Cal. 94109

3M Co., 3M Center, St. Paul, Minn. 55101

Three Rivers Aluminum Co., 718 Chestnut St., Pittsburgh, Pa. 15212

Thru-Vu Vertical Blind Corp., 615 Fenimore Rd., Mamaroneck, N.Y. 10543

Tocomc of Atlanta, Box 45167 AMF, Atlanta, Ga. 30320

Tremont Nail Co., 23 Elm St., Wareham, Mass. 02571

Triangle Pacific Cabinet Corp., 4255 LBJ Freeway, Dallas, Tex. 75234

Trion, Inc., Box 760, Sanford, N.C. 27330

Tub-Master Corp., 413 Virginia Dr., Orlando, Fla. 32803

U-Line Corp., Box 8124, Milwaukee, Wis. 53223

Ultraflo Corp., Box 2284, Sandusky, Ohio 44870

Unique Window Products Corp., 4 Taft St., South Norwalk, Conn. 06856

United Cabinet Corp., Box 420, Jasper, Ind. 47546

United DeSoto, Inc., 3101 S. Kedzie Ave., Chicago, Ill. 60623

United Gilsonite Laboratories, Scranton, Pa. 18501

United States Gypsum Co., 101 S. Wacker Dr., Chicago, Ill. 60606

United States Gypsum Co., Roofing Div., 525 S. Virgil Ave., Los Angeles, Cal. 90020

United States Metals & Manufacturing Co., 1301 S. Main St., South Bend, Ind. 46613

United States Register Co., Battle Creek, Mich. 49016

United States Steel Corp., Alside Div., Box 2010, Akron, Ohio 44309

Universal-Rundle Corp., 217 N. Mill St., New Castle, Pa. 16103

Universal Water Systems, Inc., 1425 W. Hawthorne Lane, West Chicago, Ill. 60185

Upjohn Co., CPR Div., 555 Alaska Ave., Torrance, Cal. 90503

U.S. Fiber Corp., 101 S. Main St., Delphos, Ohio 45833

USM Corp., Box 1139, Reading, Pa. 19603

U.S. Mineral Products Co., Stanhope, N.J. 07874

U.S. Plywood, 1 Landmark Sq., Stamford, Conn. 06921

Utica Radiator Corp., 2201 Dwyer Ave., Utica, N.Y. 13501

Uvalde Rock Asphalt Co., Azrock Floor Products Div., Box 531, San Antonio, Tex. 78292

Vega Industries, Inc., Heatilator Div., Mt. Pleasant, Iowa 52641

Velux-America, Inc., 80 Cummings Park, Woburn, Mass. 01801

Vemco Products, Inc., 31623 Stephenson Hwy., Madison Heights, Mich. 58071

Ventarama Skylight Corp., 40 Haven Ave., Port Washington, N.Y. 11050

Vermont Marble Co., Proctor, Vt. 05765

Vermont Structural Slate Co., Fair Haven, Vt. 05743

Vermont Weatherboard, Inc., Wolcott, Vt. 05680

Versa Products Co., Ohio St., Lodi, Ohio 44254

Verticals, Inc., 704 E. 133rd St., Bronx, N.Y. 10454

Vestal Manufacturing Co., Box 420, Sweetwater, Tenn. 37874

Victor Oolitic Stone Co., Box 668, Bloomington, Ind. 47401

Viking Sauna Co., 909 Park Ave., San Jose, Cal. 95150

Vikon Tile Corp., 130 N. Taylor St., Washington, N.J. 07882

Village Lantern, 598 Union St., North Marshfield, Mass. 02059

Vulcan Radiator Co., 775 Capitol Ave., Hartford, Conn. 06101

Wallace-Murray Corp., Box 137, Belmont, Cal. 94002

Wallace-Murray Corp., Eljer Plumbingware Div., 3 Gateway Center, Pittsburgh, Pa. 15222

Wall & Floor Treatments, Inc., Flexi-Wall Systems Div., Box 477, Liberty, S.C. 29657

Jim Walter Corp., Box 22601, Tampa, Fla. 33622

Wal-Vac, Inc., 2851 Buchanan SW, Grand Rapids, Mich. 49508

Warp Brothers, 1100 N. Cicero Ave., Chicago, Ill. 60651

Washington Stove Works, Box 687, Everett, Wash., 98201

Watco-Dennis Corp., 1756 22nd St., Santa Monica, Cal. 90404

Water Control Products/N.A., Inc., 1100 Owendale Ave., Troy, Mich. 48084

Waterlox Chemical & Coatings Corp., 9808 Meech Ave., Cleveland, Ohio 44105

Webb Manufacturing, Inc., Conneaut, Ohio 44030

Weil-McLain Co., Hydronic Div., Michigan City, Ind. 46360

Weil-McLain Co., Red Jacket Div., Box 3888, Davenport, Iowa 52800

Wellmade Metal Products Co., 860 81st St., Oakland, Cal. 94621

Wessel Hardware Corp., Erie Ave. & D St., Philadelphia, Pa. 19134

Western Chemical Co., 417 S. Fourth St., St. Joseph, Mo. 64501

Westinghouse Electric Corp., Bryant Div., 1421 State St., Bridgeport, Conn. 06602

Westinghouse Electric Corp., Central Residential Air Conditioning Div., Norman, Okla. 73069

Westinghouse Electric Corp., Decorative Micarta Div., Hampton, S.C. 29924

Westinghouse Electric Corp., IXL Div., Elizabeth City, N.C. 27909

Westinghouse Security Systems, Inc., 200 Beta Dr., Pittsburgh, Pa. 15238

Whirlpool Corp., Benton Harbor, Mich. 49022

White-Westinghouse Appliance Co., 930 Fort Duquesne Blvd., Pittsburgh, Pa. 15222

Whittlewood Corp., Box 26208, Albuquerque, N.M. 87125

Williams Lumber Co., Rocky Mount, N.C. 27801

Williamson Co., 3500 Madison Rd., Cincinnati, Ohio 45209

Wilmot Industries, Inc., RR5, Box 365, Elkhart, Ind. 46514

Wilson-Imperial Co., 115 Chestnut St., Newark, N.J. 07105

Ralph Wilson Plastics Co., Temple, Tex. 76501

Wilson Research Corp., 2001 Peninsula Dr., Erie, Pa. 16512

Wind-Wonder, Inc., Box 36462, Houston, Tex. 77036

Winter Seal of Flint, Inc., 209 Elm St., Holly, Mich. 48442

Wiremold Co., West Hartford, Conn. 06110

William Wirtz Associates, 228 Phipps Plaza, Palm Beach, Fla. 33480

J. Wiss & Sons Co., 400 W. Market St., Newark, N.J. 07107

Witco Chemical Corp., 277 Park Ave., New York, N.Y. 10017

Wolverine-Pentronix, Inc., 1650 Howard St., Lincoln Park, Mich. 48146

Woodco Corp., 3323 Paterson Plank Rd., North Bergen, N.J. 07047

Woodcraft Millwork Specialties, Inc., 10 Willow St., Moonachie, N.J. 07074

Woodcraft Supply Corp., 313 Montvale Ave., Woburn, Mass. 01801

Woodhill Chemical Sales Corp., 18731 Cranwood Pkwy., Cleveland, Ohio 44128

A. R. Wood Manufacturing Co., Box 218, Luverne, Minn. 56156

Wood-Mode Cabinetry, Kreamer, Snyder County, Pa. 17833

Wood Specialty Products, Inc., 24300 W. 60th St., Mountlake Terrace, Wash. 98043

Wrightway Manufacturing Co., 371 E. 116th St., Chicago, Ill. 60628

Z-Brick, Box 628, Woodinville, Wash. 98072